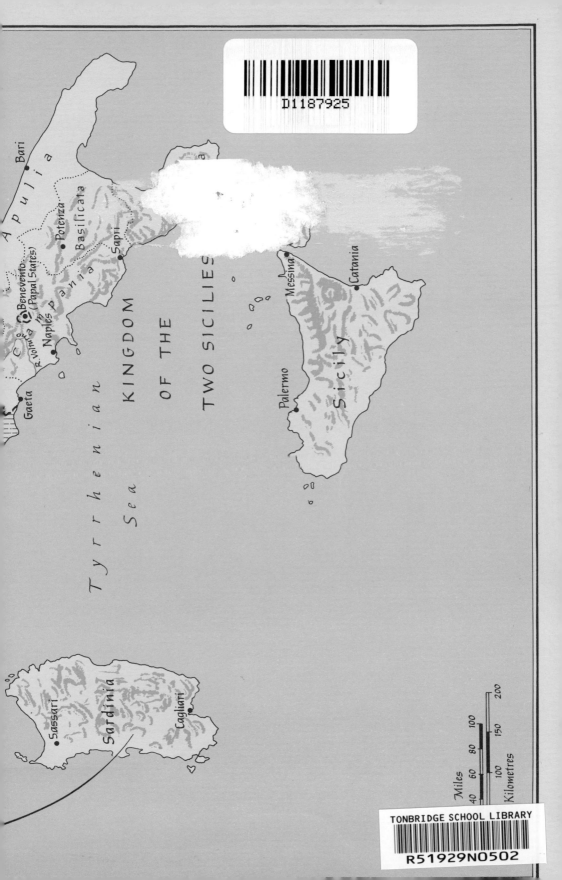

D1187925

Apulia

Bari

Basilicata

Potenza

Benevento
(Papal States)

Sapri

Campania

R. Volturno

Naples

Gaeta

Messina

Catania

KINGDOM

OF THE

TWO SICILIES

Sicily

Palermo

Tyrrhenian

Sea

Sardinia

Sassari

Cagliari

Miles
40 60 80 100

100   150   200

Kilometres

A history of
ITALY 1700–1860

A history of
ITALY 1700–1860

THE SOCIAL CONSTRAINTS OF POLITICAL CHANGE

Stuart Woolf

P 373

p 382

METHUEN & CO LTD
11 NEW FETTER LANE
LONDON EC4P 4EE

First published in 1979 *by* Methuen & Co Ltd
11 New Fetter Lane, London EC4P 4EE

© 1979 *Stuart Woolf*

Printed in Great Britain by
Western Printing Services Ltd, Bristol
Bound by
Redwood Burn Ltd, Esher

ISBN 0 416 80880 8

Contents

Preface

Big books (and some small ones too) often take far longer than anticipated. As far as I can recall, I began this history of Italy in the mid-1960s. It has formed part of my intellectual (and material) luggage ever since, written at intervals at Reading, Settignano, Cogne, Turin, New York, Paris, Melbourne and Colchester. An earlier version in Italian was published by Einaudi of Turin as part of its courageous and enterprising *Storia d'Italia*, and I am grateful to Giulio Einaudi and to the editors of this collective undertaking, Corrado Vivanti and Ruggiero Romano, for offering me the challenge of writing a foreigner's interpretation of the most 'national' period of Italy's long history. The present book, besides a substantial revision of the original Italian edition, includes four new chapters.

There are obvious disadvantages in writing a book over so many years. Knowledge deepens, so that one is inclined continuously to rewrite the same parts. But, at a certain moment, it is necessary – if the book is ever to be finished – to let the publisher prise the manuscript out of one's hands. New materials and new interpretations have continued to appear inexorably and sometimes with terrifying rapidity. I have not always been able to take them fully into account. It is true that a portion of this vast production of printed matter might appear to the disenchanted observer of Italian cultural practices as the inevitable (and often superfluous) legacy of a particular tradition of humanistic rhetoric and the consequence of the more general requirements of academic advancement. Delay has sometimes relieved me of the need to read what soon has been justly forgotten. I hope it has not led me to neglect that substantial part of Italian historical writing of notable quality and integrity which has appeared over the past fifteen years, and which has led to a radical and deep revision of the traditional interpretation of the Risorgimento as the triumphantly inevitable culmination of the previous history of Italy. Vivacious intellectual curiosity, backed up by tenacious research and sophisticated maturity of interpretation, are characteristics of the best Italian historiography of the most recent decades, one more facet of that remarkable cultural vitality displayed by the Italian people after the years of suffocating conformism of the fascist regime.

That I owe much to Italian historians, particularly of the younger generation, will be evident to the reader. My debt is not confined to their writings, but extends to the discussions we have carried on, as if without interruption, over twenty years. By chance, I have researched mostly in the three capital cities of unified Italy – Turin, Florence and Rome. But if I have been able, in this book, to share with the reader my understanding of the tormented history of Italy, I believe it is not only as a result of what I have studied and discussed with historians, in these three cities and else-where, but also because of my personal 'non-academic' life in Italy, my experiences of living with and among Italians. However pretentious an echo of Machiavelli's dictum this may sound to the 'cultured' reader, it is written with humility and gratitude. It is difficult, indeed arrogant, to write the history of a foreign people, as it presupposes an understanding of a civilization, a culture, a mentality, absorbed from earliest childhood and only observable by the outsider in fragmentary perceptions derived not only from the written documentation, but from the visible and oral evidence that surround him incessantly. I was fortunate in commencing my earliest researches in Italy before the dramatic – and traumatic – pace of industrial-ization transformed social relations and led, through the painful experience of mass migration from south to north, to what might be considered in many ways as the real unification of the Italian people.

I have been even more fortunate, through the kindness and sympathy of an ever growing number of friends, in being offered the rare privilege of a hospitable introduction into a vast and bewildering variety of groups, families and homes, in remote mountains and villages as much as in the plains and cities. It has taught me the obvious lesson that in Italy regional and local diversity runs deeper, for historical and cultural reasons, than in most western European countries and that it maintains its vitality despite the impact of apparently overwhelming national changes. It has also taught me the equally evident truth (unfortunately noted infrequently by political historians) that the history of Italy is not just – is not even primarily – the history of its cities, however resplendent they may appear as testimony of past glories. It is the history of a harsh, mountainous land, where a living has to be torn from a soil impoverished by inclement natural conditions and human neglect. These structural influences play, and have always played, a complex role in conditioning social as well as more easily visible political developments in Italy. It is difficult to understand their relationships; but to ignore them is to run the risk of writing a history that ignores as much as it explains.

The new generation of Italian historians is very aware of these slow-

moving undercurrents of long-term change, and in recent years has begun
to explore them. But the social history of Italy, particularly in the nineteenth
century, remains to be written. So that, in one sense, my rash attempt has
come too early: I cannot write where research does not as yet exist. I have
endeavoured to piece together what evidence is available, from original
sources, from my own researches and from the work of young Italian and
non-Italian historians; and on this basis I have written the pages that
discuss social structures and social changes in Italy. The gaps are evident,
and I am acutely conscious of the inadequacies of what I have written. But I
remain (indeed I have become ever more) convinced that political history,
if it is to be more than just the recounting of a story, is so far from offering
an autonomous approach that it can only be understood through the conditioning and slowly changing structures of society. Perhaps this attempt to
offer a synthesis at least will serve the purpose of indicating useful lines of
research.

Like all authors, I owe thanks to a host of people. Above all, I am grateful
to Brian Pullan and Paul Ginsborg for their patient and immensely helpful
detailed comments on large portions of the text. Eric Jones, Olwen Hufton,
Verina Jones and Maurice Aymard read chapters at different stages of the
book's prolonged birth, and I hope I have benefited from their pertinent
remarks. My thanks also to Ian Fletcher for his assistance in rendering
Italian doggerel into its English equivalent.

This book is dedicated to Anna, who will probably be glad not to look at
it again, and to Deborah, who has seen it around the house for most of her
life.

March 1978   Stuart Woolf

Note on references

I have kept the footnotes to an absolute minimum in order to avoid over-
burdening the text unnecessarily, as was requested for the earlier Italian
edition. Therefore the references are given at the end of each quotation, the
number after the author's name indicating where the full reference is to be
found in the bibliography, which is divided into sections.

Introduction:
The land and the people

Italy has always attracted foreigners, from ancient Greek settlers to present-day whistle-stop tourists, from pilgrims to mercenaries, from artists to romantic poets. Over the centuries, it has retained its hold over the imagination of the western world, an appeal perhaps varying in intensity over time, but never absent, and fundamentally explicable in terms of two different (although sometimes superimposed) images of the country: its cultural traditions, both religious and secular, and its fertility.

The theme of the natural fertility and wealth of the peninsula may surprise readers of today, only too accustomed to discussions of development and under-development, of industrialization and economic backwardness. But that Italy was 'the garden of the Empire' was an image which remained unchallenged until the seventeenth century, only aroused serious criticism in the eighteenth, and was still applied – inappropriately – to the physical potential of the southern regions in the decades after unification. It was an image composed of the historical memory of the south as the 'granary' of the Roman republic and empire and of contemporary impressions (from the eleventh until the sixteenth century and beyond) of the fertility of the landscape of the Po and Tuscan plains and the wealth of their cities.

The making of the landscape, as much as the building of the cities, were the result of countless generations of human endeavour. For physical geography has endowed Italy with few advantages. Within natural frontiers formed by the Mediterranean and the awesome barrier of the Alps, four-fifths of the territory consists of mountains and hills. Not only the great Alpine arc, sweeping west to east from the Mediterranean to the Adriatic, but the steep hostile range of the Apennines, stretching irregularly down the length of Italy, north-west to south-east, and the mountains of Sicily and Sardinia, have set permanent barriers to the possibilities of cultivation. Beneath the permanent or semi-permanent snow levels, the higher slopes of the Alpine mountains and Tyrrhenian Apennines are covered by only a thin surface of soil; the steepness of the slopes in the sub-Alpine chain and the Apennine ridge has led to erosion, not least because of the continuous deforestation; in the low hills and plains of the south and islands the humus is extremely thin. Climate has imposed another, equally rigid limit, sharply dividing the more temperate, humid environment of the northern and central plains and river valleys, with their richer soils, from the hot, arid, typically Mediterranean climate of the south and islands, marked by long months of drought, interrupted only briefly by violent rains, which swell the rivers and streams into threatening torrents. The line dividing the south from the north is an irregular one: the Tuscan Maremma can be regarded, from the point of view of physical geography, as belonging to the south, Campania to the north. But in pedological, climatic and agricultural terms, the division between the Mediterranean south and the more amenable north has constituted a permanent barrier over the centuries, explaining much of the differences in development of the two regions. Within both regions, the enormous and often abrupt changes in altitude, climate, soil and vegetation – probably greater than in any European country – as well as the presence of extensive marshlands and the constant threat of the irregular flows of torrential streams have conditioned the varying forms of human settlements and agriculture.

Over the thousand years from antiquity to the modern period, three broad trends can be discerned in human endeavours to control and exploit the environment in Italy: irrigation and drainage schemes to control and harness the permanent presence or recurrent threat of water; a more-or-less continuous process of deforestation, worsening the hydrological disorder; and fluctuations in the frontiers of the cultivated areas, corresponding to the periodic increase and decline of the population. In the course of this long period, the landscape of Italy was slowly shaped, from the carefully irrigated and intensely cultivated lower Lombard plain, with its mixed husbandry, to the vast, uninhabited wheat prairies of the Roman and Sicilian latifundia, from the great sheep runs of the Abruzzi, Lazio or Apulia to the specialized fruit and market gardens near the cities throughout Italy, from the hill-top villages of the south, in flight from the malaria-infested plains, to the isolated farmhouses of the central Italian sharecroppers. The process was slow, but occurred for the most part between the twelfth and sixteenth centuries. The deep depression of the seventeenth century, like the demographic growth of the later eighteenth, both left their mark; but not until the present century was the landscape again to undergo drastic modification.

By the twelfth and thirteenth centuries, the cities of northern and central Italy, as much as the countryside, had already acquired that characteristic physiognomy of towers and civic buildings, of markets and economic bustle, which amazed all foreign visitors and distinguished Italy from the rest of Europe. In a feudal world, with universalist ideals of Church and Empire, the supremacy of these merchants in their communes, independent city-states, represented an aberration, which imposed itself on Europe because of an undeniable economic hegemony, soon accompanied by a cultural superiority. The reasons for this secular leadership in a Christian world are not to be found in any 'national characteristics' of Italians (for, if this were the case, how can one explain the subsequent centuries of Italian 'failure'?), but – in origin at least – in the one crucial advantage with which geography had endowed the peninsula: its central location within the Mediterranean. Within the context of a general European economic revival from the ninth and tenth centuries, Italians were able to play a growing and soon a dominant role because of their virtual monopoly of trade between East and West. The products and cultures of the Orient, Byzantium, the Arab world and beyond, as far as China, were filtered through Italy to the feudal Christianity of Western Europe; spices and silks, saints' remains and heresies, ancient manuscripts and contemporary plagues, all passed through Italian ports – Amalfi, Pisa, Genoa, Venice – and inland cities – Milan, Pavia, Bologna, Florence.

The great success of Italians between the eleventh and fourteenth centuries cannot, however, be ascribed to purely geographical causes. In part it was due to the revived importance of Rome, formerly capital of a secular empire, now see of the successors to St Peter. Pilgrimages and Peter's Pence created new routes from north to south, crossing those from east to west, and assisted (even if they did not create) the fortunes of Emilian, Tuscan and Umbrian cities, such as Bologna, Florence, Siena and Viterbo. As a city, Rome – with a population of perhaps 30 000 in 1300 – was of little material importance compared to Florence and Venice, with populations of 100 000, or Milan, with 80 000. But as a myth, a symbol of continuity with the greatness of antiquity, both secular and religious, its significance cannot be underestimated in medieval Europe. Alongside the unprecedented modernity of the communes, the antiquity of Rome represented the other, contradictory image of Italy – its continuity with the glories of the past.

The independence of the communal cities of northern and central Italy was essential to their economic success. Contemporaries were startled by these Italian city-states precisely because they stood out in sharp contrast, as islands in the sea of feudalism of medieval Europe. Feudalism continued to dominate large areas of Italy as well – and was ultimately to prove the downfall of the communes. Not only in southern Italy, where the Norman and Angevin conquests suppressed communal independence, but in Piedmont, the Trentino, Friuli and large areas of central Italy, the feudal structure of society remained unchallenged. The area of communal Italy always remained confined. But within this area the relationship between the cities and the surrounding feudal territories was fundamentally transformed. Far from depending upon the feudal lords, the urban centres asserted their control over the surrounding territories. It was the requirements of the cities, with their rapidly growing populations and expanding trade, that underlay the dissolution of the manorial system and the commercialization of agriculture. It was the predominance of the urban economies that explained both the leading role played by merchants and artisans and the residence of noble families within the cities. For visitors accustomed to the unchallenged supremacy of the feudal order, the distinctiveness of the Italian communes lay in the acceptance by Italian nobles (whether willing or coerced) of the political independence and economic activities of the citizens. The development of the structures of communal government and of the guilds, as much as the characteristic and endemic struggles between the cities or between factions within each commune, took place with ever less reference to the world of feudalism, precisely because the nobles of northern and central Italy accepted the hegemony of the urban centres.

The citizens of these communes, like the foreign visitors, were conscious of their material wealth. It was a wealth based on industry – the production of high quality, mainly textile goods – but regulated according to the demands of international trade. Italian merchants and bankers dominated European trade because of their entrepreneurial skills. The technical innovations – the coining of gold and silver moneys, letters of exchange, double entry book-keeping, insurances – were perhaps less revolutionary than has been claimed. What was revolutionary was the physical presence of Italian merchants and bankers throughout Europe and beyond, their knowledge of prices over a wide geographical area, and their ability to turn this knowledge into profit by relating it to time. The basic skills of literacy and numeracy, essential for these trading activities, can be linked to the internal needs of government and administration of these independent communes. More importantly, the mobility of these merchants and their capacity to group themselves in commercial organizations – which ultimately explains their superiority over their foreign rivals – probably need to be explained in terms of family and kinship structures and in forms of 'sociability' particular to the Italian cities.

By the thirteenth and early fourteenth centuries the leadership of communal Italy within Europe was an established fact. It was a cultural, as much as an economic, leadership of which Italian citizens were wholly conscious in their contemptuous references to the 'barbarians' beyond the Alps, and their exaltation of communal patriotism in urban chronicles and civic buildings. For foreigners, Italy aroused both admiration and envy. It was the centre of culture, both religious and lay. With the formal institution of jubilees in 1300, Rome successfully asserted its role as the religious and administrative centre of Christianity, where the path to redemption could be eased by the discomforts of the long journey and the purchase of indulgences. But other cities equally exerted their appeal as centres of culture: the university towns, especially Bologna, already from the twelfth century establishing a new jurisprudence; later, supremely by the fifteenth century, the humanist cities – Florence, Venice, Milan – attracting the intellectuals of Europe in search of manuscripts and ideas.

Civic Italy reached its apogee as a source of cultural inspiration when, economically and politically, it was already in decline. The famines and epidemics that affected all Europe, culminating in the terrible Black Death of 1348, checked the expansion of the Italian economy. The land routes to the East were interrupted by the end of the 'pax mongolica' in the early fourteenth century; Venice, Genoa, Florence, Naples all experienced monetary crises; the great banking houses of Florence, Genoa and Venice ran into increasing difficulties and often collapsed; Italian merchants abroad began to be persecuted; textile production in Florence, Brescia, Pisa, Venice and Verona, declined; the urban populations fell sharply. In the countryside, particularly in Tuscany, Lazio and Sardinia, the enormous loss of life through the plague led to the abandoning of villages and cultivated areas; marshland and malaria forced a retreat from the plains, in the north as well as the south; arable was converted into sheep pasturage; ports and river deltas silted, especially in the south, but also in the lower Po valley, the Tyrrhenian and Adriatic coasts and the Tuscan Val di Chiana.

The contrast between the earlier expansive development of the economy and the deep crisis of the later fourteenth century is dramatic; it led to long-term changes within the cities and in the relationship between city and countryside. The economic activities of the Italian cities revived during most of the fifteenth century, as did the European economy. But Italian merchants no longer dominated Europe. Despite the spectacular image offered by great banking houses, such as the Medici, the urban economies remained tied to the production of luxury goods and hence particularly vulnerable to interruptions in international trade. Within the cities, the lesser guilds, the *popolo minuto,* lost their struggle for power. The urban revolts of the textile workers in the later fourteenth century, at Lucca, Siena, Perugia, Genoa, Verona and, above all, the famous revolt of the Florentine Ciompi in 1378, had failed. Production was increasingly controlled by the *popolo grasso,* the merchant-bankers. The guilds closed in upon themselves, increasingly concerned to protect their monopolies and privileges, hostile to competition, reluctant to innovate. Urban Italy remained tied to the production of high quality, expensive goods, which – after a final boom towards the mid-sixteenth century – proved ever less capable of competing with the new, cheaper textiles produced in England, Holland and France.

The triumph of the merchant-capitalists over the *popolo minuto* carried with it the destruction of the communes. Internally, the history of the communes is one of perennial instability. The endemic struggles of guilds, factions and families had blocked the development of the bureaucratic and financial instruments of government and the transformation of the cities into states through the establishment of uniform administrations. Wealthy oligarchies asserted their control over the communes, but were easily overthrown because of their lack of a broad social base. In Florence in 1343, only 3500 citizens were eligible for office in a population of over 70 000. It was always possible to challenge the authority of the ruling families by appealing to the people, especially in times of economic difficulties or after a military defeat by a rival city. As vast numbers of citizens withdrew from active participation in public life and concentrated on their economic activities, the *signori* seized power in the communes.

The transformation of the communes into *signorie* was not just the consequence of the internal weaknesses of the former. It was even more symptomatic of the isolation of the communes within a feudal world and of the close links between the urban oligarchies and the feudatories. Once food supplies and free, adequately secure communications had been assured, the communes had never attempted to challenge the continued existence of feudal holdings. Indeed, the landed purchases of rich merchants and the urban residence of magnates created multiple ties between the two groups, which became closer as the nobles – excluded from power in the thirteenth century – again asserted their right to hold public office. The convergence of interests between the two groups underlay the progressively oligarchical development of the communes; even in republics such as Venice and Genoa exclusive power was seized by limited numbers of families. Elsewhere, the *condottieri* who served the communes and the *signori* who overthrew them – the Visconti, Estensi, Gonzaga, Scaligeri and many others – often came from feudal families. Their feudal territories provided them with the base from which to seize power, or even – as with the Visconti or Carraresi – to regain it, if thrown out of the cities.

The diffusion of the *signorie* in the fourteenth and fifteenth centuries in northern and central Italy accentuated the feudalization of society, long characteristic of the south. If power was easy to seize, it was difficult to retain. The extension of the territorial authority of the *signori*, such as the Visconti or Sforza in Lombardy, was achieved at the expense of compromises with the local oligarchies, by the granting of privileges and 'liberties'. From the final decades of the fourteenth century, old and new families were granted feudal investitures, with tax exemptions and judicial rights. The feudal world reasserted itself, as the urban classes bought land, acquired titles and gradually adopted the feudal code of values, from knightly conduct and noble honour to rigid social hierarchy and reluctance to engage in 'mechanical' arts. Even the republican citizens of Venice created a feudal system of investitures for lands in their colony of Crete.

The effects of these transformations were equally profound in the countryside. The earlier expansion of the communes had led to the dissolution of the manorial system, the emancipation of the peasants and their property, the creation of semi-independent rural communes, the encouragement of a commercialized agriculture with the development of urban markets. With the crisis of the fourteenth century, the cities no longer offered an outlet for the pressure of the population on the land. Even if the disastrous plague of 1348 momentarily relieved this pressure, the peasants were only able to benefit temporarily, because of the urban demand for land: the properties around the cities were rapidly acquired by magnates and citizens. The security offered by the *signori* encouraged investment in the land. The fifteenth and sixteenth centuries witnessed a progressive transformation of property and landscape, at the expense of the peasants. Large estates were created in northern and central Italy and consolidated in the south. Rural communes lost their autonomy together with much of their commonlands. If some wealthy peasants emerged, the majority were dispossessed by this concentration of property. At the same time, agriculture in the north and centre became increasingly commercial. The estates were often rented to capitalist entrepreneurs, *fittabili*, 'country merchants', concerned to maximize production rather than increase productivity. Sharecropping contracts (*mezzadria*), introduced in Tuscany through the thirteenth and fourteenth centuries, became increasingly common, but changed in character, as growing labour demands were imposed upon the peasants in order to introduce new cultures, such as hemp, or increase profitable existing ones, such as vines. *Mezzadria* spread into Emilia in the fifteenth century, Umbria, Piedmont and the central and western Po valley in the sixteenth and seventeenth. If the shortage of livestock constituted a structural limitation on agricultural productivity, except in a restricted area of the Lombard plain, the introduction of specialized cultures reflected the commercialization of the countryside: industrial plants, such as woad in Lombardy and saffron in the Abruzzi, olive oil in Apulia, sugarcane in Sicily, rice in the Vercellese. Above all, the reclamation of marshlands and the expansion of sheep flocks and pasturages marked the changing agrarian landscape. From the late fifteenth century wealthy citizens, aided by their governments, invested huge sums in and made equally large profits from drainage schemes in Venetia, along the Tuscan coast, and near Bologna, Ferrara and Mantua. In the Tuscan Maremma, but even more in Roman Lazio, Neapolitan Apulia, as well as in Sicily and Sardinia, the great feudal landowners raised vast sheep flocks, seriously reducing the arable area and hence threatening the wheat supplies of the cities.

By the mid-sixteenth century, the fundamental differences between the commercial agriculture of the north and that of the south were apparent:

intensive farming, with a certain degree of specialization, in the north and centre; extensive wheat and sheep culture in the south. The structure of landholdings, tenurial contracts and human settlements reflected these differences: vast estates and small peasant properties or leaseholds in the south (except near the major cities), with the mostly landless populations travelling considerable distances from their large villages according to the demands of the agricultural cycle; varying sized estates, divided into smaller working units according to the size of the peasant family, with isolated homesteads or small villages near the cultivated land, in the plains and villages of the north and centre. Only in the mountain valleys did peasant smallholdings remain predominant.

What was common to all regions was the hostility of the citizens towards the peasants. The working population of the countryside is satirized in literary works between the fourteenth and sixteenth centuries as stupid, hypocritical, dishonest – and as a threat. The peasant response, after the failure of sporadic risings in the fifteenth century, was a retreat into the *paese di Cuccagna*, a fairyland, upside-down world, replete with food, where sleep, not labour, created earnings, where lords and gentlemen did not exist and peasants were free. Here too the difference between the two basic regions of Italy remained firm; for this popular literature only circulated in the north and centre.

The political crisis and collapse of an independent Italy in the early sixteenth century did not modify, but accentuated these long-term trends of Italian society. The period of the *signorie* had continued the development towards regional states within the peninsula. But the dominant cities – Venice, Milan, Florence, Rome and the smaller capitals – had proved incapable of creating solid and uniform state structures. The Sforza of Lombardy, like republican Venice or Medicean Florence, controlled large but heterogeneous territories by a mixture of force and compromise with the local urban oligarchies. In the kingdoms of Sicily and Naples the feudal barons retained their power, even after Ferdinand of Naples' massacre of those who had plotted against him. In the Papal States, the schisms encouraged the creation of abusive fiefs, only formally checked during the foreign invasions of the sixteenth century by papal exploitation of the insecurity of the other Italian rulers. The long period of relative peace from foreign threats enjoyed by the Italian rulers from the mid-fourteenth century, culminating in the apparent balance of power established by the treaty of Lodi (1454), masked the weakness, not the strength, of the Italian states. The much-lauded skills of Italian diplomacy served to hide the military impotence and fears of internal plots of the *signori* and republican oligarchies. That the wealth of Italy continued to attract foreign adventurers is demonstrated not only by the invasion of the French king Charles VIII (1494), but even more by the rapidity with which the emperor Maximilian and Ferdinand of Spain, as well as Charles' successor Louis XII, hastened to join in this division of the booty.

The collapse of Italy, consecrated definitively in the peace of Cateau-Cambrésis (1559) which established Spanish hegemony, shocked contemporaries because it contrasted so violently with Italy's ancient and recent glories. Above all, the political failure coincided with – and accelerated – Italian cultural influence throughout Europe, from France and England to Bohemia, Poland and Moscow. Italian humanism, painting, sculpture, architecture, the decorative arts, urban and garden planning, offered models to European intellectuals, artists, nobles and royal courts from the later fifteenth until the seventeenth century, from Pico della Mirandola and Leonardo da Vinci to Machiavelli and Borromini. The collapse of the *signori* and the increasingly repressive atmosphere of counter-reformation, Spanish Italy led to the exodus of innumerable Italian artists and craftsmen who left their characteristic imprint throughout the Continent. The contrast between the material evidence of Italy's great past and her present decline, a commonplace of all foreign travellers between the seventeenth and nineteenth centuries, expressed in terms of shock, nostalgia, contempt or philosophical resignation according to period and nationality, was fundamentally based upon a judgement of Italian cultural achievements.

For Italian intellectuals the shock of the collapse was obviously more immediate and overwhelming. The writings of Machiavelli and Guicciardini, their discussions of ancient Greece and Rome, reflect their constant striving for the means to adapt sixteenth-century institutions and customs into safeguards of an illusory independence. But even before the foreign invasions, as the rigidity of oligarchical control increased, the humanists had begun to withdraw from their role as public servants. Alberti could deny that honour was to be found in public service. With the wars in full course, Castiglione accepted the new realities of absolutist power, while striving to preserve the dignity of the intellectual in his new role as courtier. But already in the same years, his contemporary Ariosto gained public acclaim for his advocacy of the need to eulogize the prince and so obtain his patronage.

The change had come rapidly. By the mid-sixteenth century, Italian political writers accepted established authority; soon, they also accepted Italy's loss of independence. The steady stream of treatises on political and social behaviour published through the seventeenth century alternated between opportunistic counsels on how to manipulate 'reason of state' and open advice on the search for pensions and benefices through panegyric glorification of the prince. Anti-Spanish proclamations of the need to regain the 'liberty' of Italy merely masked a practical withdrawal from political commitment into a concern for private, and especially family, advancement.

Counter-reformation, Spanish Italy was a country of rigid social stratification. Both Church and Spanish protocol encouraged and codified this hierarchical division of society. The Church's role was twofold: suppression of dissent and consecration of a divinely ordained and fundamentally immovable social order. Its success in Italy was unusually complete, because of the structural weaknesses of the Italian states and society, but also because of the restoration of papal authority, achieved with remarkable rapidity in the council of Trent (1545–63) and confirmed by the support of that Most Catholic Sovereign, Philip II of Spain. A mere half-century separated the ill-famed political intrigues of Alexander VI (Borgia) from the fanatical authoritarianism of Paul IV and Pius V. By the later sixteenth century, heresy in Italy had been stamped out by the restoration of the moral authority of the Church, often described as the Catholic reformation, but even more by the extreme centralization of authority by Rome. Whole villages of Calabrian Waldensians were massacred while the council of Trent was still in progress. Dissent was suppressed by intimidation, the ever-present threat of the inquisition and the introduction of a general index of prohibited books. Jewish communities were expelled or forced into ghettos. The significance of the successful defiance of a papal interdict by Sarpi's Venice (1606) is not to be found in any challenge to Catholic orthodoxy, but rather in its firm rejection of papal pretensions at the political level of Church-State relations.

The counterpart to the repression of heresy was the inculcation of a set of imposed beliefs and external practices of piety upon a laity excluded from active participation within the religious life of the Church. The publication of the Roman catechism (1566) offered an effective instrument to shield the laity from the dangers of contamination through direct contact with the Scriptures. At the popular level, a flood of edifying publications on piety and the lives of the saints accompanied the 'missions' of Jesuits, Barnabites and the new religious orders, through the seventeenth century, into the cities and countryside of Italy in order to win back the people to the true religion. Superstitious practices and baroque churches were complementary aspects of this Catholic *reconquista* of Italian society.

The Church was particularly successful in Italy because of the broad identification of its vision of society with that of the ruling groups. If, at the political level, it had been forced to accept its role as a separate, albeit autonomous, organization from the secular polity, it remained intimately linked by multiple ties to the various nobilities and oligarchies of Italy. The Jesuits had replaced the humanists in the education of the noble young. The ecclesiastical hierarchy continued to be recruited from patrician families. Benefices and lay control of nomination of priests to churches, appointment of administrators of charitable institutions, were instances of the continuous, close links between ecclesiastical authorities and secular oligarchies. However separate as an organization, the Church confirmed and reinforced the aristocratic ideology of society, from its affirmation of the sovereign as the earthly manifestation of divine majesty and its hierarchical structuring of religious ceremonies and processions to its homilies to the humble on the duties of respect, obedience and resignation.

Spanish influence accelerated the aristocratic restructuring of Italian society. In the course of the sixteenth and seventeenth centuries aristocratic wealth, power and ideals definitively replaced those of communal merchants. The process is most immediately evident in the massive purchase of land by the urban ruling groups and in the inflation of noble titles. Land offered security, tax exemptions in many cases, food supplies for the family, and the most legitimate base for claims to office or titles. It could also produce a satisfactory income through supplementary seigneurial rights and, above all, through the exploitation of labour, facilitated by harsher tenurial contracts and the growing indebtedness of the peasants. Nor did possession of land exclude speculation in large-scale trade or industry, or in usury. Titles, as barons, counts, marquises, dukes or princes, legitimated the entry into the aristocracy of new nobles and confirmed – through upgrading – the superiority of the old. Both land and titles offered the structural supports for the exercise of power. The rulers of Spanish Italy could not be overturned, like the *signori* of the previous centuries. But their endeavours to create the bureaucratic and fiscal structures of absolutist states required the collaboration of the landed nobility. Excluded from – or reluctant to accept – the most influential positions in the central administrations, the patriciates of northern and central Italy retained the monopoly of local office, identifying themselves increasingly with the traditions and privileges of their own cities. It was these local nobles and notables who dominated the life of their cities, often exploiting their administration of religious and secular institutions for personal profit. In southern Italy, the financial weakness of the Spanish monarchy progressively excluded any possibilities of administrative change. The Neapolitan revolt of the populace in 1647 then forced the government to accept the expansion of feudalism as the price of political security.

Aristocratic ideals permeated Italian society to a degree probably only paralleled in Spain. The nobilities of the various states maintained their power by co-optation into their ranks of the most successful urban bourgeoisie. The one state that attempted to maintain a closed caste – Venice – was forced to change its policy in the mid-seventeenth century. Education and charity were offered to poor nobles, lest they degrade their status. The conservation of the family patrimony became a matter of overwhelming importance, to be achieved through legal entails on property, self-imposed sexual abstinence of younger sons and daughters, the careful accumulation of funds for the provision of dowries. Heredity and status conditioned the structure of noble families. Honour, military prowess, duelling, private violence and contempt for inferiors imbued their behaviour.

The triumph of this aristocratic revival was in part the consequence (as well as a cause) of the structural crisis of the Italian economy. The traditional urban industries proved unable to compete effectively against English, French and Dutch production. The output of woollen textiles declined sharply in Florence and Milan from the 1560s, in Venice by the 1620s. The guilds proved unable to guarantee employment even to their own members. New luxury industries emerged or survived – crystal glass, leather, printing, quality soaps and sweets, above all silk, which developed into the major Italian industry of the seventeenth and eighteenth centuries. But, increasingly, Italy shifted from the production of finished cloths for both foreign and domestic markets to the export of agricultural produce and semi-finished goods. The population of the cities – Venice, Florence, Genoa, Milan, Rome – stagnated or increased only marginally. But their consumption demands remained and indeed were reinforced by government legislation, concerned to ensure adequate food supplies at controlled prices. The vast capitals of the south – Palermo with a 100 000 population, Naples, the most populous city in Europe with 250 000 inhabitants at the end of the sixteenth century – became parasitical centres of government, with little or no industrial production and vast consumption needs.

The regression of the urban economies, increasingly heavy taxation and aristocratic landownership, had negative repercussions in the countryside. The rapid growth of the rural population in the sixteenth century, as earlier in the fourteenth, exerted increasing pressure on resources. By the last quarter of the sixteenth century, the difficulties became too great for this subsistence economy: heavily indebted peasants abandoned their cultivated lands, the rate of growth of the population slowed down, famines recurred, culminating in the terrible years 1590–1. In the seventeenth century, the pressure of population slackened, particularly after the plagues of 1630 in Lombardy and 1656 in the kingdom of Naples; but in most regions, agriculture remained weak.

The structural weaknesses of a rural economy – incapable of any major increase in productivity through shortage of livestock and traditionally reliant upon an extension of the cultivated area to meet the demands of an increasing population – were laid bare in the later sixteenth century. Urban landownership and consumption demands threatened the self-sufficiency of peasant family economies by a growing commercialization of agricultural products. The dominant form of landed tenure in seventeenth-century central and northern Italy, share-cropping, created limits to any significant increases in production and made the share-cropper peculiarly dependent upon the owner or his estate manager. Because *mezzadria* was based upon a division of the produce, the size of the farm and the choice of crops was necessarily structured around the consumption requirements of the peasant family. But the owner's direct control of the running of the farm and, above

all, the peasant's total dependence upon the owner for all working capital –
seed, animals and tools – rendered him acutely vulnerable to demands on
his labour. As the *mezzadri* fell into debt, the owners could improve their
land with little capital expenditure by obliging the tenants to plant
trees or vines, extend the drainage ditches or terrace the hill-slopes.
Rigidly controlled in their private lives, their right to marry, their
daily behaviour, the extended families of *mezzadri*, once in debt, were
liable to dismissal or, alternatively, could abandon the struggle through
flight.

It would be absurd to assert that all the peasantry were in the same condition. In the higher mountain valleys peasant property and extensive communal lands permitted the survival of a subsistence economy – although, in
times of population growth, at the price of annual migrations of most of the
male population. In the countryside fairly near to the cities of northern and
central Italy, the rapidly developing silk industry offered supplementary or
substitutive domestic employment to large numbers of peasants. In the
Valle Caudina, in the kingdom of Naples, the sharp drop in population after
the 1656 plague enabled the former day-labourers renting land to become
virtual proprietors and maintain a fragile subsistence economy until the
terrible famine of 1764. In the Piedmontese plain, small peasant owners
endeavoured to uphold their independence by carefully balancing size of
family, age at marriage, and purchase and sale of plots of land.

Nevertheless, there can be little doubt that, from the later sixteenth
century, the rural population became increasingly pauperized. In Sicily,
meat vanished definitively from the diet of day-labourers, to be replaced by
a growing consumption of wine. In Venetia, and slowly through the Po
plain and the less fertile hills, maize began to be cultivated because of its
high yield. Throughout Italy there is evidence of growing peasant indebtedness. When the population began to grow again in the eighteenth century,
conditions immediately worsened.

Pressure on subsistence and loss of economic independence led almost
invariably into indigence and dependence upon charity. The problem of
poverty was not new. Indeed, in a Catholic society it was the necessary
counterpart to wealth, permitting the private atonement of sin and the
public mitigation of harsh laws through charity. Socially, it was not even
necessarily undesirable, as the insecurity of dependence on alms encouraged
meekness and gratitude. Italian society had developed a sophisticated
battery of institutions to cater for the poor, from pawnshops and hospitals
to confraternities and retreats. What was new was the pressure of the poor
upon these institutions in the later sixteenth century and the harsher
response of society. Some 20 to 30 per cent of the urban populations of
Italy depended on charity, either wholly or in part. By the late sixteenth and
seventeenth centuries Italian society adopted an increasingly harsh attitude,

distinguishing between the 'deserving' and the 'undeserving' poor, identifying unemployment with sloth. Above all, both ecclesiastical and civic authorities displayed a steadily more hostile approach towards beggars and vagrants, regarded as dishonest rogues, evil and idle, carriers of disease, an embarassment to the faithful within the churches. Residence was a sign of respectability, vagrancy evidence of impiety and illwill. Beggars had to be removed from public view by their enclosure in special institutions. The 'hostels for the poor', that were created in Bologna, Milan, Turin, Venice, Florence, Naples and Genoa in the later sixteenth and seventeenth centuries, collected heterogenous populations of aged and infirm, women householders and prostitutes, orphans and immigrants, beggars and criminals.

By the end of the seventeenth century, Italy had become a country of external pomp and ubiquitous poverty. Italian society had become rigidly hierarchical and passively conformist, concerned to uphold a static social order. Its more fortunate members had withdrawn into the pursuit of family fortune and honour, if necessary by employment of 'honest dissimulation', to quote the title of a successful Italian pamphlet of 1641. But it was also a society, as the Scottish traveller Gilbert Burnet noted in 1685, 'full of beggars'.*

* *Some letters containing an account of what seemed most remarkable in travelling through Switzerland, Italy, some parts of Germany . . ., Rotterdam, 1687, p. 90.*

Part 1

The re-emergence
of Italy 1700–60

But to leave these futile lamentations and sorrowful memories, let us rather give our thanks to the divine mercy, that this year has caused the fury of rulers to cease and by their withdrawal from the states they have had to cede has restored tranquillity and cheer to so many kingdoms and principates enveloped in the calamities of war for seven years. This peace must be judged the more memorable not only because it has spread throughout all Europe, but because it has been accompanied by universal peace throughout the earth; for in these times no other war of significance has been heard of in the other parts of the world; and thus we have no reason to envy the times of Augustus. . . . But besides the thanks we owe to the supreme Author of all good, it also behoves us to send to His throne our humble prayers that the great good of peace restored to us be not a gift of a few days, and that the potentates of Europe finally sacrifice their resentments, and likewise machinations of ever restless ambition, to the repose of poor peoples, who after so many calamities are beginning to breathe. While peace reigns in Italy, what can we not hope for, since we have princes of such good will and rectitude? (Muratori, 26, t.XII)

To Lodovico Antonio Muratori, seventy-seven years old, the peace of Aix-la-Chapelle in 1748 brought an overwhelming sense of relief and a glimmer of hope – relief that the savage futility of warfare was finally at an end, hope that the rulers of Europe, on whose decisions Italy's fate rested, would at last leave her in peace, and that Italy's princes would lead their 'poor peoples' towards a brighter future. Muratori's long life had witnessed the changes which had marked Italy's slow emergence from a state of impotence and isolation to an awareness of the backwardness of the Italian 'nations' in the general advance of European civilization, to a belief in the possibility of renewed contact and integration with Europe.

This provincial abbé, of cosmopolitan curiosity and erudition, was born in 1672, a moment when Italy's 'decadence' seemed to have touched its lowest point, when Spanish rule and influence had penetrated the entire peninsula, when industrial and commercial activities had been eclipsed by the significant advances of the English, Dutch and French, when social relations had crystallized into a rigid, formal mould, symbolized by the Spanish etiquette adopted in all the local courts, manifest in the search of nobles and non-nobles for the security and prestige of landed possessions; a moment when intellectual and cultural enquiry seemed to have lost its vitality under the deadweight of the scholastic, casuistic, fossilized humanistic education inculcated by the Jesuits, when the princes, descendants of the more fortunate and successful *signori*, strove to create absolutist structures of government and the republican oligarchies withdrew into an affirmation of their privileges.

By the time of Muratori's death in 1750, the political, economic and intellectual world of the Italians – though less so the pattern and relationships of Italian society – had undergone deep transformations. These were changes which emerged concurrently with, and were at least partially dependent upon, the renewed contact with Europe; and they gave rise to that belief in the possibility and effectiveness of rapid social change within a basically static structure which was to lie at the centre of the preoccupations of the generation of reformers and intellectuals who followed Muratori. But this world of the reformers of the later eighteenth century, imbued with an optimism generated and sustained by the very diffusion and apparent reception of their own convictions, was different from that in which Muratori had worked and hoped in isolation, almost alone. How this world came about, how Italy emerged from its prolonged isolation to observe a Europe which bore little resemblance to the Europe of 'barbarians' described by its humanist writers, are the first and most immediate questions that require explanation. For it was the interactions of this new European influence with the legacies of Italy's 'Spanish' past that were to mark the course of the eighteenth century.

I

Italy, the 'pawn' of European diplomacy

The search for a new equilibrium

Italy was thrown into brutal and violent contact with Europe by the break-up of the Spanish empire. Only once, during the previous century and a half, had Italian soil offered the battlefield for European warfare – during the Thirty Years' War – and even then fighting, however savage, had been restricted to the northern plain. Spain had acted as a shield between Italy and Europe, by its direct rule of Lombardy, Naples, Sicily, Sardinia, the Tuscan garrison of the Presidi, and by its effective control of the political activities of the other Italian states.

With the death of Charles II of Spain (1700), Italy once more attracted the attention of European diplomacy as a crucial element in the overall balance of power. For both Habsburg and Bourbon the possession of Italy offered a dominant position in the Mediterranean. Half a century of wars was needed before a stable equilibrium was reached, an equilibrium based on the relegation of Italy to the periphery of European power politics, and on the achievement of a local balance of power within the peninsula through the exclusion of the direct rule of any of the great powers. During this half-century, and indeed after the peace of Aix-la-Chapelle (1748), Italy was conceived of, not as a collection of separate states, but as a single piece on the chess-board of European international diplomacy. But this piece, especially after 1748, was regarded as of no more significance than a pawn. Although Italy continued to represent an 'object' of European diplomacy, it remained, until the new conflicts aroused by the French Revolution, an object of minor importance.

How these transformations and diminution of Italy's international importance came about needs to be explained in terms of the political ambitions of the great European powers, not in those of the almost uniformly insignificant hopes, intrigues and activities of the Italian rulers. It was the extension of the struggle of the great powers to their colonial possessions outside Europe, the revival of Austria and the rise of Russia, and the new threat to the equilibrium represented by Frederick II of Prussia, that shifted the battlefield away from the Mediterranean and Italy. But during these long and bloody decades the desire for peace grew stronger among Italians, and was accompanied by a recognition by Italy's princes and ruling classes of the peninsula's insignificance in the world of power politics. Italy became neutral in 1748 because the great powers so decreed. But it was Italy's rulers who ensured that its neutrality was maintained.

The struggle over the fate of the Spanish empire in the opening years of the eighteenth century had witnessed the alignment of the Bourbons of France and Spain against the Habsburgs of Austria allied to Britain and the United Provinces. The underlying purpose of the struggle was to maintain the balance of power by a territorial distribution among the two rival dynasties which would avoid the threat of predominance over Europe by either. It was to achieve this end that Britain, the major naval power, firmly installed in the Mediterranean through the conquest of Gibraltar and Minorca, ensured the strengthening of the house of Savoy by its acquisition of the former Lombard provinces of the Alessandrino and of the kingdom of Sicily. For this stronger Savoy was to act as a counterbalance to the extension of Austrian power with the imperial possession of Lombardy, Mantua, Naples and Sardinia (treaty of Utrecht, 1713). The three wars which followed – in 1718–19, 1733–6 and 1740–8 – centred wholly or partly on Italy because of the traditional rivalry of Habsburgs and Bourbons. But the roles of the two dynasties were now reversed: it was Bourbon Spanish and French hostility to the Austrian occupation of Italy that maintained the tension and led to hostilities.

Austrian policy was divided between concern for its possessions in Germany, Hungary and the Balkans and hopes of its new Italian lands. The major impulse towards an active Italian policy came from the Spanish exiles at Vienna – the 'Catalans', who had followed Charles VI (1711–40) when he abandoned Spain – and above all from the victorious and powerful general and statesman, prince Eugene of Savoy (1663–1736). Italy was of more immediate economic importance to the emperor than his possessions in the Netherlands as a market for commercial activities, as the base for a Mediterranean fleet and as a source of taxes. As the Piedmontese diplomat, marquis Ignazio del Borgo, wrote in 1725: 'The provinces of Italy are the Indies of the Court of Vienna. For more than 25 years a good part of the silver of Italy has gone there' (Quazza, 17, p. 30). The years before and after Utrecht witnessed Austria's attempt to consolidate and expand its power in Italy by exploiting its claims as imperial suzerain of fiefs scattered in the territories of the other Italian states. The acquisition of Sicily in exchange for Sardinia in 1720, which was imposed on Victor Amadeus II, left Austria as strong in Italy as had been Spain and gave rise to hopes of power in the Mediterranean.

But Austrian influence in Italy was constantly undermined by the Bourbon threat and by the inefficiency of its government in the early years. Initially welcomed by large sectors of the ruling classes in the former Spanish provinces, as well as by heterogeneous groups in the other Italian states, who looked to the emperor as the natural and traditional leader of the struggle against the world of the counter-reformation, almost the personification of what was anachronistically regarded as the 'ghibelline'* cause (Venturi, 30, p. 18), Charles VI and his representatives failed to live up to expectations. The corruption of the 'Catalans', the exaction of heavy taxes, the lack of resoluteness in the struggle against the papacy in southern Italy, led increasingly to abandonment of the imperial cause, even to nostalgia for Spanish rule. Austria never managed to consolidate its power in the kingdoms of Naples and Sicily. Only in the duchy of Milan did the ruling classes remain firmly tied in allegiance to Vienna, not least because of their fear of conquest by the enemy at Turin, who had already annexed the duchy's western provinces.

The basic cause of the insecurity and apparent fragility of Austrian rule was the Spanish challenge. The close ties between the Italian and Iberian peninsulas had not been snapped by Utrecht. Too many Spaniards owned lands in Naples and Sicily. Too many Italians still served as Spanish diplomats, too many nobles, merchants, craftsmen, bureaucrats, and soldiers had emigrated to Spain in the previous century. Philip V's second wife was a Farnese; her chief minister, cardinal Giulio Alberoni (1664–1752), aimed to oust the Habsburgs and ensure the return of Spain. Alberoni's 'plan' was more than a mere return to the past. It was an unusual mixture of old and new. It picked up the theme – so frequently voiced by seventeenth-century publicists – of freeing Italy from the foreigner; it offered one more scheme to upset the local balance of power in favour of a single Italian dynasty. But at the same time it proposed a novel solution: that Italian states, when ruled by foreign princes, should not thereby revert to the status of provinces of the major European powers, but should remain autonomous. Spanish power was to be used to evict the Habsburgs from Italy. But the

---

* The term 'ghibelline' was a conscious re-evocation of the medieval struggles between supporters of the emperor (ghibellines) and those of the pope (guelphs). The words lost their original meaning almost as soon as they became current, and were used to describe or legitimize a multitude of factional, family or personal feuds before falling into disuse during the long period of Spanish and counter-reformation dominance. The revival of the term 'ghibelline' (to which the antiquarian studies of these years perhaps contributed) – as even more the diffuse usage of 'guelphism' a century later in the romantic and historicist environment of the post-Napoleonic period – throw an interesting side-light on the difficulties experienced by the Italian intellectual class in freeing itself of the heavy burden of Italy's past.

vacuum would not be filled by a simple restoration of Spanish power. For the new prince, don Carlos, son of Philip V (1683–1746) and Elizabeth Farnese (1692–1766), would rule over the Habsburg Italian possessions independently of Spain; the throne at Madrid would descend from Philip V to his eldest son, Carlos' half-brother Ferdinand. A new and powerful Bourbon-Farnese dynasty, closely linked to the Farnese of Parma (whose state would be enlarged) would control Italy.

Alberoni's plan survived the failure of the Spanish invasion of Italy in 1718 and the cardinal's own fall the following year, to remain as the dominant theme of Italian and Mediterranean politics until Aix-la-Chapelle. The birth of a second son to Elizabeth and Philip, don Philip, merely led to the extension of Alberoni's plan, with the proposal to create two Italian states rather than one for Elizabeth's children. If the states could not be created at Habsburg expense, the imminent extinction of two of the old Renaissance dynasties – the Farnese of Parma and the Medici of Tuscany – offered a timely alternative solution. The complex modifications of Italy's political geography in these decades reflected Elizabeth Farnese's determination – reluctantly accepted by the other great powers – to instal her two sons on Italian thrones. It would be anachronistic to ascribe 'patriotic' motivations to Alberoni's plan. The cardinal conceived it in terms of the dynastic juggling of the age. It offered a solution which requited the ambitions of both the Spanish Bourbons and the Farnesi. Even if Elizabeth's children, don Carlos and don Philip, ruled autonomous states in Italy, they were expected to remain – and for many years did remain – diplomatically, financially and militarily dependent on Spain. The relative independence and neutrality which ultimately characterized the new Italian dynasties was unforeseen and unexpected.

The initial short war upon which Alberoni embarked in 1717 only gained a promise from the Quadruple Alliance (Britain, France, Austria and the United Provinces) that don Carlos would inherit the states of Tuscany and Parma, which he would hold as imperial fiefs (1720). The following decade of continuous tension culminated in 1731 in the guarantee of this pledge by the introduction of Spanish troops into the fortresses of Tuscany and Parma. But the War of the Polish Succession (1733–8), in which French, Spanish and Piedmontese armies attacked the Habsburgs successfully in Italy, brought a new territorial arrangement: don Carlos received Naples and Sicily (he was King of the Two Sicilies from 1735 to 1759, and then King of Spain from 1759 to 1788), the Austrians were compensated with the duchy of Parma; Tuscany was to be given to Francis, duke of Lorraine, in exchange for his own state, ceded to the unsuccessful candidate for the Polish throne, Stanislas Leszczynski, with the promise of Lorraine's reversion to France on his death (1766). The War of the Austrian Succession, which lasted for eight bitter years (1740–8), led to only one further change:

the assignment of Parma to don Philip (1745–65). In 1748 the eighty-eight-year-old Alberoni triumphed, thirty years after he had first put forward his plan.

These decades witnessed a diminution of Britain's direct involvement in the Mediterranean. Italy's importance for British commercial activities had increased rapidly in the course of the seventeenth century. The control of trade with Leghorn, Genoa, Naples, Messina and Venice was fought over by the Levant Company and the Merchant Adventurers. Imports from Italy between 1717 and 1740 averaged about £500 000 annually, or nearly 10 per cent of all British imports. Strategically, Italy was of great significance for the British fleet. It was for this reason that Britain had assigned Sicily to the ruler of a small, almost land-locked state, the duchy of Piedmont-Savoy, which was bound to England as an export market for its silk produce, and wholly dependent on the British fleet: in 1713 the new king and his retinue were transported to the island kingdom on English ships.

British political intervention in Italian affairs was a response to Habsburg-Bourbon rivalry. Alberoni's adventure, while confirming British naval supremacy (Admiral Byng destroyed the Spanish fleet off Cape Passero in 1718), also led to the sacrifice of Victor Amadeus II (1675–1730) and acceptance of the Habsburg possession of Sicily in exchange for Sardinia (1720). British policy, especially under Walpole's leadership, remained tied to the traditional alliance with Austria and the United Provinces. But the advantages of a Bourbon counterweight to the Habsburgs, in the form of don Carlos, were not to be underestimated. Thus Britain was involved in Italy because of its concern for the European balance of power. As Victor Amadeus II wrote in 1729, 'to dominate Italy has been the aim both of the Emperor and Spain . . . as experience has taught that domination in Italy goes far towards upsetting the universal balance of power' (Quazza, 17, p. 136). Savoy was to be strengthened in order to check the French advance in the Mediterranean; don Carlos was to be supported as a balance to both Savoy and Habsburg Italy. Britain dominated the search for a secure solution to the Italian problem until the early 1730s, when Walpole's parliamentary difficulties enabled Fleury to seize the initiative with the Franco-Savoyard and Franco-Spanish treaties (1733). Even in the following years Britain remained deeply involved, attempting to mediate in the Polish Succession War, preventing don Carlos from attacking the Austrians in north Italy in 1742 by a threat to bombard Naples. But British interests were turning elsewhere, to Germany and, supremely, towards the colonies. The equilibrium finally achieved at Aix-la-Chapelle could hardly have proved more satisfactory for British interests.

For the French the 1748 treaty did not mark so decisive a dividing line. French influence in Italy was still to be pursued, but by the more peaceful and personal methods of marriage ties and family pacts. Even before

Aix-la-Chapelle, French concern with Italy had changed in tone. It is a matter of historical dispute whether Louis XIV – in accepting the inheritance of Charles II of Spain for his grandson – was aiming at a Bourbon hegemony of Europe, such as the earlier Habsburg union of the Spanish and Austrian empires under Charles V had seemed to threaten. But the Spanish Succession War that resulted had involved Bourbon France (whether for itself or on behalf of Bourbon Spain) in its last serious attempt as a dynasty to dominate Italy. In the two subsequent wars intervention in Italy played a subordinate part in a broader plan in which French strength and influence on the Rhine and in central Europe was regarded as of greater significance. It was in this context that the marquis d'Argenson put forward his famous plan in 1745 for a federation of independent Italian states, a 'Republic or eternal association of Italic powers, like the German, Batavic and Helvetic ones' (Quazza, in 4, vol. 2, pp. 845–6). The plan expressed an acceptance of what, by now, was strikingly clear – the futility of continuing the struggle for mastery of Italy and hence the need to achieve a permanent equilibrium outside foreign control.

Italy, 'that apple of discord, that for so long has kept wars going almost continuously' (in the words of a Savoyard diplomat, marquis d'Arvilliers) was being pushed towards the periphery of European politics (Quazza, 17, p. 157). Strategically and, even more, commercially, the peninsula retained its importance. The great powers were determined to maintain their influence – but by diplomacy and intrigue, not by war. Thus, at moments of crisis, pressure was brought to bear on the Italian princes. The princes responded with increasing reluctance. As awareness of their political impotence grew deeper, their desire for neutrality became stronger.

The Italian states

The wars had marked Italy deeply. The end of Spanish rule had aroused new hopes and expectations, and at the same time had revived memories of the past, of the glories of long-past communal independence. There was thus a search for a new political solution, but also a retreat into traditional structures. The wave of 'ghibellinism' which emerged in Italy in the years after Utrecht typically combined this anxious probing into the future with a resurrection of the past. But Charles VI betrayed these anti-curial forces and, in a desperate effort to guarantee his daughter Maria Theresa's succession to his throne, compromised with those Italian supporters regarded as his natural enemies. Yet, in these opening decades of the eighteenth century, were these 'enemies' any more substantial than the 'ghibellinism' of the emperor himself? Or were the one and the other mere wraiths from the past? The papal curia, even France, no longer represented immediate and total threats to the survival of the Italian states.

By the 1730s these early hopes had been shattered. Economically, after the apparent revival of the 1720s, Italy may have experienced a brief slowing down, curiously out of phase with general European trends. Intellectually, the spirit of enquiry, the political passions of a Muratori, a Giannone, which had emerged in the years of the collapse of Spanish rule, gave way to feelings of disillusion and disenchantment, to withdrawal into erudition or Jansenist asceticism. Politically, the Bourbon-Farnese adventure acted as a catalyst for the composite, heterogeneous forces which arose for a variety of reasons in reaction to Vienna – in vindication of their local privileges, in traditional assertion of their anti-imperial spirit, or in equally traditional defence against the threat of a single foreign ruler.

For a while there were those who hoped that an Italian prince – the king of Sardinia, Charles Emanuel III (1730–73), or don Carlos, now king of Naples and Sicily – might gain control of all Italy and free it of the foreigner. But these were voices from the past, faint echoes of Machiavelli, soon silenced by the thunder of cannon and shrieks of war reverberating through an Italy that knew little and cared less about the reasons for this new descent of barbarian armies. 'A dance of destruction' was the Udine nuncio Tartagna's description of the siege of Mantua in 1734 (Battistella, 18, p. 1422). An attempt at Rome by Spanish agents to conscript troops for the war led to popular riots that shook the authority of Clement XII. By the time the even remoter Austrian Succession War savaged Italy, the feeling of weariness and scepticism had become widespread. 'Among the ideas that sometimes pass through our head, we have also thought of composing a treatise, *Of martyrdom by neutrality*', said Benedict XIV with bitter resignation, as he tried to organize charity for his subjects in the Romagne and Marches, whose lands had been ravaged by the Spanish and Austrian armies (Venturi, 30, p. 105). As in the previous war, desertions from all armies were continuous. A new standard was set in 1742 when Charles Bourbon's Neapolitan army – consisting in good part of Austrian soldiers captured at the battle of Bitonto in 1734 – was ordered to march northwards against the Austrians, but dissolved and vanished *en route*. By the latter years of the war, weariness and scepticism began to give way to popular resistance. Already in 1742 the Garfagnana peasants in central Italy had blocked attempts by the Bourbon 'Franco-Spaniards' to build a road across their mountains. In 1744 the peasants of the Cuneese mountain valleys in Piedmont launched into a real 'guerilla' war, harassing the Franco-Spanish army, killing the enemy officers they captured. At the end of 1746 it was the turn of the Genoese populace, rising in mass against the shameful surrender of their city to the Austrians and defending their liberty in alliance with the peasants of the surrounding mountains. The people – 'the poor peoples condemned to do penance for the lofty plans of their sovereign' (Muratori, 26, t.x ii, p. 277) – were tired of war.

This weariness, this sense of the futility of the wars, took the form of a search for protection against disaster in local and traditional structures. In Tuscany the very territorial unity of the state, which had been consolidated with such effort in the previous two centuries, seemed about to break down as the Medici dynasty drew to its end. The old communes, Florence, Siena, Pisa, reasserted their claims and revived their ancient rivalries. In Genoa, the rising against the Austrians momentarily rekindled the flame of the old popular administration: the demand was voiced for the reform of the 1576 law which had consolidated the power of the oligarchy, and the pre-oligarchical Assembly of the People was revived. Elsewhere, in Lombardy and Naples, the nobles confirmed and asserted their local aristocratic privileges. Throughout Italy there was a withdrawal into the traditional structures of the city, the region, the petty state, in a desperate attempt to avoid the destruction of war and the changes imposed by foreign powers.

Not all states were successful. Few emerged unscathed. The old seigneurial and Renaissance dynasties, the descendants of the tyrants who had seized power between the thirteenth and fifteenth centuries, suffered most, for, by chance, they were reaching the end of their successions. The destiny of their states depended on their relations with the Bourbon and Habsburg dynasties. Cosimo III de' Medici (1670–1723) could only protest against the arbitrary assignation of his state to a foreign prince, 'which was just not decent with regard to our quality and the gratitude we owe our subjects' (Quazza, 17, p. 96). On the death of his degenerate heir Giangastone in 1737 the grand-duchy of Tuscany passed to Francis of Lorraine (1737–65), future husband of Maria Theresa. It was this marriage and the arrangement by which Lorraine was to revert to France that kept Habsburg and Bourbon armies off Tuscan soil in the Austrian Succession War. Francesco Maria Farnese (1694–1727), duke of Parma and Piacenza, could only look to his niece Elizabeth and Bourbon Spain for salvation. On the death of the last Farnese, his brother Antonio (1731), the duchy paid the price for its weakness: assigned to don Carlos in 1732, it was dismembered in the Polish Succession War, then to be annexed (with Piacenza) by Austria in 1738, only recovering its independence under the rule of don Philip in 1748. The Este dynasty of Modena survived with difficulty, and primarily through its close ties with Vienna. With the duchy occupied by the French from 1733 to 1736, the dynasty risked its existence in 1737 on the death of duke Rinaldo: his son Francis III (1737–80), who was far away fighting the Turks in Hungary, was only able to return through Habsburg benevolence. This was no empty risk – only twenty years earlier the Gonzaga of Mantua had lost their duchy to the Habsburgs because of their opposition to the emperor. As the marquis d'Argenson commented, 'The petty tyrants of Italy have become the prey of the great ones. Shameful image among men of what occurs among ferocious animals' (Venturi, 30, p. 5).

Nor were the larger states immune from danger. The republic of Genoa, tied financially to Spain, paid the price of its imprudent intervention in the Austrian Succession War – an intervention provoked by the threat of the Piedmontese acquisition of Finale, which would have cut its territories in two – by the surrender of the city in 1746. Genoa emerged territorially intact from the wars, but with the prestige of its oligarchy weakened, its finances imperilled, its authority eroded by the recurrent Corsican rebellions. The republic was to survive the century, but under the protection of Bourbon France, to which it ceded Corsica in 1768.

The republic of Venice maintained its traditional neutrality with apparent success. The succession wars, though costly, left its territories relatively unravaged. Its success was admired by the other states. But Venetian neutrality was hardly a free choice. Economically weak, incapable of supporting a large army, the Serenissima had been hemmed in since Utrecht by Austrian possessions. The Habsburg advance in the Balkans had deprived the republic of the commercial hinterland of Venetian Dalmatia; Trieste and Fiume were being developed as rival ports; Austrian Lombardy and Mantua pressed against the Venetian frontiers and threatened the transit trade along the Po. Venice lived on, comforted by the myth of its divine right to survival. But it survived helpless, in the claws of a grasping Austria.

The papacy's divine right to survival was even better attested. Its helplessness was as evident. Clement XII (1730–40) in 1736, like Clement XI (1700–21) in 1720, had launched an appeal for an Italian league to settle the peninsula's fate without the foreigner: 'to make us capable of supporting each other and freeing us from the outrages that foreign nations inflict on poor Italians, always vulnerable to being treated as their enemies' (Quazza, 17, p. 316). The impotence of the papacy rendered the appeals pure rhetoric. Papal territories submitted perforce to the passage of the opposing foreign armies.

The former Spanish provinces were equally helpless. The two islands were awarded as prizes by the great powers in their search for a settlement: Sardinia to Austria and then to Savoy; Sicily to Savoy, to Austria and finally to don Carlos. Naples, which had looked expectantly to the emperor Charles VI, welcomed don Carlos at least as warmly after his victory at Bitonto in 1734. The Neapolitan people had no choice. They could only hope for a king who would show concern for his kingdom and its inhabitants. The kingdom of Naples experienced the discomfort of enemy armies in both the succession wars. But the damage and devastation it suffered from the wars was insignificant compared to that endured by Lombardy. This duchy was of crucial importance to Vienna, for both economic and strategic reasons. It was the one Italian province neither Charles VI nor Maria Theresa (1740–80) were prepared to cede. Its misfortune was that it was regarded by the dukes of Savoy as the natural and traditional area of expansion. It offered, in consequence, the major battlefield for the succession wars in Italy, and suffered the loss to Savoy of some of its most fertile provinces as the price of these wars: in 1706 the Alessandrino, the Lomellina and part of the Novarese; in 1737 the Tortonese and the remainder of the Novarese; in 1748 the Vigevanasco, the Oltrepò pavese and the Val d'Ossola. By Aix-la-Chapelle, the Lombards had seen their state thrice mutilated, found themselves cut off from their traditional communications with the Mediterranean, and had been reinforced in their mistrust and hatred of Savoy.

The duchy of Piedmont-Savoy, alone among the Italian states, had acted with a certain autonomy during the wars and had emerged from them, as the kingdom of Sardinia, considerably increased in territory and prestige. The strength of its rulers lay primarily in the geographical location of their states, straddling the Alps, which made Savoyard support essential to Habsburg or Bourbon for a successful campaign in Italy. Victor Amadeus II had exploited this position in the Spanish Succession War with audacity and conviction. His son, Charles Emanuel III, attempted to continue the same policy, but showed far less ability or finesse. In terms of European politics, Piedmont-Savoy was only of importance at moments of direct confrontation between France and Austria. At all other times – like the other Italian states – it could only accept the decisions of the major powers. Victor Amedeus had been obliged to recognize this in 1720 with the enforced exchange of Sicily for Sardinia and the introduction into Italy of the new and potentially powerful rival dynasty of the Bourbon-Farnese by his protector Britain. Charles Emanuel found himself in the same helpless position with the Franco-Austrian agreements of 1735 and 1756. As the Neapolitan representative at Vienna, Di Majo, noted with a certain satisfaction on the latter occasion, 'accustomed to fish in troubled waters, the Sardinian king must sit on this occasion silent spectator of what others do' (Valsecchi, 19, p. 201).

It was as much the impotence of Turin, caught between the pincers of Paris and Vienna, as the geographical shift in interest of the great powers, which spared Italy the bloodshed of the Seven Years' War (1756–63): by then, suspicion of the ambitions of the Sardinian rulers had set deep in Italy, suspicion mingled with awareness of Charles Emanuel's weakness. It can be seen even in the popular poems which circulated in Lombardy at the time of his temporary and unsuccessful conquest of Milan (1734):

The glories of the king of Sardinia – with the replies

Already Insubria* lies in my power	*Don't we know it.*
And the gates of Milan have been broken down	*Milan threw them open.*
Caesar has lost the laurels of his crown	*Well, he jacked them in.*
He'll be Duke no longer in Milan	*Oh yes, he will.*

* 'Insubria' was the Roman term for modern Lombardy.

He'll never put foot to ground there again	*He'll be back.*
I am King and shall never leave this place	*There'll come a day.*
No one shall chase me out of here	*What about Mercy?**
Whom should I fear? There's Marshall Villars	*He's about off.*
The world indicts me. But where was I wanting?	*Double-faced.*
I was sincere. Won't they say that?	*Not on your nelly.*
Whatever they say, I rule here still	*Rule what?*
France will always stand my friend	*Couldn't say.*
Firmly and lastingly I keep my throne	*Oh dear!*
I am and will be King of all Lombards	*Hope not.*

(Battistella, 18, p. 1417)

Peace and political impotence

The treaty of Aix-la-Chapelle marked a decisive moment in Italian history. It led to almost 50 years of peace. Initially its stability was doubted by both Italians and foreigners. Would the peace offer more than yet another temporary truce to Bourbon attempts to oust the Habsburgs from Italy? The ambitions of the house of Savoy, the strength of the new Bourbon dynasty of Naples, the uncertainty over the destiny of the duchy of Parma pointed to the likelihood of a revival of the conflict. Already in April 1749 negotiations for a treaty between Piedmont and Prussia seemed to threaten Italy with involvement in any renewal of the European struggle.

Yet within a short span of years the conviction had grown that Italy had finally reached a state of equilibrium which would enable its rulers to conserve their neutrality. A balance of power had been achieved within the peninsula between the three major states of Lombardy, Sardinia and Naples. The mutual suspicions of the princes and their individual ambitions had inhibited all attempts at an Italian federation. The effect of the wars, in fact, had been to crystallize the political situation, to drive the ruling groups into a search for salvation in their traditional, local divisions. The Italy which was finally emerging was to be an Italy of different 'nations', Tuscans, Genoese and Lombards, as much as Neapolitans, Sicilians or Venetians. This composite Italy, of the many independent states and cities, each searching for its own 'liberty', emerges clearly in the judgement of the Tuscan chronicler Giuseppe Maria Mecatti on the Genoese revolt of 1746. He acclaimed

> the illustrious glories of the Genoese people, when rising above every other Italian nation they shook off that unworthy yoke of servitude that others wished to place upon their neck and that they had never been accustomed to bear;

* Mercy was the name of the Austrian commander.

when with their industry and valour they freed themselves of the outsider's oppression and resumed their prior freedom, so displaying that the ancient valour of Italians was far from spent. (Venturi, 30, p. 64)

The peoples of Italy, as much as their rulers, were tired of the senselessness of the wars, and wanted peace and the liberty of their states. Recognition of this new situation was symbolized already in 1750–1 by the readiness of the Piedmontese and Lombard governments to settle their frontier disputes peaceably and facilitate trade.

The major threat to this stability and peace was represented by the close family ties of Bourbons and Habsburgs with so many of the Italian dynasties. It was true that the major powers had decided that Italy should remain at peace. In 1752 Vienna and Madrid confirmed – and obliged Turin to agree – that Italian crowns should remain separate from those of other states. In 1756 the famous 'diplomatic revolution', which witnessed the alliance of the traditional enemies at Paris and Vienna offered a further reassurance. In 1759, when Charles of Naples succeeded to the Spanish throne, it was the agreement between France, Austria and Spain, supported by Britain, which ensured the maintenance of the status quo, by blocking the accession to the Neapolitan throne of Charles' brother, Philip of Parma.

But these same powers attempted to maintain their influence in Italy by exerting pressure on what they regarded as dependent dynasties. Charles Bourbon was only seventeen years old when his Spanish army won him the kingdom of the Two Sicilies in 1734. Until the death of his father Philip V in 1746 Neapolitan foreign policy was controlled by Spain. Even after Aix-la-Chapelle Charles and his brother Philip remained dependent on their half-brother Ferdinand VI (1746–59) at Madrid for their army, their finances, even their diplomats. Tuscany, in Habsburg eyes, was regarded in similar manner as a province. Its new ruler Francis, Maria Theresa's husband, only visited his grand-duchy once; half the Regency council consisted of foreigners from his former duchy of Lorraine, while ultimate authority was exercised by a Council at Vienna. In the Seven Years' War Tuscany was obliged to offer financial and military assistance to the empress.

This subordination was increasingly resisted by the new rulers. After Philip V's death, Charles of Naples' main concern was to conserve his kingdom for his own heirs, independent of Spain. As his own succession to the Spanish throne became more probable, he fought against the 1748 agreement which promised Naples to his brother Philip and in his search for autonomy turned to Britain, even to Austria. Tuscany's evolution was similar: on his accession to the grand-duchy, Peter Leopold (1675–90), Maria Theresa's son, dismissed his foreign ministers. The desire for autonomy, for the independence of the small Italian states, was strong.

But the pressure of dynastic ties weighed heavily on the rulers and their ministers. When Charles left Naples for his new kingdom of Spain in 1759, he seemed to be oblivious of his previous policy of autonomy and tried to make Naples join the Bourbon family pact. Bernardo Tanucci, Charles' minister who had fought for the emancipation of the Neapolitan kingdom, resisted: 'France is Bourbon, but Spain is also Bourbon, and the Sicilies are Bourbon too. France has its interests, but so has Spain, so have the Sicilies. This Holy Office of Bourbonism must be extinguished' (Valsecchi, 19, p. 258). Despite Tanucci's hostility, the Bourbon sense of family obligation remained strong: when the papacy attempted to make Parma revoke its anti-ecclesiastical measures in 1768, family solidarity emerged with the French and Neapolitan occupations of the papal territories of Avignon and Benevento and a collective demand by the Bourbon sovereigns that the pope withdraw his decree. Habsburg family ties did not differ. In the 1760s Maria Theresa attempted to extend Habsburg influence by a series of marriage alliances. In 1768 her daughter Maria Carolina married Ferdinand IV of Naples (1759–1825); in 1769 another daughter, Maria Amalia, married Ferdinand of Parma (1765–1802); in 1771 her son Ferdinand (1790–1801) married Beatrice of Modena. As a Venetian diplomat commented: 'hunting royal spouses – for her eight daughters and four sons – she pushes forward in every court, and through such kinship arranges her future claims to interfere' (Valsecchi, 19, p. 258).

Yet, despite these pressures, the Italian states remained independent and neutral. The power of foreign ministers was resented: in Bourbon Parma the reforms of Du Tillot were opposed not least because of the French nationality of their exponent; in earlier years, Richecourt's reforms in Tuscany had met with similar opposition. Ultimately the very clash of influence between Madrid, Paris and Vienna enabled the Italian states to assert their autonomy. The resentment against foreign interference, the determination to remain on the periphery of European politics, reflected a recognition by both rulers and local ruling classes of Italy's weakness, but also of its independence. For the first time in centuries, only two Italian states remained under foreign rule – Lombardy and Mantua. It was the consciousness of this independence that underlay the distress of the new political class at Genoa's abandonment of Corsica to France. As Tanucci wrote to the young Neapolitan reformer Ferdinando Galiani in 1764, 'that the desperation of the Genoese and Corsicans should call barbarians into Italy is not a good thing today when all Italy has its own princes either designated or ruling' (Valsecchi, 19, p. 226).

Corsica was lost to Italy because of the weakness of the Italian states. But for the rest of Italy this weakness was not necessarily a disadvantage. Thirty years after Tanucci's words, in 1796, a leading Tuscan statesman, Francesco Maria Gianni, could theorize and extol Italy's political divisions, its neutrality, the advantages to be gained from the smallness of its states, in terms which recalled Guicciardini's defence of Italy's lack of unity:

Italy can neither be a kingdom nor an independent national republic, and it would mean trouble for Italy and its neighbours if it became a leading actor in the theatre of European politics. . . . The admired prosperity of Italy is born of the division of its states. . . . The republics or principates of Italy have guaranteed the prosperity of their peoples in their respective areas according to the opportunities offered them by the nature of the localities, but this would not have occurred if all the activities of the small governments and small nations had not been concentrated in small zones of territory. (Venturi, 27, p. 983)

To Guicciardini, the peace of Lodi (1454) marked a significant step in the stabilization of a naturally divided Italy. To Tanucci, Gianni and their contemporaries, the peace of Aix-la-Chapelle played a similar role. But there the likeness ended. For the Italy of the eighteenth century no longer led the world.

By 1748 Italians could already measure how far Italy had moved forward. But the peace they now enjoyed only made them more aware of how far the Italian states had fallen behind the civilized world and the magnitude of the problems that awaited resolution. In the years that followed Italy's ties with Europe were to prove of increasing significance. Politically, as the wars of succession had shown, they were ties of dependence. Economically, the prosperity of the Italian states was seen to be closely linked to the European market. Intellectually, the reformers felt the need to learn from and participate in the cosmopolitan circulation of ideas which radiated outwards from France. Italy had re-emerged. There was a general belief that, to progress, it now needed to strengthen its contact with Europe.

2

The social physiognomy
of the Italian states

The countryside and landed power

The Italy which emerged from the long period of Spanish rule had undergone a profound transformation. Economically, its industrial and commercial activities had declined; the population of its cities had long remained stationary or even fallen. Socially, the nobility had grown in
strength and prestige, as the merchants and manufacturers weakened. In
the ecclesiastical sphere, the Church had increased in influence and privileges, although the papacy's political power had declined. Administratively,
the regional states had developed more centralized structures of government, that accentuated the predominance of the capital cities but were chal
lenged by the survival of local institutions and by the growth of aristocratic
and ecclesiastical privileges.

Italy, by the early eighteenth century, had become an overwhelmingly
agrarian society – to a far greater degree than two centuries earlier, or than
the societies of more advanced countries like England or Holland. The
decline of the cities accentuated this agrarian character, but did not lead to
the countryside's emancipation from its servitude to the cities. Indeed, the
increasing difficulties experienced by the cities would seem to have strengthened the bonds by which they controlled the *campagna* (countryside). In
three crucial ways the cities maintained their hold. Firstly, the obligation on
producers to send large quantities of grain to the cities in order to avert the
danger of famine, like the control of grain and other food prices by the
authorities, led to continuous, arbitrary interference with market price
mechanisms. Secondly, the prohibition of the export of grain and of certain
raw materials utilized by city guilds kept prices artificially low. Both these
systems were upheld by complex administrative structures and a multitude
of laws devised to maintain the typically mercantilist principles of low food
prices, artificially sponsored domestic industries, and a strictly controlled
balance of payments. Thirdly, the fiscal systems discriminated against the
countryside. Although direct taxes on land did not provide the major source

of state income (in the kingdom of Naples they only provided one-fifth), consumption taxes and the increasing number of exceptional taxes fell most heavily on the rural communities. The salt excise and poll-tax (*testatico*) were as onerous as the various customs duties. Thus the countryside supported the cities, whose remoteness and authority increased with the development of administrative bureaucracies and the expansion of formalized courts.

Within the countryside the structure of landownership had changed. Ecclesiastical and noble holdings had increased in size and concentration. Ecclesiastical possessions grew steadily with donations to the Church, that varied from small plots to fairly large estates. But although they increased the total areas owned by the Church, they usually did not accentuate the compactness and concentration of ecclesiastical estates, because of the variety of sources from which they were received. Because most land which fell into mortmain, or the 'dead hand' of the Church, acquired a considerable degree of exemption from secular control and was unlikely to be sold again, state authorities attempted to limit or prohibit such donations. The regulations were rarely successful, except for brief periods. Possibly of greater long-term significance was the fact that not all land received in mortmain was lost irrevocably to the landmarket. For many smallholdings were sold, according to the testator's desires, in order to raise the necessary capital to provide an annual income for masses.

Noble landed estates grew more ostentatiously, as the decline of industry and the uncertainties of trade led to an increasing investment of capital in the land, and as the social prestige of the aristocracy induced successful bankers, *fermiers* and lawyers to buy the estates which were regarded as the necessary accompaniment to their newly acquired titles. By the early eighteenth century, formerly successful merchants of such city-states as Florence or Venice were investing their wealth in the acquisition of estates. The vast increase in the landed holdings of the ruling Medici family – caused only partially by the confiscation of the possessions of rebellious rival families – was symptomatic of a far broader trend. In the feudal principates as well, such as Naples or Piedmont, the increase in titles went hand in hand with a growth in aristocratic landownership. In the south, in particular, foreign merchants and bankers – Genoese, Lombards and Venetians – established and expanded their possession of the land, alongside the great papal families and Spanish officers or courtiers.

The total area of land owned by the clergy and nobles in the early eighteenth century, and the degree of its concentration, can be reconstructed for many of the states with reasonable accuracy. There were wide variations within the different regions of each state and between the states. The areas which resisted noble and ecclesiastical penetration most effectively were, naturally, the least fertile mountainous zones along the Alpine arc and in the

Apennines. In the hills, although smallholdings characterized the system of cultivation, ownership of the land by the privileged classes was expanding, in Piedmont, Lombardy and Venetia as much as in Tuscany, the Papal Legations and the kingdom of Naples.

But it was above all in the plains that the Church and the aristocracy asserted their pre-eminence. In Lombardy, in the mid-eighteenth century, the nobility owned 42 per cent of the plateau and 46 per cent of the plain (alongside 49 per cent of the hilly areas), while the Church (including lay religious confraternities and hospitals) owned 21, 22 (and 23) per cent respectively. In the middle and lower Mantovano, the richest plains of the Duchy, the nobility owned 45 per cent and the Church 13 per cent of the land. In Venetia, in 1740, the ruling oligarchy and local nobles owned 55 per cent of the plain and 38 per cent of the hills, while the Church owned 10 and 7 per cent respectively. When considered regionally, these holdings varied considerably – from the 91 per cent of the Vicenza plain owned by nobles to the 42 per cent of the Adria plain. In Piedmont noble and ecclesiastical ownership was less overpowering: probably 10 per cent of all cultivated land was in the hands of the nobility and 15 per cent in those of the Church. No figures are available for Tuscany, but the vast estates of the Medici, Ferroni or Della Gherardesca families, like those of the Order of Santo Stefano, when considered together with the massive landed investments of the former Florentine merchant families, point to the same conclusion. The Tuscan Maremma plain was dominated by large holdings. The Papal States probably contained the greatest concentration of privileged land in Italy: in the Agro Romano 113 families owned 61 per cent of the land, and 64 ecclesiastical institutions a further 37 per cent (1783). In the Legations the position was slightly better. But the nobility owned 70 per cent of the Bolognese plain (1784), while in the Urbino Legation a contemporary lamented about the expansion of ecclesiastical properties in the coastal plain, that 'if they progress, all will be of the priests, and nothing of laymen' (Paci, 180, p. 17, n. 46). In the kingdom of Naples the baronage owned at least 20 per cent of landed income and the Church a further 20 to 30 per cent; in some areas, such as the Basilicata, the proportion of noble landed income rose as high as 42 per cent (1806). The Sicilian barons and prelates did not lag behind their Neapolitan relatives and compeers.

These bare figures reveal the strength of the two privileged classes in the *campagna*. It seems probable that – outside the Papal States – noble landed possessions were growing more continuously and more rapidly than those of the Church. Noble estates also tended to become more concentrated during the eighteenth century by exchanges with or the purchase of private smallholdings, the leasing or usurpation of commonlands, in short, by the conscious pursuit of a policy of consolidation. The size of these estates

varied enormously, from the middling properties of a few hundred hectares*
of the Piedmontese nobles to the vast *latifondi*, extending over thousands of
hectares of the papal or Sicilian aristocrats.

The predominance of these large holdings was accentuated by their concentration in the hands of a diminishing number of families. The example
of the Agro Romano has already been given. But in the duchy of Mantua
only 142 families owned one-third of the entire territory. In the kingdom of
Naples only 15 out of about 1500 titled families owned three-quarters of all
feudal lands, with the Pignatelli family in possession of 72 fiefs. The concentration was assisted in part by the fusion of family properties through
marriage or the natural extinction of collateral branches. But it was accelerated by the legal ties on estates that prohibited their sale (entails or
fedecommessi as they were usually called). Muratori was only voicing widespread concern when he attacked the negative effects of these entails whose
diffusion he dated to the seventeenth century. Noble and ecclesiastical properties thus dominated the countryside, occupying the richest lands.
Mortmain and entails, until the later eighteenth century, inhibited the
acquisition and expansion of middling and large properties by non-nobles.
The countryside tended to be characterized by great estates, alongside
small, often minute peasant and communal holdings. The possession of
middle-size estates was exceptional, although leasing of middle-sized farms
from the great owners was becoming more common in northern and central
Italy by the mid-eighteenth century.

The power of nobles and ecclesiastics was reinforced by their privileges.
These privileges derived from immunities inherited from the feudal past or
from exemptions instituted and enforced by the cities. Traditionally
'feudal' property (i.e. appertaining to a fief) and ecclesiastical lands were
exempt from the land-tax (except in Venetia). Lands owned by citizens in
some states (for example Mantua or Tuscany) originally also enjoyed whole
or partial exemption. But in the absence of accurate measurements of landholdings or cadastral registers listing their taxable value, who was in a
position to prevent these privileges being extended abusively to newly
acquired lands? Certainly not the peasant, nor the rural commune, for lawsuits were too expensive and could drag on for decades. When Victor
Amadeus II completed the first effective land measurement in Italy (the
perequazione) in 1731, one-third of ecclesiastical lands previously claimed as
privileged was regarded as abusively exempt and subjected to taxes; the
total area of similarly abusive feudal land was probably greater.

The fiscal systems further favoured the privileged classes. Those who
worked the land paid heavier taxes than those who owned it. The taxes on
goods of basic consumption, the excise on the sale of salt, the poll-tax on
every adult, the customs duties on manufactures and goods in transit, the

* One hectare equals approximately 2·5 acres.

exceptional taxes which, imposed a first time, tended to be repeated, all favoured the landowners by their method of imposition. In Lombardy in the 1720s the 200 000 people who owned three-quarters of the wealth of the state paid only 6 million lire of the total 21 million raised annually by the state. In Naples, ecclesiastical income was as great or greater than state revenues in the 1720s; it was subjected to a 'voluntary' *donativo* of 4 per cent (authorized by Clement XI and Benedict XIII), but although the tax had thus been approved in principle by the ecclesiastical order and Curia, the clergy resisted.

Possession of land and exemption from taxes or fiscal privileges thus formed the basis of noble and ecclesiastical wealth. It was augmented by the exaction of seigneurial and ecclesiastical rights. The structure of Italy's feudal past survived in countless forms, from the emperor's claims to suzerainty over northern and central Italy and the pope's similar claims over the kingdom of Naples, to the survival of minute independent fiefs which constellated every area of Italy and impeded the attempts to impose centralized, uniform administrative structures. These feudal legacies sometimes offered protection to the peasants, in the form of commonlands or grazing rights, or fixed dues paid for virtually perpetual leases or emphyteuses received by ancestors in previous centuries.

But the feudal past also survived in the form of seigneurial rights exacted from the peasants. Tithes, both feudal and lay, hunting and fishing rights, tolls, monopolies of mills and ovens, civil, even criminal jurisdiction, payments due in kind and money for a multitude of reasons provided the everyday evidence of a past which refused to die. Apart from the tithes, it is doubtful whether the other seigneurial rights yielded much in financial terms in northern and central Italy. Indeed many of them had been sold to the communes. But in southern Italy feudalism ruled triumphant: three-quarters of the fiefs in the kingdom of Naples belonged to the barons. Small wonder an anonymous writer should state in 1733 that ministers were 'quite careful not to offend the nobility, nor the other orders of the city, because of the reflection that viceroys change, but these others stay for ever and, given their inclinations and nature, are capable of a vendetta' (Marini, 89, p. 30). But even in the north there were areas, such as Friuli or the Bresciano, where the feudatories rampaged unchecked. Throughout Italy the survival of these feudal attributes of jurisdictional and seigneurial rights reinforced the noble's economic position and allowed him to dominate the local communes, often even to disregard the state administration. Far from declining, the possession of these rights had been consolidated by the eighteenth century.

In this rural world in which land represented the most prized possession, the exactions and obligations imposed by the dominant cities offered the great owners considerable possibilities of increasing their wealth. It was these proprietors, for the most part, who advanced money to peasants and rural communes when they were unable to meet their commitments. It was these proprietors who speculated on the harvests, storing their grain illegally in order to create an artificial shortage and force up prices. It was these same proprietors who used their influence in the capital to buy the special licences which permitted them to export their surplus. They were both producers and merchants, in Sicily as in Tuscany, in Lombardy as in Venetia. These great proprietors, not surprisingly, tended to support the proposals for freedom of export which emerged in the later eighteenth century. The clergy, especially the absentee prelates, had a further source of income, for they were able to import and export tax free within the law. But this legal concession offered illegal opportunities. As the papal nuncio at Naples wrote with genuine concern in 1713, 'I have written to the Capuchin Provincial and other religious heads, imploring them to observe the proprieties and not to abuse their right to import tobacco at the expense of the royal exchequer and interested parties' (Marini, 89, p. 24, n. 4). The rigidity of control over foreign trade inevitably encouraged smuggling, which remained endemic throughout the eighteenth century. Both poor and rich engaged in this illegal traffic. The poor were usually those who lived near one of the innumerable frontiers. The rich were the great landowners, collaborating – especially in the south – with foreign merchants.

The irresponsibility of these privileged classes was already roundly condemned by the mid-eighteenth century. The ecclesiastics – *abbés*, priors, above all prelates – rarely resided on their lands. They belonged to the same families as the great secular landowners and shared their concerns and outlook. They dominated the official and intellectual life of the Italian states and were attracted by the possibilities of careers at Rome. But their very dominance and riches rendered them peculiarly vulnerable. The disparity between their wealth and the poverty of the parish clergy, strikingly visible in all the Italian states (though to a lesser degree in Piedmont), created a deep division within their own ranks. Moreover, isolated voices in the early eighteenth century began to suggest that ecclesiastical possessions represented a reserve treasury for the state. This was not a new idea. It underlay the claim by state authorities to exact taxes from the clergy in exceptional circumstances. Venice indeed refused to recognize tax exemptions for the clergy. But the concept took on a more menacing form in the eighteenth century. It was voiced most clearly at Naples, where the struggle against ecclesiastical excesses had first emerged. In 1737 an anonymous writer proposed that the king should guarantee the daily requirements of the clergy, 'and as, given such a measure, it will be unnecessary for ecclesiastics to own such rich possessions, Your Majesty can attach them to the patrimony of the crown and employ them in uses that tend towards the general good of your subjects' (Venturi, 30, p. 35).

The Church was thus open to attack. But its influence and penetration of Italian society remained profound. The very number of clerics bears witness to its attraction: over 20 000 priests and religious in Piedmont in the mid-eighteenth century, 40 000 in Venetia, over 10 000 in the duchy of Modena, 11 000 in the kingdom of Naples, perhaps a majority of the 160 000 inhabitants of the city of Rome. The Church offered security, the possibility of a career, at least the advantage of a benefice. Domenico Passionei, member of a provincial noble family and future cardinal, wrote to his father in 1710 to explain why he was entering papal service: 'I hold dearest the interests of our family, and after theirs my own, and then that our posterity remember me. . . . The brightest lad in every family always takes the cloth in order to advance his family with him' (Caracciolo, 85). Muratori, Maffei, Genovesi, Galiani, Metastasio, Parini, Denina: all were *abati*. Even in the later eighteenth century, when the reforming movement to construct a lay state had gathered strength, the attraction of the Church remained strong: from clerical ranks were to emerge many of the revolutionary Jacobins. In the earlier decades of the century criticisms might grow, but ecclesiastical power could not be denied. The last *auto-da-fé* was held at Palermo as late as 1724. It needed the revolution to shift the initiative within the states decisively to the secular authorities.

The power of the nobility was to prove more tenacious. In some of the principates – Mantua, Tuscany, Sicily – the aristocracy had been excluded from public office in the previous century. In the republics Venice, Genoa – public authority was vested in restricted oligarchies, to the exclusion of the provincial or lesser nobility. But in both principates and republics the nobles retained their hold on traditional institutions and local administrations, which they turned into weapons of defence of their own privileges: the Sicilian parliament or the *sedili* of Naples, the Milanese senate or the Mantuan *congregazione*, the town councils or the nominated officials of the Neapolitan fiefs all served the same purpose. The uncertainties that followed the end of Spanish rule had given the aristocracy the chance to consolidate its power in Sicily, Naples, Tuscany, Parma, Lombardy and Mantua. Only in states where there was no discontinuity of political authority – as in Piedmont or Venice – were the pretensions of the nobles contained or even restricted in the early decades of the eighteenth century. The diversity of origins, both feudal and civic, the growth in titles perhaps confused the concept of nobility. In Tuscany Pompeo Neri could write that the nobility could only be identified 'with the class of persons treated at Florence as nobles' (Venturi, 30, p. 329). But its power could hardly be denied.

It was a power which acted as a deadweight against change. The aristocracy's idleness and inertia, its ignorance of and indifference to the public good, were constantly attacked by the reformers. Life at Court and palace building perhaps offers an over-simplified characterization of the principal concerns of the richer Italian nobles in the earlier part of the eighteenth century. Nevertheless, such activities still reflected aristocratic ideals. The Mantuan reformer Giambattista Gherardo d'Arco was convinced that the lack of investment in agriculture, which explained its backwardness, was due to the diversion of resources towards 'expenditure on ostentatious living' (Vivanti, 62, p. 179). The attack on 'luxury', a recurrent motif of the writings of the reformers, was based on this vision of the wasteful expenditure of the nobles. Their absence from their estates, their preference for residence in the cities and attendance at Court was judged equally negatively. As the Tuscan Francesco Maria Gianni wrote:

> When you find small Courts brilliant and full of luxury, judge them to be a weakness of the sovereign, draw the conclusion that the nobility which populates them ruins itself, that the civic spirit is corrupted, that a class of subjects is formed in ignorance of truth and the useful sciences which debases itself by its mannerisms of vain pride and hence of contempt for the other classes, that the administration of justice and government normally takes on a character of partiality insulting to the other classes. Birth and favour take the place of merit and reason. (Anzilotti, 64, p. 148)

Yet in areas where nobles were in possession of real feudal power – in the Bresciano, Bergamasco, Friuli, Papal States or the kingdoms of Naples and Sicily – their presence at Court was preferable to their residence within their fiefs. The limitless extent of landed power in the mid-eighteenth century could be a frightening phenomenon. The abuses that often followed upon such residence are amply described in the words of the Neapolitan Paolo Maria Doria:

> The baron has the power to impoverish and ruin a vassal; keeping him in prison or not allowing the governor or judge of the commune to expedite his case. Through his right of pardon he can murder whom he wishes and pardon the murderer; through the commutation of sentences he fills the land with rogues and assassins. He abuses his power over the possessions as over the honour of vassals. Trade, like matrimony, must submit to his whims. It is impossible to prove a baron guilty. And the government itself, which can sometimes violently repress a weak baron, has nothing but indulgence for the strong. . . . From these abuses it can be seen that some barons are like sovereigns in their lands. (Villani, 94, p. 599)

Systems of tenure and peasant pauperism

Despite the deeply negative aspects of the predominance of ecclesiastics and nobles, it was from some of their estates that the major changes in the rural economy were to develop. The absenteeism of the great landowners led to the emergence of new men who rented and ran their estates. Systems of land tenure varied widely in the different regions. In the Po valley and central

Italy the great estates were often rented in smaller units. The *fattoria*, unique to Tuscany, was an organized administrative unit, comprising several small, usually contiguous *poderi* or farms of less than ten hectares each. Elsewhere in northern and central Italy, the management of the different farms (which varied widely in size, up to fifty hectares) was far less co-ordinated. But throughout these regions, each *cascina* or *podere* was cultivated separately by a peasant family of *coloni* or *mezzadri*. Tenure by *colonìa parziaria* was more characteristic of the Po valley, while *mezzadria* (share-cropping) was predominant in central Italy. The main difference between the two systems was that the *mezzadro* paid his rent in kind, by what was initially an equal division of the crops, but cultivated his land under the more immediate supervision and control of the landlord, while the *colono* paid rent mostly in money and was more independent in the use to which he put the land. But in practice these distinctions diminished in significance during the eighteenth century, as the *colono* who fell into debt found himself under close control.

In the Tuscan Maremma, the Agro Romano and southern Italy, the predominance of *latifondi* signified different systems of land tenure: the characteristics of sheep farming and extensive grain cultivation implied a widespread use of hired labour. The survival of feudal forms of tenure further complicated the agrarian landscape. Commonlands, communal rights of pasturage – the *comunanze* of the Legations – the *usi civici*, which allowed grazing rights even on private feudal arable land after the harvest had been gathered and the collection of wood for burning, acted as obstacles (from the point of view of the landowner) to the possession of full property rights. Age-old forms of customary tenure – emphyteuses, *livelli, terziari*, tithes – which had originated in the long-lease of initially uncultivated land to peasants, now ensured the existence of minute peasant holdings, which impeded the creation of compact estates because of the impossibility or difficulty of redeeming them, not least because of the obligation to indemnify the tenant for past and present improvements to the land. These small feudal plots or wider communal rights existed throughout Italy and in some areas, such as Sicily and Naples, had become more extensive as abandoned land was brought under cultivation in the seventeenth and early eighteenth centuries.

By the mid-eighteenth century the picture began to change. The rapid rise in population in Italy from about 13 to 17 million during the century, in accordance with the general European trend, created a rising demand for food. Even more, the industrial-commercial developments in England, Holland and France from the 1740s created a growing external demand for food products and raw materials. Exports of wheat, oil, wine, citrus fruit and both crude and semi-finished silk, wool and cotton, increased. Internal and external incentives existed to produce more.

These incentives led to profound changes in systems of tenure and to minor improvements in methods of cultivation. Agriculture remained predominantly extensive. Only in the Lombard plain did any intensive cultivation exist, based on mixed farming, with the animals providing manure which gained higher grain yields, as well as the milk for a separate cheese industry. In Tuscany in the seventeenth century a very few wealthy landowners had reclaimed abandoned land. Elsewhere there was little evidence of improvement. From the mid-eighteenth century agricultural production began to increase – but mostly by the extension of the cultivable area – as landowners or their stewards looked to exports. In the south – in Sicily, Naples, the Papal States – this led to the extension of cereal crops and of pasturage. In the Lombard plain, where a capitalist form of agriculture already existed in embryo, there were significant developments which required fairly heavy investments and certain technical improvements. A new agrarian landscape was appearing. Amidst the subsistence farming that still characterized the greater part of Italy, despite the obstacles to trade presented by the pitiful system of communications and the survival of innumerable transit duties, a new commercial agriculture, responsive to the trends of international trade, established itself in areas of most of the Italian states in the later eighteenth century.

This more modern agriculture was based on changes in methods of estate management. Absenteeism of landlords was no new phenomenon, particularly in the south; but it became far more widespread throughout Italy, except probably Tuscany, during the eighteenth century. More significant was the change in the role of the steward. This intermediary, who ran the lord's estates, at first tended to limit his functions to collecting rents and dues without any personal involvement in the methods of cultivation. But, increasingly, these same stewards, or new men who rented entire estates, began to take a more direct interest, to increase the contractual obligations of the sub-tenants, to farm part of the estate directly with day-labourers, to evict peasants from rented smallholdings which impeded the expansion of sheep-farming, to encroach upon and enclose communal lands. The methods varied according to the pre-existing systems and the constraints imposed by the nature of the terrain. In lower Lombardy, large farms based on hired labour, with considerable investment in more modern methods of cultivation, aimed at raising productivity and production. Elsewhere these *fittanzieri*, or large-scale tenants, like the owners who remained on the land, were as much concerned with the trade in agricultural produce as with actual production. 'Country merchants' they were significantly and accurately called in the Agro Romano, where they monopolized the provisioning of the capital. Elsewhere in the south the stewards or *gabelloti* had close ties with foreign merchants and maintained a strong hold on production through these ties. Their power was the greater because they represented one of the few sources of capital – working capital, not capital for investment.

Thus, by the later eighteenth century, the landlords, for the most part, had become absentee rentiers. Only in Tuscany and some areas of Venetia did many of them retain direct contact with their properties. Increasingly, throughout Italy, they were being replaced in the countryside by the more active, ambitious non-noble stewards, *fittanzieri* and *gabelloti*. These stewards, as they increased their wealth, began to buy up land. The legal restrictions on mortmain and entails imposed by the reforming governments facilitated their purchases.

Relatively small numbers of non-noble landowners began to challenge the overwhelming predominance of nobles, whose rising expenditure in the cities would also seem to have led to a crisis of many family patrimonies. These new owners acquired noble and ecclesiastical lands, as much as communal and peasant property. By the eve of the revolution, new groups had arisen, which were economically of significance. Only superficially did they resemble the English tenant farmers of middling-size estates. Their numbers were far smaller. They were more concerned to exploit existing systems of tenure than to invest capital in agricultural improvements (except in the lower Lombard plain). But their attitude, alongside that of the far more powerful class of noble landowners, was to influence the course of many of the reforms and condition their success. For they formed the nucleus of an agrarian middle class, stronger in north and central Italy than in the south, which suffered from and began to fight against the system of privilege and controls, in favour of free circulation of agricultural produce, free exports and greater fiscal equality.

The effect of these transformations was to worsen the living conditions of the vast agricultural population. Until the 1740s the number of smallholdings and leases probably remained relatively stable, and even grew in certain areas of the south, as in the Neapolitan Valle Caudina or in Sicily, with the creation of the new baronial villages. But then the terrible famine of 1764–6 reversed the process; the contractual terms of the *mezzadri* and *coloni* began to deteriorate. The smallholders, often owning only minute plots and forced to lease other land, were faced with the pressure of rising taxes and the reduction or elimination of communal rights. The only real advantage gained by some of these smallholders from rising external demand was the possibility of reeling silk or spinning wool in the winter months. But even these forms of domestic rural industry tended to be restricted to relatively few regions. The absence of any cash reserves upon which to fall back in times of bad harvests, and the ignorance and inability to take advantage of the technical improvements proposed by the landowners' agrarian academies, too often led to a crisis in the family economy which forced the small owners or tenants to join the growing ranks of day-labourers. Angelo Gualandris, secretary of the Mantuan 'Agrarian Colony',

in a fictitious dialogue, offers a convincing picture of the resignation and
scepticism of the peasant smallholder when faced by proposals on how to
improve his land:

> What right have you to talk, Signor Rutilio, you who have never shared our
> life? In my old age, I can testify that my father, my grandfather, all my own
> generation, have worked as hard as possible. If you only understood what
> continuous effort we have put in, how we have tilled the soil according to the
> practices of our fathers, how we have sacrificed every comfort. If it had been
> your misfortune to experience all this, as we have, and still find that things have
> gone from bad to worse, that they have reached the point that one no longer
> knows how to make enough to live on, then in all truth, instead of blaming our
> methods of farming, you would invoke bad luck and hard times! (Vivanti, 62,
> p. 137, n. 20)

The condition of these smallholders and tenants worsened because of the
harsher terms imposed not only by the stewards, but by government fiscal
agents. As the governments began to draw together and lease their multiple
sources of income to groups of *fermiers*, these tax-farmers increased the
efficiency of the fiscal administration by ruthless methods, even reviving
dues which had long since fallen into disuse. The eighteenth century was
marked by a steady growth in the indebtedness of peasants and rural communes. As arrears mounted, the local capitalists – sometimes nobles or
ecclesiastics, more frequently stewards, merchants, lawyers, doctors,
pharmacists, notaries, even inn-keepers – loaned small sums and tightened
their hold. In the kingdom of Naples all agricultural life was dominated by
a system of loans called *contratti alla voce*: in the winter and spring months,
as peasants tried to eke out their dwindling resources by seeking other forms
of employment, the merchants offered them wheat advances to be repaid in
kind at the future harvest; the price of the wheat was only fixed at the
time of the harvest, when prices were often 30 to 40 per cent lower than
when the advance had been received. Ferdinando Galiani who initially
viewed the *contratto alla voce* as a useful instrument of credit, lamented by
1784 that its misuse had led to 'one of the greatest evils ever done to this
kingdom' (Villari, 97, p. 44). In north and central Italy no such system
existed. But most peasants found themselves pledging increasing proportions of their future income to pay interest on their rising debts.

By the later eighteenth century the general increase of the population and
worsening tenurial conditions led to a steady growth in the number of day-
labourers. The famine of 1764–6, which affected all southern and most of
central Italy, had profoundly negative consequences for the peasantry.
Wages throughout Italy remained basically stagnant, while prices rose
steadily. Few labourers could hope to be employed for more than half the
days of the year. Inevitably these casual workers consumed most of their
wages in food. There are numerous examples of employers paying labourers

a part of their wages in food at prices arbitrarily fixed by themselves. These conditions, which worsened considerably in the latter part of the eighteenth century, led to emigration and begging. Labour shortages arose during harvesting, at least in southern Italy. In the kingdom of Naples employers even made cash advances to labourers in the winter months to ensure their presence at harvest-time. All states legislated – ineffectively – against emigration.

Worsening conditions were reflected in the growth in the number of mendicants. The physical condition of the peasants deteriorated. In the words of a parish priest near Modena: 'if we want to avoid seizure of our goods for debt, for a good part of the year we have to eat bread, polenta and onions, and on very rare occasions a little soup' (Orlandi, 179, p. 65). The agrarian expert Gualandris described a smallholder's diet in the Mantovano: 'for meals, just imagine, a sardine, a salted herring, a clove of garlic, a small piece of bacon rind must satisfy five or six people; but you need more than that to put on your bread!' (Vivanti, 62, p. 227). The countryside through-out Italy swarmed with so-called 'vagabonds'. In the south brigand bands grew in numbers. The wealthy and educated classes, when travelling, took care where they stayed the night. These 'vagabonds', when caught, were accused of theft – but of objects of the most trifling value. The Modenese priest quoted above described the losses and dangers experienced by his parishioners through living near a large city in 1786:

> The parish is always full of poor, and poor from the city who, not satisfied with begging alms from house to house, steal whatever they find – the produce of the meadows and fields, vegetables, grapes, fruit, poultry; in short, the most charitable parishioners are those who then tend to be robbed by the poor and vagabonds from the city. (Orlandi, 179, p. 64)

These vagabonds represented the lowest level of the poor. For there were different categories of poor. The parish priest of Campogalliano in the duchy of Modena offered the following description of the 250 families who were his parishioners:

> There are four classes of poor: the first consists of those incapable of procuring a living; the second of those who do not earn enough from their labours to maintain themselves; the third of those who go begging from door to door; the fourth of strangers who pass by the nearby roads to Correggio, Carpi and Reggio. Of the first, for the most part there are two or three, as at present. The second increase in years of penury and diminish in years of abundance; from year to year there are about sixty such families. There are five or six families in the third class. But the strangers amount to a great number and are usually twelve or fifteen, and many times even more than twenty a day. (Orlandi, 179, p. 261)

These 'strangers', the 'vagabonds', were mostly *braccianti*, day-labourers from the plains. The description of them by a Mantuan country doctor, Giampietro Fiorio, might have fitted almost any region of Italy:

> Without a scrap of land, without homes, lacking everything save a great brood of children, they are forced to settle here and there, like Tartar nomads, changing residence almost every year with a humble train of a few sheep and baggage consisting of a tattered bedstead, a mouldy cask, some rustic tools and a few pots and pans. (Vivanti, 62, pp. 224-5)

This was the Italian countryside of the eighteenth century. It was an isolated countryside, remote from the concerns and interests of the cities. It was fragmented, grouped around the rural communes. The small, often minuscule settlements were led by those few individuals who stood out because of their education or local prestige – the doctors, pharmacists, notaries, inn-keepers, successful peasants. These were the local administrators. But they could do little against the abuses of the great owners, the nobles, ecclesiastics, stewards or merchants. Indeed, some slowly built up their fortunes by usurious loans, and crept into the class of the wealthy. Others were to be found among those who spread revolutionary propaganda in the 1790s.

The only real links between the countryside and the cities were the traders and the parish priests. The former ranged from the travelling merchants, collecting the produce of agriculture and rural industry for the cities, to the resident petty tradesmen of cheap clothing and goods and the itinerant barbers and cobblers. The latter often endured the same poverty as the peasants. They were looked to by the governments and reformers, who hoped that, as priests, they might improve the peasants' condition by practical education. An 'agricultural catechism' was what Pietro Verri advised. Less dogma and more education; an education that, as an anonymous memoire stated, should be limited to 'just reading and writing and the simplest sums, to avoid the danger of diminishing the number of labourers in the countryside'. In any case, as the writer added, it would be pointless to offer more, as 'geniuses are not born into that class' (Vivanti, 62, p. 217).

The cities: economic activities and social structure

The world of the cities was far removed from the preoccupations of the countryside. The citizens looked to the government to guarantee their food supplies and the raw materials required by the manufacturing guilds. Despite widespread poverty, life in the cities was always easier than in the *campagna*. The government controlled food prices and restrained the nobles from more flagrant abuses of their power. The distribution of alms was better organized. Service in the growing number of palaces offered alternative employment to apprenticeship in the guilds or horticulture (which was still widespread within the cities). Thus, even among the subordinate classes, there was little contact with and no nostalgia for the countryside. Among the ruling classes of the early eighteenth century the fashionable vision of the countryside was of an idyllic Arcadia, from which the harsher realities were banished. It was left to the merchants, often foreigners, and the fiscal agents to maintain the links between these two worlds.

The population of most cities rose more slowly than that of the country-side. The few cities which experienced sharp growth were administrative centres or ports: Turin rose from 44 000 inhabitants in 1702 to 92 000 by 1791; Naples, the most densely and monstrously populated city of Italy, incieased from 337 000 in 1766 to 438 000 by 1797; Genoa, Leghorn, Trieste, experienced similar expansion. Elsewhere growth was relatively slow: Milan rose from 114 000 (1714) to 131 000 (1790); Florence from 73 000 (1740) to 81 000 (1795); Rome from 142 000 (1700) to 163 000 (1800). The popula-tion of some cities, indeed, remained stagnant – Venice, for example, at about 138 000 inhabitants, and Mantua at about 20 000. But in general, compared to the preceding period, urban population was slowly rising. The cities were responding to the increase in the pace of European economic activities which developed from the 1740s. Nevertheless, compared to the surrounding countryside, their populations remained small. The eight major cities of Tuscany in the 1740s only numbered 170 000 inhabitants out of a total population in the grand-duchy of 890 000. Even the city of Naples accounted for less than 10 per cent of the population of the kingdom.

These urban centres varied in size, in privileges, in economic activities. As the cities asserted their privileges over the countryside, so the state capitals insisted on their domination of the subject cities. It was a domina-tion both administrative and economic. Venice, like Turin or Rome, con-tinued to reduce such freedom of action as remained to the subject cities. Milan asserted its superiority over Pavia, as Florence did over Siena; Naples possessed its privileged *sedili*, while Palermo remained the seat of the Sicilian parliament. The presence of the Court and of the central organs of government guaranteed a stimulus, however artificial, to the life of these major cities. It was the life-blood of such capitals as Modena or Parma. Economically, the capitals also insisted on their superiority, retaining the monopoly of industrial products as far as possible. But here they proved less powerful. Most subject cities, even small towns, possessed their own guilds, and some had long-standing reputations in specific industrial sectors – such as Brescia for iron products or Bologna for special types of silks. The pressure of competition from abroad and from rival Italian states led the governments to look beyond the capitals to all centres of industry and com-merce; increasingly they looked beyond the guilds to new, free industrial enterprises. The decline of Italian industry and commerce had led to a new orientation of the economic activities of the Italian states, in which the smaller cities and the countryside played a more positive role. Only in the smallest states where no other cities existed – such as Genoa or Lucca – did the capitals maintain their predominance. Elsewhere, as the pressure of foreign competition increased in the eighteenth century, the industrial and commercial physiognomy of the Italian cities changed.

The guild system throughout Italy had outlived its usefulness. It had become the monopoly of small hereditary groups, who looked to the government for protection and subventions to maintain the level of production and exports. By the eighteenth century the very structure of the guilds worked against increases in production. The once famous *arti* had become closed organisms that prohibited the production of cheaper goods in order to maintain the supremacy of traditional luxury goods, that restricted the number of workers and apprentices even when the demand for products was rising, that imposed prohibitive fees and manipulated examinations for admittance into their higher ranks, that blocked technical advances such as the combined use of wood and brass in furniture. Despite a tendency towards industrial concentration the guilds remained small closed shops. In Milan seven different guilds were engaged in the treatment and sale of skins.

As the century wore on, the negative effects of the guilds became of increasing concern to the reformers. In some states, particularly in Naples and Sicily, their economic significance was slight, because of the predominantly rural character of the economies. But in Sicily their political strength remained important as they offered the government a counterbalance to the baronage. The autonomy of their jurisdictions and their right to an armed militia lay at the basis of their power. Economically, the Sicilian guilds were subject to the great merchants who supplied them with raw materials and exported their products. Politically, they grew in importance as Charles III entrusted to their militia the custody of the Palermo city walls (1735) and Ferdinand allowed them to maintain public order and control the market (1773). Their number rose from 45 in the seventeenth century to 74 in the eighteenth. Elsewhere in Italy, by the second half of the century, the governments began to intervene to reform or circumvent them. If industry had any future, it lay outside the guilds. Thus, in the early eighteenth century governments began to sponsor their own industries, or to give special privileges such as exemption from guild restrictions to new industrial enterprises, like Nicola Tron's wool factory at Schio, or Francesco Tieffen's Lombard wool factory, or the various linen and cotton industries which emerged in northern Italy.

Despite these initiatives, Italy increasingly assumed the physiognomy of a producer of agricultural and industrial raw materials and semi-finished products. The period of decline during the long years of Spanish rule now took its toll. Backward industrial techniques, the isolation of the few industrial developments, inadequate capital, restricted and fragmented domestic markets, disastrous communications, all militated against effective competition with the major European powers. In this context, the Italian cities, in their weakness, fought against each other to achieve a greater share of the export demand. The only sign of positive advance was to be seen in the modest expansion of rural domestic industry for semi-finished textiles. Silk and wool remained the basic industries of all the major Italian states. But the silk industry was particularly subject to the recurrent crises of international trade. In general, Italian industries – and hence the Italian cities – found themselves, throughout the eighteenth century, in their renewed contact with Europe in a situation of subordination. Industry, in fact, was dominated by its commercial outlets, and commerce was controlled to a significant extent by foreign merchants.

It was the merchants who acted as the major channels of communication between both the cities and the countryside, and the cities and international trade. In the Papal States and southern Italy it was the 'country merchants' and the great traders manipulating the system of the *contratti alla voce* who (as we have seen) dominated agricultural activities. Although many merchants in the Italian states were native citizens, the scarcity of capital left the initiative in the hands of foreigners. For, apart from the Genoese and Venetians, it was usually the foreigners – English, French or Dutch – who possessed the financial resources and commercial contacts. English merchants dominated the wine industry at Marsala, and the export of silks from Piedmont; Genoese and French merchants controlled much of the export trade from Naples. The revival of trade strengthened their position. At Genoa, it led to the continued dominance of the aristocratic bankers who loaned money abroad, but also gained from the transit of Piedmontese and Lombard trade. In other states it strengthened the new 'free ports'.

Ancona, which was given the status of a free port in 1732, was the only really active city of the Papal States. It was a city where local merchants, such as Francesco Trionfi, retained control. Messina was given the status of a free port in 1728 in an attempt to develop its commerce. But the activities of these two cities were limited compared to those of Leghorn, which had become a free port in 1675 and which was developed by foreign, especially English, merchants. The relative success of these ports bore witness to the negative effects of the protectionist duties and internal barriers to trade. The traditional competition to Venice of Leghorn, Trieste and Ancona, which dated back to the early seventeenth century, became more threatening in the eighteenth, as they developed as free ports. Despite its Levantine trade, despite its Jewish colony, Venice – which felt unable to imitate them – continued to decline. It was in these free ports that foreign and Jewish colonies were most easily established. At Naples Charles III tried but failed to gain local acceptance for the introduction of such foreign merchants.

The major economic revival of the Italian cities thus occurred in the ports. Industry, wherever it developed, tended to base itself on the earlier stages of transforming agricultural products. Here, too, foreign capital was much in evidence. The security of land and government borrowing offered a strong rival inducement for local capital. But by the mid-eighteenth century there was a distinct, though limited, development of industry in northern Italy. The interests of the new industrialists, who favoured protective measures, conflicted with those of the merchants. In Lombardy there was a continuous clash between the two groups in the middle decades of the century. In Tuscany, a proposal was made in 1747 to create a local company which, in return for a monopoly of silk and wool production, would assume responsibility for the exaction of state taxes. But barely ten years later an enquiry among the Leghorn 'nations' of merchants asserted that 'trade flourishes where it is free and languishes where it is harassed' (Venturi, 30, p. 320). Grain production and the transit trade lay at the basis of the merchants' interests. But the industrialists, too, were hostile to the innumerable checks to internal trade. Both groups, which were growing in importance in all the Italian states by the mid-eighteenth century, offered support of one or another kind to the reformers.

The merchants and industrialists, like the bankers, remained, however, limited groups throughout the eighteenth century. The industrialists were only of real significance in certain cities of northern and central Italy – Milan and Pavia, Venice and Bergamo, Vicenza and Padua, Florence and Siena, Turin, Racconigi and Biella. The merchants spread all over Italy, in the south as well as the north, in the ports as well as the inland cities. The bankers, often foreigners, were frequently also industrialists and merchants.

Control of the cities remained primarily in the hands of the nobles. It was the nobles who set the tone of social life. It was the nobles who controlled the local administrations. Their power was strengthened by the eagerness of successful merchants, lawyers, bankers, tenants to enter their ranks. The Sicilian parliament, the *sedili* of Naples, the Milan senate were all firmly controlled by the nobility. In the smaller provincial cities, such as Treviso, Saluzzo or Siena, the situation was the same. It was usually only where the provincial cities had experienced a certain economic development that the middle class managed to gain representation on the city council. But in these cities they were often dependent upon the protection of the government. When, as at Mantua, Vienna imposed the participation of citizens and lawyers alongside the nobles in the Council of Decurions, the nobles kept control by placing their own representatives among the lawyers and by shifting the real seat of decision-making to the municipal junta, which they controlled.

The ubiquitous power of the nobility was to remain the basic feature of eighteenth-century Italian society. It was predominantly power of a negative kind, which resisted change and fought for the conservation of privileges. But by the middle of the century the attitude of isolated individuals and even small groups of the younger generation began to change. Increasing numbers of these younger nobles were to be found in the various branches of the state administration, not just in the fields of diplomacy and the army. There was probably little distinction between the older and the newer nobles. But a greater difference was visible between the nobles of the capital and the provincial aristocracy. Traditionally, the patriciate, particularly of northern and central Italy, had identified with its local city. In the provincial cities, by the latter part of the century, these nobles were to display a new interest in the agricultural world, forming agrarian academies which were profuse in technical advice about how to increase productivity, but remote from the daily preoccupations of the peasants. These same nobles were to be found in the masonic lodges which penetrated Italy from the 1730s. It was not surprising, given the predominance of the aristocracy, that so many of the reformers were to emerge from their younger scions, who were increasingly conscious of the ills that beset the Italian states and their backwardness compared to the progress of European civilization.

This change in the attitudes of a small minority of the nobilities was paralleled by a modification in the opinions of individual clerics. Despite its pervasive influence, the clergy was in a weak position, the object of attack because of the Church's wealth and its claims to exemption from secular authority. Isolated clerics, such as Muratori or Lami, criticized these claims and began to express a desire for a simpler, more purified Church. Ecclesiastics were to be found alongside the nobles in the masonic lodges: the lodges offered a point of contact with the cosmopolitan world of the foreigners and a meeting place for individuals of differing social status, evading by their very ritual the rigid distinctions of formal etiquette. In later decades, these clerics – in Piedmont and Lombardy, Tuscany and the Papal States – were to be found among the near-schismatic Jansenists, whose search for a more ascetic spiritual life and democratic Church offered support to the reforming governments.

Less support for the reformers was gained from the lawyers. These excessively numerous products of the universities, expert in canon as in civil law, who had dominated public life in the previous century, slowly lost their control in the eighteenth century. Few had kind words for the lawyers, symbol of a past age, too closely tied to the defence of noble and ecclesiastical privilege, too deeply imbued with traditional, scholastic values to rally to the new ideas. Jurisprudence, to Muratori, was 'a garden turned upside down: the more you care for it, the more the weeds and thorns grow' (Muratori, in 27, p. 164). There were exceptions. It was the Neapolitan lawyers, like Costantino Grimaldi, who had led the attack against papal claims at the opening of the century. It was a Pisan professor of law,

Giuseppe Averani, who taught many of the Tuscan reformers who were subsequently to play their part in various of the Italian states. But the lawyers, ever-present in the public and private life of the Italian states, tended to resist the introduction of the reforms.

Beneath all these privileged groups lived the 'plebs', the greatest part of the populations of the cities. Only in a few cities, where industries were developing, can one speak of a proletariat. The most compact groups were probably formed by the weavers in isolated cities of northern and central Italy, such as Vicenza. The wages of those who worked in the new, 'free' industries, tended to follow the rise in prices. The wages of guild workers remained stationary. For the most part the workers were trapped within the controlling mechanism of these guilds. Those who found employment as servants were probably better off. Their numbers were large: nearly 13 000, 10 per cent of the population of Venice in 1760. As agricultural conditions worsened, as harvests failed, the city populations increased through migration from the countryside. Some of the new inhabitants turned their experience to good use and engaged in horticulture. But the majority of the city populations depended on governmental control of food prices or alms. Begging was endemic. The 'plebs' remained a threat. As Genovesi wrote, if the state did not intervene, the people might carry out a 'reform like plundering soldiers' (Genovesi in 27, p. 625). The Genoese revolt of 1746 offered a stark warning, like the earlier Roman rising of 1736. The privileged classes retained their control. But as the eighteenth century drew on and living conditions worsened, the threat from the urban masses increased.

3

The problems of government

Administrative confusion and financial crisis

The systems of administration and government in all the Italian states in the early eighteenth century were conditioned by the social structure and distribution of authority. Spanish rule had seen the development of more centralized forms of government in which all power derived from the sovereign. This absolutist rule had removed effective political power from the nobility in most of the states – Lombardy, Mantua, Modena, Parma, Tuscany, the Papal States and Naples. In Piedmont it ensured the loyalty of the nobility, old and new, to the dynasty. In the republics of Venice, Genoa and Lucca it conserved political power in the hands of small and numerically diminishing oligarchies.

But this growth in centralization had been superimposed upon, and had not replaced, the existing structures. Nobles and ecclesiastics, cities and communes, although deprived of political power, resisted, in the name of their legal or customary rights, the encroachments of the central administrations. The territorial unity of the states was maintained only by the persons of the rulers. Even in Piedmont the sovereign ruled over a duchy of Savoy, a county of Nice, a principate of Oneglia, a duchy of Aosta, a principate of Piedmont, a duchy of Saluzzo, a duchy of Monferrat, and soon a kingdom of Sardinia, to say nothing of the differing titles of his new Lombard possessions. Elsewhere territorial particularism ran even deeper, strikingly so in Tuscany and the Papal States. In the upheavals that followed the end of Spanish rule, as we have seen, the old, local autonomies asserted themselves. In the Austrian-ruled states the feudatories often gained further concessions or consolidated their hold on their fiefs. The uncertainties of the succession in Tuscany and Parma facilitated a similar process. Only where there was continuity of rule, particularly in Piedmont and Venetia, was this centrifugal drive avoided in the early eighteenth century.

Thus, the new foreign rulers found themselves confronted by a complicated and chaotic structure and by more active resistance to administrative

change than had been apparent in the preceding century. Nostalgia for
the old dynasties increased their difficulties as, under the stress of war, it
offered the basis for organized political opposition. In Austrian Lombardy
this pro-Spanish feeling tended to disappear in the face of Piedmontese
aggression. But in neutral Tuscany Philip V's representative, Father
Ascanio, organized protests against Francis of Lorraine among the unemployed, the beggars, the city plebs. In Naples, during the Austrian
Succession War, discontent with Charles III's reforms offered the opportunity for Gregorio Grimaldi to engage in anti-Bourbon propaganda on
behalf of the invading Austrian general, Lobkowitz.

The confusion of administrative, judicial, financial and economic functions was not, of course, peculiar to Italy. But the particularism of Italian
history and the peninsula's continued division into small states rendered
it more acute. As in other European states, the political, administrative
and judicial powers of the central organs of government overlapped and
merged into one another. Officials were responsible in their person for
the widest and most unexpected range of duties. No distinction was made
between the patrimony of the state and the private possessions of the
prince.

Administration was conceived of primarily in terms of legal precedent.
The consent of subjects was a concept alien to the eighteenth-century
administrator. In so far as it had existed in limited form in some of the
states, it had disappeared with the suppression of virtually all the representative assemblies, retaining little of its original character in those
which survived in the Aosta valley, Friuli, Sicily and Sardinia. But the right
to challenge or evade governmental decrees on legal grounds – exemption
or exoneration claimed in terms of older statutes, precedents or simply
tradition – was as strong as, perhaps stronger, than ever. As every state contained a maze of conflicting jurisdictions, the competence of individual
courts could easily be challenged.

In Florence there were thirty tribunals, besides the fourteen of the guilds.
Barons and ecclesiastics, cities and communes, guildsmen and foreigners
and innumerable other estates and conditions of men insisted on their own
prerogatives and spheres of legal authority. The reformer Pompeo Neri
complained that the confusion and conflict of jurisdictions in eighteenth-
century Tuscany resulted from the transformation of a republican city-state
like Florence into a grand-duchy as long ago as the sixteenth century.
Republican governments had involved their citizens in a plethora of
magistracies in order to cement their loyalty. Once created, a tribunal was
rarely suppressed, as Neri explained:

This multiplicity derives from the fact that when the House of Medici rose to
the principate it took care not to abolish the names of the Republican magis-

tracies; in republics the number of such offices, because of the system of popular government, is always greater than necessary and than is usual in principates. (Venturi, 27, p. 38)

But the problem was not limited to republics. In kingdoms as well, government authority was constantly hampered and often rendered impotent. The cardinal legate of Bologna could not prevent this subject city negotiating directly with its sovereign, the pope, through its own ambassador. In Sicily the viceroys were incapable of breaching that citadel of baronial rights – parliament. In the kingdom of Naples royal courts failed to overrule baronial jurisdictions. A vivid image is offered by the example of an unfortunate surgeon, Antonio Casella, who appealed against his local baron. As he stated in one of his many appeals, before he lost his life:

> Not only imprisoned without right, beaten and placed in a horrible felon's cell to die there, from which he had been released by order of the Supreme Court; but imprisoned again and then a shot fired at him . . . he entreats Your Majesty to provide him with safeguards, so that he shall be secure from other snares on his life and released from other unjust imprisonments. (Villari, 97, p. 150)

This tangled legacy of laws and jurisdictions protected the privileged and nurtured the legal class. Small wonder that in the city of Naples 26 000 people were reputed to gain a living out of the law in the mid-eighteenth century. At the same time all governments were inhibited from radical change The early reforms were to reveal the strength of opposition which derived from this jurisprudential jungle. Only when, as Pompeo Neri wrote, reason and technical skills replaced legal arguments, would the reforming movement make real headway.

The urgent need for some change was apparent in all the states. Fiscal revenues were frozen at a time when military expenditure was rising. The constant wars of the first half of the century forced even neutral states, like Venice or the Papacy, to increase their taxes. For the states which were involved in these wars, the expense was obviously far greater. The decades after 1715 saw a general rise in the cost of warfare, as the arquebus and musket were replaced by the rifle and the artillery assumed greater tactical significance. The old sources of revenue proved ever less adequate.

Constant borrowing by the governments or princely largesse had mortgaged many of these revenues to private individuals. Pallavicino calculated in 1747 that half the Lombard revenues of 6 million lire were pledged as interest on past debts; in Naples it was estimated that only one-fifth of income exacted by the state reached the royal coffers. As exemptions had grown, the territorial base of the land-tax had diminished. The imposition of new, extraordinary taxes failed to raise much additional revenue, merely increasing the indebtedness of the rural communes. Taxes on land in fact, in virtually all the Italian states, had become considerably less important than revenue from excises. But the yield from these customs was also held down by the chaotic system of giving them out to contract and by the low level of economic activities which in their turn were hindered by government protection of privileged industries, private and ecclesiastical exactions, and guild restrictions. For fiscal and economic reasons, as much as for administrative ones, the governments of all the Italian states were impelled towards reforms. If state income was to be increased, economic activities had to be encouraged and the obstacles represented by privileges and jurisdictions at least reduced. Underlying these specific and concrete motives was a new sense of the state, a growing awareness among the foreign rulers and their advisers of the need to create a modern administrative structure, free of the anachronistic entanglements of the past.

These problems, which characterized the Italian states, resembled in broad terms, and often in detail, those present in other European countries in the first half of the eighteenth century. Nor was this surprising. For all states suffered from similar administrative confusion, generated by the survival of privileges, and similar financial crises, caused by the wars. But there was more than a general similarity in the choice of policies and proposed solutions. Italy had renewed its contact with Europe; increasingly it was entering into the rhythm of European life. Italian rulers and administrators looked to the experiences of other European countries, as its scholars, writers and ecclesiastics looked to their intellectual, economic and religious progress.

The new rulers were naturally those most open to foreign experiences. So it was their states – Lombardy, Tuscany, Naples – which experienced these early reforms, as later they were to experience the full flowering of the Enlightenment. The break in continuity that marked the accessions of Charles VI, Charles III, Francis of Lorraine, as later of Philip of Parma, left these princes freer to challenge the multitude of limitations to their power which bound most other governments. But all the Italian states felt the urgent need of some modifications or changes and one ruler – Victor Amadeus II of Piedmont – was responsible for the most successful reforms of the first half of the eighteenth century.

Autocracy and reform: Piedmont

The immediate stimulus behind Victor Amadeus' reforms was – as in the other states – the impact of war. Expediency – in the shape of his alliance with Protestant England and Holland against Louis XIV – explains the readiness of this wily and unscrupulous ruler to abandon the traditional counter-reformation persecution of heretics and re-admit to their valleys his Protestant subjects, the Waldensians (1694). This almost incidental act of toleration was to lead to a lengthy dispute with the papacy, in which Victor

Amadeus gradually asserted the authority of the state against the pretensions of the Roman curia. But it was the exhausting experience of the Spanish Succession War that preceded and was responsible for the intense years of reform from 1717 to 1731. The reforms were intended to eliminate the most evident weaknesses in the administrative and legal structure of the state, to limit the encroachments of privilege, to provide a firm basis for taxation, to stimulate industry and commerce, to assert the sovereign's control over the Church, to break the ecclesiastical monopoly of education, to create a broader administrative class of new men alongside the nobility, to forge a large and efficient diplomatic service and army.

The Council of State was reorganized and given responsibility for judicial matters (1717); the Secretariat of State was divided into separate departments for internal affairs, foreign affairs and war (1719); four *aziende* or departments were created with responsibility for finances, war, artillery and fortifications, and the royal household (1730). The Royal Constitutions of 1723 and 1729 offered a compendium of laws, eliminating the contradictions of previous legislation, simplifying and occasionally modifying in favour of royal authority the chaotic jurisdictions inherited from the past. The general *catasto* or cadastral register, which was finally promulgated in 1731, offered a new measurement and valuation of almost all land in Piedmont on which to base the land-tax, restricting feudal and ecclesiastical exemptions to properties with proven title of their privileged quality. Attempts were made to create a textile industry, that proved more successful in the silk than in the woollen sector. The University of Turin was reformed and given the monopoly of higher education, while provincial colleges, offering scholarships, were founded to train the new bureaucracy (1729). By the concordats of 1726 and 1727 a compromise was reached with the papacy: religious orthodoxy was reasserted, but the limitation of ecclesiastical immunities, the subordination (and, in practice, suppression) of the Inquisition, the exclusion of foreign clerics from ecclesiastical jurisdictions and the royal administration of vacant benefices were explicitly or tacitly accepted by Rome. The nobility was humiliated by the confiscation by the royal demesne of illegally acquired fiefs (1720). A highly trained diplomatic service sent representatives all over Europe. The standing army of 24 000 men (equivalent to one soldier for every 95 inhabitants) could be increased to as many as 43 000 in time of war (1734).

The reforms were impressive in their execution. They were remarkable in their technical efficiency, which ensured their completion – even of the most lengthy and complicated, the *catasto*. But they were reforms typical of dynastic absolutism. They looked back to the France of Louis XIV in both scope and nature. They were practical reforms with specific, limited ends, bearing no trace of the new ideas which were beginning to circulate in Europe and in some of the other Italian states. The ends were the traditional ones of strengthening the state for purposes of war. Hence the administrative reforms, the *catasto*, the formation of a bureaucracy of new men, the creation of a powerful army and diplomatic corps. The economic measures were equally traditional, typical of the paternalistic mercantilism of the age of Colbert. The religious and educational reforms were even more revealing, for they were inspired by purely political and practical motives. Once royal control over the Church had been asserted, there was no place in Piedmont for the heresies of Alberto Radicati, who was forced to seek more congenial company in the free-thinking circles of London and Holland. Once clerical control of education had been broken, strict limits were set to the unorthodoxy of the new professors.

It is necessary to remember that Victor Amadeus' reforms were carried out in the 1720s. To expect of them the philosophy of reason, the clash of opposing principles, the desire to abolish the past and start afresh, the optimism and confidence in man's ability to reform society which imbued the Enlightenment reforms of the later eighteenth century would be unhistorical. They were reforms of a transitional period, necessitated by the stresses and strains experienced under pressure of war by all states at the opening of the eighteenth century, but still dominated by the paternalistic absolutism of an age that had drawn to an end with the Spanish Succession War. They were pre-Enlightenment reforms, but already displayed that sense of the superior interests of the state that characterized the activities of Victor Amadeus' Prussian contemporary, Frederick William I. At the same time, the very success of the reforms set Piedmont apart from the other Italian states. They made the sub-Alpine kingdom the most efficiently organized, bureaucratic-militaristic state in Italy, with a genuine tradition of loyalty to the dynasty among the ruling classes.

There were to be no further developments. During Charles Emanuel III's long reign (1730–73), the final touches were to be given to his father's reforms, with the reorganization of local administrations (1733, 1738, 1742, 1750), the minor revisions of the constitutions (1770), the jurisdictional victory of the concordats (1741, 1742), the reforms in Sardinia (1759–65). What was missing was even that minimal recognition of the implications of ecclesiastical and cultural reforms which Victor Amadeus had sensed and utilized. The new university professors were regarded with suspicion and soon abandoned Turin for Milan or Vienna. The eccentric noble freethinker Alberto Radicati had been at least temporarily encouraged by Victor Amadeus during his struggle with the papacy; the leading Neapolitan anti-curialist writer, Pietro Giannone, by contrast, was trapped and imprisoned in Piedmont by Charles Emanuel as the price for the peaceful settlement of his conflict with the papacy. In the 1720s the reforms had placed Piedmont in the forefront of the Italian states. By the 1750s and 1760s the self-contained, limited scope of these same reforms isolated Piedmont from the new ideas and ambitions that characterized the reforming movement elsewhere in Italy. In this highly centralized state, in which nobles and bureaucrats vied with each other in their loyalty to the crown, there were few possibilities for an independent and critical intellectual class to emerge and develop. The way had been blocked by the success of the royal reforms.

The early reforms: ecclesiastical privilege, administration, finances

In the states with new rulers the early attempts at reform were less successful than in Piedmont. The sovereigns could not appeal to dynastic loyalty as a means of over-riding opposition. The renewed warfare of the 1730s and 1740s, and the strength of local opposition, compromised the reforms. The earliest attempt at a major reform – the Lombard land register, on which preparatory work was begun in 1718 – was continuously resisted by the privileged classes, who finally sabotaged it with the outbreak of war in 1733. The early hopes of the emperor in the 1720s died away during the crisis of the following decade. The cost of the Polish Succession War, the political uncertainties, the initial extravagant favouritism of the emperor towards his Spanish followers, the corruption of the local administrators, the centrifugal drive of privileged groups, the exhaustion of the states, made change imperative. But the reforms which were put forward from the late 1730s were cautious, limited, often hesitant.

The new rulers brought with them foreign counsellors and administrators. The empire in particular was cosmopolitan in its employment of administrators, who – like Pompeo Neri – moved about from state to state. Genoese of ancient noble lineage (like Giorgio Pallavicino), Tuscans of legal origin (such as Pompeo Neri) or descendants of the old patriciate (like Giulio Rucellai), nobles *de robe* (like Beltrame Cristiani) worked alongside or in collaboration with German princes (Marc de Craon, Philip of Hesse-Darmstadt) and foreign parliamentarians (Emanuel de Richecourt). In the new Bourbon states there was the same mixture: the Tuscan Bernardo Tanucci administered together with the Spanish duke Montealegre di Salas, who was later replaced by the Piacentine marquis di Fogliani. 'National' and indeed social origin was of little consequence in service to the monarch. In these years a new class of functionaries emerged, among whom administrative skill and – to a lesser degree – legal knowledge counted for more than dignity of birth or country of origin. But the very presence of so many foreigners in Italy and the ease with which they transferred their activities from state to state ensured a more cosmopolitan experience for the countries they administered. The range of this experience was more immediately visible in Habsburg Lombardy and Tuscany. But it made its impact slightly later in Bourbon Naples and Parma. This class was responsible for the early reforms. It was regarded with hostility by the local nobles and ecclesiastics and with diffidence by the new intellectual groups. At first governments and intellectuals in these Italian states struggled with their problems and groped towards their aims on different planes. Gradually, their concern with the same problems of society and their consciousness of Italy's place in Europe brought them together. At that point – in the 1750s and 1760s – the experience of the Enlightenment began in Italy.

In the preceding decades, however, the administrators worked for the most part alone. Their most successful reforms emerged from their struggle with the Church. The impotence of the papacy, internationally and internally, weakened its resistance, while the governments could count on limited support or at least little opposition within their states. Even so, the reforms offered a compromise, which limited but barely questioned the concept of ecclesiastical privilege.

Even in Naples, with its strong anti-curialist tradition, the ideological challenge offered by Giannone's assertion of the absolute authority of the secular state was avoided. A political solution was achieved by the 1741 concordat, which limited the immunity of priests from customs duties, subjected ecclesiastical lands to half the tax paid by secular owners, and gained the participation of secular authorities alongside the bishops in ecclesiastical tribunals. Ecclesiastical censorship remained strong. But the lawyers, the mainstay of this Neapolitan jurisdictionalist struggle, made the king resist an attempt by the archbishop of Naples to reintroduce the Inquisition in 1746. In Lombardy the Church was less overpowering. But even here, at a time when the reforms had gained impetus, Pompeo Neri was prevented from abolishing all ecclesiastical tax exemptions in his *catasto* by the 1757 concordat. Tuscany, closely tied by the Medici to the papacy, had no traditions of an anti-curial struggle, nor a legal class as at Naples. It was to Naples and Turin and to the new link with Vienna that Rucellai looked as he embarked on 'emancipating' the Tuscan Church from Rome. In 1743 state control was asserted over censorship and the sale of books. In 1745 the personal immunity of clerics was limited, as was that of ecclesiastical sanctuaries (Florence alone contained 243). But Rucellai drew back from restricting the Church's fiscal privileges. He went furthest in 1751 when he attempted to prevent any extension of such exemptions by prohibiting further gifts or legacies of land to religious institutions in mortmain. Rucellai's ecclesiastical reforms were more radical and successful than those of the other Italian states because he refused to accept their codification – and hence limitation – in a concordat: the Tuscan administrators were determined to find their way alone, without paying undue attention to the pope's restrictions.

The early reforms in other spheres were less successful. In Tuscany Neri's initial measures (1739, 1741) to cut through the conflicting and lethargic web of magistracies and jurisdictions by the creation of a grand-ducal court with extensive powers were not followed up until Leopold's accession. In Naples Tanucci immediately attacked baronial jurisdictions as a means of improving public order in the kingdom: a commission was formed in 1736, local tribunals were reorganized in 1739 and ordered to submit reports on homicides to the higher courts. It was an attempt to decentralize, but at the same time to assert regal control of the administration of justice. But hostility from both the capital and the barons enforced the virtual withdrawal of the reform in 1744. Tanucci's novel attempt to create a Supreme Magistracy for trade in 1739, which would expedite commercial lawsuits but also act as a model to the other courts through the speed and cheapness of its workings, was resisted with even more vigour and finally emasculated in 1746. In Lombardy attempts to reform the administration and justice only emerged after the great cadastral register of 1757. But the successful resistance of the Mantuan nobles to the administrative unification of their duchy with Lombardy – which was Vienna's declared policy – enabled the privileged classes there to escape the effects of this land register.

Legal reform also failed. At Naples a commission was appointed in 1742 to draw up a compendium of the laws, as in the Piedmont Constitutions. Its members, who included traditionally minded lawyers, such as one of Muratori's leading critics, blocked the initiative for a decade. In Tuscany Muratori's appeal for a new code seemed to meet with a response from the reforming administrators in the 1740s. But the dangers of replacing the old laws with an entirely new code were increasingly felt to be insuperable. Neri was finally prepared to compromise by issuing only a compilation of the existing laws. But the particularism which fragmented the state, 'that infamous Tuscan mentality' as Richecourt described it (Venturi, 27, p. 324), sabotaged the project.

The attempts to reform the fiscal structure and increase state revenue met with equal hostility and also resulted in compromise. But they marked a major step forward. Indirect taxes from customs, import and transit duties, from the salt and tobacco monopolies, from the excises on innumerable products and retail trade by now formed the major source of state incomes. At Naples, especially, much of the income from these taxes had been alienated in payment of debts or granted as gifts. In all the states, as elsewhere in Europe, exaction of these revenues was leased to tax farmers (*fermieri*) who advanced payment to the government for the contract. But the indebtedness of the governments, that reached new heights with the succession wars of the 1730s and 1740s, and the shortage of capital in circulation, made them turn not infrequently to the tax farmers for loans as well. The *fermieri* thus gained increasing power as creditors of the governments, while the administrations lost a significant proportion of their income from taxes because of their fragmentation among so many tax farmers and the confusion of the accounts. There was the double problem of a multitude of debts and countless separately leased indirect taxes.

The pressure of war led the Italian administrations, like those in England, France and Spain in the same years, to search for methods to fund the debts and raise more income. After Aix-la-Chapelle, popular resistance to the existing fiscal administration, in some of the Italian states as in Holland, underlined the need to find a solution. Even Venice, so confident of its stability, decided in 1735 to unify the taxes within each administrative unit of its *terraferma*. In Tuscany, after early proposals to reduce the public debt by the sale of the allodial lands of the last Medici, and possibly even of ecclesiastical lands, the Austrian Succession War and the demands for assistance from Vienna led to the more modest compromise of unifying and leasing the indirect taxes to a single company of tax farmers (1740). In Naples the war had the same negative effect. But the most urgent problem in the kingdom was to redeem incomes from the *arrendatari*, or state creditors. An attempt in 1743 failed. Charles III's scruples about the legality of the procedure weakened the initial optimism. In the end the special 'junta for repurchases' (1751), strongly under the influence of nobles and clergy who owned a large part of the alienated incomes (*arrendamenti*), paid less attention to their redemption than to increasing the existing taxes on communes and feudatories.

In Lombardy, the governor Pallavicino reached a similar conclusion. He submitted a plan to Vienna in 1747, in which he proposed that a state bank be created to repurchase the indirect taxes leased by contract; these taxes should then be reorganized, starting with the tobacco and lottery revenues, until a single 'general tax farm' could be created. The company leasing the farm would advance sufficient capital to finance further reforms, above all a new measurement of landed property, to form the basis for a revised land tax. Pallavicino had obviously learnt much from the recent Tuscan example of consolidating the indirect taxes. Many Lombard administrators remained doubtful about the plan, particularly over whether the capital raised would permit the completion of the cadastral register. When Vienna finally agreed, after peace had been achieved, Pallavicino unified the indirect revenues and, after considerable difficulties, found a group of Bergamasque tax farmers, headed by Antonio Greppi, who were ready to advance sufficient capital at a reduced rate of interest to redeem the taxes from the previous *fermieri* (1750). Three years later the Monte di Santa Teresa was created to fund the scattered public debts. Although the bank never achieved the catalytic effect of the Bank of England, it was highly successful in redeeming the most costly state debts and by the 1770s was turning to the debts of local administrations.

This unification of the indirect taxes offered no long-term solution to the fiscal problems of the states. Even where it was most successful, in Tuscany and Lombardy, it brought with it the danger of creating a powerful group of financiers who could influence the government and harass the population. In France the *fermiers*, by their long-term loans, had gained a virtual monopoly of the public debt, so making it impossible for the government to free itself from its dependence. In Naples the *arrendatari* enjoyed a similar position. The reform of the excise system was thus a compromise measure, which forced the governments to exert continuous control by close supervision and by guaranteeing the presence of an adequate number of efficient members of the Court of Accounts in the administration of the general farm. But it was a measure which gained respite for the governments and an increase in revenue.

The necessary complement to the unification of the indirect taxes was the revision of the land-tax through the completion of the cadastral register. In Tuscany such a measure was never achieved in the eighteenth century, because of the hostility of the landowners and the widespread belief in the freedom of agriculture. In Naples a cadastral register had been completed by 1742. It was a curious combination of old and new: the income of the land was calculated and then capitalized; but the figures arrived at were then transferred into rateable values expressed in the old money of account. A basis had been laid, but antiquated methods were still employed. In its methods and intentions this Neapolitan *catasto 'onciario'* bore a resemblance to Victor Amadeus II's *perequazione*. Its purpose had been to provide the basis for a system of direct taxation. But the resistance of the communes, particularly with the Austrian Succession War, hindered its application.

In Lombardy the completion of the cadastral register marked the development from individual, separate reforms, achieved often only partially, to a new more all-embracing concept of the duties of government and sense of the state. It was Pallavicino who had called Pompeo Neri from Florence to Milan to supervise this renewed attempt to compile the cadastral register. If Neri was able rapidly to complete the task, it was because the groundwork had been prepared in the previous abortive attempt (1718–33). Neri's aim was the same as that of Machault in France and La Enseñada in Spain: to uproot all privilege. By 1757 the work for the register was completed. The evaluation of landed income, as in Piedmont, was no longer based upon the declarations of owners, but had been carried out by agricultural surveyors and assessors, who measured the properties, listed the types of cultivation and estimated their yields. Land was subjected to a fixed tax, so that future improvements in productivity would benefit and so encourage the owner. The reform was not a total success, as Neri was forced to accept many ecclesiastical exemptions, the continuance of a rural capitation tax, and a separate system for the duchy of Mantua. But through its efficacy, and even more its aims, it laid the basis for a new collaboration between officials and the intellectual class.

This collaboration was to emerge increasingly in the wider field of economic activities. In Tuscany it was Sallustio Bandini's influence on Neri which lay behind the latter's support for the freeing of the export of grain from a single region – the Maremma – for a limited period (1738). In Lombardy the administration, bedevilled by the frequent and arbitrary changes in frontiers which encouraged smuggling, achieved a customs agreement over transit trade with Piedmont and Modena (1751–2). In Naples attempts were made to develop trade with the Levant, and in 1740 an edict was passed to encourage the immigration of foreigners and Jews. Popular opposition, the famine of that year, the Messina plague of 1743 and finally the Austrian invasion of 1744 made Charles III retreat. It was another example of the deep-rooted character of the opposition and the disruptive effect of the wars. But already by the 1750s the reforming administrators were gaining courage. By then they were beginning to win the respect of the new intellectual class. There was a convergence between the two groups in their awareness of the developments in Europe and the problems besetting the Italian states, in their vision of the necessary solutions. A new mentality was emerging.

4

The 'new' intellectuals

The origins of the new culture

The intellectual revival in Italy can be traced back to the last decade of the seventeenth century. Its origins are to be found in the renewed curiosity about scientific and philosophical developments outside Italy, in the spread of new critical standards of erudition and an avid 'encyclopedic' search for knowledge, in the emergence of a secular culture out of the 'jurisdictionalist' struggle to confine papal authority within its proper limits. At first restricted to isolated individuals, then spreading to small groups, even schools, the developing contacts with European culture brought a growing awareness of the advances over the classical world made by modern civilization, but also of Italy's backwardness compared to much of Europe. This backwardness was ascribed to the stifling effects of the 'official' counter-reformist culture in Italy, to a conformist mentality which led to acquiescence in the teachings of churchmen and lawyers, an acceptance of scholasticism, superstition and curialism.

In the eyes of those who resented and chafed at the restrictions which accompanied such attitudes, the defence of these traditional values was personified in the Jesuits. In fact, until the late seventeenth century, the Jesuits displayed a remarkable capacity to accommodate new ideas within their own system, allowing the discussion of Descartes and even Newton. But they remained the paladins of papal authority and ecclesiastical control of education, propagators of a casuistic theology, watchdogs of Italian purity against foreign, especially Protestant, contamination. Free intellectual enquiry was inevitably at odds with the monopoly of 'true' knowledge asserted by the counter-reformist culture of the Church. As the friction caused by this clash of ideas was transferred onto an institutional plane by the employment of ecclesiastical censorship and the Inquisition, so the intellectuals were drawn towards more direct political involvement through their growing awareness that only political measures could restrict the power of the Church.

One important source for the development of this challenge to a conformist, traditionally minded, religious mentality was to be found within the Church itself, initially outside Italy. Under the leadership of the scholarly French monks Montfaucon and Mabillon, ecclesiastical texts were subjected to critical analysis, which cast doubt on accepted traditions and aroused fresh interest in the early history of the Church and the classical world. If Montfauçon failed to arouse Italian enthusiasm for the Greek world, if Mabillon's concern for patristics did not take root, a 'Mabillon school' still developed in Italy after the great Benedictine monk's visit to the peninsula in 1685. The school, headed by the Benedictine monk Bacchini and enthusiastically supported by the bibliophile Magliabechi, was concerned to teach the new critical, philological, comparative method, to apply reason to erudite research. Bacchini's greatest pupils were Scipione Maffei and Lodovico Muratori, who displayed in their erudition and encyclopedic interests how the new methodology was applicable not only to ecclesiastical history (where it was employed, almost as a pastime, to disproving the existence of many saints), but to secular history, law and ever-wider branches of knowledge.

Muratori shifted interests decisively from the classical to the medieval world. Antiquarian erudition remained a fundamental characteristic of Italian culture throughout the eighteenth century and by its cult of the past encouraged local provincial patriotism, sometimes – as in the subject Venetian cities – becoming so obsessive a passion as to impede the later penetration of Enlightenment ideas. But this same erudition lay behind the doubts about the universal validity of Roman law, the growing interest in the German school of natural law, the belief in the need for legal codification. For the encyclopedism of the great scholars spread outwards, explaining the problems of the present times through their medieval origins, denouncing the ignorance, superstition, misery and bellicosity of the past, pointing to the progress of recent centuries, the superiority of the 'moderns' over the 'ancients', the undeniable benefits of the use of reason. Such were the beliefs of those remarkable *dotti* Muratori and Maffei, the isolated scholars who dominated the early decades of the eighteenth century and who, through their wide-ranging interests, tireless correspondence and travels, brought to Italy the new (and not so new) ideas discussed in France, Holland, England, Germany and Austria. This new critical and rational approach led them to challenge accepted values, albeit with hesitation and caution. It also made them increasingly conscious of the anomalies and ills of contemporary Italian society, but fortified them with faith in peace and humanitarianism, with hope in the possibilities of improvement through change. Above all, it slowly transformed their erudition into the conviction that study must be useful, that knowledge must benefit society.

No-one better than Muratori personified this evolution. At the opening of the century his interests were typically encyclopedist: he wished to publish a bibliographical journal to bring to the attention of Italians new foreign books, he defended 'modern' literature against the 'ancients', he was patriotically determined to publish a collection of the sources of Italian history, such as existed in other countries. As the decades passed, scarred by the bitter experiences of the wars, Muratori became ever more aware of the strident contrasts and anomalies within the Italian states. But he remained wholly convinced of the progress of European civilization, a progress marked above all by the use of 'scientific' reason and experience, the antithesis of the traditional abstract logic and deductive philosophy of the schoolmen. Deeply religious, frightened of the implications of an absolute faith in man-made reason, Muratori hovered between an almost fatalistic belief in Christian charity as the only response to the misery and poverty of this world and confidence in reform for the common good, in a more usefully educated ruling class, above all in a prince aware of his responsibilities towards his people.

If the new critical, rational approach led to the questioning of established intellectual traditions and hence to a readiness to accept, or promote, change beneficial to the commonweal, the struggle to limit the pretensions and power of the Church was to develop into recognition of the values of the secular State. Clashes between Church and State had marked the entire period of Spanish domination, supremely at Venice under Sarpi. The struggle revived with particular intensity from the 1680s at Naples, where a small group of lawyers challenged papal claims to suzerainty over the kingdom. The traditional scholastic, legalistic methods of disputation, adopted by the Jesuits in their assertions of ecclesiastical authority, began to be refuted by these lawyers in terms not only of historical precedent, but of human reason and natural law. Their interests, as reflected in the authors they discussed in the privacy of their academy, were characteristic of international European culture at the end of the seventeenth century – Gassendi, Descartes, Spinoza, the Royal Society, Machiavelli, Hobbes, Bodin. The new historical approach, with its political and religious implications of the sovereignty of the secular State and freedom of enquiry, was exploited with supreme ability in his *Civil History of the Kingdom of Naples* (1723) by the greatest of these Neapolitan anti-curialists, Pietro Giannone. Individually and as a group these lawyers were wholly dependent on royal protection. In the early 1690s they were subjected to fierce persecution by the Inquisition. As Spanish rule collapsed, they turned hopefully to Austria; disillusioned by Austrian rule, they prepared the ground through their writings for Charles Bourbon. At Naples, what had begun as a limited defence of royal independence from papal suzerainty, argued in traditional terms, had developed by the 1730s into a broader awareness of the need for secular authority and close contacts with the most advanced European culture as premisses for the creation of a modern state.

Elsewhere in Italy the juridical struggles with the Church continued. At Milan, Venice and Parma, in these early decades the disputes perhaps retained their traditional character. At Modena it was Muratori himself who denied papal claims to Comacchio (1708). In Piedmont, Victor Amadeus II deliberately extended the scope of his challenge to Rome by breaking Jesuit control of the University, inviting from abroad rationalist intellectuals, who disputed the administrative and theological claims of the Church, even utilizing the heretical Alberto Radicati. Until reduced to silence or forced to flee by the king's cynical concordat with Rome (1726-7), this small group at Turin kept in close contact with the intellectuals who were challenging papal authority elsewhere in Italy, such as Muratori and Giannone, as well as with foreign, even Protestant writers, and strove to open up this bureau-cratic, regimented sub-Alpine state to European culture.

The early eighteenth-century Italian movement to restrict papal authority embraced heterogeneous, even contradictory beliefs and personalities. The new rationalism, the new scientific ideas – even the symbolic ritual of the freemasons – encouraged scepticism about the traditional authority of the Church. But, more specifically, the movement gained in richness and com-plexity from the political and religious opposition to the papacy that had developed in varying guises outside Italy. Gallicanism – the demand for the administrative independence of the Church from papal control, which had become a major issue in the France of Louis XIV – developed in Piedmont. Many of the arguments of imperial propaganda against papal claims in Germany were repeated in Modena and Parma. Jansenism – whose austere doctrine of salvation by grace alone had been condemned by Clement XI's uncompromising bull *Unigenitus* (1713) – gained support among enlightened Catholics in Italy as opposition to such papal demands for obedience spread in France and led to the schismatic defiance of the Catholic Church of Utrecht (1723). The whole movement was held together by hostility to the Jesuits, by an anti-curialist vision of Catholicism, reminiscent of Sarpi. But, as Sarpi's campaign had relied upon the protection of the Venetian govern-ment, so this broader Italian anti-papal movement of the early eighteenth century was dependent upon the protection of the secular rulers, and hence tended to offer support to, even to identify itself with, the regalist doctrine of royal supremacy in Church affairs.

The aims and convictions of those who found themselves directly or in-directly involved in this struggle differed widely, from the practical politics of Victor Amadeus to the Jansenist sympathies of Celestino Galiani, from the protestantizing deism of Radicati to the religious obedience of Muratori. There were many who were hostile to the dogmatic intolerance of the Jansenists, few who were ready to follow Radicati, Giannone, or later Pilati,

in their progress from religious doubt to protestantism, tolerance, even
deism or atheism. Enlightened Catholics, like Muratori, even intellectuals
who accepted the implications of applying reason and experience, like the
Venetian Ortes, remained firm in their sense of obedience to the Church.
But despite differences of ideas, beliefs and personalities, the anti-curialists
tended to join forces in the struggle, not least because of the danger of
persecution. Ecclesiastical censorship and the Inquisition remained serious
threats, especially in the 1730s when the princes, seized by the political
crisis that dominated Italy, partially withdrew their protection. As late as
1739 the Tuscan poet and freemason Tommaso Crudeli could be arrested
by the Inquisition and forced to abjure, despite the protection of the leading
Tuscan minister, Richecourt. Only during the long pontificate of the open-
minded Benedict XIV (1740–58), when Jesuit influence was on the wane,
could criticism and opposition be voiced more openly. But even then the
new ideas could only be expressed freely under the protection of the prince.
Thus the struggle to limit the powers of the Church drew its intellectual
supporters increasingly onto more immediately political grounds, because
of both their dependence upon the princes and their increasing awareness that the Church's authority could only be curbed by reforms imposed upon it. And the impulse towards reform, whether political
(restricting the legal or economic privileges of the Church) or pedagogic
(through a more 'useful' education of the clergy), could only come from
the prince.

By the 1740s the new scientific mentality, faith in science's utility to man,
strengthened the belief not only in the desirability, but in the practicality of
reform. The scientific tradition had never wholly vanished in Italy, particularly in centres strongly influenced by Galileo or Pomponazzi, such as Pisa,
Padua, Bologna or Naples. But the later seventeenth-century Italian
scientists were very open to the new developments in Europe. They looked
abroad to Descartes and Gassendi, as much as to Galileo, exploring the new
horizons opened up by this experimental method based on a mathematical
intuition of reality. By the 1710s Newtonian ideas began to penetrate Italy,
spreading rapidly through the close connections of the different scientific
centres. Celestino Galiani at Rome trained many of the young generation,
who carried Newtonian experimental concepts all over Italy in their intellectual wanderings. Antonio Conti returned from France and England to
construct new apparatus for physical experiments at Turin in 1726, and to
convince Vallisnieri at Milan, Giannone at Venice, of the validity of the
Newtonian method. In these same years, Locke's empirical ideas began to
penetrate, significantly, the same circles. As early as 1713 Antonio Conti was
reading Locke's *Essay Concerning Human Understanding*. Locke's empiricism proved more difficult to assimilate than Newtonian ideas, because of its
obviously dangerous implications for religious beliefs. In 1733 Galiani was

denounced to the Holy Office; the following year Clement XII banned Locke's *Human Understanding*.

But by this time it was already too late. The interest in 'modern' ideas, in liberty of enquiry, had acquired a new character, a specific methodology applicable to the study of all branches of knowledge, inevitably challenging traditional beliefs, even religious faith. The intense personal contacts and correspondence of the early isolated scholars, Maffei, Muratori and Magliabechi, had been replaced by groups, even schools, centred around outstanding teachers in the universities and academies at Pisa, Bologna, Rome, Naples, Padua, Turin and Venice. The rapidity with which the new ideas had followed each other was vividly described by the hostile Paolo Maria Doria:

> When I began my studies, everyone followed the philosophy of Pierre Gassendi. . . . But this frenzy hardly lasted, because shortly after Epicurus' sect was banished and René Descartes' doctrine embraced. . . . Applause for this second philosophy lasted for some years, after which the modern philosophers tired of it too, and started searching for other new sciences. First they got hold of the doctrines of Mr Newton, but because that great mathematician and philosopher does not meddle much with metaphysics, many of the moderns then turned to the philosophy of Mr Locke . . . and this is now the persuasion followed by many masters in Rome, Naples and the other parts of Italy. . . .
> (Garin, 36, vol. 2, p. 898)

The success of Algarotti's *Sir Isaac Newton's Philosophy Explain'd for the Use of Ladies*, first published in Italy in 1737, reflected the degree of diffusion of the new philosophy, the new methodology of analysis, experiment and observation as the basis for the deduction of general propositions, in contrast to the dangerous abstractions of Cartesian 'systems'. Even metaphysics was placed on an experimental basis by the application of Lockeian empiricism. Newton and Locke belonged to the cultural patrimony of all 'modern' intellectual groups, even in such minor centres as Genoa or Palermo.

This widespread interest in the new philosophy among intellectual groups throughout Italy made them more critical of established traditions in any sphere -- including government, administration and law -- and more receptive to rationally based, empirical attempts at change, such as could be seen in Lombardy, Tuscany and Naples.

Italy and Europe: reason and reform

These varied, often contradictory elements -- from the new methods of erudition to the different currents that formed the anti-curial movement, to the scientific advances -- had brought Italian intellectuals into continuous contact with European culture. They all shared a strong sense of rejoining the intellectual community in Europe, after a long period of isolation. The new ideas often came from abroad and were largely disseminated by foreigners. Maffei was typical of many in the earlier eighteenth century who had thus enriched their own experiences in their travels abroad. The young Pietro Verri was not alone in searching for a career abroad and returning with a new awareness of the possibilities and methods of change. Foreign visitors on the Grand Tour or foreign residents in Italy actively spread knowledge about 'experimental philosophy' or theological dissensions. The English consul at Turin, Allen, sent a copy of Newton's *Principia Mathematica* to Sicily; at Florence, an obligatory staging-post on the Grand Tour, English visitors stimulated discussion of the scientific debates current in the Royal Society; at Rome Cardinal Polignac encouraged Jansenist tendencies. Leghorn in particular was an open gateway to Europe. The spread of free-masonry in the 1730s, in Tuscany and then elsewhere, accelerated the diffusion of the new concepts. The lodge at Florence, at first an English reserve, was subsequently opened to Italians; fairly soon foreigners and Italians were meeting without the formal impositions of social etiquette.

Above all, the increasing importation or translation of foreign books and journals – despite the vagaries of the censorship system – played a central role in the formation of the new mentality. Italian journals were closely modelled on foreign, especially French and English, journals and like their prototypes changed in character and purpose from the purely informative, bibliographical encyclopedism of Maffei's *Giornale de' letterati d'Italia* to the critical discussion used as an instrument of cultural propaganda of the Verri brothers' *Il Caffè*. But for Maffei, as for the Verri brothers, a central function of the journal was to keep Italians fully informed of the progress of European culture.

This sense of rejoining the mainstream of European civilization was to remain the predominant characteristic of the Italian Enlightenment. It was a feeling shared by reforming administrators and rulers as well as by intellectuals. The new administrative methods introduced in the foreign-ruled states owed much to the examples of Vienna, Paris and Madrid. At Parma, during the years of du Tillot's control, a virtually French court was created, headed by Condillac. In Tuscany, Leopold and his ministers felt themselves in the vanguard of European progress, alongside the margrave of Baden and the crown prince of Sweden, in introducing physiocratic reforms.

But for the intellectuals, to conceive of the European community implied a recognition of Italian backwardness. As the aged Muratori wrote to the Neapolitan economist Genovesi: 'I observed with envy, years ago, those learned men beyond the Alps who discuss a philosophy freed of the fripperies of the barbarian centuries with such acuteness and precision and so much liberty' (Venturi, 30, p. 533). A year later, in 1748, he could write bleakly: 'If one compares Italy to France, England, Flanders, Holland and some German lands, a good part of Italy remains inferior in industry and trade to those countries beyond the mountains' (Venturi, 30, p. 186). Intellectually and economically Italy had lagged behind the rest of Europe.

As the reform movement developed, the Italian intellectuals remained only too aware of their debt to foreign, especially French, culture. The classic writers of the French Enlightenment, such as Montesquieu, Diderot and D'Alembert, as well as Rousseau, were the inspiration behind Beccaria's *Essay on Crimes and Punishments* (1764). By the time of Filangieri's *Science of Legislation* (1780), alongside such classical *philosophes* as D'Alembert and Helvétius, this morose Neapolitan legal reformer was turning to later, more radical *lumières*, to physiocrats and philosophers of history, such as Mably, D'Holbach, Robertson and Hume. But by then Filangieri could also turn to such Italian writers as Genovesi and Pietro Verri. For the Italian Enlightenment had come of age; Italian writers and reformers had made a positive contribution to this cosmopolitan movement. Already in 1767 the Modenese reformer Paradisi could polemically defend Italy's contribution to the Enlightenment by listing renowned Italian scientists and *philosophes*. By the later 1770s – when the reform movement had met with a set-back in France – the continuing progress in Italy reinforced the sense of achievement, without lessening the close ties with foreign culture.

The importance of the empirical method, of the new 'experimental philosophy', derived from the belief that it offered criteria, already elaborated and successfully applied in the experimental sciences, specifically applicable to all aspects of human activity. There was a strong sense of scientific progress, dating back to the inventions and discoveries of the preceding hundred years, identifiable with the names of Bacon, Galileo, Newton and Locke. But equally, there was the conviction that this scientific knowledge, these *lumi*, were directly linked to the economic and civil progress of such countries as England, France or Holland. The new method could both be understood by all educated men who used their reason, and applied for the good of society. In this it differed from and was superior to a generic acceptance of reason or, even worse, of Cartesian or other 'systems'. For this reason Algarotti, like Voltaire in his *Lettres philosophiques*, set out with a deliberate publicistic aim to explain the new 'experimental philosophy' to a wider audience. The all-embracing erudition, the wide-ranging scientific culture of earlier decades, was deliberately restricted by a concentration on those elements which were 'useful' to man and society.

Optimism, faith in man's capacity to achieve peace and a more civilized, humanitarian existence were the keynotes of the new Enlightenment mentality. By the early 1750s Bartolomeo Intieri, the aged administrator of great Tuscan estates in the kingdom of Naples, who had followed with sympathy the regalist struggles against the Church of the Neapolitan lawyers and had participated in the cultural evolution of Italian scientific circles, was convinced of the immediate utility of the experimental sciences for the continued progress of mankind. As he wrote to the Tuscan scientist Antonio Cocchi:

> Europe has glorious achievements to vaunt over the last 350 years. If it perseveres in its noble and fine purpose of instruction, particularly in matters of use to the public good, as it has done over this period of time, then mankind can hope for all forms of goodness and happiness. (Venturi, 101, p. 448)

Despite 'those three great ills, ignorance, servitude and poverty', there was hope that even Italy 'may lead a less hard life than at present, since its life and that of all Christian Europe is far, far less miserable and unhappy than the life of Europeans until about the fifteenth century' (Venturi, 101, p. 432).

These hopes were based on a growing conviction that economic reform was the most effective instrument for progress. The major discussions of the 1740s and 1750s reveal the slow and difficult emergence of those beliefs, and the hesitations of many, particularly the older intellectuals. The disputes in the 1740s over usury and over the number of religious holidays, in which Muratori and Maffei had taken a leading part, already showed an awareness of the negative economic and social consequences of too rigid an adherence to traditional moral attitudes. A commercial interest rate on loans had to be accepted, at least within limits, asserted Maffei, as a new world was emerging with the growth of prosperity. The excessive number of obligatory religious holidays had to be reduced, maintained Muratori, as they deprived the peasants and craftsmen of work and only encouraged drunkenness and the corruption of ecclesiastical dispensations. The prince had a responsibility to carry through such a reform: 'The secular government must insist on having shops open on popular holidays. . . . The poor people here need to be instructed and disabused' (Venturi, 30, p. 158). In neither case did Benedict XIV meet these reformers' demands. In these same years Muratori attacked the abuses and privileges encouraged by the disorders of the legal system and persisted in his search for the methods to achieve public happiness. Once more he looked to the prince. Once more his urgent sense of the need for practical reform was accompanied by an acute consciousness of the overwhelming obstacles and by a groping awareness that the traditional humanistic-legal training was inadequate, that the study of political economy gave the key to the future.

The polemic over witches and magic during the decade 1745–55, which corresponded to D'Alembert's and Diderot's attack on miracles in the *Encyclopédie*, rapidly developed into a fierce debate between reason and faith, involving both the older and the younger intellectuals. The contemporaneous discussion between the French *philosophes* La Mettrie and Maupertuis on the scientific calculation of pleasure and pain, with its implications of social criteria of utility in place of religious morality, aroused a similar fierce debate in Italy. Reason and experience now challenged religion and faith.

At this point many of the intellectuals, scholars like Muratori, even some scientists, drew back: 'Does not the denial of the existence of demons open the way and even lead directly to a denial of the existence of God as well?' (Venturi, 30, p. 371), wrote the conservative Benedetto Bonelli. Muratori had already warned that reason could lead to error, and had lumped together sceptics, followers of Gassendi and Locke, deists, atheists and libertines. The scientist Zanotti refused to accept the fashionable belief of many

> who, without concern for the principles of honesty, look at society alone and want it to be born solely of profit and the individual's comfort, and derive all the duties of man from this first premise. But I believe that they deceive themselves greatly and do little honour to men, believing that they have come into society each one moved by his own interest alone, without allowing that any part can have been played by 'respect for other people'. (Venturi, 30, p. 398)

The polemic between reason and faith never developed into an open struggle for toleration such as that waged by Voltaire in France. The Church was too strong, the danger of compromising other reforms too great. The extremist religious reformers, especially those influenced by protestantism or deism, were isolated and went into exile, like Radicati and Giannone.

Nor did all men believe that economic reform could be the instrument of effective change. It required too radical a revaluation of accepted beliefs, too arduous an acquisition of new concepts, too unreserved an optimism. Zanotti clung to his belief in Christian morality, the Newtonian Ortes was too pessimistic, even the young Ferdinando Galiani, who analysed clearly the function of money in stimulating productive activities, remained too sceptical.

But in the 1750s and 1760s a new generation of young intellectuals emerged, who optimistically believed in the possibility of progress through change and turned to the princes as the only effective agencies of reform. The earlier diffidence towards the rulers, the fear of betrayal after the bitter experience of early imperial rule, the impatience at insufficiently bold reforms, so typical of the previous decades, of the Neapolitan anti-curialists, of the young Lombard Pietro Verri, gave way to new hope and a desire for collaboration. Where the princes were active, the reform movement gathered strength. Elsewhere – in Piedmont, Venice, Genoa, the Papal States – the intellectuals turned hopefully to the example of the reforming states.

The Enlightenment vision of the social bases of reform

The prince alone seemed capable of achieving reform. Little hope could be placed, as in France, in 'intermediate bodies', for such institutions as the

Milanese senate or the Sicilian parliament were the bulwark of privileged interests. Nor were the examples of the republics of Venice and Genoa very inspiring. Montesquieu's *Esprit des lois* was discussed at Naples by Genovesi, as at Milan by Verri, but decisively rejected. Montesquieu's vision of the English constitution aroused no desire for emulation, not least because English liberty seemed vitiated by licence. 'The populace of London is the most insufferable of any to be found in the world', wrote one Italian visitor on his return (Annoni, 22, p. 275), and his verdict summed up the dangers of excessive liberty. Only in Tuscany was Montesquieu of significant influence, where he seemed to offer a theoretical justification to the collaboration of ruler and landed proprietors.

Muratori had already stressed that authority should impose limits upon itself. The age-old view that the sovereign had a duty to his people acquired new significance in terms of the practical as well as the moral training required to carry out such a duty, which were reflected in the treatises on the princes' education that appeared throughout the century, written by Doria, Muratori, and others. By the later decades the princes, like such foreign contemporaries as Frederick the Great, could view themselves as delegates of the people. Indeed, the examples of foreign rulers like Frederick or Catherine the Great were frequently invoked, even by minor figures such as the Apulian writer Giovanni Presta who sent samples of the oil he refined to Catherine. The particular vision of the prince that emerged was the Voltairean 'legal despot', contrasted to Montesquieu's 'oriental despot'. As Giuseppe Gorani asserted in his derivative *The True Despotism* (1770), legal despotism is

> a formidable force, which destroys every other power, but which, far from frightening those who consider the system it creates, can be the easiest source of public prosperity – if this figure (in which so many forces are embodied) is regulated by virtue and by knowledge of the true means to stay virtuous. (Venturi, in 27, p. 484)

The task of the enlightened ruler, a task that required a knowledge of all 'useful' sciences, was seen as the removal of the obstacles that impeded the functioning of a 'natural code' of law and even of economics.

The reforms of the princes, however, would be effective only if supported by educated opinion. The early intellectuals and reformers all laid emphasis on the need for a more practical, technical education: the universities were to be reformed, new schools created, more useful subjects introduced into ecclesiastical seminaries. Even literature had to be useful, said Baretti and Alfieri, echoing Muratori and Genovesi. Reason, wrote Genovesi, 'is not useful until it has become conscious practice; nor does it become such, until it is so disseminated in our customs and crafts that we adopt it as our sovereign rule, almost without being aware of it' (Genovesi, in 28, p. 100). On a correct education, wrote Maria Theresa in the preamble to a decree, 'depends the culture of minds and rectification of hearts, and in consequence the formation and propagation of enlightened and unprejudiced subjects who can uphold and support salutary regulations' (Peroni, 61, p. 283). The emphasis was already shifting from the practical advantages of a usefully educated administrative class to the need for the support of public opinion. 'It is well known that peoples are governed by great opinions: but in lettered countries, all the great opinions are born in the schools and then spread among the peoples', believed Genovesi (Genovesi, in 28, p. 228). Pietro Verri, not so optimistic, viewed progress as depending less on actual education than on the irrational movement of 'opinion'. It was here that he saw the importance of the intellectuals – to combat prejudice and accepted beliefs, to win the support of public opinion for reform. Whatever the defects of the *Encyclopédie*, it had won public support. As he wrote to his brother Alessandro,

> With much quackery the Encyclopedists have displayed philosophy in a more venerable and luminous manner, not for your observation or mine, but for the public's. . . . At the sound of their imperious voice, sovereigns have hastened to seek their friendship. . . . The exhibitionism of the Encyclopedists is an evil . . . I agree with you; but it is an evil that has come to do great good in Europe.
> (Valeri, 57, p. 143)

Already in 1750 Pompeo Neri had urged publication of his report on the reform of the land-tax in order to win support for the new cadastral register and isolate resistance. The Milanese journal, *Il Caffè*, Verri felt satisfied, had been effective on a wider front.

The function of the writers, thought Pilati, was to prepare public opinion. Longo judged that 'it would be insufficient and without effectiveness, if one tried to repair the present ills exclusively by force of law, without prising up their roots, which lie in a public opinion nourished particularly by ignorance' (Longo, in 27, p. 245). Paradisi could idealize the figure of the new intellectual: 'The philosopher has formed the man. The philosopher orders society. . . . Fortunate is the nation which harkens to the philosopher, where philosophy acts as moderator as much of public affairs as of laws!' (Paradisi, in 29, pp. 445–6). The task of the intellectual was thus eminently practical. He was as much concerned with disseminating useful knowledge as with discovering it. Paolo Frisi, cosmopolite, mathematician and technical adviser to the Habsburg rulers, was regarded (and regarded himself) as the Italian D'Alembert, for whom practical experience was of more value than theoretical hypotheses. His eulogy of Galileo, wrote Alessandro Verri, was supremely successful as it animated 'cold geometry with some flashes of philosophical eloquence' (Venturi, 27, p. 300). As long as the intellectual accepted his subsidiary role, as long as he maintained his faith in the positive function of the prince, collaboration was possible.

There was less agreement about the identity of the ruling groups which, with the intellectuals, were to assist the prince. The traditional ruling class, the ecclesiastical dignitaries and nobles, were the prime object of attack, the former as they represented an usurpation of authority in the secular State, the latter because they displayed a blatant disregard for the public interest, both groups because their hereditary privileges had so negative an effect on the economy.

Discussions about the nature of the nobility – by Neri, Genovesi, and many others in all the Italian States – were of significance, as they revealed the inadequacies of traditional definitions in a changing society where wealth seemed more important than inherited title and where equality before the law was a fundamental aspiration. In later years, criticism of nobility by inheritance could lead to quite radical egalitarian attitudes in such writers as Mario Pagano, but could also be utilized by more pessimistic writers to demonstrate the inevitability of inequality. But already by the 1760s there was clear recognition that property, not inherited title, was the essential qualification for political responsibility, and that only a renovated nobility, purged of many if not all its privileges, could claim the right to form part of the ruling class. Property, as Pietro Verri wrote, 'is the basis of justice in every civilized society' (Valeri, 57, p. 172).

That the reforms needed the support of a ruling class imbued with, or at least ready to accept, the new approach to government was not in question, for the writers were only too conscious of their own lack of effective power and their dependence upon the prince. The Tuscan Francesco Gianni, perhaps the most practical of the reformers, described the opposition of vested interests to Leopold's reforms as an 'invisible barrier against his projects' (Venturi, 27, p. 984). Some hope was placed in enlightened landowners, especially in Tuscany where the Academy of the Georgofili seemed the expression of a new mentality. It was this hope that inspired the numerous but wholly ineffectual agrarian academies that sprang up all over Italy. The lower clergy could also be of assistance to the reforming prince not only by maintaining order and tranquillity, but by imparting 'useful' education to the peasants.

But, more than with the landowners, the Lombard and Tuscan intellectuals saw the future as lying with a rising generation of efficient administrators, equipped to deal with economic and administrative problems on the basis of an enlightened, 'philosophic' training, rather than by the traditional methods of *ad hoc* legislative interventions concerned more with juridical form than effective content. Naturally such writer-reformers as Pietro Verri did not expect the rise of this new administrative class to reduce their own personal influence, so that Joseph II's creation of a modern, relatively efficient but wholly subordinate bureaucracy came as a bitter shock. In Naples, where no such administrative class existed, Genovesi turned to the educated, 'the middle order', as he called them, consisting of 'priests, monks, teachers of the humanities, jurists and all private gentlemen' (Venturi, 28, p. 28), while his successors Filangieri and Pagano placed their hopes, less vaguely, in an idealized body of honest magistrates. Behind these specific groups of potential collaborators, the intellectuals were agreed on the need for an active 'middle class', by which was usually meant such non-privileged, (not excessively) wealthy and enterprising individuals as merchants, industrialists, craftsmen and smallholders. As the aristocratic Neapolitan reformer, Domenico Caracciolo, wrote to Tanucci, 'I have found by experience, in all the countries where I have lived, that the middle class, the class in the middle of society, is always the most capable, the most well-bred, the most virtuous' (Croce, 104, p. 96). This might well be so in England and France (where Caracciolo had lived) or even in Lombardy or Tuscany; in Sicily, where he became viceroy, such a class was virtually non-existent.

The intellectuals' vision of the agencies of change was ultimately dependent on the belief that those members of existing leading groups in society who supported the reforms would grow in number and broaden the social base, as education and practical change showed their effects. These groups were expected to play a subordinate role in supporting the prince's reforms. But in later years, as doubts about the sovereign's absolute powers increased, greater stress was placed upon the independence of their role; and the ground was thus prepared for later liberal, constitutional ideas of representation.

Production and public happiness

Change could not be achieved by traditional methods. The legislative interventions of earlier monarchs had shown their inadequacy and were in any case vitiated by their scholastic, legalistic approach. Legal systems constituted a baffling maze full of contradictions; new decrees merely added to legislative inflation. 'To put one's faith in laws is a youthful error', wrote that wise old fox Tanucci (Croce, 104, p. 29). By the 1760s many of the bolder intellectuals, such as Verri and Filangieri, felt, like Muratori some decades earlier, that the only solution was to abolish the existing system, to abandon the age-old reliance on Roman law and write new codes.

The very purpose of law had changed. The natural law tradition, the German school of Wolff, was employed to justify the firm belief in equality before the law. Modern jurists began to reject the notion that legislation had a sacred character in that it reflected the historical past, and urged the conscious adaptation of laws to fit the development of society and their exploitation as an instrument to direct that development.

The new instruments had to be based on an understanding of economics. This conviction derived partly from the belief, expressed by Genovesi and Verri as by Voltaire and the *Encyclopédie*, that civil and intellectual progress was directly linked to economic progress. But even more it emerged from awareness that economic conditions had changed in Europe, that the classic mercantilist approach had failed (and was shown to have failed by the decline of Spain), that more precise technical knowledge, a more conscious theoretical basis were required for the formulation of economic policy. The impelling faith in the pursuit of public happiness, the utilitarian belief in the possibility of achieving pleasure (for a society, not only for an individual) led to the equation of happiness with economic prosperity, with 'national wealth', as it was described by so many writers. For many of the intellectuals, with strong humanitarian feelings, the ubiquitous presence of poverty and misery could be reduced or eliminated, the increase of national wealth would improve the material conditions of the poor over an unspecified, but usually relatively short period of time, without need for further government action.

There was thus a search for new techniques, for new methods of analysis, which led to an intensive reading of foreign writers on economic policy, a study of foreign experiences. This was already clearly visible in the monetary discussions of the 1750s, which developed rapidly from an examination of purely monetary phenomena and government manipulation of coinage, still in the tradition of sixteenth-century debates, to broader, deeper analyses of the functions of money in the economy, its relationship with wages, prices, inflation, taxation and commercial policy. The sources of this and the other discussions of these years were the English, French and Spanish late mercantilists and early exponents of partial free trade, such as Mun, Cantillon and Uztáriz. For the young Verri, as for Genovesi, the development of industry and trade still required strong state support and encouragement. But a new emphasis was now placed on the advantages for national wealth of individual initiative ('private vices benefit the public interest' was Mandeville's dictum) and on the circulation of wealth as a condition of economic activity and hence of the generation of further prosperity. Economic policy meant a concern with national, as distinct from individual, output. Within this framework, it was regarded as inevitable that the State should continue to play a leading role, given the absence of a strong entrepreneurial class and the high concentration of wealth in the Italian states. These same negative features also reinforced the belief in the need for a strong sovereign to enforce public over private needs.

The transition to this new economic mentality was not easy, as could be seen in the hesitancy and slowness with which attitudes changed towards luxury, traditionally condemned by Church and statesmen alike on moral and economic grounds. The older writers, such as Paolo Maria Doria, remained hostile. Muratori, searching for a new path, remained uncertain. Even Genovesi hesitated for some time before he finally decided that luxury acted as an agent of economic (and implicitly civil) progress, as it was 'a means to propagate, perfect, stimulate the arts, the spirit and polish of the nation, and to offer a livelihood to those families that have no other capital than their labour' (Genovesi, in 28, p. 199). By the 1770s the Piedmontese writer D. F. Vasco could regard luxury as evidence of the development of civilization; for what former ages regarded as luxuries were progressively transformed into 'the needs of comfort', 'needs merely stipulated by opinion' (Levi, 45, pp. 812, 814). By then, even though there were a few writers who still attacked luxury because of its negative consequences for the poor, criticism usually came on economic grounds from physiocrats or those influenced by their thought, who regarded the encouragement of luxury as a wasteful diversion of resources from the necessary modernization of agriculture, the basic source of wealth.

All the writers and reformers were agreed on the need to unify the domestic market by removing internal hindrances to the movement of goods. The attack on ecclesiastical and feudal privileges of all types, jurisdictional rights and exemptions, tolls, tithes and private monopolies, was for economic as much as for egalitarian reasons. In the states where they were still important (particularly Tuscany, Lombardy and Venice) guilds were attacked because they were deemed to restrict production. The same concern for production underlay the drive to simplify taxation systems and redeem the accumulated debts of governments and local administrations. The notable efforts of the reforming governments in these directions inevitably won the support of the intellectuals.

Until well into the 1760s customs barriers were still regarded as necessary to protect national industry by discouraging the export of raw materials and the import of 'unnecessary' goods. In fact, the prime concern of almost all the reformers in this and later decades remained the export rather than the domestic market. Hence there was a readiness to accept tariff barriers penalizing foreign goods, despite their connotations of inefficiency and corruption. Nevertheless, as the years went by, doubts increased about both the efficacy of offering subsidies and incentives to domestic industry and the negative effects of customs duties on trading interests. As the basic importance of agriculture became clearer, particularly through the traumatic experience of the 1764 famine and the growing influence of the physiocratic writers, there was increasing belief in the need for free trade, at least for free exports, especially for agricultural produce, as higher prices would stimulate production. This faith in physiocratic doctrine was most marked among Tuscan reformers, but was also of considerable significance to Lombard and Modenese writers; it even influenced some Neapolitan, Papal and Piedmontese intellectuals belatedly in the 1780s, when the reaction to the agricultural, free trade tenets of physiocracy had already set in.

The same preoccupation with production explained the almost unanimous desire for a more equitable distribution of property. According to the reformers such a redistribution of the land, like increased production, would generate positive social changes. For both economic and social reasons, they all agreed that owners should live on and cultivate their lands, as English proprietors were alleged to do. Given the absolute belief in the right of property and the optimistic expectation of a spontaneous improvement of social conditions, it was not surprising that the reformers' proposals to obtain a less inequitable distribution of land were very moderate. For Beccaria and Filangieri the abolition of legal ties prohibiting the sale of land, such as entails, would suffice to ensure the disintegration of excessively large patrimonies. For Genovesi and Gianni, the vast royal demesnial properties, communal and ecclesiastical lands should be divided up and leased to peasants on perpetual quit-rents. For Verri, the encouragement of luxury would by itself lead to the dissipation of patrimonies (and, unknown to him, in Sicily this would seem actually to have come to pass).

Inevitably, the high concentration of property remained. Indeed, as physiocratic doctrine spread in the 1760s and 1770s, the economic and social arguments diverged. Physiocracy saw the absolute encouragement of free private initiative as necessary to achieve the 'natural' economic order. All structures that impinged upon individual economic freedom – in agriculture, industry or trade – were obstacles to be removed. For Quesnay and Mirabeau agriculture was the source of all wealth, production had to be increased (not least by investment), landowners needed the inducement of high prices to raise productivity, and this could only be achieved by free trade. It was the duty of the princes to destroy the ties that prevented such conditions from prevailing especially as land was to provide the basis for taxation. Large estates – the most productive unit in agriculture – were the backbone of this system. The sanctity of private property and the encouragement of economic individualism both underlay the attack on communal lands and customary promiscuous rights, regarded as archaic and economically pernicious relics of an earlier stage of civilization. Contempt for the stupidity and prejudices of the peasant was the counterpart to confidence in the innovating landowner. Smallholdings tended to be defended on humanitarian or social, rather than economic grounds. Doubts about physiocratic policy were to arise with the increase in the number of paupers, the sense of growing poverty, the realization that social improvement did not necessarily follow from increased production. A more explicit egalitarian spirit was needed before more radical proposals – even of enforced redistribution of property – could be voiced. By then the collaboration between reforming princes and intellectuals was already breaking down.

Part 2
Reform and authority: Enlightenment and despotism 1760–90

Looking back across the turbulence and violence, the apparent anarchy and undoubted disorder of the revolutionary years, to the peaceful and fundamentally regular rhythm of the reforming experience, some – though by no means all – of the Enlightenment writers and reformers tended to extol the progress achicved by Italy in the half-century following Aix-la-Chapelle. In like manner, long before, Guicciardini had idealized the Italy of Lorenzo de' Medici. This contrast between the experience of 'Enlightened despotism' and the shock of the years of revolutionary domination has recurred as a constant and distorting motif of subsequent historiography, too often preoccupied with later, Risorgimento disputes.

The self-conscious purpose of the *philosophes* and rulers – to reform, indeed transform the structures of the Italian states – is evident in their sustained and concentrated efforts to create by legislation more modern societies, whose civil, economic and social progress would place them on a par with civilization elsewhere in Europe. The attempt was without precedent and unquestionably left a deep imprint. Milan, Florence and Naples formed the epicentres; but there were few capitals or major cities in Italy which could totally resist the impact of the Enlightenment's reforming drive. Its strength derived from the convergences and contrasts, the tensions and misunderstandings between rulers and intellectuals, a dialogue and conflict always cast in terms of the wider experiences of contemporary Europe.

But these long years of conscious reforming effort also contained an inner rhythm of their own, generated by the very dynamic of the reforms. The reforms were undoubtedly conditioned, and often compromised, by the legacies of the past and the lethargic fabric of the societies they were attempting to modify. But, equally, they were conditioned by the ideological convictions of the 'philosophers' and rulers who led the movement. By the 1790s, when enlightened reformism had run its course, many of the

Italian states had undergone transformations. But if administrative structures had often been improved and agrarian production had increased, social inequalities and tensions had reached a new level and the 'philosophers' had lost their optimism. If the Church had been radically weakened, the landed proprietors had been reinforced in their predominance. Some major steps had been taken towards achieving equality before the law, but the widespread and sharp increase of pauperism underlined the exclusion of the poor. To a significant extent, the reformers themselves – especially the more humanitarian among them – were responsible for this new social fabric because of their faith that harmonious social change would emerge spontaneously and relatively rapidly, once the obstacles of the past had been removed by Enlightenment. These contradictory experiences, this tension between reform and authority, Enlightenment and despotism, between legal, administrative changes and their social consequences, form the central themes of our discussion of Enlightened reformism in Italy. The reforms had three specific aims: the modernization of the lay structures and machinery of the states, the development of their economic potential, the achievement of a more equitable – and hence more stable – society. The extent to which the reformers were successful in achieving these ends will be discussed in the following pages.

5

The years of collaboration : 1765–75

By the 1750s, the achievements of the reforming governments attracted the intellectuals. For the first time in half a century Italy had not provided the battlefield for a European conflict, the Seven Years War. Only the house of Savoy and the leader of the Corsican revolt, Pasquale Paoli, had hoped that the conflagration would spread to the peninsula. The new dynasties, instead, had displayed a concern for peace and reform. The Corsican revolt against Genoese domination, which by now had lasted over thirty years, aroused widespread sympathies among writers and administrators as different as Verri and Tanucci. Symbol of the struggle for independence of an Italian 'nation', Corsica under Paoli's rule appeared to combine the advantages of Enlightened leadership with an egalitarian, libertarian spirit. The sale of the island to France in 1768 was felt to be a betrayal. But it was a price that had to be paid, not only because of Italy's political impotence, but because of the need for peace if the possibilities of reform that now seemed to exist in the major Italian states were to be realized. Reform appeared to be gaining ground outside Italy as well, even in France in these years of Choiseul's ambiguous leadership.

In the 1760s the writers thus entered the administrations, the intellectuals became reformers. The numbers actively involved remained limited. There were always those whose ideas were too radical or critical to be absorbed within the princes' ambit. But there were many more, living in the provinces, preoccupied with their own local or specific problems, freemasons, Jansenists or just petty landowners or lawyers, who were increasingly aware of and responsive to the progress of the reforms and the contribution of the intellectuals.

By these years the reforming princes and their leading ministers, also deeply influenced by the new ideas and hopes, were ready, occasionally even anxious, to secure the intellectuals' collaboration. Pietro Verri could cry in triumph in 1763, after a fierce attack on government manipulation of monetary rates of exchange: 'The writings of philosophers remain without reward, but not always without effect' (Venturi, 30, p. 702). Four years later, the imperial minister Kaunitz, writing to Firmian, head of the government in Milan, could express his apprehension at Catherine the Great's invitation to Beccaria, lest the government lose 'a man who is not only well furnished with knowledge, but who would appear, at least on the basis of his book, to be well used to thinking; and this is particularly worrying, given the dearth of thinking men and philosophers in the provinces' (Venturi, 27, p. 19).

It was on the basis of these mutual expectations that a period of practical collaboration between rulers and intellectuals began in Lombardy, Tuscany, Modena and, later, Naples. Italy never experienced the wide-ranging, but less immediately effective public debate of the French *philosophes*, not least because of the attractions of administrative responsibility. The former founder of *Il Caffè* could write with satisfaction of his own metamorphosis:

> Whoever would have guessed that Pietro Verri, head of the *Accademia dei pugni*, author of *Zoroasters* and *A Fit of Spleen*, infantry captain changing the guard at the gates of the ducal palace, would become the successor of those Magnificent Magistrates [who formerly ruled Milan]? (Venturi, 30, pp. 739-40)

Collaboration never proved easy. The whole period was marked by tensions, dissatisfactions, personal animosities. Firmian, a professional administrator, could write angrily to Vienna in 1770, with a barely veiled allusion to Verri:

> For some time now I have been concealing the impertinence of certain persons with connections here; in order to exalt their own mainly chimerical ideas, they put every effort into discrediting the ideas of others, publishing biting criticisms of measures taken by the government, condemning and ridiculing them. (Valsecchi, 59, vol. 2, p. 147 n.)

The intellectuals felt disillusioned by the apparent disregard for their ideas, by their political impotence, by the labyrinthine intrigues of government circles. Verri could write to his brother Alessandro: 'I am desolate, abandoned by my friends, surrounded by the dangers of my office, I have lost my supporter at Court with the death of the abbé Giusti' (Valeri, 57, p. 135). Despite optimism that progress was being made, despite the sense of community among the reformers, despite the feeling that the petty rivalries of the Italian states were being overcome, that reform was successfully disregarding local political frontiers, a sense of constraint remained, of impatience at the insufficiently bold nature of the reforms.

For it was the princes and their ministers who remained firmly in control of the direction and pace of reform. Where the prince seemed too weak (as in Naples), where certain reforms seemed excessive (as with Leopold's Jansenist policy or Joseph II's administrative changes), disquiet and dissatisfaction were to grow and, ultimately, lead to a split between the princes and the intellectuals. But until then, for a period of ten to fifteen years, the intellectuals collaborated in the economic reforms and gave support to the princes' ecclesiastical policies.

Naples: the traditional reformism of Tanucci

It was at Naples, earlier than elsewhere in Italy, that Antonio Genovesi preached the need for urgent and radical economic reform. From his chair of political economy, created for him in 1754, for fifteen years this dedicated teacher brought to an entire generation of pupils the examples of seventeenth-century England and Holland, contemporary France and Spain, as well as nearby Tuscany. His editions of Italian and foreign economic writers, his *Lectures on Trade* (1757-8, 1765-7) and *Academic Letters* (1764, 1769), were concerned with the instruments of economic policy, the technical means of reviving trade and improving agriculture. Although Genovesi was still basically a protectionist, he was converted by the harrowing experience of the 1764 famine towards support for a free grain trade. But the provisioning system remained as strong as the other multiple impediments to economic prosperity. Genovesi died in 1769 dominated by his sense of overwhelming corruption which impeded reform and threatened catastrophe. But his faith in the possibility of change remained firm: 'nevertheless I believe that a few solid principles, if applied with real determination, could produce great good in the long run and prevent that crisis which can only be of use if a state collapses totally' (Venturi, 28, p. 29).

Paradoxically Genovesi's faith was strengthened by his confidence in Tanucci. Yet Tanucci – even after he had assumed control over economic matters on Charles III's departure for Spain in 1759 – remained deaf to Genovesi's proposals. He was suspicious of the abstractions of the French philosophers: 'you can't learn politics out of books; those who write and speak about it in depth are not those who make politics' (Croce, 104, p. 28). Tanucci was too sceptical to share the philosophers' optimism about the effects of radical transformation and only too conscious of the failure of Charles III's economic reforms (cadastral register, Supreme Magistracy for trade, redemption of State debts). In consequence, this misogynic, experienced, dedicated Tuscan ex-professor concentrated on the legal and anti-ecclesiastical reforms he best understood.

After a concentrated attack on the Church, Tanucci passed measures to limit the autonomy of baronial jurisdictions (1759, 1773), and finally launched an assault on the inconsistent and often corrupt interpretation of the laws by magistrates, demanding that they present written justifications of their sentences, insisting that 'judges are executors, not authors of the law; the law must be certain and definite, not arbitrary' (Colletta, 88, p. 221, n. 179). This major reform (comparable to Maupéou's attack on the French

parlements), supported by the young Filangieri, failed, like so many previous measures, because of the opposition of those affected. The failure
marked the division between those who relied on the traditional legal
approach and the reformers imbued with the new culture. Both Leopold
and Joseph II were critical of Tanucci when they met him at Naples. As
Joseph noted:

> Tanucci is a talented and educated man, but an arch-pedant and full of
> miserable wiles and tricks, which he believes to be acts of statesmanship; he
> magnifies all the minutiae and hence is too involved in them, lacking the courage
> to drop them in order to busy himself seriously with more important matters.
> (Colletta, 88, pp. 197–8).

The active collaboration between intellectuals and governments, which
by then had emerged in Lombardy and Tuscany, failed to materialize in
Naples because of Tanucci's dominating presence. When finally, after
Tanucci's fall, the hopes of the Neapolitan reformers revived, their efforts
were not only inadequate, but were out of phase, too late, for collaboration
elsewhere in Italy had already broken down.

Lombardy: Viennese administrators and Milanese 'philosophers'

By the time of Genovesi's death, the Lombard reformers could already
claim some success. The 1750s, a decade of inaction in Naples, had already
witnessed a series of decisive reforms in Lombardy, pushed through by
Pallavicino's successors, Beltrame Cristiani and Pompeo Neri, with the
energetic encouragement of prince von Kaunitz. Viennese control was
strengthened with the abolition of the last symbol of Spanish influence, the
Council of Italy (1757), and the confidence accorded to the imperial plenipotentiary in Lombardy, Cristiani. Genoese by birth, an able lawyer and
diplomat, Cristiani was responsible for successful frontier agreements with
Piedmont, the Papal States and Modena (1751–8) and was architect of the
concordat with Rome (1757). He played an important part in the major
reform of provincial and communal administrations (1755–8) by which the
leading role of the wealthy landowners was reinforced.

The Tuscan Neri had pushed through the cadastral register (1757) at a
moment when government finances had improved with the creation of the
general tax farm and the funding of the government debt. It was above all
the cadastral register, the *censimento*, with its reforming potential as an
incentive to agricultural improvement, that attracted the intellectuals. For
the tax was calculated on the basis of the estimated potential yield of the land
rather than on its actual revenue; at the same time, a guarantee was given
that the amount levied would not be increased. Thus the purpose of the
cadastral register was not merely to increase state revenues, but to act as an

incentive to agricultural improvement, as all future profits from a growth in production would benefit the owner. Neri's *Report on the Present State of the Comprehensive Land Survey* (1750) had aroused discussion and support, assisting him to overcome much of that local resistance which had defeated his contemporaries Machault and La Enseñada in France and Spain. An important indirect consequence was to weaken the traditional sense of purely local responsibilities, rooted in the communal era, by subjecting all landowners to a basically egalitarian system of taxation.

With Cristiani's death and Neri's departure for Tuscany in 1758 the reforms lost their impetus, as Vienna was absorbed in the Seven Years War. Indeed, the new plenipotentiary in Lombardy, the Trentino Carlo di Firmian, formerly imperial minister at Naples, could write a depressing report to Kaunitz in 1760 about the illegal multiplication of exemptions from the land-tax in favour of wealthy landowners. Only after the end of the war (1763) was Kaunitz to resume the work of reform.

By then, a new group of young, impatient nobles at Milan had put forward specific proposals for co-ordinated reforms to be based on a general philosophy; only in such a manner they believed would it be possible to build upon and surpass what they regarded as the mere improvisations of Pallavicini and Neri. At the centre of this group was Pietro Verri, who had returned to Milan after searching for adventure in the Austrian army and employment at Vienna, a convert to the new philosophy and convinced of the need to shock complacent Milanese society. The young nobles who gathered around Verri in the self-styled *Società dei pugni* ('Society of fisticuffs') between 1762 and 1766 – the apostle of penal reform Beccaria, Pietro's brother Alessandro, the mathematician Paolo Frisi and a few others – rejected the erudite formalities of the academy or the superstitious ceremonies of the masonic lodge in favour of semi-casual, egalitarian meetings. 'We are not forming a society based on a final, definite plan, but an informal gathering of friends', wrote Beccaria (Venturi, 30, p. 683).

The enthusiastic adoption of the ideas of the *Encyclopédie* affected all their writings, from Verri's *Considerations on the Trade of the State of Milan* (1763) and his *Meditations on Happiness* (1763) to Beccaria's *Essay on Crimes and Punishments* (1764) and the wide-ranging criticisms published in their periodical *Il Caffè* (1764–6). General philosophical problems were closely linked to proposals for specific reforms, as the group attacked ignorance and discussed the utilitarian basis of happiness, the achievement of equality through reforms, the inhumanity of torture, the necessity of a new legal code, the pernicious effects of noble privilege, the advantages of internal free trade, the need to accelerate the circulation of wealth in order to increase prosperity and create a happier and more egalitarian society. There was little discussion of political issues, because these reformers' cosmopolitan and pacifist beliefs meant acceptance of the existing political state of Italy and Europe. Nor did they follow their French mentors in questioning religious faith, for their prime concern was to be effective, to influence society immediately. Oscillating between reliance on the prince and confidence in the effectiveness of a public opinion guided by philosophers, between the much-quoted examples of Peter the Great and the abbé de Saint-Pierre, Verri and his companions were eager to participate in the practical task of reform.

There can be little doubt that they were successful in forcing their ideas on the attention of the government. If Firmian ignored Verri's essay on the reform of the salt-tax (1761), Kaunitz was sufficiently impressed by his analysis of the decline of Lombard trade and the need to revive it by legal reform, internal free trade and the abolition of the tax farm to appoint him to the junta investigating the farm (1764). Even when Verri abused his position the same year by publishing the figures for the 1752 budget in order to gain support for his proposals by his demonstration of a deficit, the angry Kaunitz still charged him to prepare a more accurate and recent budget (although placing a trusted lawyer alongside Verri to restrain his impetuosity).

In 1765 the position won by these young philosophers was officially recognized by the creation of the Supreme Council of the Economy to survey and make proposals about all aspects of Lombard economic policy: monopolies, the provisioning system, the cadastral register, the tax farm, the commercial code, monetary reform, technical schools and methods to increase production. Verri was a member, although the more orthodox reformer Carli was appointed president. Three years later, on Carli's advice, Beccaria was appointed to a chair of political economy at the Palatine Schools, 'to search for the surest and easiest method – taking into account the situation, quality, produce and customs of the various nations – of spreading the greatest possible amount of goods among the greatest possible number of men' (Venturi, 27, p. 19).

The following years saw the appointment of another member of the group, Alfonso Longo, as professor of ecclesiastical law, then as censor and as Beccaria's successor, and the employment of Paolo Frisi, already professor at Milan, as expert on a wide range of proposed reforms, from irrigation and technical schools to Church-State relations, as censor and as official commemorator to Maria Theresa. Even a minor member of the coterie, Giambattista Biffi, who led a melancholy life at Cremona, was employed as local administrator of the provisioning system, schools and censorship. *Il Caffè* ceased publication, the *Società dei pugni* broke up, as its members were absorbed within the machinery of government.

The decade 1765–75 – when Joseph II, now co-regent with his mother, Maria Theresa, took an active interest in Lombardy alongside, often in rivalry with Kaunitz – were the years of a new reforming drive. The

Supreme Council was the seat of harsh debates, which embittered relations between Verri, Carli and Beccaria. Fiscal needs intertwined with measures to develop industry and trade in a complex relationship that revealed the practical difficulties of reform.

An initial attack on the position of the tax farmers was made with the partial reform of customs duties in 1765. But through fear of losing income, the reform was limited to rationalizing transit dues, while maintaining protection on the frontiers. Despite frequent adjustments, transit dues were only abolished in 1781 and all customs duties unified only in 1787. The major advance, the reduction by 50 per cent of imperial tariffs on Lombard cloths in 1769, owed more to Joseph II than to the reformers. But despite the pressure of the merchants, neither the prince nor his collaborators were ready to accept physiocratic arguments in favour of free trade. National industry still needed protection.

In contrast, Verri's battle against tax farmers was wholly successful. It was the more remarkable in that the leading contractor Greppi had consolidated his position by the renewal of the farm in 1757 and his acquisition of the Mantuan tax farm in 1761. In 1765 Verri had already gained a measure of government control by the creation of a mixed farm, with a third share to the Lombard administration (represented by Verri). Five years later, despite Carli's opposition, Verri achieved the abolition of the farm and the direct exaction of taxes by the government (though not in Mantua, where Greppi retained a one-third interest). The danger had been avoided of creating a new privileged group of tax farmers, on whom the government relied for finances, as in France. Antonio Greppi had lacked the time to sink roots. Like the land-tax, the indirect taxation system had been (at least partially) reformed and was now under immediate government control.

Government solvency was virtually achieved with the redemption of Crown incomes (*regalie*), for which Verri was again responsible. A survey of alienated revenues was begun in 1766 and for the next twenty years – despite a recognition of the rising cost, not least because of determination to treat owners justly – these sources of revenue were successively redeemed by the Monte di Santa Teresa. By the late 1780s, when Vienna began to borrow money again, public revenues were once more wholly owned by the government and a capital reserve had been created. In this field the reformers, and especially Verri, had demonstrated their ability.

Attempts to develop industry were far less successful. The traditional method of subsidies was continued and, although monopolies for the production of minor goods were abolished, they were still granted as a method of encouraging major initiatives in textile production. There was no comprehensive vision of the economic system, merely concern for specific sectors. The reformers, when faced with a reluctance to invest capital (certainly available in Lombardy, in contrast to the rest of Italy), had no new proposals to make and proved incapable of modifying the existing structure. The only exception was the destruction of the guilds, regarded – in true physiocratic manner – as constituting a limitation of economic liberty. Verri and Beccaria were responsible for the dissolution of a series of guilds between 1769 and 1774; Joseph II completed their work in the 1780s.

The initiative for these fiscal and economic measures had come from the Lombard reformers. They showed the limits of their ideas. Although Verri lived in a state which owed its prosperity to its relatively modern agriculture (and not least to its livestock), his ignorance about agriculture could lead him to attack the irrigation and meadow system: as he expostulated to Joseph II in 1769, 'our country is becoming more and more a marsh' (Valsecchi, 59, p. 300). Like the other reformers and writers, Verri was certainly influenced by the physiocratic debate. But very few were really converted to physiocracy. Verri could move from the protectionism of his *Elements of Trade* (1760) to support for agricultural free trade in his *Reflections on Restrictive Laws* (1769). But, like his colleagues, he displayed a notable lack of interest in agriculture. Physiocracy obliged the Lombard reformers to focus their attention once more on the taxation system, if only to refute the French 'economists' ' demand that taxes be levied solely on the land as the only source of wealth. But Verri and his colleagues in the Supreme Council were obsessed with manufacturing and the export market. Yet it was here that their lack of technical knowledge or of an overall vision played them false. The economic realities of the country were often fairly remote from their expectations and proved remarkably unmalleable. Perhaps the responsibilities of office reduced their independence of mind. Carli certainly became a conservative administrator, all too conscious of practical difficulties, while the philosopher in Beccaria simply disappeared.

Relations between ruler and reformer were often coloured by scepticism. As Joseph II wrote in his private diary, after attending a session, the Supreme Council 'seems to be filled with naïve innovators and people of little experience, especially in legal matters' (Valsecchi, 59, p. 323). While Joseph and Kaunitz were prepared to listen to the reformers' proposals, they took care to balance them with those of professional administrators or lawyers. All reforms had to be tempered with justice: Greppi was compensated for the loss of the tax farm by the monopoly of the transport of mercury from Austria to Spain.

The reformers, in fact, frequently played only a secondary role in Austrian plans for Lombardy, this 'experimental field' of the empire. They were consulted, but the power of decision lay in Vienna. This was clearly visible in the educational and the administrative reforms.

The reform of higher education was an essential feature of the campaign against the Jesuits. Not only Carli, but radical Lombard intellectuals and

the Neapolitans Genovesi and Filangieri, drew up projects and plans about
the purpose and methods of educational reform. Unquestionably, their
ideas were influential in the introduction of modern, 'useful' subjects into
the curriculum of the reformed Pavia University (1765–71) and the new
Palatine School at Milan: empiricism in philosophy, moderate utilitarianism
in morals, natural law in jurisprudence, State authority in ecclesiastical law,
experimental methods in the physical sciences.

But there was a basic ambiguity about the purpose of education: whether
it was meant to serve the needs of culture and the people, to create a secular
mentality, as La Chalotais maintained; or whether it was to serve the prince
by enabling him to control his subjects' professions, as J. G. Heinecke had
asserted. For Maria Theresa and Kaunitz there was little doubt. The
purpose of higher education was practical, to train bureaucrats, encourage
material prosperity and prepare a new generation of more obedient –
because more enlightened – subjects. Such was the motive behind their
encouragement of the 'Agrarian Colony' at Mantua (1770) and the Patriotic
Society at Milan (1776). Kaunitz questioned the value of 'too erudite
professors' (Peroni, 61, pp. 285–6), and limited their potential danger by
substituting textbooks vetted by the government for lectures. As professors,
bureaucrats and men with technical training were preferred to pure scientists.
Paolo Frisi, mathematician turned publicist and engineer, was the outstanding example. The rulers had made the fundamental decisions. The
reformers were left to publicize them.

The major administrative reforms of 1770–1, which Kaunitz and Joseph
judged a necessary consequence of the abolition of the tax farm, accentuated
the increasing dependence on Vienna. Both Verri and Carli were involved in
the discussions, alongside the professional administrators at Vienna and
Milan, Sperges and Firmian. Verri hoped for a single administrative body
under his own direction. But Joseph II imposed a rational, uniform system
which separated administrative, judicial and financial functions and diminished local autonomies: the Supreme Council, with its wide-ranging
powers, was replaced by a Royal Cameral Court for administration, a single
Treasury supervised by the Court of Accounts, and a Senate restricted in
power to judicial matters. Once more Carli, the most conservative of the
reformers, was made president of the Cameral Court and Verri only a
member. The subordination of the Lombard administration was confirmed
by reducing the plenipotentiary Firmian's powers through the creation of a
collegiate Government Conference.

Despite this secondary role, the achievements of the Lombard reformers
attracted the interest and approval of the reformers elsewhere in Italy. In
the wide-ranging economic debate they focused attention on specific types
of reforms. The idea of the Supreme Council of the Economy, as an
institution to promote economic prosperity, was adopted by the governor

of Lombardy, Francis III of Modena, in his own state in 1766 and, much later, in Naples in 1782. The dangers represented by the class of tax farmers were discussed in almost identical terms in Tuscany (where the farm was abolished in 1768) and became a central issue of dispute in Modena and Parma in the 1770s. Neri's *censimento* was seen as a new development in its stimulation of production, and was further perfected in the Modenese and Bolognese cadastral registers of 1788 and 1789. To the moderate Tuscan reformer Giuseppe Pelli-Bencivenni, Milan, like Paris, was an almost mythical centre: 'If I were free and wealthy I would hasten to Milan to throw myself in the arms of the Verri brothers and Beccaria, and to Paris to embrace D'Alembert' (Rosa, 74, p. 227).

Tuscany: the physiocratic victory

In Tuscany the tensions between reformers and administrators so character-istic of Lombardy were far less evident. Close contact had long existed between the administration and the focal point of intellectual life, Pisa university. Not only Neri, but almost all the leading Tuscan ministers had been trained at Pisa, and with the encouragement of the Jansenist head of the University, Gaspare Cerati, the government turned there for technical advice. In the words of Rucellai, the minister responsible for ecclesiastical affairs, 'The university of Pisa has alone saved Tuscany from that state of ignorance into which almost all the rest of Italy has sunk' (Capra, 87, p. 9 n.). At the same time, most of Leopold's collaborators had a long experience of administrative or judicial posts before reaching high office.

The ruling group was thus more united in its aims and cohered more closely in its policies than elsewhere in Italy. This consensus, backed by a conscious campaign of propaganda and deliberate encouragement of the new philosophy (besides censorship of retrograde beliefs), was as much responsible for the impact of the reformers as the support received from the newly reforming great landowners. Conversely, the more down-to-earth, practical attitudes of the reformers inhibited theoretical discussions. The moderating influence of Montesquieu, deeply influential in Tuscany, blocked the bolder and more radical developments of the *philosophes*. Tuscany never produced as original or enlightened a writer as the Milanese Beccaria or the Neapolitan Filangieri. Although the Tuscan reformers acknowledged their debt to the Parisian *lumières*, they often failed to grasp the political, 'ideological' implications of their writings. Typically, when Leopold authorized the reprint of the *Encyclopédie*, Pelli-Bencivenni, a minor figure in the Tuscan reforming elite, ignored its political significance and could only regret that it had not been brought up to date by the addition of new scientific discoveries.

Pompeo Neri's return to Florence in 1758 gave renewed impulse to reform. Since the check to the early administrative and financial reforms, only Rucellai had energetically pursued his policy in the ecclesiastical field. Neri, with the prestige of his Lombard achievements, was the leading minister until the early 1770s. Gradually his influence was displaced by Angelo Tavanti, former editor of Locke's writings on money, and by Francesco Maria Gianni, ex-director of the Pisa customs and superintendent of the silk guild. But it was the grand-duke Leopold who dominated the reform movement. This second son of Maria Theresa, with his vast, eclectic reading – ranging from Leibnitz and Lorrainese Catholic reformists to Montesquieu, the *Encyclopédie*, Voltaire, Rousseau and Turgot – moved by a wider and deeper vision of the new philosophy than any of his ministers, imposed the direction and set the pace of Tuscan reformism from his accession in 1765.

The discussions of the reformers at the time of Leopold's arrival in Tuscany were focused on the effects of legal restrictions on the grain trade. The acute shortages of the Tuscan harvests between 1764 and 1767 and the contemporaneous attempts at a free trade policy in France (1763–4) high-lighted the contrasting problems of maintaining an adequate level of supplies for subsistence through the traditional provisioning system, or encouraging, on physiocratic lines, production (and consequently higher prices) through exports. The reformers, only too aware of the inefficacy of the provisioning system in times of famine, were agreed on the need to create a free, unified domestic market: all internal controls were abolished in 1766. But they differed in their attitudes to the foreign market. Gianni, voicing the opinion of the big landowners, wanted free export but protection against grain imports; Neri was a more convinced physiocrat; Leopold remained cautious. The 1767 decree, an improved version of the French decrees of 1763–4, only allowed free exports below a maximum domestic price, which – once exceeded – was to lead gradually to free imports. Concern to keep prices at a reasonable level by competition led Tavanti, the new minister of finances, to insist successfully on absolute freedom of imports in 1771: 'The owners certainly merit every consideration, but one must not favour them too much at the expense of the consumers' (Mirri, 70, p. 80). The renewed famine conditions of 1772–4 led to popular agitations against the reforms and deep divisions among the reformers: only in 1775 did Leopold and Tavanti finally agree to enact the physiocratic policy of totally free export of grains, irrespective of internal shortages which, it was believed, would be avoided by the policy of free imports adopted in 1771.

Marco Lastri, editor of the important journal *Novelle Letterarie*, expressed the Tuscan reformers' sense of triumph at this adoption of the basic tenet of physiocratic theory:

Experts in political economy spread truths and ministers and princes listened to them. . . . We hope to be believed when we point to our Tuscany as the first country to experience in practice the beneficent influence of economic science. (Diaz, 73, p. 208)

The 1770s, in fact, witnessed an explicit campaign to win support for physiocratic policy. Ferdinando Paoletti, whose *Thoughts on Agriculture* (1769), with their advocacy of technical improvement, had gained the approval of reforming landowners, was won over, and publicized the new economy with his *Of the True Means to Render Societies Happy* (1772). Bandini's much earlier *Discourse on the Maremma of Siena*, the first Tuscan work to propose free grain export, was now published at grand-ducal expense (1775). Raimondo Niccoli, Tuscan secretary at Paris, who maintained close contact with the physiocratic leader Mirabeau, emphasized the European significance of Tuscany's adoption of physiocracy in his despatches:

> All Europe, Your Excellency, awaits with impatience what will happen in Tuscany this year 1773. . . . It is known that the grand-duke has given to understand that the harvest has failed, but that he has promised not to interfere in provisioning the country. . . . It is known that Tuscany has not produced enough grain in the decade for the needs of its population. . . . If, despite all these setbacks, Tuscany does not die of hunger in the present year, if it has grain at a price below 21 lire [a sack], then all Europe will draw a favourable conclusion about the freedom to export. (Mirri, 69, pp. 102-3)

Thus, after considerable hesitations, physiocracy was finally adopted in Tuscany as the key to a total transformation of the state. The provisioning system, based upon obligatory stockpiling of grain for the cities, was abolished. Communal lands and pasturages (in practice only of marginal importance in Tuscany) were then divided up for cultivation, following the reformist faith in the productive superiority of private property. The Florentine guilds were destroyed (1779) and freedom of work asserted.

The need to co-ordinate the reforms and put them on a political footing was felt rapidly. Local autonomies were attacked by Gianni's reform of communal and provincial administrations (1774, 1776, 1779). Property, not nobility, was the new criterion for office and local owners were given greater administrative responsibilities. Learning in part from Lombard experience, the Tuscan administrators abolished the tax farm (1768), unified the multitude of taxes and eliminated privileged exemptions, and slowly redeemed the public debt by the sale of demesnial lands. Tribunals were made uniform and restricted to purely judicial functions, losing their administrative powers. 'The party of reforms', as Gianni called it, was all-embracing. The duty of government was to create the structure for the free initiative of man. Gianni, as always, was quite explicit: 'The law can forbid certain of man's actions, but it does not know and cannot teach man what to put in their place. . . . Every restriction on this absolute liberty is an insult of man-made law to the law of nature' (Diaz, 72, p. 59).

For Leopold the new policy had strongly humanitarian ends. The increase of production and the unification of the state by administrative rationalization were regarded as means to achieve the greater happiness of the people – all the people, not only the wealthy landowners and merchants. Gianni had been hostile to the great estates for both social and economic reasons: 'Vast estates, excessive wealth, lavish spending, contracts which enslave the peasant: all these things are incompatible with the precious skills of agricultural labour' (Anzilotti, 64, pp. 49–50). Nevertheless, the 1775 decision on free trade marked a decisive victory for the great landowners. For it encouraged a long-term increase in production through higher export prices at the expense of government-regulated, low, domestic prices on which a large proportion of the population was traditionally dependent. Leopold's attempts to balance the demands of the proprietors against the claims of social justice had failed, as could be seen in the disputes over the creation of smallholdings and the improvement of agrarian labour contracts.

By 1764 Gianni was proposing that the lands of religious orders and the grand-duke's demesne be divided and that they be sold to peasants by means of perpetual quit-rents. The landowners were hostile, and when initial experiments were made with the sale of some estates of the Conservatory of the Poor (1769), the Order of Santo Stefano and the grand-ducal *Scrittoio* (1772), they often turned them to their own advantage by buying up the plots. The exemption of the peasants from taxes was only accepted by the proprietors when they were forced to recognize that the peasants were too indebted to pay. In 1771 Leopold asked the Academy of the Georgofili for its opinion about the improvement of share-cropping contracts in order to guarantee minimum subsistence levels. Paoletti, mouthpiece of the landowners, rejected the suggestion as impinging upon the liberty of property. More than anywhere else in Italy, Leopold had been hoist with the petard of physiocratic non-interference. Freedom of property was of little help to the propertyless.

Modena and Parma: the limits of reformism

Habsburg reformist influence extended inevitably to Modena, with the appointment of Francis III as governor of Lombardy in 1755 and the marriage of his grand-daughter to Maria Theresa's third son Ferdinand in 1771. After his return to the duchy (occupied during the Austrian Succession War), even before his departure for Lombardy, Francis III had tried to strengthen his administration and its control over the communes by the creation of a special magistracy. In the 1760s the Lombard example began to enrich the powerful tradition of Muratorian reformism. Some fiscal exemptions, especially ecclesiastical, were restricted, as was mortmain.

Feudal entails were limited to nobles, following the Piedmontese code and Muratori's proposals. By 1771 the revision of the legislation could be published in a code.

In these same years, his Lombard experiences induced Francis to adopt new fiscal and economic measures. Belatedly in 1766 – at the very moment when Verri was successfully attacking the Lombard tax farm – Francis leased the Modenese indirect taxes to a Milanese group of financiers, including the ubiquitous Greppi. The twelve-year contract of the tax farmer, while guaranteeing the duke some increase in income, was to block the possibilities of a wide range of fiscal reforms. The same reluctance to adopt radical measures and challenge existing interests marked the activities of the Magistracy for Trade and Agriculture, created in 1762 with a wide brief to improve the economy. Its task, as interpreted by its president, Salvatore Venturini, was 'to bestir the rustics into discreet activity, without inconveniencing the owners' (Poni, 80, p. 24).

By the 1770s the examples of nearby Lombardy and Tuscany led to a change in the pace and character of Modenese reformism. Encyclopedist and physiocratic ideas were introduced by the leading minister, Gherardo Rangone. The university was reformed (1768), and a leading intellectual, Agostino Paradisi, called to a new chair of economics, with the additional duty of founding an agrarian academy. A Supreme Council of the Economy was created in 1766. Physiocratic doctrine, supported by Rangone and Paradisi, was widely discussed and a radical plan was drawn up to revise the fiscal system on physiocratic lines, with a basic land-tax, abolition of almost all indirect excises and monopolies and a drastic reduction of taxes on the peasants (1777). At this point, the resistance of the tax farmers proved too powerful and blocked the adoption of policies similar to those in Tuscany.

By the time of Francis III's death in 1780, Modena stood alongside Lombardy and Tuscany as a reforming state. But the Modenese reformers had made relatively little headway. The small size of the duchy, the deep rivalry between the only two important cities, Modena and Reggio, above all the absence of a determined prince, facilitated the resistance of local interests, in a state where 111 out of 136 districts were under feudal jurisdiction and where the duke relied on his tax farmers to pay for his extravagances as governor of Lombardy.

In the adjacent Bourbon duchy of Parma, the new philosophy appeared to have achieved greater success. This was an illusion. For the superficial sprinkling of Enlightenment culture at the Court was never transmuted into an effective reforming drive. Guillaume du Tillot, who emerged as the leading minister in the later 1750s, was determined to make of Parma a glittering Renaissance-style Court, decked out in the trappings of the latest cultural fashions. For a decade Parma seemed a miniature Paris of the *philosophes*, a salon whose most distinguished adornment was Condillac.

The great library, the proposals for university reform, the constant flow of distinguished French visitors, the incessant discussion of the latest ideas, bore witness to du Tillot's concern to make of this insignificant provincial town a cosmopolitan centre of the *lumières*.

Behind this imported façade, du Tillot's cautious moves towards reform were impelled by his urgent need of money to pay for the Court, the large army, the royal marriages. The central administration, particularly the financial branch, was reorganized. The French-owned tax farm was restricted in 1765, and was taken over by the government in 1770, the same year as in Lombardy. But in Parma the farmers were left with a one-third interest – dependence on France was too great to be ignored. The same hesitation in challenging privileged interests marked the proposed cadastral register of 1765: the aim was purely financial, not to stimulate the economy as with Neri's *censimento* (about which du Tillot was fully informed); noble titles of exemption were accepted, and the challenge to local communal immunities was dropped when resistance threatened.

Despite the examples of Lombardy and Tuscany, despite the animated discussions at Court, traditional attitudes died hard even when attempts were made to improve the economy. A protectionist customs barrier was maintained; the guilds were left undisturbed; attempts were made to create new textile and soap industries by granting special privileges and enticing foreign skilled labour. Agriculture was believed to be subordinate to industry: mulberry trees were planted for the silk industry, but freedom of the grain trade was rejected. Du Tillot's knowledge of foreign treatises on agricultural techniques, such as Jethro Tull's, did not convince him of the need to support proposals for an agrarian academy. The duke's passion for hunting in the Piacentino took priority over the pasturages required for the relatively healthy cheese industry.

Under du Tillot Parma acquired the form but not the substance of a reforming state. In only one field – that of ecclesiastical laws (which will be discussed in the following section) – did du Tillot make a genuine contribution, and it was only in this area that he could rely on earlier reforming traditions or locally trained administrators. In so small a state, divided (like the duchy of Modena) by the rivalry between the two major cities, Parma and Piacenza, he could do little against the economic strength and administrative independence of the Church and nobility, or even against the traditional autonomy of many of the communes. Du Tillot lacked support from any intellectual or social group in the country, for there was resentment of French dominance. But equally he lacked the courage to attempt radical reforms. As he wrote, rejecting Gian Rinaldo Carli's offer of his services:

> once his projects began to be examined here, it was recognized that his talent, which inclined towards producing vast ideas on the basis of principles of simple theory, could not be adapted to the limited requirements of a poor state like

this one; and so this Court politely disengaged itself from all negotiations. (Valsecchi, 19, p. 697)

When the queen, Maria Amalia, dispensed with du Tillot's own services in 1771, the foreign intellectuals carried away with them the modest reformist impulse they had brought and the duchy of Parma sunk into its habitual provincialism.

Piedmont, Venice, Genoa: the absence of reformism

The collaboration of rulers and intellectuals, so fruitful in Lombardy and Tuscany, never developed elsewhere in Italy in the 1760s and 1770s. In Naples and the Papal States faith in the implications of comprehensive change and hopes of Enlightened despotism were to come later, in the 1780s and 1790s, belatedly, when Lombard and Tuscan collaboration was already breaking down. In the other states there were specific economic or administrative changes, but no sense of the interdependence of the reforms, no will to transform the state.

Piedmont-Savoy was noticeably absent from the ferment and challenge of those years. For Charles Emanuel III and his leading minister Bogino the earlier reforms had already achieved their purpose, the state had been strengthened and rendered efficient. A barrier of hostility kept the intellectuals distant and fearful. The radical Dalmazzo Francesco Vasco spent eighteen years under arrest. Even the mild historian Carlo Denina, who had turned to foreign diplomatic representatives for intellectual stimulation in the militaristic atmosphere of Turin, was persecuted for his extremely moderate proposals of reform. Like the publicist Baretti, the renowned mathematician Lagrange, the great poet Alfieri and many others, Denina too finally emigrated, to the court of Frederick the Great. The only serious reform in Piedmont, the new version of the Royal Constitutions, published in 1770 six years after Beccaria's tract, was condemned by the philosophers: 'Who would not be scandalized like you by this new criminal ordinance in Piedmont!', wrote Auguste de Keralic to Paolo Frisi, 'It revolts humanity. If philosophy or, what is the same thing, reason, is making progress in certain countries, one must recognize that it is undoubtedly retrogressing in others' (Venturi, 60, p. 304).

The only reforming activities were in the island of Sardinia. There in the 1760s Bogino attempted to impose royal authority and even to stimulate the economy in order to cover the cost of the island to the government. The administration and tribunals were re-ordered and feudal jurisdiction attacked. Control was asserted over the regular clergy. Two universities were created at Cagliari and Sassari in order to train a new bureaucracy. The famines of 1764 and 1765 led to the creation of grain stocks to break the stranglehold of usurers by advancing the necessary seed and food to the peasants. But the vast problems of this primitive economy, still based on pasturage and periodic divisions of the commonlands, were not easily understood by Piedmontese administrators. Despite the dedication of isolated intellectuals, such as the Jesuit Father Gemelli, who put forward an idealistic picture of the possibilities of creating a profitable agriculture, based on privately owned property and a free grain trade, the reforms barely scratched the surface of Sardinia's economic structure. Bogino only succeeded in integrating Sardinia administratively within the Savoyard state. His reforms were ultimately little more than an extension of those of Victor Amadeus II. On Charles Emanuel III's death (1773), even these reforms ceased.

Venice was perhaps the most active printing centre of Enlightenment publications in Italy. But its cosmopolitan intellectual interests had as little influence on government policy as the typically Enlightened discussions of agricultural problems in the new agrarian academies that arose in many of the subject cities.

In Genoa memories of the great crisis of 1746 left the republic with an even more rigidly oligarchical structure. The war against Corsica had a debilitating effect on the Genoese economy. But even after its end, lack of territory and natural resources rendered major changes in the financial-economic structure of the state impossible. Financial investment abroad remained the major occupation of the oligarchs, accompanied by a moderate growth in maritime activities. But the provisioning system was retained to ensure an adequate food supply for the capital, as was the system of consumption taxes which formed the basis of state revenue. Discussion of Enlightenment ideas was fairly widespread, among both the commercial middle class and the leading nobles: the mathematician doge Agostino Lomellini even translated D'Alembert's *Discours préliminaire* to the *Encyclopédie*. But, as in Venice, the new ideas had little contact with the reality of the state.

In these circumstances, the intellectuals in states which seemed impermeable to Enlightenment reform could only emigrate or – like the Piedmontese Dalmazzo Francesco Vasco or the Venetian Francesco Griselini – requite their aspirations by admiration of the successful reformers in Lombardy and Tuscany. The stature of the reforming states rose, in the eyes of Enlightened public opinion, by contrast with unreformed Italy. It was further enhanced by the attack on the Church.

6

The offensive
against the Church

Rome: hopes of ecclesiastical reform

The long reign of Benedict XIV (1740–58) was remarkable for the pope's conciliatory attitude towards critics of the Church. As cardinal archbishop of Bologna, before his elevation to the papal throne, Prospero Lambertini enjoyed a considerable reputation both as a theologian and as a man of broad intellectual interests. He had read extensively among the French *philosophes*, even the anti-clerical Voltaire. He was a sincere, active and forthright man, who was reputed to have proposed to his fellow cardinals in the conclave that led to his election, 'if you want someone earthy, choose me' (Valsecchi, 19, p. 482). As pope, he attempted to arrive at settlements with the secular princes which, while recognizing the need for some concessions, safeguarded the interests of the Church. Concordats were signed with Sardinia (1741), Naples (1741) and Spain (1753), while less formal agreements were reached with Tuscany (1739–46). But at the same time freemasonry was condemned (1751). If Benedict failed to achieve more lasting settlements in Church-State relations, this was less through lack of willingness on his part than through the intrinsic weakness of the papacy (summed up in the contemptuous dismissal of his claims at Aix-la-Chapelle in 1748) and the new determination of the sovereigns to limit the power of the Church within their states. But Benedict at least achieved the ambiguous merit of praise from both English protestants and French *philosophes*.

The reform of the curial university, the Sapienza, and the publication of an important journal, the *Giornale de' letterati* (1742–54), under the patronage of Benedict's secretary of state, cardinal Silvio Valenti Gonzaga, reflected these new cultural interests of the papacy. Rome, during Benedict XIV's pontificate, became an intellectual centre. Hopes of reform within the Church, of the suppression of excesses of superstition and 'disorderly' devotion, of better-educated priests, flourished alongside Jansenist and Augustinian attacks on the laxity of Jesuit-inspired theology, morals and discipline and proposals for more vigorous doctrine. A 'school' (the

Archetto group) was formed by two leading ecclesiastics, Bottari and Foggini, in the Corsini palazzo at Rome, which brought together Enlightened Catholics, Augustinians, Jansenists and anti-curialists. The group was held together by its hostility to Jesuit influence and its belief in reform within the structure of the Church. Pietro Francesco Foggini, a scholar and erudite, propagated Jansenist ideas of an inner religiosity, in which grace was only attainable through God's choice, not through man's will. Giovanni Bottari, professor of ecclesiastical history at the Sapienza, custodian of the Vatican library, confessor to Clement XII, Benedict XIV and Clement XIII, adviser to the Congregation of the Index, fought a militant battle against the doctrine of molinism, which laid stress on the importance of free will in obtaining grace. An erudite and a philologist, Bottari was strongly influenced by Muratori, but also by the rector of Pisa university, the Oratorian Gaspare Cerati and by the abbé Antonio Niccolini, both friends of Montesquieu, who had travelled in France and Holland and set these theological disputes in the context of the broader European debate. At Rome Bottari and the Archetto group were protected in the Curia by some of the cardinals. In the rest of Italy their activities and teaching encouraged and often trained priests with reforming or Jansenist tendencies.

The essence of the dispute was theological and doctrinal, with the Jansenists condemning the positive role which, they maintained, Jesuits and their molinist allies wrongfully ascribed to man's free will. But the Jansenists and their sympathizers had by now broadened their criticisms to challenge the existing organizational structure of the Church, which the Jesuits had helped to mould in the counter-reformation, and to question the nature and respective powers of pope, bishops and parish priests. When the Jesuits began an offensive against their critics after 1750, the defence of Jansenism became part of this wider struggle for ecclesiastical reform. Benedict XIV, although defending Muratori's proposals for Church reform against accusations of Jansenism or (even worse) heresy, was hostile to the violent polemics of the anti-Jesuits. But as tension rose in France with the attacks on the Jesuits by *parlements* and intellectual groups, and at Rome with the counter-proposal to sanctify the Jesuit Bellarmine, Benedict was forced into an increasingly difficult position. Fear of Jesuit power led an increasing number of the Society's opponents within the Church, all of them loyal to the authority of the pope and many unsympathetic to the aggressive dogmatism of the French and Dutch Jansenists, towards a defence of the Jansenist cause and a refusal to accept the *Unigenitus* bull or the condemnation of the Utrecht Jansenists. The activities of the Rome group around Bottari became more intense and spread outwards to the other Italian states.

In Tuscany, the university rector Cerati and the papal nuncio at Florence, Martini, were only two of a significant number of leading ecclesiastics who offered support to these Roman anti-Jesuits. The future leaders of Tuscan,

Lombard and Neapolitan Jansenism – de' Ricci, Tamburini, Zola, Serrao – were all educated by Bottari and Foggini or collaborated with them. At Naples Tanucci and the Jansenist minister De Carlo, with the archbishop of Naples Spinelli, actively supported Bottari and protected Jansenists. In Piedmont, where Jansenist ideas had penetrated directly from France, the archbishop of Turin, delle Lanze, corresponded with Bottari. In Parma and Venetia leading Enlightened Catholics gave support. At Genoa, marquis Girolamo Durazzo, expelled from Rome for his Jansenist contacts by Benedict's successor Clement XIII, acted as protector of Jansenists. While Benedict XIV lived, the struggle remained within the Church and these ecclesiastical reformers gave no more than indirect support to the sovereigns' claims for control over the Church within their states. But the pro-Jesuit policy of the new pope Clement XIII (1758–69) and his secretary of state, cardinal Torrigiani, dashed their hopes of an internal reform of the Church.

Princes and churchmen: the subordination of Church to State

Increasingly the Church reformers and Jansenists turned abroad and to the Italian princes in their search for allies. Contacts were strengthened with Jansenists in France and Utrecht. Bottari urged the Neapolitan minister Tanucci to publish an Italian translation of Mésenguy's Jansenist catechism as a deliberate challenge to the Congregation of the Index and the curia. Tanucci needed little persuasion. As he wrote to Bottari in 1760, the Jesuits were 'a true cancer of mankind at the present time' (Passerin d'Entrèves, 39, vol. III, p. 276, n. 18). The publication of the catechism in 1758 marked the beginning of active collaboration between Jansenists and their supporters and the princes. Characteristically, it began at Naples. With the catechism's final condemnation in 1761 (which Clement XIII forced the pro-Jansenist cardinal Passionei to sign), the ecclesiastical reformers lost their battle at Rome. The philosopher Emanuele Duni, living at Rome, lamented bitterly to the English consul at Venice, John Strange: 'Here I am, not only in this depraved Italy, but in the city where pure doctrine lies deepest buried, and where – low be it spoken – one is hardly allowed to respect it even in one's own home' (Venturi, 86, p. 791).

The initiative had passed to the sovereigns, and increasingly the doctrinal-theological character of Italian Jansenism dropped from view as its exponents turned to more practical problems of reform. This was the price paid for their dependence on the rulers. But, until the final crisis, it was a price paid willingly enough, for most Jansenists retained a seventeenth-century faith in the divine right of the sovereign, 'living image of the eternal Ruler', in the words of a minor Pisan Jansenist, Francesco Salesio Donai (Passerin d'Entrèves, 39, p. 271).

The challenge to the papacy was of more than Italian dimensions. In 1759 Pombal expelled the Jesuits from Portugal; in 1764 Louis XV was forced by the *parlement* of Paris to expel the Society from France; in 1767 Charles III of Spain followed suit. By then, the Italian – and especially the Bourbon – rulers found themselves in the front line of a European battle.

The measures taken against the Church related to its juridical, economic and disciplinary powers. The range and rapid succession of the new decrees marked a new phase in Church-State relations. Moreover, the measures increasingly asserted the right of the sovereigns to intervene in the internal organization and discipline of the Church to a degree surpassing even that of Venice at the turn of the sixteenth century. Muratori's advocacy of a purified, simpler Church, limited in its temporal power, with educated priests fulfilling functions useful to society, an Enlightened Catholic attitude, which had proved so influential in the *Reformkatholicismus* of Maria Theresa's hereditary lands, now returned to Italy in Austrian Lombardy and the other Habsburg-dominated states, Modena and Tuscany. In Lombardy, the concordat of 1757 was accompanied by the creation of a Junta of Stewardship to advise Vienna on all aspects of Church-State relations; in 1762 royal authority was asserted by making the publication of papal letters subject to royal *placet*. In Modena, a Supreme Junta of Sovereign Jurisdiction was created on the Lombard model in 1758. In Tuscany, Rucellai had already attempted to check further increases of mortmain by prohibiting acquisitions of landed property by the Church (1751), and had followed Naples and Venice in limiting and restructuring the Inquisition (1754). In Bourbon lands the new phase heralded by the Mésenguy controversy developed rapidly in the mid-1760s, to culminate in both Bourbon and Habsburg territories by the end of the decade.

For a brief period the small duchy of Parma found itself at the centre of attention. It is questionable whether du Tillot intended his measures to arouse such controversy. His decree prohibiting mortmain (1764) was issued only after negotiations with Rome had failed. Although du Tillot went beyond traditional assertions of State authority to justify his measure in terms of the negative economic consequences of mortmain through the withdrawal of land from the market, the decree hardly differed in kind from similar laws passed by Lucca (1764), Modena (1763, 1764, 1770), Venice (1768), Naples (1769, 1771) or Tuscany (1769). Nor was the decree subjecting ecclesiastical land to taxation (1765) so novel, as such a measure had been proposed by local Parma administrators since the 1750s, and had already been accepted by the curia in concordats with Piedmont, Lombardy and Naples. Parma became the focal point of controversy because it was chosen by Clement XIII as the most convenient state over which to assert papal authority. The papacy claimed suzerainty over the duchy (as it did over the kingdom of Naples) and this small Italian state seemed too weak to resist. Unexpectedly, du Tillot's need to maintain his reputation as an Enlightened reformer and the family ties of the Bourbon rulers toughened this sacrificial lamb's resistance to the high priest's knife. A Royal Junta of Jurisdiction was created to assert royal power, the royal *placet* and *exequatur* were imposed to control relations between the local clergy and the Holy See, ecclesiastical courts were restricted in authority, regular clergy disciplined and a few, small convents suppressed (1765–7). Du Tillot's measures were characterized by their cautious application, not least because of popular hostility, and the piety of the new duke Ferdinand. Indeed, du Tillot hesitated for a year after the expulsion of the Jesuits from Bourbon Spain and then only issued a similar decree after Clement XIII – in his bull *In coena domini* (1768) – declared null all ecclesiastical legislation in Parma since 1764.

But Clement XIII was no Innocent III and papal fulminations echoed hollowly from his throne. The reaction was immediate. Tanucci occupied the papal territories of Pontecorvo and Benevento, Louis XV that of Avignon, and Charles III of Spain joined the other Bourbon sovereigns in warning the pope to withdraw. Even Maria Theresa refused to allow the bull to be published in her lands. Clement XIII had failed and by his intransigence started off a wave of anti-ecclesiastical measures. His weaker successor, Clement XIV (1769–74) was to suffer the consequences and in 1773 finally bowed to the pressure of the princes and suppressed the Jesuit order.

In Naples, Tanucci expelled the 650 Jesuits living in the kingdom (1768), rejecting papal suzerainty and justifying royal action in terms of the king's divine authority:

> We the King, by virtue of the supreme and independent authority that we acknowledge from God and from no other, for it was made by His almighty power inseparable from our sovereignty for the good government of our subjects, ordain that the Society of Jesus be forever dissolved within our Kingdom of the Two Sicilies and perpetually excluded therefrom. (Colletta, 88, vol. 1, p. 194)

In the following years Tanucci passed a series of anti-ecclesiastical laws: convents were suppressed, tithes abolished, mortmain forbidden, royal permission required for ecclesiastical decrees. With the expulsion of the Jesuits, the first steps were taken to control public education by the preparation of new textbooks (1768–72). In the following years, relations with the papacy worsened as Tanucci tried to prevent the election of cardinal Braschi as pope Pius VI (1775–99) and insisted on transferring the anti-curial, reformist archbishop of Palermo, Serafino Filangieri, to the archbishopric of Naples. When Pius VI, against all tradition, refused to make Filangieri a cardinal, Tanucci responded (1776) by suspending payment of the *chinea*, a symbolic annual payment to Rome, marking royal acceptance of papal overlordship.

Tanucci's measures were undoubtedly effective in fixing the path of Church-State relations in Naples until the revolution. They were supported by the reformers of the older generation, such as Genovesi and Caracciolo, whose anti-clericalism sometimes rivalled that of Tanucci himself. As Caracciolo wrote, it was essential 'to reduce to just limits the monkish rabble, the tyranny of the Roman curia, and to make the ecclesiastics pay' (Croce, 104, p. 103). But for the younger generation, attacks on the Church along traditional, Giannonian lines were inadequate to solve the economic problems of the country. Even more, the measures gained little popular support: these were the years when the followers of the pro-Jesuit Alfonso de' Liguori successfully spread his doctrines in both the city of Naples and the provinces.

In Lombardy the years 1768–9 also marked a new phase in Church-State relations, as Kaunitz and Firmian issued a series of decrees against mortmain and the other economic privileges of the Church. The refusal to publish the bull *In coena domini* was followed by the assertion of state control over censorship (1768). As the intellectuals gave support, they were often encouraged by the government to promote and propagate this new aggressive policy. Carlantonio Pilati's unsolicited, violently anti-clerical and socially radical *Of a Reform of Italy* (1767) may have gone far beyond the intentions of Vienna, but many of Pilati's proposals   suppression of most monastic orders, reduction of the number of secular clergy, creation of State seminaries, strict control over all clerical activities – were to be enacted in the following decades. Paolo Frisi consolidated his close relationship with the imperial chancellor Kaunitz by writing a treatise on the temporal power of princes which declared all concordats null (1768). Alfonso Longo, in his inaugural lecture as professor of ecclesiastic public law, was so anti-curialist that Firmian obliged him to modify the tone of the published version. The suppression of the Jesuits led to public discussions among the intellectuals over the responsibility of the State to control education and spread light among the people. From restriction of ecclesiastical privileges and control of secular education, it was a relatively short step to intervene in the internal disciplinary arrangements of the Church and the education of the clergy. Joseph II was to take this step.

In Tuscany the new measures began slightly later – in 1769. Then the same path was followed: mortmain, *exequatur*, restriction of ecclesiastical rights of refuge (1769) and ecclesiastical courts (1771), suppression of monasteries (1773). The drive towards reform from Vienna strengthened the efforts of Giulio Rucellai to assert independence from Rome and control the Tuscan Church. At the end of a long career, Rucellai displayed an open-minded approach to the new developments proposed by the *philosophes*, attacking the traditional view that pauperism could be solved by charity, even urging direct control over the education of the clergy in order to ensure that priests be well-trained. There was strong encouragement for the reforms among Leopold's ministers, as also among small groups of professors and educated clergy at Pisa and Siena. Typical of the optimistic anti-curialism of these intellectuals was the attitude of *abate* Niccoli, Tuscan representative at Paris, an intimate of many of the *philosophes*, who wrote hopefully of the suppression of the Jesuits, 'as one desires that of many other religious orders, which will come about in very few decades' (Mirri, 69, p. 79). But support in Tuscany was far less widespread than at Naples, Venice or even Lombardy. It was perhaps because of the limited number of persons primarily concerned with what should be the necessary future reforms in the ecclesiastical field that the Jansenists were able to gain increasing influence by the late 1770s. Certainly Jansenism was to impose a distinctive physiognomy on ecclesiastical reform in Tuscany in the following decade which differed from that of any other state in Italy – or Europe.

The wave of anti-ecclesiastical measures swept Modena too. Here the reforms were strongly influenced by Muratori's teaching. Laws reducing the number of religious feasts (1774) were justified in pure Muratorian terms: 'so that the poor and the rustics can provide for the maintenance of their families by regular work' (Poni, 80, p. 23). Although traditional aims were not forgotten (such as the exclusion of foreigners from ecclesiastical benefices), the economic implications of anti-ecclesiastical measures were now predominant. The Supreme Junta of Sovereign Jurisdiction, in issuing a law against mortmain (1764), only regretted 'that it has been promulgated too late, so that by this time mortmain has gained possession of at least half the landed holdings of the state of Modena' (Poni, 80, p. 19). A Junta of Stewardship was created, as in Lombardy, not just to administer but to improve the possessions of vacant benefices. Finally, the suppression of charitable institutions and convents developed rapidly, earlier than in the other states, into an ambitious plan to solve the problem of pauperism along Muratorian lines by the creation of a single General Charitable Institution for the Poor and the construction of a Great Hospice for the Poor (1764-8). Charity had been removed from the hands of private, largely religious institutions to those of the state. Two decades later, the leading Modenese minister Lodovico Ricci – like Joseph II – was to attack the very concept of charity and attempt to subject the charitable institutions to the interests of the state.

Elsewhere in Italy the Church was also under attack. Genoa quarrelled with Rome over the Apostolic Visitor in Corsica (1760-7). Paoli in Corsica refused to accept ecclesiastical tribunals. In Venice, Sarpian traditions of secular authority were revived by Marco Foscarini and by the dispute over Benedict XIV's decision to divide the patriarchate of Aquileia into separate

Austrian and Venetian dioceses (1751–8). These years of a general anti-ecclesiastical offensive witnessed Venetian laws prohibiting the Church from acquiring more possessions and restricting its tax exemptions, reducing the number of clergy and suppressing some convents (1767–72). But, in general, the Serenissima did not copy its reforming neighbours, not least because of its good relations with Clement XIII, the former Venetian cardinal Rezzonico. Indeed, an earlier decree to control the relations of Venetian bishops with Rome (1753) was virtually rescinded. Venice was content to remain within the limits of its traditional relationship with the Church – as Pilati found to his surprise when his *Reform of Italy* was banned. But precisely because Venetian measures to control the Church were so traditional and so carefully limited to the ruling class, they failed to arouse interest and support in the Terraferma. Even the Brescian Jansenists – despite the freedom with which their publications appeared – felt constricted by the Republic's caution: the future Jansenist leaders Tamburini and Zola preferred to cross the frontier to Lombard Pavia.

In Piedmont there was little need or desire for new laws. As Domenico Caracciolo wrote to Tanucci from Turin in 1759:

> Here they mock the Roman Curia, although they pretend to be obedient children of the Church and zealous for the Holy See; they do not want to tolerate abstract struggles and academic disputes over jurisdictions, but in practice they maintain an unlimited authority in their own house, and the bishops have neither armed retinue nor prisons and do not take any step without the positive approval of the prince. . . . In ecclesiastical matters [the king] has only left the priests a mere veil, but in substance has kept to himself absolute power and authority. (Croce, 104, p. 86)

As always in Piedmont, authoritarian secrecy was preferred to public discussion.

7

The crisis of collaboration:
1775–90

Princely domination and intellectual withdrawal

The struggle with the Church from the mid-1760s had undoubtedly drawn together the reforming princes and administrators and the intellectual groups, both 'philosophers' and Jansenists. Strong support was given to the princes for attempting to reform the Church without consulting Rome. As *abate* Gianfranco Cossali wrote, 'the great obstacle is Rome' (Codignola, 38, p. 221). The philo-Jansenist Giovanni Cristofaro Amaduzzi could write to the scientist Gregorio Fontana: 'May God employ the resentment of the secular princes to promote and bring to fruition the necessary reform of the Church, which cannot be hoped for from the spontaneous deliberations of the present ruling priesthood' (Rosa, 75, p. 264). Ecclesiastical reforms intertwined with economic and administrative measures. The decade from the mid-1760s was characterized by faith in the possibilities of collaboration.

The progress of the reforms was accompanied by the growing hopes and enthusiasms of the *philosophes*, even in states where there was little reforming activity. Thus in Venice Francesco Griselini endeavoured to spread the central ideas of the Enlightenment in his periodicals *Giornale d'Italia* and *Corriere letterario* in the same years as Verri's *Il Caffè* and Beccaria's masterpiece on penal reform; the Piedmontese Giambattista Vasco voiced his egalitarian, humanitarian support of the peasant in his first work, *Public Happiness Considered among the Cultivators of their Own Lands* (1769) in the year that the great Neapolitan reformer Antonio Genovesi expressed his concern with the same problem in his final writing, *Academic Letters on the Question Whether the Ignorant are more Happy than the Scientists*. The themes of discussion were naturally those of the world of the Parisian *philosophes* and their timing, often even the years of their publication, were closely linked to the succession of problems raised in this supremely cosmopolitan debate. But, equally, they were directly tied to the reforms that were being enacted in the progressive Italian states.

By the later 1770s this optimism began to be pierced by doubts. Too much depended on the attitude of the sovereign. When the radical Pied-montese intellectual Dalmazzo Francesco Vasco was arrested in Rome on behalf of the Sardinian government in 1768, Pietro Verri was scandalized: 'If philosophy is not armed with authority, it must hide itself for, if it does not do so, persecution is always at the ready' (Venturi, 27, p. 817). But even in the reforming states the intellectuals were becoming anxious about the policies of the rulers. Paradoxically, if the reformers had previously chafed at the caution of the princes, particularly over economic and administrative reforms, it was now the very determination of the sovereigns and the pace of change that often made the *philosophes* hesitate or withdraw. Even in Tuscany, where collaboration lasted longest, Leopold's ministers remained substantially opposed to his Jansenist policy.

The mid-1770s thus witnessed a change in the relationship between rulers and intellectual reformers. In these years the older generation of administrators disappeared, the new rulers emerged in the fullness of their powers. The two administrators who had dominated the early decades of reforms – Pompeo Neri and Bernardo Tanucci – disappeared in 1776; Rucellai died in 1778. Neri's influence had already declined in his final years, as the young Leopold, imbued with Enlightenment spirit, accelerated the pace of reform. Tanucci, to his surprise, was dismissed. His words of sorrow at Neri's death summed up his awareness that times were changing:

> A most just grief is felt by his friends, the sovereign, the patria, the nation for the loss of Neri, the friend of truth, wise enough to recognize it, capable of promoting it, cultured enough to recognize the quality of wisdom. I mourn the loss of an old friend. . . . I do not know the new generation and can only hope that Neri's successor will be as useful. (Venturi, 27, pp. 949–50)

The generation of practical ability, common sense, 'logic' (Tanucci's favourite word) was replaced by a generation of new, young reformers, driven on, almost daemonically, by their faith in the need for and the possibility of rapid and radical reforms, dictated by reason, experience and *lumières*. In Tuscany Leopold had already made clear his determination to transform the state. In Lombardy Joseph II intervened increasingly, even before his mother Maria Theresa's death in 1780. In Naples another of Maria Theresa's children, Maria Carolina, inspired hope in the intellectuals as she urged on her weak husband Ferdinand IV. At Rome Clement XIV was succeeded in 1775 by a vigorous new pope, Pius VI, determined to resist the attacks against the Church, but also to rescue the Papal State from its desperate financial straits by radical reforms. In Piedmont, by contrast, on the death of Charles Emanuel III (1773) the last hollow echoes of the great reforms of half-a-century earlier were silenced with Bogino's dismissal by the reactionary, bigoted Victor Amadeus III (1773–96). More than ever, by the later 1770s, the possibility and direction of reform was to depend on the will of the prince.

But these decades were also characterized by doubts about the prince's capacity to overcome resistance to change. Increasingly the civilized world – the Europe to which the reformers had looked with such optimism – appeared incapable of rising to the challenge of Enlightenment. In France the physiocratic experiment of Turgot, in whom the 'economists' had placed their faith, ended abruptly with his dismissal in 1776. England, the symbol of progress and liberty, seemed to betray its trust with the outbreak of the American revolt in 1775. In Italy, as elsewhere, the philosophers began to look outside the 'old' Europe to Frederick II of Prussia, to Catherine of Russia, to the young America, or even further afield or back in time to romanticized visions of China, the South American Incas, the pre-Roman tribes of Italy. Doubts about the present state of Europe reinforced utopistic images of an ideal future. Nobody expressed this combination of uncertainty and faith better than Gaetano Filangieri: 'The nature of things has changed', he continually repeated, 'gold has become the measuring-rod of all'; 'the present state of the nations of Europe is that everything is to be found in the hands of few. Action is needed to ensure that everything be in the hands of many. This is the goal, the remedy to be aimed at.' 'But there is no limit to one's hopes in a century in which the spirit of letters is not incompatible with the spirit of sovereignty, in a century in which the rapid course of the imagination is not checked by the obstacles which despotism is accustomed to set against it.' But Filangieri's flow of optimism was tempered by his reluctant admission that 'through heaven knows what baneful destiny the man of letters is not always admitted to the presence of princes to discuss the great affairs of state' (Filangieri, in 28, pp. 618, 667–8).

The search for a better world was nourished, as always, by the writings of the French *lumières* and now, also, of the Scottish philosophers. Erudition was dismissed in favour of a broad philosophical vision of history. Following French discussions, Italian intellectuals rediscovered the Neapolitan philosopher Vico as they debated the interpretation of myths and rites and the origins of peoples. Voltaire and soon Condorcet were cited alongside Hume and Robertson in this common search for a philosophy of history which would explain the present ills and, perhaps, point to the future happy society. D'Holbach's materialist atheism began to excite interest and even Morelly's communist utopia (previously virtually unknown except to a hostile Genovesi) attracted attention. Above all, as the difficulties of transforming society appeared more intractable and as faith in the princes faltered, the driving force of Rousseau's egalitarianism was expressed more frequently and more openly. Filangieri was but one of the many voices which now insisted on equality – and not merely equality before the law.

The prolonged struggle of the Corsicans rapidly lost the contours of reality for the more radical intellectuals as it was transformed into the symbol of a democratic, egalitarian society. Already in the final years of Paoli's resistance, Dalmazzo Francesco Vasco had written a *Suite du contrat social* which, despite its title, turned as much to Montesquieu as to Rousseau, who had himself written a constitution for the island. By 1783 the Tuscan Luca Magnanima, an impassioned supporter of the Corsicans, could see the successful American revolt as vindicating the Corsicans' fight for independence. The American revolution constituted the

> major event which will close this century. The century to come will undoubtedly count many others, because Europe is laying the foundations for such happenings continuously. The finest will be a universal light among the nations illuminating their true interests and hence a greater liberty. May the Heavens wish that it be so! (Magnanima, in 27, p. 798)

Not all shared Magnanima's optimism. The Neapolitan Francescantonio Grimaldi was convinced that the history of civilization offered perpetual confirmation of the inevitability of inequality; the Istrian Gian Rinaldo Carli in *The Free Man* (1778) violently attacked Rousseau's belief in liberty and equality; the Triestean Antonio de Giuliani turned Enlightenment optimism in progress and science on its head:

> man believes himself to be an active being when he is nothing but passive. . . . It is a deceit to suppose that science regulates events, when, on the contrary, events give motive force to science. Theories are nothing but pure luxury. . . . Rousseau proved marvellously that the sciences have not improved man's fate at all. (De Giuliani, in 27, pp. 688-9)

But for the majority of the intellectuals there was still hope – hope in an almost miraculous transformation of society or in the adoption of radical measures that would go beyond the aims of princes and inevitably restrict their power. Freemasonry, which spread rapidly throughout Italy in the 1770s and 1780s (although on a more limited scale than elsewhere in Europe) offered an ambiguous combination of faith in the prince, incarnation of the gradual progress of rationalism and Enlightenment, and aspiration towards a more transcendental Kingdom of Light, to be achieved through the mystery of its rites. But the very diffusion of freemasonry among Italian intellectuals in these years, especially in the south, was symptomatic of a diffidence towards the possibilities of open discussion, a withdrawal into secret meetings. By the late 1780s even the faith in gradual controlled change of the official masonic lodges was rapidly eroded, particularly in Naples, by the egalitarian, communistic propaganda of the extreme sect of so-called *Illuminati*. Driven out of Bavaria, their doctrines were now carried to Italy by the Danish archaeologist Friedrich Münter.

Outside the lodges as well there was a search for new approaches and new solutions. With egalitarianism spread republicanism, faith not in fossilized city-republics like Venice or Genoa, but in the new American republic, to which Filangieri turned, or in William Penn's ideal republic or even Mercier's fantasy *L'an 2440*. Machiavelli reappeared in republican clothes: the Neapolitan Galanti planned a new edition of Machiavelli's works, which were then published by the Tuscan Jansenist de' Ricci.

Criticisms and demands sharpened. Genovesi and Filangieri had believed that the evils resulting from the excessive concentration of private property would vanish with the abolition of primogenitures and entails. Now Beccaria and Gorani attacked the concept of private property, Giambattista Vasco demanded an agrarian law. Proposed reform of abuses within the Church led, in extreme cases, to rejection of the very idea of a Church except as a free democratic association. The physiocratic faith in private agricultural production and free enterprise, although it remained the official doctrine in Tuscany and retained the loyalty of some writers in Lombardy, Modena and Naples, came under increasing attack as evidence of social inequality and injustice – above all pauperism – mounted. The recession in the silk industry in Piedmont, Lombardy and Tuscany in 1782–3, the desolation of the 1783 earthquake in Calabria, played their part in the revival of neo-mercantilist doctrines, or even (in the south) of the demand for State intervention. Yet the physiocratic faith in a natural economic order remained, and gained strength from the slow penetration of Adam Smith's ideas, discussed in the Papal States, Naples and Piedmont by the 1790s. Indeed one writer, de' Giuliani, transformed this concept of a natural but basically static economic order by interpreting it as the motive force of the history of civilization: all history, for de' Giuliani, revealed a cyclical search for equilibrium between the opposing interests of classes of producers and consumers. This belief in a natural order began to imply limitations on the prince's power. The real function of 'legal despots' was seen as confined to removing the obstacles which hindered the functioning of the natural order, in order to permit (as Adam Smith taught) the free competition of individuals which would achieve a natural equilibrium.

This natural economic order could be construed as further evidence of the existence of a law of nature. Already in 1773 the Lombard Alfonso Longo could write of fundamental laws; ten years later the Neapolitan Filangieri could turn to an ideal magistracy to check abuse of power. In the following years the Tuscan G. M. Lampredi could assert contractualist limitations to despotic excesses, while Dalmazzo Francesco Vasco found himself once more imprisoned for daring to write in Piedmont a *Political Essay about a Form of Legitimate Government Moderated by Fundamental Laws* (1791). Montesquieu was revived and utilized polemically to justify the traditional aristocracy, alongside Rousseau's assertion of the rights of the people, in a common defence against the dangers of despotism.

The appeal to public opinion, of which the intellectuals were always so conscious, began to develop into an assertion of the right to greater participation. Freedom of the press, free speech, toleration, even the benefits of the English party struggle, were demands voiced by several of the more radical Italian writers. The administrative reforms in Lombardy and Tuscany, which had aimed at involving broader strata of the population in the process of government by drawing the wealthy and the landed owners into local responsibilities, pointed in the same direction.

Leopold himself had realized these implications of his reforms. Bureaucratic hostility threatened to sabotage the effective execution of the new laws. In an attempt to bypass the bureaucracy by involving local interests in the implementation of the reforms, he had urged Gianni to prepare a scheme for a national representative body (1789): 'the general purpose of the new institution', as Gianni wrote later, 'consisted in ensuring that the nation could give the throne knowledge of the needs of the small communes, the larger provinces and the entirety of the state' (Anzilotti, 64, p. 28). Pietro Verri, reflecting on the danger and damage to Joseph II's paternalistic authoritarianism, advised his successor – the same Leopold – to create (as in Austrian Belgium) a 'permanent representation of the general society of the state' protected by an inviolable law; such a body 'will be able humbly to submit its needs to the throne, and will act as an eye-glass through which the monarch can see the truth' (Anzilotti, 64, p. 29). These were no liberal constitutional schemes of the nineteenth century: the assemblies were to have no legislative attributes and nothing obliged the sovereigns to heed the appeals of their peoples. But they contained within them the germs of future constitutional beliefs. By the time Verri wrote his *Thoughts on the Political State of the Milanese Region* (1790), with his proposals for representation, the French revolution had broken out. But even before, on its very eve, the radical Giuseppe Gorani could demand that Enlightened sovereigns gain the free and spontaneous collaboration of citizens. By these last years of the *ancien régime*, the intellectuals were beginning to draw away from the princes, in whom for so long they had placed their trust.

Joseph II: the autocratic reformer

In Lombardy the ten years of Joseph II's reign led to the break between monarch and Enlightened reformers. The Enlightened despot *par excellence*, Joseph II was determined to re-order his vast states on a rational, uniform pattern for the benefit of his peoples and saw it as his task to override opposition from whatever quarter. Already before his accession in 1780, his influence as co-regent had been felt in Lombardy. In 1769, after his lengthy visit to Italy, he had played a central role in the most important customs reform in the history of eighteenth-century Lombardy – the reduction of duties on Lombard exports to the German states of the empire. Verri had appealed to him in 1770 over the major administrative reforms. But Joseph II was an aloof and independent-minded sovereign of whose support no administrator or reformer could be sure. It was not surprising that, after his succession, the Enlightened reformers should have resented his assertion of authority, his brusque disregard for their opinions.

Carli, ever more conservative, was replaced by Verri as president of the Cameral Court. But by 1785 Verri, too, found himself put aside. Even before Joseph's accession Verri had complained bitterly of the inability of the individual reformers to make their influence felt under the bureaucratic despotism created by the new administrative reforms: 'Given the present system, I see that none of the employees can have enough influence to do good: one person always proposes, another opposes, a third one modifies, and the result is then a diagonal line along which one moves' (Valeri, 57, p. 203). The Tuscan Jansenist Fabio de' Vecchi echoed Verri's disenchantment, commenting on Joseph's ecclesiastical reforms that 'the manner of executing them is more military than ecclesiastical' (Passerin d'Entrèves, 39, vol. III, p. 363).

It was in the ecclesiastical field that Joseph II first displayed his determination to create a modern secular state. In 1781 the concordat was denounced; contemporaneously an edict of toleration sounded the trumpet-blast of Enlightenment. Support for Jansenism was asserted by the prohibition of the bull *Unigenitus*. Joseph's ecclesiastical policy, 'josephism' as it has been called, already clearly visible in so many of his mother's reforms, was based on a careful balance between the intellectual, philosophical demands of the Enlightenment and the theological, moral concerns of the Jansenists. It was the integration of these two aspects within the state that explains why the important group of Jansenists from Pavia – in contrast to their Tuscan colleagues – was not hostile to Enlightenment ideas, but shared the *philosophes'* concern for natural law, individual rights, secular power.

The Junta of Stewardship was now replaced by an Ecclesiastical Commission with three departments responsible for the secular clergy, regular clergy and public education and charity. Every aspect of ecclesiastical life was to be controlled. In 1783 ecclesiastical exemption from taxation was abolished and the Holy Office suppressed. The excessive number of priests was reduced, although Kaunitz was worried that this might result in a diminution of parish priests, who 'are mediators in the frequent quarrels of citizens, for they check brawls, prevent wrangles and disputes by their authority and arbitration, generally invigilating over the moral conduct of their parishioners' (Valsecchi, 19, p. 619). The policy of suppressing monasteries and convents was accelerated (52 were suppressed in 1782), while those that were allowed to survive were separated from their mother houses. The pace and radical nature of the reforms was such that Pius VI took the desperate decision to visit Joseph II at Vienna (1782). But the emperor continued on his path, entrusting control over ecclesiastical discipline and education to Jansenists. The final step was taken with the creation of a General Seminary at Pavia, at which all new parish priests were to be trained (1786), and the preparation of a new catechism for the faithful. The duties of the citizen and the believer were to be conciliated, religion was to demonstrate its social utility.

Charity and education were inextricably linked to this subordination of the Church to temporal authority. Already in 1769 Joseph had complained to Firmian that charity – the giving of alms and assistance to all who pleaded poverty or illness – inflated the number of beggars and vagabonds: the workhouse was too comfortable, its work too light. The growth of pauperism was ascribed to the prevalence of a counter-reformist mentality of Christian charity and not to the worsening conditions in the countryside. The mainly religious institutions that had evolved to succour the poor and destitute encouraged idleness, professional begging and administrative abuses. Although an obligation remained to assist those genuinely incapable of looking after themselves – abandoned infants, the infirm, the aged without family or resources – this end could be achieved more rationally and economically under secular control. In 1786 the confraternities which were traditionally responsible for charity were abolished, and their resources unified – as in Joseph's German lands – in a new Company of Charity Towards One's Neighbour.

Measures to control education had already been taken by Maria Theresa with the reform of Pavia university and the Palatine Schools at Milan. Under Joseph a conscious effort was made to laicize education and make it an instrument of government. The Patriotic Society, founded in 1776 on Prussian and London models to stimulate interest in the development of arts and manufactures, was now closely controlled. The masonic lodges, acknowledged as effective institutions to diffuse Enlightenment ideas, but regarded as too independent through their number and variety, were prohibited and replaced by an official lodge, to which the imperial plenipotentiary Wilczek belonged. Pavia university was to create a new school of public administrators. As an unconvinced citizen wrote: 'The University of Pavia has thus become as it were the only source; whoever desires to employ himself in some way is obliged to go there; and the evidence is that the university of Pavia teaches according to the prevailing principles' (Valsecchi, 19, p. 622). Even if the teachers were still priests, education was to be strictly controlled and inspired by the new maxims of reason and persuasion, not by threats. Paolo Frisi's advice was invited on the creation of training schools for technicians. An attempt was even made to secularize primary education along the lines of the Austrian reformer Felbinger, whose regulations had been adopted in the Trentino in 1774. After a visit by

Lombard administrators to the experimental school at Rovereto in 1784 twenty new schools were founded together with a teachers' training college, as the first steps towards the creation of a communal school in each village, a principal school in each district and a teachers' training college in each province.

These measures required years to produce their effect. They were based on faith in the future – a future which failed to materialize on Joseph's death in 1790. But the emperor's administrative reforms were meant to be of immediate effect. He felt the need to centralize and render uniform the structure of government. In 1784 the noble monopoly of municipal 'congregations' was attacked by opening these councils to administrators, wealthy citizens and professional people. In 1786 all the traditional institutions that had guaranteed local autonomies – the senate, the state congregation, the Cameral Court – were abolished and replaced by a Government Council with specialized departments; the old provincial boundaries were replaced by eight uniform circumscriptions, each under a Political Intendant; almost all existing jurisdictions were abolished in favour of a simple, rational scheme of local courts, appeal courts and a supreme tribunal. In this single year, centuries of traditions and autonomies were erased, the old rivalries between Milan and the provinces, between the cities and the countryside, between the nobles and the other classes were abolished with the imposition of a uniform, centralized structure of government which, in its creator's intentions, was to be inspired by reason and the application of measures for the good of the people. Resistance was to be broken and obedience ensured by the creation of a police force and a mild form of censorship.

These major ecclesiastical, scholastic and administrative reforms were not accompanied by a similar drive in the economic field. The main reforms were the abolition of the guilds (completed in 1787) and the completion of the Mantuan cadastral register (which had dragged on from 1771 to 1784). Perhaps the reforms that followed Pompeo Neri's *catasto* had shown the limits to government action. According to Pietro Verri, Joseph's attitude towards agriculture, during his 1769 visit, had been that 'it was good for the population to be spread as uniformly as possible on the face of the earth, not crowded together' (Valsecchi, 59, vol. 2, p. 296). But beyond the encouragement of agrarian academies and treatises on agricultural techniques (such as those of Paolo Frisi on irrigation), there was probably little that Joseph could do – or possibly even felt inclined to do in view of the increase of agricultural production in the Po plain. Physiocratic doctrine was never adopted except in a limited, partial manner. This was most clear in the industrial and commercial spheres: customs duties were continuously retouched but never abolished; and if the guilds were suppressed, subsidies and privileges were still granted to individual industries. The desire to develop industry proved inadequate to overcome the reluctance of local capitalists to risk their funds. Even the most important Lombard capitalist of the century, Antonio Greppi, preferred speculation to industrial investment after burning his fingers with a silk factory at Mantua (1763–9). Capital was not lacking, but labour costs were constantly adduced as an excuse, undoubtedly encouraging the government in its view that the charitable institutions should serve a socially useful function by training the poor for industrial employment.

Unable to overcome the reluctance of entrepreneurs, disinclined by current physiocratic doctrine to interfere with the 'natural' economic order, concerned not to endanger public finances which, although healthy, were undergoing considerable pressure to pay for the reforms, Joseph II failed to change the existing pattern of agriculture, industry or trade. In the countryside, as production increased, the living conditions of the peasantry worsened. This was particularly visible in the Mantovano, where the cadastral register, unlike its Milanese model, failed because of uncertainty surrounding its completion to act as a stimulus to agricultural improvement. The peasant crude silk producers continued to be exploited by the large merchants, despite the creation of a silk bank to advance them credit, along the lines advocated by Verri and Beccaria (1781). The economic power of the Milanese patricians remained, symbolized by their private bank of S. Ambrogio which Joseph subordinated to the state's bank of S. Teresa, but did not dare abolish. Politically the power of the nobles appeared to have been broken by the administrative reforms. But local hostility remained strong. The nobles continued to dominate municipal councils. Even Joseph had hesitated over the abolition of fiefs (despite their political insignificance), as they offered the government a source of revenue. His intendant at Mantua, Giambattista Gherardo d'Arco, a solitary figure of an Enlightened provincial noble (like Giambattista Biffi at Cremona) found himself unable to carry through reforms because of the opposition of the local nobles and clergy who whipped up popular agitations. The ecclesiastical reforms – for which Lombardy had been chosen by Joseph, as the experimental ground for the empire – were regarded with incomprehension or resentment.

Perhaps with more time, with the consolidation of this new bureaucracy, with the safeguard against reaction of a police force, Joseph II might have succeeded. But by the time of his death in 1790, among the older reformers as much as among the conservatives, widespread hostility had arisen to his reforms, regarded as too revolutionary, too authoritarian, too abstractly concerned with the theories of Enlightenment to meet the political needs of the country. It was in this decade that hostility to Austria acquired substance in Lombardy, although it never erupted into revolt as in Austrian Belgium. But it was in these same years that a new, younger generation began to glimpse the revolutionary implications of Joseph's reforms. Many of this new generation were to be found in the future democratic party of the Cisalpine republic.

Leopold of Tuscany: physiocracy and Jansenism

In Tuscany, the hesitations of the reformers over the grand-duke's policies only emerged in the later 1780s and never led, as in Lombardy, to a real split. Here, as in no other Italian state, physiocratic policy had triumphed in the 1770s. Its corollary, encouragement of the rising production and profits of large private estates, had won the day and defeated the efforts of Leopold to improve the living conditions of the peasantry. The growing foreign demand for grain, combined with the adoption of free trade, discouraged the landowners from serious experimentation with alternatives, such as crude silk production or livestock breeding, which had developed in the Lombard plain where customs differentials offered incentives. The discussions on livestock breeding were confined to the academies, especially the Florentine Georgofili, and concentrated (somewhat illogically in this environment imbued with physiocratic mistrust of State actions) on State encouragement of the diffusion of techniques, rather than on the actual practices of farming. Paoletti was representative of the landowners in his pessimism about the ability of the peasant to improve the land. Like Genovesi and Verri, he turned to the parish priest, whose status, prestige and influence gave him particular opportunities to teach the peasant.

Given the strength of the landowners and their support for Leopold's physiocratic policy, as voiced by the Georgofili, it was hardly surprising that Leopold and his leading minister Gianni were unsuccessful in their attempts to create smallholdings. Proposals to divide the lands of religious orders and charitable institutions into small plots and lease them by quit-rents, *a livello*, were not confined to Tuscany. Muratori had written of the need for such leaseholds in 1749, as had Genovesi in the 1760s and D'Arco in the 1780s; an attempt in Modena in the early 1770s had failed. The policy of such a division of land (at the Church's expense) accorded well with Enlightenment ideas of gradual social change and the spread of material happiness. But in Tuscany, as elsewhere in Italy, these humanitarian aims were doomed to failure, despite the general recognition of the peasants' poverty. As a leading Tuscan reformer, Pagnini, wrote, 'fortunately for them and us', the peasants were not aware of belonging 'to the lowest and most pitiful class of their estate' (Mirri, 71, p. 188, n. 30). After the experimental and basically unsuccessful sales of land in 1769 and 1772, it was the same Pagnini who resisted Gianni's proposal for a more carefully controlled method of creating smallholdings. Gianni's plan was accepted. But even these sales, in 1784, were unsuccessful, as the entry fines and annual quit-rents were too costly for the peasants and as the execution of the project was left to the local administrators – the landowners, providentially provided with capital resources to buy out the peasants by the recent redemption of the public debt (1778). In these same years, the Georgofili requested and gained Leopold's acceptance of the right of landowners to dismiss share-croppers. As in Lombardy, the reforms increased production but failed to achieve a greater degree of social justice.

But among the educated classes the demand for such justice began to be heard. Already in 1772, as famine again struck Tuscany, the bishop of Cortona, D'Ippoliti, asserted the *mezzadro*'s right to subsistence, irrespective of contractual arrangements; for 'one must necessarily admit that the peasant is the true curator and the sole depositary of primitive wealth, which passes from his hands into those of all the others' (Mirri, 71, p. 195). Ten years later the exiled Tuscan journalist Giovanni Ristori could draw his conclusions about the need for a forced division of property, an 'agrarian law':

> What more insulting prospect for humanity exists than to see five rich men strut about pretentiously and proudly in front of a thousand poor, who are humiliated by their unhappy condition, and rendered squalid by hunger and hard labour! Ah! When inequality of fortune is carried to such extremes, would it be so wrong to think of passing agrarian laws? (Capra, 87, p. 87)

In the industrial world, physiocratic policy proved even more negative. A favourite theme, voiced for example in the mid-1780s by the publicist Aldobrando Paolini, was the liberty of labour. But the immediate result of destroying the guilds was an industrial crisis, for little private initiative existed to offer fresh employment. The violent reaction of the Florentine populace after 1790 reflected this unexpected consequence of Leopold's reforms. Whatever conventional physiocratic wisdom, destitution resulted from far deeper causes than idleness. Nor, incidentally, could the poor classes alone be accused of idleness, as the young economist and scientist Giovanni Fabroni observed. Fabroni's egalitarian spirit conflicted with his physiocratic faith.

Physiocracy also played an important part in the discussions that led to changes within the fiscal system and administrative structures. But it was not the only influence. For Leopold, these reforms were complementary to the new economic policy and necessary for the transformation of the state. The physiocratic ideal of a single land-tax as the basis of state revenues remained the ultimate aim, but the fiscal (as all of Leopold's) reforms were marked by a gradual, experimental approach. Discussions about the taxation system had begun as early as 1766. In 1781, just before his death, Tavanti had attempted to move towards a free trade system by a major reform of customs and excise duties. But the practical difficulties that arose, and Gianni's doubts about the ability of Tuscan manufacturers and commerce

to withstand foreign competition, led to the creation of a Deputation for
Finances in 1786, which was responsible for minor, experimental changes
two years later. Leopold was undoubtedly influenced by Voltaire's and
Turgot's criticisms of the unfairness of the methods of imposing taxes and
hence limited himself to rationalizing the fiscal structure. At the same time
the sovereign's private patrimony was legally separated from Crown
property and the special tribunal for demesne revenues (the *regalie*)
was suppressed as constituting an improper exception to the rule of
equality before the law. But this limited cautious introduction of partial
reforms failed to achieve the desired end, leaving a system with many
anomalies.

More striking were Leopold's attempts to reform the law and his
increasing recognition of the rights of individuals. The new criminal code
of 1786, which abolished the death penalty and torture, had been drawn up
after consultation with Beccaria. It was regarded, justifiably, as a major
achievement and confirmed Tuscany's place under Leopold in the vanguard
of the reforming movement.

By Leopold's final years this position was even clearer. Already in the
communal reform of 1787 Gianni had asserted that civil liberty, not fear of
the sovereign, ought to be the basis of legislation, echoing Voltaire's *Essai
sur les moeurs* and D'Argenson's proposals for municipal reforms. Increasingly, as resistance to reform became more entrenched, Gianni expressed his
doubts about the efficacy of reforms without broad social support. Many
years later he could look back and express his admiration for Leopold, 'a
sovereign whose dominant passion was philanthropy, of rare intelligence,
holding the most just principles of political philosophy, the most sound
maxims of government, with a heart full of humanity' (Venturi, 27, p. 984).
But even so remarkable a sovereign could not transform a state without
widespread support. Reforms would inevitably fail, 'unless the nation can
in some manner examine, suggest, clarify, discover errors and prevent
deception' (Venturi, 27, p. 985).

This conviction, which undoubtedly influenced Leopold, underlay the
preparation of a financial budget in 1787 and even more the publication of a
final financial account of Leopold's stewardship of Tuscany at the moment
of his departure for Vienna in 1790. Leopold was influenced not only by
Gianni's practical preoccupations, but by the criticisms of Turgot and
Dupont de Nemours of the inadequacy of the principle of equality before
the law. These physiocrats asserted (and the American constitution confirmed) that the individual must have protection against unjust laws.
Leopold accepted the idea of an original pact, of fundamental laws:

> I believe that the sovereign, even if hereditary, is only a delegate and employee
> of the people, for whom he exists, to whom he owes all his efforts, sufferings,
> vigil. . . . I believe that each country needs a fundamental law or contract

between the people and the sovereign, which will limit the latter's authority and power. (Tivaroni, 20, pp. 268-9)

This conviction explains Leopold's decision to encourage his ministers (especially Gianni) to prepare a constitution that would allow the election of deputies with legislative powers. In one sense, these constitutional proposals could be seen as a logical development from the reform of local administrations, involving a broader base of property owners. For 'the people' was not conceived as including the peasants, too ignorant to participate in government. But Leopold's constitutional plans, in their rejection of the medieval system of representation by the three estates of nobles, clergy and burghers (such as still existed in Italy and even more in France and Germany), in their acknowledgement of the concept of individual representation, however limited, were a recognition of the limits of Enlightened reformism.

Leopold's attempts, in these same years, to impose a Jansenist reform on the Tuscan Church contained elements of a somewhat analagous scheme of participation. By the late 1770s the Jansenists were looking to the princes to reform the Church independently of Rome. The alliance of the Jansenists with the princes had first emerged in 1774-6, when energetic emissaries of the schismatic Utrecht Church had tried to gain support in their struggle for recognition. In Tuscany the Jansenists remained far more closed to Enlightenment ideas than in Lombardy: de' Vecchi was disgusted by the publication of the *Encyclopédie* at Leghorn, and strongly opposed Pilati's regalist *Reflections of a canonist* (1787), with its proposals for royal control. At first Leopold tried to mediate between the desire for religious reforms of the Tuscan Jansenists, led by de' Vecchi and de' Ricci, and the demand for the extension of State authority of his ministers. Typically, it was Leopold, and not his ministers, who initiated discussions with the Jansenists. Fabio de' Vecchi, who had been forced to leave Rome because of his Jansenist views, was most influential in these early discussions with Leopold, but slowly found himself displaced by the more intransigent and rigid Scipione de' Ricci, who was made bishop of Pistoia and Prato in 1780. These two friends were asked by Leopold to set up ecclesiastical seminaries at Siena and Pistoia to train a new generation of priests, while a third seminary was created at Leghorn under another Jansenist Baldovinetti.

The Tuscan Jansenists were thus drawn into closer collaboration with Leopold: their earlier almost exclusive preoccupations with doctrinal issues receded, as they came to accept the need for practical, State-imposed reforms. They shared Leopold's desire to reform the Church by means of provincial and ultimately 'national' synods, along the lines proposed by the French gallican François Richer. They asserted episcopal powers against the authority of Rome, invoking the theses of the bishop of Trier Febronius (Johann von Hontheim). Soon they claimed the right of parish priests to participate with deliberative powers in the synods, going beyond the pro-positions of the Utrecht Jansenists. These demands were not based on any secular view of royal authority or egalitarianism, but on their Jansenist faith in their religious and ecclesiastical significance, as was their conviction of the need to re-establish the rigorism of the early Church. But for Leopold, as for his brother Joseph, the reforms had a primarily practical, utilitarian purpose as steps towards the creation of a reformed, subordinate Church. The divergence of aims emerged in the discussions over the creation of 'ecclesiastical treasuries' from the income of suppressed religious orders, to be utilized by the State for the maintenance of the poorer parish priests and for primary education (1783–6). The Jansenists were divided. Baldovinetti was in favour, de' Vecchi feared the total subjection of the Church to State control, de' Ricci tried to compromise by proposing the gradual creation of such ecclesiastical patrimonies as benefices fell vacant.

It was thus Leopold who forced the pace, keeping closely in touch with his brother Joseph's reforms, convinced that the papacy was too weak to resist. The same spirit of Muratorian-inspired Austrian *Reformkatholicismus* was to be found in Tuscany as in Lombardy: alongside the suppression of the Holy Office (1782) and ecclesiastical jurisdictions (1784), superstition was attacked, penitential processions prohibited (1773), begging limited (1778, 1783), confraternities replaced by a single Company of Charity in each parish (1785), simplicity of ceremonial urged (1786). The summoning of the Pistoia synod in September 1786 was typical of Leopold's method of trying out a proposed national reform within a limited area. De' Ricci's circular to his clergy for the synod admirably expressed the fusion of Jansenist and regalist hopes in its attack on 'orthodox' ecclesiastics:

> They abhor every mention of reform and falsely claim – contrary to what the Holy Ghost has announced to us – that the Church can never experience periods of obscurity and old age; they cry out senselessly against the heretic and inno-vator every time that one wants to return to the Gospel in order to purge the Church of the foulness it has accumulated through the malignity of the times. Besotted with the warped ideas that ignorance and ambition spread in dark centuries under the guise of piety, they taint as heretical novelty every revival of ancient discipline more in conformity with the Gospel. (Rosa, 75, p. 277)

The apparent success of the synod convinced Leopold that it was time to force the situation and give the reform of the Tuscan Church European resonance. Unlike Joseph, Leopold recognized the right of bishops to regulate the internal life of the Church. The synods were seen as the ecclesi-astical counterpart to the representative provincial assemblies. Nevertheless, the Tuscan hierarchy was subjected to a virtual state of siege: the bishops were only able to correspond secretly with Rome through the Spanish resident at Florence; a proposal by the bishop of Fiesole to summon an 'anti-Pistoia' synod was prohibited. But Leopold's position was weak. His ecclesiastical policy lacked the support to be found in Naples and Lombardy and his precipitate determination alienated the moderate bishops. He failed to convince Joseph to call a German national synod. Even the Tuscan Jansenists warned about the dangers of too hasty action. With support limited to his secular ministers who saw in the synod a means of asserting greater control over the Church, Leopold summoned an assembly of the Tuscan bishops in March 1787 to prepare for a 'national' synod. At the assembly the Jansenists were isolated and their theses decisively rejected.

Jansenism had reached its high-water mark in Tuscany and had failed. In the final years of his reign, Leopold reverted to the traditional policy of asserting royal control with the closure of the nuncio's tribunal and the separation of religious orders from their foreign superiors (1788). A disillusioned de' Ricci now resisted the attempts by Gianni to create ecclesiastical patrimonies.

As in Lombardy, it was the prince who had imposed a new pace on the reforms. Leopold had tried to make Tuscany the centre of a European movement. His economic, constitutional and religious reforms were often more audacious than those of Joseph, not least because he was only responsible for a single, small state, not a vast, dispersed empire. Even so, his reforms ultimately failed through their inability to gain broadly based support. His departure in 1790 on his brother's death to take up the imperial throne was marked by an immediate wave of discontent and reaction.

8

Belated collaboration : 1780–94

The Two Sicilies: Genovesi's pupils and the lack of effective leadership

With the fall of Tanucci, engineered by the young Austrian queen Maria Carolina in 1776, hopes of reform revived in Naples. The traditional policy of restricting the power of the Church had run its course. Although the dispute continued, acquiring Jansenist overtones in response to the new developments in Lombardy and Tuscany, attention was focused on improving the economic conditions of the kingdom.

The new generation of reformers, almost all pupils of Genovesi, had come of age. The years after 1776 witnessed the publication of the vast majority of eighteenth-century Neapolitan enquiries and proposals to solve the economic ills of the country. The long years of Genovesi's sermons appeared to have borne fruit, in the countryside as in the capital. A new circle of Neapolitan writers gathered together in the 1780s: their interests ranged from literature and archaeology to economics and philosophy. Scattered around the provinces, in Calabria, Apulia, Molise, Abruzzo, small groups of reformers exchanged ideas, if not in the agrarian academies on which Genovesi had placed such hopes, in masonic lodges.

In 1775 Tanucci had attempted to suppress freemasonry, as had his sovereign Charles in 1751. But now freemasonry flourished, with the open support of the queen, and enrolled the leading reformers and ministers: the prince of Caramanico was grand master of the Neapolitan masons when he departed for Sicily as viceroy in 1786. In the same year the Danish *Illuminato* Friedrich Münter reached Naples and began to convert many of the younger masons, such as Pagano and Zurlo, to the egalitarian beliefs of the Bavarian sect. It was from this group that many of the leaders of the revolutionary and Napoleonic period were to be drawn.

This new generation, only too conscious of the reforms in Lombardy and Tuscany, began to explore the economic realities of the kingdom to which Genovesi had drawn their attention in his proposals for a more energetic economic policy. Gaetano Filangieri attacked the negative consequences of

feudalism on agricultural production. Domenico Grimaldi, who endeavoured to create a model farm on his estates at Seminara in Calabria, insisted
on the need for new agricultural techniques, for adequate irrigation, for
credit to encourage investment. Giuseppe Palmieri, also experimenting in
methods to increase productivity on his lands near Lecce, put forward a
neo-mercantilist programme to stimulate national industries and urged
financial reforms. At Gallipoli, in the heel of Italy, Filippo and Domenico
Briganti searched for methods to improve the quality of olive oil. In the
Molise, Francesco Longano and Giuseppe Maria Galanti, in the Abruzzi,
Melchiorre Delfico wrote detailed analyses of the backward agriculture of
their regions, which led them to attack feudal abuses and the dominance of
the capital city of Naples. Filangieri discussed how best to convert the vast
pasturages of the Apulian Tavoliere to private cultivation. Mario Pagano
defended the cause of the fishermen, exploited by the monopoly of the
merchants.

Almost all these intellectual reformers turned to the state to take the lead.
Private individuals lacked the resources and will, or were hampered by
antiquated laws. Only state intervention could change the situation. The
terrible earthquake of 1783 in Calabria laid bare the disastrous conditions of
the kingdom and strengthened the demand for state action. Physiocracy
attracted only a minority, not least because these Neapolitan reformers
elaborated their ideas and proposals in years when physiocracy was under
attack everywhere except in Tuscany. Ferdinando Galiani, the major figure
linking this new generation with the earlier age of Genovesi, scoffed at the
abstract confidence of the French physiocrats. Even Domenico Caracciolo,
who returned reluctantly from his long years at Paris, hesitated when viceroy of Sicily over introducing a free grain trade. For Giuseppe Palmieri,
paladin of the landed proprietors, increased production was more important
than social inequality, and local manufactures needed protection against
foreign exploitation: 'I believe that general poverty is less harmful and less
of an obstacle to the general wealth of the nation than individual wealth'
(Palmieri, in 28, p. 1098). Francescantonio Grimaldi dismissed the needs of
the peasants – 'they are, in short, almost similar to savages' (Grimaldi, in 28,
p. 569) – while his more practical-minded brother Domenico relied on
social snobbery to win over the more enterprising to the cause of production:

> Once a peasant understands that agriculture gives him not only what is useful,
> but also an imaginary good – such as sitting next to the most distinguished
> personages of his village at rustic gatherings – this stimulus by itself will be
> enough to make him value his occupation and apply himself to it with the most
> fervent attention. (Grimaldi, in 28, p. 452, n. 2)

Underlying these demands for state intervention was fear of the consequences of further inaction. Economic conditions worsened for the

peasantry as grain prices rose, feudal appropriations of communal lands increased, pauperism spread, brigandage re-emerged. 'The Greeks and Romans had slavery, modern peoples have begging: two things that more than anything else dishonour the human race' (Galanti, in 28, p. 1076), wrote Galanti. Longano continued to inveigh against the deep gulf that separated the nobles from the plebs: 'The State has reached its final point of decline when it is reduced to just two classes, of which one enjoys wealth, while the other is lacking in the bare necessities' (Galanti, in 28, p. 335). Even Ferdinando Galiani admitted by 1780 that agricultural conditions had worsened. To delay longer was to invite disaster. The reformers, whether conservative like Palmieri or egalitarian-minded like Longano, voiced a common fear of impending catastrophe, perhaps presaged by the Calabrian earthquake.

For a brief period, a mere decade, it appeared as if the reformers' demands had met with a positive response. An air of activity began to pervade the Court, as a new minister, the Franco-Irish John Acton, rose in influence under the protection of Maria Carolina. Acton had followed his uncle as head of the Tuscan navy, until Leopold had 'loaned' him to Ferdinand IV to reorganize the Neapolitan navy in 1779. Minister of war the following year, Acton had also taken over the financial and commercial ministries in 1782, becoming chief minister in 1789. His rise to power marked the Queen's determination to free Naples from Spanish tutelage. Cautiously approaching the Habsburg rulers and even the pope in order to avoid isolation, determined to revive Neapolitan naval strength, actively encouraging Neapolitan trade in the eastern Mediterranean by commercial treaties, even with Russia, conscious of the validity of the reformers' demands, this active cynical foreigner – together with the unbending enlightened aristocrat Domenico Caracciolo, viceroy of Sicily in 1781, chief minister in 1786 – symbolized the contradictory nature of Neapolitan reformism. Acton's campaign for military and naval strength ultimately clashed with his desire for reform. But this was not to emerge openly until the years of revolution.

Sicily

The new drive for reform was felt in both the kingdoms of the Two Sicilies. The island of Sicily had played little part in the plans of Genovesi or his successors. These Neapolitan reformers looked back to a unified, centralized 'Regnum Siciliae', such as had existed before the successful Sicilian 'war of the Vespers' in the late thirteenth century. They believed that the reforms they proposed for the mainland would be equally effective on the island. Tanucci had attempted a few reforms to restrict the power of the Church and limit the abuse of feudal jurisdiction, but the barons had effectively castrated them. Enlightenment ideas, often brought in by foreign travellers and disseminated by masonic lodges, had begun to circulate as early as the 1730s under the patronage of isolated barons and ecclesiastical dignitaries. By Caracciolo's time they were so fashionable that the Sicilian poet Giovanni Meli could satirize the young ladies who took Voltaire and Rousseau to their summer retreats:

> Voltaire! Rousseau! What say you?
> Does the little lady understand their books?
> Oh, she's such an utter French madam,
> She has them off with the servant in the wood.   (Pontieri, 105, p. 59, n. 8)

But if these small groups of Sicilian writers, particularly in Palermo and Catania, began to discuss such typically Enlightenment themes as penal reforms and natural philosophy, rationalism and economic reforms, they drew back before the central problems of Sicilian society: 'Religion must be considered as one of the main parts, indeed as the prop of the political system' (Romeo, 225, p. 39), wrote Tommaso Natale. Those seductive French writers should be read with care, warned Vincenzo Gaglio, for they can 'easily give birth to seditions in a state' (Romeo, 225, p. 40). Above all, even when discussing the need for legislative reforms and for stimulating agricultural production and trade, none of these Sicilian writers dared attack the vast estates of extensive cultivation, the feudal *latifondi*.

In so traditional and lethargic a society, Caracciolo's activities as viceroy (1781–6) must have seemed to the Sicilians like the onslaught of yet another foreign invader. Fresh from his Parisian experiences, deeply imbued with a conviction of the efficacy of rational reform, brusquely contemptuous of all opposition, this Neapolitan grandee, after suppressing the relatively harmless Sicilian Holy Office because it represented an open challenge to Sicilian authority, could write to D'Alembert: 'To tell you the truth, my dear friend, I broke down with emotion and wept: for the first and only time I reached the point of thanking Heaven for taking me away from Paris to serve as the instrument of this great work' (Croce, 104, pp. 107–108).

But Caracciolo's main target was baronial power. By a series of manoeuvres he attempted to limit baronial jurisdiction, free peasants from their ties to the land and feudal communes from baronial interference, assert regular control over public magistracies and public finances, even subject nobles and clergy to taxes. A firm believer in the middle class (virtually nonexistent in Sicily) and defender of the peasantry ('one must save the peasantry from the fangs of these wolves, for the barons of Sicily are wolves' (Pontieri, 105, p. 200)), he hoped to break the monopoly of grain production and exports exercised by the barons and foreign merchants, as well as prevent popular risings at times of famine (as in 1773) by government

regulation of the grain trade. Against the traditional authority of the baron-
dominated parliament, Caracciolo asserted the supreme authority of the
Crown, interpreting feudal laws against the barons, and finally even
attempting to introduce a land survey as the basis for a new taxation system
that would remove financial control from parliament.

These whirlwind activities were only moderately successful. The Sicilian
baronage had an age-old experience of passive resistance to interfering
viceroys and could claim as a victory Caracciolo's recall to Naples (albeit as
chief minister). But its position had been weakened, and the Sicilian intellectuals felt encouraged to extend their criticisms to the feudal order and its
negative effects on agricultural production. In this late flowering of a
Sicilian Enlightenment, the major names of the French and Scottish philosophers became obligatory points of reference. As the antiquary Giovanni
Evangelista Di Blasi observed sarcastically:

> If the thoughts have not been turned on the lathe of Voltaire, Rousseau,
> Mirabeau, and others of similarly pure gold, if they have not been sprinkled
> with a somewhat poisonous, piquant salt, even when they deal with the most
> sacrosanct subjects, they arouse such regret and become such a bore that they
> fall from one's hands. (Romeo, 225, p. 93)

The new viceroy, the prince of Caramanico (1786–94) called for the collaboration of these intellectuals: they should collect and codify the laws of the
kingdom, found primary schools, carry out surveys of the economic conditions of the island, advise on the division of demesnial lands. Until fears of
revolutionary subversion called a halt to the reforms, Caramanico pressed
on and by his tactful persuasion advanced considerably further than
Caracciolo: the parliament was persuaded to accept the preparation of a
land survey, feudal privileges were restricted and laws of inheritance
tightened, some demesnial lands were divided into private freehold properties and preparations were made to allot ecclesiastical lands at quit-
rents.

As in the kingdom of Naples and more so than elsewhere in Italy, it was
the prince and his ministers who led the reform movement in Sicily. The
power of the Church was considerably restricted, that of the barons challenged for the first time. But support for the reforms remained limited –
even more than on the southern mainland – to isolated intellectuals, a few
young nobles, merchants and craftsmen of the Catania region. It was from
these groups that the few Sicilian Jacobins were to emerge. Among the
great barons, some of them worried by the diminishing incomes of their
family patrimonies, resentful of the attacks on their rights, hostility to
Naples grew. As the marquis di Villabianca wrote in his diary, looking back
nostalgically over five hundred years, to when the kingdom of Naples had
actually been governed from Sicily: 'The Neapolitans naturally dislike our

Sicilian nation, which in the past dominated over their nation' (Pontieri, 105, p. 113).

Naples

Within the kingdom of Naples, relatively little (though approving) attention was paid to the struggle in Sicily. The reformers were too deeply involved in their own battle and felt that their moment had come. The year after Caracciolo went to Sicily, Acton created a new Supreme Council of Finances – to advise on the economic problems of the kingdom – nearly twenty years after the formation of similar authoritative institutions in Lombardy and Modena. Leading reformers – Grimaldi, Galiani, Filangieri – were appointed members; Galanti was appointed a Visitor of the Kingdom, responsible for enquiries into provincial conditions; Delfico became military assessor in the Teramo militia tribunal; Pagano advocate of the poor in the new maritime and admiralty tribunal. Longano dedicated his analysis of the backwardness of the Capitanata to the Supreme Council. The reformers were now in office; and the times seemed long past since Pio Grimaldi should have to plead that his son Domenico be given an honorary title within the royal bureaucracy, 'as this would also contribute significantly to giving authority to his statements and to ensuring that his instructions make a deeper impression on the spirit of the uncouth' (Venturi, 28, p. 424).

A wide range of reforms were attempted, especially after the 1783 earthquake revealed the piteous state of the kingdom. The grain provisioning system was virtually abolished and the guilds attacked; the local militia was reorganized (1782) and the Tuscan criminal code adopted for the military court (1786); a series of commercial treaties were signed with Tripoli, Sardinia and Russia (1785–7) and even the high protectionist duties were reduced (1788); a free port was created at Messina (1784); proposals were made for a system of primary education, based – as in Lombardy – on the Austrian model (1784). The mere listing of these reforms is indicative of their disconnected nature: there was no overall plan nor even awareness of the interdependent character of reforms, in contrast to the movement in Lombardy and Tuscany. In their multiplicity, and often their confusion, these Neapolitan reforms of the 1780s resembled the attempts of earlier decades, of the 1730s and 1740s, but were imbued with an optimism typical of the southern intellectuals of the end of the century, a faith that the abolition of privilege and injustice was sufficient to ensure the appearance of prosperity, happiness and justice.

Alongside these reforms, Tanucci's anti-ecclesiastical policy was pursued and Jansenism encouraged: the Jansenist Giovanni Andrea Serrao was appointed bishop of Potenza in 1782, despite papal opposition, and at royal request convoked a diocesan synod. Some bishops and priests were in correspondence with the Tuscan de' Ricci. These Neapolitan Jansenists, like their colleagues in Tuscany, willingly accepted the authority of the sovereign, while remaining diffident towards Enlightenment ideas. When negotiations with the papacy for a new concordat broke down through Pius VI's refusal to accept Neapolitan demands, Caracciolo repeated his Sicilian gesture by abolishing payment of the *chinea*, an annual tribute paid to Rome in acknowledgement of its feudal overlordship (1788). It needed the fear of revolution to improve relations with Rome.

But such measures against the Church were regarded by the reformers as of secondary importance, when indeed they were not tainted by association with Tanucci's long years of authority. The central theme of the new reforms, expressed with increasing clarity and bitterness, was the attack on the baronage. The 1770s had witnessed widespread discussions and measures against feudalism in Europe, particularly in Habsburg lands and France. In Naples Filangieri launched a violent onslaught on baronial jurisdictions (1780, 1783), and was followed by many other reformers. Even a professional member of the bureaucracy, unassociated with the intellectual reformers, but eager to strengthen royal power – Giacinto Dragonetti – proposed that the laws and critiques on feudalism be published 'so that the public and private persons be informed of the true facts' (Villani, 95, p. 298). The Neapolitan reformers, like the Tuscan and Lombard, were beginning to see the advantages of popular support in the struggle against privileged groups. Their proposals, however, remained moderate, such as the abolition of feudal jurisdictions or, at most, of such fiefs as devolved to the Crown through extinction of the male line. By 1790, Delfico could make the more radical suggestion that the barons be not indemnified for their jurisdictions. In 1791 Pagano recognized that the right of property was not absolute; but when the devolved fiefs began to be sold as non-feudal, allodial lands, Pagano still demanded their exemption from taxes (1791). It needed the war against France for Ferdinand IV (not the reformers) to broaden the attack from feudal jurisdictions to fiscal exemptions.

The limited, moderate nature of this assault on the baronage was typical of the hopes and failure of the Neapolitan reformers. There was an acute awareness of Naples' backwardness compared to other Italian regions, an awareness brought home not only by the foreign experiences of some of the reformers like Domenico Grimaldi or Melchiorre Delfico, but by the very cosmopolitanism of Neapolitan life, with its constant flow of foreign travellers, freemasons, books. In these conditions, the reformers could not aspire to an economic programme on so broad a scale as in Lombardy or Tuscany. There was a primary need to break the stranglehold of privilege of the barons, of the capital city, of the merchant exporters, before there could be any realistic discussion of boosting national production or permitting free trade. Hence the limited influence of physiocracy; hence the absence of any

real attack on the guilds, as industry was too subordinate. Belief in the
desirability of abolishing all restrictions on private ownership of property
remained: Filangieri expected the division of demesnial lands to increase
production by a third. This explains the intense discussions of methods to
divide up the vast pasturages of the Apulian Tavoliere and the reformers'
approval of the 1792 decision to sell off communal lands. The division
of these lands, the abolition of grazing rights, were easier than the attack
on feudal privileges. This encouragement of private property gave support to the slow formation of new groups of small landed owners –
usurers, administrators, contractors, brokers, small merchants and local
officials.

As in Lombardy and Tuscany, the reforms that made most progress were
those that favoured, or at any rate did not damage, the most powerful
groups among the population. But in the kingdom of Naples the prince was
far less able to impose his own decisions. Delfico had attacked as anachronistic and unfairly privileged the tribunal with authority over livestock
provisioning in the Abruzzi; he thought he had achieved its abolition – but
the local administrators ensured its continuance. The customs reform of
1788 was never applied through local resistance. The destruction of the
grain provisioning system led to sharp price rises and the re-imposition of
official maximum prices in the 1790s. The weakening of the feudal strong-
hold, the *sedili* or assembly of the representatives of the city of Naples, was
achieved not by reform, but by the Bourbons' reluctance to ask for *donativi*
(only ten were requested in sixty years).

The reformers still looked to the sovereign and the state. When the
statutes for a model colony of silk workers at San Leucio were published in
1789, replete with Rousseauist doctrines of equality, natural justice and
abolition of inheritance laws, the masonic priest Jerocades and many of the
reformers published odes in praise of their sovereign – who, only two years
earlier, had prohibited the circulation of Voltaire's works in his kingdom.
But the state was too weak and incapable of ensuring the obedience of its
representatives in the provinces. Hence the reforms, proposed in frantic
haste, were not carried out. As Palmieri wrote in 1792:

> The late abbé Galiani was right to compare the Council of Finances to a
> Christmas dinner, in which too much is eaten and everyone ends up with an
> almighty indigestion. The Council has great projects, it commissions plans and
> reforms for the public good, trade, agriculture, arts and crafts, etc. And then it
> begins all over again without concluding anything; or things end up worse.
> (Venturi, 28, p. 1111)

Perhaps the most concrete result of these years was the ruin of state finances.
The balanced budget so slowly achieved by Tanucci over long years of
careful administration was rapidly destroyed by the demands of the 1783

earthquake, a disastrously expensive regal tour of northern and central Italy and three royal marriages.

By 1794, when all reforms were abruptly suspended, Filangieri and Palmieri were dead; Domenico Grimaldi and Mario Pagano were soon arrested and Genovesi's academic successor, Odazzi, died in prison. The hopes of some of these intellectuals – that the threat of revolution would accelerate the pace and efficacy of the reforms – were smashed. The Neapolitan experiment at reform had come too late, the prince had proved too weak. Even before the reaction, some of the reformers had begun to despair of the sovereign. Filangieri, Pagano and Delfico expressed growing aspirations towards liberty and equality in this highly unfree and unequal society. The successful dissemination of the egalitarian ideas of the *Illuminati* sect among the freemasons at Naples reflected the same desire for more radical change. By 1794 the Church was subordinated, the baronage on the defensive, but Genovesi's pupils had lost their faith in collaboration with the prince. Some, like Galanti, withdrew into isolation. A few – like Pagano – were to join the younger generation in the attempt to create an egalitarian, constitutionally regulated republic.

The Papal States: the impotence of reformism

At Rome, as at Naples, the mid-1770s were marked by renewal of hope and attempts at reform. The previous decade had witnessed the humiliation of the papacy, as the princes legislated against the privileges and independence of their churches without reference to Rome. In 1773 papal authority touched its nadir as the Franciscan Clement XIV finally gave way to Bourbon insistence and suppressed the Jesuit order. The revival came in 1775 with the election of the determined, efficient Romagnol cardinal Gian Angelo Braschi as Pius VI.

It was a revival only in a relative sense. There was little that Pius could do – despite his pilgrimage to Vienna – about the renewed Habsburg onslaught against the Church. The most he could achieve was a stubborn defence of orthodoxy and the suppression of Jansenism in the Holy City. The probably unexpected result was to drive the Jansenists into more extremist positions, challenging the very authority of the pope and justifying the regalism of the princes.

Renewed hope, in fact, was centred not on religious matters, but on Pius VI's determination to carry through economic reforms within the Papal States. As elsewhere in Italy, it was the prince who took the lead, it was the prince to whom the few and isolated reformers turned. Memories of Clement XI revived, but there was now greater optimism that the example of the other Italian princes could serve to overcome resistance in this most autocratic and inefficient of states.

The need for reform was urgent. Papal finances were increasingly inadequate, not least because the attack on the Church in Catholic Europe cut off foreign sources of revenue. The communes were heavily indebted and too feeble to challenge the demands for fiscal exemption of the great ecclesiastical dignitaries and nobles. Agriculture was stagnant, and in such cities as Bologna or Ancona industry and trade pitifully weak. The dead-weight of tolls and the continuous demand for food-supplies of the parasitic capital strangled internal trade and effectively broke up the Papal States into an agglomeration of virtually separate provinces. Mendicancy increased, as the 'country merchants' exploited the peasantry. Nearly 6000 of the 13 000 inhabitants of Ravenna lived wholly on charity, according to the local magistrate Marco Fantuzzi.

The disastrous conditions of the Papal States, apparently worse even than those of Naples or Sicily, had emerged tragically with the 1764 famine. The moderate proposals for reform of early writers seemed to have fallen on stony ground. In 1767 Carlantonio Pilati could 'threaten' the pope with impending catastrophe, unless he hastened to carry through reforms. By 1776 Ange Gondar could propose the imposition of a legal limitation to the size of the large estates, alongside financial and customs reforms to encourage free trade and the export of grain. Increasingly in these years foreigners with experience of the great reforming centres put forward proposals for urgent change: the Piedmontese Cacherano di Bricherasio, the Lombard Paolo Vergani, the Neapolitan Nicola Corona, the Tuscan Angelo Fabroni. Even local reformers, such as cardinal Ignazio Boncompagni, looked to Lombardy, Tuscany, France, England, even Prussia, Russia and Sweden. But the initiative could only come from the pope. Pius VI's attempts at reforms aroused public discussion for the first time: Riccomanni tried to spread technical information through new journals, in the provinces agrarian academies arose and booklets of agronomic propaganda appeared. At Montecchio – where the Benigni brothers had founded such an academy – a monument to Pius VI celebrated his achievement in disciplining vaga-bonds. But it was typical of the lack of real collaboration that the new journals were suppressed by the curia immediately discussion seemed inopportune.

Already in 1768–9 when treasurer-general to Clement XIII, cardinal Braschi had called in a Milanese tax farmer, Francesco Antonio Bettinelli, to make proposals about how to stimulate trade and so increase the state's fiscal revenues. The choice of a Lombard tax farmer, rather than a reformer, was revealing of the limits of papal initiative. Bettinelli had come forward with a vast plan: replacement of the multitude of existing exactions by land and grist taxes and an excise on salt; responsibility for communal debts to be taken over by the papal camera; responsibility for the collection of taxes to be decentralized, under the control of the local cities; all internal tolls and customs to be suppressed; the varying customs duties on the frontiers to be unified. Compared to Lombardy or Tuscany, these were extremely moderate proposals, limited to abolishing internal barriers to trade, simplifying the taxation system and protecting national production by mercantilist measures. No attack on the landed privileges of nobles and ecclesiastics was threatened, for the existing out-dated cadastral registers were to be used as the basis of the land tax. This typically mercantilist, anti-physiocratic proposal to stimulate industry and trade as a substitute for essential agrarian change was the key-note of Pius VI's reforms, as it had been of earlier papal reformers.

In 1776 a special congregation approved Bettinelli's plan. The following year edicts were passed to abolish all tolls and to co-ordinate the existing cadastral registers as the basis for a new one. But even these reforms failed in the face of local resistance, as had an earlier decree of Benedict XIV in favour of free internal circulation of goods (1748). By the 1780s, Pius turned to agriculture, initiating the drainage of the Pontine marshes, and proposing the extension of grain cultures in the Agro Romano. But resistance was again too strong, as the landowners and 'country merchants' preferred to maintain a privileged woollen industry based on pasturage. By the later 1780s the new treasurer-general, cardinal Fabrizio Ruffo, gave fresh drive to the movement for change, decreeing a reform of the customs system to achieve more uniform protection (1786). But the most profitable regions of the state – the Legations – were exempted, and the dishonesty of the officials sabotaged the reform. The only partial success was the legate of Bologna Boncompagni's new cadastral register (1789): using the Lombard and Modenese experiences, Boncompagni employed surveyors to carry out direct measurements of the land rather than relying on declarations by landowners, and abolished all exemptions from tax. Even more important was the calculation of the tax on the potential value (rather than the actual yield) of the land, which aimed at stimulating owners into improving their productivity in order to offset the weight of the new tax.

By the time of Ruffo's fall in 1794, of the initial financial plan only the customs reform remained – and even this could not be carried out because of local resistance. It was to re-emerge with the Restoration. Isolated voices put forward more radical proposals: Fantuzzi urged irrigation works in the Romagna plain and measures to aid the peasants; Spreti proposed the abolition of primogenitures and limitation of mortmain; Corona advocated moderate free trade, citing Adam Smith. But there was no hope of major change. The strength of the landed interests was such that physiocratic reforms were replaced in the Papal States by traditional mercantilist programmes. Even these proved ineffective.

Modena: Ricci, the isolated reformer

The accession of Ercole III in 1780 and the rise to power of Lodovico Ricci gave renewed drive to the reforms in Modena. The comparative success of these reforms, in contrast to papal attempts, owed much not only to the energetic drive of the government, but to the progress already achieved in the previous decade. Yet, as in the other reforming states in Italy, the effectiveness of reform was limited by the opposition of privileged groups.

In the early years the attack on the Church was continued, with responsibility for education and censorship at Reggio given to the anticlerical Agostino Paradisi, and the suppression of the Holy Office. But measures to improve the economy increasingly dominated Ricci's attention. Faith in physiocracy was no longer unlimited, a more positive role was enjoined on government. The long years of discussions and analyses of the economy, which had dominated the reform movement everywhere, had created an acute sense of the need for accurate economic information on which to base policy. Lodovico Ricci, with his untiring passion for collecting statistics, epitomized this crucial aspect of late eighteenth-century reformism.

Ricci was concerned about all aspects of economic life, but his major reforms related to agriculture. Government income was to be increased by raising agricultural production. Irrigation works and land reclamations were carried out, rice cultivation introduced, new roads and bridges built, the grain provisioning system abolished. Pressure for one or another aspect of physiocratic policy continued to be voiced: Antonio Cesi developed Venturini's earlier plan for a single land-tax, Agostino Paradisi's son Giovanni attacked all indirect taxes and urged free trade. But the possibilities of reform, particularly in freeing trade and revising the fiscal system, had been blocked, by the maintenance of the general tax farm, which Ercole III had removed from foreign control, but had conserved as a 'national' tax farm. The only possible major fiscal reform was that of the land-tax. Under Ricci's direct control a new cadastral register was drawn up (1788–91), which marked a distinct advance on the earlier Lombard or almost contemporaneous Mantuan ones: taxation rates were to be based on a combination of actual production and a calculation of the land's capacity to produce more, in order to act as a stimulus to productivity. Both Verri and Carli were full of praise, and cardinal Boncompagni was to use Ricci's new cadastral register as the model for his own even more advanced and controversial one. Even before the register had been completed, Ricci had reduced the land-tax; on its completion, he reduced the excise on salt. But the opposition of the tax farmers blocked any attempts to reduce further indirect taxes.

If little could be done to stimulate trade because of the tax farm, in the industrial field Ricci apparently had a freer hand; and he attempted to reform the guilds (1787-94). But here there was little scope, for the state was too small, with inadequate resources to develop significant industries. Yet it was in relation to industry that Ricci's reforming mentality emerged most strikingly. As elsewhere in Italy, pauperism was spreading: at Modena, 7000 of the 24 000 inhabitants lived continually off charity, at Reggio another enquiry showed that a third of the population were beggars. In his *Reform of the Charitable Institutions of the City of Modena* (1787) Ricci concluded, 'abandon all men who can engage in some activity, and you will make them industrious, useful and happy' (Giarrizzo *et al.*, 29, p. 485). Charity was regarded as a relic of a counter-reformist mentality, pernicious to society by its encouragement of idleness, imposing a heavy weight on the economy and strengthening a dishonest bureaucracy. The 'almshouses of idleness' should be offered to the guilds, to be transformed into industrial establishments, with the sole condition that entrepreneurs guarantee wages to the poor they employed. In this way charity could be reduced and the cloth industry developed. Ricci, like Joseph II, Domenico Grimaldi and so many of the reformers, confident of his freedom from religious superstition, was concerned purely with the material good of society.

Ricci's reforms were energetic, but only partially successful. The revolutionary impetus in France showed only too clearly the limits of Enlightened despotism. Feudal prerogatives and jurisdictions remained predominant. Trade and industry languished under the deadweight of the tax farm. Reggio remained resentful of Modena's dominance. As elsewhere in Italy, only the power of the Church had been successfully checked. In this small, poor state, there was not even a body of intellectuals and reformers ready to second Ricci's activities. The government remained fundamentally dependent on Muratorian inspiration. Ricci alone endeavoured to legislate amidst increasing difficulties. It was almost inevitable that this remarkable reforming administrator should join the Republic in 1796.

The consequences of Enlightened reformism

By the 1790s, as the experiences of revolutionary France imposed themselves on the attention of all Europe, the crisis of the reform movement in Italy became evident. The unreformed states – Venice, Genoa, Piedmont, Parma – were rent by local rivalries and social tensions. Venice's response to its economic weakness – growing centralization – increased the hostility of the mainland cities and the resentment of the poor nobles of the capital. As the absolute numbers of Venetian nobles fell, and the proportion of poor nobles, the *barnabotti*, grew, it became difficult to ensure even the continuity of administration. But the revolts of Angelo Querini (1761-2) and Giorgio Pisani (1780), spokesmen of the *barnabotti*, were internal squabbles of a fossilized ruling group. The provincial nobility was so hostile that when the Serenissima offered to inscribe forty families on the role of the Venetian patriciate, only ten provincial nobles came forward (1775). The Venetian republic was disintegrating internally long before the French armies reached its frontiers.

Nor was the Genoese republic stronger: the oligarchy consolidated its monopoly of power, but the tensions between nobles and people, which had exploded in 1746, remained; freemasonry and Jansenism acquired a subversive, often democratic character that was to emerge with the rising of 1797.

In Piedmont, the pale ray of light that penetrated the opaqueness of government censorship in the late 1780s flickered uncertainly only for a few years before it was extinguished by fear of revolution. Economic and social conditions worsened, with the crisis of the silk industry and the increasing exactions that accompanied the rapid displacement of landowners by managers. The reformers, such as the Vasco brothers, who had gathered around the new Agrarian Society (founded in 1785) and published in the *Biblioteca oltremontana*, attacked tolls and other checks on internal trade, the guilds, the large-scale leases of land, the counter-reformist encouragement of idleness through charity, the retrograde criminal code. But their proposals were ignored. The only cultural activities that were encouraged were those of the aristocratic academies, the Sampaolina, the Filopatria; Piedmont's past glories, its army and its rulers were exalted, and the cosmopolitanism of the Enlightenment and French influence attacked.

In the reforming states, too, the experience of Enlightenment had led to varied, contradictory and sometimes unexpected consequences. The strength of opposition had frequently checked, compromised or blocked specific reforms. The small dimensions of some states, the immediate demands of finance for dynastic or courtly purposes, the uncertain, inconsistent or superficial leadership of individual princes, the isolation of reforming ministers, the deeply entrenched historical individuality and independence of single cities or regions, the very respect of the reformers (and especially the princes) for the legal validity of certain categories of historically proven titles or privileges, help explain why the reforms made but little impact on such states as Modena or Parma, the Papal States or Naples.

Even in the two major reforming states – Lombardy and Tuscany – the hostility of the privileged groups had acted effectively to delay the reforms and dilute the intensity of the desired transformations. The administrative and fiscal reforms, the radical but not total renovation of the machinery of the state, were probably the most successful aspects, and had enabled the governments to continue on the path of reform. But the effective resistance to Joseph II's measures in the Austrian duchy of Mantua, or Leopold's hope of by-passing bureaucratic opposition and consolidating his reforms by the issue of a constitution in Tuscany, both bore witness to the limits of Enlightened despotism.

The reforms, in fact, were most effective in these states when the opposition was weak or when the ruling classes were prepared to give support. The most striking example of the first instance was the attack on the privileges of the Church, which emerged at the end of this period largely stripped of the economic, juridical and cultural positions it had enjoyed in Spanish Italy. The economic reforms, aimed at boosting agricultural production, had equally profound consequences. In some states, such as Naples, the landowners retained their feudal privileges, while being encouraged to modernize and develop production. In others, above all in Tuscany, even when certain fiscal advantages were lost, the landowners were favoured by the abolition of internal checks to production, while they effectively blocked attempts to encourage or protect smallholders or peasants. The famine of 1764–6 had had disastrous effects on the economic independence of the peasantry. With the growing external demand for grain, rising prices and a rapidly increasing population, the consequences of these reforms – for long unforeseen and ultimately accepted by the legislators and intellectuals – were to accentuate the miserable living conditions of the peasant and urban masses. The increasing number of day-labourers, the spread of pauperism, the accentuated phenomenon of internal migration and emigration, the growth of petty rural theft, the popular hostility to the reforms in the last decades of the eighteenth century, all reflected the deep level of social tension, which had been worsened and not improved by the reform movement.

Many of the reformers were left with a sense of disillusionment, a growing awareness of poverty, hostility towards inequality. The faith in economic activity often remained, leading to condemnation of idleness. But sloth was no longer regarded as an attribute merely of the poor. What Giovanni Fabroni wrote of Turin in 1775 was applicable to all the Italian states:

> The population amounts to 75,000 people, of whom 22,000 are idle: 4,000 soldiers, 2,000 monks and priests, 8,000 so-called nobles, 7,000 servants of luxury and about 1,000 beggars – the rest are engaged in activities and develop the arts. (Venturi, 27, p. 1084)

At the same time a sense of achievement remained, for Italy had undoubtedly advanced in these decades. The pride in Italy, in its past but now also in its present progress, sometimes led to resentment of French cultural influence. Carli's famous article in Il Caffè, 'Of the Italian fatherland', which looked to the progress of science as the means to the re-emergence of a single Italy such as had existed under the Romans stretching 'to the furthest frontiers', struck an unusual, even jarring note in the European debate of the Società dei pugni. As Pietro Verri commented on the article: 'It is truly excellent. But I would not like love of country to affect our impartiality as good cosmopolites' (Valeri, 57, p. 291, n. 12). But this defence of Italian culture and civil progress could be found in other writers, in Paradisi's angry defence of Italian intellectuals, in Paolo Frisi's criticisms of Lalande's neglect of Italian scientific contributions, in Alessandro Verri's reservations about the encyclopedists. It was the expression of a nascent patriotism that arose in Italy, as elsewhere in Europe, with the shock to cosmopolitan hopes of the Seven Years War. The advance of the reforms in the following decades, when set against their failure in France, strengthened the sense of pride. But Italian patriotism remained a facet, a subsidiary aspect of an overwhelmingly international, cosmopolitan feeling of progress. Except among some of the secondary Piedmontese writers there was a total acceptance of the political fragmentation of Italy.

By the 1790s the disillusionment with Enlightened reform had led to concern about how to continue to progress. As the revolution in France developed, some of the reformers, such as Carli and Galanti, drew back in horror. Others, like Verri, Pagano and Ricci, were to join a young generation in their aspirations for a fairer, egalitarian society, free of the limitations and disillusionment inherent in their earlier faith in the Enlightened princes.

Part 3
Revolution and moderation
1789–1814

It is a commonplace that the French Revolution transformed the western world. The radical nature of the break with the past, the decisive strength of the mass popular movements, the victorious drive of the 'nation in arms', the political doctrine of popular sovereignty, the romantic faith in the *patrie*, were all aspects of the sharp change from traditional assumptions of dynastic balance of power and a fixed order of society. Memories and myths of the achievements of the Revolution, as of the violence and social anarchy of the Jacobin experiment, were to haunt the nineteenth century, from the years of Napoleonic social conservatism, through the following decades of instability and upheaval, until the Paris Commune.

Amidst the precipitous and varied developments of the revolution – Declaration of the Rights of Man and Citizen, Civil Constitution of the Clergy, the Constitutions of 1791, 1793, 1795, Constituent Assembly, National Convention, Committee of Public Safety, Thermidor, Directory – two experiences were rapidly and widely regarded as traumatic: the subversive force of the revolutionary armies and the terrifying Year II of Robespierre. The successes of the revolutionary armies were to make a return to the past impossible. But the ruling classes of Europe – including the middle classes now dominant in France – were determined to prevent a recurrence of Jacobinism and the dangers of social revolution. Both faith in egalitarianism and fear of social rebellion had existed in Italy, as we have seen, before the Revolution – as they had existed in France. But the experiences of these turbulent years now tempered the social attitudes and political proposals and were rapidly to lead to a self-conscious concern for social conservatism.

To argue about the path of Italian development, had the French not invaded Italy – at one time a favoured debate of Italian historiography – is not only otiose, but profoundly unhistorical and misleading. Italy – like almost every other European country – was inevitably affected by the intensity of the impact of the Revolution and the enormous area of its diffusion. Italy's geographical vicinity, its cultural traditions, its social evolution rendered it particularly vulnerable to the shock of the Revolution.

Particularly, but not uniquely so. In many respects the Italian experience was not dissimilar to that of Holland or Belgium, the Rhineland or Switzerland. All these countries were peculiarly susceptible to the penetration of French ideas and open to French military 'liberation'. At moments, Italy may have played a prominent role in Napoleon's constant wars and incessant juggling of the European map. But in these instances, her role was as passive as in the eighteenth century. From the French point of view, Italy – or rather the Italian states – were 'liberated' or conquered territories, which offered resources and, occasionally, an 'experimental field' for constitutional or administrative innovations or developments. But so, to a greater or lesser extent, were the other 'sister republics' surrounding the *grande nation*. In so far as the Italian experience of French domination was 'unique', this derived from the particular forms of social, economic and cultural developments of the various regions, compared to those of Switzerland, Belgium or the Rhineland. Italy, in fact, had now re-entered the mainstream of European civilization and henceforth her experiences were to remain, in one form or another, closely dependent upon those of the rest of the continent.

9

Revolution and the break with the past: 1789–99

France and Europe

The Revolution initially had seemed a matter of purely French concern. At most it would severely reduce French political and economic influence, but it was unlikely to disturb the peace of Europe. Perhaps for this last reason too, as much as for the victory of the egalitarian principles of the more advanced Enlightenment, for the apparent continuation of the principles of the American revolution in the heart of Europe, it was unanimously welcomed by intellectuals and artists, from Spain to Russia, from England to Italy. The princes were hardly enthusiastic, but – despite family and dynastic ties – they were not inclined to interfere. However, as the Revolution progressed, concern increased among the privileged and propertied classes and received ideological consecration with Burke's *Reflections* (November 1790) and Pius VI's condemnation (April 1791). Even then, despite the incitements of the *émigré* comte d'Artois and the urgings of the king of Prussia, the emperor Leopold, the obvious leader of a counter-revolutionary coalition, held back, concerned about the disturbed conditions in the empire he had inherited from Joseph II and about Russian and Prussian designs on the moribund Poland. Only in April 1792, after Leopold's death, did the new emperor Francis II and Frederick William II of Prussia declare war on France. And although their formal reason was to save their fellow sovereign, in reality they had reacted to the threat of a revolutionary crusade by the French. When England and Holland joined the coalition in spring 1793 it was because of the specific threat of invasion and the opening of the river Scheldt. Thus political and economic rivalry, rather than ideological reasons, lay at the base of the first coalition. Pressure was then exerted, partly on the grounds that it was necessary to contain and defeat revolutionary expansionism, to force the smaller states to join the coalition: Spain in 1793 and then the major Italian states – Naples, Sardinia and Tuscany. Politically, Europe had been divided into two camps – of 'patriots' and 'counter-revolutionary' governments. Those Italian princes who did not join the alliance – such as the pope and the duke of Modena – broke off relations with France.

The war had been welcomed, and indeed partially provoked, by the French revolutionaries. The original Enlightenment conviction that democracy implied peace gave way to a new crusading faith. *Emigré* activities across the Rhine certainly acted as an irritant. But for the Girondins, led by Brissot, war seemed to offer a solution to popular discontents and economic crisis. From October 1791 Brissot preached an armed crusade against rulers in order to liberate the peoples of Europe. Only Robespierre and a small group of his followers questioned how far the peoples would welcome such liberators. The war had gone badly until the invading Austro-Prussian forces were defeated at Valmy (September 1792). With their armies now poised to invade Belgium and Holland, the French Convention debated whether to meet the appeals of 'patriots' in Savoy, Nice and the Rhineland to annex their territories to France. Despite considerable warnings against the dangers of a policy of conquest, Danton and the Prussian-born Anacharsis Cloots persuaded the Convention to adopt the policy of France's 'natural frontiers' along the Rhine, Alps and Pyrenees. Savoy was annexed in November, while the Convention issued a declaration that it would grant 'fraternity and aid' to all peoples who wished to recover their liberty (19 November 1792). But wars have to be paid for. And within a month (15 December 1792) instructions were issued by Cambon that the liberated territories would have to pay for their liberating armies. The new policy was completed with the doctrine of the 'sister republics' which were to surround France beyond her 'natural frontiers' and provide both protection and financial contributions.

This policy of revolutionary expansionism was not put into practice until late 1794. As England and Holland joined the coalition, the French were driven out of the Low Countries and Rhineland; and – after the fall of the Girondins – Robespierre and the Committee of Public Safety fought for the survival of France until the victory of Fleurus (April 1793–June 1794). When the French once more occupied Belgium and the Rhenish provinces, a final debate within the Directory confirmed the policy of annexation. By October 1795 Belgium had been annexed, the Rhineland placed under military government, and Holland transformed into the Batavian republic: these three alternative methods of treating the 'liberated' territories lay open to the Directory, once it finally decided upon the invasion of Italy and Switzerland.

Until 1795 Italy had been barely touched by these programmes. After the French conquest of Savoy and Nice in 1793 French agents had been sent into Italy to gather information and assess the possibilities of invasion. An army threatened Piedmont from Nice, but a stalemate situation had ensued, while an attempt to invade the island of Sardinia had failed (December

1792–February 1793). Until Fleurus Robespierre and the Jacobins had been on the defensive. After his fall, the Directory which had emerged from the Thermidorian Convention found itself unable to control the situation in France, where popular *sansculotte* agitation against inflationary rising prices and a rapidly growing royalist movement had led to two successive risings in 1795, only suppressed by calling in the army. Isolated within the country, the Directory saw the continuation of the war as the most effective method of financing France by exactions from the conquered territories. But the aim of the war, according to the Alsatian Reubell, supported by his fellow Directors Lareveillière-Lépeaux and Barras, was to achieve the Rhine frontier. Austria was the major enemy and hence the most effective policy in Italy was to bribe Austria's allies to desert the coalition by offers of territorial gains in the subsequent peace agreement.

Only in November 1795 did the Directory seriously discuss what to do with Italy and its members were then totally divided over the question of mounting a major invasion. When Filippo Buonarroti, the former Jacobin and commissar at Nice, put forward proposals, early in 1796, to invade and liberate Italy, the Directory found itself for the first time assessing advantages and disadvantages of creating a sister republic. But on both occasions, as when they finally decided to invade Italy in spring 1796, the Directors were determined, in traditional manner, to utilize Italy (or, more precisely, northern Italy) as a bargaining counter in future peace negotiations. As late as May 1796, on the eve of the invasion, Reubell's plan was to defeat Austria in Italy in order to relieve the French Army of the Rhine, but then give back Lombardy within a matter of months in return for the Rhineland. Italy was to remain a passive 'object' of European diplomacy.

Italy and the revolution

Within Italy, as elsewhere in Europe, the Revolution had aroused immediate enthusiasm among most intellectuals, followed by a more varying reaction to the social upheavals and the Jacobin experience. Carli was typical of the moderate intellectuals' horror at the 'excesses' of Jacobinism; Cesarotti would rejoice at Robespierre's execution. But for the majority of intellectuals the revolution was a positive achievement. Some, like Paolo Greppi or Giuseppe Gorani, set off for Paris where, like Tom Paine, they rapidly found themselves endorsing more-or-less moderate positions. Others, like Pietro Verri, Francesco Melzi or Francesco Maria Gianni tried to use the threat of the Revolution to put forward constitutional schemes or encourage reforms. The events in France were followed with intense interest through the widespread diffusion of French gazettes and pamphlets and the clandestine publication of revolutionary writings: Robespierre's speeches were published in Italian in Milan; the Venetian government was unable to curb the activities of the city's printers.

Interest and discussion were rather innocuous activities, although disapproved of by the Italian governments. Conscious propagation in masonic lodges of 'Jacobin' ideas, as they were loosely called, was potentially more dangerous. That it should have become actually dangerous was, at least in part, the fault of the governments which joined the coalition or broke off relations with France.

The governments had reacted with varying rapidity, but common hostility, to the dangers of revolutionary propaganda. Only mutual suspicion prevented them from creating a league, as proposed by the kings of Sardinia and Naples, until the great powers applied pressure in 1794. The Sardinian king and the pope had immediately suppressed all public discussion, while the former soon found himself engaged in war because of the French occupation of his territories beyond the Alps. The Venetian and Genoese oligarchies maintained a hostile neutrality, but the Serenissima in particular was faced with dangerous signs of discontent in the provinces. Lombardy was inevitably affected by the brusque change in policy which marked the accession of Francis II, a change symbolized by the renewed use of the secret police in Austria. In Naples, Maria Carolina and Acton dropped all pretence of reform and adopted a policy of blind repression. Only in Tuscany did a more tolerant policy prevail, but even there the popular risings which had followed Leopold's departure led to the panic abandonment of the Jansenist reforms, the introduction of partial controls on the grain trade, and the restoration of the death penalty.

Enlightened reformism had come to an end abruptly. Jansenism, the weaker and more exposed element of reformism, suffered most immediately: the General Seminary at Pavia (like the one in Flanders) was suppressed. The Tuscan Jansenists were persecuted: 'The jansenist parish priests and clerics of Prato have had to flee from several places, and are wandering about, lost and dispersed' (Codignola, 38, p. 146), wrote Antonio Longinelli to Tamburini. At Rome the Jesuits returned and the less rigorous molinist theology of the followers of S. Alfonso de' Liguori was encouraged. The freemasons were likewise condemned and repressed: the lodges were at the centre of the arrests and trials of 1794–5 at Turin, Rome, Naples and Palermo. But, in a more general sense, the reaction against the Revolution marked the definitive break with the reformers, reflected for instance in the decision of the Milanese patriciate of the General Council to restrict all office to its own members.

The reaction was not merely due to the current simplistic identification of the causes of the Revolution with Enlightenment philosophy. The Italian reformers were, after all, too small and weak a minority, divided among themselves, and incapable of seriously challenging the established governments, as they demonstrated in the conspiracies and plots which were discovered between 1792 and 1795. More worrying were the popular disturbances of these years, sparked off by rising prices and heavy taxes, but deriving from deep-rooted hostility to the feudal lords or land brokers and the perennial demand for land. The disturbances and risings were similar to those which occurred in these same years in Ireland, Hungary, the Palatinate, some Swiss cantons, and which had pushed the French Revolution beyond its initial, moderate phase. The episodes we know about, although isolated, are symptomatic of a far more general discontent that simmered ominously just beneath the surface. In the Venetian *terraferma*, in the Abruzzi and Basilicata, in Piedmont and Sardinia, the risings were directed explicitly against the lords and landowners; at Pistoia and Florence in 1790, as at Arezzo in 1795, violent protests voiced an open condemnation of the reforms, which had left the urban masses and much of the peasantry without their traditional forms of protection.

Dangerous in themselves, these peasant threats assumed a more menacing character through the imprecise but definite knowledge of what had occurred in France. In the kingdom of Naples there are instances of meetings of probably wealthier peasants proclaiming that they will 'act like the French'. In Piedmont peasants from 13 communes appealed to the king in 1792:

> Think, O Majesty, those who are ruined are we your subjects, we who are ready to give our lives to defend the State and the Crown; but Your Majesty needs to help us and act so that we can live. So provide us with foodstuffs, immediately, and decree null at the end of the year all rentals and make all the swindling Lords, Counts, Barons, Cavaliers, and Marquises pay their debts to their creditors. Then Your Majesty will see that all will be well and that there will be no more calamities in your States, that the Lords will live quietly and will no longer be so arrogant, the subjects will live in peace, and all will be well. Lacking this, there will be no need of the French, there are enough of us to rise up against these infernal wolves of Lords and stewards who believe they can grab even the figs. (Prato, 43, p. 41)

These threats and agitations remained local. With the exception of the anti-feudal, anti-Piedmontese rising in the island of Sardinia in 1794, they were not even as successful as the Swiss St Gall peasants who gained the commutation of part of their feudal dues. But amidst the general inertia and passivity of the peasantry they indicated a degree of sympathy for the Revolution and offered favourable conditions for a 'liberating' army.

Some at least of the Jacobin conspirators of these years were aware of these possibilities, although rarely in a concrete practical manner. Jacobinism had spread in the Italian states through the masonic lodges, some of which transformed themselves into revolutionary clubs. The masonic network had spread most rapidly, acquiring an explicitly revolutionary physiognomy, in

Naples and Calabria after the intimidatory visit of French ships under Latouche-Tréville in 1792. But French agents and the brief occupation of Leghorn in 1795 had encouraged the diffusion of conspiratorial clubs and 'patriotic societies' throughout Italy. For the most part these were small urban groups. At Naples and in the Venetian *terraferma* cities, they consisted mainly of nobles; elsewhere the provincial smaller bourgeoisie tended to predominate, with members of the lower clergy. The aims of these groups were disparate and often vague. For this reason alone the term 'Jacobins', applied to them by the authorities, was misleading, except in the sense that they were inspired by French example to discuss or plot changes in the existing political situation. For some, such as the Paduan noble 'Jacobins' or the Bolognese Zamboni in 1790, the aim remained purely municipalistic, to free Padua or Bologna from Venice or Rome. For others the goal was more egalitarian: a group of thirty to forty Brescians, mostly noble, swore to absolute equality and 'indissoluble fraternity'; the radical writer Francesco Paolo Di Blasi plotted in Palermo with craftsmen and soldiers to create a republic. In Piedmont the Jacobin groups were trying to establish contact with the unrest in the countryside when they were discovered in 1794.

But these 'Jacobins' remained few in number, unclear in aims and dependent upon French support to achieve any political change. In this they did not differ from the 'patriot' groups in Belgium, Holland or the Rhineland, to whose appeals the French had responded. Nor was the Directory ignorant of the situation in Italy. Since 1794 its diplomatic agents, Cacault at Florence, Eymar at Genoa, Desportes at Geneva, had sent periodic reports to Paris. They bore witness to the spontaneous growth of patriotic groups, which were increasing in number by 1796. Indeed, they had maintained contact with these groups, had protected them from persecution at Genoa, and had urged on the Directory the importance of utilizing the patriots who had been forced to flee – some 300 by 1795, according to Cacault.

But the agents were only too well aware that the success of an invasion would not depend upon the patriots. Their reports stressed far more the general state of unrest and the weakness of the rulers. As Cacault wrote in 1794:

> The Italian nation, which has only provided its princes with very weak military resources, has remained a spectator; it is new, it is virgin in the great war ablaze in Europe. The senseless princes can be overthrown and the people regenerated; it is perhaps less impossible to win them over than any other people. (Peroni, 125, p. 245)

But by early 1796, when the French minister for foreign affairs, Delacroix, had enquired whether it was possible or useful to republicanize Italy, the general response of the French agents in Italy had been negative: the

Italians were not mature enough for liberty, as they had been corrupted by religious superstition and political servitude, the patriots were too few and in any case dangerous. Cacault, before 1796, had already expressed his scepticism about the young Italian democrats, plaintively idealistic, with no practical ideas. His description of the type of supporters the French should seek – the serious, moderate Italians, at present hiding their opinions for the sake of peace and quiet – summed up what was to be the almost constant line of French policy in Italy:

> One must be extremely mistrustful of the extreme petulance and dash of the youth of Italy, excited and carried away by ideas borrowed from our revolution, who want to stir things up, without knowing how, without calculating their resources, without any clear and balanced ideas about what sort of thing they want to set up. . . . If one trusts too much in them, this party of self-interested men will do nothing but spoil matters by pushing too hard. If we come into Italy it will be necessary to utilise men who are truly ready for liberty. The serious, withdrawn individuals are the really valuable Italians. (Peroni, 125, p. 254)

It is in this context – of French scepticisms about the realism or strength of the Italian 'patriots' and Directorial concern for the Rhine frontier rather than the fate of Italy – that Buonarroti's plans for a rising in Italy need to be assessed. Son of an officer, trained in law at Pisa university, in 1789 Filippo Buonarroti had abandoned Tuscany for the revolutionary circles in Corsica in which the young Napoleon Bonaparte gained his first political experiences. After tumultuous experiences in Corsica, which included his temporary expulsion and an abortive expedition to 'liberate' the island of Sardinia, Buonarroti arrived in Paris in 1793 and became a French citizen. A strongly egalitarian follower of Robespierre, he was appointed commissar of the French-occupied Piedmontese territory of Oneglia. There he gathered together the French exiles and endeavoured to win mass support for the Revolution. The exiles were employed to start up schools and so propagandize republican, egalitarian ideas; a 'terroristic' attack on the feudatories was initiated; but aware of the depth of religious feeling, he had advised a careful, gradualist approach towards 'superstition'. His career broken by Robespierre's fall, Buonarroti was soon recalled from Oneglia and imprisoned. By the time of his release with other terrorists in October 1795, after the defeat by Bonaparte and other young generals of an attempted royalist coup (13 Vendémiaire), his egalitarian ideas had developed into a conviction of the need to abolish private property. Buonarroti took a leading part in Babeuf's 'conspiracy of the equals' to overthrow the Directory. Babeuf's aim was to create a system of collective ownership and production; but only the inner insurrectionary committee was aware of this ultimate plan. The larger groups of ex-Jacobins, whose headquarters was the Pantheon club and who were to win over the Parisian *sansculottes*, were involved in the more limited but dangerous scheme to overthrow the moderate Directory.

To this plot Buonarroti contributed the plan for a rising in Italy. Under his leadership, the exiles at Oneglia and patriots in Piedmont agreed to act as a unified group which would organize a rising in Piedmont before the French invasion, in order to create a provisional revolutionary government and so avoid military rule. The risings in Paris and abroad were conceived of by Buonarroti as integral and interdependent parts of a radical scheme to reverse the conservative trend of the Directory and return to the original purity of the Revolution. In contact with the powerful commissar Saliceti, and through him with his fellow Corsican Bonaparte, Buonarroti hoped to utilize the more revolutionary forces of the Army of Italy to support the coup in France, where a return to a Robespierrist policy would change the policy of military conquest to one of friendship for the 'sister republics' in Italy and Holland. In Italy, Buonarroti stressed the importance of gaining popular support by attacking feudalism in Piedmont, while adopting a gradualist approach towards the clergy, 'superstition' and other innovations. The aim was limited almost entirely to obtaining independence and an anti-feudal republic. As his fellow conspirator Pellisseri wrote to Buonarroti:

> I fear only one thing: that too many innovations will be wanted at the same time. . . . So rather than present a completely new system to the people, we should make sure of success by proposing certain indispensable reforms to be carried out by a provisional government. Total regeneration can be left to a Convention. (Vaccarino, 144, p. 102)

For one moment, in March 1796, Buonarroti's proposals to the Directory to accompany the invasion by a patriotic rising seemed to win their support. But the rapidity of Bonaparte's invasion and the discovery of Babeuf's plot (10 May) ended the hopes of both a revival of the Terror in France and a successful, independent patriotic rising in Italy.

To discuss whether the rising could have gained popular support and succeeded is idle hypothesis. More realistically, it offered the first example of a practical, carefully organized and clearly defined attempt at insurrection, which taught the considerable number of patriots who were involved the need to overcome local municipal rivalries. At the same time, by creating a link between the more advanced patriots and the ex-'terrorists' at Paris, it tainted all but the most moderate Italian patriots in the eyes of the Directory as followers of Babeuf.

The 'liberation' of Italy

The brief 'Jacobin' years were to leave a deep mark on future developments in Italy. But that Jacobins and patriots should have been able to play so prominent a role during these short, turbulent years was ultimately due to the success of the French armies and the clash between Bonaparte, his fellow generals and the Directory.

The Directory regarded the campaign in Italy as a war of conquest to raise finances for the French Republic. Negotiations with Turin in the previous months had broken down because of the French refusal to give up Nice and Savoy. By spring 1796, like the Directory, the coalition powers were ready to fight once more, rather than accept France's conquests. The strategy of the Directory was a simultaneous attack on all fronts: an expedition to Ireland under Hoche to threaten England, the invasion of Italy under Bonaparte as a diversionary tactic to harass the emperor in Lombardy, while the Rhine armies under Moreau and Jourdan thrust into Germany. The initial reluctance to appoint the twenty-six-year-old Napoleon Bonaparte commander-in-chief of the Army of Italy had been overcome through the assistance of Saliceti.

Not all the French connected with the expedition agreed that Italy should be treated as conquered territory, a mere source of revenue. Some advocated caution, recalling popular enmity in the Low Countries and Germany to the exactions and rough passage of French troops living off the land. Others (such as Saliceti) retained sufficient of their former Jacobin sympathies to favour the creations of 'sister republics'. Cacault saw the chance of achieving a 'model' revolution: the support of 'Enlightened' people should be won by paying careful attention to local circumstances when introducing the maxims of liberty and by avoiding the mistakes committed elsewhere; once the Italians were sure that the French were not imposing a new tyranny, they would respond, unlike 'the stupid Belgians, the besotted Germans' and war would only be needed to seize Lombardy and Rome (Peroni, 125, p. 256). The ideal of 'liberty' achieved without sacrifice was to survive in French circles, to be used as a pledge (or indictment) of Italian loyalty. Eighteen months after the invasion, Bonaparte's mouthpiece, 'The Courier of the Army of Italy', could still appeal (somewhat hypocritically) to the Cisalpine citizens: 'You are the first example in history of a people who became free without sacrifice, without revolution, without torment. We gave you liberty, know how to conserve it' (Bourgin and Godechot, 164, pp. 48–9).

But if the conquest proved surprisingly easy, French financial exactions, political interference and almost total disregard for patriotic aspirations or local conditions were soon to create the same hostility as had followed the 'liberations' elsewhere in Europe. Only Bonaparte's independent actions saved the Italian provinces from remaining under military rule.

Northern Italy was freed within a matter of months – although not entirely to the satisfaction of the patriots. After lightning victories in April 1796 over the Austro-Piedmontese armies, ignoring both the Directory and the Piedmontese patriots who had tried to set up a republic at Alba,

Napoleon signed the armistice of Cherasco with Victor Amadeus III (28 April), by which the king withdrew from the war. The chances of republican-izing Piedmont had vanished. On 10 May the young general defeated the Austrians at Lodi in a battle which was to be recorded and idealized in the iconography of the period. Four days later he entered Milan and before the end of the month had driven the Austrians out of Italy and reached Venetian Brescia. Following the instructions of the Directory to continue his con-quests and financial exactions, in June Bonaparte turned against the Papal States and freed Bologna and the Romagna.

The Directory had been taken by surprise by the rapidity of Napoleon's successes. Although gratified by the huge subsidies he sent to France, it was alarmed by his independence and ambitious plans – and especially by his encouragement of revolutionary propaganda which would make it more difficult to restore the Italian peoples to their rulers at a future peace. But as the Rhine armies ran into difficulties and were defeated (September–October 1796), Napoleon's liberty of action increased, until by January 1797 the Directory suppressed its civil commissars with the Army of Italy and gave Napoleon power to negotiate with Austria.

The creation of the Cispadane and Cisalpine republics resulted from Bonaparte's increasing autonomy. Lombardy had been kept under military and then civil administration, but denied the formation of a republic. But when the Army of Italy was forced onto the defensive in autumn 1796, as the coalition forces threatened an invasion, Napoleon saw the freedom of central and then northern Italy as a means of military defence, which would reduce the numbers of France's enemies and protect his flank. It was in these months that he welcomed Reggio's rising against its duke, occupied Modena, encouraged the formation of the Lombard and Italian Legions, and urged Reggio, Modena, Bologna and Ferrara to form a military federa-tion.

But these actions, apparently so favourable to Italian independence and future unity, were subordinate to Napoleon's overall strategy. He planned to join with the Rhine armies to strike against Vienna, and for this purpose peace in Italy was essential. Thus, within months of encouraging the Emilian cities, he rapidly made pacts with the Italian princes, blocked the proposals made at the Congress of Reggio to form a Cispadane Republic, and discarded the central Italian patriots, just as he had ignored their Piedmontese brothers at the armistice of Cherasco.

To describe Napoleon's actions in Italy as purely dependent upon his military strategy would be misleading. He had far greater sympathy for the Italian patriots than the Directory (as could be seen in his readiness to employ revolutionary propaganda) and found himself, through his own victories, facing his first experiences of diplomacy, major policy-making and administration. His close attention to the details of the creation of the

Cispadane and Cisalpine republics (in January and June 1797) is indicative of his determination to assert his political alongside his military abilities. And his negotiation of the agreement of Leoben with Austria (18 April 1797), after the victories of the Italian and Rhine armies in the spring, marked his definitive triumph over the Directory: the Rhine frontier was sacrificed in return for Austrian recognition of the Cisalpine republic. Napoleon was triumphant in Italy, and after supplying military support for the Directory's purge of the royalist majority in the French council of 500 (Fructidor, 4 September 1797), he was free to make the final peace with Austria which ended the first coalition. The treaty of Campoformio (18 October 1797), which horrified the Directory as much as it did the Italian patriots (though for different reasons), cynically sacrificed the newly created democratic republic of Venice to Austria. It was politically less favourable than Leoben and can best be explained in terms of Bonaparte's haste to conclude the Italian campaign and move on to greater affairs: in November, he left Italy (to the relief of the Directory) to head a proposed invasion of England, which soon gave way to his Egyptian campaign.

Leoben and Campoformio were not merely episodes in the struggle between Napoleon and the Directory. They were also of significance in altering the relationship between France and Europe. The Director Reubell's determination to conquer the left bank of the Rhine had remained within the relatively limited expansionist policy of 'natural frontiers'. The creation of the Cisalpine republic, far beyond France's frontiers, implied – more than the Batavian republic – France's adoption of an aggressive revolutionary policy of propaganda and expansion, a constant threat to the other European states, and most immediately to Austria. Campoformio, in fact, led rapidly to the formation of the second coalition against France.

Bonaparte had left Austria strongly entrenched along the Adige river, facing a Cisalpine republic with almost indefensible frontiers but with ambitious plans for expansion. The French army in Italy had been weakened by the withdrawal of troops for the English expedition, and by garrisoning requirements. The solid block of monarchical states to the south of the Cisalpine republic – Tuscany, the Papal States, the Two Sicilies – continued to represent a threat in the event of war. The Directory, re-asserting its authority after Napoleon's departure, found itself following his policy in order to strengthen French control of Italy: the Papal States were invaded and the Roman republic created in order to break the threat of encirclement (February 1798): the Helvetic republic, formed soon after, guaranteed communications between France and Italy; plans were laid to incite revolutions in Piedmont and Naples. Propaganda, revolution and armed conquest, followed by financial exactions, were the order of the day, to consolidate French power and open up new possibilities in the Mediterranean (occupation of Malta, Napoleon's Egyptian expedition). Inevitably, these unilateral changes frightened the princes, who remained acutely suspicious of the Directory's offers of guarantees of future stability. The equilibrium in Italy was once more at the centre of European diplomacy and led to the second coalition of Britain, Austria, Russia and Turkey (1798).

Thus the Roman republic, like the Cisalpine and Ligurian republics, owed its existence to French war policy. With Napoleon's departure, the Directors were determined to establish tight control over all three, as over the French generals in Italy. The civil commissars with the armies in Italy, responsible only to the Directory, were appointed to regularize the financial exactions and check all attempts at independent action by the generals. The Directory had owed its survival too often to the generals, and the Army of Italy – in contrast to Bernadotte's Army of the Rhine – was strongly republican and loyal to Bonaparte. In September 1797 the Directory had been forced to turn to Bonaparte to eliminate a royalist threat in France (Fructidor). But after May 1798, when the Directors purged the Assembly of Jacobin supporters (Floréal), the Italian Army represented a threat. Only by early 1799 had the Directory managed to assert full control. The generals and officers continued to play at politics, and a state of tension existed between Napoleon's former army and Bernadotte's troops which had been sent to reinforce it. The army was discontented as money was short. In February 1798 a revolt broke out among Bernadotte's officers in the Cisalpine republic, followed by the successful refusal of part of the garrison at Rome to accept the republican Masséna as commander. Successive commanders-in-chief, Brune and Joubert, too republican and sympathetic to the patriots for the Directory, were recalled. When Championnet, the commander at Rome, exceeded his orders after invading Naples by creating the Parthenopean republic (January 1799), he was arrested. The history of French power in Italy in 1798–9 is one of continuous conflict between the generals and the civil commissars, with the Directory gradually but (after Floréal) increasingly asserting its control through the latter.

Control was exerted far more easily over the republics than over the generals. As financial exactions increased and the Directors repressed patriotic protest, direct intervention in the affairs of the republics became the order of the day: in the Cisalpine republic the assemblies were purged to force them to accept a military alliance with France (April 1798); between August and December 1798 three further purges were carried out, as the civil authorities (Trouvé, Rivaud) struggled for control with the military (Brune). In the Roman republic all laws were subject to French approval and the 'liberators' twice purged the administration. Even during the short life of the Neapolitan republic the commissar Abrial restructured the government once. Immobilized in the straightjacket of French control, it is hardly surprising that the republican governments achieved so little, or that the patriots found themselves steadily driven into opposition.

By the early months of 1799 the Directory had extended control over all Italy, except the islands. Charles Emanuel IV had been driven out of Piedmont (9 December 1798), Ferdinand IV out of Naples (21 December 1798) and Ferdinand III out of Tuscany (27 March 1799). Their territories had been occupied for strategic reasons and Reubell opposed any change in their status which might complicate peace negotiations. For this reason Championnet had been arrested, Joubert forced to resign, and the civil commissar Eymar dismissed after allowing the Piedmontese provisional government to vote the state's annexation to France (February 1799). But already Reubell's moderate Directory was on the defensive: in April the coalition armies under Suvorov occupied Lombardy and then Piedmont, while Macdonald retreated hastily from Naples; on 18 June the military party in France, aided by former Jacobins, carried out a coup against the Directory (Prairial). For a few short months, until Bonaparte's coup of 18 Brumaire (10 November 1799), there was a return to the ideals of a revolutionary war: the civil commissars were suppressed, Championnet (with Joubert in support) was appointed commander-in-chief in Italy. But by then the French 'liberation' of Italy was over. With Bonaparte's return the following year a new experiment was to begin.

The Jacobins

In later historiography, the *triennio*, or three years of French revolutionary control, were to be described as the 'Jacobin' period. As such, its exponents were condemned, from opposite sides, either for their 'anarchy' and lack of realism, or because of their failure to create a peasant-backed revolution as in France. Yet the 'Jacobins' were only in a position of relative importance in the early phases following the invasion, and their actions were at all times heavily conditioned by French control.

In their actions and their ideas the Jacobins were quite distinct from the reformers of the pre-revolutionary years. Verri's dismissal of those who flocked into Milan with Bonaparte as dishonest adventurers was typical of the mistrust felt by the older reforming generation. Those of the reformers who welcomed or were prepared to collaborate with the French adopted moderate positions, in line with the France of the Directory, if not of that of the initial Revolution of 1789–91. Where reformism had been most successful, as in Tuscany, Jacobinism did not exist. Only where it had failed disastrously, as at Naples, were reformers to be found among the Jacobins and even then they were, like Mario Pagano, among the most moderate; Vincenzio Russo, with his proposals for the abolition of private property, was a unique exception.

The Jacobins, in fact, formed a new generation. Many had witnessed or participated in the great events at Paris, some had received French citizenship, far more among the exiles who had gathered at Paris, Genoa or around Buonarroti at Oneglia had fought under Bonaparte during the invasion. Others, who had plotted or conspired in Jacobin clubs or masonic lodges and had frequently been imprisoned for their opinions, now emerged in the light of day, sharing the exiles' optimism that the Revolution would liberate Italy and regenerate society. It was their political belief in the independence of Italy as a necessary step towards the achievement of a totally new society (in Italy and among humanity) that marked off the Jacobins from the reformers. The Revolution signified a sharp break with the immediate past, from which specific egalitarian elements might be salvaged (and Rousseau's name is among the few to be cited with a certain frequency), but which belonged to a corrupt age. Far better the pure and simple virtues of Sparta and ancient Rome, whose imagery colours the speeches and writings of the Jacobins.

Their total commitment to independence and a republic remained a constant of Jacobin action and was the immediate cause of official French mistrust and hostility. These had been the aims of Buonarroti's Piedmontese conspiracy and offered the dominant note in the essays written for the famous competition about the future of Italy organized by the Lombard administration in September 1796. The area of Italy which was to be included within the independent republic was disputed or left imprecise. Many of the leading Jacobins who participated in the Lombard government's competition 'Which form of free government is most fitting for the happiness of Italy?' – such as Melchiorre Gioia and Matteo Galdi – asserted the need for a unitary republic as it would offer greater military security. Others, like Carlo Botta and Marco Fantuzzi, favoured a federation of republics which would reflect more accurately regional differences or municipal claims. Few indeed thought seriously that the republic could initially comprise more than northern and central Italy, although many hoped that its example and subversive capacity would 'revolutionize' the states still subject to despotic rule. But national independence, whatever its geographical limits, constituted the framework of Jacobin ideas.

The highly individualistic Piedmontese ex-priest, Giovanni Antonio Ranza, whose evangelistic fervour and democratic views had led him to play a leading role in the Buonarrotian attempt to create a republic in Piedmont in 1796, observed that the insistence on the 'republic, one and indivisible' derived from the French example: 'This fashion, like the others, has come from France, but not all the fashions of France are good and convenient for other countries, especially for Italy' (Saitta, 128, vol. 2, p. 195). The comment merits attention, for in their political, as in much of their social programme, the Italian Jacobins were consciously attempting to relive the

French experience. Times had changed, circumstances were drastically different, but the Jacobins looked back to the most radical and democratic period of the French Revolution, its most 'heroic' moment, the revolution of Robespierre and the Committee of Public Safety of 1793–4. This inspiration lay behind their hopes and their proposals: education and terror, a more egalitarian distribution of land and control of prices, patriotic societies and free sister republics. Matteo Galdi was a Neapolitan who had fled to France in 1794, had returned with the Army of Italy in 1796 and may have been involved in Buonarroti's conspiracy. He was perhaps the most explicit of the Italians in his recognition of the debt that all patriots owed to Jacobin France:

> We have no reason at all to complain of revolutionary propaganda. If it had not existed in France, there would have been no liberty in Italy. If it had lasted for yet another year, beyond 1793 to '94, acting at an equally rapid pace, there would not have been so many negotiations and treaties about the fate of our unhappy country. By a single *fiat* of the great Convention not only our peninsula, but all Europe would by now be a republic, single and indivisible. (Cantimori, 126, vol. 1, p. 248)

In mid-November 1796, when the Austrians seemed to threaten the survival of the Revolution, the Cisalpine Jacobins tried to rally the nation – as their French prototypes had done in 1792 – holding continuous sessions in the Patriotic Society, supporting the workers' demand that the price of bread be reduced, proclaiming formally by notarial act (without French permission) the independence of the republic. Galdi could extol 'anti-moderatism' given that the moderates with their *scioaneria* (*chouannerie* or 'royalist spirit') were typically the good citizens who murdered patriots and had subverted the Army of the Rhine. By 1799, as the coalition armies advanced, these same patriots proposed taking hostages from those leading Milanese families which had secretly formed a 'Club autrichien'. Even the Neapolitan Pagano, so much more moderate than most of the northern Italian Jacobins, proposed 'extreme' measures in the last desperate days of the Parthenopean republic.

Emergency situations demanded emergency measures. But the Jacobins were convinced that the true strength of the republic was to be found in the support of the people. How to gain this support and how to define the people evoked different responses. All were agreed on the importance of education, and many were aware of French revolutionary pedagogical experiments as well as (usually unacknowledged) Enlightenment writings. The constitutional circles and popular societies were seen by the neoclassical Modenese poet Giovanni Fantoni as performing missionary work. Schools were to be set up in each municipality; Giuseppe Abamonti, who paid particular attention to schooling as the most effective means of regeneration, proposed democratically that those children who were to continue their education after the age of ten be chosen by their classmates. Matteo Galdi clearly stated that education was for all the population: 'I understand revolutionary public education to mean the instruction and education of the people as a mass in the principles of democracy' (Cantimori, 126, vol. 1, pp. 223–4). Education, in fact, was to destroy 'superstition' and thus enable the people to understand and embrace egalitarian democracy. At its lowest level, according to Galdi, it would teach the people how to hold constitutional elections. Vincenzio Russo, as always more extreme than most Italian Jacobins, saw schooling as a means to eliminate criticism based on selfish individualistic criteria and implant uniformity of mind, a necessary premise for the establishment of a propertyless egalitarian republic: 'conformity of thought signifies a great part of general equality, and is of considerable help in carrying out the rest' (Cantimori, 126, vol. 1, p. 326). But until schools could be set up, it was necessary to reach the people in different ways, through gazettes, constitutional circles, preaching of the democratic catechism from the pulpit, simple expositions in dialect, as the Neapolitan poetess Eleanora Fonseca Pimentel proposed. The Bolognese ex-noble Giuseppe Gioannetti, arrested for inciting the poor against aristocrats and bankers, wrote brief republican morality plays, to be read to the peasants in their hovels by itinerant Jacobins.

The problem of gaining peasant support was clearly felt. As Abamonti stated: 'It is essential immediately to interest the mass of the nation in its political change, otherwise our republic will be an abortion without life' (Saitta, 132, p. 236). The difficulty was that the initial sympathy, where it existed, or the more general apathy, rapidly turned to hostility through French depredations and heavy taxes. Many of the Jacobins were extremely cautious in their attitude towards religion and 'superstition'. The Piedmontese Jacobins in their draft constitution of 1796 had warned against offending the people's religious beliefs. In the following years, Jacobins from Lombardy to Rome emphasized the need for a gradual approach. But earlier experiences and those of the French revolutionaries left their mark in the general and often violent tone of anti-clericalism that characterized the debates of the Cisalpine assembly. Almost all the Jacobins were moved by religious fervour and believed that a spiritual transformation – a natural religion, a Supreme Being – would accompany the regeneration of society. This conviction, with its usual accompaniment of anti-clericalism, ill-fitted (and sometimes contradicted) the Jacobins' predication of the need to enlighten the superstitious by degrees, slowly.

The same concern to win support was an element of the Jacobin attitude towards property. But here egalitarian motives and the Spartan vision of the small, independent peasant, symbol of virtue, played their part. The principle of private property was accepted, as it had been by the majority of

French Jacobins. But the problem of the landless poor was felt acutely. The Bolognese Gioannetti, who came from a region of large estates, incited the peasants against the stewards and noble owners. Some Jacobins, like Melchiorre Gioia, wanted to divide up confiscated ecclesiastical properties among the poor. Fantoni proposed a maximum limit on income, the utopist 'Nicio Eritreo' a recurrent egalitarian distribution of the land. Only Russo opposed the concept of property.

But property division was not enough. The Jacobins were agreed on the State's duty to provide for the needy. Public assistance was a sacred obligation, hospitals and hostels were to be created and begging banished. For the visionary ex-noble Enrico Michele L'Aurora the first duty of the legislature and nation was to show the people that the revolution was on its behalf:

> Yes, representatives of the Italian people, before passing any law . . . concern yourselves with the indigent class of people, and by a wise and just law banish begging for ever, grant the destitute rightful and necessary subsistence; begin to make the people see that the revolution is really made for them, that it is made to improve their state, that it is made to relieve their poverty and assist their happiness. (Cantimori and De Felice, 127, p. 484)

The people were thus to be won to the republic and its constitution. For the Jacobins the constitution was that of the French democrats of Year II, not the far more restrictive constitution of 1795, applied with variations by the French to all the Italian republics. Giuseppe Abamonti voiced the belief of most Jacobins in the need for popular control of the legislative assembly, to be achieved by varying methods; Vincenzio Russo asserted the necessity of direct popular government.

But who were the people? Here the typically rural vision of a settled agricultural society, avoiding the corruptions of luxury and (sometimes) of the cities, combined with memories of the anarchical upheavals in France, and often resulted in a restrictive interpretation. Ranza was quite explicit that the landless should be excluded: 'the only respect that can or should be used towards them is not to leave them without bread or justice or fear' (Cantimori, 126, vol. 1, p. 439). The Piedmontese doctor and future historian Carlo Botta defined the people as 'honest farmers, industrious craftsmen, comfortable bourgeois of the towns and cities . . . cultured men and scientists' (Saitta, 128, vol. 1, pp. 25–6). The ex-priest Melchiorre Gioia, winner of the Lombard administration's essay competition, was concerned to win the support of the traditional ruling classes – noble cadets, clergy, lawyers, merchants – as the rest of society was naturally in favour of the republic, while the 'lowest classes' tend to imitate the higher:

> As I am convinced that reconciliation extorted by fear alone is neither sincere nor lasting, I have so far endeavoured to summon to the support of the republic

all classes of society by appealing to interest and reason, without hurting people's vanity or exacerbating resentment. (Saitta, 128, vol. 2, p. 101)

These were the more moderate Jacobins. For the more radical, writing in almost messianic tone, the problem of definition did not exist: independence and the republic were the first steps towards a total regeneration, which – wrote the Bellunese hydraulic engineer Giuseppe Fantuzzi – was starting in Italy and would regenerate humanity and the world.

Probably the larger part of these Jacobins' proposals were published in 1796–7 in liberated Lombardy or following the creation of the new republics at Rome and Naples. They bear the mark of the enthusiasm and freedom of discussion of the early days, before the French hand weighed down too heavily. 'Revolutions are prepared by philosophers and decided by bayonets', wrote Fantuzzi, thinking of Italian valour rather than of French troops (Saitta, 128, vol. 1, p. 260). But it was French military strength which progressively limited the practical possibilities of action by the Jacobins. In the early months following the invasion, the Jacobins were at their strongest. Many had fought with the French, they received a degree of support from the influential Corsican commissar Saliceti and at least benevolent protection from Bonaparte, who was acutely aware of the value of their propaganda. As Ranza wrote, with a deeply democratic suspicion of Napoleon, the Lombard essay competition of 1796, which brought the Jacobins into the open, had been 'an assay of Bonaparte's policy, by which he wanted to test Italian opinion' (Saitta, 128, vol. 1, p. xxxiii). The split between these revolutionary patriots and the more moderate groups was immediately visible in Milan as in the Emilian cities: at Bologna the aristocratic Senate tried to ensure that the change to the new order would involve as little disturbance as possible. Melchiorre Cesarotti, an 'establishment' poet, explaining to a friend a few years later why he had written his catechism, 'Instructions of a citizen for his less educated brothers', accurately caught the state of mind of the moderates faced by the dangers of a cataclysm:

> The aristocracy was buried: our destiny seemed fixed . . . so what was left? To teach the people about the newly established order, the nature and aims of its government, to make it loved and prized above all else in order to generate faith and peaceful support . . . to prevent excesses and abuses, above all to inculcate the virtues necessary for the conservation of the new state and indicate the vices which could spoil it radically and turn it, from the best of governments which it could become, into the worst. (Romagnoli, 151, pp. 7–8)

In moderate eyes, 'excesses', 'abuses', 'vices' were connotations of the Jacobin.

The Jacobins were only too aware of the dangers of the revolution dying on their hands. In Lombardy they were initially assisted by the massive absenteeism of the patricians, who withdrew to their country estates and dismissed their servants. The patriots, gathered in the Popular Society, seized their chance and gained appointment by Bonaparte to the Municipality and Congregation of State. But when they realized their impotence under tight French control, they tried to regain the initiative by forming a military force, the Lombard Legion (with a 'Proclamation to Italian Youth' to cease being 'idle spectators' (Peroni, 148, p. 66)), and by appealing for unity.

In these initial months of uncertainty, the underlying contrast in mentality of the Jacobins and moderates was overshadowed by or summed up in the wholly political issue of unity. The moderates and many of the more advanced patriots had asserted the independence of their own cities and reluctance to unify. The Jacobins, incited by former exiles such as Galdi, saw the major hope for the expansion of the revolutionary movement in unity: once the French had left, the revolution could only be continued in a large unified state, capable of defending itself under the direction of the Jacobins. The deputation to Paris, which presented Galdi's memoir on the diplomatic advantages to France of an independent Italian republic; the Lombard Legion; the offer of a prize essay on the best form of government for a free Italy; the continuous propaganda; were all episodes in this struggle for independence through unity.

By the end of 1796 and early 1797, as neither the Directory nor Bonaparte seemed ready to listen, the Lombards were becoming desperate, especially when Napoleon refused to allow them to take an official part in the Reggio congress which was to lead to the Cispadane republic. Porro could write that within two months they would either be republicans or abandoned and sold back to Austria. In Emilia the Jacobins and patriots – the distinction was becoming blurred precisely because of the issues of independence and unity – had been favoured because of Bonaparte's desire for a military bloc and hence his belated readiness to permit the creation of the Cispadane republic. Then, with the decision to create the Cisalpine republic, the Jacobins seemed to have won their battle. But they were soon disillusioned.

Within the Cisalpine republic the Jacobins lost influence at once. For Bonaparte their function was purely subsidiary – to gain support for the new regime by their propaganda. Few Jacobins reached high office. Assertions of independence or radical social change were suppressed: in January 1797 Bonaparte had tried (unsuccessfully) to create a more malleable Patriotic Society. In February leading Cispadane Jacobins, such as L'Aurora and Gioannetti were expelled or harassed. By 1798 Milan had lost its position as the centre of Jacobinism, as many of its leading exponents, tacitly acknowledging their defeat in the Cisalpine republic, moved to Rome and later to Naples. By then their hopes of influencing the course and character of the French invasion had vanished, and what freedom of expression they still possessed was dependent upon the protection of individual French generals – Brune, Joubert and Championnet. They had been defeated by the moderates because of French (and Napoleon's) support for the latter. Equally, they had failed to gain widespread popular support because of French rapacity, with which they were associated as collaborators.

A hostile patriot critic of the revolution, writing under the pseudonym of Francesco Becattini could describe the Jacobins in his *Portrait or Summary Essay of the System of Liberty Proclaimed by the French* as

> hangmen of the people, cowardly and lying patriots who were the first to betray the common cause by selling themselves to the whims of the iniquitous [French] emissaries, dividing the spoils of their fellow citizens with them, and lending them a hand to complete their ruin. (Peroni, 148, p. 98)

The Neapolitan *lazzaroni* could chant:

> To the sound of the violins
> Ever death to the Jacobins.   (Croce, 158, pp. 39–40)

Forced into opposition, Jacobins and unitarian patriots were pushed towards each other by the Directory's persecution. For the Directory they were all tainted with Babeuf's 'anarchism'. As Bignon, a French diplomat attached to the Cisalpine republic wrote: 'The French Directory is convinced that the anarchy repressed in France has fled to Italy and wants to make its home there' (Vaccarino, 144, p. 188). Certainly the Jacobins included some – such as Fantoni, Jullien, perhaps Galdi – who had connections with Buonarroti and Babeuf's conspiracy. But the Directory's obsessive panic over Jacobin anarchy in practice served to strengthen the links between these extreme Jacobins and the more numerous unitarian patriots. It was French policy which was responsible for the formation of the mysterious Society of Rays, whose plots were worrying French representatives in 1798. By then French hostility was once more leading the Italian Jacobins and patriots to seek links with the extreme Jacobin opposition in France. But the Prairial coup of June 1799 came too late to strengthen the Italian Jacobins.

The Italian republics

If unitarian aspirations developed during these three years, city and regional rivalries remained prominent. Once liberated in 1796 most cities sent deputations to Paris to appeal for the expansion of their own territories as independent republics. The Milanese claimed that, for economic and political reasons, the republic should be extended to include Mantua, the Venetian *terraferma*, even Venice and Dalmatia, the former Lombard provinces which had been acquired by Piedmont, Genoa or at least another out-

let to the western Mediterranean, as well as one to the Adriatic; the frontiers
of the proposed republic were to extend as far as those of the old Visconti-
Sforza duchy. Milanese hostility to separate republics – 'three republics
equals no republic' (Peroni, 125, p. 8) – often masked hopes of hegemony.

The other cities were less ambitious, but as anxious to extend their
economic power and avoid subjection by their rivals. Bologna wanted its
republic to include Ferrara, Ancona and the Romagna; Ferrara hoped for
control of nearby Cento and Pieve, but preferred union with Milan to
domination by Bologna; Modena claimed Ferrara, while Reggio was anxious
to remain separate from Modena. When Ancona gained independence
briefly, it wanted control of the Marches, but hoped for union with the
Cisalpine republic to avoid renewed subjection to Rome. The Roman
patriots had ambitions on Neapolitan territory; the Neapolitan Lauberg
thought the Roman republic should be merged into the Parthenopean
republic, if the French occupied Sicily. It was against these deep traditions
and widespread sentiments of local mistrust and municipal avidity that the
more determined patriots, especially the exiles, asserted the need for unity
as the only means to achieve independence.

Inevitably, these particularist tendencies remained strong within the
republics. Melchiorre Gioia could comment of the Cisalpine republic in
1798:

> Sabatti wants the guns to be bought at Brescia, whereas the interest of the
> Republic demands that they be put up to tender open to all sellers, Codde
> wants the Mantua lottery to be introduced into Milan in defiance of justice and
> good faith; the inhabitants of Reggio want the court of appeal to be located at
> Reggio, the Bolognese struggle against the excise on foodstuffs as it did not exist
> in their department. (Gioia, 129, p. 124 n.)

To many of the cities, in fact, union meant immediate loss of administrative
or economic activities.

These structural weaknesses were inevitably (and, some said, deliberately)
encouraged not only by French hostility to all unitarian aspirations, but by
French determination to keep the republics weak. The frontiers of the
Cisalpine republic remained vulnerable, with the Austrians entrenched on
the Adige, the Tyrol and Grisons borders open to enemy spies and infiltration, and the remote area of the Garfagnana isolated between the Parmigiano
(denied to the republic), Lucca and Tuscany. The frontiers of the Roman
and Parthenopean republics were never clearly defined.

For the French the purpose of the republics remained that of providing
finances for the Army of Italy and for France itself. The exactions were
heavier than in the previous period of peace and were exacerbated by the
private plundering of the generals. The seizure by the French of part of the
biens nationaux confiscated from the Church led to continuous disputes, as

the republican administrations attempted to limit or at least specify precisely their total value and extension in order to facilitate the sale of the remainder. The Cisalpine republic was forced to sign a commercial treaty favouring French products. These depredations, the arbitrary behaviour of so many of the French officers, were responsible, more than anything else, for the insurrections in the Roman republic and lay behind much, though not all, of the general rising which accompanied the French retreat in 1799.

The choice of personnel and the imposition of constitutions formed part of the same French pattern of obedient collaboration. The Directory and Bonaparte were agreed that the two major sources of opposition to French policy in Italy were the pro-Austrian reactionaries and the extremist patriots; where they differed was in their assessment of the potential danger of the latter. The French commander at Modena who threatened pain of death 'to whomsoever by word or deed shall seek to favour the monarchy, the French constitution of 1793 or any other form different from the present one' (Turi, 160, p. 299) was accurately expressing official policy. The strength of the republics was to be based upon the moderates, men of a certain standing and wealth, whether noble or bourgeois, who were ready to serve in the new governments, or whose name would give prestige.

Bonaparte was quite explicit about the need to restrain the *exaltés*. But initially, impressed by the enthusiasm of the Reggio patriots, who had risen spontaneously and successfully (26 August 1796), yet convinced that their exaggerated democratic ideas would be contained by the influence of the Emilian landowners and patricians, he was prepared to encourage the 'congresses' of the four cities (Bologna, Ferrara, Reggio, Modena), – although advising the nomination or (indirect) election of priests, nobles, landowners, merchants and professional men. Only when these apparently moderate representatives decided to overcome their local rivalries and create the Cispadane republic (second congress of Reggio, December 1796– January 1797), nationalize ecclesiastical lands, abolish primogenitures and feudal services and decree internal freedom of trade, did Napoleon suspend the 'united' government until a constitution had been passed. And he personally modified the constitution elaborated by the elected congress of Modena (January–March 1797), although it was already a conservative version of the French constitution of 1795.

The difficulties of controlling the situation, without nominations and careful checks, were shown in the elections following the constitution (April): Bologna and Ferrara returned large numbers of nobles and priests, while Modena and Reggio were riven by the disputes between moderates and democrats. For Napoleon this first experiment in self-government had proved too dangerous, as the moderates were too weak and fear of the Jacobins favoured the reactionaries. He did not hesitate to carve up the Cispadane republic, incorporating Modena and Reggio (and later Bologna and Ferrara, as well as Bergamo and Brescia) in the Cisalpine republic (29 June 1797). The 'immaturity' of the Italians seemed proved. As the Directory wrote in July 1796, after a general enquiry among French diplomatic representatives in Italy: 'All the information we have received about the attitude of people in Italy, shows that they are not yet ready for liberty, or rather that they have been rotted by slavery and the vices it brings in its train' (Vaccarino, 144, p. 40).

The failure of the Cispadane republic marked the end of any official pretence of allowing the Italians freedom of choice. When Napoleon overthrew the Genoese oligarchy (6 June 1797), he personally nominated all the members of the new administration, balancing the different social groups and the different cities of the Ligurian republic. He displayed the same concern to achieve a social and geographical balance in the Cisalpine republic, where he was particularly worried by the strength of the Milanese democrats. At Campoformio (18 October 1797) he ignored the expressed desire of the Venetian patriots to join the Cisalpine republic.

After Napoleon's departure, the Directory was determined to mould the republics in its own moderate image, to the exclusion of the more democratic patriots. In the Roman republic almost all democrats were kept out of office. In the Cisalpine republic, as Talleyrand instructed the ambassador Trouvé, sent to Milan to 'revise' the constitution: 'The interests of the Republic do not permit the Directory to tolerate that those individuals who loudly expound principles of unity should obtain the least employment in the administration, so far as this is possible' (Vaccarino, 144, p. 51). For the same reason the civil commissars blocked the exchange of diplomatic representatives between the Italian republics.

The constitutions, which were imposed on the republics after the Cispadane experience, were all based on the moderate French constitution of 1795; modifications, where they emerged, were of minimal importance and usually reflected a strengthening of the executive at the expense of the legislature. The two chambers were elected by restricted indirect suffrage, the executive consisted of five directors who nominated the ministers, the judiciary was elective; the three powers were rigidly separated, the chambers and executive could only communicate in writing, and the ministers were only responsible to the Directory; the administrative structure was rigidly centralized. As with the French constitution of 1795, the overriding concern was to prevent the possibility of a recurrence of 'anarchy': the primary electoral assemblies were forbidden to assume any representative functions, electors at the second grade were restricted by age and income qualifications, collective petitions were prohibited, liberty of assembly was subject to public order, political associations were forbidden to acquire a formal structure with their own officials or to communicate with other associations. But liberty of person and domicile was emphasized. And property was defined as a sacred right, at the basis of human activities and the social order. Moderate constitutionalism was the order of the day, and fitted in well with the Italian public law tradition. Pagano had drafted a constitution on similar lines at the moment of the Neapolitan republic's fall; Compagnoni lectured on representative democracy as meeting the needs of modern peoples 'to unite in great masses' (Cantimori, 126, pp. 418–19) and began to publish a 'democratic dictionary' to define the new ideas.

Thus, having embarked upon the experiment of creating subordinate republics, the Directory spared no effort. Yet the results, from the French viewpoint, were by no means wholly satisfactory. The constitutions – like the French prototype – proved unworkable, as there were no means of settling disputes between the executive and legislature, or between the two chambers. Even worse, despite the various precautions, the representative assemblies were easily infiltrated by reactionaries and extremists. This was particularly true of the most important and long-lived of the assemblies – the Cisalpine – whose political history is documented in detail in the minutes of these bodies.

Despite Bonaparte's personal nominations to the assemblies, the Council of Seniors, with a primarily noble and ecclesiastical membership, proved strongly conservative, the Council of Juniors, on the other hand, showed a revolutionary tendency as it was rapidly dominated by patriots and Jacobins because of the resignation of the moderates. Nearly 60 members had left the two councils within six months; after the Trouvé *coup* of August 1798 there were mass resignations from the assemblies and the administration. A few of the old generation of reformers – Ricci, Pagano, or Gianni during the brief French occupation of Tuscany – were willing to collaborate; but many more – like Melzi d'Eril – resisted French pressure. As with the Jacobins, the moderates whom the French supported were usually new men. The patriots at Pavia, who were placed on trial during the Austrian reaction, were lawyers, notaries, priests and monks, writers, university professors, doctors, engineers, as well as a certain number of tenant farmers, land-owners and artisans (Soriga, 152, pp. 106–23). Inevitably, a number of these patriots, in all the republics, were more concerned with their own fortunes than with responsibility towards the state: the history of the republics is coloured by the frequently justified accusations of the corruption of those in office.

In these conditions of subordination, mutual distrust, unrest and almost continual war, it is hardly surprising that the republican assemblies and governments, during their short span of life, should have 'achieved' so little. But it is worth glancing briefly at their discussions, as they reveal the continuing pursuit of many pre-revolutionary ideals and the sharp difference in aims and mentality between moderates and Jacobins, north and south.

The debates in the Cisalpine Council of Juniors continued the classic themes of Lombard reformism: anti-clerical attack on the Church, with confiscation of ecclesiastical property and Jansenist proposals of legislation to control the Church, a physiocratic vision of the economy, exaltation of the peasantry, but concern for the cities, internal freedom of trade, a simplified taxation system and moderate customs barriers at the frontiers. But within the context of these discussions, dominated by the need to meet French financial demands, the differences between the moderates and Jacobins, the consciousness of poverty and the demands of social justice emerged in a clear-cut manner. The Jansenists, with their respect for established authority, were inevitably to be found among the moderates, in the Cisalpine as in the Ligurian republic.

The moderates continuously warned against the negative financial effects of democratic reforms and their violation of sacred rights: a progressive land-tax discouraged prospective purchasers of the *biens nationaux*, owners of confiscated demesnial rights should be entitled to indemnity, abolition of consumption taxes would bankrupt the republic. For Alfonso Longo, one of the last of the *Caffè* group of reformers, the proposal to fix minimum wages for day labourers

> would be to violate the most sacred of rights, that of personal property and freedom of contract. Let us leave these daily wages to free competition, to the variety of circumstances of each village, to the whims or needs of men, and let us remember that the legislator's most important policy consists in leaving industry free to act, in *laisser faire*, and not in multiplying with ridiculous frenzy the pedantic and frivolous regulations of ministers of monarchical governments. (Montalcini and Alberti, 145, vol. 6, p. 452)

Giuseppe Compagnoni defended free export of grains as offering encouragement to the owner to employ labour. Bovara, a Jansenist who had played a leading role in Joseph II's ecclesiastical reforms, proposed to reintroduce the grist-tax, on the grounds that the peasants did not eat wheat. Salimbeni defended the salt-tax, as 'it is wholly false that the rich man pays the same as the poor. For the poor man a pound of salt lasts a week; in the rich man's home, as much salt is consumed in one day as the poor man uses in perhaps twenty days, because the rich man's home needs ice-creams and salted meats and well-seasoned foods'. (Montalcini and Alberti, 145, vol. 5, p. 657).

For the Jacobins, the ubiquitous presence of poverty and begging proved the case for price controls in order to ensure subsistence. Giuseppe Valeriani proposed to provide poorhouses with obligatory work for beggars and so 'raise every pauper, as far as possible, out of his reprehensible and wasteful mendicancy to the level of an honest producer' (Montalcini and Alberti, 145, vol. 2, pp. 252–3). This attitude towards the able-bodied destitute, condemned for their idleness, was shared by Jacobins and moderate reformers (as was faith in the regenerative qualities of education). But the radical members of the Council of Juniors had no doubts that economic and social inequality was widespread and would worsen with the indiscriminate sale of *biens nationaux*, free export of grain, consumption taxes on agriculture. Pietro Dehò, a country doctor, summed up the Jacobin challenge to reformism:

> What is the first, what is the most sacred, what is the sole right of man? Subsistence. . . . Ever since I have had the use of reason, I have always seen that the rich, even when they have repeatedly sold their goods at quite a high price, not only have never increased their workers' wages, but indeed have always sought to harass them and pay them as little as possible, so attacking that very right to subsistence that nature cannot deny to those unfortunates. (Montalcini and Alberti, 145, vol. 2, p. 145)

The Jacobin challenge was defeated on grounds of financial and political exigences. With its defeat vanished the only possibility of gaining more widespread support. The major changes enacted by the Cisalpine republic – abolition of feudal privileges, tithes and entails, confiscation and sale of ecclesiastical lands – strengthened the landowning classes, whether noble or bourgeois. By the time the republic fell (28 April 1799), over half the *biens nationaux* had been sold.

In the other republics the Jacobins never managed to mount so major a challenge. In Rome, their activities were confined to the Constitutional Circle and political newspapers, where they attacked the venality and ostentatious wealth of the moderates, invoked a popularly elected priesthood as the basis of a democratic Church, and warned of the need for 'bread, onions and Liberty' (Giuntella, 155, pp. 59–60) as the only solid basis for the republic. The indigenous Jacobins, such as Angelucci, were far more moderate than the unitarian exiles who abandoned the Cisalpine republic for Rome, like L'Aurora and Pagano.

At Naples, where the patriotic movement had attracted so many of the former reforming intellectuals, the brief life of the republic (January–June 1799), its rapid loss of control of the provinces, and the overwhelming power of the baronage led to far more moderate proposals than in the Cisalpine republic. The only effective law passed by the provisional government was the abolition of entails. The Neapolitan Jacobins, often imbued with so deep a respect for property as to negate the possibility of the radical reform required to break the hold of the baronage, divided over whether feudal demesnes could be expropriated without indemnity. The reform of the government by the French authorities Macdonald and Abrial (14 April 1799) eliminated the more democratic leaders, such as the ex-priest Lauberg.

Outside the capital, the failure of the patriots in the provinces was even more marked. In the Calabrias, in contrast to the Abruzzi and Molise, 'democratization' had occurred peacefully. Inevitably the leaders consisted of the local *galantuomini* – lawyers, notaries, doctors, some priests, a few nobles – often educated and open to the new ideas, always acting for local reasons: against the local feudatory, to achieve administrative independence from another commune, to wrest control from rival families. The Revolution had been accompanied by peasant refusals to pay taxes and occupations of the land. Once in possession of an unstable authority, opposed by the vast majority of the barons, traditionally distrusted by the peasantry, these republican *galantuomini* remained inert, concerned above all 'to protect their own' (Cingari, 159, p. 298). The contrast to the Cisalpine republic was total: where the northern Jacobins pushed for measures to assist the poor and win mass support, the deep class hatred in the south inhibited the republicans even from contemplating legislation in favour of the peasantry. In the north, the Jacobin defeat had consolidated the power of the moderate landowners; in the south, the 'Jacobins' – or patriots, as more accurately they should be described – could only leave the legacy of their martyrdom.

The two Italies

The collapse of French power in Italy was rapid and dramatic. Already in February–March 1799 cardinal Ruffo's 'Sanfedist' army had occupied the Calabrias, and by April the Basilicata too. The coalition armies drove the French back across the Rhine and in north Italy, under Suvorov's command, forced the Adda in April and entered Milan on the 28th. Macdonald secretly withdrew his troops from Naples in mid-April and hurried north to reinforce the main French army. His defeat by Suvorov at the Trebbia (17–19 May) led to the collapse of French control of Piedmont and the occupation of Turin on 26 May. Naples fell before the combined attack of Ruffo's army and the *lazzaroni* on June 22; Florence was occupied by the insurgents on 7 July. By the end of August, the French ambassador at Rome, Bertolio, could write: 'We are stranded at Rome as if on Robinson Crusoe's island; but our position is far more tiresome' (Giuntella, 155, p. 37 n.); once the French troops had left, the Roman republic collapsed on 30 September. Only Ancona and Genoa, besieged by the coalition armies, remained under French control.

The victory of the coalition armies had been greatly facilitated by the strength of anti-French feeling. But it is necessary to distinguish between the hostility and conspiracies of the 'unitarians', which evoked so exaggerated a concern among the French, and the mass insurgence, whose scale and ferocity would seem to have taken the French by surprise.

Popular disturbances had marked the entire period of French domination and had effectively denied the French control over large areas of the Roman and Neapolitan republics. That these almost exclusively peasant risings were always exacerbated by French exactions and behaviour cannot be denied. But the nature of the risings, as indeed their continuation after French withdrawal, revealed far deeper and more complex causes than merely anti-French hostility. There was a profound difference between the risings in Lombardy or the later insurrection in Tuscany and the massive movements in the south of Italy. In northern and central Italy, where the reforming movement had gained the greatest impetus, few of the patriots had moved beyond a generic, usually physiocratically inspired vision of the desirability of smallholdings. Only the Jacobins, for the most part, faced by the ubiquitous evidence of pauperism and indigence, were aware of the social dangers of reformism, but some of them, as we have seen, were inclined to offer restrictive definitions of the 'people' and to exclude from the immediate rights of 'active' citizenship the poorest sectors of society. In this they were undoubtedly influenced by the evidence of the close ties between hostile clergy, nobles and their peasants.

In Venetia in April 1796 the peasants and 'plebs' of Verona rose against La Hoz's 'liberating' legion; in May the peasants of Binasco had tried to march on Milan, and immediately after 5000 peasants and craftsmen momentarily captured Pavia; in July the peasants at Arquata Scrivia, a former imperial fief, massacred a column of French troops. In July 1797 there was a rising of the Garfagnana peasants, followed by the resistance of the peasants of the Bergamasco; in July 1798 a more serious insurrection occurred in the Valtellina. In most of these risings the patriots accurately pointed to the instigation of the local lords and priests, whose influence remained strong in mountainous, remote areas barely (if at all) touched by the reforms. But the risings were often more than a mere reaction to the new order of events. They revealed the depth of social tensions, the antipathy of the peasantry to their lords, the resentment of seigneurial exactions and appropriation of the commonlands. Not all the risings were directed against the patriots: at Bricherasio (in Piedmont), for instance, the commune had initially supported them against the feudatories; in February 1799 the Langhe peasants who rose against Piedmont's annexation by France had connections with Jacobins of babouvist tendencies.

These were undoubtedly isolated episodes amidst the general hostility which harassed the French retreat in 1799. But by then the Jacobins were only too well aware that they had failed to gain popular support. Buonarroti had insisted on the need to free Piedmont before the French invasion. As early as the end of 1796 Fantoni lamented to the Lombard administrators and Reggio deputies that the moment had been lost:

> Everything favoured an imposing gathering of forces, if the people of Italy had had the courage to proclaim their own liberty and sovereignty at once. In front of the triumphant French army they could have appealed to the sacred rights of nationhood and chased out the defeated German army. Their example would have roused the neighbouring cities; soon the French army and Italian patriots would have decreed by arms that Italy was free. . . . Aristocratic intrigues by those who, least of all, should have engaged in them suppressed the appeals of

the patriots, and the most favourable moment for the liberty of Italy was squandered. (Saitta, 132, pp. 242–3)

But few of the patriots had so clear a vision, and most were hostile to radical demands of property redistribution. In Tuscany, where Jacobinism did not exist, the former minister Gianni typically expressed the desire of the patriots to utilize the French occupation primarily in order to continue the Leopoldine reforms. Nowhere did he reveal more clearly the limited aims of the most moderate patriots than in his definition of the purpose of the national guard:

> We are of the opinion that the public should be informed that the purpose of the guard is only to defend the property and persons of the citizens against criminal aggressions. Sentiments of patriotism excite the patriots, but the safety of goods and persons will attract everyone, and so we believe that membership of the Guard should also be open to the proprietor who has a shop of some worth to protect or to the wealthy who wish to safeguard their houses. (Turi, 160, p. 163)

But in the reaction of 1799 even such moderate collaborators as Gianni were to be disqualified by the taint of 'Jacobinism'. The accusation, arousing reactions of fear and hatred, was exploited within the Tuscan cities by the conservatives who had opposed not only the French, but earlier Leopoldine reformism. But if the urban educated happily vindicated their anti-French feelings by such accusations of 'Jacobinism', the massive risings in the Tuscan countryside revealed far deeper economic and social tensions.

The Tuscan risings of 1790, 1795 and 1799 had been directed against the reforms by peasants and craftsmen who had suffered directly from rising prices and increased unemployment. Like those in east Piedmont, where large rented farms were the norm, the risings were centred on areas which had experienced major transformations – the Valdichiana and Valdarno. When popular tumults and threats against the rich continued in Cortona in 1799, the local notables, hostile to the French, still preferred to call back French troops. These risings in Tuscany, and especially the general insurrection of 1799 led by Arezzo, acquired the character of a religious crusade – more so than the insurrections in Venetia, Lombardy and Piedmont. But the cry of 'Viva Maria' ('Long live the Virgin Mary'), the sudden flood of miracles, masked a deep hatred against the landlords who had been responsible for the reforms. As an Arezzo 'Notice to the Public' stated in 1795, inciting disorder:

> So rise up, long live the faith and let the temple and divine worship be respected. And when the signal is given by the churchbell of the Pieve let all those who have suffered from the greed of bastard barons and their kind wreak vengeance with speed and savagery. Let them spill the iniquitous blood and carve up the bodies of those who have sought only our ruin and despair. (Turi, 160, p. 91)

In the north, the popular risings had been relatively limited before the French collapse and had often reflected both the traditional ties which still linked the ex-feudatories to the peasants and the negative effects on the craftsmen of the abolition of the guilds. In Tuscany, the conservatism of the reforming landowners gave the risings a more distinctive social and economic character, despite the personal link between owner and peasant which the *mezzadria* contract was supposed to offer. In the south, the risings were even more of an explicit class nature and developed into virtual *jacqueries*, often under the pretext of a religious crusade.

The French were very conscious of the dangers of a religious rising, particularly after their recent experiences in their homeland. At Rome, they had taken great care not to meddle with the position of the Church and Catholicism, but had inevitably aroused hostility by the pope's exile and by the granting of civil rights to Jews. At Naples, general Macdonald had immediately ensured that San Gennaro perform his customary, albeit (on that particular day) unscheduled miracle. But their efforts were to no avail. At Rome, in Trastevere the populace rose against the Jews to the cry of 'Long live Mary, long live the pope', followed by the people of the nearby region of the Castles: 'It is a complete Vendée', wrote general Girardon (Giuntella, 155, pp. 32–3). In Calabria, cardinal Ruffo led his 'Christian Army' to defend the Holy Faith.

But if popular religiosity cannot be discounted in these southern insurrections, it was never the predominant element. In the two southern republics of Rome and Naples, virtually no attempt was made by the patriots to meet the demands of the landless peasantry and urban populace for land, to end state and seigneurial fiscal exactions, to control prices. The suppression of ecclesiastical charitable institutions worsened the situation. 'We do not want republics, if we have to pay as before', protested a peasant from the Calabrian village of Cirò (Cingari, 159, p. 300). French interference and lack of time might have explained the patriots' failure. But in practice the gap between the owners and the mass of the populations was too great for the problem even to be considered as a practical possibility. The French Championnet had written: 'In general, all who own something are for us' (Rambaud, 181, p. 533). The very identification of the owners, the *gentiluomini* and lords, with the patriotic movement condemned it in the eyes of the masses:

Whoever has bread and wine,
  Must be a Jiacobine.   (Croce, 158, p. 46)

In the south, where the pre-revolutionary reforms had failed or had never been attempted, the gulf between the educated, privileged classes and the rest was too deep. Even in Bourbon Sicily in 1799 an urban militia of peasants and craftsmen threatened a rising, refusing to pay taxes and murdering 'Jacobins'. The small group of patriots – nobles, lawyers, intellectuals, professional men and lower clergy – were too isolated. In many instances they had only become republicans for local, personal, family reasons – and were soon to regret their choice. The mass insurrections in the Trasimeno, Circeo and then the Marches, in the Abruzzi, Molise, and Calabria, were soon exploited by a wide variety of clergy, royalist nobles, Austrian agents – but also by bandits and local notables anxious to settle old feuds. Insurrection turned into organized revolt, with 'mass troops' led by ferocious bandits known only by their nicknames – Brother Devil, Mammon, Big Sabre, Black Belly, – but equally by *galantuomini*, priests, officers of the defeated Neapolitan army and petty nobles. Ruffo's spectacular success owed much to his awareness of the need to abolish some of the hated taxes, a measure described by the exiled queen Maria Carolina as: 'most wise, worthy of a shrewd and deep thinker; by not relieving the peoples of fiscal pressures all in one go, any advantage gained has to be in proportion to merit and always leaves something to hope for' (Cingari, 159, p. 191). But the degeneration of the 'crusade' into theft and murder, the settling of personal vendettas, soon left little to 'hope for', and Ruffo found his army disintegrating as the peasants returned to the villages to protect their homes and families. Banditry in the south had been widespread before the reaction of 1798–9. Momentarily encouraged, it was now to prove difficult to suppress, and exacerbated the seething discontent. The violence and bloodshed which swept away the patriotic movement in the south – in sharp contrast to northern and central Italy – was to condition future democratic initiatives there.

Patriotic conspiracy

Compared to these massive but shapeless peasant movements, the anti-French conspiracies of the 'unitarians' were of little immediate practical significance. To state this is not to underestimate their longer term importance as contributory elements in the emergence of a national consciousness, but to place them in their historical perspective.

By mid-1797 the Jacobin unitarians had been forced onto the defence, but still hoped to condition the French policy of conquest. The French Jacobin Jullien de la Drôme, who had fled to Milan after the failure of the Babeuf conspiracy, advised caution and secret union as the most effective method to achieve power: caution over religion and property, the avoidance of clubs and factions, republican austerity and discreet unified action to force the pace of revolution in Italy. The Lombard Legion, under the leadership of the ambitious La Hoz, formed a focal point for the unitarians, whether Jacobin or more simply patriotic. Agitation and propaganda was kept up by the Venetian exiles who had flocked to Milan after Campoformio. La Hoz, head of a mission to Paris in July 1798 to block Trouvé's conservative modification of the Cisalpine constitution, was suspected by the Director Reubell of being leader of an elusive organization of anti-French unitarians, the Society of Rays. The links between these patriots and the French generals Joubert, Championnet and Brune were clear, and the Directory suspected – correctly – contacts with the French 'extremists'. By October 1798 the commissar Faipoult could write in alarmist manner to Talleyrand:

> Following the letters written from Turin, Rome and many places in Italy, there can be no doubt that at this moment a vast plot is being hatched to assassinate Frenchmen from Susa to Terracina. Scoundrels are planning new Sicilian vespers against the Italian governments. They have been listened to by many people, and mystery still shrouds part of the horrors that have been prepared to make the war more deadly for the hated [French] nation, if fighting should start again. (Vaccarino, 144, p. 38, n. 2)

By 1798–9, in effect, many patriots, particularly among the exiles, had begun to conceive of unity as the only means of defence. Among them, Jacobins such as Fantoni, protected by the commander-in-chief Brune, were plotting with survivors of the Babeuf conspiracy to exploit discontent in the occupied territories and contemporaneously overthrow the Directory in France. In Italy the members of the Society of Rays were based on Modena, Reggio and Bologna; at Milan La Hoz, assisted by his contacts in the police, was to lead his troops in the insurrection.

The moderate Floréal *coup* in France (May 1798) and especially the Trouvé and Rivaud *coups* in the Cisalpine republic (August, December 1798) presumably checked these plans. The only attempt at a rising for unity, with strong babouvist connotations, occurred in Piedmont in February 1799. The French civil and military officials were taken by surprise by the decision of the Piedmontese provisional government to demand annexation by France in order to avoid the depredations of a continuing French military occupation. A plot was discovered of clear babouvist character: a secret central committee directed other committees, unaware of its existence, and was responsible for exploiting the discontent in the provinces among those Piedmontese who opposed annexation. The plot, led by Fantoni and the head of the Cisalpine police Mulassano, was easily suppressed, but the *anarchistes* had succeeded in making contact with the peasants: in the ensuing rising in the Langhe peasants were found carrying miniature portraits of the French 'extremists' Marat and Lepeletier.

The connections of these patriots with the French Jacobins who carried out the *coup* of 30 Prairial (18 June 1799) against the Directory seem conclusive. But the *coup* had come too late. With the Austro-Russian occupation of Lombardy and Piedmont, the patriots, both moderate and Jacobin, had been forced to flee to Genoa or France. The mutual distrust between moderates and Jacobins now burst into the open. The Cisalpine Directory at Chambéry and the Piedmontese General Administration at Grenoble found themselves in a weak position in the revived Jacobin atmosphere of these months in France. The Jacobins at Grenoble, led by Fantoni, drew up a harsh indictment of the moderates, the 'Cri de l'Italie', which accused them of responsibility for the collapse of the republics. The 'Cri', like other appeals drawn up at Genoa and Grenoble by exiles from all over Italy, was directed to the French Council of 500, where the Jacobin Briot used them to attack the entire system of the former Directory, and to draw the conclusion that the liberated peoples had to be treated on terms of absolute equality, creating one or more truly free republics in Italy.

The appeals, which varied in tone, all agreed in blaming the former French Directory for the disaster, and in seeing the only hope in a unitary Italian republic. For the 'Glance at the Causes which have Degraded the Public Spirit in Italy' the basic mistake had been to try to impose a French revolution instead of following the 'genius of the nation' (Peroni, 161, pp. 52–3), humiliating the attempts of Italians to arm themselves, despoiling the populations and dividing the country into small, vulnerable states. For the 'Cri', the loss of popular support was to be attributed to the discriminatory policy of the moderate leaders, like Melzi, supported by the French ambassadors. Despite Campoformio, despite his ambiguous policy, these patriots represented Bonaparte as an honest patriot, deceived by the Cisalpine moderates. In this moment of hope induced by the convergence of generals and Jacobins, Napoleon regained prestige.

The Jacobins enthusiastically co-operated with the French in preparing for the renewed invasion of Italy, which this time was to assure them real power. The liberation of Italy, they urged, should be followed by a national Convention at Florence.

The Cisalpine general Giuseppe Lechi formed an Italic Legion at Dijon, but not all Italian patriots agreed with them. One renowned leader – La Hoz – had deserted to the Austrians to fight for Italian independence. Other Piedmontese, worried that a successful invasion would be followed by the absorption of Piedmont by the Cisalpine republic, drew back.

The invasion was successful, but the Jacobins were again disillusioned. The generals in whom they had placed their trust – Joubert and Championnet – were killed in battle. The allied coalition collapsed even before the end of 1799, with Suvorov's defeat at Zurich, the Anglo-Austrian withdrawal from Holland and tsar Paul I's defection. Bonaparte's return from Egypt and the *coup* of 18 Brumaire (9 November 1799) marked the definitive end of Jacobin hopes. The crossing of the Alps and the victory of Marengo (14 June 1800) were to mark the beginning of a new, moderate experience, once more closely dependent upon the rhythm of French life and Napoleonic ambition.

10

Rationalization and social conservatism : 1800–14

Italy's frontiers were altered more frequently during the fifteen years of Napoleonic domination than at any time since the Wars of the Signorie in the fourteenth and fifteenth centuries. Perhaps only German diplomatic geography suffered more from drastic strokes of Napoleon's pen – but then the German empire had retained an infinitely greater degree of medieval fragmentation before the Revolution. The political changes were marked, in classic eighteenth-century manner, by total disregard for the opinions of the populations involved. Italy – like Switzerland, the Low Countries, Germany – remained an area whose fate was decided by rulers and diplomats. But in two ways, of significance for the future, the political modifications imposed upon Italy differed from those of the pre-revolutionary period: on the one hand the brief years of the 'Jacobin' republics had left a strong political consciousness among patriots of the need for independence, if not of unity; on the other, respect for the sacred rights of dynasties was swept away. Both elements were to play an important role in the final years of the collapse of Napoleonic rule, and underlay all the aspirations, movements and conspiracies of the following years.

Napoleon and Italy

The battle of Marengo had freed Lombardy and Piedmont of Austrian troops and Austria, which also evacuated the Romagna. But the settlement of Italy depended upon the final outcome of the war with the second coalition. Although the Cisalpine and Ligurian republics were once more proclaimed, in the following months of diplomatic negotiations a variety of proposals were produced in official and unofficial circles. Lomonaco's 'Coup d'oeil on Italy', which appeared in July 1800, expressed the renewed hopes of the unitarians. Napoleon himself asked at least two of the more ardent patriots – Jullien and Paribelli – for their opinions. Jullien's memoir, proposing the creation of a strong north Italian state (Lombardy–Piedmont–Genoa) as an effective barrier against Austria, but also that of three or four other states (Venetian and Neapolitan republics, and one or two states in central Italy under the rule of Spanish princes) reflected the unitarians' growing awareness that hopes of unity could no longer be entertained. The central problem now was the future of the former Habsburg lands in Italy. The Spanish Bourbons, who had cautiously kept out of the coalition, were to be rewarded by French benevolence towards their family in Italy. The kings of Naples and Sardinia seemed protected by tsar Paul I, who had abandoned the coalition because of his suspicions of Austria and England, but who remained intransigent in his defence of the rights of these two sovereigns.

Austrian hopes of continuing the war were ended by Moreau's victory at Hohenlinden (2 December 1800). The peace of Lunéville (9 February 1801) between France and Austria, at which Cisalpine representatives were spectators, followed the same pattern as Campoformio, but marked Austria's acceptance of French predominance in Italy. The Batavian, Helvetic, Ligurian and Cisalpine republics were recognized, and the Cisalpine republic was strengthened by including within its frontiers the former Venetian territories up to the line of the Adige river (left to Austria in 1797), half the city of Verona and the surrounding area, and Rovigo; already in September 1800 the Cisalpine republic had been given the Piedmontese provinces of the Novarese, irrespective of formal treaty agreements. At Lunéville and the following treaty of Aranjuez between France and Spain (21 March 1801) the Habsburgs of Tuscany and Modena were sacrificed and despatched to Germany in the interests of the Bourbons of Parma: Ferdinand of Parma retained his duchy until his death (1802), while his son Ludovic was given Tuscany with the title of king of Etruria. Alberoni still cast his shadow over central Italy. Spain, in exchange, sold its American possession of Louisiana to France. The Bourbon Ferdinand IV of Naples, who had occupied Rome and had hoped to expand his kingdom at Tuscan expense in the months of political fluidity which preceded Lunéville, was only saved from Bonaparte's vengeance by the intervention of Paul I. Threatened by Murat's army, Ferdinand was forced to sign the treaty of Florence (28 March 1801) by which he renounced his Tuscan garrisons, the state of the Presidi (annexed to Etruria), pledged himself to free all political prisoners and accepted French garrisons along the Abruzzi and Apulia coast until England agreed to peace. The new pope Pius VII (1800–23) – in contrast to his predecessor Pius VI, who had been imprisoned by the Directory–was treated with full respect by Napoleon.

A delicate settlement had thus been reached in 1801. Bonaparte had acted the role of peacemaker, regaining France's 'natural frontiers', but confining French influence beyond these frontiers to the restoration of some of the former revolutionary republics. He had deliberately rejected both the hopes of Italian unitarians and the plan of the moderate Lombard leader Melzi d'Eril for a north Italian state, to be ruled as a constitutional monarchy by the grand-duke of Tuscany, strong enough to remain independent of France and Austria and so help maintain the equilibrium in Europe. Austria, although still in possession of Venice and lands east of the Adige, had lost all influence in Italy, Naples had been curbed and Piedmont militarily occupied (12 April 1801) after Charles Emanuel IV had lost his protector Paul I who had been assassinated on 24 March. The Cisalpine republic, while strategically stronger, was balanced by the new kingdom of Etruria and a friendly pope, with whom Napoleon signed a concordat (15 July 1801). Only England, which had occupied Malta and destroyed the Danish fleet (2 April 1801), remained at war. But by 1802 even England required a breathing-space. Despite concern at Napoleon's assumption of the presidency of the newly created Italian Republic (25 January 1802), England and France signed the peace of Amiens (25 March 1802), which – while ignoring the changes in Italy – tacitly acknowledged France's control of the Continent and England's control of the seas and hence the colonies. Bonaparte could claim to have brought peace to Europe.

If the settlement of Italy had proved the main difficulty, delaying peace with Austria before Lunéville, it was to become one of the major reasons for the renewed outbreak of war between England and France in May 1803. The insertion of the title of 'Italy' in the name of the new republic seemed to portend renewed attempts at expansion and hence disturbances in the peninsula, while the First Consul's assumption of the presidency was a direct denial of the Republic's independence. After Charles Emanuel IV abdicated (4 June 1802) in favour of his brother Victor Emanuel I (1802–21), Napoleon ignored the protests of the tsar Alexander I and annexed Piedmont to France (11 September 1802). The occupation of Parma then followed the death of its duke (October 1802), while Elba and Piombino were annexed. Italy remained at the centre of Napoleon's attention, although he also asserted France's power on its north-east frontiers. Thus French troops continued to occupy the Batavian republic, while in Germany, at the congress of Rastadt (February–March 1803), Napoleon created a clientele of minor states. The purchase of Louisiana was followed by an expedition to San Domingo and the English suspected Napoleon of planning a new attack on Egypt and India. Worried at this redress of the balance in France's favour in so short a space of time (1802–3), concerned to develop their colonial ambitions, the English refused to surrender Malta and declared war (May 1803).

The renewal of the war marked the end of hopes in the Italian republic of a stable and peaceful settlement. Melzi was clear about the need for 'a free Italy, really independent and independent of all' (Zaghi, 162, p. 113). Even

before he became vice-president of the Republic, he had constantly maintained the need to distinguish north Italy's fate from that of France. He had
failed to gain separate diplomatic representation for the Republic. But he
had persisted in his aims, proposing to the semi-official Austrian representative at Milan, baron Moll, a grandiose plan for the creation of a large north
Italian state, stretching from Piedmont and Liguria to Venice and the
Trentino-Southern Tyrol, ruled by the former Tuscan grand-duke and
guaranteed by both Paris and Vienna; Austria would be compensated at
Prussian expense, and Prussia with English Hanover. In this way, not only
would Italian independence be assured, but the new kingdom would form
an element of stability and equilibrium in Europe by acting as a barrier
against French or Austrian expansion. Vienna, in a weak position, seemed
prepared to listen. Napoleon, not surprisingly, was totally hostile and
categorically ordered Melzi not to engage in any further diplomatic
initiatives.

The Italian Republic, in fact, however great the autonomy left to Melzi
over internal affairs, was closely subject to the changing directions of
Napoleon's foreign policy. As an anonymous Brescian diarist had written
on the morrow of its formation at the Lyons assemblies: 'I say nothing
because I understand nothing; while people were saying that the Republic
was independent, I instead see it entirely dependent on France, while its
arbiter is also the arbiter of France' (Zaghi, 162, p. 142).

May 1804 inevitably meant a change in the status of the Italian Republic.
Despite Melzi's delaying tactics, the Republic became the Kingdom of
Italy (19 March 1805). Napoleon's decision to assume the crown himself,
after some hesitation and his brother Joseph's refusal, was an open challenge
to the Austrian emperor Francis, soon to abandon the millennial title of
emperor of the Holy Roman Empire. Napoleon was presenting himself as
heir to Charlemagne, with the right to dispose of Italy, even if he agreed
that the two thrones of France and Italy should be separated under his
successors.

Imperial Italy

The creation of the Kingdom of Italy was the most spectacular, but not the
only, measure which transformed Napoleon's war against England into a
more general war against the third coalition of England, Austria and
Russia. The policy of 'natural frontiers' began to move towards that of the
'Grand Empire' in these years. Italy was the first area to be affected: the
Ligurian republic was induced to vote its annexation by France (25 May
1805); the principate of Piombino was given to Napoleon's sister, Elisa
Baciocchi, and the former republic of Lucca to her husband Felice Baciocchi
as a principate (23 June 1805); the states of Parma, Piacenza and Guastalla,

directly administered from Paris, were placed under the honorary rule of Napoleon's sister, Paolina Borghese (21 July 1805). The first signs of a Napoleonic family empire had been marked out – appropriately in the Bonapartes' country of origin.

Napoleon's crushing victories in the years 1805–7 were to lead to the extension of the 'Grand Empire' to all Europe. It was accompanied by, and closely linked to, the imposition of the Continental System. Napoleon's original plan, after the renewal of war with Britain, had been to revive the former revolutionary attempts to invade England. The 'Army of England' had been assembled at Boulogne at the end of 1803. After the death of the only outstanding French admiral, Latouche-Tréville, the plan had been delayed, but was revived after Spain's entry into the war as France's ally (1804). The Italians, like many nationalities, had contributed their contingent. But inability to break the English hold of the Channel and the final defeat of Trafalgar (21 August 1805) definitively buried the scheme.

The failure of the invasion was to be followed by the attempt at an economic blockade. The Continental Blockade was originally conceived as a development of measures adopted by the Convention in 1793 to protect French industry, particularly textiles, against English competition. It was a retaliation against English naval 'harassment' of the coasts of France and allied countries. After the outbreak of war in 1803 protection was extended beyond France's frontiers along the coasts it controlled: it was imposed on the Batavian republic and north Germany as far as Hanover. It lay behind the annexation of Genoa, a crucial port in the struggle to weaken the English in the Mediterranean and facilitate French exports to Italy; it was extended to the Kingdom of Italy with the prohibition of English imports (27 July 1805); it was the cause of the French occupation of Ancona (1805) and Civitavecchia (1806), when the pope opposed the ban on trade with England.

The military victories of 1805–7 led to the full development of both the Continental System and the 'Grand Empire' scheme. Austria had finally entered the war in summer 1805, after Napoleon's unilateral actions in Italy and his challenge in Germany through his alliances with Bavaria, Württemberg and Baden. The French Grand Army, withdrawn from Boulogne, captured the main Austrian army at Ulm (20 October 1805) and defeated the Russian-Austrian army at Austerlitz (2 December). The following year, after Prussia's incautious entry into the fourth coalition, Frederick the Great's army was cut to pieces at Jena and Auerstädt (14 October 1806). The less decisive victories over Russia at Eylau (8 February 1807) and Friedland (14 June) brought the wars once more to an end. Austria had already been forced to sign the humiliating peace of Pressburg (26 December 1805). Alexander of Russia now made peace and an alliance with France at Tilsit (8 July 1807), by which the two emperors agreed to divide Continental Europe into two spheres of influence.

With Pressburg and Tilsit, Italy declined in importance as Napoleon's attention centred increasingly on Germany. Europe was to be reshaped into a confederation of states tied to France. Italy's function was now to provide territories for France and Napoleon's family; total control was essential in so sensitive an area as the Mediterranean to ensure the functioning of the Continental System. The Austrian emperor was expelled from both Italy and Germany: Venice and the *terraferma* lands ceded at Campoformio and Lunéville were now annexed to the Kingdom of Italy; the Tyrol and Trentino were given to Bavaria, elevated to a kingdom; Austrian Swabia was divided betweenWürttemberg and Baden (treaty of Pressburg). In 1806 the Batavian republic was transformed into the Kingdom of Holland for Napoleon's brother Louis, while Napoleon decreed that the Bourbon dynasty of Naples 'had ceased to exist' and replaced it, with Masséna's army, by his brother Joseph (30 March 1806). Apart from the pope, all the old dynasties had been swept out of the peninsula, and the houses of Savoy and Bourbon Naples only survived through English protection on the islands of Sardinia and Sicily. In Germany, the emperor was deprived of all authority by the creation of a Confederation of the Rhine of 16 princes under Napoleon's presidency.

With Tilsit, it was Prussia's turn to suffer humiliation: its lands west of the Elbe formed the nucleus of the new kingdom of Westphalia under Jerome Bonaparte; its Polish territories were formed into a grand-duchy of Warsaw under the faithful elector of Saxony; Alexander of Russia was offered visions of expansion into the Baltic and Turkish empires.

The final changes in Italy's frontiers in 1808–10 and the annexation of a large part of the peninsula to France were the direct consequences of the Continental Blockade. Until 1806 Napoleon had imposed protectionist measures, but had been open to the protests of French manufacturers that the use of the blockade as a weapon of war, imposed upon neutral countries, would damage French interests. With the conquests of 1806–7 it seemed possible to seal off the Continent from British ships. In the Berlin decree of November 1806 Napoleon declared the British Isles 'in a state of blockade' and ordered the seizure of all British and colonial goods. Austria and Russia gave their support after Tilsit. As the British reacted with threats against neutral countries (November–December 1807), Napoleon replied with the decrees of Fontainebleau and Milan (13 October, 23 November, 17 December 1807), imposing the seizure of all neutral ships obeying the British orders. For Napoleon the crucial aim now was to seal off the entire Continent to all British trade, and above all to stamp out contraband. The system aroused immediate and increasing protests and opposition; already in 1810 Napoleon granted special licences to Frenchmen to trade with

Britain; in the following years the breakdown and evasion of the blockade became increasingly clear. But by then, Napoleon, in his desperate attempts to make the blockade effective through direct control, had remodelled Italy and north Germany and sparked off the wars which were to lead to his downfall.

The invasion and division of Portugal (1807), followed by the enforced substitution of Charles IV of Spain by Joseph Bonaparte at Bayonne (May 1808), were the immediate results of the attempts to extend direct French control over the Iberian peninsula. Their repercussions were felt in Italy: at Naples Joseph, against his own wishes, was replaced as king by Napoleon's brother-in-law Gioacchino Murat. In central Italy Napoleon extended the blockade to the Papal States (ignoring Pius VII's assertions of his neutrality) with Miollis' occupation of Rome, Lazio and Umbria (2 February 1808), and then the military occupation and annexation by the Kingdom of Italy of the Papal Marches (2 April 1808). In Tuscany, where smuggling had proved rife, Leghorn and Pisa were first occupied and then the whole of the Kingdom of Etruria was annexed to the French empire (December 1807), together with Parma and Piacenza (May 1808). The following year, after the defeat of Austria in the fifth coalition at Wagram (6 July 1809), Dalmatia, and Istria and part of Carniola and Carinthia were transformed into the Illyrian provinces under French administration, while the Trentino and south Tyrol, where Bavaria had proved incapable of suppressing an anti-French revolt, were ceded to the Kingdom of Italy (treaty of Schönbrunn, 14 October 1809). The annexation by France of what was left of the Papal States (17 May 1809) was accompanied by that of Louis Bonaparte's Kingdom of Holland, the German Hanseatic cities and Oldenburg and the Swiss Valais canton (1810). The Grand Empire had been created, and through its incorporation of the greater part of Europe was intended to maintain the Continental System.

This Grand Empire, divided into 130 departments, stretched from Hamburg to Rome. Around its frontiers had been created a host of client states, which included the kingdoms, principates and duchies assigned to the Bonaparte family and the more successful generals and civil servants, the new feudatories of the empire. The entire complex was subject to the direct control or heavy pressures and interference of the emperor Napoleon. The populations of both empire and vassal states were forced to contribute money and soldiers to maintain the impetus of France's wars. Their rulers, often only so in name – like Elisa Bonaparte, grand duchess of Tuscany – were subjected to the rationalizing zeal and administrative uniformity imposed by Napoleon.

Within this empire Italy was assigned a formally important role. Napoleon's son by his second wife Maria Luisa of Austria was given the title of king of Rome (1811). Rome was to represent the second capital of the empire, while the other major cities – Milan under Napoleon's step-son Eugene Beauharnais, Naples under his brother-in-law Gioacchino Murat, Florence under his sister Elisa, Turin under his sister Paolina – were elevated to imitations of the petty royal courts of the eighteenth century. But beneath the trappings of this new Carolingian empire, Italy was totally subordinated to the emperor's policies, to his wars and his economic blockade. Imperial duchies with state endowments for French generals and ministers were carved out of the incomes of the kingdoms of Italy and Naples. French prefects ruled directly over Piedmont, the entire Tyrrhenian coast to further south than Rome, and much of central Italy. Napoleon personally controlled the details of the administration of the Kingdom of Italy. Only Murat at Naples was, to a limited degree, able to take decisions independently. But both he and Beauharnais were swept up in Napoleon's final wars in Germany and Russia. Italy, like Holland, Switzerland and the other frontier areas, was subjected to the full impact of Napoleonic rationalization and social conservatism.

The Italian Republic

Northern Italy, reoccupied after Marengo, was the region most immediately affected by the new climate that prevailed in France. Lombardy, in particular, which had provided the field for Napoleon's first military victories and administrative experiments, was to find itself closely tied to the rhythm of political changes and legislative transformations imposed by Napoleon during his years as First Consul (1800–4).

Brumaire had marked the end of Jacobin hopes; Lunéville signified the defeat of unitarian aspirations. Bonaparte had decreed the end of the Revolution. Factions and parties were to be banned; reconciliation and unanimity, respect of property, persons and religion were to be the keynotes of the new regime and the basis of Napoleonic legislation. The aging Jacobin Ranza, imprisoned after Brumaire, commented bitterly on the regressive character of the new French constitution of 1799, with its exclusion of popular control and restrictions on the liberty of the press, public assemblies and religion: 'this complex of aristocracy and oligarchy, this ladder to monarchism' (Cantimori and De Felice, 127, p. 526). The moderate Ferdinando Marescalchi, Cisalpine representative at Paris, noted after Bonaparte's bloody purge of the French Jacobins in 1801: 'There is absolutely no toleration anymore of anything that implies even the shadow of revolution' (Roberti, 168, vol. 1, p. 244). Ferdinand of Naples' ambassador at Paris, marquis del Gallo, wrote to Acton in indignation ill-becoming a turncoat who was soon to join the Napoleonic settlement as Neapolitan foreign minister:

These French personages, who today are moderate and yesterday were Jacobin;
who earlier preached independence and today preach subordination; who
plotted revolutions before and now suppress them; they, I say, are men who act
according to circumstance rather than to character.   (Croce, 158, pp. 417–18)

The new structure of society, which Napoleon imposed on and consolidated in France, admitted of no opposition. The Jacobins had been
proscribed; liberal constitutionalists such as Madame de Staël and Benjamin
Constant, who looked to a legislative assembly with effective control, were
exiled or silenced; Bourbon royalists were terrorized by the execution of the
duc d'Enghien. Obedience was the prerequisite of service in the Napoleonic
state and Fouché's police ministry kept close check on potential rebels. But
excluding these fringe oppositions, service to Napoleon and the state was
encouraged. Moderate republicans and conservative royalists, former
Jacobins and nobles of ancient lineage merged in the *amalgame* which
Napoleon transferred from the mass armies of the Revolution (where the
term was first used in 1793) to civil society. Authority and equality before
the law, an orderly social hierarchy and destruction of privilege, consecration of religion and property and assurance of adequate food supplies, were
the keystoncs of Napoleon's policy. In these fruitful years of peace (1800–3),
Napoleon hastened through major legislative measures and settlements –
bank of France, civil code, *lycée*, concordat – which were aimed at enshrining
many of the conquests of the Revolution in a conservative mould. Inevitably, Napoleon's settlement in northern Italy closely resembled that in
France.

The creation of the republic

Whatever the antipathy towards the Cisalpine republic in 1799, the thirteen
months of Austrian financial exactions, degradations, persecutions and
threats to revoke the sales of the *biens nationaux* had prepared the ground
for the French return. Napoleon remained the hero of the battle of Lodi,
the liberator of Italy, untainted by the anarchy and speculation of the
Jacobin years. Hence the guarantee of peace and security that he seemed to
offer was welcomed.

The second Cisalpine republic was intended by Napoleon to assume a
moderate political physiognomy, such as now existed in France. The
Extraordinary Government Commission and Consultative Assembly were
filled with personalities who had played a moderate part in, or had withdrawn from, the first Cisalpine republic. The anticlerical laws of the first
Cisalpine republic were immediately cancelled and the archbishop, who had
fled from Milan, was welcomed back. But the weaknesses of the first
republic soon re-emerged, and with them discontent and criticisms. The

abuses and enormous exactions of French military occupation were repeated, the republic's finances lapsed into a state of chaos as the government found itself unable to impose its authority on the local administrations. Bologna refused to pay taxes to Milan and began to re-form its national guard. Each city acted as if it were the centre of a small independent republic. The exiles of 1799, including many Jacobins, returned and gained posts in the local municipalities; the triumvirs at the head of the Cisalpine republic, Visconti, Sommariva and Ruga, used their positions for their own private profit: '[a] mockery of proconsular thieves, petulant citizens, timorous magistrates', was Foscolo's disgusted comment (Roberti, 168, vol. 1, p. 60). Irrespective of the international situation (which contributed to the uncertainty before Lunéville), a reorganization of the republic was essential to achieve stability and win acceptance for a permanent settlement.

The discussions over a new constitution were dragged on by Napoleon during 1801 until the peace of Lunéville and the military occupation of Piedmont ensured that the Cisalpine republic would remain independent. Although the official leaders of the republic, such as Marescalchi and Aldini, were formally consulted, Napoleon summoned Melzi d'Eril from his voluntary exile in Spain to act as his collaborator in the structuring of the new state. Francesco Melzi d'Eril had been a prominent figure among the reforming nobles close to Verri before the Revolution and for this reason had been sent by the city of Milan to welcome Bonaparte in 1796. Deeply hostile to the Jacobins, he had emerged as leader of the 'landowners', author of a pamphlet demonstrating the natural right of property. Untainted by involvement in the two Cisalpine republics through his repeated withdrawals from political life, valued by Napoleon for his diplomatic skill after his participation in the Rastadt negotiations of 1798, but above all for his belief in order, tranquillity, and rational controlled reform, Melzi expressed the new moderate programme of the Italian Republic. Melzi had absorbed two distinct lessons from the experience of the Jacobin years: belief in the need for independence and fear of the Jacobins.

His ideal was the creation of a strong independent north Italian state, preferably under a monarch, but with an effective constitution based on property. The new state was to acquire solidity and a national identity by efficient administration, by winning the support of national 'sentiment' and by cautious territorial expansion to achieve more homogeneous frontiers:

No, we are not yet a people; and we must become one and form ourselves into a Nation, strong through unity, happy through wisdom, independent through true national sentiment. We have no ordered government; and that too we must create. We have no organized administration; and we must organize it. (Melzi d'Eril, 165, vol. 1, p. 45)

The dangers represented by Jacobins and republican unitarians were to be avoided by gaining the collaboration of the landowners, by prudent reforms and by the achievement of a European peace which would recognize the new frontiers of France and so prevent any further revolutionary upheavals. Internal and international proposals thus closely intertwined in a moderate vision, which strongly resembled that of Madame de Staël and the French liberals, but which easily slid – through fear of popular 'anarchy' – into a social conservatism neglectful of the achievements of the revolution.

The creation and life of the Italian Republic could be described, without excessive simplification, as the history of Melzi's mainly unsuccessful attempts to impose this programme on Bonaparte. Melzi was unsuccessful because he was dependent on Napoleon for the restoration of internal order and on a powerful France for the achievement of independence. Internally and internationally the Italian Republic was thus tied to France and Melzi was forced to accept Bonaparte's decisions. But although he failed to achieve his programme, Melzi was given enough independence and support by Napoleon to weld together the structure of a unified north Italian state.

The weakness of Melzi's position was already revealed in the genesis of the new Republic. After tortuous discussions of the proposed constitution, on whose moderate character all parties agreed, Bonaparte unexpectedly called an assembly of notables to Lyons (January 1802), both to test the nature and strength of Italian support and to legitimize the formation of a new allied state in the eyes of Europe by the apparent convocation of a constituent assembly. As Talleyrand noted:

> The coincidence of the meeting of the powers at Amiens and of the friendly nations at Lyons will, by their contrasting impression, heighten the grandeur of the rule of the First Consul, whose single-minded purpose it is to create the federative system of France at the same time as reestablishing the system of public law in Europe. (Pingaud, 166, vol. 1, p. 295)

Melzi agreed with Napoleon on the need to manipulate the selection of candidates. Roederer, who drafted the constitution (having participated in the 1798 'correction' of the Cisalpine constitution) proposed the division of electors into professions: ecclesiastics, judges, merchants, intellectuals, departmental and municipal representatives, army and national guard officers, the members of the existing councils of the second Cisalpine republic, as well as a large contingent of local notables. The high proportion of government nominees (notables and officers), the method by which the leaders of certain categories selected their representatives (bishops, university professors and learned societies, local administrators, tribunals, etc.), the explicit choice of the notables on the basis of their 'morality' and landed holdings, the disqualification of the election of undesired deputies (such as the poet Pindemonte, suspected of involvement in a plot against Napoleon), all these ensured the presence of a preponderantly moderate body. But the very assembling of so many distinguished figures also conveyed the impression of a 'national' gathering.

These much-vaunted Assemblies of Lyons revealed themselves a parody of a constituent assembly. The agenda and presidents of the sessions were imposed on the deputies, discussions were cut short, the members were divided into regional groups voting separately, and open pressure was used to achieve the creation of the Republic, Roederer's constitution and the final election of Napoleon himself as Head of State. In like manner, the ecclesiastics present at Lyon were bludgeoned into accepting Bonaparte's 'organic law of the Italian clergy', Catholicism was recognized as the religion of the state (although private worship remained free for other religions) but the nomination of bishops and control of the Church remained firmly in temporal hands. Bonaparte's only concession to the bewildered and muted opposition in the assembly was to agree to the name of 'Italian' for the Republic.

A Republic had thus been created, tied to France in the person of its president, committed to pay for French troops, obliged to abandon earlier revolutionary anti-ecclesiastical measures. This Republic was subjected to a heavily moderate constitution, weighted towards the landowners, but with a complicated structure which soon appeared to check the authority of the executive. As negative were the territorial frontiers of the Republic: virtually the same as those of the Cisalpine republic, they remained indefensible and facilitated contraband. Napoleon's refusal to give the former duchy of Parma to the Republic cut its territories into two, linked by a narrow corridor of 30 kilometres between Legnano and Guastalla. Despite this clear defeat of his hopes, Melzi accepted his appointment as vice-president of the Italian Republic, regarding its weakness, its republican constitution and its alignment with France as lesser evils, which still left open the possibility of creating an independent moderate state.

Melzi and the republic

Melzi's immediate and constant aim was to create a state and a 'nation' out of the upheavals of the previous years. He was clear about the method required to achieve this end: the selection of a strong, honest body of functionaries, chosen for their 'morality' and social standing, and the creation of an efficient centralized administration. The example offered by the administrators and legislators would have an immediate and deep effect on the conduct of the people, as Melzi explained to the Legislature:

> On that day in which we were turned into a people, obliged to rule and govern itself, we had neither the practical ideas, nor the customs and habits of a people, nor that national sentiment which is the first element of the strength and greatness of a nation. . . . It is precisely this state of affairs which, while giving

the first magistrates an immense influence of opinion over the people, imposes on them great and extraordinary duties, because it makes them the guiding light of the people's first steps on their new path. . . . The magistrates' words in assemblies form the comment which normally determine the people's judgement about the laws that must govern them; and even their private speeches act as that prism through which the people see and form their opinion about matters. (Melzi d'Eril, 165, vol. 2, p. 339)

The difficulties, as Melzi constantly complained in his letters to Napoleon and the Republic's ambassador at Paris, Marescalchi, were infinite. The second Cisalpine republic was an 'epoch in which faction took off its mask and plundered all gentlemen' (Roberti, 168, vol. 1, pp. 81–2). In contrast to France, it proved almost impossible to persuade the landowners to accept appointment as prefects and move away from their homes to a different department. At the lower level, the bureaucracy had been inflated by the employment of exiles: a full purge was carried out in the provinces, especially of secularized priests, which tended to leave in office the employees of the pre-revolutionary regimes; at Milan Prina, the new minister of finances, dismissed 133 employees in one day.

The difficulties of replacing and reducing the number of personnel were accentuated by Melzi's almost obsessive hatred of the Jacobins and unitarians. Although constantly protesting his impartiality and exclusive concern for honesty and his preoccupation to replace parties and factions by the new solidarity of the *amalgame*, Melzi discriminated constantly against the patriots, and tended to favour the landowners and pre-revolutionary public servants. Only one patriot, Somenzari, was nominated as prefect; apart from two professional men, all the others were large landowners. The appointment as a minister of Vismara, a republican and ex-priest, was an exception which Melzi felt the need to justify. Most of the other ministers, such as Spannocchi, Prina and Bovara had served the pre-revolutionary states, or – like Marescalchi – had assumed very moderate positions during the Cisalpine republics. Some few patriots and even Jacobins were accepted, but almost on trial: Gioia was employed as official writer, Custodi as publisher, Compagnoni in the legislative department, even Salvador as a spy; Foscolo was recommended for the diplomatic service. In the army, where democratic feeling had been more widespread, it was necessary to give official posts to La Hoz's colleagues, generals Pino and Lechi. But the great majority of those compromised by the past were dismissed or kept out of office.

As in France, the powers of the police department were increased: arrests were made on suspicion, passports were only gained with difficulty. Melzi was violently opposed to giving the Venetian exiles citizenship of the republic, as 'the greatest number of ex-Venetians is in good part un-adulterated dregs' (Roberti, 168, vol. 1, p. 341). He proposed a prison camp and deportation for the political refugees, and an agreement with Austria and Tuscany to ensure throughout Italy the impotence of the former Jacobins and unitarians. His sectarianism was so acute that Napoleon objected. Its effects were to accentuate the social conservatism of the Republic and to drive the opposition into open rebellion at Bologna in July 1802. The insurrection, which owed much to municipal resentment against Milan and the French dissolution of the local national guard, took on social tones, with attacks on grain speculators; led by a secret society of the *stilettanti* ('stiletto-holders'), it provided the occasion for the last Jacobin rising, involving both Italian and French exiles. Its suppression by French troops marked the effective end of the Society of Rays and of a Jacobin opposition, despite Melzi's tendency to see Jacobins behind every murmur of discontent.

The creation of an efficient structure of the state, Melzi was convinced in true Enlightened manner, was the touchstone to resolve past evils and forge a national edifice. The difficulty, apart from lack of personnel, was Melzi's ultimate dependence on Napoleon. The First Consul, although insisting on almost daily reports, rarely interfered in matters of administration, and indeed gave Melzi far greater autonomy than his successor Eugene Beauharnais or any of the later nominees in Italy, except Murat. In the early years Napoleon gave Melzi full support against the intrigues of Sommariva and Aldini, and tried to attenuate the animosity between his military commander in the Republic, Murat, and Melzi. But the vice-president inherited the constitution imposed by Napoleon, and was forced to accept an understanding with the Church which went against the josephine tradition.

The constitution, modelled on French experience, was constantly criticized by Melzi. It was a deeply conservative document, although Melzi accused it of being too liberal and democratic. The electoral body was divided – according to Bonaparte's belief society was composed of these three significant sectors – into colleges of landowners, merchants and intellectuals, with weighting in favour of the landowners. The legislature, only half of whose 75 members were elected from the colleges, had extremely limited powers and in practice was only able to reject, and not to amend, the government's proposals. The president (or vice-president), with the assistance of a small consultative assembly of state, was responsible for initiating all laws and nominating the council of ministers. A consultative legislative council of 10 was meant to link the executive with the legislature. A censor controlled the elections of the colleges and senior magistrates.

In practical terms, Melzi – always deeply respectful of the formal procedures of the law – objected to the criticism of an opposition to his proposals, which he ascribed (as always, touchy and susceptible) to personal animosity: 'There is not even a dog here who would support me if I moved fractionally outside the established forms: consultative assembly, council, legislature, tribunals have not been made by me, as they well realize' (Roberti, 168, vol. 1, p. 106, n. 3). As tension increased, Napoleon sent a senior French official, Jacob, to Milan to investigate. Jacob agreed that the personal opposition of Aldini and Cicognara in the council and the revival of the old Cisalpine opposition in the legislature hampered the government. But he criticized Melzi for his rigidity and inability to delegate.

Despite this nervous reaction to all criticism, Melzi went far towards creating an orderly and uniformly organized state. He was torn between his faith in efficiency – which made him prefer the local departmental administrators of Milan to those of the other regions, against Napoleon's insistence on an accurate regional distribution of posts – and his desire to involve as broad a segment as possible of the respectable landowners. The local administrative laws of 1802 and 1804, based on the French example, created a uniform hierarchy of communes, districts and departments, each of which possessed a permanent executive and a consultative council responsible for the distribution of taxes. But the councils only met twice yearly, and the structure proved too complicated and costly. Typical of the landowners' attitude was the bitter comment by Lodovico Vernazze from Ferrara that proprietors felt obliged to attend these local assemblies to please the prefect. Melzi complained: 'To cure a people of laziness and guide it step by step towards a larger exercise of its powers, creating new habits and more noble attitudes is a superhuman task' (Zaghi, 162, p. 186).

Melzi's reforms, in fact, were more effective at the central level. Crime and brigandage, which were rampant during the second Cisalpine republic, were ruthlessly suppressed by the use of special tribunals and the creation of the *gendarmeria*. The preparation of legal codes, already begun under the second Cisalpine republic, was pushed forward by Spannocchi. An Italian civil code, for Melzi, was evidence of the individuality and separateness of the Italian Republic from the French, and two drafts had been prepared before the delays of Spannocchi's successor Luosi led to the imposition of the French civil code (1805). The codes of civil and penal procedure and the penal code, well advanced by the end of the Republic, met the same fate through delays. But by then the groundwork had been completed and a uniform judicial structure was functioning, no longer conditioned by the tangle of past laws and precedents. Abolition of privilege and equality before the law, the conquests of the Revolution, formed an integral part of the conception of the new state. The Legion of Honour, introduced into the Italian Republic, conferred personal and not hereditary titles.

Civil equality was employed to the advantage of the landowners. Already in 1803 allodial (in distinction to feudal) lands of nobles that had been appropriated by the state or the local commune during the revolutionary period were restored to their former owners. The sale of the remaining *biens nationaux* was renewed, with little attempt to assist smallholders, but with the explicit intention of reducing the public debt by sales to the wealthy owners who had been subjected to forced loans during the Jacobin years. There was a close identity between the members of the electoral colleges of 1804, all local notables, and the major purchasers of the 'national properties'. Any uncertainty about future rights of possession was removed with the papacy's formal recognition of all sales in the Concordat (1803).

The public debt was consolidated (March 1803), so restoring confidence in the state's credit, although no Italian state introduced a national bank, as had Napoleon in France. Above all, the taxation system was drastically recast, simplified and modernized by Prina. Although the land-tax remained heavy, particularly on smallholders, the customs tariffs were designed to encourage the export of agricultural produce and the import of manufactures. Domestic manufacturing, in fact, was neglected, and with the rise in price of grains and rice during these years of peace, the large landowners could express their satisfaction with the Republic. Melzi, indeed, wished to go further, and allow totally free export of grains. He was only blocked by Napoleon, too realistic to risk the dangers of popular risings for abstract physiocratic ideals:

> Of the thousand questions which divide the proletarian and the proprietor in opinion and interest, the price of grains is that which arouses the greatest opposition of interests. It is also the issue, perhaps the only one, in which the government must always favour the proletarians against the proprietors · if this is not done, there is tyranny by the proprietors and revolt by the people. (Melzi d'Eril, 165, vol. 2, p. 85)

By the time Napoleon decreed the end of the Italian Republic, Melzi had succeeded in creating a modern and reasonably efficient structure of the state, based on the interests of the landed proprietors. If his achievements stopped there, this was due to Napoleon's direct intervention and to public apathy. The most clamorous failures came with Melzi's attempts to assure the long-term independence of the Republic, whether internationally or against the Church. A Lombard reformer by upbringing and belief, Melzi had bitterly opposed Napoleon's settlement with the Church. In 1802 he had deliberately created a ministry of religion under the Jansenist, regalist Bovara. State control of education and charity was asserted, along with strict regulation of mendicancy. When Napoleon finally published his Concordat with Pius VII (26 January 1804), it followed the lines of the French Concordat: re-establishment of the authority of bishops over parish priests and of the Catholic religion in the Republic, in return for papal recognition of the loss of the Legations, state control over the nomination of bishops and the sales of ecclesiastical lands. Unable to prevent the Concordat, Melzi, of his own initiative, immediately published an executive decree reaffirming the Republic's laws over religious matters. His action achieved a stalemate, partially blocking the execution of the Concordat, at least until he fell from power.

Melzi had retained a certain degree of autonomy over the Concordat, because he was supported by the leading ministers in the Republic on an issue which could be regarded as falling strictly within the internal competence of the state. He failed totally in his attempts to gain diplomatic independence and expand the republic's frontiers. Britain, Russia and Denmark refused to recognize the Italian Republic. But of deeper import was Napoleon's refusal to allow the Republic to exchange diplomatic representatives with other states. French diplomats acted on behalf of the Republic and all decisions on international matters were taken by Napoleon at Paris. The full implications of this dependence were displayed when the Italian Republic found itself involved in the war against Britain in 1803 and obliged to send a contingent of soldiers and ships for the proposed invasion.

By then it was clear that Napoleon was hostile to expanding the Republic's frontiers, despite the aspirations and even official approaches made over annexation by the Republic of the duchy of Parma, the Ligurian and Lucca republics, the Ticino and Trentino. Melzi's main hope lay eastwards, in the former Venetian lands, where Austrian military rule, followed by the highly centralized administration of the Habsburg empire, had aroused widespread discontent. Joseph de Maistre, passing through Venice on his way to Russia as ambassador of the king of Sardinia, had noted: 'The Austrians are defeated and do not know how to recover. When will they understand that, when one acquires new subjects, the only thing to change is the title of the edicts?' (Pingaud, 166, vol. 2, p. 76). A short-sighted statement in view of the changes occurring contemporaneously in French-dominated Europe, but revealing of the dangers to Austrian-Italo-French relations of the expansionist pressures (shared by Murat) at Milan. But these ambitions were only to be partly fulfilled at Pressburg.

Independence and the creation of a national consciousness lay behind Melzi's determined efforts to create an army. Lack of homogeneity and of professional instruction characterized the army which had emerged from the Italic Legion. Even worse was the general contempt for the military qualities of Italians, expressed, for example, by the Cisalpine general Milossewitz at the Lyons assembly in his misquoted Tacitean epigram 'Ignavis et imbellis [sic] manet squalor' ('Dirt sticks to the cowardly and unwarlike'). Against enormous difficulties, desertions, conscript rebellions, and the hostility of the population and clergy (who hid the birth registers), a small Italian Legion was formed of deserters and vagabonds, followed by a conscript army of over 20 000 during the war against England. The significance of this achievement was noted by contemporaries: it broke down local municipal spirit, enabled the new state to resist Austrian attack –

in 1805 as later in 1814 – and encouraged patriotism to the Italian flag. Military valour – not on an individual basis, but with the modern techniques of the revolutionary armies – was seen, both then and later, as the essential corollary for independence. The young officer Ermelao Federigo, enrolled in the Grand Army at Boulogne in 1804, expressed this new pride succinctly:

> I never disapprove of those means which can help to make Italians good soldiers. I believe that military training must be the main aim of every good Italian. . . . What does it matter if one serves the ambition of this man or that? The principal task must be to learn warfare, which is the sole profession that can make us free . . . I see the matter in this way. I serve my patria when I learn to be a soldier, and even if I served the Turk it would be the same. Our Republic will certainly gain more reputation and glory from its few soldiers than from all the sessions and laws which the legislature might pass. We are still too young to think of liberty. Let us think of being soldiers, and when we have a hundred thousand bayonets, then we can talk. Meanwhile, let us thank heaven that they have not cut off our only means of being free at a future date, that is by being soldiers. (Federigo, 173, pp. 17–18)

But it was precisely this close association between military capacity and the desire for political independence that worried Napoleon. He took care to divide the Italian corps among his armies and send them to garrison or fight in distant areas – as he did with the Polish volunteers. In the longer term, over the entire period of Napoleonic domination, Melzi's hopes of arousing patriotism by military experience proved well-founded. But the Italian army proved of little immediate use to gain independence for the Republic. It constituted the focal point of patriotic aspirations, the haven for small secret urban conventicles, drawn together by a common desire for independence and hence, usually, muted hostility to the French. Murat, always worried at symptoms of opposition, wrote anxiously to Napoleon:

> The great majority of those one might call Italian patriots want the independence of all Italy and, without considering their present inability to preserve and defend liberty, they simply regard the French on their territory with displeasure. This party is the more dangerous because it is the party of all the Italian military, and it is on the increase. (Pingaud, 167, pp. 192–3)

But, in reality, the danger was slight, as few, after the Bologna rising, were prepared to take action. There existed, as Melzi noted, 'a decided preference for a different order of affairs, extremely vaguely conceived, but still desired by the majority, which just cannot understand what is a nation, what is the price of independence, and which is anything but willing to give a penny to achieve it' (Pingaud, 166, vol. 2, p. 387, n. 1). Far more general was the sense of indifference, mixed with antipathy. If the landowners reluctantly collaborated with Melzi, and a new class of functionaries slowly emerged, the vast majority of the population, whether peasant, urban populace or bourgeois, resented the financial and military burdens, but passively accepted the arduous construction of a new state.

The Grand Empire

The independence enjoyed by Melzi in the Italian Republic was not conceded by Napoleon to any other Italian state or department and was only partially seized by Murat at Naples in the final years of Bonaparte's domination. With the transformation of the Italian Republic into the Kingdom of Italy (1805), control over Italy was exercised in a direct and often brutal manner, as over the other peripheral areas of the Grand Empire. Napoleon's viceroy at Milan, Eugene de Beauharnais (1805–14), was warned to give priority to French interests:

> Italy must not make calculations separate from the prosperity of France . . . it must blend its interests with those of France: above all, it must take care not to give France an interest in annexing it; because, if France had such an interest, who could prevent it? So take as your motto: France before all. (Zaghi, 162, p. 469)

Maria Luisa of Etruria was abruptly removed for failing to enforce the Continental Blockade. Pius VII was imprisoned. Murat was threatened with the deposition imposed on Louis Bonaparte in Holland. The regions annexed to France – Piedmont, the Tyrrhenian coast, Parma, Umbria and Lazio – were ruled from Paris as integral parts of the empire, subject to its laws. The Tuscan prefects corresponded directly with Paris. The Kingdom of Italy was equally subordinate, with Aldini following the emperor on his continuous itineraries across Europe to obtain his decision on even minor matters of administration. The reforms and restructuring in Italy – as in the Low Countries, Germany or Switzerland – were thus direct emanations of Napoleon's will, although no single Italian state was subjected so systematically to the entire range of Napoleonic reform as the 'model' Kingdom of Westphalia.

Napoleon's belief in an integrated, centralized and uniform empire was reflected in his insistence that French diplomats represent the satellite states, in order (in Talleyrand's words) to 'sanction in the opinion of Europe the establishment of the great federation' (Rambaud, 181, p. 480). But even more revealing was Napoleon's employment of senior administrators and civil servants successively in the various parts of the empire, in a manner strikingly reminiscent of that of the eighteenth-century Habsburg emperors. Gioacchino Murat alternated as soldier and administrator in the Italian Republic, Germany (where he became ruler of the duchy of Berg) and Spain, before receiving the kingdom of Naples; Roederer, constitutional and financial expert, was minister successively in Switzerland, Holland,

Naples and Berg; Saliceti was minister at Lucca, Genoa and finally Naples; general Menou was administrator of Piedmont and then Tuscany. This despatch of administrators from state to state was almost certainly most common among Frenchmen. But Cesare Balbo's youthful career in these years was certainly not unique: acting as Menou's secretary general in Tuscany in 1808, and secretary to Miollis' consultative body at Rome in 1809, he was appointed auditor of the Paris consultative assembly in 1811, to be sent soon after to the Illyrian provinces.

Napoleon's conviction that, ultimately, what was French and had worked in France was valid everywhere, irrespective of local conditions, was not always shared by the rulers and administrators of the satellite states. An undercurrent of tension accompanied the close collaboration between Paris and the regional capitals. At a technical level, a civil servant like Melchiorre Gioia frequently sought advice about the new and rapidly developing statistical methods. But at the political level Beauharnais and Murat – like Louis of Holland and Jerome of Westphalia – tried to moderate Napoleon's insatiable demands for money and troops, while Elisa in Tuscany, Joseph Bonaparte at Naples and even Aldini in the Kingdom of Italy were reluctant to apply Napoleon's Concordat. The administrators, whatever their nationality, were strongly aware of local conditions and hesitated to enforce the French system in too rigid a manner. The Tuscan Junta in 1808 felt the need

> to study with care not only the localities, but also the system of the old administration of this country, in order to determine with precision the analogies or differences that might exist among them, and utilize this parallel to introduce the legislation of the Empire with greater ease, simplicity and smoothness. (Catoni, 177, p. 19)

The introduction of the French penal code, with its death penalty, was much resented in Tuscany and the Kingdom of Italy.

This underlying conflict between Napoleon's rigidly centralizing instructions, which subordinated all local requirements to France's demands, and the instinctively 'autonomistic' reaction of the satellite states, became acute by 1810–11 as Napoleon indulged in an increasingly feudal and hierarchical vision of the Grand Empire and as the negative consequences of the Continental Blockade and the wars began to be felt. But if this was the moment when Murat's relations with the emperor reached a point of crisis, they were also the years when the major reforms were imposed in almost uniform manner on Italy.

About the need for, and the broad lines of these reforms, there was little disagreement among the Napoleonic ruling class in Italy. The states had to be modernized in their structures by those who were enlightened enough to judge what constituted the 'happiness of the people'. The earlier faith in democratic processes of government had definitely disappeared. Two active participants of the 'Jacobin' years, now both Napoleonic bureaucrats, the Neapolitan Vincenzo Cuoco and the north Italian Melchiorre Gioia, could justify absolutism through its necessity. Consultation of responsible elements was to be encouraged, but not elective representation. 'It is not the authority of the legislature that I want, but its opinion', Napoleon told Beauharnais in 1805 (Roberti, 168, vol. 1, p. 302 n.). The powers of this moderate body were drastically restricted, and at the first sign of opposition it was suspended:

> A prince must never suffer the spirit of cabals and factions to triumph over his authority, or allow a miserable spirit of flightiness and opposition to discredit his prime authority, foundation of the social order, executor of the civil code, and true source of all the happiness of peoples. (Roberti, 168, vol. 1, p. 296 n.)

The constitutions confirmed this virtual return to despotic authority. The 1805 constitution of the Kingdom of Italy explicitly followed the French constitution; the 1808 Bayonne statute for Naples (which was never applied) was a replica of the statute about to be issued for Spain and, like the West-phalia constitution of 1807 and that of the Kingdom of Italy, severely limited the electoral powers of the colleges, while giving modest encourage-ment to their activities at the local departmental level.

The reforms were intended to centralize and render more efficient the individual states. The rationalization of the central administration was accompanied by the creation of an ordered structure of departments, districts and communes with nominated officials and consultative councils. Internal customs barriers, where still existent, were abolished and frontier customs unified. Great emphasis was placed on the construction of roads, canals and bridges, of which the Simplon pass remains the greatest legacy. Unified systems of weights, measures and moneys were introduced. The taxation system was reordered, simplified and carefully controlled to ensure the reduction of government expenditure and an increasing yield. The public debt was consolidated in each state and virtually extinguished by 1814 in Tuscany and Naples by the sale of ecclesiastical lands.

The French civil, penal and commercial codes were introduced. The civil code, in particular, with its insistence on equality before the law, civil marriage, secular education, abolition of privileges, primogenitures and entails, marked – with the granting of civil rights for Jews and religious toleration – the definitive break with the *ancien régime*. Uniform schemes were drawn up for public health and the provision of hospitals and charity at the local level, but under central control. Education was reorganized, but typically the greatest attention was paid to the higher levels and more resplendent initiatives, such as the Bologna National Institute or the agrarian academies. An official culture was encouraged (like the officially sponsored freemasonry and even official Jansenism), with government patronage and propagandists, but carefully delineated boundaries. These years witnessed the final flowering of the literary encomium, the counterpart to censorship. As Napoleon instructed Beauharnais: 'I want you wholly to suppress the censorship of books, the country already has a narrow enough spirit without restricting it further. Naturally the publication of all works contrary to the government will be stopped' (Roberti, 168, vol. I, p. 381 n.).

Reading the collections of decrees and laws issued in these years creates the impression of a total abolition of the past and the writing of a new page in the history of the Italian peninsula. But too little is still known about the effectiveness and consequences of this flood of legislation, and all assessments must remain approximate. It is fairly clear that the reforms were, in general, more effective at the central than at the local level; and that the longer the period of French rule the deeper the mark it left: the Piedmontese departments were far more deeply transformed than those of Umbria and Lazio, and the kingdom of Naples than the Trentino. It is also clear that, in contrast to the period of Enlightened despotism, when the reforms were often blocked or sabotaged by the hostility of the propertied classes, the decade 1805–14 witnessed the collaboration of these same groups. Napoleonic rule reinforced their social position, while at the same time destroying feudal privileges.

It is probable that the Achilles' heel of Napoleonic administration in Italy was the inadequate preparation of the personnel and the reluctant participation at the local level. The great statistical enquiries carried out after 1810, although more accurate than previous surveys, convey a misleading impression of precision and efficiency, belied by the occasional glimpses we can catch of local life. The arbitrary method of dividing the demesnes in Calabria, the failure to create the local committees for hospitals and charity in the department of Ombrone (Siena) despite imperial decrees, the high degree of communal indebtedness in the Trentino with the consequent inability to fix communal budgets according to the laws reorganizing the fiscal system, are but a few of numerous instances of reforms carried out on paper rather than in practice. The ultimate responsibility for communal administration had deliberately been placed in the hands of the *estimati*, the listed tax-payers; too often indifference, local rivalries or corruption (a frequent complaint in the kingdom of Naples, but also in the Kingdom of Italy in the final years during Eugene's absence in Russia) distorted the intentions of the governments. Nevertheless, there can be little doubt that where French rule lasted, as in Piedmont, these weaknesses were in good part overcome, while in all areas of Italy a larger class of civil servants was created, based on talent and not heredity.

The social basis of Napoleonic Italy

As in France and elsewhere in the empire, Napoleon's policy in Italy aimed at winning the support of the propertied classes. The theory of 'amalgamation' was the political counterpart to a vision of a harmonious social structure: factions were to be banned, able-bodied mendicants placed in workhouses. As the provincial council of the Terra di Lavoro in the Neapolitan kingdom wrote somewhat ingenuously:

> It is of the greatest interest to the State that individuals, who form a people, should act, speak, think in the same manner. In this way, their sentiments acquire that unity which, by tightening the social bond, will impress upon them a sort of national mark, suitable to distinguish them from all others. (Valente, 185, p. 32, n. 2)

In practical terms, as the imperial procurator in Tuscany, Chéry, spelt out, this meant respect for the laws, which were 'inseparable from customs; if the latter are corrupt, the laws grow lax. Religion is the queen of customs, it purges, propagates and upholds them' (Catoni, 177, p. 50, n. 123). But, equally, it meant respect for property.

The sale of the 'national lands' was the most significant method of gaining this support. But whereas in France the richer peasants had gained substantially and permanently from these sales, in Italy the *biens nationaux* benefited the existing owners, wealthy merchants and civil servants, magistrates and army provisioners, the provincial bourgeoisie, and only to a very small extent the smallholders and peasant proprietors. In the revolutionary years the ecclesiastical lands had been used to pay back the forced loans and credits raised from the wealthy. But some attempts had been made to ensure that lands would be divided among the less wealthy, while some of the old noble families had been ruined. Now the sales led mostly to a progressive concentration of property in the hands of small groups of nobles and upper bourgeoisie: in Piedmont typical purchasers of national properties were the great noble families whose names were to figure so prominently in the later period of the Risorgimento – Cavour, Lamarmora, Balbo, D'Azeglio; in the Kingdom of Italy, leading administrators – Aldini, Guiccioli, Massari – created their huge patrimonies in the last years of Napoleonic rule. In some areas, such as central Piedmont, with a tradition of smallholdings and *mezzadria*, the wealthier peasants gained. But in others, such as the Vercellese, Novarese or parts of Emilia, where high-farming or rice cultivation expanded, an inverse process of creating landless labourers was evident.

The abolition of feudal ties and division of inheritances encouraged the rapid redistribution of land. The unification of the internal market, protection, rising prices and export demand from France which accompanied the Continental Blockade, as much as official encouragement and subsidies for agricultural experiments (such as those of Michele di Cavour or Vincenzo

Dandolo), consolidated the position of a new landowning class, in which bourgeoisie and new nobles asserted their claims alongside the old noble families.

The effects on the peasant masses of these deep and rapid transformations were, almost everywhere, negative. In some areas the change of frontiers created a crisis: the annexation of the Trentino to the Kingdom of Italy in 1810 closed its traditional German export market for wine, tobacco and silk, while contemporaneously subjecting it to the competition of Lombard and Venetian produce. Elsewhere the international market for rice and silk upset the traditional relations in the countryside. The effects of the general European economic crisis of 1810–11, the sharply rising prices, lay behind the sporadic popular risings of these years, as much as resentment against taxes and conscription. Pauperism was certainly rising, and communal indebtedness would seem to have increased in most areas by the final years. Nothing as yet is known about the conditions of the urban workers, but the creation of a free labour market can hardly have improved their standard of living, given the negative effects of the Continental Blockade on most Italian industries and Napoleon's encouragement of employers.

The Continental Blockade aroused increasing hostility because of the closure of the traditional English markets and the deliberate attempts to tie Italy – like Spain, Portugal and Holland – to France as a supplier of raw materials and an export market for French manufactures. Cereal, vegetable and silk production certainly benefited, while probably Italian manufactures, already weak, did not suffer significantly. But France increasingly turned to Italy and Spain as its major export markets, and in 1808 imposed a discriminatory trade treaty on the Kingdom of Italy, lowering customs on manufactured goods between the two countries. By 1811 the French general council of commerce and manufactures could report to the emperor that Italy was the only market left to France and was virtually supporting French industry. The effect of the Blockade was to ruin the traditional patterns of trade, especially of colonial goods: there were a series of commercial and banking failures in the years after 1810. Along the coasts the ports were ruined. Smuggling became a major activity. Murat broke away from Napoleon on the specific issue of the Blockade.

Against this background of growing distress and popular discontent, rising prices, heavier taxation to subsidize France, and finally massive conscription, the Napoleonic regime increasingly gained the collaboration of the old and new ruling groups. As in Belgium, Holland or the Rhineland, the educated middle classes in Italy had quickly entered Napoleonic service. In the former 'Enlightened' states, such as Lombardy or Tuscany, Napoleonic centralization seemed a natural, and effective continuation of the eighteenth-century reforms. Indeed, the Tuscan reformers – such as Fabroni and Fossombroni – who had opposed the Etrurian settlement for both patriotic and ideological reasons (the loss of Tuscan identity and the subsequent re-introduction of obligatory grain-stocks), had no hesitation in joining the new government in 1808. The Napoleonic settlement, in fact, was a guarantee of moderation.

Moreover, despite the Concordat, Napoleon soon showed himself in Church-State relations a worthy heir of the reforming princes. If the Concordat, from the pope's point of view, had prevented a schism in France, for Napoleon it had secured the allegiance of Catholic opinion. In the Kingdom of Italy, as in France, Napoleon virtually ignored the Concordat once it had been signed: ecclesiastical property continued to be confiscated, parishes were reorganized, the civil code (with its assertion of civil marriage and divorce) was introduced, a single form of catechism was imposed, as in France. Jansenism lost its remaining theological content and was transformed into a defence of State authority under official encouragement. Religion meant respect and obedience and had little to do with the authority of the pope – especially after his imprisonment in 1809. In all these measures, Napoleon was encouraged and supported by anticlerical, often masonic ministers, such as Aldini; the Jansenist minister Bovara exercised careful administrative control over the clergy and, although with some hesitancy, even attended the Council of French and Italian bishops summoned by Napoleon in 1811.

As Napoleon's conservatism increased, the support of the old nobility was won in all the Italian states. A conscious policy of *ralliement* was followed, particularly in Piedmont and Naples, where leading members of the old families were offered posts in the bureaucracy, armies or at Court. After momentary hesitation, the nobles came forward. By 1814 the Cavours, who made their fortune in these years, were hardly different in their devotion to the Napoleonic family from the Pignatellis or Carafas at Naples. To the chagrin of the exiled monarchs, the courts at Turin and Naples were resplendent with the most distinguished representatives of the aristocracy. The official establishment of the French branch of freemasonry in 1805, like the creation of primogenitures and imperial titles (1809), had the function of merging old and new nobility with upper bourgeoisie in a single bond of loyalty to the person of the emperor.

A new ruling class had been forged, whose power and influence, based fundamentally on land, stood out the more clearly through the withdrawal at the local level of the vast majority of smallholders, peasants and craftsmen who possessed the right to political participation. A report of 1814, noting the absenteeism at the cantonal assemblies of the department of Sesia could only regret 'the thoughtlessness of the people', who, 'out of ignorance, fettered by habit, not yet fully impervious to the sinister threats made against them by the enemies of the present system, remain apathetic in exercising their rights' (Davico, 174, pp. 144–5).

But the equilibrium between the groups composing this new social order remained precarious. In the final years of Napoleonic rule, as Italy was dragged into Bonaparte's last, disastrous wars, and as the emperor's penchant for nobility and property became more pronounced, criticisms began to be voiced secretly. They were the criticisms of the moderate liberals, who were to emerge fleetingly in 1814 and to pursue their aims after the Restoration. Deeply influenced by their vision of England, or by the French liberal opposition to Napoleon, they looked to a constitution to curb the dangers of autocracy. But middle-class intellectuals who owed their careers to these years – such as Gioia – were also critical of the influence of the conservative landed owners and spoke for the commercial and professional classes. All landed owners and middle-class civil servants were agreed over the exclusion of the great mass of the people. But in the renewed political-civil structure of northern and central Italy, Gioia's vision of the social bases of progress, with its awareness of English developments, was to survive the Restoration as a challenge to the superior prestige of landed power.

The Kingdom of Naples

The kingdom of Naples occupied a particular place in the Napoleonic settlement of Italy, because of its strategic importance in the Mediterranean, but also because of the social tensions that characterized its life after 1799. It was the one Italian state which was subjected to virtually no territorial modifications by Napoleon and which consequently retained traditions of territorial unity and historical patriotism. The kingdom formed an outlying area of the Grand Empire, whose communications were only assured after the occupation of the Papal States. Threatened by the Anglo-Bourbon presence in Sicily, hemmed in by the English fleet, harassed by Barbary corsairs, it remained a crucial area for Napoleon for control of the Mediterranean and as a base for his grandiose schemes for the Orient: the occupation of the kingdom was followed a year later by the conquest of Corfu.

No other Italian state had suffered so savage a repression at the end of the Jacobin experience; nor anywhere, with the exception of the Papal States, had the 'restoration' lasted so long. 1799 had been followed in the kingdom by a larger emigration than elsewhere in Italy. The reaction left a deep and permanent split between the Bourbons and the leading nobles and intellectuals. Ferdinand IV had punished the nobles for their support of the republic by suppressing their traditional representation in the *sedili*, the assembly of the city of Naples (1800). The private vendettas and confiscations, most savage in Calabria, ruined some families. Royal attacks on feudal privilege and encouragement of the *galantuomini* who had remained loyal left the feudatories in a state of crisis, while the middle-class landowners rapidly developed a sense of their own strength. But royal control of the country remained uncertain, not just because of the constant fear of a French invasion: the 'Sanfedists' had of necessity been pardoned, bandit 'companies' threatened the countryside, the peasants who had not followed Ruffo in 1799 also refused to pay taxes and occupied the land. The *galantuomini* remained terrified of social risings. Order was re-established by armed force. The years of Bourbon rule passed in an atmosphere of spying, denunciations and fears of plots, although no real opposition existed any more. But nor was there any real loyalty: despite Ferdinand's illusions, the people failed to rise against the French in 1806.

That the Napoleonic kingdom of Naples managed to retain at least semi-independent status was due to the determination of Joseph Bonaparte and even more of Gioacchino Murat. For Napoleon Naples was a conquered country, which should pay for itself and for the large French army of occupation; like other states drawn into the orbit of the Grand Empire, it should be subjected to the necessary radical reforms without respect for precedent. Joseph, who had previous administrative and political experience and prided himself (as a former pupil of Pisa university) on being a philosopher-king, was acutely aware of the difficulties of welding together this superstitious society, riven by class hatreds. He oscillated between confidence in his own popularity and a sense of the impossibility of his task. Supported by his ministers, he tried to find the manner of introducing reforms, while winning local support. Hence his concern for religious sentiment, which evoked Napoleon's ironical comment: 'I congratulate you on your reconciliation with San Gennaro, but despite all that I imagine that you have armed the forts' (Rambaud, 181, p. 532). But the *lazzaroni* of the city of Naples were not a threat, and in fact never rose against the French, even in 1814.

The real difficulty was to win the support of the peasantry by giving them land and reducing taxes. But in so divided a society as that of the kingdom, this implied revolutionary democratic reforms which were inconceivable to a Napoleonic monarch. Popular disillusionment and the offensive nature of the military occupation, the flouting of local customs and the disregard for the traditional place of women in Neapolitan society, all these were responsible for the mass rising in Calabria two months after Joseph's tour of the region. It took the French two years to defeat the organized guerrilla movement in the Calabrias, which was secretly supported by the English in Sicily. And the following years witnessed the revival of brigandage on a massive scale, with no political motivation, but sufficiently serious to represent a constant embarrassment to the government and require the adoption of ruthless repressive methods by general Manhès.

Popular unrest and risings, which occurred throughout Italy during the empire, were thus on a far greater scale in the kingdom of Naples. Indeed, the guerrilla warfare left a tradition which was to inspire later Risorgimento democrats such as Fabrizi and Pisacane, to turn to Calabria as the classic land of popular risings. Among the educated classes, the policy of reconciliation, which Joseph pursued actively, also proved more difficult than elsewhere because of the bloodshed of 1799. The patriots who had survived and returned were eager for vengeance and demanded a monopoly of office. In true Bourbon tradition, most Neapolitans continued to regard an administrative post as a favour rather than a function: 'it is the division of leisure', commented Roederer in disgust (Rambaud, 181, p. 376).

In the higher levels of the administration, an uneasy balance was achieved between the patriots (such as Abamonti and Galdi) and the moderates (like Zurlo and Ricciardi). At the lower levels, the chronic lack of trustworthy personnel – a constant complaint of the new French governments throughout Italy – led to the employment of the patriots of 1799. The same divisions existed among the French ministers appointed by Joseph: former Conventionists and Jacobins – Saliceti, Briot – were balanced by the constitutionalists of 1789, like Roederer and Miot. Republicans and royalists, chastened by their past experiences, were only united in their sense of the need to revise the entire structure of the state and society. Slowly, in the pursuit of this end, the political differences faded away. Joseph could leave Murat a small but homogeneous administrative class. Between this group, supported by the landowners, and the great mass of the peasantry, the petty bourgeoisie of the capital remained apathetic: 'a quiet man must live by himself', Carlo De Nicola confided to his diary (Valente, 185, p. 11, n. 1).

The reforms imposed by Joseph and his ministers followed the general pattern of Napoleonic rationalization: uniformity and centralization of the administration, reform of the judicial system along the French pattern, abolition of feudalism, reordering and simplification of the taxation system. But the difficulties in carrying out these reforms were immensely greater than elsewhere in Italy, because of the chaotic state of the Bourbon administration in its final years, the endemic corruption, and above all the negative effects of feudal penetration of almost every aspect of the state structure.

Thus, while it was relatively easy to abolish all baronial and private courts, to ostracize former baronial governors, to appoint energetic intendants (the former Jacobins Briot and Galdi, and Pietro Colletta in the Calabrias), sub-intendants and even local notables in the district councils, the poor communications, the lack of education or adequate income and especially the fear of attacks on life and property made it almost impossible to find candidates for communal office: 'the most honest, most enlightened, most notable among the citizens refuse to accept such office, because they know it carries with it all the contempt, insults and humiliations that the lowest of the low would refuse to suffer', complained the provincial council of Calabria Citra in 1808 (Caldora, 184, p. 79). The *decurioni*, the communal representatives, failed to attend meetings, communal income was mis-appropriated, the local baron often managed to reassert his domination. The judicial reform suffered from the same weaknesses: with the abolition of baronial courts, the local municipalities were responsible for tribunals of the first instance, and justices of the peace chosen among the proprietors (and, later, *decurioni*). As late as 1810 the judicial system was still functioning badly, in contrast to the rest of Italy.

The financial reforms proved even more difficult. Roederer, funda-mentally a physiocrat, imposed a single tax on land and industry, without exemptions, in place of the 104 Bourbon taxes divided into 30 separate administrations. Roederer was convinced that, with the abolition of feud-ality, the new land-tax would free the peasants and the landless and encourage smallholdings, without damaging the owners. But, as Ricciardi and Zurlo warned, the tax was crippling for the small owners and so worked against any social improvements. Murat, like Prina in the Kingdom of Italy, was forced to diminish the land-tax and increase the personal tax, a poll-tax imposed on all adult males. The new *catasto*, the land register, compiled hastily by Roederer, was vitiated by the hostility and corruption at the communal level. The reform and unification of the customs proved even more arduous, as the previous system was particularly vulnerable to corruption: Roederer's nephew Gentil wrote bitterly: 'Stealing and theft by employees is unbelievable; the vice has passed into their blood and they carry the marks on their faces like smallpox' (Valente, 185, p. 332). By 1808 it had only proved possible to unify the customs tariffs of the city of Naples; internal excises in the kingdom were only abolished in 1810.

The foundation stone, on which ultimately all the other reforms rested, was the attack on feudalism. The law of 2 August 1806 abolished the personal and jurisdictional rights of the barons (with indemnities for the jurisdictions), but confirmed their landed rights. In 1807 entails were abolished. The moderate character of the reform, aimed at freeing the communes and peasants from their juridical dependence on the barons, but not at re-distributing property at the expense of the nobles, reflected the limited ends of Napoleonic reform. The other reforms concerned with the redistribution of the land were likewise intended to encourage the mobility of circulation of the land and cultivation rather than to increase smallholdings at the expense of large property. The sale of ecclesiastical lands, decreed on 2 July 1806 and pursued in the following years, reflected the need to sell small lots in favour of 'the indigent class'. But the dominant concern was to settle the public debt, enormously inflated through the resumption by the state of the *arrendamenti*, government and crown revenues alienated to private families in the preceding centuries. The division of the demesnial lands, decreed on 1 September 1806 (with further laws on 8 June 1807 and 3 December 1808), perhaps went furthest towards a social redistribution: these commons were to be divided between the barons and the communes, with the obligation on the latter to fix quotas for their inhabitants.

Nevertheless, if Joseph seemed reluctant to challenge the landed power of the nobles too directly (and the virtual civil war in Calabria certainly acted as a constraint), the consequences of the abolition of feudalism were more far-reaching than the law had seemed to promise. A special feudal commission had been formed to decide the immense number of lawsuits pending between the feudatories and communes. Until Murat's accession in 1808, this – like the other reforms – seemed to make little impact. But from then on, the small group of feudal commissioners, including the former Bourbon reformer Winspeare and the former revolutionary Cuoco, supported by the minister Zurlo, incited the communes to assert their claims against the feudatories; by the time the commission's powers expired, it had judged over 2000 cases. The commission aimed at confirming the right of property against all feudal ties and customary rights. Baronial lands, the legality of whose possession was not challenged, were recognized as free property. Fiscal prerogatives and monopoly rights were abolished. Where customary rights of pasturage existed, the commons were split between barons and communes, with an obligation on the latter to divide them among the poorest inhabitants. Tithes and mortgages were reduced or suppressed when judged exorbitant, or in any case made redeemable. The feudatories, the great majority of whom had limited resources, found themselves in acute financial difficulties, less through the loss of lands than through the abolition of their administrative, legal and political powers and rights. The communes, won over by the determined approach of such former Bourbon Enlightened administrators as Zurlo and Winspeare, began to accept the state. The rural middle classes, the *classe colta* ('educated class'), now entered the communal and provincial administrations more readily, collaborating with the intendants and central government. General Pignatelli di Strongoli, a typical representative of the feudal families which had rallied to the Napoleonic settlement, commented bitterly in later years that the baronage had been treated worse than Jews.

Zurlo and Winspeare had broken the stranglehold of the feudatories, but, working against time, they were unable to achieve the division of the demesnial lands among the poorer inhabitants. The task was left to the intendants and had barely begun before it was caught up in the financial and military crises which accompanied the break with Napoleon and the Russian campaign. Zurlo was aware of the hostility towards distributing the commons among the peasants, and fought to prevent the wealthy owners from appropriating the demesnial lands. Some smallholdings had been created with the abolition of feudalism. But the major advantage was gained by the rural middle classes. In Calabria, where the division of the demesnes began late in 1810, the small plots of land which were offered were often refused or sold to speculators because the peasant owners lacked the resources to buy seed or pay the low rental.

The abuses and illegalities of the *gentiluomini* often merely replaced those of the feudatories. The commune of Albidona (Calabria) in 1821 sadly recounted the story of the effects of the reforms:

> The extremely large territory of this commune was only feudal and ecclesiastical. . . . We were happy to be present at the destruction of the baron and the celestial religious order. The properties passed through various hands, and from the Holy ones and the barons re-entered into the hands of the commune administered by the despot Bassà from the provinces. With this administration, the invincible strength of two was concentrated in the hands of one. And we citizens, instead of enjoying advantages, are even further humiliated. (Caldora, 184, p. 172)

The sale of the ex-ecclesiastical lands, after the initial, customary assault of court nobles, generals, high functionaries, large merchants, financiers and speculators, spread from Naples to the provinces after 1810 and confirmed the formation of some medium-sized properties in the hands of the provincial middle classes.

By 1810 the reforms passed by Joseph and pushed through with vigour by Gioacchino had begun to take effect. The regime appeared consolidated. The strong sense of independence had been met by Murat's deliberate policy of employing Neapolitan ministers and then by his decree requiring Neapolitan citizenship for the holding of office (1811), by his adoption of a national flag and creation of a large army. But despite the government's encouragement of the provincial middle classes, the increasingly heavy taxation on land, the wholly negative consequences of the Continental Blockade – in contrast to its more varied effects on the Kingdom of Italy or Tuscany – created resentment and discontent, which began to be expressed in the secret groupings of the *carboneria*. Murat's absolute intolerance of criticism in the provincial councils and his refusal to call the parliament promised by his predecessor in the Statute of Bayonne further stimulated opposition.

The revolt against Napoleon

Popular risings marked the whole period of Napoleonic domination in Italy, as elsewhere in the empire. They were directed against taxation, especially the personal tax, but even more against conscription in the Kingdom of Italy and the annexed departments: in the Parmigiano in 1805, at Padua and Vicenza in 1806, in the Maremme in 1808. Some regions – Romagna, Marches, Abruzzi, Calabria – were subject to continuous unrest, often led by bandit companies and incited by local priests and English or Austrian spies. As the pressure of Napoleon's wars and the Blockade made themselves felt more directly, the risings became more frequent and widespread.

The massive peasant rebellion led by Andreas Hofer in the Tyrol in 1809, which had been sparked off by the French defeat at Essling, led to peasant risings in the Polesine, Mantovano, Veronese and Emilia, and the destruction of taxation records and the civil registers. The police were thankful that the risings had lacked any co-ordination or leadership. The general economic crisis of 1810–11, the unemployment, poverty and growing pauperism, the immense demands for money and troops – Beauharnais reported 40 000 desertions in four months in 1810 – all deepened the gulf between the Napoleonic regime and the great mass of the population. A French official in 1810 could report on the department of Marengo:

> It is fortunate, from one point of view, that the state of almost continuous illness in which these people languish has not allowed them to show their strength; they were the only ones who would have had some reason to take part in the popular insurrections which took place in the years 1797 and 1798 in Piedmont; they were the only ones who had nothing to lose; nevertheless, this department is perhaps the only one in all Piedmont where no insurrection has occurred. (Davico, 174, p. 159)

These peasant risings represented a constant and growing embarrassment to the French in Italy, as elsewhere in Europe. But they never became a 'national' rising for Church and King, as in Spain, Tyrol or Russia in these years. The fear of risings under the pretext of religion, as in 1799, remained strong. Secret Catholic sects – the 'Society of the Heart of Jesus' in the Romagna, the 'Trinitarians' and *Calderari* in Calabria and Apulia, 'Christian Amity' in Piedmont – which explicitly evoked the Sanfedist tradition, tried to incite such rebellions. *Carbonari* were responsible for a forged papal bull in 1814 which circulated in southern Italy. But during the final collapse of Napoleonic rule in Italy in 1813–14, there was no mass religious or 'patriotic' rising, partly because famine and the extreme hardship caused by Napoleon's continuous wars worked against the spread of any sustained revolt. The bandits and disbanded soldiers, who constituted the most widespread and organized resistance in the Abruzzi, Apulia and Calabria, had more mundane and limited aims. Except for isolated incidents, such as the rising in Milan in April 1814, there was little contact between those popular movements and the members of the patriotic sects, who remained – particularly in the south – fearful of the dangers of social rebellion.

The secret societies

The revolt against Napoleon in Italy thus developed at two levels – popular risings and secret sects – which, as in Germany, remained distinct. But the comparison with Germany ended here, for the patriotism of the Italian sectarians never acquired such violently nationalist overtones as in Germany. The sectarians shared, in common with the members of secret societies of other countries conquered by Napoleon, an unequivocal desire for independence. Frequently, they also shared a moderate form of liberalism which expressed itself in the desire for a constitution, as a protection against the arbitrariness of despotism and 'tyranny'; and, if Napoleon was the personification of despotism at that moment, a liberal constitution was regarded as a necessary barrier after his overthrow.

The origins, relationships, composition and strength of the various sects remains obscure. With an organizational structure and symbolism derived from eighteenth-century freemasonry, the sects inherited a conspiratorial, activist spirit from the revolutionary clubs and plots of the 1790s. Their hierarchical structure and the secrecy which enveloped their rites, as well as their penetration of Napoleonic freemasonry, facilitated their diffusion internationally, from France to Spain, Italy, Germany and Russia. The sects in Italy (with Spain, the major area of their expansion before 1815) – whether Catholic, patriotically liberal, or more determinedly egalitarian – were agreed in their opposition to Napoleon, and the very immediacy and generality of this aim facilitated the fluid formation and re-formation, merging and superimposing of one group upon another, which obscured their distinctiveness and increased the ambiguity of their goals, ultimately rendering them all instruments of English propaganda, and the anti-Napoleonic coalition.

The traditional Catholic sects looked back to pre-revolutionary traditions (Jesuit sects formed after the Order's dissolution), as well as to the Sanfedist experience and the romantic return to the faith which marked the early decades of the new century. The liberal sects emerged specifically as forms of opposition to Napoleon. Their members were often ex-Jacobins or republicans, opposed to Brumaire and even more to the empire, so that initially they retained an egalitarian element, which was only to be submerged by the emotional patriotism of the final struggle against Napoleon. Active Jacobin opposition in Italy had vanished with the dissolution of the Society of Rays after the Bologna rising of 1802. But the early membership of the liberal sects probably owed much in northern and central Italy to the survivors of the Rays, republican unitarians, perhaps some Jacobins, certainly linked to the French Jacobins dispersed and driven into secrecy by Napoleon's dictatorship.

The army and national guard had remained the centre for unitarian ideas in Italy, as Murat had observed in 1803, but it also offered a haven for anti-Napoleonic opposition in France. French officers carried this opposition over Europe, and it was one of Championnet's officers, general Malet, who led a plot against Napoleon in Paris in 1812. These French officers, usually too young to have been involved in the Jacobin plots of the previous decade, reacted against the official character of Napoleonic freemasonry of which they formed part. They joined with Jacobin elements, possibly from *illuminati* lodges, to form the *filadelfi* sect. The *philadelphie* or *filadelfia* was carried by these officers through the empire, and into the masonic lodges of the Kingdom of Italy. The *adelfia*, which emerged in north Italy and France, was probably a derivation from the 'filadelfia', but subsequently absorbed many of the *filadelfi* groups. The leaders of both the *filadelfi* and 'adelfi' in Lombardy and Piedmont, of Jacobin or democratic formation, possibly survivors of the Rays, probably influenced by the Scottish-rite masonry of the *illuminati*, gave a democratic egalitarian orientation to the sects. When Buonarroti, on his emergence from prison in 1809, began to spin the threads of renewed conspiracy, he worked within the *adelfi*. At Paris, Luigi Angeloni, a democratic exile from the Roman republic, who in 1810 refused Fouché's offer of a post at Rome, was a leading figure in the *filadelfia* and was involved in Malet's plot.

The *carboneria*, which developed in southern Italy, may have been another derivation from the *filadelfia*. It was obscurely linked to the example of the *compagnonnage* of *charbonniers* in the Franche-Comté and its diffusion certainly owed much to French officers and dissident groups within freemasonry. Perhaps it came to Naples from Spain; more certainly, it was propagated in the early years of Murat's reign by the former Jacobin Briot, intendant at Chieti and Cosenza. The *carboneria*, which penetrated to some degree Neapolitan freemasonry, appeared to work more widely in southern Italy (with its deeper traditions of secret societies) than the *filadelfia – adelfia* in the north.

In the former papal Legations, with its centre at Bologna, another secret sect emerged – the *guelfia*. Possibly a derivation from the Rays, the *guelfia* was more moderate than the *carboneria* or the *adelfia*, to which it was certainly linked. Little is known about the composition of any of these sects before the Restoration, but the *carboneria* would appear to have gained supporters among the local landowners and intellectuals as well as among some petty nobles and officers. The *adelfia* possibly included a greater proportion of officers, nobles and merchants as well as intellectuals.

The existence of 'patriotic' groups was certainly known to the authorities, at least in the kingdom of Naples, by 1808. These may not yet have been organized into *carbonari vendite* ('conventicles') but in any case they hardly represented a real threat. The secret societies, in fact, only spread with a certain intensity with the news of the disastrous end of Napoleon's Russian campaign, announced in the official bulletin of the Kingdom of Italy on 23 December 1812 and confirmed by Murat's abandonment of the Russian army and precipitous return to Naples in January 1813. By 1814–15 the *carboneria* was spreading into central and northern Italy, where it came into contact with the *adelfia*; the latter, smaller but more compact and organized more secretly, was to penetrate and influence the *carboneria* in the years after the Restoration.

But in these last agitated years of Napoleon's collapse, the sects were unable to offer an effective alternative to Napoleonic rule and mainly served as channels of agitation for English propaganda. Their earlier egalitarian and democratic spirit tended to be displayed by patriotic demands for independence and a constitution. This liberal formulation had gained strength from the examples of the constitution announced by the Spanish Junta in 1812, and even more of the Sicilian constitution of the same year.

The rulers of Sicily and Sardinia, like the other sovereigns outside the Grand Empire, had been forced, by reaction to the Revolution and Napoleon, to introduce reforms. In Sardinia, Victor Emanuel I had centralized the administration, gaining some control over feudal jurisdictions, and had partially liquidated the public debt by the sale of ecclesiastical lands. The Bourbons in Sicily were in a weaker position, as they were wholly dependent on the English forces occupying the island. The traditional struggle between the king and the Sicilian barons, claiming to represent the entire people of the island through Parliament, reached a deadlock in 1810 over the king's demand for a *donativo*, a tax requiring the assent of the three estates in the assembly. The barons, led by Belmonte and Castelnuovo, refused. The barons were influenced by their contact with English liberal officers and supported by the small commercial middle class centred on Catania. They were concerned not only to obtain Sicilian ministers in place of Ferdinand's Neapolitan ones and to gain confirmation of the autonomy of the kingdom of Sicily by the convocation of annual parliaments, but to save their own weakening financial position through the abolition of feudal ties prohibiting the alienation of land. The barons were victorious because of the support of the English commander Lord Bentinck, a liberal whig convinced that the English system was the panacea for all European countries.

A firm believer in the independence of the island – which would consequently need English maritime support – Bentinck asserted that its future hopes lay with the nobility, purged of its privileges, but confirmed in its political predominance. He intervened in dictatorial manner, exiling the queen (suspected of plotting with the French, as well as with the anti-Murattian Catholic sects) from Palermo and then from Sicily. By forcing the king to hand over the government to his heir, Bentinck was responsible for the Sicilian constitution of 1812. The independence of Sicily was confirmed, together with freedom of speech and the press. The lords were guaranteed control over the Commons. Feudal rights were abolished without indemnity. Belmonte's conservative interpretation of the method of abolishing feudalism triumphed over Castelnuovo's more liberal view, and the Sicilian baronage retained its predominance and its incomes.

But the myth of the Sicilian constitution was influential in the kingdom of Naples, where it reinforced *carbonari* demands for a constitution, as promised in the Bayonne Statute. Murat had always opposed these demands. In 1813, during his renewed absence from the kingdom to fight in Germany, the *carboneria* spread rapidly into the Molise and the former papal lands of the Marches and Abruzzi. An attempt was made to suppress the *carboneria* in the army. The government, in Murat's absence, was divided over what attitude to adopt, because of the danger of losing the support of the rural middle class. Ricciardi, indeed, stated that 'the entire class of proprietors of the kingdom wanted the fulfilment of the promises, repeated many times, to establish a constitution' (Valente, 185, p. 73). Zurlo and Pignatelli were for military suppression and by 1815 repression had won the day; the official freemasonry hastened to expel *carbonari* from its ranks. The *carboneria* was too weak to offer any real resistance: a revolt at Cosenza was suppressed by Manhès, as easily as had been an earlier plot against Saliceti in 1807. But Murat's hostility possibly weakened his army and certainly lost him the support of the provincial mainstay of his regime by driving the *carboneria* towards the Bourbons: in April 1815 the *carbonari* could rise at Polistena in Calabria to the cries of 'Independence of Italy' and 'King Ferdinand, Republic or Constitution' (Caldora, 184, p. 423).

The sects in both southern and northern Italy had been actively encouraged by English and even Habsburg propaganda. The image of a liberal constitution, which (it was believed) would ensure a political settlement such as existed in England, had widespread appeal among the educated classes of the nations subject to Napoleon. Bentinck was among the first to attempt to spread these ideas in Europe. On landing in central Italy in 1814, he had urged the Italians, like the Dutch, to fight for their independence; and against Castlereagh's orders had recreated the Genoese republic. He had even proposed to create a British protectorate over Sicily, which could thus act as the model for and instrument of Italian independence. Bentinck was disowned by Castlereagh because of the dangerous practical consequences of his proposals. But the British government was itself responsible for this propaganda based on promises of independence, a constitution and even unity.

In the early years of the struggle against France, the English had adopted the classic arguments of the counter-revolution, synthesized supremely by Burke. Now, aware of the hostility to France of the educated populations of the subject lands, the English Foreign Office organized an anti-Napoleonic press from Sicily, Malta and London which was distributed by political agents. An early agent had been Vittorio Barzoni, who had emigrated to England out of disgust with French rule. By 1813–14, Augusto Bozzi Granville, who had fled from Pavia and served in the British fleet, was publishing a government-subsidized journal at London, *L'Italico*, which indicted the aulic emptiness of life in the Kingdom of Italy ("There are Academies and Sub-Academies like Prefectures and Sub-Prefectures, but they are trees without fruit' (Soriga, 152, p. 193)) and proclaimed the need for independence and unity: 'All the provinces now must form a single kingdom, and on its throne a Prince must be placed, it matters not of which royal stock, so long as he is endowed with virtue and valour' (Soriga, 152, p. 191). Bozzi, in London and during his secret mission to Italy in 1814, used his masonic contacts to persuade many, including Confalonieri and the small group of 'Pure Italians' in Lombardy, that if not all Italy, at least the Kingdom of Italy could maintain its independence, or if not its independence, at least union with Piedmont to prevent the return of Austria.

Bentinck and Bozzi, in their different ways, help explain the widespread hopes placed on England. It seemed possible, with the rapid disintegration of the Napoleonic empire, that Italy could finally achieve independence and a constitution. Not only England, but Alexander I seemed to promise a constitutional future for oppressed peoples. But the very ambiguity of the promises were indicative of the weakness of the sects: for the sake of independence, any prince would suffice, whether English, Bourbon, Murattian, Savoyard, or even Habsburg; the conspirators oscillated between hopes of unity or a federalist solution, and often – as with the Milanese provisional government which overthrew Beauharnais – proclaimed independence as a guise for narrow municipalistic ambitions. But, even more than the absence of a single, clear programme and a unified organization, the sects failed totally because of their lack of military force and Italy's dependence, as so often in the past, on the great powers.

The collapse of French rule

Two Italian armies existed and had proved their valour on the battlefields of all Europe. But the best and many of the most patriotic of the officers had been lost fighting for Napoleon: 30 000 from the Kingdom of Italy and 8000 from the kingdom of Naples had joined the Russian campaign in 1812, and a further 24 000 left for Napoleon's final German campaign in 1813. As Napoleon was forced to retreat into France after the defeat of Leipzig (October 1813), Eugene Beauharnais, slowly withdrawing before the Austrian advance to the Adige (November 1813) and then the Mincio (February 1814), still commanded an army of 45 000.

Melzi, once more at the head of the government, desperately sought to convince Eugene to abandon Napoleon, as had Murat and so many other of the emperor's relatives and marshals. For Melzi, supported by officers and civil servants, the one hope for Eugene was to proclaim the kingdom's independence and convoke the electoral colleges, so confronting the allies with a *fait accompli*, backed by a strong army. When Eugene finally agreed, after the news of Napoleon's abdication (11 April 1814), and summoned the

Senate, Melzi's plan was sabotaged by the overwhelming hostility expressed by Confalonieri to any connection with Napoleonic France. The Senate's revolt and the violent tumult which culminated in the lynching of the minister of finances, Prina (20 April 1814), meant the end of all hopes of a military resistance and total reliance on allied promises. The Austrians rapidly dispersed the Italian army and sent it across the Alps. As the Austrians restored the former dynasts – Ferdinand III of Tuscany, Pius VII, Francis IV of Modena, Victor Emanuel I of Sardinia – and established garrisons in the Romagna, Legations and the Novarese as a pledge for the future peace settlement, the plots of former protagonists of the Cisalpine republic, such as general Teodoro Lechi and Giovanni Lattuada, were destined to failure, as they lacked any effective military support.

The only Italian army still in existence was that of Gioacchino Murat. In 1813, after some hesitation, Murat had joined the Austrians and English to save his throne. Tormented perhaps by a sense of loyalty, attracted undoubtedly by hopes of enlarging his kingdom at papal or Tuscan expense, increasingly worried by Bentinck's hostility and the Austrian emperor's slowness in offering guarantees, Murat had acted in an equivocal manner in the 1814 campaign against Beauharnais, marching into central Italy but avoiding any real attack on Eugene's forces. With the collapse of the Kingdom of Italy, Murat found himself as the one surviving Napoleonic ruler in Italy, the 'Italian Bernadotte', as he was called with reference to the king of Sweden, the first Napoleonic marshal to betray his master in order to conserve his kingdom.

When the congress of Vienna opened in November 1814, Murat's representatives were not admitted and the king began to plot once more with what remained of a Napoleonic party in Italy. When Napoleon escaped from Elba to France (1 March 1815), Murat staked his fortunes on a final gamble and tried to rouse the support of the Napoleonic and liberal elements in Italy by launching a proclamation from Rimini (his army had remained in occupation of the Marches) for the independence and unity of Italy (30 March); the promises of a constitution remained vague. Too much suspicion existed after Murat's previous tortuous behaviour and open hostility to liberal ideas for any national insurrection to occur in Italy. In like manner in France, Napoleon's proclamation of a constitution failed to arouse popular enthusiasm. Defeated at Tolentino (2 May), Murat's army rapidly dissolved during its retreat south. Murat was to pay for his gamble with his life, but – like Napoleon – was to leave behind him the myth of a patriotic king, defender of the independence of the Italian people.

The possibility of independence had, in fact, virtually vanished before Murat's military challenge. Only discord and the revival of old disputes among the allies had kept alive the hopes of the Italians, as of the Poles and populations of the Rhineland and Saxony. With Napoleon's return, the allies once more united and, long before Waterloo (18 June 1815), the Austrian occupation of Milan (28 April 1814) had been accepted by the English. Confalonieri and the anglophile Lombard conspirators for independence were left without support. Confalonieri's famous mission to Castlereagh at Paris was merely one episode in a series of deputations which these 'Italian Poles' sent around the courts of Europe. Austria was to remain in possession of northern Italy, while Ferdinand IV returned to Naples.

But Italy had been transformed. Confalonieri had based his plea to Castlereagh on the profound effects of the changes wrought during the years of French dominion. They were confirmed by a more hostile observer, the Sardinian ambassador at London, count d'Agliè, who tried to persuade his monarch to take advantage of the situation:

> This nation has altered considerably in fifteen years. . . . The changes which have taken place since the beginning of the century, the cessions and exchanges of different parts of the country which have been made on various occasions, and above all the military habits which have been introduced there, have given a new impetus, a new spirit to our land. (Soriga, 152, p. 220)

This new spirit and the sense of military valour were to prevent a total return to the past.

Part 4
The search for independence 1815-47

It was on the eve of the 1848 revolutions that Metternich described Italy as 'a geographical expression'. It formed part of his appeal to the other great powers of Europe to recognize that the settlement of Italy was 'a major European question', guaranteed by public law at the treaty of Vienna and hence immutable (Metternich, in 298, pp. 77-8). For Metternich, the Italian peninsula, like the German states, represented a passive object of European diplomacy: as in the eighteenth century, Italy's importance lay in its territorial divisions, essential for the maintenance of the balance of power.

By 1847 such a viewpoint could only be upheld in the narrowest sense of international diplomacy. It denied the transformations experienced by Italy, as by other states, during and since the years of revolutionary and Napoleonic domination. It ignored the development of national and liberal ideologies which had formed a central feature of European life since the Restoration. No longer were Italy's ties with Europe restricted to purely dynastic arrangements – although these retained a certain importance. Opposition to the settlement of Vienna, which was responsible for the continuous unrest and sporadic revolutions and insurrections which characterized Italy's history in these decades, was evidence of Italy's participation in and identification with the main currents of European thought and action. From the early liberal revolutions to the Mazzinian dream of democratic national emancipation or the opposing, moderate vision of gradual, peaceful economic and civil progress, Italian patriots thought in European terms and saw Italy's future as forming part of – indeed being dependent upon – the progress of European civilization, which they identified only too easily with the cause of humanity.

The difficult elaboration of these ideas, and their translation onto the plane of political programmes and actions, form the main theme of the following pages. The total number of persons actively concerned to transform

Italy's condition and, if possible, achieve independence never amounted to more than a minute fraction of the population of some twenty millions. But they represented a growing proportion – although always a minority – of the educated classes and they displayed an increasing concern – usually expressed in rhetorical or generic terms – to win the support of the 'multitudes'. If these groups, both democratic and moderate, failed to arouse active mass support before 1848, it was not because they were unaware of the need, but because of their ignorance of the world of the peasantry or their fear of social anarchy. The rapid economic transformations in Europe in these decades, which affected Italy so directly, bore home to the more perceptive Italian patriots an acute awareness of social problems. But the division between city and countryside remained deep and few were able or willing to interpret the inarticulate claims of the peasants. As the varied and antagonistic experiences of these groups culminated in the 1848 revolutions, this division and ignorance was to influence profoundly their behaviour and chances of success.

11

Legitimacy and
conspiracy: 1815–31

Restoration in Europe

The upheavals of the previous quarter of a century required a settlement even more far-reaching than that of the peace of Westphalia in 1648. The statesmen of Europe who gathered at Vienna in November 1814 were aware of the immensity of their task, but – like the publicists who were busily elaborating the ideology of this restoration – they were confident of their ability to prevent the recurrence of revolution and French imperialism by their carefully balanced modifications of the political geography of Europe and by their assertions of the principles of legitimate authority and territorial security. Metternich and Castlereagh, like Alexander I and Talleyrand, held no illusions about the possibility of a simple return to the world of the *ancien régime*. Their agreements and treaties, which culminated in the final treaty of Vienna (9 June 1815), were not merely concerned to construct a barrier of sufficiently large states to prevent a renewal of French aggression, but implicitly recognized that the dynastic egotism which had characterized international relations in the eighteenth century constituted a persistent and undesirable threat to peace. The Congress of Vienna was thus also an attempt to regulate international relations by the exclusion of force, 'to work for a political system to consolidate and uphold the public order in Europe' (Hinsley, 191, p. 197), in the words of its publicist, Friedrich von Gentz. These two aims – to achieve a stable balance of power and to ensure the settlement of future disputes by international agreement – were rendered explicit in the treaties of 1814–15 and the congresses of the following years.

The territorial resettlement was complicated by the rivalry between the two major powers, Great Britain and Russia, as well as by the ambitions of Austria and Prussia. Castlereagh's policy was based on his determination to retain the most strategic colonial conquests made during the Napoleonic wars (and so British command of the seas) and to block all Russian threats of hegemony on the continent of Europe; the former aim had already been achieved by a series of bilateral treaties before the Congress of Vienna met. Alexander I had likewise extended his empire by the acquisition of Bessarabia and Finland (treaties with Sweden, Turkey and Persia, 1809, 1812, 1813) and at Vienna sought to increase his possessions in Poland. At the same time, the treaty of the Holy Alliance (26 September 1815), a document imbued with mystical language, appealing to sovereigns to consider themselves a 'real fraternity', 'all members of a single Christian nation', was initially invented by Alexander both to ensure the respective powers of monarchs and constitutions and to gather all rulers in a single international organization which could be used as a check on England. This rivalry dominated the congress at Vienna, as the other major issue – the definition of the frontiers of France – had already been definitively settled after Napoleon's 'Hundred Days' along the boundaries of 1792 (treaty of Chaumont between England, Russia, Austria and Prussia, 9 March 1814, revised and confirmed 25 March 1815). Austria and Prussia, as well as some of the smaller powers and later France, were obliged to act within the restrictions imposed by this Anglo-Russian antagonism; but they were also able to exploit it.

Because of the treaties preceding the Congress of Vienna the great powers were concerned primarily with the determination of territory in central and southern Europe. The underlying principle, successfully introduced by Talleyrand, was that of 'legitimacy', that is the confirmation of the legitimate rights of sovereigns. The principle, however, was capable of elastic interpretation and was never used directly against the interests of the great powers. Thus there was little hesitation in sacrificing the republics of Venice and Genoa, the duke of Saxony or innumerable smaller German princes in the interests of the balance of power and the creation of strong barriers against France. The immediate effect of Anglo-Russian rivalry was to strengthen Austria's position on the Continent through English support. The congress had almost broken down over the division of Poland and Saxony, with Prussia and Russia against England, France and Austria. In the end, most of Poland was given to Russia and nearly half Saxony to Prussia, which was compensated for its loss of Polish lands with territories on the Rhine and in Westphalia.

A stronger Prussia thus stood as guardian against France, whose frontiers were blocked to the north by the merging of the former Austrian Belgian provinces with the kingdom of Holland, and to the south by the restitution of Savoy and Nice to the king of Sardinia, who also received Genoa. In Germany Talleyrand ably exploited the differences between the powers to ensure the survival of many of the small and middling German principates and protect them against the dominance of either Austria or Prussia with the creation of the Germanic Confederation (Frankfurt agreement, 1819).

Austria was compensated for its losses in Belgium and western Germany by the sacrifice of Italy and the northern Adriatic.

Italy's fate – like that of Poland and Belgium – was thus settled by the powers without regard to the appeals of many articulate sectors of the population, as it had been in the eighteenth century and during the years of French domination. The only limits to the extent of Austrian domination were those achieved by the skill of individual diplomats in gaining the support of one or other of the powers: the Sardinian minister Vallesa replaced Castlereagh's tepid attitude with Russian support to resist Austrian claims on the upper Novarese; while cardinal Consalvi successfully asserted the principle of legitimacy to achieve the restoration of the Papal States (except Avignon), despite Austrian ambitions on the Legations. Italy thus emerged from the congress of Vienna wholly under Austrian control. Besides Lombardy, Austria was given possession of the former Venetian republic, the Valtellina and the Trentino, merged into a kingdom of Lombardy-Venetia, territorially compact and contiguous to the Habsburg lands on the other side of the Alps. The grand-duchy of Tuscany was restored to the emperor Francis' younger brother, Ferdinand III of Lorraine (1790–1801, 1815–24); the duchy of Modena was given to Francis IV of Austria-Este (1815–46); the duchy of Parma was assigned to the former empress of the French, the Austrian emperor's daughter Maria Luisa (1815–47) (although its subsequent reversion to the Bourbons of Parma, now given the former republic of Lucca as a duchy, was agreed in 1817). The Bourbon Ferdinand IV of the Two Sicilies (1815–25) was restored to Naples after the overthrow of Murat, but only after signing a permanent defensive alliance with Austria (12 June 1815). Finally, Austria gained the right to garrison the citadels of Piacenza (in the duchy of Parma) and Ferrara (in the Papal States). Only Victor Emanuel I of Sardinia (1802–21) retained his formal independence, because of the importance assigned to this kingdom by the great powers in the international equilibrium. But the maximum assertion of this independence was marked by the Sardinian rejection (together with the Papal States) of Metternich's proposal for an Italian confederation under Austrian presidency, similar to the German Confederation.

The settlement of Italy had aroused no real disputes at Vienna and the frontiers were to remain unchanged until 1859. But Italy was to prove one of the focal points of opposition to treaties which were regarded by many contemporaries as a consecration of the *ancien régime*. It was precisely to prevent or suppress such 'dissidence' that the great powers had elaborated their philosophy of the 'Concert of Europe'.

In the treaty of Chaumont the victorious allies had already expressed their intentions of continuing to maintain the peace, once France had been defeated. The Holy Alliance, although originally intended by Alexander I to serve religious, humanitarian and pacifist purposes, had aroused Castle-reagh's hostility as it could be 'prostituted to the support of established power without any consideration of the extent to which it was abused' (Webster, 189, p. 171). It could, incidentally, also be used as a powerful weapon against English interests, which had undoubtedly gained the better of Russia at the congress of Vienna. Castlereagh's reply was the Quadruple Alliance (20 November 1815) by which the allies renewed the treaty of Chaumont but also arranged to meet occasionally in conferences in order to agree on necessary measures for the preservation of peace and the happiness of peoples. The alliance, to which France was allowed to accede in 1818, was conceived by Castlereagh as a limited method of settling disputes diplo-matically. Conservative but not reactionary, Castlereagh was keenly aware that too rigid an assertion of the status quo would arouse opposition and conflict. The congress system, in his view, was a means whereby differences of interest among the powers could be adjusted, irrespective of public opinion. But this Concert of Europe, as it evolved in the following decade, was transformed by Metternich into a weapon to suppress all attempts at national emancipation.

Metternich's 'system', which dominated Europe (although with increasing difficulty) until 1848, was an extension to the entire Continent of the principles upon which his master, Francis I, based his rule of the Austrian empire. Monarchy was the only sure foundation of order, and although the prince could no longer claim divine approbation (especially given the im-perfect application of the principle of legitimacy in the interests of the balance of power), his authority remained absolute, only subject to his recognition of the requirements of justice and humanity. Constitutional monarchy was thus inadmissible in principle and a subversive threat in practice. At most, carefully delimited and politically impotent consultative bodies could be accepted, as indeed could conservative constitutions, sanc-tioned by tradition and alien to all concepts of popular sovereignty, such as existed in Hungary.

'Nations' existed only in so far as they had shown themselves capable of maintaining their political independence over the centuries. 'Subjects' were not interested in chimeric ideas of nationalism proposed by revolutionary sectarians, but only in their material well-being and the efficient administra-tion of just laws. Hence all threats to these true interests of subjects must be suppressed, by censorship, secret police (and Metternich maintained a private spy service in Germany and Italy) or international intervention. Europe constituted a unity, a 'society of states', which implied as its corollary that disturbance in one part inevitably affected the whole, that domestic policy was closely dependent upon international considerations. Leadership in opposing such disturbance naturally belonged to Austria, as the hege-monic power on the Continent, concerned to preserve the balance of power against the threat of Russia. The means to achieve the conservation of the political and social status quo consisted of periodic congresses in which governments could be made to assume their responsibilities by adopting necessary preventive measures against subversion.

Metternich was able to apply this 'system' successfully in the early years of the Restoration not only because of Alexander I's rapid conversion to absolutist principles from his earlier enthusiasm for a religious regeneration of peoples, but also because of France's impotence and Castlereagh's hesitations between his broader concern for Europe and the specific interests of Britain. Already at the Aix-la-Chapelle (Aachen) congress of 1818 Alexander wanted the Holy Alliance to act as formal guarantor of European peace. Castlereagh opposed this, and managed to prevent discussion of European intervention against the Spanish American colonies which had revolted. But the following year at Carlsbad (Karlovy Vary), after Kotzebue's murder by a radical student, he was prepared to accept Metternich's repressive measures against 'revolutionary intrigues' in the German Confederation.

When revolutions broke out in Spain and Portugal in 1820, followed by those in the Two Sicilies (1820) and Piedmont (1821) and then in Greece (1821), Castlereagh's opposition became explicit as the Mediterranean concerned British interests directly. Although he managed temporarily to avoid intervention in Spain by his note of 5 May 1820, he could only protest against the Troppau (Opava) congress protocol (19 November 1820), in which Metternich persuaded the powers to establish the principle of European intervention against any state in revolution. Italy, like Germany, was regarded as of immediate Austrian concern, and at Laibach (Ljubljana) (January 1821) England did not oppose, but merely abstained from the congress's decision to authorize Austrian intervention in Naples at its sovereign's request, whereas – supported by Austria – it prevented Russian intervention against Turkey over the Greek rebellion. At the congress of Verona (October–November 1822) an isolated England was unable to prevent authorization of a French expedition against the Spanish liberals.

The Verona congress was the final instance of Metternich's undisputed hegemony. Castlereagh, while affirming the principle of non-intervention, regarded the concert of powers as too important to break and was in any case reluctant to turn to English opinion for support. But the right of intervention, once recognized, increased the mutual suspicion among the powers. Russian spying activities in Italy, the Balkans, even Spain; Austrian interference in Germany; French intervention for purposes of prestige in Spain, all strained the earlier sense of agreement. After Castlereagh's suicide (August 1822), Canning, as moderate a tory as his predecessor but indifferent to the idea of European collaboration, displayed a narrower concern for specifically British interests. But, more open in his support of constitutional liberalism and his readiness to appeal to public opinion, Canning deliberately split the unity of the congress system. Following President Monroe's warning to the Holy Alliance against intervention in Latin America, Canning gave official British recognition to the new republics (January 1825). The following year a British fleet ensured the introduction of a moderate constitution in Portugal. But the destruction of the congress system was achieved by Canning's leadership of European liberal and romantic opinion in favour of the Greek war of independence: the British foreign secretary won the support first of the new tsar Nicolas I (4 April 1826) and then of a French government frightened by the strength of public opinion (6 July 1827). The congresses began to be replaced by lower level conferences usually held at London. It was such a conference which – after the destruction of the Turco-Egyptian fleet by the allied navies at Navarino Bay (October 1827) – guaranteed independence to the Greeks (1829-30). By the time the July revolution of 1830 broke out in France, the congress system lay in shambles.

The ideology of the Restoration

By 1830 the more extreme forms of Restoration culture had also begun to disintegrate, although their partial absorption into the forms of government and administration of most European states still seemed firm.

The fall of Napoleon was regarded as marking the end of an historical period by both conservatives and progressives. Civilization had reached one of those turning points which periodically marked its path. The era of individualism and rationalism had given way to a new 'organic' age, in which the individual was replaced by the community, anti-historical abstract rationalism by morality, religious faith and an historical sense of the past. Amidst the confusion of this Restoration revulsion against Enlightenment and dictatorship, these vague but potent ideas could be utilized, with opposing intent, by both reactionary and visionary progressive thinkers, by de Maistre and Saint-Simon. Romanticism, widespread among the new generation of intellectuals, accentuated this common heritage, with its credo of instinct, tradition, faith, 'human nature', non-rational 'true' reason, the 'genius' of heroes and peoples. Democratic, socialist and liberal writers, as different as Mazzini, Fourier or Gioberti, were to retain specific but numerous threads of the romantic culture of the Restoration.

But if many ideas were shared initially, conservative and progressive thought differed fundamentally over the concept of progress and the significance of history. Progress, in the sense of the advance of civilization, did not exist for the traditionalist writers. For Joseph de Maistre and Louis de Bonald experience demonstrated the emptiness, inefficacy and indeed impiety of attempts to create a new society by the abstract use of reason.

The only hope was to revert to an earlier, uncontaminated society, in which order and hierarchy were respected and the theocratic basis of monarchy consecrated by an infallible pope or divine revelation. De Maistre and de Bonald, like Ludwig von Haller with his vision of the State as a family ruled by a patriarchal monarch, represented the extreme and isolated fringe of a broad spectrum of anti-progressive thought. But, like the German 'historical school' of jurists such as Savigny and Eichhorn who emphasized historical continuity against revolution, or German romantics such as Novalis or Schlegel, they assigned a dominant role to the Church and Christianity. *Christianity OR Europe*, Novalis entitled a famous work. But, in fact, a 'Christian Europe' was the ideal of these writers, a Europe such as had existed in the Middle Ages, which led them to glorify the roles – indeed, the missions – of the papacy and the Austrian empire. To revive this ideal, it was necessary to attack and refute the corrosive influences of more recent ages, the uncertainty which derived from free rational enquiry, the individualism of political liberalism and a materialist economy.

The revival of faith in Catholicism was the most visible aspect of these anti-progressive attempts to justify intellectually and influence in practice the order and hierarchy of the political Restoration. Pius VII emerged from his imprisonment in Savona with the halo of the martyr. The return to the faith of the educated classes (in contrast to the growing trend of secularization among the urban labouring classes) was accompanied by a readiness on the part of most monarchs to abandon the anticlerical attitude of their eighteenth-century predecessors. The Church was an important support in the reconstruction of legitimate order and hierarchy, even for Protestant princes, such as the kings of Holland, Prussia or England, with large Catholic minorities. The old national churches had disappeared under Napoleonic despotism, offering a unique opportunity, as cardinal Consalvi realized, to assert papal supremacy and reduce the local churches to mere emanations from Rome. For the 'ultramontanes', led most vocally and effectively by Lamennais, the only way to restore the moral and social order destroyed by the individualist reason of the *lumières* was total submission to the Church:

> When Christianity promulgates, with authority and without hesitation, the truths which are necessary to man, it does not require man to understand them fully, because man understands nothing in this manner; but it wants the motives of his faith to be evident to reason, *rationabile obsequium vestrum*.
> (Omodeo, 193, p. 110)

The restoration of the Jesuit Order, the 'missions' of young priests into the French countryside, the introduction and diffusion of semi-superstitious practices – the rosary, the Marian month, the cults of the Sacred Heart of Jesus and the Sacred Heart of Mary – all reflected a passionate desire for religion, which, by its very emphasis on the external trappings rather than on internal conviction, was symptomatic of a search for a secure and immutable authority in which both individuals and society could place their trust.

This resurgence of Catholicism and the papacy was weakened, however, by the very enthusiasm of its most ardent supporters, both within the curia and in the lay world. The total faith of a Lamennais was based upon his conviction of the precedence of religion over all human institutions and implied an integral theocracy. The formula of 'throne and altar', for which the princes were ready to pay the price of an accommodation with the papacy, was soon threatened by the intransigence of the ultramontanes. But, equally, within the curia, the sense of triumph (even vindictiveness) of the 'zealots', personified by cardinal Pacca, threatened to arouse renewed hostility through their refusal to forgive and forget the past. The papal nuncio at Vienna, Severoli, voiced Consalvi's concern when he wrote to the pope: 'His Holiness in his wisdom will do what is most fitting. It seems to me that a dispensation for the past, given the circumstances, is equivalent to a prohibition for the future' (Omodeo, 193, p. 374). Consalvi was acutely aware of the papacy's fundamental weakness, its inability to impose obedience: 'The worst trouble is the impossibility (so, alas, I believe) of upholding and realizing in the future what we said we wanted' (Omodeo, 193, p. 379).

By its intransigence, the curia lost the sympathy the pope had at first enjoyed, aroused the hostility of the emperor Francis I, firm in his assertion of the josephine tradition, and identified the organized Church too closely with the Restoration settlement. Although cardinal Consalvi was successful in preventing the re-emergence of national churches subject to their monarchs, he had separated the papacy, aligned with the most retrograde of Restoration governments, from educated Catholic opinion. First in France and then elsewhere in western Europe, as liberal ideas increasingly challenged the anti-progressive, hierarchical philosophy of the Restoration by their emphasis on progress, liberty and the positive achievements of the Revolution, so many educated Catholics turned away from the papacy towards an interior, individual faith or a utopian reconciliation of Catholicism and liberty. These new ideas emerged slowly within the leaden structures that characterized most Restoration governments before 1830.

Restoration in Italy

The great powers at Vienna, far from advocating a return to the pre-revolutionary situation, had recognized the massive changes in private property occasioned by the sales of ecclesiastical and demesnial lands, and had accepted the existence or possibility of granting constitutions – for instance in France, the German Confederation and individual German states. Indeed, concerned to prevent an immediate revival of opposition, many rulers had been advised (and some obliged) to abstain from a purge of the administrators and officers of the Napoleonic years. France offered the most striking example of a compromise between the pre-revolutionary forces, represented by the person of Louis XVIII, brother of the king guillotined in 1793, and the demands for popular sovereignty which had triumphed during the Revolution. On Talleyrand's advice, the new king asserted his personal authority by revising and decreeing the constitution proposed by the French Senate; the years of the Restoration witnessed a struggle between the opposing forces over the liberties guaranteed by this *Charte octroyée*. But France, as the epicentre of the Revolution, had experienced the deepest transformations, which continued to dominate the political, social and cultural life of the country in subsequent years. Elsewhere, either because the Revolutionary period had made less impact, or because the restored monarchs refused to recognize the implications of the preceding decades, the intentions of the great powers at Vienna to negotiate a peaceful settlement by acceptance of social changes but rejection of political claims were often defeated. The attempts to achieve an authentic restoration were most visible in Spain – where Ferdinand VII revoked the constitution of 1812 and reintroduced the Inquisition – and the Italian peninsula.

Habsburg Italy

The kingdom of Lombardy Venetia (created by imperial decree on 7 April 1815) offered, by contrast, an example to most of the Italian states of an attempt to accompany absolute authority with a just administration. More than elsewhere in his empire, Francis I felt the need to offer at least a symbolic appearance of self-government to his Italian subjects: as viceroy he appointed his brother, archduke Rainier, whose functions however soon emerged as purely ceremonial. Two central congregations at Milan and Venice, with subsidiary provincial congregations, were formed of wealthy tax-payers nominated by the emperor, with limited consultative functions, particularly over the distribution of new taxes. At the local level, the communal law of 1755 was revived, by which a general council of tax-payers met twice annually to approve the local budget and nominate to local office. Although this law gave slightly greater autonomy to the communes than under Napoleon, the entire structure of the administration was broadly similar to that of the Kingdom of Italy, with its heavy centralization and its emphasis on the wealthy members of the population, whether landowners or merchants. The judicial and financial structures also tended to follow the pattern of those of the Napoleonic kingdom, with the introduction into the kingdom of the recent Austrian codes. Relations with the Church, in contrast to almost every other Italian state, retained the josephine and Napoleonic imprint of strong state control, with imperial nomination of bishops and confirmation of the sale of ecclesiastical lands. Concern for education, again a Habsburg trait, placed Lombardy-Venetia far ahead of the other Italian states. Nearly all the Italian civil servants of the Napoleonic government retained their positions, and at first very few 'foreigners' were sent from Vienna.

Austrian rule in Lombardy-Venetia thus consciously avoided any abrupt break with modifications wrought by the Napoleonic years. It attempted to satisfy the population by a fair and basically honest administration, which for many decades remained undoubtedly more modern than that of such other Italian states as Piedmont or Naples. Nevertheless, discontent and opposition arose almost immediately among far broader sectors of the population than the small groups who had attempted to retain the independence of the Kingdom of Italy in 1814.

In two major respects the new administration altered or worsened the arrangements of the preceding government. Firstly, conscription was imposed for eight years (double the time of the 1802 law) and enforced more strictly than in the imperial possessions north of the Alps. Service in this multinational army, nearly always outside Italy, removed all patriotic motivation such as had inspired the officers of the former Italian army. Secondly, the commercial links with France and the west were abruptly cut off by the imposition of the Austrian 'prohibitive system' of customs barriers on imports, exports and transit goods, erected for fiscal purposes. Even after the removal of the barriers dividing Lombardy from Venetia and the whole Kingdom from the rest of the empire (1822, 1825), Viennese economic policy continued to direct the trade of its Italian possessions towards the imperial market by the maintenance of protective barriers against France and Piedmont. Venice suffered most, given Austrian determination to boost Trieste as the major imperial port. But the Lombard commercial classes felt handicapped in their trade with the 'natural' outlets of Genoa and Lyons, despite the compensation of improved road and postal communications with central Europe across the Gotthard and Splugen passes.

Resentment against Austria spread with the sense of foreign domination. Venice was humiliated by its continued subordination to Milan through Austrian decision. But the ruling classes in both Lombardy and Venetia were hostile to the presence of a 'foreign' army of occupation. The extreme centralization of the administration at Vienna, typical of the whole empire, soon revealed the emptiness of the local concessions and the limited possibilities of a career in the civil service. Initially Austria was understanding about the cost of winding up the Napoleonic administration and installing the new one, and even more about the fiscal consequences of the tragic famine which affected Italy, as all Europe, in 1816-17 (Venetia had already experienced a famine in 1813-14). But soon there was a widespread conviction – confirmed by the secrecy which surrounded the budgets – that Vienna was exploiting its Italian kingdom financially to subsidize the regular and growing annual deficits of the imperial budget.

Bellegarde, governor of the kingdom until 1816, warned Metternich:

> Even in this moment in which I cease to hold influence over the administration of this country, I shall not tire of repeating that it is absolutely necessary wholly to abandon the idea of a future, albeit slow, assimilation of these provinces within the German body of the empire, and similarly to abandon that plan of complete fusion, already attempted with total lack of success by the emperor Joseph II at a time when the ties of affection and obedience to the house of Austria were extremely strong. (Sandonà, 210, pp. 359–67)

Four years later, after revolution had broken out in Naples, the new governor Strassoldo sent an identical danger signal to Metternich:

> The Lombards have been and always will be unable to get used to the Germanic forms imprinted on the government of their country; they loathe them, and they detest the system of uniformity by which they have been put on a par with Germans, Bohemians and Galicians.

But Metternich's regular response was to tighten the system of censorship and espionage. After the failure of a clumsy attempt to subsidize, secretly, a cultural journal, the anti-intellectual character of Austrian censorship alienated a further sector of the population.

If Habsburg rule failed to gain public support in Lombardy-Venetia, it appeared to achieve greater success in two other Italian states. In the small duchy of Parma, Maria Luisa, assisted by her lover (and subsequently morganatic husband) general Neipperg, maintained Napoleonic legislation, only substituting the French civil code by a carefully prepared and generally admired new one (1820). As in Lombardy-Venetia, no concessions were made to the Church and clergy, whose subordination by the Napoleonic concordat was confirmed. Concern for public education and economic activities, typically Enlightened Habsburg traits, were accompanied by only mild police controls.

The grand-duchy of Tuscany (now enlarged by the annexation of the former Neapolitan state of the Presidi, or 'garrisons', Piombino and Elba) was the only state in Italy where the Napoleonic years had not created a sense of rupture. The Tuscan ruling class, which had collaborated with Napoleon in furthering the Leopoldine reforms, now ensured that there was no break in this tradition. Vittorio Fossombroni, a leading administrator during the French years, who virtually ruled Tuscany until his death in 1844, personified this continuity. Although Leopoldine legislation was in general substituted for that of Napoleon, the latter's major improvements, directed against landed privileges or to further commerce, were maintained:

laws abolishing fiefs and entails, establishing the land-tax register, the commercial code, the regulation of mortgages. Similarly, the Napoleonic administrative system, which had practically abolished communal self-government, was essentially adopted. Ecclesiastical legislation was restored, negotiations with the papacy over ecclesiastical property broken off, and the Jesuits prohibited entry into Tuscany. Alone in Italy, Fossombroni and Ferdinand III returned to Leopold's free trade legislation, despite popular discontent during the famine years of 1816-17. Censorship and police spying were of less importance than anywhere else in Italy in this state whose rulers were convinced that there could be no real advance on its particular form of eighteenth-century Enlightened reformism.

Southern and central Italy

Hatred of the ideas and men of the immediate past inevitably exerted a strong influence in the capitals of Restoration Italy. Metternich and Castlereagh had been concerned to prevent precisely such a reaction and Metternich imposed specific conditions on Ferdinand of the Two Sicilies as the price of Austrian support for his restoration to Naples (treaty of Casa Lanza, 20 May 1815; Austro-Bourbon treaties, 29 April, 12 June 1815). As Metternich wrote: 'We proposed as our goal to enchain and smother the spirit of partisanship and vengeance, to ensure respect for the right of property based upon the laws, and finally to forestall all dangerous reaction which could compromise the peace of the country' (Romeo, 221, p. 53, n. 5).

Ferdinand, more cautious after the experiences of his first restoration, agreed to grant a full amnesty for the past, guarantee all purchases of lands and titles made during the Murattian years, and accept full parity of treatment between legitimists and Murattians in the army and administration. He also pledged himself not to grant a constitution. The retention of the entire body of former civil servants and officers implied in practice acceptance of the deep transformations of the Murattian period and an effective check on any attempt at a full restoration. The threat of such an attempt was serious, given the influence and vindictiveness of the nobles who had followed the king from Sicily and gained the appointment as minister of police of the almost mystically reactionary prince of Canosa (January 1816). For five months Canosa endeavoured to unleash a massive repression against the *carboneria*, now hostile to the Bourbon dynasty because of its refusal to grant a constitution. He was even ready to ignore legal procedures and employ the reactionary sect of the *calderari* in order to create himself a broader base in the country. Only after Canosa's dismissal through Austrian and English pressure was the leading minister Luigi de' Medici able to apply the policy of administrative absolutism which he had unsuccessfully attempted during the first restoration and during the years of exile in Sicily.

Luigi de' Medici, like Fossombroni, had gained his early experience in the Enlightened tradition, but in the very different circumstances of Naples. Only too conscious of the divisive effects of the revolutionary years, he now aimed at restoring the authority of the Crown by a policy of 'amalgamation' between the Murattians and the most able diplomats and administrators of the exiled government in Sicily. The reforms of the French period were to be accepted, with modifications, and the efficiency of the administration increased by a rigid centralization of the two parts of the kingdom. Separation in the past had been the ruin of Naples, and now 'if the two kingdoms are once separated, the kings of Naples and Sicily will become the dukes of Parma and Modena of the south of Italy' (Romeo, 221, p. 87). The unification of the kingdom was symbolized by the change in Ferdinand's title from that of Ferdinand IV of Naples and III of Sicily to Ferdinand I of the Kingdom of the Two Sicilies (8 December 1816).

The practical consequence was the application to Sicily of Neapolitan legislation and administration: the constitution of 1812 was suspended, the island's offices in Sicily and a quarter of those in the united kingdom were reserved to Sicilians and the direct tax contribution remained fixed at the level decreed by the 1813 parliament. The new administrative and judicial structures, like the new codes, substantially maintained those of the Murattian decade on the mainland. In Sicily, the effect was to cut through the local traditions and customary practices of the island in one sweep. But it also opened up new careers in the administration. The abolition of entails, like the attempted abolition of communal customary pasturage rights, was aimed at completing the destruction of feudalism in Sicily, as had for the most part been achieved on the mainland during the previous decade. Small groups of Sicilian middle-class liberals (mainly from Catania and the east coast) were attracted by these reforms. But hostility grew steadily among many sectors of the population. The dominant noble ruling class resented the loss of the influence and power it had achieved with the 1812 constitution. The inhabitants of Palermo saw the former capital reduced to merely one of seven administrative centres. Conscription was imposed for the first time and aroused widespread opposition. The merchants objected strongly to the new internal customs barrier erected between the two parts of the kingdom, which favoured Naples. These very different grounds for opposition to Medici's centralizing policy began to coalesce in the demand for a separate Sicilian kingdom under the constitution of 1812.

The counterpart to administrative centralization for Medici was to be a balanced fiscal policy which would not burden the people. The huge bribes which had been expended to ensure Allied confirmation of the Restoration and the cost of the Austrian army of occupation led to a financial crisis by 1817. To obtain a balanced budget, Medici insisted on the withdrawal of Austrian troops, gained large foreign loans, cut expenditure on public works and revived confidence in the public debt. The total budget was kept at a level lower than in Murat's final years, but without shifting the burden onto indirect taxes or local finances. The principle was clear: 'under constitutional governments the people strain at the leash, but tolerate exactions; under absolute governments they do not tolerate them' (Romeo, 221, p. 73). For the same reasons, in the face of the economic crisis which followed the end of the Continental Blockade, with the collapse of local industries and the competition of cheaper grains from the Black Sea, Medici adopted measures to protect the poor classes by a customs system that favoured imports at the expense of exports. The pattern of Bourbon finances laid down by Medici was to remain unchanged until the final collapse of the kingdom in 1860: low taxes, constant concern not to burden the poor classes, but a withdrawal of the State from necessary public expenditure to stimulate the economy.

Fair taxes, good laws and administration seemed to Medici a sure method of winning public opinion. But his freedom of action had been limited in two crucial areas – foreign trade and ecclesiastical policy. Under pressure from Britain and France, he had been obliged to grant a 10 per cent reduction on customs duties paid on goods carried in British, French and Spanish ships to compensate them for former privileges (1816–18). Local producers, especially the smaller landowners, already hit by the agricultural crisis and the heavy weight of the land-tax, became increasingly critical. Intellectual opinion grew equally hostile as Medici was forced by Ferdinand to conclude a concordat with the papacy (1818), which ran counter to the entire struggle for secular sovereignty of eighteenth-century Naples. Although Medici negotiated quite favourable terms, along the lines of Napoleon's 1803 concordat (confirmation of the sales of ecclesiastical lands, royal nomination of bishops), ecclesiastical courts and censorship were re-established, monasteries were refounded and the growth of the ecclesiastical patrimony encouraged. Clerical interference and an air of the confessional began to pervade the government. Medici's remarkable tolerance towards the secret sects, based on his conviction that the State was superior to parties and 'extremes', merely increased the suspicion of the conservatives (even of Metternich) and the optimism of the sectarian liberals. The 'administrative state' and policy of 'amalgamation', far from bridging the gap between government and people, in many ways had increased tensions and opposition.

In the Papal States the power of the 'zealots' reduced Consalvi's attempts to create an 'administrative state' to an empty shell. Absolute in power by tradition and apostolic inheritance, stimulated by the wave of ultramontanism, rendered arrogant by the imposition of concordats on at least the weak Italian states, exempt as a non-signatory from the treaty of Vienna, the pope wasted no time in eliminating all traces of the impious French regime, from the restoration in the Lazio and Umbria of all the old legislative and administrative practices (municipal statutes and customs, ecclesiastical and noble privileges) to the abolition of vaccination and street lighting.

Consalvi, on his return from Vienna, managed to retain part of the Napoleonic legislation in the provinces he had saved from Austrian cupidity (Marches and Legations) and then, by the *motu proprio* of 6 July 1816, to modernize the administrative, judicial, financial structures of the entire state, so reducing the sharp differences between its two parts. Except for Rome, the state was divided into 17 administrative provinces ruled by cardinal legates or apostolic delegates, assisted by government-nominated, partly lay, consultative congregations. Lay or ecclesiastical governors were in charge of the cities and districts, with similarly mixed councils over each commune. The individual statutes of the communes were thus abolished, as were most baronial privileges, while baronial judicial powers and entails, where still in existence (in the provinces first restored to the pope), were severely limited. Past alienations of ecclesiastical lands were recognized, but the State assumed responsibility for paying indemnities to the former owners. The land-tax was imposed without immunity, but on the basis of Pius VI's land register which contained all the irregularities of earlier registers; only the personal tax and the tax on trade and professions were abolished. A uniform, moderately protective customs duty was applied to the whole state, aimed more at increasing State income than developing domestic industry. In 1818, after the famine of the previous years, export of grain was prohibited when it reached a fixed price, anachronistically following the lines of the system first adopted and then revoked by Peter Leopold in the 1760s. The Napoleonic codes were abolished, but only two new codes were prepared (civil procedure and a 'regulation of commerce'), in all other respects leaving in existence the former pontifical legislation.

The reforms, bitterly opposed by the 'zealots', represented a far less positive compromise with the Napoleonic changes than Medici had achieved in Naples. Pontifical fiscal policy proved wholly inadequate and from 1818 the burden of taxation increased steadily as the State passed many charges to the provincial administrations. The customs tariffs created disputes between the few industrialists and the traders of the ports of Ancona and Civitavecchia; the exemptions granted to cardinals and foreign ambassadors defeated even the fiscal purposes for which the duties had been imposed. Agriculture declined, unable to meet the competition of Russian grain, and this worsening situation aroused the hostility of the new landed middle classes of the Legations and Marches, and even that of the landed nobles, resentful of the restoration of ecclesiastical privileges. The crisis of the once-important fair at Senigallia became acute, as did that of the (mainly Roman) craftsmen. Clerical-dominated public education proved inadequate and charity failed to stem the growing number of beggars, an endemic feature of papal society remarked upon by all foreign visitors. But worst of all was the revival of the ecclesiastical monopoly of the administration, which Consalvi had been unable to prevent. It led to inefficient and corrupt government, particularly after Pius VII's death (1823) and Consalvi's dismissal. 'A cardinal is a prince in Rome, a pasha in the provinces' (Demarco, 216, pp. 26–7), wrote Pellegrino Rossi some years later. The anachronistic administration of the restored Papal States appeared immediately to both foreign statesmen and Italians as an inevitable incitement to opposition and rebellion. The temporal power of the pope was well described as the 'plague' of Italy.

No Consalvi held power in Modena or Piedmont. In consequence, although the lay administrations of these states proved more efficient, their rulers imposed a more complete restoration than elsewhere in Italy. Francis IV of Modena, relying on Austrian support, abolished almost all Napoleonic legislation, returning to the eighteenth-century administration of the house of Este. The civil service was purged of all who had served the Italic Kingdom and the major offices, at both central and local level, were reserved for faithful nobles. Ignoring the pre-revolutionary, Enlightened reforms of Rangone, Francis considered the state as his private patrimony, which he administered absolutely but with a certain ability. The most reactionary Catholic tendencies were encouraged, the Jesuits welcomed and religious orders restored (1821), even at the risk of a clash with Metternich. 'Throne and altar' was the keynote of this ambitious prince's rule, and his obscure contacts with reactionary Catholic sects, such as the 'consistorials', fitted both his temperament and his hopes of territorial aggrandisement at the expense of Lombardy or Parma.

Piedmont

The Restoration in Piedmont was as integral as in Modena. An edict of 21 May 1814 stated that: 'without regard to any other law, from the above date the royal constitutions of 1770 and other provisions issued up to the period beginning 23 June 1800 [i.e. the French occupation] shall be observed' (Romeo, 199, p. 10). The Napoleonic codes were replaced by the previous Piedmontese legislation and judicial order, to the extent of driving the Jews back to the ghetto, harassing the Waldensians and suppressing the public notification of mortgages. An attempt was made to dismiss or humiliate all who had collaborated with the French, although by 1817, with the appointment to the government of two Napoleonic administrators, Prospero Balbo and San Marzano, this was recognized as impracticable. Although the French fiscal institutions were retained (as elsewhere in Italy), protectionist barriers were restored at the frontiers and within the Sardinian state: the customs duties between Piedmont and Genoa tragically aggravated the famine of 1817 and were abolished the following year. The restoration of guilds and industrial privileges worsened the economic crisis of these post-war years. Politically, administratively and economically Victor Emanuel and the Court thus attempted to return to what they conceived to be the pre-revolutionary traditions and practices of the house of Savoy.

Like the rulers of Naples and Modena, the king of Sardinia regarded the Church as a necessary ally: although the sales of ecclesiastical lands were accepted, the religious orders were recalled and endowed, the Jesuits given control of education and censorship, a concordat was signed with Rome which re-established ecclesiastical courts (1817). On de Maistre's advice the semi-secret sect 'Christian amity' was transformed into a public lay organization, 'Catholic amity', which propagandized the most retrograde aspects of Catholic culture. So out of touch with the changed times was the Court that San Marzano could express hurt surprise at the critical reception of the government's policy:

> So what do they complain of? The censorship of books, entrusted to the old inquisitors, most respectable men, without the re-establishment of the inquisitor? The order that our most holy religion be observed and respected? The bishops' examination of the conduct of clerics? Oh really, there is no reason to make a noise about these measures, so essential to religion and the state. (Omodeo, 193, p. 359)

In so far as Victor Emanuel attempted to win public support, he did so on the basis of loyalty to the dynasty, with its long-standing military traditions. A vastly disproportionate part of the budget was spent on the army, and assertions of the 'Italian role' of the house of Savoy began to circulate widely for the first time. Did not the possession of Genoa prove that Savoy's future lay south of the Alps? But even this dynastic, 'Italian' policy proved ineffective in winning support (except among the already converted), as the king refused to press the traditional anti-Austrian policy of the Savoys beyond cabinet intrigues. For the Court, absolutism with a centralizing administration was the only method of holding together a state composed of so many disparate parts as the kingdom of Sardinia. But the king and his ministers, emerging from the semi-feudal atmosphere of the island of Sardinia, seemed unable to recognize that at least a modern form of absolutism was required. This sense of bewilderment at the depth of social change, as typical a trait of Piedmont in these early Restoration years as the militarism and clericalism, is poignantly revealed in the ingenuous complaint in the early 1820s by the Turin council of commerce that in the olden days people dressed according to their social rank:

> A more useful separation arose from this distinction. As no regular communication or correspondence took place between these classes, the customs of the different orders were maintained, and in consequence there was a greater respect for the more distinguished people in society: in short, honour was the

most effective stimulus of those happy times of the past. . . . Among the innumerable other ills produced by the revolution was the destruction of this basis and the introduction of a total confusion among the different classes. . . . Everyone dresses in the same manner, the noble cannot be distinguished from the plebeian, the merchant from the magistrate, the proprietor from the crafts-man, the master from the servant; at least in appearances, the woeful prin-ciple that created the revolutions is regrettably maintained. (Fossati, 230, p. 55)

Opposition to Restoration

The depth of the social transformations of the revolutionary period and the confused character of the anti-Napoleonic movements made it inevitable that the Restoration should have aroused opposition from the moment of its installation. This opposition, with strong ties of continuity with that ex-pressed during Napoleon's 'Hundred Days', assumed two different and antagonistic forms – open, lawful liberal criticism and secret sectarian liberal-democratic plots. Whereas the sects which had formed against Napoleon in such different countries as France, Spain, Switzerland, Italy, and Germany continued and extended the geographical range of their activi-ties, the liberal opposition developed initially in France, where past ex-periences, the present political settlement – the *Charte* – and the intensity of ideological discussions offered the most suitable conditions. France thus continued to exert its political and cultural influence on Europe in the decades following the overthrow of Napoleon.

The constriction of public opinion and free discussion by Napoleon's imposition of an imperial 'official' culture had led during the 'Hundred Days' to remarkably open demands for constitutional guarantees of liberty, which continued after the Restoration through fears that the 'ultras' would reduce the *Charte* to an empty formality. In these early years the liberals, of whatever hue, agreed in abandoning all theories of popular sovereignty and universal suffrage, regarded as the source of anarchy. Madame de Staël, whose posthumously published *Considerations on the Principal Events of the French Revolution* (1818) opened the way for a positive assessment of the revolutionary years, offered an ode to individual liberty as the ideal of life, destroyed by the egalitarian Revolution, which had led inevitably to the degenerations of 1793 and Napoleon: 'the only permissible reflection is that the remedy for popular passions is not despotism, but the rule of law' (Omodeo, 193, p. 223). The independent Benjamin Constant and the minute but effective group of 'doctrinaires', such as Guizot and Broglie, equally stressed 'legal liberties' against the dangers of reactionary legitimacy. The 'doctrinaires', consciously rejecting the revolutionary experience, asserted the organic nature of society. This required the unity and com-penetration of powers in order to avoid the disastrous consequences of their separation in the revolutionary years; the monarchy was to be raised above political strife, to act as the conscience of a nation protected by the full exercise of liberties, and so inhibit the degeneration of differences of public opinion into factions. Bulwark of these liberties was the constitution, an ideal whose physiognomy remained imprecise, not least because of the universal ignorance of constitutional practices outside France. After disillusionment with England's part in the Restoration, the 'doctrinaires' supported a form of constitutionalism which left the monarchy as the centre of power guaranteeing, together with parliament, freedom of speech, freedom of vote, freedom of the press and freedom of religion.

The French *Charte*, with its nominated hereditary senate and its high age and property qualifications for the chamber, offered the model for more conservative liberals in Europe throughout the Restoration. But for the constitution to be effective, the exercise of liberties by the citizen required guarantees. An intense political struggle developed in France, particularly during the reaction following the murder of the duke of Berry (February 1820), to conserve these liberties against administrative centralization and pressure from the 'ultras'. The method of defending these liberties – especially freedom of the press and protection of the individual against administrative abuse – by winning public opinion through the formation of legal associations, constituted the essence of the new liberal ideology, which opposed the hierarchical-Catholic ideology of the Restoration and offered an alternative, politically more effective and morally more valid, to the illegal plots of the sectarians. The young generation of liberals, such as Jouffrey and Guizot, saw itself as the herald of a new progressive civilization, natural and sole heir of a Revolution and Empire accepted and romanticized in the historiography of Thiers, Mignet and Michelet, superior to both the prejudices and egotisms of the old order and the individualist scepticism and Jacobinism of the revolutionaries. It was the ideology of the wealthier bourgeoisie which had triumphed in France, and which was as much concerned to exclude the direct political participation of the masses as to conserve its own liberties.

The secret sects, which had been encouraged in their struggle against Napoleon by allied promises of constitutional liberties and national independence, inevitably turned against the Restoration settlement and its guarantor, the Holy Alliance. The sects varied in ideology, structure and methods. Their goals ranged from simple political demands for independence or a constitution to the egalitarianism or social aspirations of democrats such as Luigi Angeloni or ex-Jacobins and babouvists such as Buonarroti; their structures went from the hierarchical masonic pattern of the 'sublime perfect masters' to the decentralized concentric network of local 'churches' of the *adelfi*; their methods extended from attempted military coups by ex-Jacobin officers to insurrections based on broad sectors of the population.

Under the Restoration the sects maintained and expanded their organizations within the armies, among the students and educated classes and, in some states, among the craftsmen, lower clergy and popular classes. Their activities spread internationally, united only in their common opposition to the international settlement imposed by the European concert.

In France the sectarians, aiming at a more liberal constitution, or a republic, or Jacobin ideals, were groups in the 'Union', founded by the ex-Jacobin Joseph Rey in 1816, and in the *adelfi*, where Angeloni and Buonarroti played important roles. In Germany, pro-independence and republican sectarians in the *Tugendbund* and *Unbedingten* tried to influence the student *Burschenschaften*. In Russia the liberals, mainly officers, formed the 'Union of Salvation', of masonic derivation (1816). In Belgium and Poland the liberal sectarians plotted for national independence. In Greece the *etairìa* planned a rising for independence and religious liberty. In Spain the more moderate liberals were grouped in the freemasonry, the more democratic in the *comuneros*, but both agreed on the need to restore the Cadiz constitution of 1812. In Italy a similar division existed between the moderate and democratic sectarians, but the two main sects – the *carboneria* in the south and the 'sublime perfect masters' in the north – were accompanied by a multitude of smaller secret associations, continuously changing name and organization to avoid detection, and often controlled – without their knowledge – by one or the other of the major sects.

The existence of the sects, periodically infiltrated by spies, was known to the governments, who tended – on the basis of police reports – to exaggerate the efficacy of their international links. Two centres did, in fact, attempt to co-ordinate the activities of the sects: a 'Directive Committee' at Paris, consisting of all shades of French opposition, Orleanist, Bonapartist, republican, Jacobin, and including the aged Lafayette, the financier Laffitte, the republican Angeloni and the Buonarrotian Voyer d'Argenson; and an even more mysterious 'Grand Firmament' at Geneva (probably personified by Buonarroti alone), which attempted to direct in a centralized and hierarchical manner an international network of republican sects, with secret socialist goals. But the risings, conspiracies and insurrections of these years at Lyons (1816, 1817), Macerata (1817), Wartburg (1817), Fratta Polesine (1818), Valenza (1819) and in the Balkans – broke out spontaneously, outside the control of either centre.

Liberal opposition in Italy

Opposition to the Restoration in Italy, whether liberal or sectarian, was closely influenced by and often directly connected to the opposition in France and elsewhere in Europe.

The liberal philosophy was expressed most clearly in Lombardy, where the initial mildness of the Austrian administration and the close intellectual contacts with France enabled former exponents of the Napoleonic regime and the new younger generation to elaborate a cultural programme that combined a romantic sense of political independence with an intuition of the practical need to keep up with the level of English and French technological progress. In eclectic manner, both parts of this programme found expression in *Il Conciliatore, The Conciliator* (September 1818–October 1819), a journal much vaunted but of questionable efficacy (given the restricted, almost family groups within which it circulated), except for the clamorous manner of its suppression by the Austrian censor. As Silvio Pellico, a major contributor, soon to be imprisoned by the Austrians, wrote after it had been banned:

> The provocations we suffered, the delays imposed by the double censorship on the publication of *The Conciliator*, the continuous rumour that we were about to be suppressed, opened the eyes of even the blindest; *romantic* was recognized as a synonym for *liberal*, and nobody dared to call himself a classicist, except for the ultras [i.e. reactionaries] and spies. (Branca, 211, vol. 1, p. xli)

For Pellico, Confalonieri and the other members of the group responsible for *The Conciliator*, the tradition of a 'civil literature' expounded by the poet Ugo Foscolo offered the most effective basis for the revival of Italy. Despite the constant emphasis on romanticism, both literary and historical, regarded as the expression of the most modern form of European culture, this literary patriotism was curiously traditional and even anachronistic for a people whose political consciousness had already been deeply stirred by the transformations of the revolutionary period. More realistically modern, and in the tradition of *The Conciliator*'s illustrious Enlightenment predecessor, *Il Caffè*, was the sense of European progress: 'in our country progress in all matters is such that it seems as if the son always knows more than his father' (Branca, 211, vol. 1, p. 194). Progress was viewed above all in terms of industrial society: Benthamite utility, technological innovations in hydraulics and steam engines, political economy and Sismondi's criticisms of the negative social consequences of industrialism, private charity and the Lancaster-Bell system of 'monitorial' instruction for the poor, were constant themes of *The Conciliator*, which contained in embryonic form much of the liberal philosophy of the Italian moderates of the following decades.

Of longer term significance than the essays of this small group of mainly aristocratic intellectuals were the writings of the former Napoleonic administrators, also contributors to *The Conciliator* – Giuseppo Pecchio, Giandomenico Romagnosi and Melchiorre Gioia. Pecchio and Gioia, combining their direct experience of administration of the economy in the Italic Kingdom with close observation of English development, offered the elements of a vision of a progressive, capitalist society, in which economic productivity, based on free industrial and commercial enterprise and an efficient, rapid and cheap administration, was accompanied by controlled political liberty and absolute respect for persons and property. Still tied to his Napoleonic experiences in his belief in a restricted ruling class and his suspicion of public opinion, Gioia was critical of the bias favouring landowners in the French *Charte*: 'great landowner is often the synonym for great ignoramus' (Gioia, 212, vol. 2, p. 111). He emphasized experience as the criterion for public service, the practical experience of the entrepreneurs, merchants, bankers, professional and administrative classes, the groups most character-istic of an industrializing society, such as was emerging successfully in Napoleonic Lombardy.

Romagnosi, although perhaps less often read than Gioia and Pecchio (not least because of his contorted and verbose style), lent the support of his vast reputation to this defence of progress, and elaborated the foundations of a moderate philosophy of 'civilizing progress' (*incivilimento*). Economic pro-gress, free trade and just laws were interdependent; progress was inevitable, given the nature of man, so long as reforms were enacted by those with the necessary wisdom: 'in every age of society there will always be a most numerous class which needs to be led by means of authority' (Sestan, 172, p. xvii).

Compared to these Lombards, the Tuscan and Piedmontese liberals were far less progressive. The Tuscans – Capponi, Lambruschini, Ridolfi – remained somewhat isolated figures, although in contact with Lombard and Piedmontese liberals until organized by Vieusseux around his journals in the 1820s. The young Piedmontese liberals – Cesare Balbo, Luigi Provana, Santorre di Santarosa – formed an even more aristocratic group than the Lombards, closely connected by friendship and family relationships. But in the provincial, dynastic environment of Turin they represented the natural and sole ruling class, consolidated by the Napoleonic policy of *ralliement* and only temporarily excluded from power by youth and Victor Emanuel's attempt to rely on wholly 'loyal' nobles. As Cesare Balbo wrote:

> I had not experienced public disgrace . . . because of family circumstances, and principally because of my father's merits. . . . Finding myself in such a situation, I – and others – believed that, once I came of age, a necessary condition in our country, I should not always be distant from public affairs. (Passerin d'Entrèves, 205, pp. 39–40)

Other Piedmontese, such as Massimo D'Azeglio and Silvio Pellico, had escaped to Milan from the suffocating atmosphere of Restoration Turin. But for Balbo and his friends dynastic loyalty, wishfully identified with Italian patriotism, remained overriding. Sharing the Lombards' romantic vision and their belief in a moderate constitution as the guarantee of liberty, these Piedmontese nobles retained a distinctive pride in Savoyard destiny. The house of Savoy was exalted not just as the only truly Italian dynasty, but because of its military traditions. Santarosa could point to Prussia as an ideal model; for Balbo, the recreation of the army distinguished Piedmont from the other Italian states. The Napoleonic military epic retained its appeal for these young noble officers, even if the army was now idealistically transformed (as it had been by the Prussian officers) into the major instrument of a war for national liberation. Inspired by a heroic vision of the Spanish resistance, Balbo dogmatically asserted the precedence of national independence over internal freedom, an independence that could only be achieved by the monarch assuming his natural role at the head of an anti-Austrian crusade. But to fulfil this role, the monarch should guarantee his subjects their rights by the spontaneous concession of a constitution, such as existed in England: 'The English constitution has spread and will spread in Europe, principally because, while the name and authority of the king have been upheld, even those most devoted to the prince have had no scruples about desiring and promoting the constitution' (Passerin d'Entrèves, 205, pp. 124–5).

The task was thus to reconcile patriotism and the monarchy, the rights of the people and the public spirit of the nation. To achieve these ends, history was endowed by these young Piedmontese nobles with the same essential function as literature for *The Conciliator* group: its purpose was to achieve the regeneration of the Italian people. History meant the history of Italy, a national 'epos' to arouse imitation by past example, in which the glorious episode of the Italian communes was accompanied by a De Maistrian vision of the Christian Middle Ages, in which the role of the papacy was exalted. In their Catholicism, as in their local patriotism, the Piedmontese liberals displayed a closed mind towards the most modern and progressive currents in Europe. *The Conciliator* writer, Ludovico di Breme, spoke for the Lombards when he caustically told these Piedmontese nobles: 'To rise again, to intimidate its executioners, Italy needs to know the immense truth that radiates in Europe. You do not read European books, because you are convinced that everything, is to be found in our own books' (Romeo, 199, p. 19).

Cultural opposition, however valid in France where it accompanied an open political struggle guaranteed by the *Charte*, was politically impotent in Restoration Italy. In Lombardy the suppression of *The Conciliator* was indicative of the ever-more restricted boundaries of permissible criticism. In Piedmont the 'reformist' party around the minister Prospero Balbo (Cesare's father) limited itself to removing the more retrograde aspects of Restoration civil and judicial legislation and suggesting the reformation of an advisory council of state. By his hostility towards a constitution, Prospero Balbo alienated the liberals outside the government; he thus isolated himself and was impotent against the attacks of the intransigent absolutists. Liberal opposition in both Lombardy and Piedmont, as elsewhere in Italy, increasingly conscious of its lack of influence, began to turn towards the more extreme and direct methods of the sectarians.

The sects in Italy

In Piedmont and then in the former Italic Kingdom the dominant sect in the early Restoration years was the *adelfia*, which remained strong within the army but now attracted members of the banned Napoleonic free-masonry. Like the separate 'Delphic Order', organized among the free-masons of the Italic Kingdom by the former Napoleonic officer, general Gifflenga, the *adelfia*, of democratic, republican tendencies, was ultimately controlled from Geneva by Filippo Buonarroti. In 1818, at a sectarian meet-ing at Alessandria, the *adelfia* was transformed into the new, or reorganized sect of the 'sublime perfect masters', the major instrument through which Buonarroti hoped to co-ordinate and direct all sectarian activity. By 1820 Buonarroti, with the aid of a conspirator from Trent, Gioacchino Prati, a French ex-Jacobin, Joseph Rey, and the German ex-Jacobins, Karl Follen and Wilhelm Snell, had gained control of a large sector of the French sects through the 'Union' and the German sects through the *Männerbund*, besides infiltrating the 'Directive Committee' at Paris. In Italy, the 'sublime perfect masters' created, as a subordinate organization, or 'economy', the 'Italian federation', which spread in Lombardy under Confalonieri's leadership among the anti-Austrian nobles and middle class and in Piedmont particularly among the army officers. Thus many of *The Conciliator* group and nearly all the young Piedmontese liberal officers (with Cesare Balbo as the most notable exception) had become 'federates' by 1820. Besides the 'federation', Buonarroti managed to infiltrate the *carboneria* in northern and central Italy, introducing into it a third grade of 'grand master' equiva-lent to the first grade of the 'sublime perfect masters'; and to control the 'Latin constitution' in the Legations, which had been created in 1818 through the fusion of the *carboneria* and the *guelfia*.

The Restoration had ended hopes of returning to 1793 or the early Directory by a military coup. But Buonarroti retained his traditional approach to sectarian activities. Ritual symbolism, rigid hierarchical struc-ture and gradual revelation of aims, typical of eighteenth-century free-masonry, characterized his endeavours to direct his cosmopolitan network of sects through risings for political independence and a constitution towards the ultimate end of an egalitarian social revolution. The 'sublime perfect masters' were divided into three strictly separated grades, each with its own organization, structure and symbols, and controlled territorially in pro-vincial 'churches' by a member of a higher grade. Members of the lowest grade, of 'sublime masters', knew only of their oath to deism, fraternity and equality; the second grade of 'sublime elects' responsible for controlling the first grade, swore to a unitarian republican constitution based on popular sovereignty; and the highest grade of 'mobile deacons', an extremely small group directly responsible to the 'grand firmament' or Buonarroti in Geneva, swore to the abolition of private property and achievement of a full communion of possessions and labour. Despite the adaptation of methods to changed circumstances, Buonarroti's aims remained those of the years of Jacobin and babouvian conspiracy: hostility towards princes, aristocrats or wealthy oligarchies; the creation of a republic, single and indivisible; revolutionary dictatorship of the virtuous initiates (the 'mobile deacons') until the people had achieved their regeneration; ultimate creation of the messianic new Jerusalem, a communistic society. In the words of the oath sworn by members of the highest grade:

> Property boundaries shall be erased, all possessions shall be reduced to communal wealth, and the one and only mistress, the patria, most gentle of mothers, shall furnish food, education and work to the whole body of her beloved and free children.
>
> This is the redemption invoked by the wise. This is the true recreation of Jerusalem. This is the manifest and inevitable decision of the Supreme Being. (Saitta, 131, vol. 1, pp. 91–2)

But the very secrecy that surrounded the higher grades inevitably restricted the diffusion of Buonarroti's aims to their more limited and immediate political aspects. Michele Gastone, as 'mobile deacon' at Turin responsible for the organization in Italy, spread its network of 'sublime perfect masters' through the urban centres of northern and central Italy (from Alessandria and Asti in Piedmont, and Milan and Pavia in Lombardy to Mantua and Venice, Parma and Modena); but the 'sublime masters', each responsible as 'guelph cavalier', 'grand *carbonaro* master' or 'grand masonic master' for the control of dependent 'economies', converted their initiates on the basis of simple and limited political demands. Thus the Buonarrotian-controlled 'federation', which achieved a wider diffusion than the *carboneria* in Piedmont and Lombardy between 1818 and 1820 because of the modernity of its organization with the elimination of grades and rites, aimed solely at war with Austria and the formation of a constitutional kingdom in north Italy; neither the social nor the unitarian aims of Buonarroti were known to the 'federates', and even the choice of constitution – the restricted French *Charte* or the more democratic Spanish constitution of 1812, based on indirect universal suffrage and a single elective chamber with broad legislative powers – remained open.

It was left to the 'sublime masters' to guide the insurrection in a democratic direction at the opportune moment. As a directive stated in July 1820:

'In the event of favourable circumstances leading to a revolution, the presidents of the meetings must strive to ensure that the direction of the revolution fall into their own hands or into those of individuals dependent upon them.' (Soriga, 196, p. 123.) Thus aristocratic moderate officers and more democratic junior officers and NCO's could plot together as 'federates' or *carbonari*, hoping to impose their own constitutional preference on their fellow conspirators. The differences in mentality and depth of antagonism masked by these constitutional slogans were to reveal themselves during the abortive Piedmontese rising of 1821.

In the duchies and the Papal States the sects spread rapidly after 1815, influenced by both Buonarroti's organizations from the north and the *carboneria* from the south. Only in Tuscany were the sects limited to scattered *carbonaro* 'conventicles' in Leghorn, Florence and a few other cities. The aims of the very numerous sectarians in the Papal Legations and Marches were extremely vague and contradictory, ranging from *guelfia* hopes of a constitutional monarchy and an independent federation of Italian states to *carbonaro* demands for reforms, a laicization of the administration, a constitution and possibly a separation of the Marches and Romagna from papal rule. This ambiguity and adaptability of goal was also typical of the Neapolitan *carboneria*, an organization as widespread as Buonarroti's sects in the north, but which had spread wholly independently of his influence.

The *carboneria* had developed rapidly in the struggle against Murat. The practical effect of the reactionary minister Canosa's attempt to set up the *calderari* as a rival Catholic sect had been further to strengthen the *carboneria* through fears of a return to 1799. In the following years, particularly after the departure of the Austrian army in 1817, the sect spread ever-wider, tacitly tolerated by Medici because of his conviction that opposition would evaporate as the effects of good administration were felt. The strength of the sect lay in the mainland provinces, where discontent with Medici's economic policy, the concordat, and above all his administrative centralization combined with hatred of the feudatories. The *carboneria* was a movement of the provincial middle class, which had emerged during the Murattian decade in opposition to feudal structures, but which had retained its distrust of Murat's administration. It had spread among the small proprietors, professional classes, merchants, craftsmen, lower clergy and especially the lower officers of the army and provincial militia. In some areas, the *carboneria* gained the support of the peasants, who hoped it would requite their demand for land. It had contacts with brigand bands and was regarded with sympathy by the wealthier bourgeois landowners, although few actually joined its ranks. Its demand for administrative decentralization explained the hostility of the Murattian bureaucrats, although contacts existed with senior Murattian officers.

The political programme of the *carbonari* remained vague, but centred on the demand for a constitution as an effective means of combating Ferdinand's absolutism. The Spanish constitution, rather than the more aristocratic Sicilian or French constitutions, assumed the value of a symbol, accepted on faith rather than direct knowledge. But serious differences existed between more moderate and more democratic *carbonari*, as between the 'conventicles' of the different regions. No centralized direction existed, such as that of Buonarroti, although the 'conventicles' of the Salerno region, Lucania and Naples had agreed on an insurrection in 1817. The plot was infiltrated, delayed and finally suppressed the following year. From then on, the *carbonari*, particularly of Salerno, awaited their chance to achieve their revenge.

Revolution and reaction

The Spanish revolution, which broke out on 1 January 1820, revealed – like the successive revolutions in the Italian states and Portugal – both the intrinsic weakness of the Restoration regimes and the hostility that divided the moderate from the democratic liberals. These divisions among the liberals, which permitted the easy extinction of the revolutions by foreign armies, were to deepen in the following decades into antagonistic ideologies, explicitly opposed over the method of achieving independence, but implicitly containing contrasting visions of the form of society and relationship of power which, it was hoped, would characterize the liberated nations.

The myth of the Spanish guerrilla war against Napoleon, even more than that of the Russian or Prussian resistance, had exerted a powerful influence on the formation of Italian opposition to the Restoration. The Alfierian image of a heroic Spanish people uncorrupted by wealth, voiced by northern moderates such as Balbo and Pecchio, was the counterpart to the Neapolitan *carbonaro* sense of common destiny and the obscure links between democratic sects in Spain and Italy. For the Italian opponents of the Restoration, with their vision of a common European civilization, Spain – like Russia or the former Spanish colonies – was a country regarded as displaying an even lower level of progress than subservient Italy. In consequence, the Spanish revolt could not but act as a spur to action. *The Romagnol Collector* wrote on 30 March 1820:

> But the Russians, Spaniards, Americans, how far have they not flown in a few years, not to say in a few months? Italy! Would you ever dare believe yourself worthy of taking a seat – I will not say alongside Russia, Spain, the great peoples of America – but merely alongside the nation of Haiti? Oh, most unhappy Italy! The Russian, the Spaniard can with reason call you superstitious, ignorant, savage and base. The Russian and the Spaniard? ... Yes, yes; they, they have full right to call you the last nation of Europe. (Spini, 197, p. 9, n. 2)

The Neapolitan revolution, 1820–1

The Spanish revolution was sparked off by a military rising led by an officer belonging to the democratic sect of *comuneros*. In like manner, the Neapolitan revolution was started at Nola, after months of plotting among the *carbonari* and in the army, by a group of junior officers and a handful of *carbonari*, led by a priest, Luigi Minichini (1–2 July 1820). Within a week the revolution triumphed, Ferdinand granted the Spanish constitution and nominated his son Francis as 'Vicar' (regent) of the kingdom. This rapid victory, certainly aided by the desertion of part of the army under the former Murattian officer, general Guglielmo Pepe, displayed the intrinsic weakness of the Restoration regime in the face of a movement organized within the *carboneria* but supported generally throughout the country. That the revolution was neither a military coup nor the work of a small group of intellectuals like the Parthenopean republic in 1799 was demonstrated by the support even of groups of the peasantry, alongside the provincial land-owning middle classes and craftsmen, and by the absence of any Sanfedist reaction among either the peasants or the *lazzaroni* of the capital.

The democratic drive behind the revolution was instantly revealed by the reduction of the salt-tax by half, which the government was forced to accept, and by the *carbonari* creation of decentralized provincial governments in Basilicata and Capitanata which attempted to assert their autonomy against Naples. The intendant of Basilicata explained the local reasons for the revolution and the dangers it now represented:

> Through fear of compromising themselves with the many police agents, a great number of proprietors had refused to take an active part in the meetings and work of the *carboneria*. That gave the chance to the landless and people worth nothing, who risked little, to play a major part in the meetings, and to make them serve their own plans; thus the Senate [the new provisional government of Basilicata] now consists for the most part of non-proprietors, or owners with insecure property, who in consequence have barely any interest at all in public order, hope for much in changes, and can profit from disorder. Now, that such a class of persons should claim to be the representatives of the province against the public vote is a strange thing, and at the same time most dangerous for its tranquillity. (Lepre, 220, p. 143)

The democratic *carbonari* were thus initially successful and managed to impose the Spanish constitution on the more moderate *carbonari* and Murattians who formed the new government. Indeed, although the local *carbonaro* proposals for a federalist form of regional self-government were rejected and the Capitanata and Basilicata forced to submit, the radical Salerno *carbonari* obliged the moderates to accept elections to parliament by universal male suffrage, including even illiterates. But as the initial unity crumbled and the different groups began to consider how best to continue and consolidate the revolution, the democratic elements rapidly lost control. The new government and provisional junta appointed by the regent Francis consisted of men of a past generation, who had played leading parts in the Revolution of 1799 or the Murattian decade: Zurlo, Ricciardi, Winspeare, Guglielmo and Florestano Pepe, even the eighty-year-old Enlightened reformer Melchiorre Delfico. These Murattian administrators, convinced of the virtues of an efficient, centralized administration, suspicious of all popular initiatives, hostile towards the *carboneria* since the years of King Gioacchino, had resented Bourbon absolutism and shared with the agrarian middle class its faith in liberty and legal security of persons and property as the only means by which the kingdom could progress towards the level of European civilization. In parliament a majority of landowners or Murattian administrators had been elected, although the democratic representatives and *carbonaro*-organized pressure from the country in the form of petitions to the assembly and demonstrations maintained an uneasy balance.

The opinion of the most moderate landowners was expressed clearly by one of their deputies in parliament, Federico Tortora, in his definition of who could claim legitimately to represent all the people in the Neapolitan nation: 'The comprehensive word 'nation' here means the proprietors who, according to the principles of economy of our kingdom, are equal to one sixtieth part of the number of inhabitants' (Lepre, 222, p. 310). But others, following the Lombard Gioia's criticisms, opposed the landowners' domina-tion in favour of merchants, magistrates, officers, civil servants; and the majority of these 89 almost exclusively middle-class deputies shared a general if somewhat indeterminate desire to improve the lot of the poor. Compared to the Murattian dominated bureaucracy and army officers, parliament remained relatively open to popular pressure and resisted government attempts to control the press and public meetings. When the peasants at Vallo in Calabria occupied the land to conserve their customary rights (December 1820), parliament rejected the government's proposals of severe measures, on the grounds that no violence to persons had been com-mitted, and recommended that the peasants voice their grievances through legal channels. But this sense of humanitarianism and spirit of constitutional legality marked the limits of the Neapolitan parliament.

In contrast to their belief in European civilization, neither moderates nor democrats displayed any desire for a united or independent Italy – at least until, in desperation, they turned to the sects elsewhere in Italy against the advancing Austrian army. The 'patria', for Dante Gabriele Rossetti and all the constitutionalists, meant the Kingdom of the Two Sicilies. Like the Spanish moderates, the Neapolitan liberals displayed a remarkable insensi-tivity towards the international political situation and were convinced that so long as the revolution was contained within the boundaries of the kingdom, the great powers would not interfere. This optimism, like their typically Enlightened, rationalist and law-abiding faith in Ferdinand's oath of loyalty to the constitution, explains why they only appealed belatedly to Spain for support and even failed to prepare the army for a defensive war, sending the most experienced troops to suppress the revolution at Palermo. The entire defence of the revolution on the mainland thus rested on an unreliable army, which even Guglielmo Pepe was unable to galvanize, as the original popular drive had by now disappeared; no Spanish-type guerrilla war was possible.

If moderate control of the government was responsible for this dwindling of popular enthusiasm, the disintegration of the *carboneria* played its part. After the initial success of the revolution the more moderate bourgeoisie entered the ranks of the *carboneria*, with the tacit encouragement of the local intendants. The sect, always divided by ideological and regional differences, now lost its incisiveness, despite attempts to maintain its organizational structure. The rivalry between the radical Salerno 'conventicle' and the more moderate Naples 'high conventicle', which masked long-standing internal hostilities between different masonic groups, was now complicated by splits within the Naples *carboneria*, which ranged from the extremely conservative aristocratic group headed by Zurlo to democratic republicans. Metternich's analysis of the sects, written in 1817, now appeared only too accurate: 'In design and principle divided among themselves, these sects change every day and on the morrow may be ready to fight against one another' (Mack Smith, 110, p. 31). Three democratic sectarians from Naples, who attempted to create a '*carbonaro* army' in the provinces, were arrested.

Only after the news of the Troppau decision approving foreign intervention, and Ferdinand and Zurlo's attempted coup against the constitution (7 December), did moderates and democrats sink their differences. But even then the liberals refused to abandon their faith in a monarchical-constitutional programme and allowed Ferdinand to depart for Laibach. The concessions towards democratic demands for administrative decentralization, like the dispatch of missions to northern Italy and Germany, came too late. After Pepe's defeat by the Austrians at Rieti (7 March 1821), the revolution collapsed virtually without resistance (23 March).

The Sicilian revolution, 1820

The Neapolitan moderates and democrats, mutually hostile about the course of the revolution, were agreed on only one matter – the suppression of the Sicilian revolution. Warnings of the resentment in Sicily towards conscription and the administrative reforms, a resentment aggravated by the economic crisis, had become increasingly frequent by 1820. The revolution which broke out at Palermo on 15–16 July, after news of the Neapolitan revolution, was a spontaneous mass rising of the guild craftsmen and workers, accepted, if not encouraged, by the separatist nobles. The 72 Palermitan guilds or *maestranze* possessed a greater independence than those of any other Italian city, but in their industrial decline were isolated and hostile towards both barons and government. They displayed a violence against royal troops and conservative barons unknown in Naples. A provisional junta, consisting of both nobles and non-nobles who had been active in the constitutional movement of 1812–14, while ready to endorse the assertion of the island's independence, was also forced to accept the demands of the guilds for the Spanish constitution and abolition of conscription, as well as the guilds' power of veto over all future decisions. The delegation sent to Naples with these claims was formed of two nobles, two ecclesiastics, two non-nobles, and two consuls of the *maestranze*. Despite the insistence on the democratic Spanish constitution in preference to the conservative Sicilian constitution of 1812, the Palermo revolt was an unusual mixture of a popular rising against the economic depression and Bourbon reforms (tax offices were regularly burnt by the insurgents) and an anachronistic defence of corporative privileges.

This specific combination explains why the revolt failed to spread throughout Sicily. Only Girgenti, of the other six administrative centres, joined Palermo in the demand for independence. The democratic middle class of Catania and the east coast had favoured the anti-baronial Bourbon reforms as a stimulus to local industry, and now opposed the demands for independence, especially of so anarchical a character. A virtual civil war developed as the Palermo *maestranze* sent out armed bands to 'conquer' the areas that remained loyal to Naples: Caltanissetta was sacked. When the Neapolitan government, supported by the *carboneria*, rejected the demands for independence and sent an army to Sicily under general Florestano Pepe, the Palermo barons, now terrified of the social dangers of the revolution, joined the opposition to the guilds. As the prince of Paternò explained: 'the patria would have been exposed to the fury of plebs without check, because the national guard, still in its infancy, would have proved inadequate for the task' (Romeo, 225, pp. 150–1).

An agreement was reached secretly by Pepe and the noble-bourgeois junta (22 September), by which the demand for a separate parliament was made conditional on the approval of all the Sicilian communes. The Palermo populace fought on against the civic guard and Pepe's troops, but finally accepted Pepe's proposal for the election of deputies from all the island to decide on the separatist issue (5 October). The struggle was only prolonged by the refusal of the Neapolitan parliament to accept this agreement, convinced that the revolt was a plot of the Palermo barons. If the harsh suppression of opposition by general Colletta was still supported by the Catania democrats and the newly formed *carbonaro* groups of the east coast, its consequence was to deepen the separatist spirit in western Sicily.

The Piedmontese revolution, 1821

In Piedmont, unlike Naples and Sicily, the revolutionaries displayed a strong desire for the independence of Italy. But the divisions between moderates and democrats were even sharper. By 1820 discontent among the liberals had spread ever wider as the absolutist Court party blocked Prospero Balbo's moderate proposals of reform. With the news of the Spanish and then the Neapolitan revolutions the pressure for a constitution grew stronger, encouraged by the influential ambassadors of Spain, France and Bavaria. The most moderate liberals, such as Cesare Balbo and Federico Sclopis, refused to engage in disloyal sectarian activities: for Balbo a constitution was to be supplicated from the king by ministers on their knees. But an increasing number of the young aristocratic officers tried to reconcile their dynastic loyalties with their constitutional, independentist aspirations by turning to the ultimate heir to the throne, Charles Albert, prince of Carignano, a man of their own generation, who had shared their Napoleonic experiences. Young, uncertain of himself, ambitious, resentful of the snubs imposed upon him by the ultra-royalist Court because of his family's acceptance of the usurper Napoleon's regime, Charles Albert was also suspicious of Francis of Modena's intrigues to gain the succession to the throne of Sardinia of his wife (Victor Emanuel's daughter). Charles Albert willingly accepted – and encouraged by his very silence – the reputation of a liberal prince thrust upon him by the young aristocratic liberals. Through his mediation the king was to be persuaded to grant a constitution and lead the war against Austria.

By the autumn of 1820, as rumours spread of Austrian intervention against the Neapolitan revolutionaries, Cesare Balbo's friends began to organize a military rising and intensified their contacts with the *carboneria*. For these young officers, who saw themselves as the representatives of the nation, a military *pronunciamento*, as in Spain and Naples, was the only conceivable and legitimate method of persuading the king to realize his true interests. Hostile to popular pressure, favouring the French *Charte*, the youthful noble conspirators, Santarosa and Boffa di Lisio, San Marzano and Dal Pozzo della Cisterna, were nonetheless impressed and increasingly convinced by the organization and broader support of the *carbonari* and 'sublime perfect masters' and ultimately, reluctantly, accepted their demand for the Spanish constitution as the only way to maintain unity among the patriots. The turning point came when an innocuous protest by university students was enthusiastically repressed by aristocratic officers (12 January 1821). Santarosa noted despondently that the feeling of class hatred, immediately revealed, signified the end of all hopes of a hereditary chamber of peers as in France. Anonymous verses warned the king:

Either you check your nobles' proud tone,
Or search for the affection of the plebs,
Or fear one day to fall from your throne.   (Romeo, 199, p. 27)

In the following weeks the plotting in the army continued feverishly and close contacts were maintained by the conspirators with Charles Albert, sectarians at Paris and 'federates' in Lombardy. The army was to be roused by the promise of a royal war to evict the Austrians from Lombardy and the concession of a constitution.

'We aim at two things', declared Santarosa and Lisio at the moment of the insurrection, 'to place the King in a position to be able to follow the movements of his truly Italian heart, and to allow the people the honest liberty of manifesting their wishes to the Throne like children to a father' (Torta, 202, p. 945). Once the Piedmontese army crossed the Ticino, the confederates under Confalonieri were to take advantage of the Austrian expedition against Naples and start an insurrection in Lombardy. The rising was delayed because of Charles Albert's equivocal behaviour and ultimate refusal to declare himself. But on 9–10 March *carbonari* officers and civilians at Alessandria proclaimed the Spanish constitution and the formation of a provisional government until the achievement of an independent Italian federation.

As at Naples, the initiative had been seized by democratic sectarians, who forced the moderate 'federates' to follow them. The insurrection spread to major cities in Piedmont (Ivrea, Asti, Vercelli, Biella, Casale) and even over the Alps into Savoy, but not all the army followed the revolutionaries. Cuneo remained in the hands of royalists, Sardinian troops at Nice refused to participate in a purely Piedmontese matter, the Novara garrison under La Tour remained undecided, and only after the arrival of a constitutionalist regiment from Savoy was it possible to send the unreliable *carabinieri* away from Turin.

The strongly militarist character of the insurrection perhaps explains the general indifference of the population. But the revolution was compromised at the outset by Victor Emanuel's decision to abdicate rather than grant a constitution, despite the urgings of Prospero Balbo and Charles Albert (13 March 1821). The illusion that dynastic loyalty could be reconciled with the revolution was irreparably destroyed, despite Santarosa's subsequent pretence that the new king, Charles Felix, was a 'prisoner' of the Austrians at Modena. Charles Albert, nominated temporary Regent by Victor Emanuel, further weakened the determination of the moderate leaders at Turin by granting the Spanish constitution subject to Charles Felix's approval, refusing to lead a war against Austria, and secretly preparing a counter-revolution with such troops as had remained loyal. His flight to Novara on 21 March, in obedience to Charles Felix's peremptory orders, left the revolutionary leaders facing a threatened invasion by Austria and Russia, with an army rapidly disintegrating through desertions and a wholly passive population.

The moderate Turin junta, manifestly ready to capitulate, was unable to gain the obedience of the democratic Alessandria junta or of the provisional government at Genoa, set up after a genuinely popular rising incited by the Alessandria *carbonari* and other sectarians (23 March). Santarosa, the sole moderate leader who remained totally committed to the revolution, tried to organize resistance to the Austrians, winning the support of the Alessandria junta. But the defeat of the constitutionalists at a skirmish at Novara (where only ten soldiers were killed) led to the occupation of Alessandria and then Turin by the Austro-Savoyard army (10 April 1821).

The years of reaction, 1821-30

The revolutions, whether sparked off by military *pronunciamento* or popular rising, had been a direct response to the Restoration settlement and the Holy Alliance. For the sectarians, who had played the leading part in their instigation in Spain, Naples and Piedmont, as in Portugal and then in Greece and, later, Russia (1825), the response had been a conscious one, conceived in international terms because all oppressed nations formed part of a common European civilization. Santarosa could appeal to the Piedmontese soldiers and national guard: 'Comrades in arms! This is a European epoch' (Torta, 202, p. 157). But the temporary success or abortive failure of the various revolutions had not really depended upon the sects: the Neapolitan *carbonari*, like the Spanish *comuneros*, had lost the initiative, while Buonarroti had been taken by surprise and was unable to control the Piedmontese movement. As a general insurrection of peoples the revolutions had failed miserably, displaying no ability to convert rhetorical appeals to a common culture into practical attempts to create political or military ties on a European scale. In the following years, the Greek revolutionaries alone were to make such an effort. But even in this instance, as in 1820-1, the international relations of the European governments were to prove the determining element. In Italy the readiness of the great powers to accept Austria's right to control the peninsula conditioned the activities of all opposition for a decade.

The years following the failure of the revolutions are traditionally regarded as marking the most severe repression of the entire period of the Risorgimento in all the Italian states – except perhaps for the Papal States and the Kingdom of the Two Sicilies where the continuous and steadily oppressive hand of the government makes such qualitative judgements both

difficult and superfluous. But the consciousness of this repression was probably rendered the more acute by its coincidence with the worst phase of the
economic crisis.

The sharp fall in prices from 1818 to 1826, in an agriculturally dominated
region such as Italy, led to greater pressure on the landowners as the
Napoleonic land-tax, maintained by the Restoration governments, remained
at a constant figure. Far worse, the crisis led to a steep rise of pauperism in
all its aspects – begging, peasant mortality, pellagra, abandoned children.
Only in Lombardy-Venetia, where Austrian financial needs and worry
about the protective Prussian customs law of 1818 led to an encouragement
of industrialism in the early 1820s, and where silk production benefited
from sustained prices, was the impact of the crisis blunted. But in Lombardy-
Venetia, as much as in the other Italian states – particularly in the south
where the rigid structure of landownership and production accentuated the
agricultural crisis – the response of the governments was protective tariffs
against foreign imports. In Tuscany alone, and then only after considerable
discussion, was free trade in grains preserved, and even there the government intervened to sustain other agricultural prices. In Piedmont and
Naples the customs tariffs of 1818 and 1823–4 were imposed in order to
stimulate domestic industry (textiles in Piedmont; cotton, metallurgy and
shipbuilding in Naples). But the weakness of the internal structures in the
kingdom of Naples and the enormous dependence of both countries on
agricultural exports to England and France neutralized any notable immediate benefits. Indeed, they accentuated the hostility between agricultural
producers, supporting silk and cotton exports alongside grain protection,
and entrepreneurs, who wanted the export of raw materials prohibited.

All states favoured the protection of their internal markets, as elsewhere
in Europe, but where grain culture was dominant the large landowners
demanded both protection against foreign grains and free exports, which
conflicted with the needs of public finance. In the Papal States the prohibitive tariff of 1824 neither improved the Treasury's deficit nor checked the
steady decline of agriculture. In the kingdom of Naples the tariffs assisted
the Sicilian corn producers, but indirectly damaged the large number of
Neapolitan oil producers by provoking English retaliation against their
exports. In both countries, as in all the Italian states, smuggling thrived.
But in the southern states in particular the inability to counter the effects of
the crisis led to heavier reliance on indirect, consumption taxes. It was in
these states that popular agitation and sectarian conspiracies remained most
active, despite the repression. Elsewhere opposition tended to revive only
in the later 1820s, as the solidity of the European conservative front began
to break up – but also at a moment when relative economic stability had
again been achieved.

The political reaction was severe throughout Italy, except in Tuscany where sectarian activities remained limited. Inevitably it was the Austrian reaction in Lombardy which attracted most international attention and set the tone for the other Italian governments. Already in 1818 the government had arrested over 30 *carbonari*; between 1821 and 1824 the network of conspiracy was unravelled in four mass trials, involving over 90 *carbonari*, 'federates' and 'sublime perfect masters', over 40 of whom were condemned to death, a sentence subsequently commuted to long terms of imprisonment at the Spielberg. The trials attracted attention because of the distinction of many of the condemned, some of whom – such as Confalonieri, Pellico, Maroncelli and Pallavicino – suffered long terms of imprisonment, while others – like Porro-Lambertenghi and Pecchio – had managed to escape abroad. In Piedmont, because the revolution had involved friends or relatives of the entire ruling class, the vast majority of the conspirators had been encouraged or assisted to escape: 90 of the 97 death sentences were delivered in the absence of the accused. As in Lombardy, legal procedures in Piedmont were carefully observed, in contrast to Modena, the Papal States and Naples.

In the Papal States, where *carbonari* in the Legations had tried to follow the example of the Neapolitan revolutionaries in 1820–1, Consalvi was dismissed by the new pope Leo XII (1823–9) and a full purge carried out in the Romagna: over 500 persons of all classes were accused by the legate extraordinary, cardinal Rivarola (1825); but *carbonaro* plots continued unabated and now spread for the first time to the city of Rome.

In Naples the desire for revenge was symbolized by Canosa's return to power. His employment of the *calderari* to strengthen the *spurgo*, as he called this persecution, once more led to his dismissal, imposed by the Austrian ambassador. But fear of the revolution continued to dominate the actions of the government, again led by Medici: a vast purge of the army, administration, judiciary and intellectuals revived old hatreds, deprived the State of its most experienced civil servants and weakened its control over the provinces. Francis's accession to the throne in 1825 brought no relief. After insisting on the departure of the expensive Austrian troops in 1827, the government asserted its authority with the savage suppression of a revolt in the Cilento in 1828. Real or suspected sectarians were once more purged at every level, with the recommendation to the authorities to 'use a just partiality against them' (Cingari, 223, p. 219). The *carboneria* was not eliminated, but survived under countless names and rites and spread to Sicily. But the 'conventicles' now consisted of the petty bourgeoisie and members of the popular classes, craftsmen and peasants, whose activities often merged into those of brigand bands. Large numbers of the former *carbonari* had fled into exile or been imprisoned. The convergence of interests which had assured victory in 1820 was broken and the liberal and democratic members of the agrarian middle class, now mutually hostile, maintained a more cautious attitude.

Political persecution was accompanied by a reversion to the most negative aspects of Restoration administration. Absolutism became identified with the concentration of all power in the hands of princes, now deeply suspicious of the loyalty of their collaborators. In Piedmont the purge of the administration, army and intellectuals had been based on the principle that: 'It is of the greatest importance that employees . . . should not think even a little differently about the nature of the government, but should be entirely devoted to it' (Corbelli, in 203, vol. 2, p. 746). For Charles Felix only the army and clergy could be trusted: 'In a word: the bad are all educated and the good are all ignorant. What choice is there in a world in which no-one anymore is made of good stuff?' (Lemmi, 204, p. 182). In the Two Sicilies, the centralization of the two parts of the kingdom was maintained, despite Metternich's opposition, and Ferdinand's suspicion of collaboration not only led to his successful resistance to Metternich's demand for the creation of two consultative bodies for Naples and Sicily, but to his division of authority between the secretary of state and the other state councillors in order to prevent a repetition of Medici's earlier 'ministerial despotism'.

Clerical pressure became ubiquitous. Under Leo XII the Jews of the Papal States were once more driven back to the ghetto. Ecclesiastical censorship, Jesuit dominance of education and official piety became the characteristics of the governments. Lamennais' visit to Italy in 1824 stimulated attempts to spread an utramontane form of culture. The Theatine father Gioacchino Ventura, called to Naples by Canosa to found the *Ecclesiastical Encyclopaedia*, moved to Rome after its suppression by Medici, where he was appointed professor at the Sapienza and directed the *Ecclesiastical Journal*, until diplomatic pressure enforced his dismissal. Modena and Turin became the cultural centres of clericalism and the Piedmontese 'Catholic amity', like Cesare D'Azeglio's 'Friends of Italy', attacked every symptom of liberalism until it was suppressed at the instigation of the Russian ambassador.

In this authoritarian, clerical, repressive environment the sectarians in Italy lost their earlier optimism and turned their hopes to Europe. Opposition to the Italian governments was revived outside Italy, where it now formed part of a more consciously international movement of opposition, which identified itself with the cause of European progress.

Disintegration of the Restoration

The collapse of the revolutions and the repression had led to a mass emigration, probably greater than in 1799: Spain, Switzerland and France, the centres of sectarianism before the revolutions, attracted most exiles. As long as the constitutional regime survived in Spain, the democratic exiles, with their faith in the international, European character of resistance, remained optimistic about the possibilities of continuing the struggle. The *carboneria* was carried to Spain and introduced to France by Neapolitan patriots. Buonarroti, from Geneva, tried to reorganize the 'sublime perfect masters' in Italy, until the arrest of his delegate Andryane enabled the Austrian police to destroy his patiently constructed network of conspiracy. At Paris the new *charbonnerie* (like the traditional masonic 'Grand Orient') plotted actively, although its initiatives were frustrated by the rivalry between the Orleanist 'high conventicle' and Bonapartist military 'conventicles'. Guglielmo Pepe's abortive sect of 'European constitutional brothers' was typical of the fleeting hopes of an imminent revolutionary revival. With the congress of Verona and the French expedition to Spain, over 1000 Italians, mostly Neapolitan but including many of the Piedmontese democrats from the Alessandria junta, remained to fight for the constitution they had lost so rapidly in Italy.

The collapse of the Spanish constitutionalists in 1823, followed by that of the Portuguese, the discovery and persecution of the French *charbonnerie*, the harsh conclusion of the trials in Lombardy, the arrests in Germany, the expulsions from France of Angeloni and Santarosa and from Switzerland (under Austrian pressure) of Buonarroti and Prati, led to a crisis in the sectarian movement which exacerbated the differences between democrats and moderates. The moderates, pessimistically convinced by the recent events that only a radical change in the international situation could offer new opportunities, concentrated on theoretical discussions and propaganda for the Italian cause. The democrats, now based on Brussels (Buonarroti) and London (Angeloni, Prati), slowly renewed their conspiracies.

Little is known about their activities in these years – the 'sublime perfect masters', for example, vanished with Buonarroti's expulsion from Switzerland and only re-emerged as the new sect of 'The world' by 1828. But the sense of crisis and even more the new experiences the exiles absorbed in their foster-countries led to re-elaborations of their credo. For the moderates, deeply influenced by the political struggles and ideology of the French liberals, faith in the formula of the Spanish constitution was rapidly replaced by the belief in the French or English constitutions. For the democrats, increased distrust in all princes led them to a firmer republicanism.

The need to avoid disunity, regarded as a major cause of the failures of 1820–1, was felt acutely by all the more active exiles and led to a search for common grounds and avoidance of issues of dispute. The most explicit instance of this was the declaration of 'principles' in 1823 of the London *carbonaro* 'conventicle', a grouping of exiles of all tendencies but controlled by the democratic Angeloni and the Buonarrotian Prati: although the declaration asserted popular sovereignty and the abolition of hereditary privileges, the question of the ultimate form of government was left to be decided by the Italian people after liberation. Only Buonarroti and his closest followers remained convinced of the need for a revolutionary dictatorship in order to achieve an egalitarian republic and the abolition of private property. But he too – as in the past – was ready to conceal these aims in the search for unity. Despite his disagreement with Angeloni's assertion of man's natural inequality and the need for small peasant landholdings, Buonarroti could write to him:

> On some points however we agree. These are: the sovereignty of the people, hatred of tyrants, love of liberty, the overthrow of monarchical and aristocratic power and the use of force, which you call opportune and natural and I call a legitimate, natural and necessary appeal. Now these agreements are of no little weight. . . . What I say I judge to be true and I believe the same of you; let us not search further, but regulate our actions, basing them on the above points of agreement. (Romano-Catania, 134, pp. 176–7)

But compromises with princes in the cause of independence were not ultimately excluded except by the most convinced republicans. The experiences of the Greek struggle in these years, in which European public opinion only became really effective when backed by the English government, seemed to prove that liberal forces, however strong, could only succeed when supported by established powers. The alternative – gaining popular support – led to no significant modification of the revolutionaries' theories, as it was assumed to be natural and inevitable by the democrats and was only half-heartedly welcomed by the moderates. Although many were aware of the absence of sustained mass support during the Italian revolutions, few were prepared to admit with the marquis di Salvo that the reasons might lie in the abstractness of appeals to liberty and independence:

> Notable writers, who believe that they must dedicate themselves to the interests of peoples, become their defenders and tribunes, often fail in the mission they have assumed because they use a language based on theories and systems. Thus they speak, in the style of proclamations, of the rights of peoples . . . but rarely indicate the means needed to guarantee and consolidate them. . . . Nobody bothers to examine up to what point liberty can be upheld and defended by the peoples for whom it is claimed. . . . Now since what is neither well understood nor strongly desired can be neither upheld nor defended with enthusiasm, it is a wholly false idea to imagine that there is a great moral force in the peoples, just because the human spirit has made great progress in the arts, sciences and reasoning. It would be much better to search up to what point civilization and enlightenment have given the peoples a real strength, capable of creating what is called a national character. (Omodeo, 193, pp. 85–6)

Di Salvo's analysis, in the very ambiguity of its appeal to both democrats, searching for the means to win popular support, and moderates, restricting the definition of the 'people' according to the level of civilization, was to be developed in the following decades. But it was ignored with the revival of sectarian activities which were to culminate in the revolutions of 1830-1.

The renewal of active conspiracy coincided with the disintegration of the Holy Alliance over the Greek war (1827-30), the success of the French liberals in the 1828 elections, and the end of the agricultural crisis. In the previous years sectarian activities had tended to group around the 'phil-hellenic committee'. To promote the international cause, this was transformed into a 'cosmopolitan committee', consisting of members of the *charbonnerie*, and French political opposition and exiles from various countries.

Buonarroti, with the publication of his *Babeuf's Conspiracy for Equality* (1828) rapidly gained adherents among the most democratic elements. He was possibly influenced by the German *illuminati* concept of the erosion of society through the formation of a fine network of sects. He certainly modified his ideas from his earlier faith in the efficacy of the moment of insurrection to a conviction of the need for a supreme authority, supported by widespread organizations, to lead the revolution and then maintain power until the people, corrupted by their past slavery, had regained the path of virtue. In his Jacobin vision of an egalitarian, agrarian world, polemical against the Saint-Simonian eulogy of 'industrialism' and the unlimited development of individualism, Buonarroti reconstructed his own sect – 'The World' – in which four new 'grades of observation' were added to the characteristic three higher grades of the earlier 'sublime perfect masters' to act as a seedbed of future leaders and to infiltrate society. He now extended his contacts in Belgium and France, where a new revolutionary movement was anticipated. In Italy, a new sect of *militi apofasimeni* ('militia of the condemned'), founded by Bianco di Saint Jorioz with Buonarrotian motives, attracted the support of Greek students, as well as Italians, at Bologna, Pisa and in the Romagna, while the young Giuseppe Mazzini revived the *carboneria* in Liguria and Leghorn.

The three revolutionary days of July 1830 took Buonarroti, like all the conspirators, by surprise. Villèle's government in France had aroused increasing opposition by its encouragement of the Church, its compensation to *émigrés* for the confiscation of their lands during the Revolution, and its attempts to curb press liberty. Abandoned by the extreme right, Villèle had been brought down by the constitutional opposition after a carefully organized pamphlet and electoral campaign (January 1828). Unable to regain popularity with a successful expedition to capture Algiers, Charles X dissolved the chamber once more. On the return of a massive liberal majority, he signed the famous four ordinances of 24 July, suspending the freedom of the press, restricting the suffrage in favour of landowners, and calling new elections. Popular discontent, exacerbated by the industrial crisis, exploded into a revolt led by republicans, who resurrected the aged figure of Lafayette.

After three days of barricades, the parliamentary liberals turned to Louis Philippe, duke of Orleans, as the only way to check the revolution. The popular revolution was channelled into a mere change of dynasty, in which the revised *Charte*, now a contract between king and nation, increased parliament's powers, but continued to rest on an extremely restricted franchise. The closed, class character of this *pays légal*, dominated by elites of wealth, intelligence or birth, often of Napoleonic origin, was to become increasingly clear in the following years. But initially both the legal 'party of movement' and the semi-legal or secret republican associations and sects retained their optimism that the revolution could be resumed in France and revived abroad.

The July revolution, in fact, marked a decisive break with the past. It was regarded as a national revolution, a vindication of France's humiliation in 1815 and a successful challenge against the Holy Alliance. France's mission to liberate other peoples, as the natural repository of the most progressive forms of civilization, was taught by Michelet and Quinet, and accepted first in France, then abroad. French romantics abandoned their penchant for Restoration and Catholic order and turned towards the causes of national liberty and revolution; the Napoleonic legend acquired substance and solid support. The new French king, son of the revolution, seemed to symbolize the demand for the revision of the 1815 treaties. As a revolutionary wave once more swept through Europe, it was in Louis Philippe that both liberals and democrats placed their trust. In Belgium, Switzerland, some central German states, Poland and central Italy, revolutions broke out in 1830–1. The Belgian revolution (August–October 1830) reinforced the faith in France, as its success had been guaranteed by Louis Philippe's assertion of the principle of non-intervention, backed by England and Prussia, and the subsequent defence of the new state against Dutch aggression by a French army and English fleet (August 1831).

But the success of these revolutions depended upon the determined support of at least one great power (Prussian support of the liberals in Brunswick, Cassel, Dresden and Hanover), or the tacit recognition by the opposing powers that the cause, whether liberal or legitimist, did not merit the dangers of intervention (Switzerland, the Iberian peninsula). In Poland (November 1830–September 1831) and Italy (February–April 1831), where Russian and Austrian hegemony were directly threatened, no great power was prepared to risk the destruction of the European Concert. Louis Philippe, concerned to gain recognition from the other powers, rapidly abandoned his foreign minister Laffitte's policy of 'movement' and endorsed his new premier Périer's declaration of order at home and peace abroad (13 March 1831). At the most, France was prepared to offer mediation over Poland and the Papal States, promptly rejected by Russia and Austria. The sectarians, once more, proved unable to resist the decisions of the powers.

The revolution in central Italy, 1831

The Italian revolution of 1831, although like the other revolutions inspired by French example, had been preceded by a lengthy and obscure conspiracy which marked the renewal of active contacts between the Italian sectarians and the exiles and the readiness of both to continue to accept compromises with the princes, despite the bitter experiences of 1820–1.

In the midst of the general lethargy of the sects in Italy, which followed the repressions of the early 1820s, Enrico Misley, a young Modenese *carbonaro* or freemason, elaborated a plan which, in its political opportunism, shocked even the broadest-minded of the liberals: to persuade the reactionary Francis IV of Modena to assume the leadership of a national liberal movement. Misley counted, not illogically, on the well-known ambitions of Francis to gain a larger state and on the continued frustration of his attempts to exclude Charles Albert from the succession in Piedmont. But, given the deeply anti-liberal, clerical policy of the duke, Misley's proposal made a mockery of the moral principles on which the sectarians based their actions. Suspected until his death of acting as an *agent provocateur*, Misley would seem to have fused patriotism with a spirit of intrigue, reducing the cause of the patria into a Court plot. It was the ultimate consequence of the *carbonaro* mentality. In the words of the democrat Nicola Fabrizi, in contact with Misley in these years:

> Perhaps Misley believed that the period immediately following the failures and bloody repressions of 1821 (a period which in fact ill-corresponded to any hopes for a rapid revival) would lend itself more easily to intrigues which, rather than relying on popular support, would seek sustenance from factions able to offer room for manoeuvre and new chances of agreement. (Candeloro, 1, vol. 2, p. 164)

Whether moved by ambitious hopes of exploiting Russian–Austrian differences over Greece to his own advantage in Italy, or merely by the possibility of unmasking sectarian activities, Francis IV accepted Misley's approaches in 1826 and authorized him, in successive journeys, to make contact with Russian agents in Switzerland and the Austrian empire and with the Italian exiles at London and Paris. In 1828–9 Misley and his fellow-Modenese, Camillo Manzini, gained the somewhat diffident support of the Paris 'cosmopolitan committee', while the London Italian 'conventicle' conditioned its support to Francis' acceptance of the principle of the creation of a single representative monarchy over all Italy; suspicions that the Piedmontese exiles at Paris still placed their hopes in Charles Albert certainly made the London group move away. But almost all the exiles – except the republicans – seemed prepared to make a political compromise.

The July revolution aroused hopes of French help among the Italian exiles. A variety of committees and associations were formed, which centred on the democratic 'society of Italian patriots' and a moderate group around Salfi. Buonarroti, on his arrival in Paris, proposed to work for the spread of revolution at two levels, through his own sect, 'The world', and through French republican associations. Typically, Buonarroti conceived of the revolution in European and egalitarian terms and was active in support of both French and Belgian republicans. A co-ordinating committee of the Italian exiles was formed under Linati, Maroncelli and Salfi, which considered a range of names as future constitutional king of Italy (Francis of Modena, Charles Albert, Beauharnais' son, the duke of Reichstadt). Buonarroti opposed it through the *société des amis du peuple* in Europe and the *apofasimeni* in Italy. The committee was soon split by personal differences, which were accentuated by mistrust of Misley after his arrival in Paris.

In January 1831 the exiles tried to create a unified front by the creation of a 'liberating Italian junta' of all political opinions, with a restricted 'executive directory'. The 'junta' consisted for the most part of the exiles of 1821, but Buonarroti and his follower Pietro Mirri were members of the 'directory', together with the old Federalist Salfi. The aim of these organizations was to mount an invasion of Italy through Savoy in support of an insurrection prepared in the duchy of Modena. But both 'junta' and 'directory' rapidly collapsed because of sharp differences over the purpose of the revolution. Many of the exiles, particularly the Piedmontese of the former Turin junta supported by moderates such as Pellegrino Rossi and *carbonari* like Pisani Dossi, wanted to restrict the Savoy expedition to a local revolution based on a constitutional programme, possibly with Charles Albert as future king. Buonarroti, rigidly egalitarian and republican and always suspicious of aristocrats and the rich, was totally hostile to all appeals to monarchs or to the limitation of the revolution to restricted political oligarchies. Strongly unitarian and convinced of the need for a transitional revolutionary dictatorship, when entrusted with the responsibility of drawing up a form of federal constitution, Buonarroti published an intransigent statement of his philosophy, in which federalism was reduced to administrative autonomy in a state based upon equality of property and power and the unity and indivisibility of popular sovereignty. With his cosmopolitan vision of the revolution, he remained convinced – as in 1796 – that conditions would only be mature in Italy when the republic had been achieved in France. With Lafayette, he now opposed the Savoy expedition (soon forbidden by the French government), as also the subsequent attempts of Pepe, Linati and Misley to invade the Tuscan coast. The totally negative practical contribution of the exiles to the Italian revolution left as its legacy a trail of personal and ideological animosities.

In Italy too the insurrection had collapsed miserably. It never spread beyond central Italy, as persecution in the states involved in the earlier revolutions kept sectarian activities at a low ebb. At Modena Misley's place had been taken by Ciro Menotti, a young merchant-industrialist whose patriotic enthusiasm and energy rapidly dissolved the suspicions that had surrounded Misley's equivocal activities. Wholly mistrustful of Francis IV, sceptical of the patriotism of the 'old liberals' and rich nobles, but still ready to utilize all available elements in typical *carbonaro* manner, Menotti had created committees of insurrection at Bologna, Parma, Mantua and in the Romagna by December 1830. Adopting the slogan 'independence, union and liberty', current in patriotic circles (already employed by Bianco di Saint Jorioz and Domenico Nicolai, it was soon after to be repeated by Mazzini for the *Giovine Italia*), Menotti proposed to create committees of 'intellectuals' in all the Italian cities to act as 'rays' dependent upon a central committee at Paris. The aim was to form a representative monarchy, whose head would be chosen by a national congress at Rome, 'that Rome which had no equal, and which shall never have it in the opinion of our and future generations'. In ingenuous manner, Menotti proposed to add a cross to the patriotic tricolour: 'With this sign, which combines with liberty, Italians will be unanimous in supporting it' (Solmi, 217, pp. 142-4). Typically sectarian in his faith in a constitutional monarchy, in his concern with the technique of insurrection and his assumption that popular support would automatically be forthcoming once the revolution proclaimed its Catholicism, the only element that Menotti added to patriotic discussions was his emphasis on Rome as capital; and even this was hardly new, given the earlier classicist and present romantic belief in the unique character of the city.

The revolution broke out through Menotti's meticulous preparations, despite his treacherous capture by Francis IV of Modena (3 February 1831). At Bologna, Modena, Reggio and Parma the governments collapsed, once more showing their inability to resist without Austrian arms (4-12 February). The long conclave after Pius VIII's death (30 November 1830-2 February 1831) offered an ideal opportunity for conspirators in the Papal States. A Bonapartist plot at Rome, headed by the future Napoleon III, had been discovered. But now the insurrection spread rapidly from Bologna through the Legations and Marches, expression of the widespread discontent and demands for a lay administration and reforms.

But if Menotti's plots had facilitated the outbreak of the revolution, his cry of union was immediately drowned by municipal rivalries, traditionally strong among the Emilian cities. Numerous minor cities set up their own governments and only after considerable dispute was it possible to form a 'provisional government of the states of Modena and Reggio' under the 'dictatorship' of Biagio Nardi. Parma and Bologna insisted on retaining separate governments. Bologna, indeed, after the Austrian invasion, was to refuse entry to Modena's troops under the former Napoleonic general Zucchi unless they first disarmed.

This civic particularism, so reminiscent of 1796, reflected mutual fears of hegemony, particularly of Bologna. But it also masked serious social differences. The provisional governments of all the cities expressed the hostility of the middle classes to the high tariff barriers by reducing custom duties. But whereas at Modena Nardi accompanied a programme to revive agriculture and commerce and diminish the land-tax with specific measures in favour of the poor (abolition of the poll-tax, exemption from judicial taxes for the poor, free restitution by pawnshops of small pledges), the extremely moderate Bologna government, consisting of 'the old liberals' of the Jacobin *triennio* and the Italic Kingdom headed by Giovanni Vicini, limited itself to few measures almost wholly in favour of the landowners and merchants. The old differences between moderates and democrats were repeated. But, unlike at Naples in 1820, the democrats never seized the initiative, with the result that the 1831 revolution displayed a distinctly conservative character. Vicini even justified the revolution in terms of past violations of Bologna's historical liberties and present papal misgovernment, rather than on the basis of the people's demand for liberty. The hastily summoned assembly of notables, nominated by the provisional governments, which appointed a 'government of the united Italian provinces' – limited to the regions that had revolted – displayed the same moderate character and traditional civic rivalries.

It was hardly surprising that these governments should have failed to attract popular support, except to a limited extent within the cities, or to offer effective military resistance. A former Napoleonic officer, Giuseppe Sercognani, of his own initiative had led a body of 3000 volunteers in a march on Rome, advancing beyond Terni to the Umbria-Lazio border. But here he had been forced to stop, not for military reasons (although the Lazio failed to rise) but because of the Bologna government's fear of international complications. Like the Neapolitan moderates of 1820–1, Vicini and his colleagues seemed convinced that the powers would not interfere, unless provoked by revolutionary aggression, particularly in view of France's repeated assertion of her readiness to defend the principle of non-intervention. At the very moment that Austrian troops, with some encouragement from the peasantry, were occupying Modena, Reggio and Parma (9–12 March), the Bologna government could appeal to the population: 'Citizens! The Modenese circumstances are not ours; the sacred principle of non-intervention imposes its laws no less on us than on our neighbours. Let us beware of damaging the public interest by acting suddenly. . . . Citizens! Remember that we are not at war with anyone abroad!' (Catalano *et al.*, 121, p. 368). When Austria, after hesitating through fear of international complications, finally advanced on Bologna, the government retreated to

Ancona, despite the desire of the citizens to resist. Until its end, this revolution was marked by contrast between the readiness of the young students and middling bourgeoisie to fight, and the acceptance of defeat by this government of old men. Zucchi's volunteer forces attempted to stage a strong resistance at Rimini, but the government hastily capitulated to papal authority (25–6 March).

12

The society of
Restoration Italy

The countryside

In the century between the 1740s and the 1848 revolutions, Italian rural
society experienced major transformations. The underlying causes were
growth of the population and the long rise in prices of agricultural produce,
followed by a sharp slump during the Restoration. Population growth –
from 13 million in 1700 to 18 million in 1800 and 22 million in 1840 – was
an almost exclusively rural phenomenon, for the cities, with few exceptions,
remained static; the rate of growth was highest in most of southern Italy,
the islands of Sicily and Sardinia and the north-eastern provinces of Venetia.
The effect of this demographic rise was inevitably to increase pressure on
land and agricultural resources.

The contemporaneous growth in prices accentuated these pressures on
the rural population by its commercialization of agriculture. The demand
for agricultural produce, both internally and for export, acted as a constant
incentive to raise the levels of total production, not just in the capitalist
estates of lower Lombardy and Venetia, but equally in the *mezzadria* farms
of northern and central Italy and the vast *latifundia* of Lazio or Sicily. In
very few areas did higher production result from increases in productivity,
for the structural weaknesses of Italian agriculture – inadequate livestock
and meadows, shortage of capital, inadequate irrigation, often primitive
tools – remained unchanged throughout this period in the greater part of
the peninsula and islands, most markedly in the south. Production levels rose
through extension of the cultivated area and, above all, exploitation of
labour. Where productivity increased, it was normally through specialization in particularly profitable agricultural products, and then usually only
in fairly restricted areas. Mulberry trees to provide leaves for silkworms
were grown increasingly in most of Italy, especially in the north and some
parts of the centre; olives multiplied in the later eighteenth century in
Tuscany, Liguria and Apulia; vines were planted, often promiscuously with
cereal crops, in the most productive soils in both hills and plains; orchards

of citrus and other fruit trees aroused the admiration of foreign travellers in the vicinity of the major cities and ports in Liguria, Campania and Sicily.

The years of Napoleonic rule, at least until the crisis of 1811–12, had maintained these expectations of high profit, because of the opening of larger markets, especially for the regions of Italy annexed by France, but also because of the ideological and practical encouragement of private property. The eagerness with which the 'national properties' were acquired by nobles and bourgeois, established landowners and new ones, is evidence of this optimism. Commonlands and communal rights were eroded with the extension of private property, at the expense of peasant proprietors and small tenants. Government incentives encouraged speculation in specialized production. In Piedmont, leading noble families – such as the Benso di Cavour and Provana di Collegno – raised sizeable flocks of merino sheep; in Naples and the Roman provinces, attempts were made to introduce large-scale cotton plantations; in many of the annexed regions, the government subsidized experiments to introduce plants for industrial purposes, such as indigo or sugar-beet.

The experiments usually failed, partly for climatic reasons, but primarily because of the economic crisis of the final years of Napoleonic rule. The imposition of new frontiers – and hence of customs barriers – had negative as well as positive effects by closing traditional markets, as for instance in the former duchy of Parma-Piacenza, annexed by France and no longer able to export to its Lombard market, now within the Kingdom of Italy. The military conquest of Spain ruined the owners of merino sheep flocks, because of the sudden abundance of Spanish wool. Above all, the crisis of the Lyons silk industry had disastrous consequences for the Italian suppliers of crude and semi-finished silk. Speculative profits suffered, except for the staple cereal crop of Italy – wheat – whose price soared with the famine of 1811–12.

With the Restoration, the prolonged slump in prices of the 1820s and 1830s led to stagnation in agriculture, except in the few areas of intensive cultivation. The mixed husbandry of the lower Lombard plain, the rice-fields of Piedmont and western Lombardy, the vineyards of the most commercially minded owners of Tuscan hills, such as baron Ricasoli, were oases in a generally arid landscape. Even in these restricted areas, the maintenance of profits was achieved primarily through an intensification of labour. Elsewhere, the slump compounded the negative effects of the backward conditions of agriculture on the standard of living of the peasantry.

Within this broad framework, the response of different sectors of the rural population to these hostile conditions varied considerably, according to region and type of agriculture. In the south, in Sicily and large areas of the kingdom of Naples, the extensive wheat culture of the *latifundia* employed much labour, but little capital. In later eighteenth-century Sicily, contemporary economists estimated that the capital invested was only one-quarter to one-sixth of that employed by 'improving' English farmers for an equivalent area. Rented in large blocks by absentee landowners to urban-based *gabelloti*, the land was then sub-rented in small lots on short-term contracts to day-labourers or owners of minute patches of land. The climatic conditions of near drought meant that the area required to feed beasts of burden, such as oxen, was three to five times higher than in northern Europe. Hence, even if these peasants had possessed the capital – which they never did – they could never rent enough additional land to feed even one animal. The size of the plot they could cultivate was conditioned by the number of working adults and children. For a period of a century after the plague of 1656, in at least one Neapolitan area, the Valle Caudina, the fall in consumption and shortage of labour had enabled the peasants to acquire their lands on quit-rents and transform them into a more balanced subsistence economy by a mixed cultivation of cereals, oil, wine and fruit. But the terrible famine of 1764 and high wheat prices destroyed this fragile equilibrium. Over the following century consumption once more out-distanced production, and birth rates began to drop slowly. In the specialized wine-growing region of the Amalfi coast, the famine of 1816–18 and the fall in wine prices between 1822 and 1832 had the same consequences: peasant families could no longer earn enough to buy their subsistence, even when they integrated their highly intensive cultivation with fishing, domestic textile production or work in the local paper factories; during the nineteenth century, these Neapolitan smallholding families began to be replaced by *braccianti*, whose chances of survival depended upon their labour and who consequently raised larger families.

In the Papal States, the hills and slopes of the Apennines surrounded the vast plains of the Maremma and the Agro romano in a semicircle from north to south. In the plains, endemic malaria had driven away any stable population, whereas the hills were over-populated with peasant owners and tenants, exploiting holdings as small as two hectares, with the typical mixed crops of a subsistence economy. The vast Agro, exploited by a small group of 'country merchants' – only 54 in 1813 – required heavy working capital because of the lack of a resident labour force. Thousands of migrant workers arrived from the mountains of the Abruzzi, Terra di Lavoro, the Marches, Tuscany and Umbria at regular intervals of the agricultural cycles, to plough, sow and harvest the wheat. A vivid description of the harvest scene is offered by the Napoleonic prefect of Rome:

> It's not unusual to find six to eight hundred harvesters in a field in a line half a league long; from time to time they let out great shouts, which run down the line. Forty to fifty overseers ride among their ranks on horseback urging them to work harder and cut the wheat as low as possible. Mules loaded with wine,

bread and cheese bring constant refreshment. At night-time they sleep in the field. (Archives Nationales, Paris, F. 20.435, Rome, 7 January 1813)

The shortage of labour explained the highly particular system of agriculture, in which the soil was sown with wheat only once every four to five years, and otherwise left as pasturage for the more profitable sheep flocks, migrating in hundreds of thousands each year from the mountains to the plain.

Sheep, both transhumant and sedentary, were to be found in most areas of Italy. Moving in flocks of two to four hundred, sometimes for a hundred or more kilometres, as between the Abruzzi and Apulia, they were owned in part by the capitalist 'country merchants' and *gabelloti*, in part by the shepherds living in the mountains. The cost of renting pasturage necessarily limited sheep-raising as a commercial undertaking, to the wealthier groups among the peasantry or to those with ample communal grazing rights in the mountains. The handful of sheep owned by most smallholders, tenants and even *mezzadri* of Umbria, Tuscany, and the central and northern Apennines were usually of poor quality and utilized exclusively within the family economy, for their wool, cheese and meat. The only attempt at mixed sheep husbandry was in Piedmont, where the shepherds, owners of their flocks, descended from the Alps for the winter and were given free pasturage in the plain by the landowners, in return for their manure.

In central and much of northern Italy, the characteristic form of *mezzadria* or *colonìa parziaria* ostensibly gave the tenants more security. The mixture of cultivations – wheat, maize and cheaper cereals, vines, olives, fruit trees – was based essentially on the need to meet the consumption needs of the *mezzadro* family. A structural link existed between the size of the farm and that of the family group, in the sense that a balance had to be achieved between the optimal number of working members and the number of mouths to feed. Farms could be as small as three hectares, but the more usual size, between ten and twenty-five hectares, required the presence of extended and multiple households, of six to fifteen members. But the *mezzadri* were wholly dependent on the landowners or their stewards. Usually subject to annual contracts, they could be dismissed if their family grew too large or too small, if a son or daughter married without the landlord's permission, if they failed to cultivate the land in the prescribed manner, if they fell too heavily in debt. There can be little doubt that during the eighteenth century their conditions had worsened. Their contracts stipulated increasing labour obligations in a type of agriculture which was already highly labour-intensive: more vines and trees were to be planted, more ditches cleaned or dug. The owners reserved to themselves a larger share of the more profitable crops, the monopoly of mulberry leaves. But above all the *mezzadri* fell easily and more frequently into debt, a debt for which the whole family was collectively responsible. Despite the apparent stability of these extended families and the paternalistic image – dear to the Tuscan agronomes of the Restoration – of a personal relationship with the owner, the status of the *mezzadro* remained precarious. The tensions of enforced cohabitation in extended households, as much as the dangers of excessive debt through poor harvests, could easily lead to the *mezzadro*'s dismissal and replacement. For eager families, in constantly growing numbers, were waiting to offer their services. In the earlier nineteenth century, *mezzadria* continued to act as a cushion against famine. But low prices further diminished the possibilities of accumulating a reserve against hard times and rendered the farmers even more vulnerable to the demands on their labour.

Small proprietors, in theory, were more independent. But their independence was fictitious unless they owned an adequate quantity of land. Most small proprietors lived on the edge of subsistence. The size of their families, smaller than those of the *mezzadri*, were similarly dependent upon the balance between adequate production and labour. In at least two periods of the family's life cycle – when the children were too small to work or the parents too old – the balance between consumption and labour was particularly endangered, and the head of the household endeavoured to maintain viability by extending the family to include relatives. Inadequate land, technical backwardness and excess labour were the conditioning elements of a family organization structured to ensure subsistence and the conservation of the family inheritance through generations, by temporary emigration, accumulation of minute plots of land or cash for dowries, and co-operation within the community in the use of common lands or irrigation. Small proprietors, like the tenants of smallholdings, continued to exist in every region of Italy throughout the nineteenth century. They formed a large but fluid sector of the rural population, with constant formation of new families and extinction of old ones. Only families with adequate land or animals were likely to survive through many generations. For a few families, and usually only in particularly remote areas, were really self-sufficient. Almost all, to a lesser or greater degree, were dependent on the market, a dependence that increased through this period with the growing commercialization of agriculture. Temporary emigration and domestic production of crude and spun silk for an expanding market assisted survival. But interruptions of trade or poor harvests easily destroyed a precarious equilibrium. The Napoleonic wars and Continental Blockade had forced many families to join the thick ranks of the day-labourers. The disastrous famines of 1812, 1816–17 and 1846–7 (like the earlier ones of 1764–6 and the 1790s) wreaked even greater havoc, driving these peasant families in tens of thousands towards the cities. 'The peasants of the provinces follow the cereals which have been seized from them, pouring into Naples', had written the French ambassador during the 1764 famine (Venturi, 102, p. 405). During these final famines of the nineteenth century, contemporaries wrote with horror of corpses with grass in their mouths.

The plains and hills of the vast Po valley were intensely cultivated by peasant owners and tenants, *mezzadri* and capitalist landowners. The unhealthy rice-fields of the Vercellese and Novarese, dependent on migrant labour, expanded rapidly during the later eighteenth and nineteenth centuries. As the Napoleonic prefect of the Sesia department commented:

> The obsessive manner with which some of the inhabitants of the plain in this department create new rice-fields, with disastrous consequences for the population, derives from three causes: the near-certainty of a good harvest, the certainty of its sale, and the present increase in the price which the owners are certain to obtain. (Archives Nationales, Paris, F. 11.474-5, Sesia, 26 brumaire, an 14)

The expansion of the great estates of lower Lombardy and Venetia in the later eighteenth century had been achieved at the expense of the small owners and tenants. The corollary of their presence was the existence of a large number of *braccianti*, day-labourers. Whereas in Lombardy heavy investment resulted in a sophisticated and modern form of farming, in Venetia the *fittanzieri*, capitalist tenants, were responsible for few improvements; grain, maize and wine continued to characterize this region of backward agriculture. In Lombardy these great estates were cultivated in *masserie*, substantial sized farms, structured around patriarchal households of four to five families, with forty or more persons directed by a head of household, the *reggitore*. In Venetia, the estates were either divided into smaller *masserie*, with about twenty persons, or exploited directly by the *fittanzieri*, paying wages to the resident families of *bifolchi*. Throughout the region of the great estates, the *braccianti* supplied the additional labour requirements. Some were hired for the year and given in advance a small amount of cash and enough maize for the winter, as well as housing and occasionally a plot of land to cultivate for themselves; others paid a rental for their lodging, but were remunerated in kind, rather than in cash, with a proportion of the crops. Far more *braccianti* were paid by the day for the periods when their labour was needed; some worked their own smallholdings, or migrated during the slack periods, to work as porters or builders in the cities; others, unable to find employment, swarmed around the *masserie* and large estates, searching for the means to survive, often by theft from the fields.

The *braccianti* constituted the lowest level of the peasantry, a rural proletariat created by and dependent upon the great estates, in both southern and northern Italy. With the fall in agricultural prices in the earlier nineteenth century, their possibilities of employment and wages fell as their numbers rose. In the Vercellese, it has been estimated, a casual labourer working 260 days a year was unable to earn enough for his subsistence between the 1770s and 1820s.

In this overwhelmingly subsistence economy, cottage industry and migration represented two essential aids to survival. Many families, particularly in the remoter mountain areas, raised sheep or cultivated hemp, to provide for their own clothing and rope for their work; rudimentary tools were constructed at home. But the raising of silk cocoons and spinning of thread represented the major rural industry. Here, too, the commercialization of agriculture meant that owners rather than tenants gained most of the benefits, as tenancy contracts stipulated strict controls over peasant silk production. Although market demand rose, mechanical innovations in weaving and spinning almost certainly had negative effects on the resources of many families.

Emigration had always existed. For many families it represented a regular phase of the life cycle. Skilled artisans – masons, roof-layers, carpenters, plasterers, barrel-makers, miners, metal-workers – left their villages for a few months each year, sometimes moving in groups, usually following an itinerary established over the years. The agricultural equivalent to these artisans were the scythers and sowers, the tree-pruners and terrace-repairers of hillside vineyards, as well as the shepherds. Others left for some years, between adolescence and marriage, emigrating to the cities as servants, or abroad to Spain or France as porters, in order to accumulate a dowry. But alongside these regular patterns, temporary or permanent migrations were the inevitable consequence of bad harvests or the collapse of the family economy. 'In bad years', noted the prefect of the Stura department, 'the number of emigrants increases very considerably, and in some places even doubles or trebles' (Archives Nationales, Paris, F.20. 435, Stura, 20 June 1811).

The evidence of the worsening conditions of the rural population is continuous from the mid-eighteenth through the nineteenth century. Migration became vagabondage, as families finally collapsed under the weight of debt, took to the road and became beggars. Maize cultivation, with its far higher yield compared to that of wheat or other cereals, spread rapidly through the later eighteenth century, from Venetia, through the Lombard plain, into the hills and mountains of Piedmont, Liguria, parts of central Italy, as far south as the Calabrian mountains. 'Maize is the basic food of the great mass of the peasantry in the plains and mountains, as wheat is the basic food in the cities', noted the prefect of the Sesia department in 1812 (Archives Nationales, Paris, F.10. 420, Sesia, 1 June 1812). Where maize did not grow well, as in the Ligurian or Pistoiese Apennines, chestnuts acted as a substitute. When the chestnut crop failed in the mountainous hinterland of Genoa, the entire population of 40 000 would abandon their villages to seek survival in the ricefields of Piedmont and Lombardy. In the duchy of Parma-Piacenza, pigs were raised everywhere, by 'farmers, land-owners, traders, day-labourers', but were sold by the peasants unfattened, as a supplementary form of income. Goats were raised wherever allowed in the mountains and valleys. Fresh meat had vanished from a peasant diet, heavily deficient in proteins and vitamins and dominated by maize in central and northern Italy. Only wine compensated for the inadequacy and mono-tony of the food, and in Restoration Lombardy was even given to children from their earliest years.

The dwellings of the great mass of the rural population were little better. The solid houses of the Tuscan *mezzadri* and Lombard *masserie* were much admired; but they were occupied only by the more fortunate families. Smallholders and tenants usually lived in houses built of stone or brick, with roofs of slate or tiles, which were often damp, and invariably small. The windows were sealed with dry dung from the animals, which shared the rooms with their owners. Among small proprietors of the Valtellina, pro-perty rights led to the division among sons and grandsons of 'the same room, the same kitchen, the same courtyard, in quarters and sixths' (Della Peruta, in 243, p. 326). In Lombardy and Piedmont, these families were forced to give up all their living space, even their kitchen, for the period when the voracious, heat-loving silkworms were raised. The huge numbers of wage-earning peasants and day-labourers lived in huts or hovels, some-times built of bricks, but often only of wood or reeds, thatched with straw or merely covered with maize husks. In the Agro romano, the day-labourers were given no shelter at all to protect them from the sun.

Throughout the period of the Risorgimento, the standard of living of the peasantry deteriorated in all regions, but most disastrously in the south. Indebtedness, resulting in pauperism, became ever more common. At moments of food shortages and sharp price rises, spontaneous riots broke out in markets, often led by women. The riots followed a familiar pattern: demand for reduction of cereal prices, attacks on bakers' ovens, or against the houses of local notables; in the south, demand for land. Little was different in these tumults during the famines of 1816–17 and 1846–7 from those of the *ancien régime*.

What was different was the attitude of the landowners in northern and central Italy. In contrast to the harsh hostility towards the poor of the Enlightened reformers, the religiosity of the Restoration encouraged a more humanitarian approach. A growing concern for public hygiene, particularly after the cholera epidemics of 1835–7, led to investigations which revealed the appalling living conditions in the countryside. The Genoese Cevasco, in 1838, suggested the need for public inspection and instruction, not just in the city workshops, but 'in the huts of misery, the hovels of our peasants' (Cevasco, 229, t. 1, p. 267). Such discussions and proposals, a constant theme of the social literature of the decades of the Risorgimento, were more frequent and intense in the regions of the north and centre, which in this, as in so many other respects, displayed their distinctiveness from the south.

The structures of peasant family economies tend to possess an inbuilt resilience to hostile external conditions, based upon an ability to exploit the labour of the family to the level necessary to achieve subsistence. The apparent immobility of these structures in Italy masked the innumerable minute changes and personal tragedies that accompanied the degradation of an increasing proportion of the peasantry into a rural proletariat. Unlike England in the eighteenth century or France in the nineteenth, agriculture failed to modernize in Italy, except for very restricted areas of the Po valley. The *latifundia* in the south, *mezzadria* in the centre and north, worked against such modernization, as they presupposed a low level of capital investment. During the Risorgimento, the competition of these more advanced agricultures caused a slump in prices, which worsened the situation. Indeed, the half century from the 1820s to the 1870s marked the final stage of a secular structural crisis of Italian agriculture. Given this situation, the virtual absence of the peasantry from the political movements of the Risorgimento requires little explanation. In the south, the desperate condition of the peasants led to constant rebellion and the demand for land. In the centre and north, Tuscany and Umbria, Lombardy and Piedmont, the Catholic humanitarianism of the landowners could do little to modify or check the increasing weaknesses of a peasant world structured around the ever-less protective shell of the family subsistence economy. But it played a role in insulating this world from the political movement of the cities.

The cities

In contrast to the countryside, many of the major Italian cities of the 1830s–40s were visibly different from a century earlier. In the later eighteenth century, the cities, with few exceptions, had remained immobile, administrative centres, the urban residence of noble landowners, with substantial artisan populations producing mostly luxury products, in some instances – as at Venice or Rome – dependent upon tourism, in all cases exerting a heavy pressure upon the countryside in terms of food provisioning and landed income. By the mid-nineteenth century, the contrast in economic vitality between some of the northern cities and the major centres of the south was already reflected in their differing rates of demographic growth and social composition.

The population of some cities remained static or even declined, through the loss of their role as independent or semi-autonomous capitals. Venice, now part of the Austrian empire, sacrificed administratively to Milan and economically to Trieste, dropped from a population of 137 000 in 1797 to 122 000 in 1845; Palermo, rigidly subordinated to Naples, fell from 210 000 in 1815 to 194 000 in 1861. Naples, after its increase in population in the later eighteenth century, oscillated around 430 000 to 450 000 throughout the period of the Risorgimento. Rome only recovered its 1800 population of 150 000 in the 1830s, then rising slowly to 184 000 in 1860. Genoa, mistrusted by its new masters at Turin, barely rose from 100 000 in 1814 to 114 000 in 1838. At the other extreme, Turin and Milan in the north and some of the smaller ports grew rapidly: from 86 000 in 1796 Turin increased in population to 137 000 by 1848 and 204 000 in 1861; Milan grew from 139 000 in 1814 to 189 000 in 1847 and 240 000 in 1861; Leghorn rose from 46 000 in 1814 to 61 000 in 1834, Catania from 45 000 in 1798 to 69 000 in 1861.

These differences in population movements masked a more general change in the relationship of the cities and the countryside. In the eighteenth century, the urban centres of Italy were 'closed' cities, usually surrounded by walls. The walls, constructed and often expanded in the communal, seigneurial and Spanish periods, served a fiscal rather than a military purpose by the eighteenth century, facilitating the exaction of customs duties on goods entering and leaving the gates. But they also acted as a clear demarcation line between the cities and the countryside. The cities were consciously and deliberately closed in upon themselves. The walls might (and usually did) include unbuilt areas, often intensively cultivated, but above all they acted as a visible boundary, within which space could be planned according to aesthetic criteria, food supplies ensured, public order policed and vagabondage excluded.

By the end of the eighteenth century, some wealthy noble and bourgeois residents had already begun to leave the city centres and construct their villas and palaces in the periphery of the city or outside the walls. At the same time, speculative housing for renting began to surround the walls, both inside the city and in the immediate suburbs. The period of French rule led to the destruction of the walls and bastions in some cities, such as Turin and Milan, and to grandiose projects of town planning. More importantly, a new functionalist concept of the city, already well developed in France, began to make its appearance in Italy. The city was viewed as a centre of exchange, as well as an administrative capital and a place of residence. Entire quarters were to be developed or remodelled in the interests of commercial activities, public services were to be improved, above all the city was to be opened outwards towards its hinterland. Privacy and comfort gained in importance, and apartment blocks were constructed with these aims in mind. For those insufficiently wealthy to own or build a country residence, easier and more pleasant social contact was assured by the conversion of the fortifications into promenades.

This new urban ideology emerged far more slowly, hesitantly and incompletely in Italy than in France during the decades of the Risorgimento. It hardly touched the small provincial towns, which continued to exert their traditional administrative and cultural influence over the surrounding countryside. Nor did it affect the dominance of the great noble families in economically stagnant capitals such as Rome or Palermo. But its presence underlay the discussions and decisions about the role of the city in developing urban centres, such as Turin, Milan or Leghorn. Civic authorities began to play a more active role in ensuring the rational planning and provision of services in the development of new urban areas, because of their confidence in the 'natural' growth of the city, in contrast to former assumptions of its static quality. The debate over public hygiene, which accompanied the recurrent outbreaks of cholera and typhus, and led in some instances to the destruction and rebuilding of the most unhealthy quarters, was directly related to preoccupations about the negative consequences of epidemics on commercial activities. The provision of water supplies and fire brigades, street lighting and paving, municipal slaughterhouses and new cemeteries outside the walls, were as much reflections of the increased importance of the urban merchant capitalists, as was the growing speculation in city housing.

The abolition of the old food provisioning regulations by the French administrations, confirmed by the Restoration rulers, encouraged a more open relationship with the countryside. But more significant was the development of new *borghi* outside the walls, often located near road or river communications with the hinterland. Industrial and trading activities, avoidance of customs duties and cheaper rentals, as well as the increased privacy of more spacious dwellings, were the prime reasons for this rapid growth. By 1837 there were as many houses outside the walls of Leghorn as within. At Milan, the *corpi santi* or suburbs outside the customs wall housed 18 000 people in 1816 and 48 000 in 1861.

The landowning urban nobles had not lost their power in the cities by the mid-nineteenth century; indeed, in Turin and Milan, as in Florence and Venice, they continued to dominate the civic administrations. But by the 1840s, in tune with the expansion of the international economy, the urban bourgeoisies had asserted their leading role and impressed upon the administrators their interpretation of the requirements of modernity. In the guide-books of the 1830s and 1840s written by patriotic citizens, the manufactures, trade, commerce and banking of the major cities, dominated by the bourgeoisie, were described in detail, with as much pride as the historic monuments and institutions of charity.

The composition of this bourgeoisie offers an indicator of its relative importance in the different cities. In Milan in 1838, there were 42 bankers, as well as 25 money-changers; the silk industry and textiles in general dominated manufacturing, with 76 silk merchants and 40 silk-weaving factories, 196 manufacturers of silk and cotton goods, and 106 traders in cloths, besides 48 textile dyeing and printing workshops. There were also 146 wholesale traders of colonial goods, 46 merchants in hides, and 155 wholesale merchants in cereals, oil, wine and foodstuffs, as well as 150 general merchants and five sugar-refineries. In this city of 148 000, with 4700 landowners (including 3000 resident nobles), this wealthy manufacturing-commercial bourgeoisie, certainly well over one thousand in number, represented a powerful force, closely backed by the professional groups – 500 engineers and 170 lawyers (232, pp. 5–7).

Milan was the wealthiest and economically most active city in Italy in the 1840s. But in most other major cities, the bourgeoisie played a similar role. At Genoa in 1838 the traders were numbered at over one thousand. At Venice, glass, woollen products, sugar refineries, a mechanized felt factory, were owned by the same upper middle class. Even in Naples, the small group of 300 bankers and merchants who controlled the trade in agricultural staples and the speculative activities surrounding the state administration – tax-farming, contracting public works, marine insurance – were 'new' men, Neapolitans and Sicilians, French and Swiss bankers and manufacturers who had remained after the French débâcle.

The example of Naples is revealing precisely because of the contrast it offers to the economically developing cities of the north. Despite government encouragement in the 1830s, on a far more substantial level than that offered by the Austrian or Piedmontese governments, the financial oligarchy refused to support the joint-stock companies or to invest in the isolated industrial ventures: the cotton factories, engineering workshops, railway building and steamship companies, which constituted the sum of Neapolitan industrialization in these decades, were financed by foreign investment and remained isolated from the rest of the economy. In Naples the behaviour of the financial-commercial oligarchy was as influential, negatively, on the role of the city as that of the Milanese or Turin bourgeoisies.

Beneath this wealthy and powerful upper middle class, the economic life of the cities continued to be structured around the petty traders and artisans. In Genoa in 1838, there were over 21 000 masters and apprentices, as well as another 1300 without a specific calling, and 6400 shopkeepers, small traders and their employees (Cevasco, 229, t.1, p. 164 bis). At Venice in 1848, there were 76 silversmiths, goldsmiths and jewellers, 108 carpenters, 61 shops selling iron, brass and copperware, 65 tailor shops, over 70 hosiery and glove shops, over 100 shops selling silk goods, 25 antique dealers and over 30 shops selling glass objects (Ginsborg, 311, pp. 37–8). At Milan in 1838, there were over 100 watchmakers, 150 jewellers, nearly 400 shops selling silk and cotton goods, 65 glove and headware producers, 16 embroiderers, 13 artificial flower-makers, over 300 tailors and 188 shoemakers, and over 1200 house and palace renovators and carriage makers (232, pp. 5–7). In all the large Italian cities manufacturing continued to be based upon

artisan skills. The suppression of the guilds had not led to an overall collapse of employment, but to its restructuring around the demands of a more
widely based wealthy clientele, partly resident, partly provided by a
growing flow of tourists.

The evidence of this growing opulence was ubiquitous – in the new
houses, the furniture, the carriages, the clothing, the new theatres, the
landaus and gondolas, the hotels and cafés. Cafés had catered for an
exclusive clientele in the eighteenth century. In Turin, by 1852, when they
numbered 150, they had 'democratized themselves, by adding the name of
restaurant to that of café' (Stefani and Mondo, 228, p. 33). Above all, the
demands of fashion and the materialism of the new age required the
employment of servants. Even if it is impossible to compare their numbers
to those of the eighteenth century, it seems likely that they had increased,
for few comfortable families did not have one servant living in. At Genoa in
1838 there were over 8000 servants, chambermaids, doormen and cooks.

As always, such visible changes in social behaviour aroused contradictory
responses among their observers. The anonymous author of an *Historical
Topography* of Milan of 1846 denounced 'the ridiculous and unnecessary
exaggeration of comforts and conspicuous consumption for purposes of
pure caprice, which is increasingly softening character and corrupting
public morality' (235, vol. 3, p. 155 n.). But for Angelo Cossa, writing in the
same years, taste and fashion, requiring frequent change of interior decora-
tions, had beneficial effects, for 'the lesser classes and even the lowest nowadays possess decent furniture, because they can buy cheaply what the upper
classes have discarded' (Cossa, 233, p. 18).

Cossa's optimism is hardly borne out by the descriptions of the living
conditions of the 'lowest' classes. Beneath the small craftsmen and traders,
often difficult to distinguish from them, lived the urban 'working class'.
The term obviously carried different connotations than in an industrialized
society. There were few factories in town or countryside, although within
the textile industries of Piedmontese and Lombard cities by the 1840s those
that existed were sufficiently large, mechanized and dependent upon child
and female labour to arouse the denunciations of leading Italian moderates.
Glassworks, tobacco factories, dockyards, engineering shops, state arsenals,
employed large workforces: 800 carpenters, caulkers and similar worked in
the Venetian arsenal in 1848, 1800 in the Neapolitan naval dockyard of
Castellammare. But apart from these isolated agglomerations, the workforce
was still highly dispersed, as in previous centuries. The bulk of this working
class produced and sold goods and above all food for an extremely localized
market, and hence, in the first instance, for their peers. The distinction
made by contemporaries between the 'people' and the 'plebs', while difficult
to define at its extremes, is thus not purely subjective, but also reflects the
different social standing of the craftsmen and shopkeepers producing

primarily for the wealthy classes and those providing for the most part for a more popular demand. The tinkers, coopers, carpenters, brass and copper-smiths, cobblers and tinsmiths, listed in the guidebooks and topographies of all the major cities, alongside the carters, porters, fishmongers, petty shop-keepers, grocers, greengrocers, bakers, pasta-makers, cheap butchers, fruit-sellers, candle-makers, and so on, all formed part of this urban working class. Food processing and selling, porterage and building skills encom-passed the major sectors of their economic activities.

It is often difficult to distinguish these petty traders and craftsmen on the edge of subsistence, from the destitute. It needed little to drop beneath the level of subsistence and hence become at least temporarily dependent on charity – the birth of an extra child, a prolonged illness, a period of indus-trial stagnation. This 'menu peuple' tended to marry early, as both partners worked. As the acute Genoese observer, Michele Cevasco, noted, the chil-dren were abandoned in the streets until they reached the age of seven or eight, when their parents tried to discipline them into helping in the shop or workshop; but as soon as a boy earned enough, he would marry and start another family. These were the 'shamefaced' poor, who depended upon the pawnshops, where they pledged their marriage rings, kitchen pots and pans, even their bedclothing, in times of difficulty. Precisely because they were the respectable poor, they were the object of particular concern to the charit-able institutions, who provided them with medical aid, mattresses and blankets, even the tools of their trade, in a continuous endeavour to enable them to regain their independence. As the administrator of a Florence charity wrote in the early nineteenth century, assistance was essential for

> the indigent families of our city, who despite their work are unable to earn enough for their entire subsistence, because of the size of their family and the young age of their children, or because of the illness of a member, or some other critical circumstance, which often forms part of the misery of the poor. (Archivio di Stato, Florence, Prefettura dell'Arno, 508, 26 April 1809)

Alongside this working class of essentially independent families, certain other groups were to be found in all the large cities. The servants ranged considerably in the economic opportunities open to them, from the relatively protected butlers, cooks, grooms and doormen of the large, wealthy house-holds to the chambermaids who had often immigrated from the countryside. The clerks and assistants of the lawyers, large merchants, administrative offices and hospitals, like the public and private schoolteachers – over 3000 in Genoa – could often be distinguished by their literacy and social standing, rarely by their earnings. In the ports, the dockers and porters – over 2000 in Genoa – formed a separate, tightly-knit category.

At the bottom of the social scale were the large numbers of the poor with-out any fixed occupation. Their numbers varied enormously, and were certainly far higher in the massive capitals of the south, Naples, Rome, Palermo, than in the cities of northern and central Italy, smaller in size, economically more prosperous and administratively better organized. Some scraped a living by hawking trinkets or foodstuffs, such as offal or chestnuts. Far more were regularly dependent on charity, when unable to find work as building labourers or in the public works projects of the municipalities, levelling the new squares and roads, paving the streets, by the 1840s building the first railway lines. Their numbers were swollen by the regular flow of temporary, as well as permanent, migrants from the countryside. As a Milanese observer noted:

> A great number only spend a few months in the city, as chimney-sweeps from the valleys of Onsernone, Canobbio, Valvigezzo, as fruit and wine vendors from the Ossola valley and the Lago Maggiore, as porters from the Bergamasco and Valtellina, pot-makers from the lake of Lugano, builders and painters from the Ticino canton, Varese, the Comasco, woodcutters from the Ligurian mountains, etc. (Gaspari, 236, p. 7)

There is little evidence about the attitude of the resident working class and casually employed towards these immigrants, but it was almost certainly hostile. In mid-nineteenth century Naples, over 50 per cent of servants were immigrants, but only 4 per cent found a living as porters (Petraccone, 256, p. 240).

A large proportion of the inhabitants of the major Italian cities thus lived in a state of indigence or destitution. The problem was certainly not new, but the numbers had increased through the eighteenth century and would appear to have continued to grow in the nineteenth. In Genoa in 1838, in a population of 113 000, less than 4000 were liable to pay either the personal or land-taxes. Contemporaries were extremely conscious of the problem of poverty and of the squalor of living conditions.

The diet of the urban 'menu peuple' was almost certainly an improvement on that of the peasantry. In the southern cities, bread continued to be made of wheat, although in Milan it was made of a mixture of wheat and maize. Fruit was of crucial importance as food for the poor in the south. At Milan, meat formed part of the popular diet, alongside pasta and rice, but consisted of offal, new-born calves, sausages, contraband horse-meat, often in a state of near putridity; between 1810 and 1862 the daily ration of meat diminished as prices rose. Little milk, butter, cheese or eggs were consumed, but salted fish, beans, potatoes and cabbages were important components, with lard as the only fat; coffee (often adulterated) and a heavy consumption of wine and cheap spirits compensated for this ill-balanced diet (Della Peruta, 243, pp. 322–5).

Hygiene and housing conditions were little better. Italian cities in the first half of the nineteenth century experienced a revival of epidemic diseases, after a long period of relative tranquillity. The last terrible outbreak of typhus, which affected all Italy, occurred in 1816–18. Despite vaccination, introduced on a broad scale by the French, smallpox was still a serious threat, sweeping through the cities of Piedmont and Liguria in 1829. But above all, cholera epidemics ravaged the urban populations in 1835–7 and Del Panta, 16, 1854–5. Local municipal authorities took urgent administrative measures to ensure an uncontaminated supply of water and some form of drainage. But hospitals, too often still characterized by 'that filth of poverty and squalor' (234, p. 820), remained filled with the indigent, suffering illnesses – respiratory ailments, dysentery, rheumatism and permanent headaches – directly linked to their conditions of housing and labour.

Housing conditions were extremely poor, because of the pressure of population and the high rentals. Few cities were yet segregated, in the sense of a division between separate residential quarters of the prosperous and squalid working-class slums. But all cities possessed popular quarters with a high density of habitation. The reputation of Naples was notorious, because of the concentration of population since the seventeenth century. In the mid-nineteenth century, in the densely packed dwellings of the *bassi* near the market, life expectancy for the 'plebs' was only 24 years; even in the residential area of Chiaia, the fishermen lived 'massed together in the side-streets' (De Renzi, 254, p. 221). As the open spaces vanished, the building speculators constructed houses of eight or nine floors, totally ignoring hygienic regulations:

> Houses were built without regard for symmetry, order, light or sun; small and narrow passage ways, some without exit, others twisting in labyrinths; an arch here, a corner there; and everywhere, dirt and filth. Towering houses, with narrow, smoke-blackened stairs, leading to one or more small rooms on each floor, which looked out on those passage ways or onto a small courtyard like a well. . . . Every type of wretch gathers in these hovels; often a variety of persons, by no means belonging to the same family, adults and children, spend the night together amidst the stench produced by every sort of filth, and then emerge onto the streets in the morning to see the sun and breathe a more wholesome and less corrupt air. (De Renzi, 255, p. 211)

The popular classes already lived for the most part in zones geographically separated from the wealthy quarters at Naples, as at Palermo, with its dense population around the port, and Rome, where the *popolino* lived in Trastevere and the area near the Tiber (while the nobles lived in their palaces on the hills). But even in these cities, noble residences in renaissance and baroque palaces in popular quarters were evidence that segregation, in the sense of Victorian English industrial cities, did not yet exist.

In the northern cities, the degree of separation was far less, or even non-existent, where lack of space – as at Genoa and Venice – or the tradition of urban development – as at Turin – led to cohabitation in the same streets and buildings. But in these cities too, some more 'popular' quarters were more densely populated. At Turin, where the great baroque palaces had been built with the intention of renting the upper floors and rooms, an average of fourteen families, or over sixty-three persons, inhabited these vast edifices in 1838; but in the new suburb of Dora there were over sixteen families and nearly eighty persons to a house; and in the 'old' quarter of Moncenisio over sixteen families (Bertolotti, 227, p. 15). At Genoa, where there was an average of nearly four families, or over twenty persons, to a house, the population density was higher around the port. At Venice, where the poor lived in the basement and attics of the well-to-do buildings, there were similar concentrations of *popolani* at Castello, Cannaregio and the island of the Giudecca. At Milan, where the medieval and Spanish artisan quarters had been left intact for the most part by the grandiose restructuring of the Napoleonic years, the same contrast appeared between dense unhygienic popular quarters and the housing of the urban bourgeoisie.

Contemporaries in these northern cities laid stress on the improvements of recent years. The authors of a guide to Turin in 1852 pointed to the 'decency and cleanliness' of the city, without beggars, 'those filthy figures dressed in rags, whom you find at every turn in the other cities of Italy'. But even in sober, industrious Turin, 'the less well-to-do, who live on the fourth or fifth floor or in the attic, feel an irresistible need of air and movement' – which accounts for the evening stroll! (Stefani and Mondo, 228, pp. 32–3). In Milan, the guide books pointed to the enterprise of the municipality in providing drains and gutters, removing the slaughterhouses and smelly soap workshops from the centre, prohibiting open closets and the discharge of water onto the streets. But here too, crowded, unhygienic housing remained the norm for the poor.

Urban poverty, if undesirable, was nevertheless regarded as inevitable. Urban conditions were sometimes regarded as being responsible for, or at least directly linked to, the consolidation of poverty, above all through the increase of rentals. But for the most part the existence of the poor was explained in Malthusian terms: too early marriage, too many children.

Assistance for the poor was regarded as religiously and socially necessary. 'The charitable institutions are the first and major marvel of Turin . . . the charities of this city would honour a metropolis three times its size', wrote a proud citizen of Turin in 1840 (Bertolotti, 227, p. 145). At Milan, the 66 institutions were described in detail, with considerable satisfaction. But it was recognized that charity would not make poverty vanish:

> Rather than pretend that, through our charity and our institutions, we can eliminate begging, we only propose to lessen the need and pretence for begging. . . . Rather than presume to substitute Providence by the works of public charity and government regulations, we wish to assist the infinite wisdom of Providence by a balanced and advantageous employment of our social strength

and resources, and so thin the ranks of the idle, the vagabonds and the do-nothings, accustoming them to a laborious, profitable and exemplary way of life! (235, vol. 2, p. 164)

Divisions between rich and poor have always existed in cities. It would be historically inaccurate to exaggerate these divisions in the class terms of an industrialized society. For although the hostility of the 'lower orders' was expressed at moments of crisis, usually in the form of verbal threats against the wealthy, it rarely developed into organized structures. Catholic charity certainly did not forge such strong bonds as its promoters believed. But it reinforced the ties that derived from the daily contacts of different social groups in their manner of living in the cities. It is probably not purely casual that the risings of the 'menu peuple' in 1848 occurred in cities where a greater physical separation had developed – in Palermo, Naples, Milan, Rome. Even in Venice, where rich and poor lived for the most part together, it was the isolated body of *carsenalotti* who rose. In Turin, the only major city where a rising did not occur in 1848, the social cohesion implicit in residence on different floors of the same palaces is not without significance. The topography, as well as the social structure of the Italian cities in the mid-nineteenth century offers an essential dimension for understanding the political movements that were to culminate in 1848.

13

Alternative paths
towards a new Italy: 1831–48

Political and economic change in Europe

The decisive effect of the July revolution in destroying the Restoration settlement became ever-more visible in the following years. The uneasy unity of the congress system had been irrevocably broken and the settlement of Vienna modified in France, Greece and Belgium. Austria and Russia, the most authoritative defenders of the 1815 treaties, had been successfully opposed by an informal agreement between England and France, supported by Prussia. Prussia's attitude towards the revolutions in Germany in 1830–1, like Russia's support of the Greeks in the preceding years, was indicative of the more flexible relations between the great powers, each concerned more openly with its own interests than with the maintenance of a rigid unity of action. The congresses, in which heads of governments or foreign ministers 'settled' the affairs of Europe, were replaced by less formal conferences of ambassadors to resolve specific problems as they arose: eight such conferences were held between 1830 and 1856, when the unique instance of a conflict between the great powers – the Crimean War – occasioned a new congress at Paris. The recognition by the powers that it was beyond their capacity to intervene *manu militari* in the internal affairs of states was acknowledged until almost the end of the 1848 revolutions, when Russia intervened in Hungary. Nevertheless, their readiness to meet in conferences and settle disputes diplomatically reflected their continuing belief in the Concert of Europe, as much as their fear of acting alone. This restraint, which derived from a rough parity of power (except for Britain), mutual diffidence and a general worry about revolutionary discontent within their own countries, bore its fruits in the avoidance of any war between the great powers from Napoleon's fall until Crimea.

The emergence of two groups of leading states – the western, liberal powers of Britain and France and the eastern autocratic regimes of Russia, Austria and Prussia – was to exert a deep influence upon the forces of opposition, whether liberal or revolutionary. But in reality, the contrast was never very clear-cut nor long-lived. Disquiet about French ambitions was common to all the powers. Nicholas I had been sufficiently worried by the Anglo-French *entente* to attempt to revive the solidarity of the eastern powers with the Münchengrätz agreement (October 1833), to which Palmerston replied with the Quadruple Alliance between England, France, Spain and Portugal (April 1834). But the latter alliance was restricted to the Iberian peninsula, where the two groups of powers attempted to give support, without direct interference and with alternating success, to the local absolutist and liberal factions.

Traditional Anglo-French rivalry soon divided the western powers, as Austro-Prussian diffidence in Germany and Austro-Russian hostility over the Ottoman empire divided the eastern ones. The 'eastern question' represented a constant source of potential conflict between the powers and ultimately, accidentally, led to their only major war. Britain, by far the strongest power in the world, was worried lest the disintegration of the Turkish empire threaten its control of the Mediterranean and the approaches to India. After Russia forced Turkey to close the Dardanelles Straits to foreign fleets (treaty of Unkiar Skelessi, 1833), British distrust of French expansionism in Algeria was almost replaced by officially encouraged Russophobia in England. But if England and France had collaborated in restraining the Egyptian Pasha Mehemet Ali's aggression against the Turkish Sultan in 1833, Palmerston did not hesitate to isolate France by reaching agreement with Austria, Russia and Prussia to settle the renewed Turco-Egyptian war in 1840 (London convention); and then to re-admit France to the Concert of Europe with the Straits convention (1841), closing the Dardanelles to all warships, including Russian.

Palmerston, who dominated English foreign policy from 1830 until his death in 1865, thus reasserted Britain's active role in Europe in order to maintain the divisions among the other great powers and so conserve the balance of power, the necessary condition for British commercial expansion. Relations with Russia were fundamentally dependent upon the preservation of the Ottoman empire and implied support of a strong Austria. But relations with France were corroded by fears that the 'revolutionary' monarch Louis Philippe would follow public opinion in attempting to revive the Napoleonic tradition of expansion; this distrust remained, despite awareness of Louis Philippe's hostility to republican and revolutionary opposition at home. Already in 1820–1 traditional diffidence towards France lay behind England's passive acceptance of Austrian intervention in Italy; and ten years later the suspicions revived when the French ruler proposed his second son as king of Belgium and sent troops to defend the new state against Holland. The Egyptian crisis of 1839–40 marked the nadir of Anglo-French relations, with Palmerston's public humiliation of Thiers; but English determination to prevent the expansion of French political and economic influence in Spain by dynastic marriages between the French and Spanish royal families (1843–6) soon ruined Guizot's attempts to restore the *entente* between the two countries. As in the late 1830s, when Louis Philippe had attempted to win acceptance and legitimation from Austria, so in the final years before the 1848 revolutions Guizot once more drew closer to Metternich, accepting Austrian annexation of the Republic of Cracow (1846) and proposing intervention in Switzerland in support of the Catholic cantons of the *Sonderbund*.

British policy towards Italy naturally formed part of its overall European policy: to maintain and encourage commercial expansion and block all potential threats from France. Sicily was virtually an economic colony for Britain, Naples was tied by a special commercial treaty, while Piedmont with the port of Genoa opened up the Po valley and the potential of central European markets for British goods. In Italy, as elsewhere in Europe, Palmerston was more concerned to maintain the existing system of treaties than to advance liberal, national causes. British diplomacy, worried about possible French intervention in Italy after the July revolution, had played an active role in settling the consequences of the revolution in the Papal States: Louis Philippe's occupation of Ancona in 1832 (a belated attempt to appease French public opinion after his failure to aid the revolution the year before) had been accepted by Palmerston because of the discredit it threw upon French prestige in Italy. In 1838 Britain had intervened to prevent Naples granting France a monopoly of Sicilian sulphur production. During the 1840 crisis, in order to isolate France, England had deliberately improved relations with Austria and Naples, while contemporaneously dangling before Piedmont the carrot of support for expansion of its territories. If Palmerston constantly urged administrative and political reforms on the Italian rulers, particularly on the pope, his purpose was to settle the continuous unrest and strengthen the *status quo*. By 1848, his readiness to consider a territorial adjustment in Italy, with the withdrawal of Austria from the north and the creation of a separate kingdom, was based on his conviction that this was the most effective method of blocking French intervention and strengthening Austria. Until the 1848 revolutions, Palmerston's policy was notably successful: Guizot was unable to establish an independent policy of support for moderate reforms in the Papal States, while maintaining friendly and close relations with Austria. Such prestige as France maintained in Italy was limited to moderate liberal circles and was based upon admiration for the controlled conservative character of the French political system rather than upon its frontier policy.

Austrian policy in Italy, as in the rest of its empire, was opposed to all change. Austria relied on England for effective support against Russian ambitions over the Turkish empire, but was consistently hostile to Palmerston's proposals for reforms in Italy. Palmerston could complain in 1832, after the failure of a joint memorandum of the five powers to the pope recommending reforms, that:

> It is certain that the Government of Rome is not likely to try to remove discontent by improvements, so long as it can hope to put down the expression of that discontent by the prompt assistance of Austrian troops.
>
> It is evident, however, that it is only the Governments of England and France who have made any real efforts to induce the Pope to put into practice the improvements recommended by the ministers of the five powers in May 1831; and that the other three Courts have either been passive in this matter, or else have used their influence to discourage rather than to promote these measures. (Morelli, 215, p. 214)

Austrian policy in Italy, already severely criticized for the harsh trials of 1821-4 and the suppression of the 1831 revolution, was subjected to outraged comment with the publication of Silvio Pellico's account of Habsburg justice in *My Prisons* in 1832.

The July revolution had undoubtedly destroyed confidence in Metternich's 'system', despite the absence of rebellions in either Lombardy-Venetia or Austrian Galicia. The bitter personal rivalry between Metternich and Kolowrat, the minister responsible for internal affairs from the 1830s, led to increasing immobility of the central administration under Francis' weak successor Ferdinand I (1835-48). The quality of Austrian administration in Italy declined, with the growth in the number of 'foreign' civil servants (often from the Italian Trentino province), and the centralization of all decisions, in highly bureaucratic manner, at Vienna.

While the imperial administration and institutions remained immobile, Italian and Hungarian resentment of Austrian domination now began to be accompanied by Czech and Slovene cultural revivals, linguistic and historico-literary movements tolerated and indeed encouraged as counterweights to Hungarian obstreperousness by the Austrian government, which was apparently as unaware of the danger of their development into political demands for independence as of the temporarily dormant nationalism of the Galician Poles. These national movements dominated the political life of the Austrian monarchy during the period of the so-called *Vormärz*. But, behind them, increasing demands were voiced by both peasants and landlords for the abolition of serfdom and feudal ties in Hungary, Lower Austria, Styria, Moravia and Galicia. The government remained deaf to all demands.

By the 1840s, because of its immobility, the government had lost contact with the rapidly changing realities within the empire and in Europe. The deficitary state of the imperial finances, now further weakened by the decision to underwrite the introduction of railways, had reached the point where interest on the state debt almost equalled the total yield of direct taxation: by underpayment of civil servants and retrenchment in the army, the government attempted to stave off bankruptcy. Clerical influence increased and Jesuits were readmitted to parts of the empire, while the old feudal aristocracy finally gained control of the civil service itself. As the 'system' ground to a halt, Austria's influence in Europe waned and Metternich's subordination to the tsar became more apparent. Already before 1848 the government's resistance to opposition had become half-hearted. As the poet Grillparzer recalled:

> The feeling of decency [of the Austrian statesmen], thinly as it flowed, yet brought down the March Government in Austria. The Emperor Francis's system of government could only be carried on if accompanied by his police system. As the pressure relaxed, the springs shot up automatically. (Macartney, 192, p. 304)

The 'commercial revolution'

Little contact existed between Lombard-Venetian opposition to Vienna and national movements elsewhere in the empire; nor did the archaic problem of feudal serfdom relate to the Italian Kingdom. But Lombardy-Venetia was affected, like all the Italian states, by the profound changes in the European economy. The 1830s and 1840s witnessed a startling acceleration in the pace of economic development: technical innovations, growth in population, vast increases in the length, speed and carrying capacities of communications (roads, canals and the early railways), mobilization of capital and development of investment banking, all contributed to the massive industrialization of England, Belgium and parts of France, and the transformation of Britain into the 'workshop of the world'. Free trade for England, which triumphed with the abolition of the corn laws (1846), was an economic necessity as well as an ideology. The protectionist barriers erected by the Continental states during the post-Napoleonic crisis had to be eroded or abolished, as Europe offered a unique market for British goods, far more important than the poor South American republics or even North America, where United States protection blocked British penetration.

All states were affected by this 'commercial revolution', as partially closed national economies, with their small markets and high costs of production, could not develop at the same rate as the industrialized countries. In Germany Friedrich List had successfully propagandized the need to create a large regional market, with internal free trade but external customs barriers to protect national industries. Prussia had followed such a policy since 1818, gradually extending the customs union to other German principates, until in 1834 it finally succeeded in creating a *Zollverein*, including the vast majority of German states with 26 million inhabitants; only Austria, the Hanseatic ports and a group of states around Hanover remained outside the union.

The implications of this inter-regional union, as much as of the process of industrialization, were fully realized by contemporaries. As Cattaneo noted, the *Zollverein* represented the most effective challenge to English commercial expansion. All states would be obliged either to enter into or form such unions, or to develop their own economies on the basis of their complementarity with the leading international economies on a more or less free trade basis. Austria had refused to enter the *Zollverein* in 1834 because of hostility towards Prussia; successive discussions in 1841–2, when southern German states invited the empire to join in order to balance Prussian dominance, led to nothing because of the opposition first of Austrian industrialists, then of Hungarian nationalists. In spite of the government's encouragement of textile and heavy industries in Lombardy-Venetia, Lower Austria and the Bohemian Lands, by the 1840s the Austrian empire, in its isolation, had fallen far behind the economic development of the advanced countries. Plans to develop the empire as a separate economic unit broke down in the face of mistrust between the different Länder and Prussian opposition.

The hostility of the most progressive sectors in Lombardy-Venetia, the most industrialized region of the Austrian monarchy, increased with their awareness that the Italian Kingdom was supporting a stagnant economy and subsidizing imperial finances. By 1847 Cesare Correnti could write:

> The country does not refuse to pay; it is not the financial sacrifices which frighten it, but the ignorance of the administrators, the stinginess over useful things, the penchant for damaging and harmful ones . . . thirty three millions are taken out of the country every year without it receiving anything in exchange except contempt and insults. These thirty three millions, together with the rich takings of the sister provinces of Venetia, sustain the dying credit of the empire. (Correnti, 276, p. 109)

The other Italian states, economically independent of the Austrian empire, tended to gravitate around the Anglo-French commercial orbit. But it was England that forced the pace of industrialization and of trading relationships. To counter the protectionism of the large states (France, Austria, *Zollverein*), British policy in these decades concentrated on establishing bilateral commercial treaties with the states 'of secondary importance' which surrounded the major protectionist powers, as an indirect means of penetrating the entire European market and of persuading the large states (especially France) to abandon protection. As Correnti noted:

> English power cannot withstand the superabundance of the great Continental states by itself; hence, in order to continue, it needs to return to the arts and efforts of liberty, and find in clienteles and lasting friendships that basis of stability which geography denies the loose and scattered bulk of the Indo-Britannic empire. (Cavour, 283, p. lxxvi)

Early trade treaties with Denmark, Hanover and the Hanseatic cities (1825) were followed by pressure on the Italian states, as British trade turned towards the Near East (Anglo-Turkish trade treaty, 1838) and the Mediterranean route to India (the P and O steamship service, with a land crossing over Suez, was established in 1840).

Piedmont, where customs tariffs had been raised between 1819 and 1825, and again in 1830, responded to the new conditions by reducing the barriers on foreign grain (1834, 1840, 1847), repealing the prohibition on the export of crude silk (1835), and concluding 26 commercial treaties with European and American states (1832–46), including an important treaty with France (1834). Silk, wool and cotton industries, producing mostly semi-finished products for export, had been sufficiently developed and modernized, with the aid of foreign capital and expertise, to meet foreign competition in the 1840s. Agricultural exports, especially crude silk, received a sharp boost. Naples, by contrast, attempted to meet the international challenge by a conscious policy of industrialization behind protectionist barriers. But, already in the 1840s, as soon as customs barriers were partially lowered (1845–6), the absence of a strong supporting agriculture and the total dependence of both parts of the Kingdom of the Two Sicilies on trade with Britain revealed the artificial character and technical backwardness of Neapolitan industry.

The major Italian states had thus been drawn into the mainstream of the international economy, where they constituted subsidiary but significant elements because of the renewed importance of the Mediterranean. For the liberal opposition to absolutism, in Italy as in central Europe, there were obvious lessons to be drawn from the ever clearer contrast between the economic power and political structures of the western powers and the stagnant autocracy of the eastern empires.

Liberal and democratic opposition

As in so many other spheres, the July revolution left its mark on opposition to the established governments of Europe. The myth of French primacy, of its mission to aid the oppressed peoples of Europe, was proclaimed more forcefully than ever and was accompanied by a revival of the Napoleonic legend, personified (albeit somewhat farcically in these years) by the nephew Louis Napoleon. 'Almost every great idea, every great principle of civilization has passed first through France in order to spread elsewhere' (Saitta, 113, p. 208, n. 99), proclaimed Guizot complacently. And foreign liberals, from the Polish Adam Mickiewicz to the Piedmontese Camillo Cavour, were ready to agree. The most serious reservation that a liberal like the Swiss Philippe-Albert Stapfer was prepared to make was that France itself seemed to have derived scarce benefits from its privileged position:

The role which the Gallic race has played since remotest times, and to which we have seen it remaining faithful in our days, is to agitate the world, to prevent peoples only inclined to till their own back garden from falling asleep and from closing themselves up within the boundaries of their needs and civilisations. . . . It is clear that providence has endowed the French with qualities and resources that have fulfilled a great European, even a cosmopolitan end; but so far these have not ensured the French real security in the enjoyment of such advantages and of uncontested common rights. They are excellent cooks for others, who make thin broth for themselves. (Saitta, 113, p. 208, n. 9)

The cosmopolitanism of a Buonarroti or a Lafayette was now replaced by a romantic belief in the 'fraternity of peoples', a religious faith in the individual patria. The 5000 Polish exiles, who had fled mostly to France after the harsh suppression of their revolution in 1831, together with the large numbers of Italian and German exiles, transformed this national faith into a messianic vocation. The democratic exiles at Paris could proclaim: 'Renascent Poland must propagate the democratic idea among the Slavs and give the signal for the general emancipation of the European peoples' (Saitta, 113, p. 213). They were echoed by Mazzini's assertion of the need

to redeem the peoples by their consciousness of a special mission entrusted to each of them, whose achievement – necessary for the development of the great humanitarian mission – must constitute their individuality and acquire for them a right of citizenship in the Young Europe which this century will establish. (Mazzini, 257, vol. 4, p. 180)

Each nation had its mission in the inevitable march of progress towards a peaceful Humanity, the creation of the Kingdom of God on earth. The opposition, whether liberal, democratic, Catholic or socialist – from Guizot to Lelewel, Lamennais to Comte – was agreed on the need to reorganize Europe by liberating its peoples in order to achieve a permanent peace. But for the republican democrats and socialists, in contrast to the liberals, peace could only be achieved by the overthrow of the existing governments.

The immense sympathy aroused by the exiled Poles explained the generic acceptance of a Slav mission. But, in western eyes, eastern Europe remained an uncertain, ambiguous frontier area because of the presence of autocratic Russia. In general, the future was regarded as lying with the socially more developed countries of western and central Europe. And here, the assertion of individual national missions against dependence on the French initiative again revealed the differences between democrats and moderate liberals. Acceptance of French primacy in these years was a predominantly liberal prerogative. Mazzini, in political terms, could write: 'The progress of peoples today consists in their emancipation from France. The progress of France consists in its emancipation from the XVIIIth century and the old Revolution (Mazzini, 257, vol. 4, p. 178). Pierre Leroux, in class terms, could deny the primacy of France (or England) because of the negative social effects of capitalism: 'I see the nations enchained, labouring under the lash of capitalism. . . . The spirit of speculation and lucre which animates England and France today is a spirit of conquest, equal to that of the Norman invaders of the XIIth century' (Saitta, 113, p. 212).

The polemic over the primacy of France, in fact, overlay and in part reflected deeper divisions between the liberal and democratic oppositions over the significance of the July revolution. The revolution, the result of political crisis and popular unrest, had once more revealed the strength of the 'labouring poor', the artisans, skilled craftsmen, domestic workers of Paris. A revolutionary working-class movement emerged in both France and England, and with it Blanqui's socialist theory of the seizure of political power, and the dictatorship of the revolutionaries. Until the failure of the Owenite General Union movement (1829–36) and the suppression of the Lyons silk-workers' risings (1831, 1834), extreme democratic revolutionaries – such as Buonarroti – could retain their faith in France. But in subsequent years, the closed class character of the July monarchy reinforced the diffidence of the democrats towards a France which socially was oppressive and politically had betrayed the revolutions in Poland and Italy. The vast Chartist agitations in England (1838–48) confirmed the divisions between moderates and democrats, whether radical or socialist.

The emergence of distinctive and often antithetical moderate and democratic ideologies after 1830 depended ultimately on the stable appearance of moderate liberal regimes in England, France and Belgium and on the concern about (or, for the democrats, hopes of) a politically conscious working-class. For the upper middle class and aristocratic liberals the English Reform Act of 1832 corresponded to the July revolution and the triumph of the moderate Belgian party: all three countries were now governed by a constitution open to both birth and wealth, which guaranteed liberty with order. Guizot's earlier theorizations of the need to achieve mobility and fusion between the successful bourgeoisie and old aristocracy appeared a reality. Even if the Orleanist regime soon displayed its closed character and the egotistical determination of restricted social groups to conserve power, its stability and parliamentary democracy (with its concern for outward forms and constitutional procedures) offered a model for the liberals of less fortunate countries. Indeed, the extensive personal influence of the king, the ministerial instability, the concentration of power by a handful of politicians, the employment of corruption and pressure at elections, were perhaps regarded as inevitable and 'natural' features of parliamentary liberalism, and so the more easily tolerated in such countries as Spain or Piedmont where a constitution was ultimately granted. If England offered a more advanced form of liberalism, the France of Louis Philippe and Guizot was a more immediate applicable model for the social conditions of the countries of western Europe. The *juste milieu*, the happy mean between reaction and subversion, with its connotations of religious tolerance and philosophical eclecticism, represented the political practice and ideal towards which moderate liberals aspired.

The counterpart of political liberalism was economic progress. Here, too, Guizot, with his belief in the adequacy of material benefits and his encouragement of railway construction, offered a reassuring example. English capitalism was even more convincing. If the cyclical crises of capitalist expansion in these decades and the human misery they caused cast doubt upon some of the tenets of classical economy, the liberals remained suffused with optimism about the benefits increasing wealth brought to all the people. Private enterprise and free trade, an efficient bureaucracy and moderate taxes, public education and recognition of talent, appeared as the enviable characteristics of English society, only threatened by the popular mass demonstrations and petitions of Chartist unrest.

Where poverty existed, it was to be alleviated and ultimately eliminated by charity and co-operation between the classes. As Guizot stated: 'There is no longer legitimate cause nor specious pretext for the maxims and passions so long placed under the banner of democracy. What was formerly democracy would now be anarchy; the democratic spirit is now and long will be nothing but the revolutionary spirit' (Hobsbawm, 188, p. 148).

Fear of revolution and of the revolutionaries' exploitation of popular unrest divided the liberals sharply from the democrats. But if the democrats were more open to the discontent of the masses, their views about resolving the 'social question' were generally not so different. For the nationalist democrats, such as Lelewel, Kossuth or Mazzini, the support of the poor was to be won by proposing material advantages: peasant smallholdings in such feudal-dominated countries as Poland or Hungary, lower taxes and 'fair' wages in Italy. But these proposals were consistently subordinated to the higher aims of national independence and (sometimes) a republic, and conceived of as a means of avoiding class conflict. Even the socialist democrats made comparatively little impact among the working masses. The Saint-Simonians and followers of Fourier were aware of the need to appeal to 'the most numerous and poorest class'; Owen tried to organize it in his General Union. But, in general, the urban masses were regarded as too ignorant and unconscious of their plight. Socialism was to be achieved by propaganda directed at the educated classes, by 'association' and co-operation. For the most part the democrats consisted of relatively restricted groups of the lower middle class, smaller landowners, intellectuals and, sometimes, new manufacturers, living in a world apart from the poor. Whether in exile or plotting in their own countries, in industrialized states with an urban proletariat or peasant societies, they retained their optimism that the 'people' would rise to their cry of revolution. In fact, it was less the democrats' identification with the poor that divided them from the liberals than the latter's fear of such a common cause. The real distinction between liberals and democrats was a political one: change by reforms or by revolution, dependence upon favourable international circumstances for pacific progress or national initiative as a preliminary to the regeneration of humanity.

Mazzini and the democratic initiative

For the European democrats the revolutions of 1830–1 had ended in failure, even in France and Belgium. Nevertheless, the power displayed by the republicans during the revolutions, and the constitutional regimes created or enlarged in these two countries, kept alive hopes of a revival of the democratic movement until the violent repressions of the mid-1830s. France inevitably formed the centre of the renewed campaigns and conspiracies, in which the veteran democrats and republicans were joined by the vast new wave of exiles from Poland, Italy and Germany. Buonarroti's immediate decision to move from Brussels to Paris after the Three Days of July was symptomatic of the interdependence which all democrats saw between developments in France and those in Europe. As in the final years of dense conspiracy before the outbreak of the July revolution, so now the exiles who asserted their ideas and programmes most successfully were those who forged links and gained the support of political forces in France: the young Mazzini, like the aged Buonarroti, owed much of his initial influence to his ties with French republican leaders.

Buonarroti was in a unique position: living symbol of continuity with the Jacobin revolution, respected for his intransigent incorruptibility, as untiringly active now as in the 1790s, he inevitably became one of the central figures of republican conspiracy. Only one other person enjoyed a comparable standing – the marquess of Lafayette, whose reputation was still based on his participation in the American war of independence rather than on his subsequent, mostly moderate and masonic-*carbonaro* activities. Buonarroti, indeed, reserved some of his most violent attacks for Lafayette, because of his traditional influence on the republican *carboneria*. But, although deeply opposed to his social moderation and his support of an American-type federalism, Buonarroti still shared with Lafayette his eighteenth-century vision of cosmopolitan progress, his antipathy towards exaggerated forms of nationalism. As the aged republican aristocrat proclaimed in the French Chamber in 1832: 'We are reaching the epoch in which the peoples will end up understanding that the advantage of one is the advantage of all, and that one conquest of liberty affects all the other nations' (Saitta, 113, p. 211, n. 108). Amidst the agitated hopes of these years, Buonarroti turned naturally to renewed conspiracy in France, the centre of the coming European revolution.

Buonarroti's techniques had not changed: employment of his own secret society, *Il mondo* ('The world') as the central organ of control; and infiltration of other sects. But the initial freedom of association in Orleanist France led Buonarroti to extend his activities to the legal republican societies, especially the 'Society of the Friends of the People', in order to gain the support of public opinion by a campaign for universal suffrage and progressive taxation. Even after he reverted primarily to conspiratorial activities, from 1832, Buonarroti continued to exert his influence through a small but compact group of friends in the French republican party and the important 'Society for the Rights of Man and Citizen'; his aim was to unite the republicans on the basis of a typically Jacobin-socialist programme, open to the demands of the Lyons workers. Contemporaneously, he endeavoured to extend his secret network into the moribund French *charbonnerie* by the creation of a 'Reformed *Charbonnerie*', and then of a 'Universal Democratic *Charbonnerie*'. Although now more openly republican and egalitarian and with a less complicated system of initiation, this new *carboneria* retained the characteristically Buonarrotian traits of absolute obedience to a hierarchical structure of leaders and total secrecy surrounding the 'high universal conventicle'. Buonarroti's influence was undoubtedly spreading, in Italy and Belgium, as well as in France, where divisions among the Saint-Simonians gained him further supporters, despite his open criticisms of Saint-Simon's 'industrialism'. Lamennais, by now converted to a Christian form of democracy, could write in 1833:

> The men of '93 are becoming most menacing in their activities and audacity. . . . At Paris they have managed to take control and subject the working class to their discipline. As the working class has found nothing elsewhere but indifference towards its all too real deprivations, it has almost been forced to throw itself into their arms. (Della Peruta, 258, p. 96)

The young revolutionary Giuseppe Mazzini (1805–72) inevitably established contact with Buonarroti during his first exile in France. Born and educated in Genoa, where hatred of the Piedmontese and the republican tradition encouraged sectarian activities, Mazzini had actively and successfully propagated the *carboneria* in Liguria after his initiation in 1827. A lay, democratic form of romanticism, with Foscolian overtones, characterized his early writings. Mazzini saw a 'European' literature as the expression of the progress of modern civilization and the alliance of peoples; employing a widespread romantic motif of these years, he looked to the 'genius', perhaps with echoes of Napoleon, as a figure capable of interpreting the future destinies of peoples and humanity through his superior qualities and intuition. Until the revolutions of 1830–1, Mazzini combined his practical conspiratorial activities with an open cultural campaign in local Ligurian newspapers, in which his romantic faith in progress and in the function of the writer as the expression of public opinion was accompanied by his affirmation of the existence of God and his exaltation of patriotic martyrdom.

Once exiled, after his imprisonment at Savona (November 1830–February 1831), Mazzini threw himself into the endeavours of the Italian *émigrés* to assist the revolutions in central Italy by expeditions into Savoy and from Corsica. Already disillusioned, according to his later accounts, by the timidity and lack of leadership, cult of secrecy and complex ritual of the *carboneria*, his analysis of the failure of the revolutions led Mazzini to elaborate his own proposals for achieving 'liberty, independence and union' through the *Giovine Italia* ('Young Italy'). But during these intense, creative months of June–July 1831, Mazzini remained close to the sectarian world of Orleanist France, making contact with republican groups at Marseilles and democratic leaders at Lyons and Paris. The degree to which he was still influenced by that sectarian mentality he was soon to condemn so roundly is revealed in his famous appeal to Charles Albert at the moment of his accession to the throne; written at the same time as the original programme of the *Giovine Italia*, it displayed a typically *carbonaro* readiness to abandon republican, democratic aims for the support of a royal army, even if its immediate purpose – as Mazzini subsequently claimed – was to destroy the illusions of the moderate Piedmontese exiles.

The first version of the 'General instruction for the brotherhood of Young Italy' (1831) showed Mazzini's uncertainty about the capacity of the embrionic organization to affirm itself against the traditional sects. Even more, it displayed the proximity of many of his ideas to the Jacobin-*carbonaro* tradition represented by Buonarroti. Mazzini had established contact with Buonarroti through Carlo Bianco di Saint Jorioz, a patriotic Piedmontese officer, now in exile. Saint Jorioz, under Buonarrotian influence, had founded a secret society of the *apofasimeni* (the 'condemned'), which Mazzini joined. The draft of the 'General instructions' began with typically revolutionary-Jacobin motifs: declaration of rights and natural laws, abolition of aristocracy and privileges, substitution of 'a simple parish system' for the upper ecclesiastical hierarchy, proclamation of a 'single, indivisible republic', unlimited sponsorship of public education. The future structure of the *Giovine Italia* was already outlined – membership restricted to the under 40s, a central congregation with provincial congregations in Italy and a reduction of the complex, macabre sectarian rituals to simple secret passwords. But, most significantly, members of the *Giovine Italia* were obliged to belong to other sects in order to direct them towards the aims of the new association. As Mazzini wrote to an early follower Giuseppe Giglioli:

> We must prepare rapidly to present a single front to enemy and friend. *Young Italy* must structure itself not so much to carry out the revolution alone, as this will come inevitably through the work of the other Societies, which we also

head; but rather to direct the revolution, to watch over the men of power, to express the vows of youth, to make the revolution suddenly become united, fraternal, harmonious as the National Association of *Young Italy*. (Mazzini, 257, vol. 5, p. 45)

This early draft, so revealing of the laboured process of Mazzini's detachment from the traditional sectarian models, was rapidly replaced by the definitive version of the 'General instructions' (July 1831). These offer perhaps the first illustration of Mazzini's remarkable self-confidence and sense of mission, and contain the nucleus of his ideology. The entire philosophy of natural rights was tacitly rejected and replaced by Mazzini's ethical-religious vision of God revealing himself through the indefinite, continuous progress of humanity, which was constituted by the creation of nations: 'Where God has wished there be a nation, the necessary forces exist to create it'; 'the progressive series of European changes inevitably guides European societies towards forming themselves into vast unitary masses'. In this preordained pattern of progress, to each nation belonged its mission, to each man his duty as a 'believer in the mission entrusted by God to Italy, and in the duty of each man born Italian to contribute towards its fulfilment'. Bound by this faith and duty, members of the *Giovine Italia* could not but reject the philosophy and practice of the sects: '*Young Italy* is neither sect nor party, but belief and apostolate. We precursors of Italian regeneration must lay the first stone of its religion' (Mazzini, 257, vol. 2, p. 51).

Mazzini's programme and method, in fact, were outlined in explicit polemic against the lack of principles, the gradualism and federalism of the old sects. Italy was to be republican because sovereignty resided in the nation and because Italy's past was wholly republican; it was to be unitarian because federalism weakened the nation. This programme of republican unity was to be propagated openly, as education was the most effective means of achieving the regeneration of the nation. *Giovine Italia* thus required a homogeneous body of members who were naturally forbidden to belong to other sects. Education was a necessary preparation for insurrection. The insurrection was to be followed immediately by guerrilla warfare, a 'war by bands' for national liberation, according to Saint Jorioz's theory which circulated widely among Italian democratic circles before 1848. The insurrection, which would give the signal to Europe, was to depend not upon foreign aid, but upon the faith and activity of the members of *Giovine Italia*. Mazzini's programme was thus conceived in antithesis not only to the *carbonari* but to some of Buonarroti's central ideas: infiltration of other sects, secrecy of the association's aims, France's natural leadership. But in other respects Mazzini was still ready to borrow from the Buonarrotian ideal patrimony: his defence of unity against federalism was framed in Buonarrotian terms; he distinguished clearly, as did the aged revolutionary, between the initial insurrection and the subsequent revolution after Italy's liberation; he was prepared to admit to the need for a small dictatorial group in the first stage, although subsequently a 'National Council' would be the source of all power.

In the following years (1831–4), as he prepared for the insurrection and entered into a troubled and ultimately negative relationship with Buonarroti and his followers, Mazzini fully elaborated his ideology. Against the 'men of the past', responsible for the failures of the 1820–1 and 1831 revolutions, the members of *Giovine Italia* represented a generational change; against these materialist, individualist propagators of constitutional monarchy and theories of the balance of power, the youth of *Giovine Italia*, moved by faith and the 'word', were herald-bearers of the new age. Strongly influenced by Saint-Simonian ideas, Mazzini elaborated on the dusk of the 'critical' age of individualism and scepticism and the coming dawn of the new 'organic' age of the people, which would be characterized by 'association', a universal principle which marked the progress of humanity.

But the central theme, which linked this ethical-religious philosophy of history to the practical realization of the Italian revolution, was Mazzini's analysis of the role of the 'people'. Deeply conscious of the absence of the 'multitudes' in the past Italian revolutions and of their present strength in France and England, Mazzini sought for the means to arouse their support. Defining the people, in Saint-Simonian terms, as 'the most numerous and poorest class' (Mazzini, 257, vol. 2, p. 69), Mazzini recognized that their support could only be won by pointing to the material benefits they would gain. The people had been corrupted by centuries of servitude, they were unaware of the new transitional age in which they lived.

> The multitudes are never doctrinaire, they know nothing of the epoch of transition. . . . They know of being well off or badly off – of liberty and slavery – of poverty and improvement – that is all. . . . The initiators of insurrections in Italy will always be masters of the multitudes in their appeals – so long as behind their appeals come material improvements. (Mazzini, 257, vol. 1, p. 139)

No revolution could succeed without the masses. But, equally, these 'multitudes' could not achieve the revolution without proper leadership. For Mazzini the initiative had to come from the 'intellects', the 'middle class', the educated young. In an early, extreme form (in the letter to Charles Albert), he could theorize a triad of powers which, once united, would prove irresistible: 'The strength of society, action, operations, true force lie elsewhere: in the genius who thinks or directs, in youth which interprets the thought and commits it to action, in the plebs who overcome all obstacles they encounter' (Mazzini, 257, vol. 2, pp. 26–7).

Even when Mazzini omitted the transcendental 'genius', he consistently maintained the need for educated leadership of the people. In the *Giovine Italia* the 'illiterate members' were forbidden to engage in propaganda activities; the direction of the association was explicitly limited to the middle classes. And if material advantages were necessary to gain the irresistible impetus of the masses, they remained subordinated to the higher aim of national independence, for the spiritual regeneration of nations necessarily preceded the material.

Inevitably, Mazzini was hostile to all class conflict because of its divisive (and diversive) effects. It was on this issue, perhaps more than on any other, that he was to break definitively with Buonarroti. Although Mazzini was ready to admit that 'the history of the progressive development of the popular element through eighteen centuries of events and wars' was the history of '*the war between individuals and the universal, between the fractionizing and the unitary system, between* PRIVILEGE *and the* PEOPLE', he concluded dogmatically: 'We abhor fraternal bloodshed. WE DO NOT WANT TERROR ERECTED INTO A SYSTEM: we do not want the subversion of legitimately acquired rights, nor agrarian laws, nor useless violations of individual faculties, nor usurpations of property' (Mazzini, 257, vol. 2, pp. 193, 210). In fact, 'if you convert a revolution into a war of classes, you will come to ruin, or you will not survive without unheard-of violence, without acquiring the reputation of usurpers, without accusations of a new tyranny' (Mazzini, 257, vol. 2, p. 195).

Preoccupied with the danger of alienating the crucial support of the middle classes, Mazzini was also convinced that there was no justification for class warfare in Italy. Although at moments he recognized the abject poverty of the peasantry, which rendered it 'disposed towards the most desperate attempts, merely if it is comforted and guided' (Mazzini, 257, vol. 3, p. 228), his propaganda was directed exclusively towards the urban poor. He himself recognized the difficulties of penetrating a world of illiteracy by his method of written propaganda. The one Mazzinian attempt to write popular dialogues – that of his follower Gustavo Modena – soon collapsed. As Mazzini admitted to Niccolò Tommaseo in a letter of 1834: 'As for speaking to the people, you are right – and I would speak: but the paths are lacking, and we wander around in a circle without breaking out of it. The people cannot read' (Mazzini, 257, vol. 1, p. 159).

It is hardly surprising that Mazzini's proposals for the multitudes should have been extremely moderate: typical eighteenth-century Enlightened measures, such as limitation on wills, donations and successions to prevent an excessive concentration of property, or a mortgage system to facilitate circulation of property, progressive taxation on net profit, state intervention to ensure public works and proportionate 'recompense' for labour. But Mazzini justified his action by his conviction that, in contrast to both feudal or more industrialized countries:

In our country, although the people are servile, the patriciate has by now renounced all caste feelings and has fraternised. The clergy, except for the higher aristocracy, always incorrigible, has begun to understand, and will understand ever more clearly, that it is the laughing stock rather than the support of thrones and Roman tyranny. Thus we only have to fear cowardice and inertia; and one takes care of the former by wisdom of choice, of the latter by energy of action; and since action has an omnipotent effect on the multitudes, when our few enemies become aware that we are able and determined, they will side with us or adopt a cowardly silence. (Mazzini, 257, vol. 3, pp. 185–6)

Mazzini and Buonarroti

Through Mazzini's untiring energy, his personal magnetism, the undoubted attraction of his idealism and the simplicity of his propaganda and conspiratorial methods, *Giovine Italia* spread far more rapidly than the previous sectarian movements in Piedmont, Liguria, Lombardy, Tuscany and partially in Romagna, creating the structure of the first modern party in Italy with many thousands of members. Although the direction of the association remained in the hands of lawyers, officers, engineers, shopkeepers, doctors and landed proprietors, it recruited significant support in these early years among the urban poor at Milan (where there were over 3000 craftsmen and lower class members), Turin, Genoa, Florence, Siena, Leghorn and even among the traditional 'papal poor' of the Trastevere, Regola and Ponte quarters of Rome. The simplicity of its organizational structure and the ease of initiation aided its diffusion, as a police report of 1832 noted at Rome: 'it spreads the more easily both because it requires no formality beyond the swearing of the oath, and because one person can on his own initiative recruit another' (Demarco, 216, p. 259).

Despite this diffusion, confronted by the determined hostility of the Italian governments and the increasing alertness of their police, Mazzini recognized the need to reach an agreement with the sects, particularly those of Buonarroti. The two revolutionaries had inevitably turned for proselytes towards the same environments and social groups: democratic ex-*carbonari* of the middle class and petty bourgeoisie, with some support among the craftsmen and workers. Buonarroti had converted many of the democratic exiles of 1821 and 1831. Some of these, like Giovanni La Cecilia and Carlo Bianco di Saint Jorioz, had collaborated closely with Mazzini in the formation of the *Giovine Italia* and oscillated in their loyalties. In Italy Mazzini had successfully absorbed the Buonarrotian *apofasimeni* within his own association. But the *Giovine Italia* was not strong enough to ignore the old sectarians, nor did Mazzini wish to risk fratricidal divisions during the preparation of the insurrection:

> I do not feel so strong as to be able to launch my movement by myself, at full speed, and say to my brothers: I have done it alone! – So I unite with them, I receive and welcome proposals – but under my breath – I swear. (Mazzini, 257, vol. 5, p. 73)

Buonarroti, anxious to maintain his influence in Italy, had created a new society of 'True Italians' by 1832, with 'families' among the exiles in France, Corsica, Malta, north Africa, London, and Brussels and in Italy at Leghorn (where Guerrazzi gained support among the dockers), Florence, Pisa, Bologna and the Legations. Learning from Mazzini's success, Buonarroti abandoned the mysterious rites and grades of initiation of his earlier sects in favour of a simple organization under the control of a central junta at Paris, consisting of representatives of the 'families', with a clear programme circulated in bulletin form among the members. The programme was classically Jacobin (explicitly citing Robespierre) and egalitarian and reflected Buonarroti's concern in these years to gain popular support by legal or semi-legal propaganda. The society, open to all nationalities, aimed at creating a democratic, unitarian republic, with 'perfect equality of rights among the citizens, with adequate settlement of possessions and work and its inherent sovereignty exercised by the people'. The 'multitudes' were to be won by explaining to them that:

> The most tangible injustice is that a small number enjoy idleness, while a great number work, wear themselves out, suffer and often lack bare necessities. This horrifying disorder exists because matters are so arranged in this world that possessions of all sorts accumulated by some are not distributed among others except with cruel parsimony. . . . One of the fundamental conditions of the Republic can be so defined: social order in which the just distribution of wealth is established and maintained by the laws which the People give themselves. (Francovich, 135, pp. 132, 134)

To achieve this end, a provisional dictatorship of virtuous men would be needed.

This confrontation between two opposing concepts of revolution offered, momentarily, a reflection in Italy of the fundamental division which was emerging with increasing force among the European democrats. Spurred on by the prospect of the imminent revolution, in September 1832 Mazzini and Buonarroti agreed on a pact of unified action, each convinced of the superiority of his own organization. The *Giovine Italia* was to act as organ of the two associations (and indeed published articles by Buonarroti and his supporters), while – according to Mazzini – the 'True Italians' 'would take care of the constitution and emigration; we would look after the interior' (Mazzini, 257, vol. 5, p. 299). But by the end of 1833, the agreement had collapsed: the statute proposed by the Buonarrotians, although deliberately softening the more extreme points of Jacobin doctrine so as to avoid frightening the exiles, was opposed by Mazzini as preempting a decision about the future form of government which could only be made by the Italian people after the liberation; the active political organization of the 'True Italians' in Tuscany threatened the predominance of 'Young Italy'. But the fundamental reasons for the split were ideological. Mazzini denied a revolutionary dictatorship and terrorism in place of a popularly elected national assembly, he refused to accept French primacy for the outbreak of the European revolution, he opposed Buonarroti's gradualist, conspiratorial approach. But above all Mazzini was totally hostile to the Jacobin egalitarianism of Buonarroti's programme, for the people, drawn together by association, formed a 'great unity which embraced everything' (Della Peruta, 258, p. 216).

The split between the *Giovine Italia* and the 'True Italians' proved disruptive for Buonarroti's organization. His Tuscan followers, like Carlo Guitera, were disoriented and many abandoned the sect for the *carboneria* or the *Giovine Italia*. At Mazzini's direct instigation, members of the society of 'True Italians' were individually approached and absorbed within his own association. In Italy Buonarrotism, as an organized movement, disappeared, unable to resist the challenge of Mazzini's idealistic and purely political appeal to the middle classes, incapable of transforming its Jacobin egalitarianism into a direct link with the masses on a class basis, outdated in its cosmopolitanism in these years of faith in the destiny of individual nations. Deeply sceptical of the adequacy of Mazzini's aims, as always convinced that the republic in France was the necessary premise for a successful international insurrection, Buonarroti used his prestige and leadership of the 'high conventicle' of the 'universal democratic *charbonnerie*' to warn against participation in Mazzini's proposed Savoy expedition, thus certainly contributing to its failure (1834). Mazzini's immediate reaction – the creation of the association of 'Young Europe' – was a deliberate attempt to challenge French primacy and destroy the influence of the Buonarrotian *carboneria*; and by 1835 he could proudly claim to have caused its disintegration.

By the time the 77-year-old Buonarroti died (1837), Mazzini's own movement was undergoing a crisis. *Giovine Italia* had spread rapidly in northern and central Italy and by 1833 Mazzinian ideas even inspired isolated groups in the Neapolitan provinces. But Piedmont was the state where Mazzini counted most support at Genoa, Alessandria and Turin, among the young officers and soldiers. Mazzini was later to explain his difficulties:

> With an abundance of similar elements, and given the dangers brought on by the double role of conspiracy and apostolate, which the Association was obliged to assume, it was necessary to utilize the growing enthusiasm before persecutions came to kill it, and to think seriously of *action*. (Mazzini, 257, vol. 77, p. 143)

Insurrections at Genoa and Alessandria were to be accompanied by an invasion through Savoy, to link up with the Lyons republicans, while the association's network in central and southern Italy was to act as a reserve force. But the discovery of the plot in Piedmont and its bloody suppression by Charles Albert, followed by similar, though milder, persecutions of *Giovine Italia* cells in Naples, Tuscany and Lombardy (1833) threw the organization into crisis. Mazzini persisted, convinced of the imminence of the revolution. With subsidies from wealthy and aristocratic exiles, he planned an invasion of Savoy to coincide with an insurrection at Genoa, in which the young Giuseppe Garibaldi gained his first hapless experience. The Savoy expedition, hampered by the Swiss authorities, corroded by internal dissent and uncertainty, aborted miserably. Garibaldi found himself the sole insurrectionary of the Genoese rising (3-4 February 1834).

Young Europe

In the general reflux of European democracy (1834-5 witnessed the defeat of the working class and republican movements in England and France), Mazzini's attempt to create an international revolutionary movement had few hopes of success. *Giovine Europa*, formed in April 1834 by a handful of Italian, Polish and German exiled intellectuals, was an attempt to replace the vague internationalism and cosmopolitanism of the *carboneria* (even under Buonarroti after 1830) by a democratic supra-national organization, in which the national associations, on wholly Mazzinian principles, pledged themselves to work for the independence of their peoples and, consequently, the progress of humanity. 'Young Italy', 'Young Poland' and 'Young Germany' were soon joined by 'Young Switzerland', the sole organization not based on exiles. 'Young Europe' was of little practical consequence, and after Mazzini's withdrawal (1835) was dissolved following persecution by the Continental powers (1837).

But *Giovine Europa* was of significance in that it represented Mazzini's successful affirmation, within the European democratic movement, of his philosophy of national initiatives over the classic revolutionary tradition of an internationalism dominated by France. For Mazzini, the leading role of the French had ended in 1814; in the new epoch of association, each people could mark out its own path for the future: 'each man and each people possesses a *particular* mission which, while constituting the *individuality* of that man or that people, necessarily plays its part in the fulfilment of the general mission of humanity' (Della Peruta, 258, p. 443). This denial of French hegemony was not merely an abstract or personal assertion of cultural nationalism. It was a conscious political attempt to replace the prevalent attitude of subordinating revolutionary activities to favourable international circumstances (particularly French foreign policy) by autonomous initiatives. To achieve this end, it was necessary to free European democracy of the myth of the French Revolution:

> The past kills us. I state with conviction: the French revolution crushes us. It weighs on the party, like a nightmare, and hinders its growth. It dazzles us with the lustre of its gigantic struggles. It hypnotises us with its victories. – We go down on our knees before it. We ask everything of it, men and things.... Now, our fathers did not ape anyone. They drew their inspiration from contemporary sources, the needs of the masses and the nature of the elements that surrounded them. They belonged to their time. (Mazzini, 257, vol. 6, p. 267)

Within this vision of individual national initiatives, sometimes interpreted as the mission of guiding nations within great ethnic agglomerates (Slav, Germanic, Greek-Latin), Italy possessed a unique place in the regeneration of Europe because of the universal function of Rome: 'The call for modern unity can start for the third time from Rome alone, because the absolute destruction of the old unity can begin from Rome alone' (Mazzini, 257, vol. 3, p. 246). The 'third Rome' became the symbol not only of Italian independence and unity, but of the overthrow of the old Europe and the consolidation of the new social epoch. Mazzini successfully appropriated for the democrats the age-old Catholic, universalist image of the Holy City, and offered an alternative to the negative judgement of Rome as the major obstacle to Italian unity, enshrined in the lay intellectual tradition since Machiavelli and Guicciardini.

The democratic movement in the 1840s

The repressive measures of the Italian governments in 1833–5, which led to the rapid disintegration of *Giovine Italia* as a united, co-ordinated organization, and the subsequent pressure exerted by the Continental great powers on the Swiss governments to deprive the democrats of their main base, led to a pause in revolutionary activities. Some exiles, like Mazzini, emigrated to England (1837); others – like Fabrizi and Durando – tried to continue the struggle in the Spanish and Portuguese wars (1832–9), or – like Garibaldi – fought for the republican cause in South America. Many withdrew from political activity, for personal reasons or because of their sense of failure, like Bianco di Saint Jorioz who committed suicide at Brussels in 1843. Mazzini, after a long crisis, returned to his apostolate as he detected the apparent signs of a revival of conspiracy in Italy (1839–40).

The intervening years had led to developments in his own beliefs as well as in the Italian situation. Moderate ideas, based upon faith in English and French progress and the possibilities of pacific reform, had begun to offer the embryo of an alternative programme to that of the revolutionaries. The Italian rulers, while firm in their political repression, had engaged upon partial, hesitant economic reforms, which perhaps promised distant prospects of progressive change. The initiative of the democratic revolutionaries was threatened.

Within the democratic camp Mazzini's hegemony was now challenged. The collapse of *Giovine Italia* had led to a proliferation of minor sects in Italy which, while often Mazzinian in inspiration (as for instance in Sicily), displayed a deep diffidence towards centralized control from outside the country. Among the exiles, some – like Gustavo Modena – maintained their absolute loyalty to the prophet; but others – like Nicola Fabrizi or Giuseppe Ricciardi – began to question his infallibility or oppose his intransigence. Fabrizi, confident of his military experiences in Spain, proposed to separate the organization of the insurrection from the educative propaganda of the *Giovine Italia*. The Italic Legion, which he founded in exile at Malta in 1839, was to spark off the revolution by a 'war by bands' in southern Italy. The Two Sicilies and the Papal States, rather than Piedmont, were now to take the insurrectionary initiative, not only because the continuous unrest in these states reflected a revolutionary situation which merely required a lead, but because their distance from the Austrian enemy would give the revolutionaries time to consolidate their positions against a counter-attack. Ricciardi was convinced that Mazzini's exclusive rigidity alienated support. He proposed a 'fusion' of the different groups of exiles, ranging from Mazzini to more moderate *émigrés*, such as Terenzio Mamiani or Niccolò Tommaseo, based on a common programme of the struggle for independence, which would deliberately make no mention of the divisive issue of the future form of government (1837). Unable to convince Mazzini, Ricciardi subsequently proposed a reform of *Giovine Italia*, with election of the leadership and absolute autonomy for the groups in Italy to decide the timing and method of insurrection (1840).

Faced by these threats from left and right, in 1840 Mazzini determined to regain the initiative by reforming 'Young Italy' on a less centralized basis, but with a firm adherence to the original programme. He was hostile to Fabrizi's separation of the twin duties of education and insurrection, as this would deprive the revolution of its moral purpose. But Mazzini also rejected Fabrizi's proposals for a southern initiative, because of his habitual insensitivity towards the peasant world and his conviction that the northern cities were more mature and closer to the European democratic movement. Nor was he ready to accept Fabrizi's theorization of the 'war by bands' as the means to start the insurrection: citing the example of the 1831 revolutions in central Italy, he asserted the need for the prior preparation of insurrectionary conditions, which would enable the revolutionaries to seize power – 'to hold government' – and systematically organize the 'war by bands' against the inevitable Austrian counter-offensive.

Far more important than Fabrizi's reckless proposals, for Mazzini, was the need to gain the support of the working class. In partial agreement with Fourier's class analysis of capitalist society, impressed by the success of 'Young Germany' in gaining proselytes among the German emigrant workers in Switzerland, but above all convinced by his direct observations of the English Chartist movement of the urgency of offering effective leadership to the working class, Mazzini proclaimed the need to create a special union of Italian workers, such as existed in England and France. The stress he placed on the popular, democratic character of *Giovine Italia* was offered as a deliberate contrast to the moderate idealization of liberal capitalism, to Guizot's exaltation of the bourgeoisie and Saint-Simon's justification of the domination of capitalists.

Like Angeloni, Buonarroti, Ricciardi and other democrats, Mazzini rejected the moderates' eulogy of English progress in terms of the deep class divisions there, which he believed, like many European democrats in these years, would soon result in revolution. In Italy class conflict, such as existed in France and England, had been delayed because of the absence of national independence and unity, which had left the workers isolated. Although republican unity would benefit both middle classes and workers politically and economically, the particular vulnerability of the working class justified the creation of an independent organization – the 'union of Italian workers' – through which it could express its needs to the middle class.

For Mazzini, the 'social problem' thus remained strictly subordinated to the political aim of unity. Indeed, worried by the influence in France, Germany and Switzerland, of socialist and especially communist doctrines (such as those of Fourier, Blanqui, Cabet, Weitling), he deliberately accentuated his rejection of class conflict and his religious ideology of faith and duty. 'Few men of genius' and the 'intellects' were the herald-bearers of the apostolate, the natural and inevitable guide of the people. 'For us the word *worker* bears no implication of *class* in the sense commonly attributed to the noun. . . . One day, we shall all be *workers*' (Mazzini, 257, vol. 25, pp. 110–11). The middle class would abandon its individualism and egoism and spontaneously accept the workers' demands, once these had been expressed, through the association 'of *capital, intellect* and *labour*' (Della Peruta, 258, p. 235). But the new, just society, like the achievement of republican unity, rested – as always with Mazzini – on the moral regeneration and sense of solidarity of the middle classes.

Mazzini is often dismissed as a failed revolutionary. That he should be singled out in this manner is a tribute to his exceptional organizational capacities and the loyalty he evoked. For his social ideas were not exceptional in revolutionary circles in these decades. His co-operative vision of society was typical of pre-Marxian socialism, and differed little – except possibly in its stress on duties rather than rights – from the socialism of

Buchez, Louis Blanc, Proudhon, Lassalle or Robert Owen in his unionist phase. Equally, his identification of the working class with the artisans was that of other revolutionaries of these years and reflected the distinction made in England and France – not only by the middle classes, but implicitly by many of the artisans themselves – that the craftsmen, as the 'labouring class', were separate from the casual labourers, the migrant workers and the permanently poor.

Neither the reborn *Giovine Italia* nor the 'union of Italian workers' enabled Mazzini to regain hegemony of the democratic movement in Italy between 1840 and 1846. Small sectarian groups continued to agitate in the Two Sicilies and the Papal States, even after the savage repression in 1837 of risings in Sicily, Calabria and the Abruzzi.

Despite Mazzini's constant warnings against inadequately prepared insurrections, he was unable to check Fabrizi's growing influence. In 1843 Fabrizi's attempt to link the Neapolitan, Tuscan and Romagnol conspirators resulted in an abortive rising of middle-class conspirators and artisans in the Romagna. The following year Mazzini was unable to dissuade the Bandiera brothers, Venetian officers in the Austrian navy, from attempting to start an insurrection in Calabria, according to Fabrizi's theory (although against his advice). In 1845 another rising under Luigi Carlo Farini, indirectly linked to Fabrizi, failed miserably after the momentary seizure of Rimini. Mazzini's sense of impotence was now reflected in his readiness to abandon his intransigence over the republic. Unity, liberty and independence were offered as a more limited programme, capable of uniting the democratic front, as Ricciardi had proposed. Mazzini's weakness was such that he was excluded even from the preparations of the 1845 Rimini insurrection. He had lost control of the democratic initiative. But by this time increasing dissatisfaction with insurrectionary methods and the growing influence of the moderates had assumed far greater importance.

Political liberalism and economic progress

The insurrectionary attempts of Mazzini and the democrats reinforced the determination of the Italian rulers to assert firm political authority. In a Europe now divided between defenders of the absolute power of sovereigns and constitutional regimes, the Italian princes were more dependent than ever upon the military strength of Austria. Every Italian government, except Lombardy-Venetia and Tuscany, had collapsed before the revolutionaries in 1820-1 or 1831. The France of the July revolution was regarded as a constant threat to all established authority, a haven – like Switzerland – for revolutionaries and republicans.

Charles Albert (1831–49), moved by hysterical fanaticism tinged with mystical overtones, was unique among his fellow princes in his determination to act as paladin of every Catholic legitimist cause in Europe. He had atoned for his involvement in the Piedmontese revolution (and gained the nickname of 'hero of the Trocadero') by serving in the French army that crushed the Spanish constitutional regime in 1823. Through the 1830s he supported legitimist plots in France, Spain and Portugal, so isolating Piedmont from France and England, the only powers capable of guaranteeing Piedmontese independence from Austria. As late as 1847, on the eve of his half-hearted conversion to the national cause, Charles Albert seconded Austrian proposals of intervention in support of the Swiss Catholic *Sonderbund*. His savage repression of the Mazzinians in 1833 was based upon his apocalyptic vision of the inevitability of a decisive struggle between revolution and the forces of order. As he wrote in 1834 to that more coherent personification of reaction, Francis IV of Modena:

> The great crisis can only be more or less delayed, but it will undoubtedly arrive; it will be terrible, because one of the two parties must then yield entirely. Your Royal Highness will then be able to render great service to Italy: as for me, you can rest assured that, if we cannot triumph, I am resolved to die then, for I shall never come to terms with the revolution, even in the smallest matter. (Romeo, 199, p. 44)

1833–4 marked the high point of repression in Italy, with arrests and trials in Piedmont, Lombardy, Tuscany, the Papal States and Naples. In the following years, as the revolutionary tide receded in Europe and Italy, the Italian rulers regained their self-confidence, although spying and strict censorship remained the rule of the day even in so liberal a state as Tuscany under Leopold II (1824–59). In 1838 an amnesty in Lombardy-Venetia allowed some of the exiles to return, and by the 1840s even Charles Albert reluctantly accepted that not all liberals were necessarily revolutionaries.

Only in the Two Sicilies and the Papal States, where endemic unrest in the provinces encouraged sectarian activities, did Ferdinand II (1830–59) and Gregory XVI (1831–46) maintain the need for continuous repression, imitated in this, for temperamental rather than objective reasons, by Francis IV of Modena. Resentment of Austrian patronage led Ferdinand and cardinal Bernetti to attempt to assert the independence of their states. Ferdinand's personal creation of a strong army and his consistent policy of neutrality enabled him easily to suppress internal opposition and to substitute the by now traditional link with Austria by an isolationist emphasis on the 'Neapolitan nation'. But Bernetti's creation of a militia of 'centurions' as the instrument of papal independence rapidly degenerated into a semi-legal weapon of internal repression, whose illegalities and ultimate ineffectiveness left the Legations in a condition of constant and increasing unrest, which continued to arouse the preoccupations of the great powers. Both Neapolitan and Papal governments tried to insulate their states from the 'subversive' doctrines circulating in the rest of Italy. But while Ferdinand initially gained some support, particularly among the former Murattians, for his centralized administration and respect for the formal procedures of justice, Gregory XVI offered only inefficient ecclesiastical administration, corrupt justice, the exclusion of young talent from career prospects and so disastrous a financial policy that for a decade after 1835 the government abandoned all attempts to prepare a state budget.

But if the defence of political absolutism remained the predominant preoccupation of Italian rulers, all the major governments (with the inevitable exception of the Papal States) were obliged to recognize the need to align their economic policies with the new requirements of the international economy. Although the propertied aristocracy remained important and influential (and indeed dominant in the islands of Sicily and Sardinia), the landed bourgeoisie by now had consolidated its position. The antagonism between the two groups, while still important in terms of political influence and social prestige, had lost its economic significance, as substantial landowners, of whatever class, were now producing for a market economy; the ties between agriculture and commerce had become ever closer, and the very conflicts between producers, traders and industrialists over the export of raw materials reflected the new level of 'commercialization' of agriculture. The benefits of a unified internal market were now generally recognized, as were the negative consequences of internal excise duties and customs and feudal barriers to the free circulation and exploitation of land. This secular process of structural change towards more capitalist forms of agriculture was encouraged by the Italian governments despite the ubiquitous evidence of the negative effects on the smallholding peasantry. In southern Italy (and especially in Sicily from the late 1830s) Ferdinand II's determined destruction of feudal vestiges led to dramatic consequences: the peasants were despoiled of their traditional communal rights, while the division of the demesnial lands into small plots – which was decreed as compensation for the peasants – was blocked by the owners of the vast grain estates and sheepruns, or misappropriated by the bourgeois and noble landowners.

Governments thus responded to the demands of agricultural producers and traders. Although agriculture remained backward, characterized in a period of ample labour supply, low prices and rising external demand by extension of the cultivated area rather than by increase in productivity (except for areas of Lombardy and Piedmont, where capitalist agriculture continued to develop), governments sought to encourage the new balance between agriculture and trade by facilitating internal circulation of produce, stimulating exports and protecting mainly craft industries. Their measures were crude, often contradictory (because of the constant preoccupation with state fiscal requirements) and revealed a notable ignorance about the economic resources of their states; but these very limits reflected the timidity, restricted sectoral mentality and general backwardness of the vast majority of Italian producers. Preference for investment in land, the public debt, private finance houses and savings banks was as marked in Lombardy and Piedmont as in Naples and the Papal States. Thus even in the economically more advanced northern states, the tendency towards 'safe' investment remained as symptomatic of a fundamental lack of entrepreneurship as the striking reliance on foreign capital and expertise for industrial development. The governments, indeed, were in advance of the business community both in their active encouragement of industry in Lombardy (from the 1820s) and Naples (from the 1830s) and in their sponsorship of railways in Lombardy, Piedmont, Tuscany and Naples (in the 1840s). But their measures, while displaying a general awareness of the new interdependence between international trade and the development of the domestic economy, remained unco-ordinated and incapable of modifying the structural weaknesses of these economies. Italy remained an agricultural-trading country. Governments could create the nuclei of modern industries by protection or state orders. But the ability of these industries to withstand international competition and their subsequent development did not depend upon government economic policy, but upon the elasticity and modernity of the agricultural infrastructure. By the 1850s, it was the absence of such an agricultural base that explained the relative failure of Neapolitan industrialism, compared to the success of northern industries.

An awareness of these deficiencies and a demand for more co-ordinated and organic policies were formulated by small groups of mostly moderate intellectuals, who tried to spur on the governments, in classic eighteenth-century reformist manner. It was among these moderates that theories of economic progress were most fully elaborated. Because of their conviction that the weaknesses of the Italian economies derived primarily from the inhibitory effects of political authoritarianism, their proposals turned increasingly from purely economic measures to political reforms. Only in this manner, according to these moderate patriots, could Italy reach the level of the progressive nations of Europe.

The Tuscan liberals

The analogy between the eighteenth-century reformers and the nineteenth-century moderates (an analogy of which the historically minded moderates were very conscious) was most marked in Tuscany, where the major elements of what was to become the moderate programme were elaborated as early as the 1820s. The Tuscan government was traditionally the least oppressive in Italy. After the failure of the 1821 revolutions it inevitably attracted both southern exiles – like Guglielmo Pepe and Pietro Colletta – and northern liberals or democrats, such as Niccolò Tommaseo and Massimo

D'Azeglio. Gian Pietro Vieusseux founded the *Antologia* (*Anthology*) in Florence in 1821 because he was convinced that the Tuscan authorities would not prove as oppressive as the Lombard censorship had been with the *Conciliatore*.

The aim of this cosmopolitan and exceptionally widely travelled Swiss merchant – like that of the promoters of the short-lived *Conciliatore* – was to open Tuscan and Italian culture to the most progressive European ideas. 'Here at least publication is possible for any book, unlike in that "most happy" Kingdom of Lombardy-Venetia', wrote Mario Pieri, a minor habitué of Vieusseux's 'Scientific-literary Circle' (Ciampini, 213, p. 109). Always hostile to local patriotisms (the *Anthology* is 'an undertaking which has nothing, absolutely nothing municipal about it; it is wholly Italian' (Ciampini, 213, p. 217)), Vieusseux conceived of Italy in a classically Enlightened cosmopolitan manner. As he wrote to the Piedmontese Giuseppe Grassi, soliciting articles: 'I would particularly ask the writer to enter truly into the spirit of the *Anthology* and show himself Italian rather than Tuscan or Piedmontese, European rather than Italian' (Ciampini, 213, p. 200).

The explicit sense of continuity with Leopoldine reformism was symbolized by the collaboration in the *Anthology* of the aged Enlightened reformer Aldobrando Paolini. But if belief in progress had also characterized the philosophy of the eighteenth-century reformers, its significance – in this age of rapid technological innovation and scientific discovery – now became more precise: 'We live in the century of moral, economic and political sciences, of natural and exact sciences' (Ciampini, 213, p. 197). In contrast to *The Conciliatore* group, with their predominantly romantic and literary interests, Vieusseux deliberately eschewed the contemporary romantic-classicist polemic, not only because he considered it by now an antiquated subject of debate, but because of its divisive effects on the Italian cultural world.

For Vieusseux and his small group of close collaborators – Capponi, Lambruschini, Ridolfi and Tommaseo – as for Confalonieri and Balbo and their friends at Milan and Turin, the leadership of Italian culture belonged to a minute group of friends and acquaintances, always willing to open their ranks to new acolytes, but acutely conscious of their own duties and responsibilities as the formative influence on public opinion. Vieusseux and his friends, with their Tuscan tradition of paternalistic reformism and their Catholic liberalism, were perhaps more openly determined than the Piedmontese and Lombard groups, at least until the 1840s, to reinforce the solidarity of the Italian intellectual elite and avoid divisive disputes. But all were imbued with a deeply moral conviction of their duty to enlighten and lead public opinion by the diffusion of progressive ideas, which would raise the level of Italian culture and prepare the future ruling class in a spirit of *amor patriae.* Apart from the typically Piedmontese class consciousness, there was a close parallel between Cesare Balbo's youthful scheme (1816) to prepare a new ruling class by public education and Vieusseux's project (1825) for an institute of higher education to 'form a nursery of honest, intelligent manufacturers and shopkeepers, administrators and farmers, of active citizens, devoted to their country' (Ciampini, 213, p. 121). The success of these groups in arousing interest and support for their ideas among the culturally more open sectors of the middle class and aristocracy increased steadily during the 1830s and 1840s: the *Anthology* had over 500 subscribers, Lambruschini's *Guide for the Educator* over 800, the congresses of Italian scientists attracted increasing attention and over 2400 members by 1845.

Progress through education and an enlightened economy remained the basic aims of the *Anthology* until its suppression in 1833. A sincerely religious sense of life and work, a highly personal form of liberal Catholicism – Florence was the centre of Lamennaisian ideas in Italy – inspired the actions of the entire Tuscan group. But until the years of Giobertian influence it remained an all-embracing religious philosophy without giving rise to specific proposals for reform. Popular education and economic progress represented different aspects of a single whole, the more closely linked because of the predominant and traditional Tuscan preoccupation with agriculture. The sharp fall in agricultural prices of these decades gave rise to animated discussions within the Academy of the Georgofili and in Vieusseux's *Tuscan Agrarian Journal* about the effects of free trade, the *mezzadria* (share-cropping) contract and the poverty of the peasantry, in part echoing and continuing discussions of the Leopoldine and Napoleonic periods, but now displaying a new emphasis on moral duty and individual initiative. The sanctity of free trade was reaffirmed. But although the personal relationships and self-contained nature of a *mezzadria*-dominated agriculture perhaps softened the worst effects of the crisis, the most advanced Tuscan landowners – heads of the most distinguished noble families, like Ricasoli, Ridolfi and Peruzzi – recognized the need for a structural transformation of Tuscan agriculture by increased investment, the adoption of modern technical-organizational methods of cultivation and raising the educational level of the peasants. Ridolfi at Meleto, Ricasoli at Brolio and Lambruschini at San Cerbone, offered examples of that personal initiative to achieve religious, moral, civil and economic progress which was to regenerate Italy. Salvagnoli applauded Ricasoli for demonstrating that:

> Tuscan agriculture cannot be truly worthy of civilization until educated and moral proprietors apply the sciences and practise their virtues on the farms, as teachers and landlords and examples for the peasants, not by words without deeds, and not by theatrical deeds without fraternal charity. (Ciampini, 213, p. 140)

Echoes of Paoletti and the Leopoldine discussions of the need to educate the peasant for economic as well as moral reasons accompanied Lambruschini's attempts to transform into reality Pestalozzian theories of popular education. Tuscany, with Lombardy, was the major centre of infant nurseries and schools of 'monitorial' instruction, created by private initiative. Lambruschini, in his *Guide for the Educator*, conceived of education in a paternalistic manner, as a force for social cohesion. Typical of this moderate Tuscan attitude was his recommendation to 'stewards, farm bailiffs, landowners' to study the news contained in the *Agrarian Journal*, which 'must help you and, through you, reach the peasant. It is your task to distinguish those matters which most meet their needs; and to show them what to read, or read to them yourselves' (Mack Smith, 110a, p. 171).

This cult of the peasant and the countryside, of strongly Sismondian tone, was based upon the conviction that Tuscany's wealth and social stability lay in its agriculture. Although isolated voices such as those of Salvagnoli or the Prato textile industrialist Mazzoni might question this primacy and its corollary – absolute free trade – the Georgofili and *Anthology* writers repeated Sismondi's accusations against the degrading effects of industrialization. As Lapo de' Ricci wrote:

> But at all events we have avoided the pauperism which afflicts England and to a greater extent those other nations which have taken upon themselves to imitate her; we have avoided the distress, the convulsions, the uncertainty which torment France today, because of an artificial system [of protection] which is breaking down. (Ronchi, 320, p. 18)

The Tuscan moderates did not deny the existence of an agricultural crisis, nor that foreign protection and competition created acute problems, which revealed themselves in the low wages, increasing difficulties of the craft and new textile industries (straw hats, silk and wool) and the growing unemployment in the countryside. But the solution was not to be found in desecrating that sacred cow of Leopoldine legislation, absolute freedom of trade, which favoured the export of agricultural products, nor in preferential treatment of any sort for industries, but in greater attention to the technical problems and moral duties of agriculture.

Ridolfi, a harsh observer of Tuscan stagnancy in this age of rapid economic development, criticized the predominance of *mezzadria*,

> a *conservative*, not a *progressive* system; whereas nowadays the problem for us is not to *conserve* but to *progress*, as otherwise we shall not meet the demands of the times and circumstances, especially in a system of full commercial freedom for agrarian products. (Ciampini, 213, p. 152)

But his proposed remedy consisted in a reform of the *mezzadria* system, teaching the peasants the methods of modern farming, and the creation of subsidiary rural industries to absorb the threatening unemployment:

> Let us be moved at least by the threat of the proletarians whose numbers are growing daily. And if begging is on the increase because of the lack of customary, normal employment, let us find the solution ourselves; let us open more country schools; let us form associations of provident charity and industriousness, and let us remember once and for all that in this voracious century he who does not look to his own preservation marches straight to his ruin. (Ronchi, 320, p. 11)

More conservative moderates, such as Capponi or Lambruschini, warned against dangers of increasing unemployment by too rapid a capitalization of agriculture. 'Do not forget the peasants', wrote Lambruschini to Ridolfi, 'when you propose systems that are more beneficial for the owners. The interests of the two do not always go together' (Ciampini, 214, pp. 51–2).

The Tuscan moderates, proud of their traditions, stood apart from moderate voices elsewhere in Italy through their identification with a purely agrarian paternalism. But in their cultural patriotism, their faith in their function as the necessary link between government and people, and their increasing awareness of the political implications of their economic and social proposals, they were representative of Italian moderatism in the 1830s and 1840s. Convinced supporters of the Tuscan government's Enlightened reformism, Vieusseux and his colleagues followed with interest and wished to propagandize such government initiatives as the reclamation of the Maremma marshes:

> To overcome ignorance, to dissipate the doubts of the public is only possible through the press. It is not fitting for the government either to instruct the ignorant directly, or to reply to their adversaries; this is the task of the writers, this is the task of a journal well known for its love of truth and utility. (Ciampini, 213, p. 137)

But the government, embodiment of the Leopoldine tradition, remained indifferent to public opinion. As the multiple problems discussed in the *Anthology* repeatedly revealed the dependence of reforms upon political decisions, the political character of the journal became more marked, particularly after the July revolution. Successful administration required collaboration:

> The administration can and must do a lot, and in certain cases take the initiative; but it is equally necessary that it be understood and supported by those it administers; it is necessary that an explicit spirit of association respond to the enlightened and beneficent views of the government and assist their execution. (Ciampini, 213, p. 218)

As the July revolution once more revealed the revolutionary force of the masses, the *Anthology* group became ever-more convinced of the need for collaboration between government and public opinion. The disorders of society derived from the ignorance and poverty of the 'inferior classes'; but the demands of the people were bound to increase: 'It is up to us to decide if the people are suddenly to win their emancipation like a mischievous child; or, with our assistance, are gradually to be prepared for it' (Ciampini, 213, p. 228), wrote Vieusseux. Not surprisingly, the explicitly political implications of this preface to the *Anthology* of 1833 led to its suppression.

Industrialism and social order

Vieusseux's new consciousness of the threatening march of the people was common to the Italian moderates of the 1830s. It resulted from their observation of class conflict in England and France and their reading of Tocqueville's theorization of the inevitable advance of democracy. As Cavour wrote, closely following Tocqueville's analysis, two contradictory forces were produced by modern society: an enlargement of political democracy through 'the general and equal distribution of political rights among an ever-growing number of individuals', and 'a proportionately increasing concentration of wealth in a small number of hands. . . . This anomaly cannot last long without grave danger to social relations' (Berti, 282, p. 178).

For the moderates of northern Italy, such as Cavour, economic progress on the capitalist models of England and France was not only inevitable, but desirable. In the new interdependence of national economies Cavour saw a convergence between the trend towards liberalization of trade and the movements of oppressed nationalities. Free trade and civil progress were encompassing an ever larger area of Europe. Hence governments, while necessarily centralizing their powers and often obliged to intervene in order to facilitate credit and assist the creation of adequate infrastructures, should remove legislative obstacles (such as protectionist barriers) to the process of capital accumulation. The increase of productivity would automatically generate an equilibrium between growth of population and of means of subsistence. Given the difficulties of competing successfully against English industrial products, the economic future of small states such as Piedmont – according to Cavour – lay in agricultural exports, based upon specialization of products and advanced agronomic techniques. The rising agricultural prices of the 1840s favoured this theory of an international division of labour where a real complementarity existed, as between England and Piedmont.

Cavour was among the most widely read and travelled of the moderates of his day, and more attentive than most of his contemporaries to the structural changes of the western economies and the post-Ricardian developments of economic theory. Following Malthus, Nassau Senior and Mill's criticisms of Benthamite utilitarianism, he was far less dogmatic than Francesco Ferrara and the new group of Sicilian economists about the reduction of the role of the State in a free trade economy. But his conviction that Italy's future in the international economy was basically agricultural reflected the general opinion of moderates, such as the Bolognese Marco

Minghetti – an opinion which was reinforced by the growing trend of agricultural trade and the slow increase of prosperity of almost all the Italian states (except the Papacy) in these decades. Industry and commerce were to be encouraged, but their role remained subsidiary and often tied to that of agriculture. Cattaneo, alone among the Italian economists, maintained the absolute primacy of commerce and its leading role in capitalizing agriculture. His contemporaries, such as Cesare Correnti, Stefano Jacini, Ilarione Petitti, even Camillo Cavour (despite his earlier interest in industrial development) and even more the Tuscan or Bolognese economists, extended their initial interests in agriculture to study the problems of industry and the infrastructure (roads, canals and railways), but remained conditioned by their more direct knowledge of the rural economy.

This hesitant attitude towards local industrial development, which accompanied a constantly positive vision of the English model of progress, derived in part from the economic backwardness of the southern Italian states, in part from preoccupations about the social implications of industrialism. There was a broad similarity in the themes that attracted the attention of contributors to moderate journals and memoirs in all regions of Italy, at Naples and Palermo as much as at Bologna or Florence, Turin or Milan: canals, machines and technological innovations, steamships, roads, railways, agronomics and agrarian instruction. In this they reflected both the pace of economic change in Europe and the growing contacts and cohesion of moderate writers in Italy. But there were profound regional differences in the manner in which these arguments were treated. While Lombard and Piedmontese moderates were basically optimistic about the relative benefits and implications of industrial developments, the Tuscans deliberately rejected modern industry in favour of agrarian paternalism; and moderate intellectuals in the Papal States and Two Sicilies displayed a predominant concern to achieve, as a prior necessity, effective unification of the domestic market and an improvement of agricultural productivity.

The discussions about economic progress and the dangers of industrialism thus differed according to the levels of economic-social development of the Italian states. But they also continued an older, reformist preoccupation with social justice. Sismondi's criticisms of the negative effects on distribution and consumption of the classical economists' obsession with production, developed by Romagnosi in the *Annals of Statistics* into a critique of the separation of economics from legislation and politics, were widely adopted by Italian moderates. The humanitarian strands of eighteenth-century Italian political economy were strengthened by contemporary evidence of the degrading effects of the factory system: child labour was deplored by the congress of Italian scientists (nearly 40 000 children were employed in Lombard industries in 1840), the right to subsistence was urged against the low level of wages. Industrialism was regarded as encouraging speculation and causing pauperism in both city and countryside. The Piedmontese Petitti di Roreto expressed a general opinion in preferring craft or domestic industry to the evils of factories:

> To the wealth which causes a great number of citizens to suffer or worsens their conditions of life, we prefer a poverty that at least keeps them healthy and honest. If such is the choice before us, and such are the consequences, we place the crude and scarce products of individual labour before the marvellous and multiple achievements of ingenious engineering. (Cavour, 283, p. L)

This humanitarian concern, habitually identified with a sense of religious duty, was revealed in the intense frequency of discussions of pauperism and almsgiving, prison conditions and poor laws, elementary education and savings banks, petty rural theft and pellagra, unemployment and mutual aid societies, popular morality and charitable institutions. These were the counterpart to the articles on trade and industry, steamships and railways, statistics and finances which documented the moderates' assiduous attention to the epiphenomena of foreign capitalist development. The increasing unemployment and ubiquitous evidence of acute peasant poverty could not easily be ignored by a ruling class aware of its moral duty, with still fresh memories of the terrible famine of 1816-17, soon to be repeated (for the last time in western European history) in 1846-7.

But if pauperism was a theme common to all the moderates, their attitudes varied about the social dangers it implied. Cavour could oppose the substitution of factories for domestic silk cultivation, 'because it would break the ties of sympathy and affection which exist between those who own and those who cultivate the land; ties which, in this century more than ever, we must strive to maintain and strengthen, even at the cost of some sacrifices' (Cavour, 283, p. 49). But he remained fundamentally optimistic about the relations between classes in Piedmont. The destruction of feudalism and the relative economic backwardness of the country had avoided the emergence of a class struggle, such as in France; the formation of a conservative liberal party (as he was to define it in 1847), through the fusion of the aristocracy with the bourgeoisie, was an adequate safeguard of social peace, if backed by 'legal charity' – so long as this ruling class remained open, in this age of rapid change, to the need for reforms. Charity and reforms: by the 1840s the formula was widely accepted by the Piedmontese moderates as an adequate remedy for the ills of a society in the throes of economic development. Significantly, two priests from Piedmont, Giuseppe Cottolengo and Giovanni Bosco, were responsible for giving institutional forms to charitable activities by creating, alongside private family almsgiving, institutional homes for society's more hapless members. In like manner, it was two northerners, Ferrante Aporti and Lorenzo Valerio, who actively propagated the corollary to private charity – popular education – by creating nursery schools and publishing *Popular Readings*. In Lombardy, where the official system of primary education was the most advanced in Italy and the government encouraged savings banks for the lower classes (albeit utilized, as elsewhere in Italy, mainly by the more comfortable middle classes), Romagnosi, Cattaneo and their followers were similarly optimistic.

In Tuscany, distrust of industrialism and worry about the emergence of a 'social question' went hand in hand. Here Sismondi's influence had penetrated most deeply. The dogma of free trade and the myth of a patriarchal rural life in an economy based upon wine, silk and oil ill-concealed an intolerance towards the problems of Prato's industries or an antipathy towards the speculation which accompanied railway construction and mining, sectors regarded as symptomatic of the dangers of industrialism. Education and philanthropy were the essential elements of a programme which deliberately sidestepped the problems of tumultuous, uncontrolled economic growth (despite the theoretical encouragement of individual initiative) by the attempted conservation of a world that had passed.

In southern Italy, and especially the Papal States, the overwhelming evidence of poverty and the continuous agitations made the moderate intellectuals less optimistic about the adequacy of charity and more aware of the immediate need for reforms, both civil and economic. In Naples the government's determined espousal of internal free trade, in a country which remained divided because of the desperate inadequacy of its communications, provoked the demand for state intervention to avoid the dangers of a famine caused by the activities of grain speculators. In the Legations, Terenzio Mamiani was expressing the opinion of the most advanced moderates in the Papal States when he claimed that 'the protection of the plebs by governments cannot consist solely, in economic matters, in removing every manner of obstacle to free trade and free competition' (Demarco, 216, p. 253). Positive measures were required to guarantee subsistence, such as the abolition of the most burdensome indirect taxes, the creation of schools, hospitals, workshops and charitable institutions. In a polemically anti-Mazzinian catechism of the 'rights' and 'duties' of the people, Mamiani went far beyond the broad confidence placed by the northern and Tuscan moderates in charity and education to demand specific economic and administrative reforms as the necessary, and only, means of resolving popular agitation.

Mamiani's proposals revealed the close ties between the moderates' worry about social dangers and their preoccupation with the political influence of the 'extremists', whether clerical or democratic. The humanitarian and religious motives underlying the propaganda and initiatives in favour of charity and popular education, and the economic calculation behind the creation of technical institutes, were accompanied by an awareness of the need to combat, on the one hand, clerical encouragement of ignorance and superstition and, on the other, democratic (or, even worse, socialist) penetration among the people, 'that numerous and inert mass that has no political predilections' in the young Cavour's words (Ruffini, 289, vol. 1, p. 251). Love of work and resignation were to be instilled in the masses. As Mamiani wrote in his 'catechism':

> The duty of the people is to labour assiduously, with diligence and zeal. . . . The duty of the people is to accept submissively the instructions and warnings of those who far surpass them in education and science. . . . The duty of the people is to practise moderation in their desires, not to disdain their condition, not to envy the rich, to behave in a frugal and sober, obedient and disciplined manner. (Demarco, 216, p. 253)

The moderates had little difficulty in distinguishing themselves from the clericals and Jesuits, who launched a massive attack against their nursery schools and pedagogic initiatives, regarded as responsible for the corruption of the masses with their modern subversive doctrines and methods. Despite this hostility, the moderates made steady progress, at least in northern and central Italy: by 1846, with the support or toleration of the governments, some 18 000 children attended the infant nurseries in Tuscany, Lombard-Venetia and Piedmont.

The democratic, Mazzinian appeal to the masses, which so worried the moderates, proved more of a fear than a reality. Unlike many of these northern and central moderates, Mazzini displayed a total disregard for the peasant masses. Apart from the short-lived attempt of Gustavo Modena to write popular dialogues with a strong democratic content (1833-4), the Mazzinians barely tried to enter the field of popular education, or else – like the Tuscan Mazzinians Atto Vannucci and Pietro Thouar – accepted and supported the moderate lead. This was hardly surprising, given the faith of both Mazzinians and moderates in the Saint-Simonian doctrine of association. But the continued agitations and renewed democratic risings in the early 1840s, inaccurately attributed to Mazzini, kept alive the moderate worry about the possibility of popular support for such initiatives in southern Italy. Once more it was in the north that the moderates remained optimistic, convinced that class conflict had been removed with the abolition of feudal privileges. Indeed, Mazzini and these moderates complacently, if unexpectedly, agreed that social relations were fundamentally satisfactory. As the moderate 'Italian League' stated in February 1848 in words which could have been written by Mazzini: 'In Italy at present (thanks be to God) we do not know those savage motives which inflame and envenom the lowly classes' (Cavour, 283, p. xxix, n. 95).

Cavour was more clear-sighted than most of his colleagues in recognizing the basically middle-class character of the democrats, although he underestimated the force of popular feeling which was to explode in 1848, even in Italy. In 1846 he stated confidently:

In Italy a democratic revolution has no chance of success. To prove this, it is enough to analyse the elements which form the party favourable to political novelties. This party does not attract great sympathy among the masses which, with the exception of a few of the urban poor, are in general strongly attached to the old institutions of the country. Its strength lies almost exclusively in the middle class and in part of the upper class. Now both of these have very conservative interests to defend. ... If social order were truly threatened, if the great principles on which it rests were subjected to a real danger, we are convinced that one would see a fair number of the most determined *frondeurs*, of the most extravagant republicans, in the front ranks of the conservative party. (Cavour, 283, p. 245)

But for Cavour, as for the other moderates, reaction and revolution were both responsible for Italy's slowness to progress. Reaction and revolution provoked each other in a continuous closed circle. The only hope was 'the just mean', *le juste milieu*, such as existed in Orleanist France. Progress could only be achieved by reforms and by convincing the princes that collaboration with the enlightened classes was in their own interests. Reason and the objective evidence of English and French economic and civil progress would ultimately lead to the slow conversion of these paladins of obscurantism. Indeed, the administrative and economic reforms of Ferdinand II and Charles Albert demonstrated that reason and progress were asserting themselves in Italy, too, however hesitantly and partially.

The formation of a moderate movement

The foreign emperor in Lombardy-Venetia and the retrograde pope in central Italy constituted the main obstacles to the achievement of Italian independence. But if the latter represented an apparently insuperable difficulty and was the cause of scandal throughout Europe, the influence of the liberal powers and favourable international circumstances – such as the periodic crises over the 'eastern question' – might ultimately oblige Austria to withdraw pacifically from Italy in exchange for an extension of her empire at Ottoman expense in the Balkans. Cesare Balbo, when he formulated these proposals in his famous book *Of the Hopes of Italy* (1844), was merely expressing ideas which had circulated in Piedmontese circles since the Restoration and which Gioberti was already proposing privately. But they reflected the liberals' conviction that Italy's future was dependent upon external circumstances, upon the European balance of power. However optimistic about the ultimate triumph of the liberal cause, this attitude was far more passive than the voluntaristic action of even the moderate liberals in the revolutions of 1820–1. It displayed an analogous faith in the international sphere to that of the moderates in the Italian governments' willingness to accept reforms internally. The Concert of Europe – it was believed – was capable of adjusting the treaty of Vienna peacefully to changing circumstances, as it had shown over Greece, Belgium and above all the eastern crisis of 1839–40. This contrast to the popular internationalism of the democrats was rendered the more acute by Balbo's denial that all nations could aspire to independence; indeed, according to these moderates, for historical and religious reasons only Italians and Poles could justifiably claim to act as representatives and defenders of western Christian civilization.

But until such favourable international circumstances emerged, the task of the moderates was to create a national, liberal body of opinion. Municipal particularism was to be combated by historical and literary writings which evoked the country's former independence and the unity of Italian history. In most of the moderate writers – the novelist Manzoni, the historians Troya, Balbo and Cantù – this cult of history, so typical a trait of these decades, tended towards an identification of Italy's past independence with the papacy. But in all the moderates, whether Catholic (like Balbo) or Protestant (like Vieusseux) it was intensely patriotic: the numerous monographs and dramatic works, the collections of documents, culminating in the Tuscan-inspired journal, the *Italian Historical Archive*, the historical institutions, such as the Piedmontese 'Society for Patriotic History', all aimed at arousing an historical consciousness among the educated classes and so moulding public opinion in favour of Italian independence. 'Before achieving primacies, one should achieve parity; and . . . the first parity with independent nations is independence', wrote Balbo, displaying his preoccupation with Gioberti's denial of the unity of Christian Europe (Romeo, 199, p. 64). And the diffusion of Balbo's *Summary of the History of Italy* (1846) was indicative of the moderates' success in gaining ever-wider cultural support.

By the 1840s moderate liberal opinion in the different states began to converge through personal contacts and recognition of a common philosophy and interests. The annual congresses of Italian scientists from 1839 strengthened these contacts and tended to direct the interests of the noble and middle-class participants towards specific limited economic reforms, given the impossibility of open political discussion and the explicit desire to utilize public opinion as a means of influencing the princes. The moderates possessed no political programme. Nor indeed were they yet so united in their ideas as their leaders pretended: distrust of Piedmont was implicit in the Tuscan moderates' attempt to monopolize the publication of Italian historical documents as much as in the Neapolitan and Sicilian assertions of independentist traditions; federalism was a means of checking Savoyard hegemony, as well as the only 'realistic' method of achieving independence.

But, if privately discussed political aspirations barely masked undercurrents of regional and traditional diffidence and hostility, the moderates were able to achieve a broader consensus on their economic proposals. A customs league among the Italian states (even without Austrian Lombardy-Venetia), uniform commercial and navigation codes, uniform moneys, weights and measures, the construction of a single railway network for all Italy, were proposals which reflected in part the achievements of Napoleonic Italy, destroyed by the Restoration, in part prominent themes of discussion in the Europe of these decades. The debates about customs leagues in the 1830s, following the creation of the *Zollverein*, and about railways in the 1840s, following the rapid extension of the European network and the prospects of increased traffic with the Far East across the Suez isthmus, displayed the moderates' characteristic and dominant interest in foreign examples of progress rather than in the specific nature and development of the Italian economies. Production within the individual Italian states was oriented increasingly towards foreign markets, rather than within Italy: and if free trade and free circulation within the confines of each state were generally accepted, there was little to show that Italian producers preferred the far less secure prospects of a unified Italian market, and considerable evidence that they regarded investment in railway construction as a purely speculative venture.

The campaigns for an Italian customs league and a unified railway system, in fact, were waged by the intellectual moderates for political ends, as the first steps of reform towards the achievement of political federation and future independence. That they should have succeeded partially in imposing these reforms on the Italian princes after 1846 was indicative less of their direct correspondence to the specific demands of the agrarian, commercial and industrial producers in Italy than of their ability to gain support among these strata for their general vision of regulated, restrained progress based upon social stability and pacific change, which – ultimately – was to gain the independence of Italy. The moderates, especially of northern and central Italy, had succeeded by the mid-1840s in creating a climate of opinion, rendered the more susceptible to their liberal and free trade ideas by the failure of the democratic attempts at insurrection. Economic progress and social paternalism offered an alternative to Mazzinian democracy and unity. But to transform public opinion into an effective instrument required political changes. And these still depended upon the consent of the princes.

Cattaneo: the idealization of the Lombard middle class

The northern moderates' optimism about the beneficial consequences of economic progress owed much to a writer who consciously avoided their facile political deductions and always opposed the romantic patriotism of their historical vision and the conservatism of their social attitudes – Carlo Cattaneo (1801–69). In contrast to Mazzinian attempts to create a unitarian party, the development of liberal ideas remained fundamentally regional (despite the centripetal intentions of the congresses of Italian scientists); and Lombardy-Venetia's appurtenance to the Austrian empire accentuated its separateness from the other states within the Italian peninsula. Nevertheless Cattaneo's writings in the Milanese *Universal Annals of Statistics* and the *Polytechnic* in the 1830s and 1840s undoubtedly influenced both moderate and radical intellectuals throughout the Po valley, with their constant flow of information about economic developments throughout the world, their analyses of the historical reasons for western progress and their incessant, rational application of these empirical data to the prospects of the Lombard, and northern Italian economies. By 1843 the *Polytechnic* had reached a subscription figure of 700, while Cattaneo himself had achieved a reputation and respectability such as to merit official recognition and governmental requests for his collaboration as the acknowledged expert in a variety of fields, from prison reform to agriculture, from education to technology. His position as an influential independent reformer, open to – even desirous of – collaboration with the Austrian government, was in many ways similar to that of Pietro Verri nearly a century earlier. But the Europe and the Lombardy of Cattaneo's days were far from those of the 'Enlightened despots', and the revolution of 1848 was to find this jeweller's son, an isolated figure, in the forefront of the struggle of the Milan populace against Austrian rule and aristocratic domination.

Until the eve of the revolution, this dedicated scholar, the most serious, penetrating and versatile intellectual of the Risorgimento, had carefully avoided all manifestations of political activity. In part, this can be ascribed to the temperamental reasons of the scholar. But there can be no doubt that Cattaneo felt little sympathy for the aristocratic cliques which had formed the backbone of the 1820–1 conspiracies, and which continued to predominate among the subdued, fringe criticisms of the moderates in Lombardy. In contrast to Cavour's vision of a fusion between aristocracy and middle classes, Cattaneo saw the future as lying with the middle classes, destined by their autonomous action to replace the aristocracy, and further progress. In 1844–5 he let the *Polytechnic* die rather than merge it with the *European Review*, which was supported by a group of Milanese nobles soon to be found among the moderate leaders of 1848.

This antipathy, revealed in all its force during the revolution, was supported and theorized by Cattaneo in these earlier years in his interpretation of the history of civilization as a struggle between the feudal aristocracy and the entrepreneurial middle classes, herald-bearers of progress. But it also reflected his deep repugnance towards both organized conspiracy and the emotional rhetoric of patriotic propaganda. And if, in later years, Cattaneo vehemently criticized the futility and negative consequences of Mazzini's obsession with action, he never ceased his caustic attacks on the complacent moderatism and idealistic spiritualism of the Piedmontese-led ethic of the 'happy mean'. Conspiracy and rhetorical patriotism were not merely irrational and of little practical effect; they were deceitful substitutes for the study of real and immediate problems whose resolution constituted progress: 'We have become a bit block-headed by dint of studying economics and statistics and, worse still, remain boorishly in favour of the progressive system; at all costs we do not want to move backwards' (Bobbio, 266, p. 75).

Progress and liberty could only be achieved, as the history of past civilizations showed, by the study and rational application of useful sciences. In his constant reiteration of reason, utility and the innovatory effects of the experimental sciences, Cattaneo harked back, as in so many aspects of his writings, to the Enlightenment. Literature he eschewed as a mere pastime and metaphysics as neither useful nor rational. But Cattaneo was fully aware of the limits of the Enlightenment, as of romantic culture. The former was excessively individualistic and interpreted the past as marking linear progress towards man's achievement of the 'light'; the latter placed an emotive stress on intuition and the cult of past traditions. Strongly influenced by Romagnosi's concept of 'sociality', Cattaneo was convinced that man could only be studied in society: there was only 'the study of the *individual* within the bosom of *humanity*, i.e. *social ideology*' (Cattaneo, 262, vol. 1, p. 328). Peoples and civilizations were the object of study, as contemporary romantic historiography taught – but without transcendental implications. For history was the history of peoples' interactions with their material and physical environment, which displayed the variety and multiplicity of human experiences. Cattaneo thus rejected both the metaphysical connotations of romantic historiography and the Enlightenment belief in the linearity of progress towards ultimate perfection. He favoured instead a study of humanity and nature by systematic, empirical research on a range and scale which only a polymath, such as himself, could dominate. His multiple, invariably acute writings on history, linguistics, physical geography, geology, vulcanology, astronomy, physics, chemistry, agriculture, engineering, economics and statistics, all bear witness to his constant striving towards the elements of a 'universal history'.

But these writings were equally marked by Cattaneo's concern for their utility, both educationally and morally. He was determined to reveal the constant variety and struggle of the diverse principles which constituted the motive forces of indefinite (but not deterministic) human progress. For Cattaneo, the examples of eastern civilizations – India, China, Japan – disproved the theory of linear progress. But, by their very contrast to the progress of western civilizations, they offered the key to the understanding of past experiences. The eastern civilizations had died through the stifling of conflict and diversity: 'Variety is life and inscrutable unity is death' (Cattaneo, 262, vol. 2, p. 358). History, in the multiplicity of its manifestations, displayed a constant dialectic between progress and regression:

> An immutable and universal State would be the common grave of progress and intelligence, and in the end of every moral value; there would be no other hope than civil wars, and out of this dismemberment of society the principle of emulation could be rekindled, and the subjection of the backward and dominance of the progressives could be renewed. (Catteneo, 262, vol. 2, p. 73)

The progress and liberty of societies were thus dependent upon conflict and variety: Cattaneo was inevitably opposed to the reconciliatory aspirations of the moderates' politics and philosophy, as he was to the uniformity implied in Mazzini's programme.

If the decadence of eastern societies derived from their uniformity and traditionalism, western civilization had progressed because of the constant friction of rival ideas and institutions, stimulated by the innovatory effects of the experimental sciences and the continuous application of the scientific method. The cradle of the experimental sciences were the Italian communes; here were to be found the origins of modern civilization, the transformation from feudal barbarism to the process of *incivilimento* ('civilizing'):

> This passage from feudal barbarism to civilization is a fact. It is the faithful abstract of that real history which in our privileged country took place seven hundred years ago, but which in Prussia, Scotland, Denmark, Switzerland, Saxony, Bohemia, Moravia, Russia only occurred a few generations or even a few years ago; and it will spread from one end of the world to the other. (Cattaneo, 262, vol. 1, p. 32)

The experimental method was thus the guarantee of an open system, of a progressive society, which respected the variety of the universe and the spontaneity of the individual, and thus human freedom.

In the more immediate terms, the study of the experimental sciences was essential because of its practical utility. In his pieface to the first issue of the *Polytechnic*, Cattaneo stated his intention:

> To offer to our fellow citizens the most rapid knowledge of that part of the truth that can be transferred easily from the arduous regions of science to render fertile the field of practicality, and to give increasing support and comfort to common prosperity and civilised life . . . because we are persuaded that the most speculative sciences, even in their driest branches, must sooner or later germinate some unexpected fruit for human society. (Cattaneo, 262, vol. 2, p. 55)

Science, material progress and the process of 'civilizing' were inextricably linked. Following Romagnosi and the English classical economists, Cattaneo saw civil progress as accompanied and marked by economic progress, which was dependent upon free competition. Like all the progressive political economists of northern and central Italy of his day, he was opposed to protection and a dogmatic supporter of free trade, although he recognized that the coexistence of the two systems required a cautious approach towards free trade on the part of statesmen. Like Cavour and Ricasoli, but on a more penetrating theoretical level, he recognized the crucial function of a capitalist agriculture in a modern economy and wrote a hymn of praise to the achievements of Lombard agriculture in his *Natural and Civil Notes about Lombardy* (1844). But unlike all other Italian political economists (except Melchiorre Gioia), he recognized the primacy of trade and industry as providing the motor force of economic growth through the rapid generation and accumulation of capital.

Cattaneo's historical investigations and contemporary researches converged in a vision of the process of *incivilimento* as embodied within the urban middle classes. In Italy, where the communes gave birth to modern civilization, the urban bourgeoisie and the experimental sciences, agriculture developed from the cities through the transference of commercial and industrial capital to the land:

> Our cities are the ancient centre of all the communications of a large and populous province; all the roads lead there, all the country markets are there, they are like the heart in the system of veins; they are the terminals towards which *consumers* turn and from which *industry* and *capital* branch out. (Cattaneo, 262, vol. 1, p. 39)

In modern times, English commerce and industry had played a similar role, forcing the pace of economic progress and civilization.

Probably no Italian in the 1830s and 1840s, not even Cavour, understood and analysed so well as Cattaneo the profundity and range of the transformations resulting from the British domination of the world economy. The triumph of capitalism became for Cattaneo the inevitable march of progress, which legitimized even such moral or social injustices as the enforced emigration of the British poor to colonize the world, or the Chinese Opium War; although his deep sense of human liberty and his denial of racial superiority made him question at moments whether

> the valiant and able peoples, whose nationality was sacrificed to raise the vast edifice of Britannic unity, whose blood was spilt, whose lands were stolen, whose memory was persecuted and suppressed, did not perhaps have good cause to complain of their destiny? Was so much evil necessary for the triumph of civilization? (Cattaneo, 262, vol. 2, p. 53)

His response to this moral problem, which he sensed more acutely on the scale of world civilization than on that of class divisions within Italy or Europe, led him to conclude that:

> We are sure that historical evil is not necessary to effect progress, but that progress prevails notwithstanding all the inroads of evil. (Cattaneo, 262, vol. 2, p. 54)

The urban middle classes were thus identified with progress, in terms of both their economic function and their moral responsibility. They were the natural leaders of the multitudes, replacing the feudal aristocracy. Cattaneo's idealization of a progressive, entrepreneurial middle-class and his faith in the self-regulating mechanism of capitalist development were so total that, alone among contemporary Italian political economists, he ignored the dangers of increasing pauperism and class conflict which so worried the moderate exponents of industrialism. The 'people', for Cattaneo, comprised all elements of the urban bourgeoisie – property owners, industrialists, merchants, lawyers and others in free professions, craftsmen; he did not distinguish among their component parts, and in class terms only saw a struggle between this category and the feudal aristocracy or patriciate. The material conditions of the 'multitudes' or plebs would be improved by public charity, hygiene, savings banks and, above all, by example and education. Significantly he had nothing to say about the peasants. In his optimistic portrait of Lombard progress, he dismissed the problems of the poor in a few brief sentences: infant nurseries had removed 'the abject ferocity and uncouthness of plebeian children'; 'the poor receive a more generous share of aid than elsewhere'; 'property is widespread in all classes; hence, all things considered, of all the countries of Europe this one presents perhaps the greatest number of civil families in proportion to the uneducated plebs' (Cattaneo, 262, vol. 2, pp. 460, 467, 468). Cattaneo's vision of future progress through industrial and commercial development left no place for class conflict:

> Within the adventurous harmony of all civil orders, a new society of industrious, shrewd, respectable men is being woven, in which every attitude has its place, every merit its reward. No longer will there be uncouth, foul, bloodthirsty plebs, downtrodden by insulting and greedy dominators. The new society moves like a well-ordered army, in which intelligence, duty, honour embrace the lowest of soldiers and the highest of officers. (Cattaneo, 262, vol. 2, p. 481)

This overwhelming sense of the rapidity of change, of the irresistible outward expansion of the nineteenth century in all directions, explains Cattaneo's dominant concern to inform and educate Italians about the developments of this new world:

> Tradition can perhaps guide peoples in the use of ancient and ordinary arts; but when it is a question of learning new arts, or meeting the competition of new industries, or embellishing the country with the gifts of modern civilization, then it is wholly necessary that there be an abundance of trained minds, with a solid knowledge of progressive doctrines. (Cattaneo, 262, vol. 2, p. 69)

Failure to understand the interdependence of this new world economy could only prove disastrous. When England lowered duties on imported spun silk, 'the other unions must either conform to its example, or be beaten on neutral markets and close down their factories' (Cattaneo, 262, vol. 1, p. 28). Patriotic nationalism was irrelevant in the face of these truths and symptomatic of inadequately trained minds:

> We are convinced, however, that Italy above all must keep in unison with Europe, and not cherish any other national sentiment than that of retaining a worthy place in the scientific association of Europe and the World. Peoples should act as a permanent mirror to each other, because the interests of civilization are mutually dependent and common; because science is one, art is one, glory is one. The nation of scholarly men is one . . . it is the nation of the intellectuals, which inhabits all climates and speaks all languages. Beneath this nation there is a multitude divided into a thousand discordant patrias, castes, dialects, into greedy, bloodthirsty factions, which revel in superstition, egoism, ignorance, which sometimes even love and defend ignorance as if it were the principle of life and the basis of customs and society. (Cattaneo, 262, vol. 2, p. 59)

This classically Enlightened cosmopolitan, elitist attitude explains much of Cattaneo's pedagogic influence on the progressive groups in northern Italy, but also of his political isolation. As an instructor he had no rival. He played a major part in raising the level of technical and economic information of the progressive sectors of Italian society to that of the advanced countries of Europe with his constant flow of articles on steam power, gas lighting, silk cultivation, modern agricultural techniques, hydraulics, geological research, banking systems and monetary questions, railways, technical training, popular education and public hygiene. He was a central figure in the campaign for a railway between Milan and Venice, which would link the major cities of the kingdom; he was a strong supporter of customs reforms, free trade and a unified system of weights and measures.

But in his deliberate refusal before the revolution to engage in emotional patriotic propaganda, Cattaneo was inevitably isolated from both Mazzinian democrats and moderates in the romantically nationalist atmosphere of the 1830s and 1840s. Convinced that Lombardy constituted the *avant-garde* of progress in Italy, he lent little support to the moderates' campaign for a customs league among the Italian states. On the eve of the revolution, he still saw the future of Lombardy-Venetia within an Austrian empire which would abandon its stultifying centralization and revert to a federation of free and equal nation-states united under the Habsburg crown; Lombardy-Venetia would dominate in this federation as the most progressive and civilized nation, and would be able peacefully to transfer to an Italian federation – but only at such a time as the other Italian states had raised themselves, by the introduction of economic, administrative and political liberties, to the level of civilization in Lombardy. Almost certainly, with these ideas, he was disparagingly comparing the aristocratic, Jesuit-dominated Piedmont so vaunted by the moderates with the relatively efficient secular Austrian administration in Lombardy. But, unwittingly, it was these very moderates that his publicist activities aided. Absorbed within his scientific-economic vision of the progress of civilization, remote from and diffident towards the more restricted and closed atmosphere of national patriotisms, Cattaneo's teaching had few points of contact with the Italian democrats before 1848 and, in practical terms, added seriousness and prestige to that moderate ideology he so disliked.

Gioberti: the neo-guelph illusion

By the early 1840s the moderate writers had won the support of sectors of educated public opinion by their cultural patriotism and their social and economic proposals for gradual, peaceful change. But their strength derived as much from dissatisfaction with the plots and attempted insurrections of the democrats as from their own initiatives. These moderates comprised loosely-linked, regionally based groups, not a political party with a national political programme, as Mazzini had tried to create. It was Vincenzo Gioberti (1801-52) who gave them such a programme, around which they rapidly built the rudimentary structure of a party offering a concrete alternative to Mazzini and the democrats.

Gioberti presented his programme with spectacular (and, given the turgid language, surprising) success in his book *Of the Moral and Civil Primacy of Italians* (1843). The programme was not original. It derived its main ideas from the writings of many progressive Catholics concerned to reconcile religion with the cause of oppressed peoples and liberty, as well as from the traditional national-humanist cult of Italian cultural primacy. Indeed, in his deliberate rejection of the common heritage of European civilization in favour of a closed, autochthonous form of Italian primacy, in his identification of religion with the retrograde Papacy, in his contemptuous dismissal of the 'people' and his polemical attacks on writers such as Lamennais who were by now predominantly concerned with the relations between religion, liberty and the masses, Gioberti tended to express the most superficial and conservative aspects of European liberal Catholic and Italian literary-humanist thought of these decades.

Liberal Catholicism in Europe was one more facet of the disintegration of the Restoration from the 1820s. Descendants of the reaction against the Revolution and the religiosity of romanticism – like the ultramontane movement – the liberal Catholics rejected the reactionary ideological connotations of the alliance between Throne and Altar and the practical subordination of the national churches to the State. An antierastian* tendency, hostility

---

* According to the ideas of Erastus (a Swiss doctor of the period of the Wars of Religion), ecclesiastical power was subordinate to civil power.

towards State encroachments on the liberty of the Church, was the major common trait of this extremely heterogeneous grouping of Christian romantics who ranged from Catholics like Manzoni or Protestants like the Swiss Vinet, concerned with the revival of religious values on the individual level, to ecclesiastics like Sterck or laymen like Keble or Chalmers, preoccupied with the organization of the Church. In Protestant countries, religious revivalism led to the growth of sectarian movements and occasionally, as in Scotland, to the creation of free churches, independent of the State. In Catholic regions, reluctance to accept either the ecclesiastical hierarchy's subordination to the secular authorities or the Papacy's determined identification with the Restoration lay behind both the romantic search for a deeper individual religious morality and the explicit appeals for Catholicism to accept the legacies of the Revolution – liberalism and nationalism.

Lamennais, formerly the most persuasively articulate of the ultramontane writers, was equally influential in young clerical circles when he transferred his theocratic ideas in the late 1820s from support of the monarchy to the new cause of liberalism. The Belgian revolution, which witnessed the victory of a tactical union between the Malines Catholic party and the liberals on the basis of mutually acknowledged liberties and rights, confirmed him in his conviction that only through such an alliance could the Church win its freedom. The French liberal Catholic movement, centred on Lamennais, Lacordaire, Montalembert and Gerbet, won widespread interest and sympathy among Catholics in France, Belgium, Italy and even Germany, although the Münich group of Catholic romantics still tended to stress the conservative, anti-Enlightenment basis of their faith. But there was a basic ambiguity in the demand for the freedom of the Church. It could form part of a broader liberal programme – as in Lamennais' demands for freedom of education, the press, association and worship – and implicitly prepare for the total separation of Church and State. But it could equally represent a purely tactical utilization of part of the liberal philosophy – as by the Jesuits – to reinforce the Church's position within the state and confirm the authority of a centralized papacy.

The years of the Restoration had witnessed a total separation between the reconstruction of the 'official' Church and Catholic religious life. The liberal Catholics, in their attempts to achieve the freedom of the Church and a more genuine religious consciousness, were ultimately dependent upon the pope. Gregory XVI's encyclicals *Mirari vos* (1832) and *Singulari vos* (1834), condemning the errors of 'indifferentism' and particularly freedom of conscience and freedom of worship, enforced the silent submission of most Catholic liberals. Few were prepared to follow Lamennais in his later advocacy of a republican, socialist regeneration of the multitudes according to the teaching of the Gospels. In the following years a movement for liturgical and theological reform gathered strength among the younger clergy in

France and Germany. Among the liberal Catholic laity, looking to the successful example of the Belgian Church, obedience to the pope was reconciled with the desire to accept the beliefs of the new age by concentrating on the struggle for freedom of education from State control and the duties of charity towards the poor: popular education formed a common meeting ground for Catholics and liberals, while Ozanam's Society of St Vincent de Paul spread even more rapidly than Cottolengo's or Bosco's organizations.

But if education and charity represented the most visible activities of liberal Catholics in western Europe, Lamennais' linking of the liberty of religion with the liberty of peoples as aspects of the general struggle for freedom retained its influence among some of the young clergy and laity. The successful example of the Belgian Catholic party could not be denied, and even Gregory XVI had not condemned it. By the 1840s it was possible to point to the support of the local clergy for the Irish and Polish national causes.

In Italy, as we have seen, the leading moderates combined a deep Catholicism with patriotism. Here liberal Catholics had been concerned with a moral, cultural revival rather than with an explicitly political involvement, as in Belgium or France. Disputes about the relationship between religion and society remained on moral grounds: Rosmini or Capponi could assert the priority of an inner religiosity against the concerns of Tommaseo or Lambruschini for the social obligations of Catholics. There were few conscious meetings between Catholics and lay or anti-clerical liberals, except on an individual basis. But, equally, Italian liberal Catholics, by and large, maintained their separateness from the Jesuits and reactionary Catholic culture, avoiding such ambiguous alliances as between Montalembert and Veuillot in the French Catholic struggle for independent education. The small and heterogeneous groups of Italian liberal Catholics, based on Florence, Milan and Turin, could thus reconcile their religious beliefs and their patriotism by avoiding directly political discussions or embarrassing considerations of the position of the papacy. Their links, particularly those of the Tuscan moderates, with French liberal Catholics dated back to Lamennais' campaign within the Church and grew stronger by the 1840s through personal contacts with Ozanam and Rendu. The habitual ties with French culture and their sense of participating in a broader, European religious movement reinforced the beliefs of Italian Catholic liberals and encouraged the vague messianic hope in the emergence of a new Gregory VII who would renovate the Church and re-establish its prestige.

Gioberti, in exile at Brussels, was facilitated in his personal and cultural relations with Italian Catholics by this common feeling of belonging to a general European movement. A typical representative of Catholic romanticism of the Restoration years, with his belief in Christianity as a discipline necessary for the good of society rather than as an act of individual faith,

Gioberti, while court chaplain at Turin, had adapted his Christianity to a form of rational pantheism reconcilable with his early Mazzinian loyalties. Ironically, this Piedmontese priest, while sharing Mazzini's messianic faith in Italy's destiny, rejected the Genoese agitator's ultimate aim of the religious regeneration of humanity, reducing religion, in an almost calculating manner, as the means to a secular end, transforming Christianity into a moral philosophy cut to size for Italian culture:

> When religion is humiliated, deformed, faded in its splendour, vacillating, a degeneration of its native purity, unfit to gain the assent of intellects and the veneration of hearts, then – in order to conserve the idea of duty and keep alive its dominion – the moralist must prop up religion with reason and philosophy, that is to say with itself. (Gioberti, 293, vol. 1, p. 180)

Religion was to remain for Gioberti, as for the French restoration writers whose cultural influence he so angrily denied – De Maistre, Lamennais and the Saint-Simonians – a necessary component of peoples and society. But, unlike the Saint-Simonians or Mazzini, he rejected the concept of a new religion, relying on a renovation of the traditional institutional form of Catholicism.

After his exile from Piedmont (1833) and a short period in Paris – where he lived in isolation and cultivated a deep resentment of French claims of natural superiority, expressed particularly vocally in these years – Gioberti moved to Brussels, where he gradually (and polemically) elaborated his philosophy of the universal function of the Church as the repository of Christian principles. For the Church to maintain its civilizing mission in western culture it needed to accept the progressive civil ideas of the nineteenth century, and so give back to society a consciousness of its religiosity. Gioberti's debt to De Maistre and the Catholic legitimist writers in his interpretation of the historical mission of the Church, as to the recently liberal Lamennais in his vision of the alliance of religion and progress, needs little emphasis. Indeed, Gioberti was so conscious of the parallel between his own career and that of Lamennais that he engaged in violent attacks on Lamennais in the press of the French ultramontane party, displaying the contiguity of and the facile transition from politically orientated liberal Catholic thought to that of reactionary Catholic culture.

For Gioberti, more than for any other Italian writer, the alliance of religion and liberalism was inextricably linked to the Italian national problem. His hopes of a liberal papacy had developed out of his disillusion with the *Giovine Italia* over the Savoyard expedition of 1834. His break with Mazzinianism was not on moral or religious grounds, but because of its ineffectiveness: even if the invasion of Savoy succeeded in starting a revolution in Piedmont, he wrote to Mazzini, this would only provoke the intervention of the great powers. Gioberti prided himself on his political realism.

But this realism consisted of an anachronistic mixture of short-term political proposals which evaded consideration of the major obstacles to Italian independence and petty, pseudo-Machiavellian Jesuitical calculations which degraded the moral force of his ambitious and idealistic programmes. The conclusion he deduced from the failure of liberal revolutions and Mazzinian plots was that no reliance could be placed on the people or on insurrections, and that in consequence the only hope lay in reconciling the various groups of patriots in support of the princes: 'The princes are weak, cowardly, egoistic, soft, ignorant, contemptuous of virtue and glory; but at least they *exist*; whereas the Italian people is nothing but a voice, an abstraction' (Gioberti, 293, vol. 3, p. 161).

There was little that was new in this reversion to the *carbonaro* mentality of the revolutions of 1820–1 and 1831, except the appeal to the pope – which during the pontificate of Gregory XVI could only represent a pious illusion, a myth, as Gioberti himself soon called it. His manner of welding Christianity to patriotism reduced religion to a purely utilitarian weapon for political ends:

> Who cannot see how useful and effective would be this spring [of religion], if only there were people who knew how to utilize it to arouse the oppressed peoples and establish liberty, instead of relegating it and tampering with it, as did the philosophers of the last century, so leaving the field free for the super-stitious, the Jesuits, the tyrants to adopt it for their own benefit. (Omodeo, 296, pp. 39–40)

There was thus little that was original and much that was unrealistic or backward-looking in Gioberti's ideas. Nowhere was this more apparent than in his proposals to make the pope the saviour of Italian independence. This neo-guelph illusion, deeply embedded in the Italian literary-humanist tradition and based on the myth of the papacy's historical role as defender of the 'liberty of Italy', had begun to circulate with greater insistence with the Catholic romantic revival, despite the contrary evidence offered by successive popes. In these decades of an apocalyptic vision of politics and national missions, it had already become wedded to an assertion of Italian as against French primacy, which easily slipped – as with Gioberti – into a closed form of nationalism, hostile to the common heritage of European civilization, of which the more sensitive moderate intellectuals, as well as the democrats, were so conscious. As early as 1835, Pietro di Santarosa had expressed the central idea of the *Primacy of Italians* in a letter to Gioberti:

> I have not given up hope that in a distant future Italians should perhaps again become the apostles and founders, or restorers of civilization. I require two things for this; the first is absolutely indispensable, the other should follow easily from the first: that the Pope should make himself independent and give back to the Church its liberty and hence its natural dignity; in short, that a new

Gregory VII arise, as needed by the times; then we shall soon have the second thing, i.e. a second Saint Thomas Aquinas, who will teach the learned of the century not to blush when they confess themselves Christian. (Gioberti, 293, vol. 2, p. 238)

Gioberti's correspondence after the publication of the *Primato* reveals his unlimited ambition and his unwarranted belief in his political abilities. He saw himself as the new Saint Thomas, companion to that equally improbable new Gregory VII – Pius IX. But by the time he wrote these letters, Gioberti had already acquired his position as leader of the moderates.

The Primato

The publication of the *Primacy of Italians* in 1843 was undoubtedly a major success: the first 1500 copies were rapidly followed by reprints and Vieusseux proposed a popular edition of 5000 copies. As Balbo wrote to Gioberti: 'You arc now leader of a school' (Anzilotti, 297, p. 112). The *Primato* had been written explicitly with the intent of attracting moderate and clerical support: hence its omissions, as well as its propositions. Nothing was said about the problem of Austrian rule (although the work was dedicated to that martyr of Austrian repression, Silvio Pellico), nor about the reform of the administration of the Papal States. Gioberti's proposals were carefully formulated to assuage Catholic and moderate worries, offering a programme of national reconciliation to oppose the national revolutionary aims of the democrats. Reason and moderation were fused with a rhetorical idealization of Catholicism, practical political calculations with a vision of the redemption of Italy's mythical primacy. Unity was rejected as unhistorical: 'to suppose that Italy, divided for centuries, can peacefully be brought under the power of a single state is madness' (Gioberti, 292, vol. 1, p. 55). Only a federal union fitted Italy's traditions and development, as both the moderates and Cattaneo maintained. Municipal self-government was asserted against administrative centralization, following the arguments in defence of individual rights of French and Italian liberals and progressive Catholics since the 1820s. But power was to be retained in the hands of princes, aided but not restricted by 'elective aristocracies', an open class based on intelligence and experience. Gioberti had deliberately kept his brief discussion of internal government to the moderates' more limited proposals for reform, avoiding all suggestions of constitutional rights and restricting participation in this 'administrative monarchy' to 'the healthy and reasonable part of public opinion' (Gioberti, 292, vol. 1, p. 93).

But all these suggestions pale before Gioberti's main proposal: the assertion of Italian primacy, the freeing of the peninsula from French tutelage through the creation of an Italic confederation under its natural leader, the pope, aided by the military force of Piedmont. Rome and Piedmont were the particular house of Italian charity and strength. In as much as the union of Italy must be consecrated by religion as idea and protected by patriotic arms as fact, so it seems that it must start where faith and militia are mainly nursed, that is in the holy city and the warrior province. (Gioberti, 292, vol. 1, p. 114)

In this image of Italy's future path, the almost total absence of discussion of the nature of the reforms, particularly of economic reforms, was as significant as the refusal to suggest a solution to the Austrian presence in Italy. Detailed proposals might arouse dissent. Gioberti's aim was to reconcile all shades of moderate opinion by a clear and simple message, based upon rhetoric about Italy's great past and future rather than upon more realistic discussions of its place in the contemporary world. That he should have aroused such enthusiasm was revealing of the superficiality of the Italian educated classes, nurtured on literary humanist, Catholic romantic myths of grandeur.

By the time his book appeared, it is questionable whether Gioberti himself still believed in the neo-guelph myth he had created so successfully. Certainly his correspondence immediately after its appearance displays his predominating concern to explain the practical purpose for which he had written the *Primato*: he justified his deliberate silence over Austria and the secularization of papal administration by his desire to gain the widest possible circulation of his book in Italy and attract the broadest support. But this very silence implied acceptance, if not approval, of papal misgovernment and left progressive intellectuals suspicious that Gioberti was still tainted by identification with the ultramontanes with whom he had consorted in earlier years. While he had provided a programme for the Piedmontese moderates and attracted support among young Neapolitan priests, the Tuscan and central Italian moderates remained critical of his theocratic ideas. Partly to refute these accusations, but even more to exploit his popularity and extend and strengthen the movement he led, Gioberti now turned his violent and prolix polemic against the Jesuits.

By the 1840s the Jesuits, under their able general Father Roothaan, had become the spearhead of resistance to liberal ideas in Europe, supporters of the Restoration formula of 'throne and altar', violent opponents of such lay initiatives as nursery schools. Still excluded from Tuscany, parts of the Austrian empire and some German states, threatened by secularist and liberal trends in France, the Order had consolidated and extended its power and influence in the most absolutist and conformist Italian states – Piedmont, Naples, Modena and (naturally) the Papal States. Rashly, Jesuits took a leading part in the French Catholic party's attack on the State monopoly of education, provoking a violent anti-clerical offensive led by Michelet and Quinet and the demand for their expulsion from France. Guizot was under pressure from the opposition but reluctant to break with the Papacy. He sent Pellegrino Rossi, long a voluntary exile from the Papal States and now a French citizen, professor at the Sorbonne and member of the upper chamber, to negotiate at Rome the closure of most Jesuit houses in France (1845). By then the recall of Jesuits to the canton of Lucerne had led to increasing tension and clashes between Protestant liberals and Catholics in Switzerland and was soon to develop into the formation of the Catholic *Sonderbund* and its defiance of the Swiss Confederation.

The *Primato* had attracted even some Jesuits, such as the Neapolitan Father C. M. Curci and Massimo D'Azeglio's brother Father Luigi Taparelli, while some moderates maintained that liberals and Jesuits could be reconciled, as in Belgium. But in Piedmont, where Gioberti had aroused the greatest support, Jesuit power represented the major obstacle to reform. In his *Prolegomena to the Primacy* (1845), the five volumes of the *Modern Jesuit* (1846–7), and the *Apologia of the Book Entitled the Modern Jesuit* (1848), Gioberti launched a frontal attack on 'Jesuitism', by which he successfully separated himself from the ultramontanes and appealed to the lay or anti-clerical liberals. Reviving the eighteenth-century accusations against the Jesuits as a corrupting influence on true Catholicism, Gioberti tried to meet criticisms that the *Primato* encouraged clerical dominance by a deliberate appeal to the moderate groups and to Charles Albert as the leaders of Italian regeneration. The lay middle classes were the natural ruling class in Italy:

> the middle class expresses the idea and essence of the popular spirit, perfectly characterized and formed in the fullness of youth, for the most substantial, alive and industrious part of the nation is located in this class. . . . When an exceptional virtuous spirit arises in the privileged or vulgar classes, it is normally enticed and drawn powerfully towards that intermediate class in which the greatest social energy is gathered, and there it settles down sooner or later, becoming part of it, and correcting by choice the chance of birth or error of fortune. (Gioberti, 294, vol. 1, p. 26)

As always rapidly adapting his theories to the changing situation in Italy, Gioberti now tried to force the pace of reform, making an open appeal to Charles Albert to accept representative institutions and lead the struggle for the independence of Italy:

> The ruler who enters first into the national arena will be arbiter of opinion, he will be morally lord of Italy without others having the right to complain, and he will carry out the functions of head and arm of the headless and dismembered patria . . . he will be tribune of the people . . . delegate of the nation . . . dictator. (Gioberti, 294, vol. 1, pp. 108–9)

As tome after tome appeared, Gioberti adjusted his arguments to control and direct the ever broader sectors of opinion he had aroused. Balbo and the other moderate leaders were alarmed by his attacks on the Jesuits, which they saw as endangering his earlier success in reconciling 'Catholic

Christian with liberal opinions' (Omodeo, 295, p. 65). But if individual clergy and some lay moderates like Silvio Pellico withdrew and supported the Jesuit counter-offensive, Gioberti had accurately assessed the attraction of his new campaign for anti-clericals and even for some democrats like Lorenzo Valerio and Giuseppe Montanelli. Neo-guelphism now represented a national movement which offered an alternative to Mazzinian republicanism, based on a programme of gradual reforms in collaboration with the princes patriotically linked in a federation and socially responsive to the requests of educated opinion. By his denunciation of Neapolitan repression, Gioberti ably consolidated the Piedmontese moderates' claims for their leadership of the movement, while forcing them to adopt a more active attitude rather than wait upon favourable international circumstances. By his advocacy of a liberal papacy and his attack on the Jesuits, he broke the traditional alliance between clergy and absolutism which had dominated Italy since the Restoration.

For three years, from 1845 to 1848, neo-guelphism seized the initiative in Italy and, with the election of Pius IX, mobilized wider sectors of opinion than Mazzini had ever reached, eroding even the democratic ranks. But the very success of its programme, with its rhetorical assertion of Italy's primacy against France and its reliance on the princes, weakened the ties with Europe which both democrats and moderates had slowly forged and left Italy lagging behind the revolutionary forces which in these same years were developing strongly elsewhere on the Continent.

The years of moderate hopes

In these final years before the outbreak of the revolutions of 1848 a sense of the imminence and inevitability of change dominated Europe. Political opposition and economic crisis within all the major European states threatened the stability of international relations. Metternich, supported by the tsar Nicholas I, fought hard to check the growing pressure of liberalism and nationalism. In Galicia, in 1846, Metternich was even ready to tolerate the savage rising of Ruthenian peasants against their Polish noble landowners who had attempted an insurrection. Austria's prompt annexation of the republic of Cracow (1846), in agreement with Russia and Prussia, accentuated the differences between the absolutist and liberal powers.

With the worsening of relations between England and France over the Spanish marriages, Guizot and Louis Philippe had once more drawn closer to Austria. But if England seemed isolated, it remained the most powerful European state; and Palmerston, once more foreign secretary (July 1846) took an active part in challenging Metternich's assertion of absolutism. Palmerston publicly denounced the annexation of Cracow, warning that the settlement of Vienna 'constituted a single whole which, if not valid on the

Vistula, can be declared invalid on the Rhine or the Po' (Macartney, 192, p. 309). When Metternich and Guizot tried to support the Swiss *Sonderbund* in 1847, Palmerston successfully sabotaged the scheme. Guizot's attempts to mediate between the opposing forces, by urging administrative reforms on the absolutist Italian states through his representative Pellegrino Rossi, only aroused Austrian and Russian mistrust and hostility in France. Palmerston was worried about the friendly relations between Austria and Russia and France's approach towards the eastern empires, and preoccupied lest the rigidity of the absolutist states provoke revolution. He openly expressed support for national feeling and liberal opposition, even sending a Cabinet member, Lord Minto, to Italy on a much publicized visit to Turin and Rome (1847). As Palmerston told the Austrian ambassador Dietrichstein (ironically at the moment of Metternich's fall):

> Prince Metternich thinks he is a conservative, in clinging obstinately to the *status quo* in Europe; we think ourselves conservative in preaching and advising everywhere concessions, reforms, and improvements where public opinion demands them; you on the contrary refuse them. (Taylor, 299, p. 32)

Liberals, perhaps more in Italy than elsewhere in Europe, could justifiably think that the favourable international circumstances they had long evoked had at last arrived, although many now recognized that Metternich's ostentatious measures to conserve Austrian control implied war.

Liberal and national pressure within the European states also encouraged Italian hopes. In England free trade won its greatest triumph with Peel's abolition of the Corn Laws, under pressure from Cobden's Anti-Corn Law League and confronted by the tragic consequences of famine in Ireland (1846). The struggle for Irish independence proved a symbol for Italian liberals. In Ireland, national and Catholic sentiment had united under the strictly legal banner of O'Connell, even though the movement was endangered by both the massive emigration from Ireland with the famine and the emergence of alternative insurrectionary methods. O'Connell's death during a visit to Italy (May 1847) was commemorated by padre Ventura in an impassioned 'Funeral eulogy' at the church of S. Andrea della Valle in Rome.

In Belgium, the liberal victory in the 1847 elections was followed by an enlargement of the suffrage to satisfy the most discontented members of the lower middle classes. In France the economic crisis and increasing signs of corruption within the restricted ruling group made Guizot's reliance on purely material progress ever-more precarious. The liberal opposition groups united in a campaign for parliamentary and electoral reforms, while a democratic republican opposition headed by Ledru-Rollin, a socialist movement under Louis Blanc and the Catholic party under Montalembert threatened the government from both Left and Right. By late 1847 a 'banquet campaign' which spread from Paris to the provinces channelled the vast discontent into demands for major institutional reforms that threatened Louis Philippe's regime.

In Germany the intellectual liberal opposition of the Rhine provinces converged with that of the liberal Junkers of the East Prussian *Landtag* in the demand for constitutional government and reforms to end the arbitrariness of absolutist rule. Frederick William IV of Prussia decreed a mockery of a reform, summoning a purely consultative *Landtag* consisting of the deputies of the provincial Diets (February 1847). The effect was to radicalize the Prussian opposition. Italian liberals, suspicious of the Germanic temperament, were worried about the outcome. As Ilarione Petitti wrote:

> Balbo is content, *hoping* it foreshadows something better. I believe on the contrary that it will accelerate the Germanic revolution, which God forbid should be more successful than the others; because if these Germanic heads get excited, it's trouble. God help us! (Codignola, 302 p., 268)

In the Austrian empire, nationalist and liberal opposition became ever-more pressing. In 1847 the Hungarian opposition groups, ably led by the lawyer Kossuth, united in demanding radical reforms which ranged from a national ministry with control of finances, representation in local government for non-nobles, legal and religious equality and freedom of the press, to redemption of peasant servitudes and abolition of feudal ties on noble estates. Czech and Croat nationalism, the direct result of Slav resentment against their Magyar and German masters, rendered the government of the empire even more impotent.

To Italian moderates these rapid developments elsewhere in Europe in 1846-7 undoubtedly pointed to the growing success of the liberal claims. But, equally, the desperate effects for the masses of the economic crisis of 1846-7 and the growing evidence of republican and socialist opposition urged the Italian moderates, like liberals elsewhere, to press for reforms in agreement with the rulers, lest a social revolution break out. The consequences of the last terrible agrarian crisis in the history of modern western Europe, when the total destruction of the potato crop in 1846 was followed by a miserable grain harvest the following year, had been worsened by an industrial depression caused by excessive speculation and lack of credit, which multiplied unemployment. This crisis of overproduction led to multiple bankruptcies and closures, driving many traders and bankers into the moderate camp for the first time. More worrying for the liberals, economic distress also appeared to go hand in hand with extreme political movements. Chartism in Britain, socialism in France, the organized hostility of the craftsmen of the old centres of domestic industry like Lyons, the Silesian textile workers' rising, the outbursts of Luddism in Bohemia, lower Austria, Rome or Naples, were all aspects of the 'spectre of communism' which appeared so menacing to liberal eyes on the eve of the 1848 revolutions. Behind this seething discontent of the urban masses, which was so immediately linked to the precipitous, unregulated, development of capitalism, loomed the shapeless menace of peasant revolts in central Europe, as in southern Italy. The Galician rising made great landowners tremble throughout the Austrian empire. Concessions were needed before time ran out, political institutions had to be reconciled with economic and social change.

The moderate movement in Piedmont

The Piedmontese moderates were the most active in consolidating the initiative seized by Gioberti with his *Primato* and the attack on the Jesuits. In these years of intense publicist activities by the moderates, the writings which gained the widest diffusion in Italy were for the most part by Piedmontese: Cesare Balbo's *Of the Hopes of Italy* (1844), followed by his *Summary of the History of Italy* (1846), Massimo D'Azeglio's *The most Recent Events in Romagna* (1846) and his *Proposal for a Programme for Italian National Opinion* (1847), Ilarione Petitti's *Of Italian Railroads and their best Organization* (1845). Moderates from all regions of Italy (many still in exile) were publishing books and pamphlets on similar historical, literary, economic and political arguments. But the Piedmontese had unquestionably managed to establish their hegemony over the moderate movement by their successful identification of Piedmont with the cause of Italy. Despite 1821, despite the religious orthodoxy and political absolutism of the Sardinian monarchs, the loyalty to the dynasty of these mostly aristocratic moderates remained firm and unwavering. A comparable loyalty existed in only one other Italian state – Tuscany. But the fundamental difference between the two dynasties lay not only in the foreign origins of the Tuscan Habsburg-Lorraine family, but in its traditionally neutralist policies. The house of Savoy, by contrast, symbolized a secular policy of expansion, and for the Piedmontese moderates, whether Balbo or Gioberti, D'Azeglio or Durando, Petitti or Cavour, the extension of Savoyard rule was ambivalently linked to the independence of Italy.

The hopes of these moderates rested on Charles Albert, whose slow, grudging, partial conversion to their ideas seemed apparent, particularly after Pius IX had set the pace of reforms. Until Gregory XVI's death, Charles Albert had little need (or desire) to satisfy the moderates, as he had no rival in Italy. Despite his early administrative and economic reforms, Ferdinand II of Naples had failed to win the support of his subjects: his obsessive suspiciousness and consequent refusal to delegate power blocked the formation of a new ruling class; his driving preoccupation with material progress alienated the Neapolitan intellectuals, particularly open to currents

of romantic idealism in these years; his determined centralization consolidated Sicilian opposition. Sectarian activities, deeply rooted in the kingdom of
Naples as in the papal Romagna, obscured the differences between moderates
and democrats and led to sporadic rebellions, heavily repressed.

Leopold II of Tuscany, of complacent, passive temperament, utterly
reliant on his ministers Fossombroni and Corsini until their deaths (1844,
1845), concentrated on maintaining the traditions of the great Peter
Leopold. In part, he regained the sympathy of the Tuscan moderates in the
1840s by his jurisdictionalist resistance to papal pressure and his encouragement of the congresses of Italian scientists. But his antipathy towards military matters and his recognition that the survival of the Lorraine dynasty
was dependent upon Austrian dominance in Italy precluded him from any
role as national leader. Francis V of Modena's attitude is most easily
characterized by the popular verse which circulated in his duchy in 1847:

> Here things are sticky
> Radetzky* my dear,
> Brace up and forward
> With your grenadiers,
>
> These swine snouts
> Of a crackbrained people,
> It seems they're after
> Running me out,
>
> Just for following
> The dear old Daddo,
> Of tender memory,
> God rest his soul.
>
> So I keep order
> With cannon and mortar,
> With simple piety
> And the butcher's axe. (Mercuri and Tuzzi, 187, vol. 1, p. 79)

Charles Albert himself was hardly a figure to excite the progressives, at
least until the mid-1840s. His ambitions, until then, seemed to have concentrated on imposing a fanatical façade of piety on his states and leading a
crusade for military repression of anything he included in his extremely
broad category of revolution or subversion. His most congenial pastimes
were cutting out paper images of saints and playing with toy soldiers.
Dominated by a belief in his own heroic destiny, his favour towards the
Church perhaps masked his search for the finger of God in a never-ending
attempt to cull divine favour. But all contemporaries agreed about his
personal weakness, his inability to reach firm decisions or live up to his own

* Commander-in-chief of the Imperial forces.

ambitions. His former tutor Gerbaix de Sonnaz, who was probably as close to him as anyone, admitted his 'total absence of moral strength and firmness of character' (Omodeo, 206, p. 132). The savagery of his repression of the Mazzinians in 1833 was probably as much due to this weakness and political ineptness as to his personal predilection for oriental forms of despotism.

Charles Albert's policy was based upon an attempt to maintain his freedom of action and control by balancing reactionary with mildly progressive ministers, Solaro della Margarita with Pes di Villamarina. But his reforms were incoherent and contradictory, attempting to reconcile the restoration of the Napoleonic administrative systems with an intransigently legitimist, Jesuitical policy. The legal codes were modernized, but at the same time feudal primogenitures were confirmed and ecclesiastical courts reintroduced; feudal privileges were abolished in Sardinia, but ecclesiastical tithes were left; guilds were abolished as a hindrance to industrial development, but were allowed to survive for religious purposes. Federico Sclopis, a Catholic and opponent of Cavour over the Siccardi laws in 1855, later admitted the deeply negative influence exerted by the clergy and especially the Jesuits over Charles Albert's policies:

> Reason could certainly exercise its rights over any matter of legislation or the economic and civil administration of the state; but whenever it was a question of ecclesiastical affairs, most times that malignant [Jesuit] influence prevailed over the counsels of knowledgeable and courageous ministers . . . public opinion, which was easily listened to in so many other parts of the government of the state, could not gain a hearing in matters which touched an interest or prejudice of the clergy. (Omodeo, 206, pp. 78–9)

By 1840 Charles Albert's policies had failed. He had isolated Piedmont internationally through his legitimist foreign policy and was regarded internally with deep suspicion by all progressives. He had failed, as totally as Ferdinand of Naples, to gain the support of his country, and to outside observers even his cherished army, on which he had lavished money and reforms, was not so effective as Ferdinand's. Only his hesitant approach towards the moderates' proposals in the following years regained him popularity. His retreat from economic protectionism had attracted the moderates and – as they preached – had once more drawn him closer to Great Britain. But it was his adoption of the neo-guelph programme that really aroused hopes. Characteristically, the king took Gioberti too literally, mistaking utopia for reality: at last, he could reconcile his Catholicism with his destiny as the hero of Italy. The famous interview granted to Massimo D'Azeglio late in 1845 symbolized this meeting between the Piedmontese moderates and the Savoyard ruler, a meeting full of diffidence and ambiguities on both sides. Charles Albert urged a doubtful D'Azeglio to assure the Romagnol patriots that 'my life, the life of my children, my arms, my treasure, my army, all will be spent for the Italian cause' (D'Azeglio, 303, p. 555).

The revival of Piedmont's traditional anti-Austrian policy presented few problems for either side, and Charles Albert rapidly won support in the country by his deliberate resistance to Austria over the Lombard imposition of heavy customs duties on Piedmontese wines (1846) and by his attempt to act as defender of Italian liberty when the Austrians occupied Ferrara (July 1847). But his reluctance to concede the internal reforms demanded by the moderates or to adopt too close a relationship with the other Italian rulers remained firm and left the liberals uncertain and mistrustful. He was only forced towards these reforms by Pius IX's rapid changes. Even then, as Petitti wrote pessimistically late in 1846, referring to Charles Albert's repressive role in 1833: 'It is clear that the pope's liberalism, excellent in itself, frightens some who are stained with the blood of patriots' (Omodeo, 206, p. 82).

Pius IX

The unexpectedly rapid election as pope of cardinal Mastai-Ferretti (16 June 1846), barely two weeks after the long-awaited death of the octo-genarian Gregory XVI, precipitated the movement towards reform. As public pressure built up over the following eighteen months, the moderates partially lost control over the very forces they had invoked and were unable to prevent the outbreak of the revolution they had so consistently opposed. For the accession of Pius IX set off an explosion of excitement and discontent, inextricably mixed with the patriotism which both moderates and Mazzinians had insistently propagated in the previous fifteen years.

The new pope's assumption of the name Pius, in homage to the persecuted Pius VII who had received him twice while he was studying for the priesthood, indicated his desire to assert the papacy's independence from foreign interference. Genuinely religious, with a firm faith in charity, of open character, susceptible to public expressions of popularity, this descendant of a minor noble family of Senigallia had spent the past twenty years as bishop in the Romagna, where he had witnessed the seething discontent and had made friends with a local moderate noble, Count Giuseppe Pasolini. Whether or not he had read Gioberti, D'Azeglio or Balbo, as legend has it, he was certainly influenced by Giobertian ideas and could not but be aware of the need for reform of the papal administration.

The last insurrection, which had momentarily led to the seizure of Rimini in September 1845, although democratically instigated, had resulted in a 'Manifesto of the peoples of the Roman State', which voiced moderate proposals inspired by Mamiani's ideas and the memorandum of the great powers of 1831: political amnesty, modern legal codes, secularization of administration and education, election of local government organs, a Council of State with control over finances, civic guards, relaxation of censorship. At the moment of the conclave local moderate leaders, such as Minghetti and Pepoli, had organized petitions with some thousands of signatures from Bologna, Forlì, Ravenna, Ferrara. Disaffection was universal and had spread even among the artisans and populace of the Trastevere, the traditionally loyal quarter of Rome. In the Legations the cardinal-legate Massimo wrote hysterically in 1845 of:

> the licentiousness of every age, every class of person . . . *the coalitions which extend without end from the patrician down to the apprentice of the obscure workshop, unite interests, connections and money*, always for purposes of crime and delinquency, and *against the Government.* . . . For the moment it is enough to say that, except for *the old, the women and the adolescents of the city*, and a *very small* part of the agricultural class, not yet wholly corrupted, *the rest of the population from 18 years upwards, except for very few, frightened legitimists, is on principle totally hostile to the government.* (Demarco, 216, pp. 267–8)

Behind the demands for ever-more specific administrative and economic reforms, the pressure of the mass of the population for social change was dangerously near the surface.

Pius IX's reforms and the moderates' campaign represented separate and ultimately contradictory attempts to channel this pressure into controllable paths. While accepting the need for some reforms, and ready to enjoy the wave of patriotic enthusiasm which followed his election, Pius was reluctant to admit the lay moderate leaders into papal government, lest they compromise the spiritual standing of the Church through their identification of the pope with the national liberal cause. He was wholly opposed to constitutional concessions which might violate the papacy's traditional policy of absolute neutrality. At most he was prepared to accept the aims of the liberal cleric, monsignor Corboli-Bussi to 'take over control of national sentiments, as of the sentiment for internal reforms, in order to utilize both in favour of the established order' (Anzilotti, 297, p. 209). But, entrapped by his mythical image of the 'liberal pope', created by the moderates and accepted by the Mazzinians, increasingly worried by the threatening pressure of public demonstrations, Pius IX was reluctantly forced into a series of concessions which regularly arrived too late to requite the growing demands of public opinion.

The political amnesty (16 July 1846) and the nomination of the liberal cardinal Gizzi as secretary of state were only followed after some months and a silent demonstration, on 4 November, by the appointment of commissions, including lay members, to revise legal procedures and study measures against vagabondage and for the provision of education, work and the building of a railway. With equal tardiness a cautious relaxation of censorship was only granted on 15 March 1847, the proposal to nominate a consultative assembly was only announced on 19 April, the creation of a Council of Ministers on 12 June (and then with only one lay member), the creation of a civic guard at Rome with a promise of similar bodies for the provincial cities on 5 July. After Gizzi's resignation and a violent clash at Rome, which the liberals regarded as a reactionary plot, negotiations for a customs league with Florence and Turin were only begun late in August and concluded on 3 November 1847, after Pius' explicit refusal of a political alliance. When the consultative assembly was finally convened on 15 November Pius warned it 'not to detract minimally from the sovereignty of the pontificate' ('Diario di Roma', 16 Novembre 1847). When the central administration was restructured on 23 December, all the new ministers were clerics. Disorder had broken out in the provinces already in 1846. By mid-1847 Pius IX had lost control and was rapidly losing popularity.

By then the pope's example and the moderates' campaign had forced the rulers of Tuscany and Piedmont to make similar concessions. Already in February 1846 Giuseppe Montanelli, a moderately democratic professor at Pisa now converted to neo-guelphism, had successfully organized public opposition against the establishment at Pisa of the sisters of the Sacred Heart, notoriously linked to the Jesuits. Tuscany, and especially Leghorn, had remained the major centre of democratic groups, with a strong current of socialist and egalitarian ideas, the legacy of Saint-Simonian groups and Buonarroti's 'True Italians'; a secret society proposing communist ideas was discovered in November 1846. The dangers of socialist propaganda undoubtedly worried the Tuscan moderates, who had even been prepared to unite with the demagogic democrat leader Guerrazzi to isolate the most dangerous critic, Enrico Montazio. The moderates, in fact, in Tuscany as in Piedmont and the Papal States, were divided over the extent to which they should encourage popular support in order to put pressure on the rulers. In Tuscany the example of the neighbouring Papal States and the success of the clandestine press (both moderate and democratic) in exciting public opinion led to a split among the moderates early in 1847: Salvagnoli, Ricasoli and Lambruschini refused to accept the passive trust in the prince of Capponi, Ridolfi and Galeotti. In May 1847 public pressure, supported by Ricasoli and Salvagnoli, gained the partial abolition of censorship. In August–September, after demonstrations and clashes in many cities, the consultative assembly was enlarged and a civic guard formed. On 28 September Leopold II, worried about the continued agitations at Leghorn, entrusted the government to the more conservative liberals under Ridolfi in an attempt to avoid the growing demands for a constitution.

Moderate leadership and democratic pressure

The papal and Tuscan developments revealed the difficulties the moderates experienced in maintaining control of a situation they had themselves created. The spontaneous demonstrations of enthusiasm for Pius IX had rapidly become organized, in Tuscany and Piedmont as well, as a means of exerting pressure for reforms. But the moderates had no means of preventing democratic infiltration of these demonstrations. At Rome in particular the active participation of craftsmen and shopkeepers was organized by former *carbonari* and Mazzinians, now partially converted to neo-guelphism: the wholesale merchant Ciceruacchio, the doctor Pietro Sterbini, the lawyer Filippo Meucci.

Mazzini, only too well aware of the strength of neo-guelphism, had welcomed Pius' amnesty as a means of reviving his organization in Italy. He encouraged his followers secretly to create 'a chain of new men, to spread our word from one point to another, wherever necessary' (Mazzini, 257, vol. 30, p. 157). Scornful of the moderates, but increasingly worried that concessions by the princes would strengthen a federal solution, he urged his supporters not to stress their republicanism but to push public opinion in a national direction and incite Austria to intervene so as to discredit the moderates and regain the initiative. As he wrote on 29 September 1846:

> The tactics to be adopted are these: without revealing vexation or hostility, to push expectations of the Pope to the limit, use Austria as the cause of his inaction, cautiously introduce as much of a national political character as possible into demonstrations of enthusiasm, act so that Austria becomes ever more worried, sends notes, makes demands, in order that the Pope, by withdrawing, clearly displays his impotence, and that spirits are prepared for a violent, and hence national, reaction against Austria. (Mazzini, 257, vol. 30, pp. 193–4)

As the princes reluctantly moved forward, Mazzini's worry about losing the initiative, and hence his activities, increased. He threw himself into frantic attempts to unify all the Italian exiles in an organization with Polish and other European democrats in order to strengthen democratic feeling in Italy. But even more he urged his followers in Italy to provoke Austrian intervention and so smash the moderates' deceitful claim that federalism could achieve reforms and free Italy without war. By September 1847 he was ready to abandon republicanism temporarily for the overriding cause of unity:

> Republicanism matters very little for the moment: much, indeed everything, depends on Unity: today the only enemy we have is Federalism. Let them give us a pope, one king alone, a dictator: we shall have time to come to terms about the rest: we cannot come to terms with Federalism. (Salvemini, 116, p. 258)

It is impossible to estimate how many followers Mazzini had in this period. But there can be little doubt that democratic and popular pressure, able to give vent in the demonstrations to the discontent created by the economic crisis, forced the moderates to move more rapidly than many wished. While agreed on specific economic and administrative reforms, the moderates differed over openly political changes and over the attitude to adopt towards public pressure. Until they had the opportunity to put their proposals into practice – until Pius IX's election – these differences had retained a rather abstract air – as for instance in the 1845-6 discussions about the reform of the Papal States, following D'Azeglio's pamphlet: Galeotti proposed a constitutional reform along the lines of Gianni's pre-revolutionary Tuscan scheme, while Torelli regarded the papacy's temporal power as unreformable and proposed its abolition. But from mid-1846 the stresses threatening a uniform programme became increasingly apparent. The awareness of belonging to a single group was overt: D'Azeglio circulated the manuscript of both his Romagna pamphlet and his *Proposal for a Programme for Italian National Opinion* among the leading moderates in Turin, Florence, Pisa, Bologna and Rome. The very title of the latter pamphlet reflected the moderates' claim to represent national opinion. As D'Azeglio wrote to Minghetti from Rome during its preparation:

> We meet every week to talk, discuss and fix our ideas about events. We have also thought it useful to prepare a programme for our party, in which we put forward our opinions, means and aims. It will serve to fix ideas in Italy and abroad, to show that we are not always talking in abstractions or poetry or secret societies. (Minghetti, 325, vol. 1, p. 263)

But by the time the *Proposal* appeared in summer 1847, it was already out of date, although it included demands for popularly elected local administrations and a uniform military system, along with legal reforms, less censorship, uniform moneys and weights, abolition of customs and a single railway system. Pressure over censorship, the civic guard and consultative assemblies, now began to build up over the introduction of constitutions. Even more, Austrian threats, culminating in July 1847 in the occupation of Ferrara (over whose citadel Austria possessed garrison rights through the treaty of Vienna), made war seem ever more likely, so threatening the very philosophy of the moderate programme. Balbo in Turin, like Capponi and Ridolfi in Florence and Pellegrino Rossi in Rome, represented the conservative wing of the moderates, increasingly worried by the way events were precipitating and war-threatening. Other moderates in the reforming states, and even in Austrian Lombardy-Venetia – such as Cavour, Ricasoli, Casati, Manin – were more confident that public support represented no threat and some even saw in it a unique opportunity to free Italy. For them, public pressure remained the most effective means of forcing the reluctant princes to commit themselves.

Nowhere was this more apparent than in Piedmont. For a year after Pius' election, Charles Albert stuck rigidly to his attempt to keep anti-

Austrian patriotism separate from the demand for reforms. Solaro della Margarita, who had visited Rome in August 1846, fought hard, with the support of much of the aristocracy, bureaucracy, army officers and clergy, to check the growing influence of the liberals. But as the pope and grand-duke granted reforms, pressure mounted in Piedmont. By 1847 Gioberti from Brussels was advising the leading moderates – Petitti, Santarosa, Boncompagni, Balbo – on the tactics to follow: win over Charles Albert and obtain the dismissal of Solaro, gain English benevolence by pointing to the economic advantages of a free Italy. But despite Lord Minto's encouraging presence at Turin, Charles Albert's hesitations left the liberals with a sense of impotence.

The liberal programme of economic and administrative reforms, now absorbed into Giobertian visions of Piedmontese expansion at Austrian expense, had made deep inroads among the Piedmontese landowners and urban middle classes. At Genoa the economic boom of 1846–7, which marked the end of a long period of stagnation, had brought home to the merchants an awareness of the structural changes in the city's economy, which now depended predominantly on exports to the neighbouring Italian states. In the island of Sardinia the weak groups of middle-class liberals wanted administrative and legislative unification with the mainland provinces in order to increase their autonomy from feudal and clerical dominance. But class divisions in Piedmont remained deep. Many professional men and clerks, particularly in the provincial cities, resented the aristocratic dominance of society and were attracted by democratic ideas of a more advanced form of liberalism: Valerio, Brofferio, Lanza opposed the moderate leadership and even among the liberals the progressive wing – Cavour, Pinelli, Castelli – exerted constant pressure on the more cautious leaders like Balbo. In the Agrarian Association, whose two thousand members had done much to spread ideas of reform, these divisions led to open hostility between the opposing groups, which rapidly became identified with class factions. Contemporaries were only too aware of these differences, which were due to the 'dislike which is beginning to come to a head among us, the bourgeoisie, against the nobility' (Romeo, 199, p. 77). Charles Albert was forced to intervene to settle a dispute between the two groups in the Agrarian Association in 1846 and, following his normal policy of balancing opposing tendencies, supported the Valerio faction against the nobles, led by Cavour. For these aristocratic moderates, only Charles Albert's commitment to reforms could unite the country.

Until autumn 1847 Charles Albert tried to divert liberal pressure by his openly anti-Austrian attitude. He ostentatiously backed the pope when the Austrians occupied Ferrara, but – lacking the support of Britain and France, the 'liberal' western powers, because of their differences – found himself isolated when Pius limited his opposition to verbal protests. He informed a congress of the Agrarian Association of his readiness to lead a war of independence. He proposed an anti-Austrian alliance to the papacy, which Pius rejected. But he firmly refused reforms. By early October the moderates were becoming desperate, as agitations seemed likely to strengthen the democratic opposition. Even the dismissal of Solaro (11 October) brought little hope, as Charles Albert balanced it by the elimination of Villamarina and the appointment of uncommitted ministers. Domenico Carbone's popular verse, 'The King of Swings', began to circulate widely:

In *diebus illibus*, in Italian lands
An old great parchment tells it all,
A King was so maddened by his nurse's milk
That he passed his days in swaying on swings.
A rare case, I'd say, among Kings.
So what did they call him? King Swing the First.

Biagio pushed first, Martino then,
One pushed fast, the other slow,
And slow or fast the King crowed out,
Bravo Biagio, Martino bravo.

Swing there, swing here, what a delicate thing
To dandle-O, dandle-O in the lap of a swing:
Faster – a little – less now – now more,
Sway there, sway here, sway up, sway down.
(Mercuri and Tuzzi, 187, vol. 1, p. 57)

It needed ever-more threatening demonstrations and the news from Naples (where a rising at Reggio and Messina had been suppressed but where the situation remained explosive) for Charles Albert finally to give way and grant a series of administrative reforms (29 October). The most important were elected communal councils, provincial councils nominated from lists prepared by the communal councils, an enlarged Council of State, and some limitations on the powers of the police and press censors. But the privileged ecclesiastical courts remained. Piedmont was still behind the other reforming states and Charles Albert's tardy concessions only aroused further agitations for more substantial reforms. By their dependence on the prince, the more conservative moderates had been caught in a trap of their own making. Democratic opposition was making itself heard.

By the end of 1847 tension had risen throughout Italy. The danger of war loomed ever closer as Metternich gave unmistakable signs of his determination to check the tide of liberalism. In early September the Milan police had attacked a peaceful demonstration. In October one of Metternich's most trusted collaborators, Ficquelmont, formerly ambassador at Naples, was sent to Milan. With Pellegrino Rossi at Rome and Lord Minto travelling between Turin, Rome and Naples, Austria, France and England displayed their concern with the Italian situation. In October–November, war – and Austrian intervention – seemed likely over a frontier dispute between Tuscany and Modena following on the cession to Tuscany of his state by the indebted duke of Lucca.

This typically and anachronistically dynastic dispute proved threatening only because it revealed the hostility which now divided Italy between reforming and absolutist states. The division of Italy was marked all the more clearly by the signing of the customs league between the Papal States, Tuscany and Piedmont (3 November). While Parma remained separate (with the death of the aged duchess in December 1847 the state reverted to the former duke of Lucca, Charles Ludovic), the rulers of the Two Sicilies and Modena were determined to resist all concessions and looked to Austria for support. But Giobertism and the reforms had aroused the hopes of the opposition in these states, too. The inability to express this opposition in legal form encouraged secret preparations for a rising in both Naples and Sicily, in which the distinctions between moderates and democrats were blurred by their common hostility to Austria and their determination to obtain a constitution.

In Lombardy, the inevitable battleground of a war against Austria, the physiognomy of the moderate and democratic groups was becoming more distinct. The noble moderates, led by Gabrio Casati, Vitaliano Borromeo and Cesare Giulini, turned to Piedmont, as had their predecessors in 1821. Indeed, the dying Federico Confalonieri reminded them: 'if we can hope for safety from anyone, it is from Piedmont and Charles Albert' (Salvemini, 116, p. 48, n. 71). Worried by the Galician massacres, these noble landowners had actively organized charity for the peasants during the famine of 1847, winning their support and that of many country priests against the Austrians. The democrats, led by Cernuschi, Terzaghi and Maestri, and acknowledging Cattaneo as their master, violently opposed Piedmont as a backward, confessional state but were not prepared to sacrifice Lombard civil progress in the cause of Mazzinian unity. The strength of these democrats lay among the Milanese craftsmen and middle class and, as in the reforming states, attracted some of the more independent intellectuals, such as Correnti, while exerting increasing pressure on the moderates.

Within the reforming states, the slowness and evident reluctance of the rulers to grant concessions strengthened the democrats and more radical moderates. The prospect of war worried many moderates, while Charles Albert's open hopes of expansion revived the traditional mistrust of Piedmont. If neo-guelph enthusiasm allowed the moderates to maintain their hegemony and so blunt the revolutionary drive developing elsewhere in Europe, there was nevertheless a growing feeling of losing control of the situation. In Piedmont the radicals felt no fear of invoking popular support; at Genoa Giorgio Doria's 'Society of Order' openly appealed for such collaboration by its demand for a reduction of the salt-tax. In the Papal States democratic agitations converged with popular demands for substantial economic and social reforms. In Tuscany some democrats were making an open challenge to the moderates' initiative. Indeed, it was in Tuscany that the moderate philosophy was most clearly refuted by isolated, but influential extreme democrats like Montazio who denounced 'certain fabricators of articles and pamphlets dedicated, as they say, to the instruction and education of youth and the people . . . certain impassioned speculators of savings banks, nursery rooms, popular schools of foreign stamp' (Ronchi, 320, pp. 107-8). 'The people do not want your alms, you aristocratic cads masked as plebeians', wrote Niccolini (Ronchi, 320, p. 108, n. 51). Here socialist undertones coloured the democratic critique of the moderates.

Until the actual outbreak of the revolutions, Mazzini's tactics of encouraging popular support for the reforming movement, while attempting to turn it into a unitarian war against Austria which would regain the initiative for the democrats, undoubtedly assisted the moderates. But this unwanted support and the pressure of the non-Mazzinian democrats turned these moderates into hostages of fate, forced to move ever faster along paths which were increasingly removed from their original itinerary. Their economic proposals almost vanished from sight as political demands came to the fore. Popular pressure had become too strong. It revealed the contradictions which accompanied the confusing superimposition of the Giobertian on the moderate programme: peaceful internal reforms within the separate states could not be reconciled with a united (albeit federal) war against Austria. These contradictions were to be revealed in full in the following months.

Part 5
The cost of independence 1848–61

The 1815 settlement of Europe was shaken to its foundations by the revolutions of 1848–9 and definitively destroyed by the unifications of Italy and Germany in 1861–70. In Germany the revolutions immediately revealed a profound conflict between liberal values and the urge towards national independence and power, which prepared the ground for the sacrifice of liberalism by Bismarck's triumphantly militaristic concept of unification. In Italy no such open clash occurred between the liberal creed and the struggle for national independence: the unification of Italy was achieved by, and confirmed the survival of, a liberal democracy, however fragile its structure, however limited its base.

Fundamental among the reasons which explain the differences in the process of formation of these two new states was the strength of the democratic initiative in Italy. By imposing themselves on the latter phase of the revolutions, after the failure of the moderates, the democrats aroused a spirit of patriotism, which – if still not touching the vast mass of the peasantry – penetrated widely among the literate classes and the urban workers. That monarchical Piedmont was able to exploit this situation in the famous *decennio* was due to the radical transformation of the international scene and to the capacity of the most sensitive and technically equipped liberal leader, Cavour, to learn from the lessons of the revolutions. The new fluidity of international relations, which resulted from the breakdown of the Concert of Europe, permitted the development of national initiatives, even by war, provided they remained confined within the bounds of international diplomacy and so avoided the dangers of uncontrollable revolutionary conflagrations. Cavour's determined enactment of the liberal programme of reforms offered an effective, modern alternative to the democratic initiative, and ultimately succeeded in diplomatizing the democratic revolutionary drive for unity. This fortunate coincidence of international and national developments and this antagonism between democrats and moderates resulted in the – unexpected – unification of Italy. The new Italy emerged out of the basic conflict of the opposing patriotic forces and the personal hostility of their leaders, not out of what traditional historiography was long inclined to interpret as the complementary and implicitly harmonious roles of the four 'heroic' leaders – Victor Emanuel, Cavour, Garibaldi and Mazzini – walking arm-in-arm towards a preordained unified state.

The accomplishment of unification, at the same time as independence, was achieved only at considerable cost. The growing concentration of both democratic and moderate leaders upon purely political change deflected attention away from the social, economic, administrative problems accompanying and consequent upon the creation of a new state. Among the democrats, Mazzini's insistence upon unification rendered impotent the criticisms of a Cattaneo or a Pisacane; among the liberals, even Cavour increasingly subordinated his economic-administrative reforms to the overriding demands, first of political independence, then of unification. The economic-social preoccupations of earlier years were poured into an exclusive mould of patriotic fervour, exemplified in its purest form by the heroic figure of Garibaldi, at its most mundane by La Farina. As the drive for independence was transmuted into the belief in the possibility of unification, national patriotism and liberal ideals began to draw apart: new demands arose for a 'strong state'. Liberalism and patriotism were not yet in open conflict, as in Germany. But the cost of their separation was to be revealed, after the successful end of the struggle for independence and unification, in the overwhelming problems confronting the new Kingdom of Italy.

14

The contradictions
of revolution : 1848–9

Le printemps des peuples

Expectation of revolution was widespread in Europe by 1848. Democratic
and socialist spokesmen had long preached revolution, liberal critics and
absolutist statesmen feared it. Italian and Polish patriots felt their moment
had come, Metternich combated their efforts by diplomatic measures to
win the support of Guizot and tsar Nicholas.

Yet the revolutions, when they broke out, took everyone by surprise.
Metternich had been prepared for trouble almost anywhere in Italy except in
the Two Sicilies. The Palermo rising (12 January 1848), even when it
spread to the mainland and led to Ferdinand's unexpected capitulation,
nevertheless remained a local affair, without significant repercussions outside Italy. It was the revolt of Paris (22–4 February) which set off a chain
reaction, as in 1830, but this time on a far wider scale. Within weeks demonstrations and the threat of revolution had led to the concession of constitutional government in western Germany – Baden, Hesse-Darmstadt, Nassau,
Frankfurt, Württemberg, Brunswick, Thuringia – a region geographically
close to France and radically influenced by the years of Napoleonic rule; the
absolutist rulers of Piedmont and the papacy, like the oligarchic regimes of
the Hanseatic cities, were forced to follow suit. With the startling collapse
of absolutism at Vienna (13 March) and Berlin (18 March), the revolution
spread like wildfire throughout the Continent to the borders of Russia and
for a moment – with the preparations for a mammoth Chartist demonstration (10 April) – seemed likely to be blown across the Channel. Risings in
the Prussian cities were followed by bloodless revolutions in Saxony,
Hanover and all the central German monarchies, as well as in the Danish
duchies of Schleswig-Holstein; Milan, Venice, Prague and Budapest simul-
taneously shook off the centralizing bonds of Vienna; Poznan prepared to
launch a war of liberation against Russia. By the beginning of April revolution appeared triumphantly and definitvely to have smashed the restoration.

The very rapidity of the spread of revolution confirmed suspicions of a prepared and co-ordinated plot. But despite the distinguished ancestry of theories of conspiracy (dating back at least to Barruel's explanation of the French Revolution) the railways, telegraph and improved postal services offered a more convincing explanation. Revolution spread by imitation, not by plan. The immediacy of its success was indicative of the internal weaknesses of the absolutist regimes and the widespread discontent rather than of conspiratorial organization. The rulers at Vienna and Paris, Berlin and Rome, had already lost their self-confidence in the preceding years and now accepted their defeat without resistance. Whatever their differences, Guizot and Metternich agreed that their time was over, when they met in exile on the steps of the British Museum. This defeatism of the governments ensured the victory of the standard insurrectionary techniques: barricades in the narrow, tortuous streets of the capital to keep the garrison troops in small isolated groups, seizure of the palace or town hall, hoisting of the tricolour and proclamation of a provisional government or exaction of a constitution. Beyond this initial stage of insurrection – itself based on memories of the past and the example of Paris – the revolutionaries shared certain common beliefs, developed in the public discussions and secret intrigues of the previous decades, but displayed little capacity to co-ordinate or reconcile their often contradictory programmes even within their national boundaries, let alone at a supranational level.

The revolutions, in fact, had taken the enemies of absolutism as much by surprise as its exponents. The spectacularly fast diffusion of revolution bore witness to deeper social causes than the plots and programmes of the middle-class democrats and liberals. The strength of the risings in Palermo, Paris, Vienna, Milan and Berlin, was based in good part upon the craftsmen and workers, concerned about the sharp rise in unemployment through the introduction of machines and the economic crisis rather than about nationalism or liberalism. The peasants, whether in southern Italy, Lombardy, the Austrian empire or Germany, were determined to obtain diminution of taxes, abolition of feudal dues and labour services and legal tenure of the lands they cultivated.

But both urban workers and peasants were regarded with distrust and fear by the revolutionary 'activists'. In Italy and Germany the peasants were ignored or repressed; in the Austrian empire, memories of the recent Galician massacres urged on both opposition and government to free the peasants of their feudal ties and grant them their lands. In cities such as Paris and Vienna, where the 'proletariat' could not be ignored– especially as it frequently formed a common front with university students – some initial measures were taken, such as the creation of national workshops to offer employment or workers' trade unions. But as socialism developed rapidly with the revolution in France and Germany, the fears of the liberals and of many democrats increased. The attempted coup of 15 May, in which

Barbès and Blanqui played a significant part, provoked the purge of the Parisian workshops and the bloody suppression of the workers by Cavaignac and the republican government (22–6 June); a 'general congress of workers' at Frankfurt, set up against a rival 'social parliament' of craftsmen demanding a return to the guild system, led to the repression of popular agitation in Berlin, Silesia, Frankfurt and west Germany (June–September); in Vienna the workers were put down when they resisted a cut in wages for public works (23 August). Almost everywhere workmen were excluded from the national guards which were set up to protect person and property. Even in October 1848, when nationalist radicals were fighting alongside the Viennese proletariat for the survival of the revolution against Windischgraetz's army, Smolka, the president of the Austrian parliament, felt the need to praise the workers for not looting the city. Except among minute groups of socialists, under leaders such as Louis Blanc or Marx, the habitual fear of a breakdown of social order accompanied the political revolutions of 1848. The 'spectre of communism', as Marx was soon to describe it, was deliberately exaggerated and exploited by reactionaries and Jesuits in order to discredit the national risings.

The example of France was crucial in influencing the European liberals in their attitude towards the social threat. Despite Mazzini's philosophy of individual national missions or Gioberti's xenophobic glorification of Italian primacy, France had retained its cultural leadership and position as the repository of the revolutionary tradition. Opposition on the Continent to the existing structure of power, whether liberal, democratic or socialist, had been constantly and deeply influenced by the French opponents of Louis Philippe. It had needed the Paris February revolution to spark off the revolutions throughout the Continent. It needed the June Days for the moderate leaders, of similar social stock and intellectual attitudes, to take courage and put down the expressions of social unrest.

Yet the revolutionary forces in France, and in consequence the course of the revolution there, retained a distinctive physiognomy, separate from elsewhere on the Continent. France had long existed as an independent, unified nation; a form of constitutional government, however moderate, had prevailed since the Revolution of 1830; the experiences of the Revolution and Napoleon had left an indelible imprint, a belief in, an almost religious cult of, the possibilities of grandiose change, a 'mental disease', as the practical, materialistically minded Guizot described it. The revolution in France had already advanced beyond the point to which the revolutionaries aspired in the other countries in 1848. The February revolution, as Tocqueville saw, was not a political struggle but a class war; in the June Days the war was won by the bourgeoisie. All that was left of the revolution, on the polital level, was the assertion, with the republic, of universal suffrage and the sovereignty of the people; and these too were soon to be distorted, repeating the classic experience of the first revolution in accelerated form, with the plebiscitary republic of Louis Napoleon (19 December 1848).

Elsewhere on the Continent the liberals seized the opportunity offered them by the popular risings to press for parliamentary government and political and civil liberties. At first this initiative seemed successful: the revolutions appeared to have given the necessary drive to fulfil the liberal campaigns of the previous years. As in Italy – Sicily, Naples, the Papal States, Tuscany, Piedmont – so in Germany and the Austrian empire, constitutional assemblies were demanded and usually accepted in a host of large, small and petty states. Thus, 1848 witnessed the development towards more modern forms of constitutionalism: from representation by estates or economic interests to representation of individuals. In Germany, Hungary and the 'Austrian' Lands, popular pressure led to the erosion and virtual abandonment of proposals to modernize the traditional system of estates by increased representation for the third estate; in Italy moderate liberals, such as Petitti or Pellegrino Rossi, were forced to give up their schemes for representation of interests or 'pure' constitutional forms. Regular periodic parliamentary meetings and control of taxation, the classic liberal demands, seemed to have been accepted. In many states the radicals and democrats, appealing to the masses for support, obtained universal suffrage. In Germany and Austria they accompanied liberal with national demands and gained constituent assemblies in April–May, an achievement to which Italian democrats aspired unsuccessfully in later months.

Liberalism and nationalism thus seemed to go hand in hand in this 'printemps des peuples'. But, outside France, the character of the revolutions remained ambiguous – for power had been achieved only passively, through the collapse of the old governments and central authority. In the Italian states and Hungary the liberals could claim to have forced the governments to give way. But even there, and far more so in Germany and Austria, the liberals found themselves in power unexpectedly. The revolutions had been created by mass pressure; successive governments in the various states were now overturned with bewildering rapidity by renewed street demonstrations. As at the outbreak of the revolutions, so in their development, the liberals were pushed along by events for which they were not responsible and which they were unable to control. Only so long as a power-vacuum existed were they able to offer a semblance of leadership – and this soon degenerated into provincial and ethnic squabblings. In the Austrian empire the various oppositions only retained command while the imperial army was engaged in Italy; in Germany they remained only until the Prussian king Frederick William IV – so similar in character to Charles Albert, except for his loquacity – summoned up courage to turn against them.

Such strength as these middle-class intellectuals and local gentry could claim to have derived from the masses who had caused the revolution. But the liberals' remoteness from and fear of the peasants in central Europe and Italy, and their suppression of the urban workers, deprived them of this very strength. In central Europe the peasants rapidly withdrew from the revolution, once their basic demands had been met – when indeed they did not turn against the landlord revolutionaries as conscripts in the regular armies. Only in the later stages of the revolution did Kossuth try to win peasant support for his national army of defence against Austria – and then with limited success. Except in Hungary, volunteer forces were disdained, as by the royalist liberals in northern Italy. Only when the initiative had been lost and the more radical groups tried to seize their chance, were belated appeals made for popular support in Berlin, Vienna, Hungary, as in Rome and Venice. But by then the rulers had regained their nerve and the army leaders, always hostile to the revolution, were given their head. Prussian and Piedmontese officers, encased within their dynastic loyalties, had reluctantly followed the wavering patriotic antics of their weak and greedy sovereigns and some perhaps had been momentarily enticed by the prospects of conquering the dominion of Germany or Italy. But for the Habsburg generals no such mirage existed, and for dynastic or ethnic reasons Radetzky, Windischgraetz and Jellačić disobeyed their sovereign and crushed the rebels.

The great powers and the revolutions

Army intervention, which proved decisive in ending the revolutions, was possible because of the determination of the great powers to maintain the peace in Europe. The February revolution had aroused traditional fears of French aggression. Metternich, indeed, claimed that the situation was a repetition of 1792 and demanded that France confirm her recognition of the existing treaties. But even before he was swept from power, Palmerston and Nicholas I displayed far more restraint. When Lamartine issued his flamboyant manifesto to Europe on 4 March, repudiating the legality of the 1815 treaties in the eyes of the French republic, he cautiously hedged it by declarations that the territorial provisions of the treaties would nevertheless be accepted provisionally and that France would only take up arms against interference in Switzerland and Italy. Despite repeated declarations of revolutionary fraternity and support for the rights of oppressed peoples by French democrats, up to the attempted coup of 15 May, French governments refused to assist Poland: when the German patriots conceived of a foreign war against 'barbarian' Russia, on the pretext of the liberation of Poland, as the most effective means of achieving German unity, Lamartine carefully avoided any French commitment (March–April). When Austria seemed to have lost northern Italy, the major concern of French foreign ministers was to avoid any expansion of royalist Sardinia. Even after Charles

Albert had been routed at Custoza, Cavaignac and Bastide did not dare risk war alone against Austria, even in defence of the Venetian republic, and with a sigh of relief escaped from France's self-projected image of defender of oppressed nations and republics by grasping at Palmerston's proposal of joint Anglo-French mediation. If France directly influenced the revolutionary conflagration in Europe, this was never through an aggressive foreign policy in support of the principles of the 'Great Revolution'.

This restraint was partly due to the disastrous financial position in France and the disorganization of its army. But it was also a response to the carefully moderate attitude of the only two great powers unaffected by revolution – Great Britain and Russia. Dislike of or concern about the revolution had been tempered by universal complacency (when not open satisfaction) over the fate of the upstart Louis Philippe. Palmerston and Russell were on excellent terms with the new revolutionary leaders and accepted Lamartine's pacifying assurances. As in 1830–1, Palmerston was determined above all to conserve the peace in Europe, and employed his representatives on the Continent – Minto, Stratford Canning, Normanby – to dissuade both absolutist rulers (in the early days) and former absolutist princes who had suddenly discovered a patriotic vocation (Charles Albert, Frederick William) from rash, aggressive adventures. As in the previous revolutionary upheaval, he was concerned to maintain the existing territorial arrangements with as little modification as possible; and while he believed that Austria should abandon Lombardy, this was because he was convinced (like the Piedmontese moderates) that Austria would be far stronger without so troublesome a province. He intervened unofficially to dissuade Prussia from waging war on Russia (whether or not on account of Poland), and exerted heavy official pressure on Frederick William to make him desist from his invasion of the Danish duchies of Schleswig-Holstein (a region about which Britain was traditionally sensitive in order to keep open the Baltic). Following the same consistent line, Palmerston was ready to allow Russia to assist Austria in the suppression of Hungary in 1849. British interests required a balance of power on the Continent and, preferably, divisions among the great powers. This was best achieved by inhibiting or at least circumscribing local clashes which risked sparking off more general conflict; otherwise states should be allowed to settle their own internal affairs without interference.

Nicholas I, the symbol of reaction and 'barbarity' to all western progressives, suppressor of the Decembrist officers in 1825 and the Polish patriots in 1831, displayed equal caution. A weak Austria and a weak Prussia could only benefit Russia in central and eastern Europe. Poland alone had not to be touched. But Nicholas, despite his dynastic links with so many German rulers, agreed with Nesselrode, his chancellor, and Meyendorff, his ambassador in Berlin, that a war against Prussia over

Poland risked uniting Germany and possibly inciting France. He avoided all provocation and gave time for the deep hatred between Germans and Poles to deflect the projected crusade into pan-Germanic assertions of Teutonic rights over Poles. Once this initial crisis had ended by May 1848 Nicholas stood aside, welcoming the restoration of order and conservatism, only intervening during the final stand of the revolutionaries in 1849, to reply positively to an Austrian request for aid against Hungary and especially to ensure that neither Austria nor Prussia should dominate Germany.

The revolutions thus remained circumscribed by the determination of Britain and Russia, followed willingly enough by France, to avoid a general rising of the peoples. The messianic predictions and promises, which had circulated with increasing fervour since the last revolution, were belied by the separate development of each national revolution and its rapid degeneration in central Europe into ethnic hatreds. If liberty and independence had seemed inseparable and mutually dependent values of the patriotic programme before 1848, only in Italy did they retain a visible, though somewhat tenuous relationship by the end of the revolutions. In Germany the drive towards unity immediately overshadowed cries of liberty. That characteristically Teutonic urge for power assumed concrete form as German liberals and democrats at Frankfurt asserted the claims of a *Gross Deutschland* to include all areas where German-speaking peoples lived: west Prussia as well as German and Austrian-ruled Poland, Schleswig as well as Holstein, Bohemia as well as the Austrian Lands, the Trentino as well as Trieste. The liberation of the Poles was rapidly replaced by proposals for renewed partitions of Prussian Poznania to the advantage of the Germans; the war against Denmark was urged on the Prussian king until Britain enforced his withdrawal; Palacký's insult to the German Confederation by his assertion that Czechs were not Germans was joyfully avenged, in the eyes of these Frankfurt liberals, by the reactionary Windischgraetz's bloody repression at Prague. Like Italian moderates, these German liberals conceived of federation as the only means of unifying the country and turned to the princes; and, as in Italy the liberals looked to Charles Albert, so the Frankfurt assembly offered the throne of Germany to Frederick William (April 1849). But whereas Charles Albert, to save his reputation, renewed war and abdicated, Frederick William – loyal to his sense of dynasty, if nothing else – disdained this offer from the 'nation' and ended by accepting his humiliation at the hands of a triumphant Austria, restrained only by Russia (agreement of Olmütz, November 1850).

The re-establishment of the equilibrium in Germany was the epilogue of the upheavals of 1848–9. By then the Austrian emperor had fully asserted his authority. In the Austrian empire, held together by the Habsburg dynasty, a movement towards unification was inconceivable. The fall of

Metternich had marked a centrifugal drive in the Italian provinces, Hungary, Bohemia and even Galicia. But the momentary protestations of friendship between the different races were soon transformed into bitter ethnic enmities. Beyond freeing the peasants and granting certain civil liberties (often restricted by requirements of education or its concomitant, wealth), the 'master' races – German Austrians, Magyars, Poles – could not envisage granting equal rights to the other nationalities. The most articulate of these, the Bohemian Czechs, laid claim to Moravia and Silesia – which promptly rejected all attempts at union – and summoned an ineffective conference of the subordinate Slav races, where the presence of non-Austrian Poles and the revolutionary Bakunin threatened the attempts to conserve the dynastic tie; ethnic opposition, mixed with democratic claims, was used as an excuse by Windischgraetz to suppress Prague and Bohemian resistance (12–17 June 1848). In Hungary, Croats, Slovenes and Serbs resisted Magyar dominance; in Galicia, the Ruthenes resented Polish rule; in 'German' Austria the Alpine lands opposed Vienna. The German Austrians were unable to choose between their loyalty to the Frankfurt or the Vienna constituent assemblies; between visions of a greater Germany or a greater Austria.

In this inextricable and insoluble conflict of ethnic claims, the dynasty survived through the loyalty of its military commanders and reliance on the Habsburg monarchy of the subordinate populations to protect them against the 'master' races. The Czechs developed a philosophy of 'Austro-Slavism', which inevitably foundered against the rock of the Austrian Germans' refusal to turn away from Germany; the Croats under Jellačić invaded Hungary and forced Kossuth's break with Vienna. With the victory in Italy, Schwarzenberg's government was once more able to take the offensive. Democratic and Hungarian liberal opposition, which had little in common except nationalism, were forced ever closer together by the polarization between revolution and autocracy in autumn 1848. After Windischgraetz's ruthless suppression of Vienna (October 1848) and the dispersal of the radicals at Berlin (November), Hungary stood alone, only able to ally with the impotent republic of Venice (April 1849). In August 1849 the last flickering embers of resistance in Hungary and Venice were extinguished. The struggle for national power and dominance, in which the peasantry was ignored, and the help of the urban workers was only accepted sporadically and reluctantly, had led to the total failure of revolutionary nationalism in central Europe and had silenced the initial appeals to liberty.

The Italian revolutions differed sharply from those in central Europe, as no open conflict between national independence and the liberal creed emerged. But in all other respects Italy formed an integral part of the revolutionary movement. The war for national independence dominated the entire course of 1848–9 in the peninsula and was almost as dependent upon developments in other parts of the Austrian empire as were those regions upon the war in northern Italy. The liberal and democratic beliefs, the illusions and ideologies of the Italians did not differ broadly from those of revolutionaries elsewhere. To the diplomats in London, St Petersburg or Paris the outcome of the struggle in Italy was as important as it was in Germany or Austria. Indeed it was more important, as the 'Italian question' was a greater threat to European peace than any other issue.

Some few Italians were aware of these interconnections, although usually they were conceived of in purely diplomatic terms. But, as elsewhere in Europe, the Italian revolutionaries, whether liberal or democratic, never really moved beyond generic, platonic expressions of solidarity, initially optimistic, ultimately despairing. Manin alone concluded an alliance with Kossuth, and this itself was revealing of the total lack of international collaboration that characterized the revolutions.

Even more, the revolutions in Italy were out of phase with developments elsewhere. In late April–mid-May 1848 the revolution was still progressing outside Italy; in France socialist pressure was still strong, in Germany (despite the suppression of the Poznan Poles) elections had taken place for the constituent assembly, in the Austrian empire the radicals were pressing their claims at Vienna, while the Magyar and Czech movements were gaining impetus. But in these same weeks in Italy Pius IX pronounced his famous allocution withdrawing from the war against Austria and Ferdinand of Naples carried out a coup against his parliament. The date of Ferdinand's coup, 15 May, aptly symbolizes this contrast: on this same day the Vienna government granted a constituent assembly, peasant dues were abolished in Galicia and the Parisian socialists attempted to seize control of the revolution. The Italian revolutionaries had lost their initiative too early, and when a radical democratic drive emerged late in 1848, it was again out of phase. Social risings in Germany had been suppressed, Prague, Vienna and Berlin had been subdued, France had elected Louis Napoleon president of the republic. This last burst of democratic revolution in Italy could not look for support elsewhere in Europe.

The high tide of revolution in Italy

In Italy by the end of 1847 tension had risen to a level that made agitations and insurrectionary attempts inevitable. In Lombardy-Venetia, the democrats Correnti and Manin forced the moderate-dominated central and provincial congregations of the two parts of the kingdom to petition the emperor for self-government and civil liberties. A public campaign to abstain from smoking – and hence cause a drop in state revenue – gave the authorities, especially the bellicose eighty-year-old marshal Radetzky, the excuse to provoke clashes, which led to injuries among the civilian population (3 January 1848). In Tuscany, three days later, the democratic exiles at Leghorn (La Cecilia and Fabrizi) organized a rising among the unemployed dockers and involved the Leghorn democratic leader Guerrazzi in an unsuccessful attempt to force the moderate Ridolfi government into war with Austria. But it was in the south, where Ferdinand's total hostility to reform effectively disqualified moderate influence, that the continuous plotting of the secret societies finally led to a major rising. The successful revolt of Palermo (12–27 January) was immediately followed by peasant rebellions on the mainland, in the Cilento (17 January). Thus already in January, and even more after the February revolution at Paris, popular pressure forced the moderates far beyond the limits of legality and finally dragged them into a patriotic war.

The constitutions hastily granted after the revolutions in Sicily and Naples signified a tardy recognition by the princes of the need to support the moderates before matters got worse. Ferdinand of the Two Sicilies granted a constitution on 29 January, Leopold of Tuscany on 11 February, Charles Albert on 4–5 March, Pius IX on 14 March; even Charles II of Parma attempted to save his throne by promising a constitution at the last moment (29 March). They were all based on the French constitution of 1830, even those granted after Louis Phillippe's downfall. Their concession by sovereigns, deliberately recalling Louis XVIII's *Charte octroyée* (in contrast to the French assertion of popular sovereignty in 1820 and 1848) reflected the princes' determination to give way as little as possible to democratic pressure. Nomination to the upper chamber and full executive power remained in the hands of the prince; the lower chamber was restricted by wealth, although in Piedmont the requirements were less than in the other states. Catholicism was confirmed as the religion of the state, although Tuscany and Piedmont granted tolerance and civil rights to members of other cults (Jews and Protestants). In like manner, freedom of association and the press were guaranteed more fully in Piedmont and Tuscany than in Naples or the Papal States. Indeed freedom of association was not mentioned in the Neapolitan constitution, while the Pope gave the College of Cardinals an absolute power of veto and excluded from the Councils all matters of 'mixed' civil and ecclesiastical jurisdiction. The grant of a Statute may have been, in the words of Cavour (who had played a prominent part in the Piedmontese campaign), 'indispensable to check the rising tide of passions and block the radical party, whose aim was nothing less than the creation of an ultra-democratic constitution, on the basis of local government institutions' (Cavour, 284, vol. 5, p. 174), but for the highly reluctant princes the constitutions were intended to impose the minimum possible limitation on royal authority. Hence the appointment of extremely moderate ministers: Balbo and Pareto in Piedmont, Ridolfi and Serristori in Tuscany,

Recchi, Minghetti and Pasolini in Rome, Serracapriola and Bozzelli in Naples.

By mid-March 1848, before the outbreak of the revolution in Vienna, the political struggle which was to dominate the course of the revolutions in Italy was thus already taking form. Popular pressure, only partly instigated or controlled by the democrats, was bursting the bonds of moderate 'legality'; the patriotic cry of war against Austria, ably fomented by the Mazzinians, was dividing the moderates among themselves; hostility to the democrats and fear of widespread social revolution was strengthening the moderates' determination to retain power, but revealed the conservatism, both political and social, of their programmes.

The revolution in Sicily

In Sicily class divisions and the deep traditions of separatism assisted the moderates' bid for power. The revolution, although instigated by the democrats, had resulted from a rising of the urban masses at Palermo, supported by the peasants of nearby villages and released prisoners and led by popular *capisquadre*; at Catania, Trapani, Caltanissetta and Messina, the urban populace had similarly seized control. Throughout the island, in both city and countryside, the administration and public order had vanished, as the people attacked government officials and taxation records and began to occupy the land. La Masa, a democratic leader of the insurrection, turned to the nobles and middle classes to lead the revolution. The General Committee, which assumed the powers of a provisional government, included both moderates and democrats, momentarily united in their anxiety to protect property and maintain order. The appointment as president of Ruggero Settimo, prince of Fitalìa, minister in Bentinck's time, vice-president of the 1820 junta, like the demand for the 1812 constitution 'brought up to date', were explicit indications of the sense of continuity from the earlier anti-Bourbon struggle.

Class solidarity, in fact, was only maintained during the fighting against the Bourbon troops, who were evicted from the island (except for the citadel of Messina and, temporarily, Siracusa) by mid-February. The democrats, few in number and with a purely political programme of Sicilian independence within an Italian federation and a constitution, were as terrified as the moderates of the popular squads. The decision to create a national guard (28 January), from which workers were excluded, 'was born of the eternal diffidence of the owner towards the non-owner', as the democrat Giuseppe La Farina recognized (Romano, 226, p. 87). Under the dictatorial leadership of baron Pietro Riso, the national guard became the most important force during the revolution, exempt from parliamentary control, with privileges over the army. After breaking up the urban squads, it exerted increasing pressure on the government and began to persecute the democrats, forcing their leaders to resign from office. The peasants continued to occupy the demesnial lands. But the democrats, debating ineffectively in the Palermo parliament, were incapable of offering leadership and proved unable to organize even electoral support among the urban populace.

The moderates thus rapidly regained social and political control and wrested the initiative from the democrats. They were united in their demand for independence from Naples and relied – with little basis – on English support. Memories of Bentinck and those triumphant years of Sicilian independence coloured their discussions. Precisely because of this rose-water image of the past, they failed to appreciate that Palmerston – and Minto as mediator – wanted to retain the unity of the Two Sicilies, although ready to support wide constitutional concessions. Even after the breakdown of negotiations with Naples (22 March), the moderates hoped to retain English favour and responded to Minto's plea against a republic by proclaiming Sicily to be a constitutional monarchy (13 April). But, once the issue of independence had been decided, the moderate middle classes successfully asserted their claims against the old aristocracy, eliminating the 1812 limitations on the voting rights of the professional and merchant classes and ensuring the supremacy of the lower house. Mariano Stabile, a former administrator of the sulphur mines, secretary of the provisional government, and now head of the government, consciously distinguished himself from the 'noble vestiges of '12 and '20' (Romeo, 225, p. 325). In this respect, and in this respect alone, the Sicilian ruling class had 'brought itself up to date', and the upper middle classes accepted the benefits of the lengthy Bourbon attack on the feudatories.

For the rest, hostility to social change and insistence on autonomy seemed only too familiar a repetition of Sicilian attitudes during the previous half-century. Radical liberals and democrats gained the extension of the suffrage to all except illiterates. Cordova abolished the grist-tax and proposed to utilize ecclesiastical lands to create a class of smallholders. Ferrara insisted on free trade. But the majority of the moderates, firmly backed by the national guard, resisted these insidious attacks on their property and positions, sabotaged national loans and reduced the authority of the government by factious squabbling. The autonomy of the communes, confirmed according to the tradition of the 1812 constitution, rapidly degenerated into the anarchic independence of local notables. In like manner, the traditional spirit of separatism effectively defeated the attempts of the democrats and the more 'nationally' minded moderates to strengthen their ties with the Italian patriots on the mainland. A symbolic contingent of volunteers left late in April under La Masa to fight against Austria. But the contradiction implicit in the contemporaneous assertion of Sicilian independence and an Italian federation was left deliberately ambiguous in parliament's decree of 1 April 'that the executive power declare in the name of the nation to the other states of Italy, that Sicily – already free and independent – intends to take part in Italian union and federation' (Romano, 226, p. 92).

The revolution in Lombardy-Venetia

As at Palermo, so at Milan and Venice workers and artisans started the revolution. The rising at Vienna and the dismissal of Metternich (13 March) led to the instant collapse of authority in what had been a highly centralized empire. The lack of directives from Vienna undoubtedly disorientated the imperial authorities in Lombardy-Venetia, while the presence of large numbers of Italian troops in the army of 70–80 000 men (perhaps one-third of the total) weakened the military command. Nevertheless there can be no doubt that the success of the revolution at Milan was entirely due to the courageous street-fighting of the artisans and workers, led by a group of young democrats against Radetzky's well-disciplined garrison of 13 000 non-Italian troops. Radetzky himself, in his dramatic despatches to Vienna during the *Cinque Giornate* (18–22 March), revealed his amazement, wrongly ascribing the tactical skill of the revolutionaries to foreign military leaders:

> The character of this people has been altered as if by magic, and fanaticism has taken hold of every age group, every class, and both sexes. . . . My information from the provinces, though slight, is very alarming, for the whole country is in revolt and even the peasants are armed.
>
> The armistice is not concluded and the fighting continues with unabated fury . . . all communications are interrupted, a number of messengers have been shot or taken prisoner, and my units meet strong resistance in the barricaded streets and villages. Reconnoitering is impossible, since all communications are broken. (Mack Smith, 110, pp. 143–4)

At Venice too, after the release of Manin and Tommaseo from prison, the rising of the Arsenal workers and the mutiny of the Italian troops in the garrison were responsible for the success of the revolution (21–3 March). In these same days all the major cities of Lombardy and Venetia, except Mantua and Verona, freed themselves. In Lombardy the Milan insurrectionaries aroused support and volunteers among the peasants, as well as the neighbouring cities, by launching balloons appealing for a rise to arms. This initial phase of the revolution witnessed a war of the people, even if in Venetia the provincial cities liberated themselves without fighting as the Austrian troops withdrew. With the defeat of Austria, their dependents, the rulers of Parma and Modena, abandoned their governments (21–6 March).

The revolution at Milan had taken all the political leaders by surprise. Even Cattaneo, on the eve of the insurrection, thought that Metternich's fall and Vienna's disastrous financial state would assist Lombardy to achieve self-government within the framework of the empire by peaceful means; he warned against the rising because the people lacked arms and leaders. Only on the third day of the fighting, 20 March, did he assume the direction of the battle, forming a war council with the young democrats Cernuschi, Terzaghi and Clerici. His activities were then divided between improvising remarkably effective military tactics and preventing the moderate town council under Casati from accepting Radetzky's repeated proposals for a truce.

Leadership had been thrust upon a reluctant Cattaneo as the moderate nobles kept to their palaces during the street-fighting. But his failure in these crucial hours to create a provisional government, perhaps even to proclaim a republic, revealed the effective hegemony which the moderates had acquired over the democrats in the previous years. When two of the more radical nobles, Litta and Cusani, refused to join a democratic provisional government half-heartedly proposed by Cattaneo (20–1 March), he immediately abandoned the attempt as, in Cernuschi's words, the proposed government would not have had 'enough credit and influence to establish a strong, respected and lasting centre' (Della Peruta, 242, p. 81, n. 3). Cattaneo, the ideologue of an entrepreneurial middle class, remained sceptical of the 'people's' capacity to maintain its revolutionary drive once the fighting ended, and thus recognized that the inter-class character of the patriotic rising implied leadership by those with most local influence – the Lombard moderate nobles.

These aristocratic moderates of the town council who transformed themselves into a provisional government on 22 March were anxious to rectify the 'unexpected absence of authority', but even more to check the danger of 'anarchy'. The February revolution at Paris had dampened the moderates' patriotic ardour, as the English consul-general at Milan, Dawkins, wrote to Palmerston: '*The majority of those who have something to lose consider these events with dismay. Hatred against the Austrians*, although it cannot be considered appeased, was at least *thrown into the shade*' (307, vol. 1, p. 447). The Five Days confirmed the moderates in their belief that salvation could only be found in Piedmontese intervention. Already on 23 March Casati wrote to Charles Albert's personal secretary, Castagnetto: 'Do not lose a moment, because if I am at the head of the Government, this is simply to avert anarchy or something which resembles it' (Ferrari, 308, p. 13). To survive, the moderate government required the support of the regular Piedmontese army.

But the strength of the popular movement and the prestige of the democrats in Milan made any political proposals for annexation by Piedmont extremely dangerous. Casati was only able to retain control in these first perilous days of government through Charles Albert's commitment of Piedmont to a 'national' war of independence and through the democrats'

anxiety to avoid dissension. The acceptance by a suspicious Cattaneo and soon after, on his arrival in Milan, by a fervently patriotic Mazzini of Casati's appeal that 'once the war is won, our destinies will be discussed and settled by the nation' (Cattaneo, 262, vol. 3, p. 77), lost the democrats their initiative and compromised the conduct of the war from the outset.

The absorption of the democrats within the resolutely moderate government and the systematic curbing of popular pressure, the rejection of proposals by both Milanese craftsmen and Lombard peasants to cut off the retreating army, the subordination of the impetuous volunteers from other Italian states to the lethargic orders of the Piedmontese military headquarters, were vividly described by Cattaneo in the bitter days following the final defeat. The provincial governments in the liberated provincial cities – Pavia, Como, Cremona, Bergamo, Lodi, Brescia, Sondrio – were inevitably composed of local persons of prestige, thus confirming the weakness of the democrats: civic guards had been formed to protect order and property, excluding craftsmen and peasants. The creation of a central provisional government in place of these city governments (8 April) accentuated the control of the moderates, who identified themselves increasingly with the great landowners, whether noble or bourgeois. Although salt and stamp duties were immediately diminished, the personal tax, tithes and consumption taxes remained, while a forced loan favoured land at the expense of industry and trade. It was not surprising that popular enthusiasm for the revolution rapidly diminished, especially in the countryside where requisitioning by the Piedmontese army soon alienated peasants.

As the moderate leaders and Piedmontese agents campaigned ever-more openly for 'fusion' with Piedmont, the democrats, who had deliberately restricted their criticisms to the lethargic conduct of the military campaign, were divided over how to counter this breach of the initial pledge to delay political decisions until after the war. Cattaneo, strongly influenced by the republican federalist Ferrari, who had returned from long years of exile in France, proposed to appeal for military aid from the French republic and overthrow the provisional government, summoning a republican assembly. Mazzini, obsessed by the need for unity among patriots, hostile as ever to French interference, convinced of Italy's initiative, successfully used the prestige of his name to reject Cattaneo's proposal (30 April). Mazzini's appeals to patriotic unity and the demands of the war against Austria, which thus momentarily triumphed over Cattaneo and Ferrari's assertion of the prior demands of republican democracy, merely confirmed the inability of the democrats to challenge the moderates' claim that they alone were responsible and realistically patriotic. The proclamation of a plebiscite over the fusion with Piedmont (12 May) marked the defeat of the democrats.

The cry for a plebiscite in Lombardy compromised the hopes of the republicans in Venice as well. In a city where rich and poor lived unusually closely together and paternalism was exceptionally strong, Manin's popularity ensured the immediate creation of a republic. This convinced supporter of the classic political demands of the democrats – manhood suffrage, equality before the law, a free press and freedom of assembly – saw the Venetian republic as the first step towards the creation of an Italian federation and, mindful of earlier hostility towards the Serenissima, was more aware of the dangers of municipalism than Cattaneo or that visionary enthusiast for guelph city-states, Tommaseo. Like Ferrari and most democratic federalists, Manin turned automatically towards the French republic for fraternal and, if necessary, military support. But like all the Italian democrats of 1848 he saw patriotism and political democracy as adequate to attract the support of the masses, and remained diffident towards their social demands. In the opening days of the republic attempts were made to explain this philosophy of the revolution to the people. As Gustavo Modena wrote in a handbill:

> Not communism – Not social subversion – Not government in the streets – Respect for property – Equality of all before the law – Full freedom of thought and speech – Free discussion without rioting – Improvement of the condition of the poor who wish to live off their own work. (Ginsborg, 311, p. 115)

The composition of Manin's government, although it excluded the Venetian nobles of the town council who had opposed his incitement of the revolution, was calculated at removing disquiet. It consisted of business and professional men, like Castelli and Paleocapa, rather than of convinced republicans like himself and Tommaseo. Within a week the obvious hostility of the government to 'anarchy' won the support of the merchants and reluctant acceptance by the nobles.

Manin's government appealed more openly to popular support than did the Lombard moderates, now reassured by Charles Albert's army. The abolition of the personal tax and diminution of the salt duty won approval in the countryside; the abolition of customs duties on cotton goods and the affirmation of religious equality and freedom of the press confirmed the support of the middle classes; the appeal to the provinces and local cities (each of which had created its own provisional government) to join the Venetian republic with equal rights removed suspicions of Venetian domination. But, as at Milan, the democratic cause was compromised within days by Manin's agreement, under pressure from the Milan provisional government, to delay a definitive decision by the people over the political structure of the country until the war was over (30 March).

This decision by a republican federalist, undisputed leader of a city with republican and anti-Piedmontese traditions, was taken in the euphoria of apparent military victory against the Austrians and the expectation that a wholly liberated Italy would soon be able to decide on its future. But it confirmed the undoubted effectiveness of moderate Piedmontese propaganda in rehabilitating Charles Albert as a patriotic leader and in proclaiming the necessity of a regular army to evict the foreigner.

Many republicans remained hostile to Charles Albert and were optimistic about the possibilities of creating a republican Italy. As a Florentine democrat, Berlinghieri, wrote to the Venetian republican, Giovanni Carrer, on 27 March:

> If we are not deceived, Sicily has already proclaimed a republican government, and the Revolution should be imminent at Naples. Genoa can only delay a few days before imitating its sister Venice. We Democrats and Republicans shall personally look to events in our country. . . . Above all, do not, in God's name, let yourselves be taken in by Charles Albert and the Princes – Be steadfast and you will triumph. We are all anxiously awaiting the decision which Milan will take. God forbid that the Milanese . . . should throw themselves into the arms of a man who now perhaps wants to enjoy the fruits of their heroic efforts. . . . But even if this were so, if Venice holds firm, Italy will be saved. (Ginsborg, 311, p. 145)

But by the time Berlinghieri wrote, republican hopes had already been lost. Despite the demands of Tommaseo, Castelli and Paleocapa that Venice proclaim a republican constitution, Manin refused and even delayed passing an electoral law to form a constituent assembly of representatives from Venice and the provinces.

The decision to rely on Charles Albert precluded the possibility of appealing to the French republic. Resentment grew in the provinces with their exclusion from an effective voice in the government and, as in the Lombard provincial cities, monarchical propagandists pressed for fusion as the price of Piedmontese aid. Occupation of estates by peasants and rioting by artisans, such as coachmen and hatters, against the competition of railways and technical innovations, aroused the never-distant fear of anarchy. In the words of a priest in Mestre: 'To improve conditions, enjoy cheap prices, live at the expense of the rich, is the first thought that comes into the mind of the plebs. To let them do it, would mean immediately putting to the test the law of communism' (Renier, 310, p. 20). Above all, a spirit of complacency as the Piedmontese army and contingents from the other states advanced sapped away a sense of urgency, so that the Italian soldiers who had deserted from the Austrian army were allowed to return home, the munitions of the Arsenal were distributed haphazardly, and no attempt was made to conscript an army from the peasants. By mid-April, as the Austrian counter-offensive made headway, Manin had lost control of the provinces and had left himself entirely dependent on Charles Albert.

Piedmont and the revolution

The Milan rising caused an immediate crisis at Turin. The February revolution at Paris had dampened anti-Austrian patriotic feeling in Piedmont, as in Lombardy, among 'that cautious herd of liberals, who fast in imitation of the Court, listen to sermons on Sunday, and every Friday recite Count Balbo's rosary of Catholic progress', as the democrat Filippo De Boni jeeringly described them (Della Peruta, 258, p. 967). The violent wave of anti-clericalism and attacks on the Jesuits, which had accompanied the popular demonstrations for reform, increased Charles Albert's religious scruples about identifying himself with patriots who were already tainted by association with democracy and republicanism. The concession of the Statute had not placated radical public opinion, whose middle-class leaders now demanded a purge of the army, judiciary and administration. With the news of the Milan revolution agitation for intervention immediately broke out in Piedmont, led by democratic federalists, with a dangerous Mazzinian groundswell at Genoa.

Charles Albert – characteristically – hesitated. Intervention meant not only disregarding English advice to maintain peace, but a deliberate violation of the treaties of 1814–15. The attitude of the other Italian princes might prove hostile. Furthermore, the army had been mobilized on the western frontier in February in a panic reaction to the Paris revolution. But fears of a republican victory in Lombardy and the distinct possibility that democratic agitation in Piedmont and Genoa might take on an anti-dynastic character ultimately decided the king. Cavour's much-quoted article in the journal *Risorgimento* of 23 March implicitly played on these fears in order to sway the king:

> The supreme hour for the Sardinian monarchy has sounded, the hour of major decisions, the hour on which depend the fate of empires, the destiny of peoples. . . . Hesitation, doubt, delays are no longer possible. . . . Woe to us if, in order to strengthen our preparations, we do not arrive in time! Woe to us if, at the moment we are about to cross the Ticino, we receive the news of the fall of the queen of Lombardy [Milan]. (Cavour, 287, pp. 106–7)

But by the time the article appeared, even the prudent Balbo and his ministers were ready to support Charles Albert's decision (23 March) to fulfil what he believed to be his heroic destiny. Their support was determined, as the minister Sclopis wrote,

> particularly by the internal condition of the State, where disturbances were threatened if arms were not openly taken up against the foreigner, by the inevitable decision of either placing oneself at the head of the national movement or being dragged along by it under the direction of demagogues. (Romeo, 199, p. 109)

Charles Albert was forced into identifying himself with the national cause by his fear of democracy and of French intervention – even at the price of accepting a political truce until the war was over. His proclamation to the peoples of Lombardy and Venetia, in which he affirmed that Italy was 'able to go it alone', was consciously worded in order to exclude any appeal to France. His explanations to England and France justified his intervention in terms of the need to avoid a republican victory in Lombardy, which would have disturbed the peace in Italy and threatened the Savoyard monarchy.

This excessive fear of republicanism and Charles Albert's explicit intention of limiting the national war by turning it into a war of dynastic conquest led to a hesitant and indecisive military campaign. Inadequate supply lines, a general headquarters so unprepared that it did not even have the appropriate maps of Lombardy, lack of well-trained officers for the reserve troops, bickerings among the Piedmontese generals, hostility towards the volunteers, were all evidence of the disorientation of an army trained to fight in defence of dynastic absolutism, not to lead a movement of national liberation. Charles Albert's piteous ineptitude as supreme commander compounded these serious weaknesses and, during the campaign, generated continual confusion in the communications between the military headquarters and the two governments at Turin and Milan.

The slowness of the Piedmontese advance into Lombardy allowed Radetzky to withdraw without hindrance to Verona and the fortresses of the Quadrilateral, where he waited for reinforcements. Radetzky's retreating army was not attacked and subsequently his lines of communication with Austria were not cut off; no attempt was made to conquer the Trentino and hence block the Brenner, the major pass over the Alps. The Piedmontese army did not even try to link up with the Papal troops or the Venetian volunteers. In this war of lost opportunities, both the regular armies preferred to remain on the defensive or engage in sieges rather than attack and destroy the enemy. The first serious clash between the Piedmontese and Austrian armies only occurred on 30 April at Pastrengo; after fighting again with little result at Santa Lucia on 6 May, the Piedmontese definitively lost the tactical advantage. In the meantime, Nugent's army of reinforcement from Austria had reconquered Udine, Belluno and Feltre, and once it had joined up with Radetzky's forces, threatened the Venetian mainland. Three more weeks of inaction, used by the Piedmontese royalists to further the political campaign for fusion, allowed Radetzky to defeat the Tuscan division at Curtatone and Montanara and unsuccessfully challenge the Piedmontese at Goito (29–30 May). The capture of Peschiera (30 May), the one major Piedmontese success of the war, hardly compensated Radetzky's capture of Vicenza, despite the resistance of the populace and the papal contingent under Durando (11 June), and the consequent Austrian occupation of Padua, Treviso, Mestre and Palmanova (14–25 June); Venice and Oseppo alone remained independent. Radetzky's final reckoning of accounts with Charles Albert was only delayed by the news of a revival of the revolution at Vienna in late May. The war had been lost long before the battle of Custoza (22–7 July) as Cattaneo cruelly commented, by Charles Albert's concern to collect votes, while Radetzky collected soldiers.

Social and political divisions

Well before Custoza Charles Albert's open policy of aggrandizement destroyed the momentary wave of common purpose which had united patriots of all tendencies in the Italian states. The traditional mistrust of Piedmont revived among the other princes, and the moderates were precipitated into the crisis. The revolutions in Austrian Italy had the dual effect of increasing popular pressure on the moderate governments and princes and of bringing to the fore the exiles and conspirators of the sects and earlier revolutions who now flocked back. Agitations in central and southern Italy spread beyond the middle classes to the urban craftsmen and even the populace, and in all the states led to a peremptory demand for participation in the war for Italian independence. In the weeks following the Five Days the traditional divisions and parochial jealousies which had so characterized the earlier risings appeared to be submerged by the general desire to evict the foreigner; student and worker volunteers left for the war. Mazzini's tactics at last seemed to be justified.

But the exiles and conspirators who dramatically re-emerged and whose presence constellated the entire course of the revolutions of 1848–9 brought with their enthusiasm political beliefs and convictions which, as in the French revolution of this year, belonged to an earlier age and which were to lead to dispute and conflict once their collaboration was rejected by the moderates and above all by Charles Albert. The countless officers of the Napoleonic years, from Guglielmo Pepe to Carlo Zucchi, from Teodoro Lechi to Pompeo Litta, found their advice ignored and their help despised. The moderates of 1820–1 who reached office, like the aged Ruggero Settimo in Sicily or Francesco Bozzelli in Naples, once more displayed their hostility to the democrats and revealed their conservatism and (in Bozzelli's case) readiness to compromise with the prince against what they judged to be the threat of social anarchy. The loyal Mazzinians, like Gustavo Modena or Filippo De Boni, clashed with the new generation of democrats, federalists like Manin or Cattaneo's followers, demagogues like Guerrazzi, socialists like Montazio. The patriotic fervour of most was rapidly tempered by the extent of social upheaval accompanying the revolutions; but some among the democrats learnt from the bitter experiences of these early months to search more consciously for popular support.

Confronted by the new situation and by the excitement of the people, the moderate governments lost control. They lacked time to establish themselves after the concession of the statutes, to consolidate their power as political parties and sink roots within the institutional structures. Forced to adapt their actions to the rapid succession of events, their failure in previous years to elaborate an effective common national programme – despite D'Azeglio's claims – rapidly led to divisions among themselves and antagonisms among the different regional groupings. In Tuscany no moderate could attain to national leadership, as Ricasoli, Salvagnoli and Lambruschini joined democrats in criticizing Ridolfi's government for its lukewarm attitude to the war. In Rome, the moderates had only too recently been admitted to share power with the ecclesiastics. In Naples the deep distrust between king and liberals led to uncertainty over how to make the constitution work; the conservative Serracapriola was finally dismissed over the Sicilian question and replaced by a more progressive moderate, Troya (3 April), who was determined to make constitutional rule effective and involve Naples in the war for independence.

Behind the dominant issue of the war, concern grew among the moderates over the social threat. As always, it was less acute in Tuscany than in the Papal States and Naples, where class divisions ran deeper. In Tuscany the democrats, long subordinate to the moderates, were divided over the priority to assign to the national struggle. An attempt, headed by the democrats Mordini and Mazzoni, to overthrow Ridolfi's government was sabotaged by a counter-demonstration led by another democrat, Cempini. The progressive newspaper *Alba* now insisted on concord, denying social divisions:

> National liberty and independence from the foreigner is the aim. Communism is a fad, a jest which does not amuse even the most eccentric minds. . . . The Italian movement . . . has a wholly national individuality, like the physiognomy and language of the people. (Ronchi, 320, p. 75)

Social agitations recurred in both city and countryside, particularly at the port of Leghorn, but the small group of democrats demanding the 'right to work' and the 'organization of labour', as in republican France before the June Days, remained relatively isolated. It needed the disenchantment following the collapse of the war for the democrats to gain from the growing social tension.

In the Papal States the economic crisis in both city and countryside nourished the agitations which had given so much force to political demonstrations since the accession of Pius IX. The concession of a limited constitution had done little to quieten discontent which – urged on, as elsewhere in Italy, by Gioberti's polemics – turned against the Jesuits. Pius IX, frightened by and hostile to this new turn in popular violence, found himself obliged to warn the Jesuits that he could not guarantee their safety. With the outbreak of revolution in Europe, tourism in Rome dropped sharply, and so worsened the economic distress. It only needed the pope's decision to withdraw from the war (29 April) for social and political agitation to become one in both Rome and the provinces. The new patriotic government of Mamiani, in continuous conflict with the pope, proved wholly incapable of re-establishing order within the Papal States or maintaining support for the war of independence. The situation had become explosive long before Charles Albert's defeat.

In Naples neither moderates nor democrats were able to unite and organize themselves throughout the kingdom. Unlike 1820, parliament never acted as a unifying catalyst for the different classes and groups, each of which pressed for its own aims. The contradictory demands of the moderates and radicals, of the various incompatible groups in the capital and in each of the provinces, reflected the disorganic nature of Neapolitan civil society, which erupted with the breakdown of state authority. Both the provincial bourgeois landowners and the merchants and industrialists had supported the new constitutional regime and initially their attention focused upon the struggle to apply the Statute and ensure Neapolitan participation in the war. The more radical leaders wanted to abolish the nominated upper chamber and the restrictions of the suffrage by wealth. But the peasants seized upon the grant of the Statute as a signal to agitate throughout the kingdom, occupying demesnial lands misappropriated by landowners, while craftsmen in Naples and near Salerno engaged in Luddist demonstrations. The bourgeoisie at Naples, both moderate and radical, took fright, only too conscious of the dangerous example of France. For these constitutionalists, 'One method alone exists to diminish the distances between the most dissimilar social conditions: that method is education' (Lepre, 220, p. 213). An attempt by Conforti, the minister of the interior, to settle the trouble by inviting the peasants to appeal to the law-courts, while instructing the local notables to maintain public order, failed in face of the peasants' determination. The frightened moderates, who predominated in the provinces, often tried to protect themselves through the national guard. Only some radicals supported and even led the peasant occupations. Political opposition to the king and social agitations remained on wholly separate planes and facilitated Ferdinand's decision to end the radical opposition in the new parliament by storming the barricades set up in Naples by provincials who had flocked to the city, and by local members of the national guard (15 May).

Ferdinand's coup was the first major success of the reaction against the revolution, and demonstrated the weakness of the moderates when not supported by the prince. It also confirmed the total breakdown of the initial hopes of a federal war against Austria. Charles Albert's appeal for support was, not surprisingly, received with suspicion by the other princes. Before the revolution, Piedmont had dragged its heels over the conclusion of a league. Now Charles Albert asked for immediate military aid in a war which, if successful, would ensure Sardinian domination of Italy, while proposing to delay discussion of the terms of a political league until after the war. The Tuscan grand-duke had only reluctantly agreed to send a regular contingent under popular pressure, 'in the clear interest of all Italy, but also to maintain order and tranquillity within his own states and to conserve his throne', as the foreign minister, Corsini, frankly admitted to the Austrian *chargé d'affaires* (Pischedda *et al.*, 304, pp. 129–30). Ferdinand of Naples only promised to send troops because his leading civil servants were unsure of the loyalty of the national guard and some army regiments; they warned him of the risk of alienating all support among the patriots in favour of Charles Albert. Even so, Ferdinand delayed sending a naval squadron and military contingent under general Pepe until the end of April. But the greatest resistance was put up by Pius IX, fearful of the international consequences for the Church of military participation in and moral leadership of a national, liberal war against Austria, a Catholic power. A small regular force under Durando was sent, ostensibly to protect the papal frontiers. An ill-judged attempt by Durando and D'Azeglio to commit the pope by a proclamation to the soldiers provoked Pius publicly to disassociate himself from the war in an allocution on 29 April.

Gioberti's neo-guelph illusion was finally shattered. With Ferdinand of Naples' decision to withdraw Pepe's expeditionary force immediately after 15 May, the façade of agreement among the princes was irrevocably destroyed. Even Tuscany, although unwilling to follow the papacy and Naples, now concentrated more on resisting Piedmontese expansion than on furthering the war. Whatever the illusions which had encouraged belief in the possibility of a national war of the princes, Charles Albert's by-now open ambitions of territorial aggrandizement left Piedmont isolated against Austria. Even the volunteers and those of the papal and Neapolitan contingents who had followed Durando and Pepe in defying their princes' orders were to turn increasingly to republican Venice.

The campaign to merge the Lombard provinces with the kingdom of Sardinia into a constitutional kingdom of northern Italy ended triumphantly for the royalists (8 June), with 550 000 of the total 650 000 votes in favour of annexation. Piacenza, Parma, Modena and Reggio had already voted in favour of joining Sardinia (8–29 May). In Venetia Manin and the republicans had fought a losing battle against royalist propaganda. The Lombard provisional government had earlier proposed a single Lombard-Venetian constituent assembly which Manin – despite misgivings about Charles Albert's plan for annexation – had been forced to accept (11 May). The decision of Casati's government at Milan to hold a separate plebiscite (12 May) precipitated the committees in the Venetian provinces of Padua,

Vicenza, Treviso and Rovigo into a similar plebiscite without awaiting elections to a constituent assembly: as the Austrian troops began to occupy the Venetian mainland, they too voted heavily in favour of annexation (5 June).

Venice now stood alone as a republic, and Manin was attacked for his apparently separatist policy. Only too conscious of the collapse of his ideal of a federation of Italian states, fearful lest Charles Albert repeat Campoformio and restore Venice to Austria in exchange for Lombardy, Manin was even prepared to contact Mazzini and then consider a new appeal for French aid. But ultimately, still hopeful that the Piedmontese army would advance into Venetia, he took no action and watched in impotence as the Austrians reconquered the mainland and isolated Venice. At this late stage, despite the continuing support of the Venetian populace for the republic, blackmailed by an offer of Piedmontese military and financial support, threatened with the danger of civil war by the civic guard, Manin was forced to convoke the assembly elected in June, which voted for annexation (4 July). For three brief weeks, until Custoza, Charles Albert nominally ruled all northern Italy.

The effectiveness of the fusionist campaign owed much to the massive propaganda of the royalists and their exploitation of the presence of the Piedmontese army, the only force now capable of defeating the Austrians. The use of plebiscites, limiting the choice to immediate fusion without mention of a republican alternative, obviously increased the size of the royalist majority. Indeed, voting was held openly in the presence of the communal officials appointed by the previous Austrian government or (for enrolled troops) of military officers. But the republicans also proved incapable of organizing a serious opposition. Mazzini had led a public protest of democrats against the announcement of the plebiscite and had immediately begun to campaign in L'Italia del Popolo against federalism and the Kingdom of Northern Italy, in favour of unity and a republic. But the republicans, in both Lombardy and Venetia, now paid for their failure to organize support in the countryside. Remote from, sometimes even hostile to the demands of the peasants, they were unable to free themselves from the accusation of 'communism' and 'socialism' thrown at them by both reactionaries and moderates terrified by the Paris February revolution. Perhaps because of the very effectiveness of these accusations, which were to touch notes of hysteria with the June Days, Mazzini and Manin refused to adopt insurrectionary tactics and insisted on conducting their opposition within the limits of legality.

The size of the vote in favour of annexation ultimately reflected the disaffection of the peasants from the revolution. The initial enthusiasm in the countryside had been discouraged immediately by both Piedmontese army officers and the Lombard provisional government. Agitation became widespread in April and May, as the peasants demanded the abolition of the consumption and personal taxes and the restitution of communal lands, contesting the inequality of the new financial measures and the abuses of the troops: 'is the right of the poor man less than that of the rich one?', protested some peasants (Della Peruta, 242, p. 91). The vote in favour of Charles Albert was a vote of protest against the 'signori', against the rich, as an anonymous contributor to *L'Italia del Popolo* subsequently explained, putting words into the mouths of the peasants:

> If the rich, who already squeeze us through their rentals, should also have the right to make laws, they would squeeze us even more arbitrarily, with impunity: it is in our interests to nominate a king who, dictating the laws and ensuring they are respected, protects our interests a little and sets a limit to the greed of the rich. (Della Peruta, 242, p. 100)

As conscription was extended in June and July the peasants were increasingly to turn against this war of the *signori*. A new cry began to be heard: 'Viva Radetzky'.

The effects of annexation were not merely to alienate the other Italian governments, and to divert attention from the active military prosecution of the war, but to deepen the crisis within the Sardinian state. Like the moderate governments in the other constitutional states, the Balbo-Pareto ministry found itself swept along by the tide of events. The withdrawal from the war of the papacy and Naples confirmed the Piedmontese moderates in their belief that they were sacrificing themselves in vain. The army obeyed without enthusiasm: the officers, from the first setbacks, inveighed against principles they opposed, allies they despised. The Milanese government proved incapable of organizing supplies. The volunteers were regarded with the distaste which Charles Albert displayed in his account of his meeting on 5 July with Garibaldi, whose support he rejected:

> The antecedents of these gentlemen and above all of the so-called General, his famous republican proclamation, make it absolutely impossible for us to accept them in the army and above all to make Garibaldi a general: if there should be a maritime war, one could employ him as leader of the privateers, but otherwise he would be a dishonour to the army. (Spellanzon and Di Nolfo, 3, vol. 4, pp. 521-2)

Paradoxically, the annexation of Lombardy provoked a violent reaction in Piedmont against involvement in this war of independence, threatening to disrupt the entire structure of the state. In Turin, the oldest Piedmontese provinces and Savoy, municipal loyalty revived through fear lest Milan become the capital of the new kingdom. By contrast, Genoa, the newer provinces adjoining Lombardy, and even public opinion in the island of Sardinia, were strongly in favour of the enlarged kingdom which would diminish the dominance of the Piedmontese. The arrangement by which the future organization of the state would be decided after the war in a constituent assembly elected by universal suffrage – the terms of the plebiscite – were violently opposed in the Turin parliament by the Piedmontese moderates, including Cavour, and only passed after significant modifications through the support of the radical opposition. Balbo's government fell. Even in Piedmont dynastic expansionism had destroyed the fragile unity of the moderates and encouraged local municipal feeling against the initial national enthusiasm of the revolution.

Abandoned by the other Italian rulers, confronted by local hostility and republican opposition in the newly annexed provinces, threatened by a dissolution of loyalty to the dynasty even within his own states, awaiting a decisive confrontation with a re-animated Austrian enemy, Charles Albert sought to salvage his gains by diplomatic means. The great powers had been active diplomatically since the outbreak of the war. The weak Austrian governments, overwhelmed by the Vienna revolution in March and its revival in mid-May, were ready to acknowledge the loss of Lombardy, but not that of Venetia; but they wanted Lombardy – like Hungary – to take over part of the national debt. Direct negotiation with the Lombard provisional government was attempted on this basis, but foundered over Milan's refusal to separate Venetia's fate from that of Lombardy. Palmerston, convinced that Lombardy was lost to Austria, anxious to restore peace rapidly, but above all preoccupied about the dangers of French intervention, extracted from the special Austrian envoy Hummelauer a proposal to grant independence to Lombardy and the Duchies and a self-governing constitution to Venetia (24 May).

French intervention had seemed imminent early in April. But as no official request for aid came from any of the various north Italian governments and the Piedmontese annexationist campaign revealed the weakness of the republicans, the French foreign minister Bastide sought for territorial compensation (Savoy and Nice) in exchange for support for an enlarged monarchy of northern Italy. Opposition to a diplomatic settlement which would sacrifice Venetia came from the French constituent assembly and, more surprisingly, from Palmerston's colleagues, Russell and Minto, now wholly converted to the cause of Italian independence. But, characteristically, the European diplomats in general paid little attention to the desires of the peoples of Lombardy and Venetia. Until late June it seemed possible that Italy's fate would once more be settled by the great powers, as Vienna accepted Palmerston's terms and Bastide and Cavaignac, after suppressing the Paris workers' rising, sought a peaceful solution. Then the crushing of Prague, renewed support for Austria in the German Confederation and Radetzky's victories in Venetia, led to a hardening of Vienna's attitude. The recent offer of an armistice (17 June) was withdrawn.

Charles Albert remained optimistic, encouraged by the support of

England and France. On 7 July, only three days after he had obtained the annexation of Venice, he wrote privately to Franzini, his minister of war:

> I believe, in all conscience, that if, through English mediation, we can obtain the cession of Lombardy up to the Adige, together with the two Duchies, we shall have waged a glorious campaign; a state as small as ours faced by the colossal Austrian empire will have made superb acquisitions, almost unheard of in history. . . . To desire more . . . would be, I am prepared to state, almost madly foolhardy. (Spellanzon and Di Nolfo, 3, vol. 4, p. 672)

Charles Albert was ready to sacrifice Venice already at the moment of its annexation in exchange for his other gains, ignoring the protests of all – even his own ministers, such as the Genoese Pareto – who turned to him as the leader of the national cause. But on this occasion diplomacy was to be confounded by the fortunes of war, with Radetzky's victory at Custoza.

The ebb of revolution

Custoza sparked off the crisis of moderatism. The battle itself, although a defeat for the Piedmontese, had left the army intact. But the demoralization of the troops, the defeatism of the generals, and above all Charles Albert's immediate fear of a revival of republicanism in Lombardy led to a precipitous retreat and the unexpected desertion of Milan by the king in order to avoid the political dangers of popular resistance. The armistice hastily signed by general Salasco (9 August) confirmed the withdrawal of the Piedmontese army behind its former frontiers. Faith in Charles Albert, as earlier in Pius IX, immediately collapsed.

The abandonment of the national war by the princes inevitably recoiled on the moderates throughout Italy. Constitutional government had facilitated the organization of the democratic opposition, while the pressure of war and popular demonstrations had impeded the moderate governments from gaining either stability or prestige. Their weakness was revealed in the rapidity with which they were overthrown or dismissed: there were three governments in the Papal States between Pius' allocution of 29 April and Pellegrino Rossi's murder on 15 November, six governments in Piedmont between Balbo's fall (6 July 1848) and the aftermath of the defeat of Novara (March 1849), three governments in Tuscany between Custoza and the flight of the grand-duke (30 January 1849). The failure of the war and the conduct of the princes made it impossible to develop constitutional government in the manner conceived of by the moderates.

In the Papal States Mamiani's patriotic foreign policy was frustrated at every step by the curia's interference. After a brief interlude under the insignificant Fabbri, during which public order disintegrated, Pellegrino Rossi endeavoured to retreat into a rigidly restrictive and anti-democratic interpretation of constitutionalism, based on public order and an executive virtually independent of parliament. In Piedmont the resurgence of local rivalries and Charles Albert's autocratic indifference towards parliament accentuated the divisions among the moderates. The Milanese Casati's government (which succeeded Balbo early in July) was opposed by the Piedmontese moderates because of their exclusion: with two Milanese, one Piacentino, one Venetian, two Genoese and two representatives of the 'new' provinces annexed in the eighteenth century (one of whom, Rattazzi, belonged to the constitutional opposition), the government only included two 'genuine' Piedmontese, both exiles of 1821. This 'Italian' ministry, explicitly representative of the new kingdom of upper Italy, resigned when Charles Albert abandoned Lombardy and signed the armistice without consulting it. But the 'Piedmontese' governments which followed – Alfieri and Pinelli, Perrone and Pinelli, Gioberti and Rattazzi – were less dependent upon a parliamentary majority than upon the attitude of the king, who displayed his authority by imposing rapid changes of their ministers of war.

In Tuscany Ridolfi, the one survivor of the early moderate premiers, was forced to resign with Custoza because of his tepid support for the war. His successor, Gino Capponi, faced a growing threat from democratically organized popular demonstrations. Even in Sicily, where neither the war of independence nor the presence of a prince affected the moderates directly, the social disorder and financial chaos, the abortive expedition in support of a rising in Calabria, the failure to attract a constitutional ruler (the throne had been offered to Charles Albert's second son, the duke of Genoa), led to the collapse of Mariano Stabile's moderate government after the Salasco armistice and its replacement by a coalition between moderates and democrats. In Naples, where Ferdinand's coup of 15 May had been followed by widespread but unco-ordinated provincial risings, especially in Calabria, the most conservative moderates, led by Bozzelli, collaborated in the restoration of royal absolutism, suppressing the risings and suspending parliament.

When parliaments were in session, as in Tuscany and the Papal States in July–August 1848 or Piedmont in October–November, the moderate governments were unable to rebut the attacks of the opposition; when the sessions were suspended, the governments were at the mercy of the princes, as at Naples. Only too conscious of their weakness, hysterically worried by the news of the workers' rising at Paris in June, the constitutional moderates became increasingly conservative, ever-less easily distinguishable from the 'retrograde' supporters of autocracy. Bozzelli and the moderate liberals at Naples, terrified of social anarchy, sought the support of king and army; Cavour and Petitti were haunted by visions of a revival of the republican Convention; Stefano Jacini could justify his acceptance of the return of Austria in Lombardy as preferable to a peasant rising:

God help me and may He always uphold my repugnance towards every form of despotism! But I am comforted by the hope that of the two evils towards which we were moving, Providence chose to afflict us with the present one, in order to give us a useful lesson, in order to conserve us, in the more beautiful future which it is preparing for us sooner or later, from the evils of anarchy. (Della Peruta, 242, p. 105, n. 5)

In the months following Custoza these moderate governments, worried by the possible consequences of their previous defiance of Austria, placed their hopes in Anglo-French mediation or tried to protect themselves by the formation of a league. French intervention – despite suspicion of monarchical Piedmont – seemed a real possibility at the end of July as help was requested separately by Casati's government at Turin and the Lombard provisional consultative assembly, whose envoys at Paris won considerable support in the French republican assembly. Cavaignac and Bastide were only dissuaded from intervention by Palmerston's offer of joint mediation to obtain the independence of Lombardy by sacrificing Venice (8 August). When Tommaseo and Mengaldo, the envoys of republican Venice, reached Paris, where they were soon joined by Cattaneo representing Mazzini and the republicans, pressure for intervention built up again in late August, as Austria had refused to accept Anglo-French mediation. British refusal of support and Austrian determination not to give way induced Cavaignac to back down (29 August–4 September).

The Austrian foreign minister Wessenberg's simultaneous loss of nerve through fear of a general conflict (2 September) led him to accept the principle of mediation. Palmerston was now only anxious to end all disturbance in Italy and warned both Venice and Sicily to reach terms with their respective sovereigns. But the Austrian military occupation of its reconquered territories, the new minister Schwarzenberg's determination to cede nothing and his readiness to abandon traditional English friendship by an approach to France, together with Palmerston's refusal to use force in support of his diplomacy, combined to nullify the attempt at mediation. Louis Napoleon's election to the presidency of the French republic through the support of Catholic voters (2 December 1848) further weakened the influence of the mediating powers. For the prince-president was more concerned with the situation in Catholic Rome than in Lombardy. Little could be expected of France by the patriots, despite Manin's conviction, which he expressed to the English representative Dawkes in December, that 'France after what she has said regarding the liberation of Italy can hardly abandon us, and even if her Government should do so, surely the French people cannot desert us' (Taylor, 299, p. 201).

Republican federalists like Manin or Cattaneo placed their hopes on French intervention, as Charles Albert relied on Anglo-French mediation. But the governments of the other states were far less enthusiastic. Capponi.

concerned to guarantee the integrity of Tuscany and worried by Piedmontese claims, sought to achieve a political-commercial league and confederation of the Italian states and hoped – somehow – to achieve independence for Lombardy-Venetia, while dividing the duchies of Modena and Parma between Piedmont, Lombardy and Tuscany. Pellegrino Rossi, while ready to support a defensive league, was hostile to both a renewal of the war of independence and Piedmont's expansion: 'The enlargement of Piedmont and the autonomy of Italy are certainly not equivalent terms nor identical questions; and the second can exist without the first' (Farini, 322, vol. 2, p. 344). The Piedmontese government sought to gain military aid for a renewal of the war and a guarantee of its annexations in return for acceptance of Capponi's proposals. Divided among themselves, almost as frightened of Piedmontese domination as of Austrian power, these moderate governments withdrew into a defence of the territorial integrity of their own state under the guise of protracted and ultimately futile discussions to create an Italian confederation.

Democratic pressure after Custoza

The continuing zeal for the independence of Italy displayed by the moderates in varying and conflicting forms resulted not only from the undoubted patriotism of some, but from democratic pressure. Charles Albert's abandonment of the struggle after his defeat, while approved of by the more cautious moderates – who were usually preoccupied with the dangers of republicanism and social disturbance – had provoked a revival of popular resistance. The Milanese had prepared to defend their city, until abandoned by Charles Albert, and many peasants of upper Lombardy responded to the appeal for a mass levy of a republican committee of public defence which virtually supplanted the provisional government in the days before the armistice. After the armistice Garibaldi tried to continue the struggle and occupied Varese with a column of volunteers, until forced out by 15 000 Austrians. Friulan volunteers resisted in the fortress of Osoppo until mid-October. At Venice the Piedmontese commissars were forced to withdraw hastily as the citizens conferred dictatorial powers on Manin. The populace of Bologna successfully beat back an Austrian attempt to occupy the city (8 August).

These isolated episodes were symptomatic of the success of the 1848 patriots in infusing into broad strata of the population their faith in the cause of independence, or at the very least their intense reluctance to return under Austrian rule. The revival of the democratic initiative after Salasco became possible through the strength of this popular support. But the support, although on a far broader scale than in the years before 1848, was for the most part confined to the urban populations, ranging from wealthy bankers and merchants (as at Leghorn) to lawyers and shopkeepers, crafts-men and the poor. The democrats attempted to organize this popular feeling. But, as in the past, they were unable (often unwilling) to search for support outside the towns among the peasants, and for long remained determined to act within the bounds of legality and avoid the breakdown of public order.

As always, the effects of these self-imposed limitations were felt most profoundly in southern Italy where the peasantry offered the only mass base for the democrats – albeit a difficult one to guide. The constitutional asso-ciations which developed after 15 May in the provinces of the kingdom of Naples were as opposed to the peasant danger as to Ferdinand's coup. Only in Calabria did such democrats as Musolino and Ricciardi seize the initiative, and even there Ricciardi's innate sense of legality inhibited him from espousing the peasants' demand for immediate practical justice by the occupation of demesnial lands, many of which were now in private hands. In northern Italy Mazzini himself had refused to break with legality in his campaign against fusion in May, while Manin, frightened by the June Days, showed himself almost obsessively concerned with the maintenance of public order.

Mazzini headed the democrats in their attempt to revive the revolutionary cause after Charles Albert's failure. The Italian National Committee, which he formed with Cattaneo and Restelli at Lugano (as successor to the patriotic, non-republican Italian National Association he had founded in March), launched an appeal to Italians in August for an insurrectionary war.

> the royal war is over; the war of the people begins; that war of the people, of
> Italians, which created America and Greece; which in Spain extinguished the
> flower of the Napoleonic army in hundreds of thousands; which made of France,
> assaulted by all Europe, the strong and dreaded power towards which you
> yourselves turn your glance today for assistance. (Mazzini, 257, vol. 38, p. 216)

Conscious as ever of the need to avoid internal disputes, Mazzini did not exclude French help, but subordinated it to a popular insurrection in Italy or interpreted it as a diversionary tactic to weaken Austrian and German claims on the Tyrol in the context of a general European war of republican states.

In Venice, support for Mazzini was widespread among the 12 000 volunteer and regular troops from all Italy, as well as among leaders like Tommaseo. The Mazzinian ideas proclaimed by the Friulan Francesco Dall'Ongaro and the Venetian Gustavo Modena in their journal *Facts and Words* were now developed by the Lombard Giuseppe Sirtori, the Tuscan Antonio Mordini and the Genoese Nino Bixio in their Italian Circle. These democrats had made an unsuccessful bid for power in Venice with the news of Salasco and steadily built up their strength in August–September, attacking the class basis of the civic guard. Mazzini planned to make Venice the seat of a pan-Italian government to co-ordinate the revolution through-out the peninsula. But Manin's increasing conservatism and fear of a popular war, his passive reliance on France and a renewal of Piedmontese inter-vention, frustrated Mazzini's plans: with the support of the commander-in-chief Guglielmo Pepe, Manin expelled the 'foreigners' Mordini and Dall'Ongaro, prohibited soldiers from attending the Italian Circle and received Garibaldi coldly on his arrival in November. Democratic hopes of Venice, which were expressed as far afield as Siena, Leghorn and Genoa, were truncated by the dictator's hostility to Mazzini and the Venetian people's faith in 'our dear father Manin'.

Mazzini continued to search for the spark to light the fire of a general insurrectionary war. A rising in the pre-alpine Val d'Intelvi in late October offered momentary hope. But his failure to interpret the aspirations of the peasant masses in Lombardy and Venetia, as much as Manin's hostility, left him without a base in northern Italy. By October–November Mazzini turned to Tuscany and the Papal States, where popular pressure in the cities had forced the collapse of the moderate governments.

The failure of the war had led to immediate bitter recriminations and to the revival of antagonism towards the moderates in cities where popular agitations had frequently broken out – Leghorn, Genoa, Bologna. Social demands coloured these protests, particularly in Tuscany and the Legations. But they merged into the patriotic appeals diffused by the democrats. Most democrats in the months after the Salasco armistice were convinced of the possibility of renewing the war of independence by forcing the princes to replace the existing governments by more energetic and patriotic ones. They sought to organize popular feeling through the formation of popular associa-tions or circles. The circles, which had been created at Rome, Leghorn and other cities in 1847, were conceived of as semi-official pressure groups, whose aim was to influence the decisions of parliament by their organized expression of public opinion. Their public meetings were meant to offer platforms to win the support of the people, both educated and illiterate, for the causes of 'liberty' and 'independence' and unspecified 'democratic principles'. Although Mazzinians, such as De Boni at Genoa, sought to direct the circles towards republicanism, most leaders of the circles which sprang up in Tuscany, the Papal States, Piedmont and Venice attempted to avoid divisions and create a broad coalition of political forces. Not many were ready to transform the circles into political 'clubs', on the French model, as instruments of direct popular control of the political life of the country.

But the moderates and political authorities feared that this was precisely their purpose. The prefect of Florence warned the minister of the interior, when the Florentine People's Circle became a public association in July 1848, that: 'these circles can turn themselves into clubs, and should they become numerous and reach the point of moving into the streets, they could prove to be a serious embarrassment to the governmental movement' (Ronchi, 320, p. 148, n. 25). Farini, representative of the government in the four Legations, was fearful of the dangers of a convergence of social and political agitation at Bologna in September:

> I know that the riff-raff hold secret meetings, in which they speak of taking their revenge at the first opportunity, which they hope will be soon; I know that they are collecting arms in their hiding places; I know that they are speaking of bands and guerrilla warfare in the mountains; and I know that they link these projects with proposals of political insurrection, republicanism and social upheavals. Thus the city cut-throats, the countryside robbers, the high-waymen are merely the last link in the chain of the discontented . . . and theft and murder are merely the final material expression of a moral fact, the result of deeply rooted causes. (Farini, 323, vol. 2, pp. 617–19)

The circles, under determined democratic leadership, exploited and led the popular unrest which culminated in the overthrow of Capponi in Tuscany (12 October), the murder of Pellegrino Rossi in the Papal States (15 November) and the appointment of Gioberti as head of the government in Piedmont (15 December).

Capponi's fall resulted directly from the government's incapacity to control the demonstrations at Lucca, Arezzo and Pistoia, after an insurrection at Leghorn (25 August–4 September). As Capponi recorded: 'I am convinced that, had it not been for Leghorn, Tuscany would never have begun the revolutions just like that; but as the government wholly lacked defensive forces, it only needed that city to subvert our State' (Capponi, 314, vol. 2, p. 101). But if Leghorn, with its compact radical, socialist-influenced bloc of small merchants, craftsmen and proletariat, represented the shock-force of the democratic initiative, it was Giuseppe Montanelli, wounded and captured at Curtatone, who on his return sounded the battle cry which rallied the democrats throughout Italy.

Montanelli's appeal for a constituent assembly with unlimited mandate, elected by universal suffrage, aroused immediate enthusiasm among the democrats, as it seemed to offer a valid alternative to the ineffective and dilatory diplomatic negotiations of the princes for a league. Moreover, its proponent was not compromised – like Mazzini – by the distrust and personal animosities of his earlier political activities. Mazzini had already launched a similar cry for a national constituent assembly at the moment he began to campaign for an insurrectionary war. He had formulated his entire programme more intransigently than at any time since the early days of *Giovine Italia*. He underlined his total opposition to the proposals of the moderates, 'the homoeopaths of politics, who contended that Austria could be conquered with railways and scientific congresses', who had betrayed the people in the war and now relied 'on the terms of a *mediation*, on ideal leagues of princes who each quake with fear of the other and all with fear of their peoples' (Mazzini, 257, vol. 38, pp. 266–7). Montanelli, by contrast, deliberately avoided a republican challenge to the existing governments. His constituent assembly, although elected by universal suffrage – 'because the nation wants to reconstitute itself by self-interrogation' – was intended as an immediate, practical step to create a national government, 'a permanent Diet, to be the living personification of Italy', which would offer unified leadership in the renewed war of independence (Candeloro, 1, pp. 303–4). As he explained three years later, the constituent assembly 'empowered constitutionalists and republicans, federalists and unitarians to shake hands without betraying themselves on the terrain of existing legality in order to contribute jointly towards the task of enfranchising Italy' (Montanelli, 316, p. 12). His indictment of the separatism of the different governments enthused all patriots: 'Unity of direction was lacking, so that not having a national government, fighting as Piedmontese, Tuscans, Neapolitans, Romans and not as Italians, was the prime reason why this great enterprise failed' (Candeloro, 1, vol. 3, p. 303).

Montanelli's appointment as head of the Tuscan government in succession to Capponi (27 October) marked the first success of the democrats in breaking the moderate monopoly of political power in the monarchical states. The moderates had lost control of the movement for independence by their retreat into a defence of constitutionalism within their separate states, by their apparent abandonment of the Italian cause. Even Gioberti, who had brushed aside the disastrous failure of his earlier advocacy of a papal-led Italy without apparent damage to his prestige and turned for support to the Piedmontese democrats and Lombard exiles, was unable effectively to challenge the Montanellian constituent assembly with his own proposal for a federal constituent assembly to be elected by the different parliaments. His challenge was only to come when he was finally appointed premier in Piedmont.

Tuscany became the focal point for democrats, as had been Milan and then Venice during and immediately after the war. Leading Mazzinians, such as Filippo De Boni and Pietro Maestri joined the local Tuscan democrats like Antonio Mordini and Atto Vannucci in forming an Association for the national constituent assembly, which was to convoke an assembly at Rome, elected by universal suffrage, with full powers. Although Montanelli had intended to play down differences between both parties and states, the Mazzinians and the most determined democrats saw the possibility of opening up the path towards the creation of a unitarian republic. It was fear of this that led other democrats, like Guerrazzi, and some moderates, like Gioberti and Mamiani, to ally themselves with the democratic initiative in an attempt to restrict its drive and contain the dangers of an uncontrollable popular revolution.

Guerrazzi's entrenched position as democratic leader in Leghorn had enabled him to regain control of the city in the August insurrection and to obtain his appointment as minister of the interior in Montanelli's government. He had expelled the popular leaders at Leghorn, who had wanted to proclaim a provisional republican government, and he immediately attempted to confine the dangers of Montanelli's constituent assembly. Rejected by the Florentine moderates as a demagogue, Guerrazzi retained the support of the Leghorn moderates (who initially provided the ministry with its finances), but was forced to rely on popular support, while contemporaneously inhibiting a revolutionary outlet. His initial success was displayed in Montanelli's reformulation of his proposals along lines more similar to those of Gioberti: the creation of the constituent assembly was to take place in two stages, the first of which was to be concerned exclusively with the war against Austria, whilst the second – to be summoned after independence – would decide upon the institutional structure of the country (7 November).

The crisis of the Papal States culminated a week later in the murder of Pellegrino Rossi by a mob at Rome, supported and probably instigated by local democrats and sectarians. The moderates' hold on power, already so fragile, now collapsed. With Pius IX's flight from Rome (24 November) and his repeated denunciations of the government, Mamiani's attempts to restrain the democrats failed. Led by the Roman prince Carlo Bonaparte, the assembly appointed a provisional state junta (11 December). Mamiani's earlier success in limiting the dangers of a constituent assembly by defining it along the lines of Gioberti's confederation, without powers to change the form of government in the separate states (1 December), was challenged by rising democratic pressure organized by the political circles in the provinces and at Rome. The rapid succession of events in the Papal States strengthened pressure in Tuscany for an Italian constituent assembly. Gioberti, after his appointment by Charles Albert, persisted in his attempt to confine a constituent assembly to a federal pact of monarchical states, with the limited aim of pursuing the war. But the drive towards a republic seemed on the point of realization as the leading democrats and republicans moved from Florence to Rome.

Republican Italy

By December 1848 the contradictions of the moderate constitutionalist movement had exploded. The constitutions at the beginning of the year had appeared both as the triumphant culmination of a campaign for reforms and political and civil liberties, and as an effective method of diverting public opposition to absolutism away from dangerous and negative insurrections into open, legal expression of opinion in parliament. But constitutionalism, to take root, required the loyal collaboration of the princes and at least an initial period of peace. Moreover, it presupposed that civil society possessed sufficient cohesion to accept a parliamentary assembly as an adequate guarantee of the interests of the different sectors and social strata within the state. The patriotic enthusiasm surrounding the war of independence had offered the appearance of such cohesion. But the precipitous events of the war had not only blocked the furtherance of internal reforms – and hence the consolidation of monarchical constitutionalism among the people – but had deprived the moderates of the always grudging support of the princes.

Although Ferdinand of Naples' coup of 15 May did not lead to an immediate suspension of the constitutional assembly, it rendered its operations ineffective and provoked among the opposition to the King a return to sectarian, insurrectionary methods. Pius IX's withdrawal from the war and Leopold II's reluctant participation sowed doubts about the effectiveness of the constitutions to further a war for which they had been neither conceived nor granted. The pope's flight, together with the evidence of the restoration of absolutism in Naples, forced both the democratic opposition and some of the more patriotic moderates to question monarchical rule. Only in Piedmont had Charles Albert's assumption of the leadership of the war ensured support for the constitutional system, despite the king's obvious determination to restrict its development. But after Custoza and Salasco the clash of opinion about whether to renew the war and the revival of long-standing antagonisms between the different regions of the kingdom reduced parliamentary government in the Sardinian states to a fragile and insecure existence.

The future of royal constitutionalism had thus become ultimately dependent, to a large degree, on the choice made by the opposition whether to pursue its objectives in parliament (assuming the responsibility of office) or to press for a revolutionary – that is, a republican – solution. It is questionable whether a republic could have emerged in the Papal States without Pius IX's flight, and even more doubtful whether a similar attempt could have succeeded in Piedmont against the strength of Savoyard military loyalty. But the willingness of the Piedmontese democrats to contain the expression of their opposition within parliament reflected the far greater cohesion of civil society in the sub-alpine kingdom, compared to the Papal States where Pius' flight merely served to spark off the deep-rooted hostility to temporal rule of virtually all strata of society.

The strength of the republicans derived from the identification of Montanelli's cry for a popularly elected constituent assembly with the pursuance of the war against Austria. All Mazzinians and democrats were united in their support of the Montanellian constituent assembly against Gioberti's proposal for a confederation with a nominated diet. But Mazzini, judging the immediate creation of a national constituent assembly to be unrealizable, seized upon Pius' flight to insist on the need to form a republic in the Roman States before convoking an Italian assembly; this would avoid the danger of the creation of a kingdom of central Italy (supported at that moment by Montanelli), while offering a republican base for a future Italian constituent assembly:

> The initiative of the Italian *Costituente* coming from a republican power could not be accepted by Charles Albert. The Austrian invasion would unite the Central and Lombardo-Venetian provinces; it would widen the sphere of operations of the Austrian army and facilitate the rising of upper Lombardy. The war, once led by an insurrectionary power, would arouse the Sardinian populations and lead them to revolt. (Mazzini, 257, vol. 37, pp. 251-2)

The less extreme democrats, now congregated at Rome, who controlled the Roman Popular Circle, at first supported Mamiani's proposal for a federal assembly. But the most radical democrats wished to push further than Mazzini and proclaim an Italian constituent assembly immediately. They included Mazzinians like De Boni and Mordini, former Buonarrotians like Niccolini, Cattanean federalists like Cernuschi, all convinced that a 'popular' revolutionary solution was the necessary premise for radical social change. Although a minority among the leaders of the Roman circle, De Boni, Maestri and other democrats initially built up pressure for the rapid convocation of a Roman Constituent Assembly, to be elected by universal suffrage. Out of fear of further popular demonstrations, the provisional junta and ministers agreed (29 December). De Boni at once led the campaign to make the Roman assembly the nucleus of a future Italian constituent assembly. Despite the opposition of federalists like Cernuschi, De Boni created a Committee of Italian Circles, to which the leader of the Roman populace, Ciceruacchio, and other Roman democrats adhered (1 January 1849). As Cernuschi, Maestri and other Lombard exiles were drawn in, the Committee again imposed its will on the government, which decreed that the hundred deputies elected with the greatest number of votes would represent the Roman State in an Italian constituent assembly (16 January).

After the elections, which attracted an enormous vote of 250 000 (21 January), the Mazzinians gained further support from the strong body of democratic deputies; De Boni and Cannonieri (another old Buonarrotian), again a minority within the Committee of Italian Circles, pressed for the proclamation of the republic. The support given them by Garibaldi and Carlo Bonaparte, prince of Canino, both elected deputies, led to the proclamation of the Roman republic by 120 of the 142 members present at the debate (8 February). The first step of Mazzini's life-long struggle had been achieved with decisive popular support – but because of the particular local circumstances. The development he envisaged – towards an Italian constituent assembly and a republic – directed, in typically Buonarrotian manner, by a small group 'at a secret level' (Mazzini, 257, vol. 37, p. 141), was, however, soon to flounder.

Mazzini and the drive for a united republic

Mazzini's hopes lay in the rapid extension of the republic to Tuscany. There the extreme democrats, in control of Leghorn and the popular circle at Florence, had attempted to force the Montanelli-Guerrazzi government to accept universal suffrage for the elections of 20 November. They had been defeated by the insistence of Guerrazzi and a majority of the democrats that such immediate demands be sacrificed in order to conserve unified support for the Montanellian constituent assembly and the renewal of the war. The elections – by limited suffrage – had confirmed the moderate majority in the assembly. As Guerrazzi continued to stress internal public order as the necessary corollary to the resumption of the war in alliance with Piedmont, Montazio and the extreme democrats led an unsuccessful insurrection of the Leghorn workers (13 December).

But as a revolutionary situation developed at Rome in January, the extreme democrats and Mazzinians gained the initiative in Tuscany for the first time. 'Our principle', wrote Montazio on 8 January, 'is that of social regeneration by means of a republican regime' (Ronchi, 320, p. 195). Following the Roman example, Mordini led a mass demonstration of perhaps 30 000 at Florence which forced parliament to agree to the election by universal suffrage of 37 Tuscan deputies to the Italian constituent assembly (23–30 January). With Leopold's flight from Tuscany (8 February), the most radical democrats seemed in control: Montanelli now seconded their demand for the proclamation of a republic and immediate union with Rome, while Guerrazzi was dependent upon their support to ward off the dangers of an internal reaction incited by the moderates and an external invasion by Piedmont. Echoes of the 'great revolution' of 1793, with trees of liberty, phrygian caps, and anti-papal evangelical propaganda coloured the attempts of the 'red republicans' in the circles, supported by Mazzini on his arrival in Florence in mid-February, to supplant the assemblies by the revolutionary proclamation of the republic by the people. In the words of a craftsman, interrogated after the restoration:

> What do you expect? In those days everyone behaved like this and acted directly in these matters. As you well know, everything then was in the hands of the people, whereas now the people no longer count. When I overheard a hostile word, I went and arrested the person. . . . And in any case, who was it who made the arrest? Not I, but the people. (Ronchi, 320, p. 160)

This momentary seizure of the initiative by the republicans, in Tuscany, made possible – as in the Papal States – by the flight of the prince, was soon lost. The landowning moderates' firm hold over large sectors of the peasantry revealed itself in loyalist risings in the countryside. Guerrazzi successfully staved off the demands of the circles by despatching Montanelli and Niccolini to organize the military defence of the frontiers and by decreeing constituent powers to the new assembly called for by the provisional government (6 March). 'The gradations of republican opinion were not few' wrote the *Popolano* (Ronchi, 320, p. 205). As Guerrazzi arrested Montazio and Pigli, and as many democrats were frightened by these popular agitations, the more moderate democrats regained control of the Florentine circle, while the enthusiasm of the people for the democrats (whether of the government or the circle) began to wane. The new assembly rejected proposals of the Mazzinians and Montanellians to proclaim a republic and unite with Rome. With the news of the Piedmontese defeat of Novara and the spread of loyalist peasant risings, the assembly adopted emergency measures of defence and voted dictatorial powers to Guerrazzi (27 March), who attempted secretly and unsuccessfully to reach agreement with the moderates over Leopold's restoration. On 12 April the moderates of the town council assumed provisional powers and recalled the grand-duke.

Rejected as a demagogue by the moderates, abandoned by the republicans whose revolution he had systematically bridled, Guerrazzi ultimately fell because he had isolated himself. But his consistent efforts to resist popular pressure for a republican revolution and direct it towards a renewal of the war against Austria were symptomatic of the reaction of some democrats and all patriotic moderates towards the proclamation of the Roman republic. The Mazzinian republican appeal for an Italian constituent assembly aroused only a cautious response even in Sicily and Venice. In Sicily, despite the enthusiasm of the weak group of democrats and even of some moderates for the Italian constituent assembly and the young democrat Crispi's awareness of the European dimensions of the revolution, separatism predominated among the great majority of liberals, irritated by the lack of understanding displayed for their cause by moderates throughout Italy. The general opinion of the Sicilian revolutionaries was unequivocally expressed by a deputy in the assembly in February 1849: 'The constituent assembly will do what it wants, and we shall not worry about that. I should like to ask the Chamber to tell me what aid we have received, in fourteen months of war, from those gentlemen?' (329, vol. 4, pp. 844–5).

At Venice, an increasingly cautious Manin, worried by the pressure exerted on the government in the new assembly by Sirtori and other 'foreigners', refused to participate in the proposed constituent assembly through fear of compromising Venice in the eyes of the great powers by association with republican regimes. Mazzini's offer of a regular subsidy in return for a defensive alliance with the Roman republic came to nothing. As Manin wrote to the Venetian representative at Rome already on 16 February:

We have urgent need to maintain friendly relations with everyone, and principally with Piedmont, the only state which has an army ready to fight Austria, which wants to make us slaves again. Piedmont keeps a fleet in our seas to protect us from blockade. We must move very cautiously in the choice of a particular political party. So we judge it our duty to temporise. (Cessi Drudi *et al.*, 309, vol. 2, p. 592)

Piedmont, indeed, continued to play a crucial role in inhibiting democratic feeling from developing more widely in Italy into republicanism. With the betrayal of Salasco, the democrats in Piedmont appeared as the only genuine supporters of the national war of independence. Casati's 'Italian' government, supported by the democrats, had resigned, as 'the armistice strengthens the accusation that the sole reason why Sardinian troops entered Lombardy was to impede the establishment of the republic there, and then return those provinces to Austria' (Rodolico, 208, vol. 3, p. 460). Republicanism gained support, particularly at Genoa where a popular movement won over the troops sent to suppress it. As Gioberti mobilized the democrats and Lombard exiles in a massive attack on the Pinelli governments, the moderates retreated into steadily more conservative attitudes, fearful of the anti-aristocratic and revolutionary character of the popular demonstrations. 'Here the democrats wage war more pitilessly on the aristocrats than on the [Austrian] Croats', complained D'Azeglio (Rodolico, 208, vol. 3, p. 528). Cavour saw revolution behind every democratic utterance, even in the proposal for a progressive tax. There was little to distinguish the moderates from the 'retrogrades', as the democrat Brofferio later recalled: 'in those days Count Revel's famous periwig close to that of Count Cavour was a mere trifle' (Cavour, 284, vol. 5, p. cccxxviii).

But if Gioberti's leadership encouraged democratic pressure, it also directed it against Piedmontese municipalism, and towards a revival of his barely updated *Primato* programme of a federal war of independence. His Society for the Italian Confederation, which held a congress at Turin in October, aimed at channelling all efforts into the war against Austria (prospects seemed favourable with the resurgence of revolution in Vienna in October) and explicitly excluded institutional changes within the states or unitarian developments. Gioberti attacked the Piedmontese nobility as provincial and consorted with democrats. But he was no less opposed to internal revolution and drastic social change than Charles Albert, who began to intrigue with such ambiguously democratic figures as the 1831 revolutionary Enrico Misley in an attempt to regain popularity and redeem his destiny as national hero. It was only Charles Albert's personal dislike of the vain-glorious, intriguing, unscrupulous philosopher that delayed the formation of a democratic government under Gioberti until mid-December. Like Guerrazzi, Gioberti then immediately displayed his hostility to the Mazzinian, republican initiative by attempting to increase his own support among the democrats. His election campaign, after his dissolution of parliament, exploited the democratic circles in a deliberate attack on the moderate aristocracy, whom he accused of responsibility for the failure of the war (January 1849). Cavour, defeated in the election, commented contemptuously to Castelli:

> The provinces really are the limit. There is hardly a petty chemist or second-rate village friar, brandishing his *Gazzetta del popolo*, who does not believe that he has the right to treat you and me and all who write for or read the *Risorgimento* as narrow-minded, limited spirits, stupid and retrograde. (Castelli, 342, vol. 1, p. 23)

As the republican tide swelled in central Italy, Gioberti was forced to abandon his initial plans to stall Montanelli, while persuading the pope to return to Rome and convincing Ferdinand to join an Italian league. Ingenious as ever in improvising grandiose schemes, he seized upon the proclamation of the Roman republic and the flight of the grand-duke to elaborate a new and far more dangerous plan to reassert Piedmontese leadership and prepare for the war of independence: in order to forestall a probable Austrian attack on central Italy, Gioberti proposed to obtain English and French diplomatic support for a military invasion of Tuscany to restore Leopold, to be followed by intervention in the Roman States to restore Pius. For Gioberti no contradiction existed between using Piedmontese democrats and troops against Tuscan and Roman democrats and then subsequently waging a united war of independence against Austria. The scheme never materialized, not only because the western powers refused to commit themselves, but because Piedmontese democrats led by Rattazzi and Charles Albert regarded the Tuscan expedition as a distraction from the preparation of the war in Lombardy. Gioberti was dismissed (21 February). But the entire course of his temporary alliance with the Piedmontese democrats revealed, as clearly as Guerrazzi's policies, the determination of all except the 'extreme left' leaders to impede the transformation of a patriotic war into a popular republican revolution. Mazzini's ideal of an independent Italian republic remained confined to Rome; and here too its existence – like that of every revolutionary government in Italy since 1815 – was soon threatened by foreign arms.

The triumph of reaction

The isolation and vulnerability of the republicans at Rome and Venice became the more apparent with the final collapse of Anglo-French attempts to mediate in Italy. In September–October 1848 Palmerston and Cavaignac had gained Austrian agreement to a negotiated peace with Sardinia and had imposed an armistice on Naples and Sicily. But in February 1849 the proposed conference between the two mediating powers, Sardinia and Austria finally broke down before Schwarzenberg's refusal to enter into discussions unless Palmerston first publicly recognized Austria's possession of Lombardy. The consequences were felt immediately in Sicily and Piedmont. Ferdinand of Naples, now sure that the western powers would not intervene by force and encouraged by the support of the Russian tsar, suspended the Neapolitan parliament and resumed the reconquest of Sicily. Despite desperate popular resistance, once the leader of the national guard, Riso, led the moderates to surrender, Palermo was occupied within six weeks (15 May).

In Piedmont the failure of mediation convinced even the moderates of the need to resume the war, lest internal revolution threaten the dynasty. The democrats still held power, although Charles Albert had appointed a general, Chiodo, to head the government. The king had identified himself irrevocably with the war. Isolated in dreams of grandeur or self-immolation, he endeavoured to reconcile Savoyard traditions with the cause of Italy by inviting exiles and democrats to royal dinners. As his loyal follower Sonnaz sadly recalled: 'The only change was the admission to these truly monarchical dinners of a crowd of Ostrogoths in tail-coats, something which the royal table had never seen. There was a crowd of *Italici*, of political foreigners' (Omodeo, 206, p. 151).

Despite the wholly inadequate preparation of the army, the moderate nobles rallied loyally around their sovereign with a somewhat misplaced sense of dramatic tragedy. Even the normally prosaic Cavour could write in a private letter: 'At any rate, should we succumb, it will be in a glorious manner, and without falling into the gutter, as at Rome and Florence' (Cavour, 285, p. 265).

The hopes which revived at Venice and Rome were soon dampened by the news of the defeat of Novara (23 March). Only Charles Albert's instant abdication, Schwarzenberg's fear of French intervention should Austria invade Piedmont, and Radetzky's concern not to provoke a democratic or, worse, a republican revolution by imposing too harsh an armistice, salvaged the somewhat battered dynasty. Even so, Genoa rose in a revolt, supported by the *menu peuple*, which required for its suppression the recall of La Marmora's army.

With Novara the Austrian reconquest of Italy seemed inevitable. The moderates, who had so totally lost control, now began to compromise their principles in order to retain their sovereigns. In Naples many liberals had accepted Ferdinand's restoration of absolutism; in Sicily they had hastily capitulated to Ferdinand's army; in Tuscany they had supplanted the popularly elected constitutional assembly and had recalled Leopold in an unsuccessful attempt to forestall an Austrian invasion. As the Austrians savagely repressed a tragically mistimed democratic rising in Brescia (23 March–2 April), the dying flames of the European revolutions flickered on in three isolated centres – Venice, Rome and Hungary.

Diffidence towards the overwhelming domination of Italy by Austria, as much as internal Catholic and clerical pressure, led to Louis Napoleon's decision to restore the pope by military force. The papacy was, after all, of international concern, as Louis Philippe had shown in 1832. Austrian proposals of joint action were rejected not only because of fear of hostile English reactions and an initial reluctance to engage in open repression, but because of Napoleon's belief that he could mediate between pope and republican Rome and guarantee the continuance of the constitution. But after the unexpected defeat of the first small French expedition (30 April), Louis Napoleon – the revolutionary who had participated in the insurrection of the Legations in 1831 – allowed himself to be trapped in the name of French prestige and was committed to the forcible restoration of temporal power. Rome, where the leading republicans had gathered – Mazzini, Garibaldi, Cernuschi, Pisacane – resisted the French forces until 3 July. Venice, where the most determined republicans like Sirtori and Ulloa took over control from Manin, was only occupied by the Austrians on 27 August 1849.

The democratic legacy

The democratic initiative, like that of the moderates up to summer 1848, had failed. Mazzini's plans for a provisional revolutionary dictatorship to make Rome the spearhead of a national Italian revolution aborted with the containment of the popular republican drive in Tuscany and the royalist renewal of the war in Piedmont. The republicans remained divided in their aims, with unitarians like Mazzini and Saffi, federalists such as Cernuschi and Manin, utopian socialists like Montazio and De Boni. Even more, they remained a minority among the democrats and only succeeded in Venice and Rome because of particular local conditions. Military emergency, rather than any Jacobin concept of a provisional dictatorship, explained the nomination of Mazzini, Armellini and Saffi as triumvirs at Rome, as it explained the powers given to Manin and Guerrazzi at Venice and Florence.

Nevertheless, the democrats emerged from the revolutions of 1848–9 with considerable prestige and popular support. In part, this was due to their courageous determination to fight on in Rome and Venice even after all hope was lost. Noble ladies, like Costanza D'Azeglio, as hostile as any moderate to Mazzini, were enthused by the defence of Rome. As important were the administrative measures of the provisional revolutionary governments. These governments in Venice, Rome and Tuscany had resisted the pressure of the 'extreme left' to adopt radical social measures and had imprisoned or expelled the most 'dangerous' leaders, especially 'foreigners', like Mordini, De Boni and Montazio. The triumvirates at Venice and Rome had rejected proposals that the republics assume their duty to guarantee employment and wages, along the lines of the French revolutionary *ateliers nationaux*. But they were responsible for programmes of reform which developed the liberal themes of earlier years in a more open and democratic manner. The two elections at Venice, like the elections for the constituent assemblies in the Roman states and Tuscany, were held by universal suffrage. Attempts were made to obtain equality before the law by the abolition of distinctions of status or jurisdiction and to impose legislative, administrative and fiscal uniformity. Ecclesiastical tribunals were suppressed in the Roman States and religious equality decreed at both Venice and Rome. Feudal residues – demesne lands, customary communal rights, emphyteuses – were abolished in the Roman States and Tuscany, as slightly earlier by the constitutional assemblies in Sicily and Naples. Attempts were made to replace and renew administrative personnel. Freedom of the press was ensured. The most unpopular taxes, like the personal tax, were eliminated; desperate financial straits led to attempts to tax previously exempt possessions and introduce progressive taxation. Public control of budgets through the assemblies encouraged the sense of participation. Confiscation of ecclesiastical lands in the Roman republic was followed by decrees proposing their division into smallholdings. Emergency measures were adopted to assist the poor in the cities.

Many of the proposals of the provisional or revolutionary governments were never carried out, as time proved too short. The Roman constitution, the most democratic of these two years, was only decreed symbolically on 4 July 1849 at the moment of the republic's fall. The reforms, whether proposed or enacted, were never revolutionary in implication and often tended to look back to the experiences of the Napoleonic years. Because of their liberal basis they were often difficult to distinguish from the moderate programme, except in the emphasis placed on popular sovereignty and more democratic fiscal measures. But they attracted far wider strata of the middle classes and craftsmen, whose support for the governments at Rome and Venice remained solid until their fall. And they were to remain, after the collapse of the revolutions, as evidence of a viable alternative to the policies of the absolutist regimes.

15

The compromises
of diplomacy: 1850–61

The breakdown of the European concert

The failure of the revolutions led to the triumph of reaction, the apparent consolidation of a second restoration, symbolized by Metternich's return to Vienna in 1851. No territorial changes had been achieved; the constitutions, with rare exceptions, had been abolished. Russia and Britain, by their careful circumscription of international conflict during the revolutionary years, seemed to have re-established the Concert of Europe, which successfully employed the traditional instrument of a conference to impose a peaceful settlement of the Danish duchies in 1852.

Schwarzenberg and the young emperor Francis Joscph drastically overhauled the structure of the Austrian domains in an attempt to create an autocratic, centralized, uniform empire: the limited constitution, *octroyée* in 1849, was never brought into effect and was finally abolished in December 1851; traditional institutions, like the Hungarian parliament, were suppressed and replaced by a German-speaking bureaucracy responsible to Vienna. Alone among the conquests of the revolution, the emancipation of the peasants was confirmed, in an endeavour to win popular support against the refractory feudal gentry and middle classes. On Schwarzenberg's unexpected death (1852), the emperor rapidly established a personal autocracy, assuming direct control of the ministry of war and reducing the role of his ministers of foreign and internal affairs, Buol and Bach, to that of mere executors of his policies. Military control, relatively efficient if heavy-handed bureaucracy, censorship, police-spying, a concordat with the Church at the expense of josephine traditions (1855), were the characteristics of this decade of Austrian absolutism, which was only to collapse under the weight of financial indebtedness and military defeat in 1859.

The determined autocracy in Austria and Russia inevitably influenced the semi-independent regions of central Europe. Absolutism and reaction became the norm in Italy, except in Piedmont. Although Ferdinand of Naples, proud of his unaided coup, retreated into an isolation resentful even of Austrian influence, the other princes, reliant on the continued presence of Austrian troops, turned to Vienna for leadership in abolishing their constitutions, and even sought to establish an Austrian-dominated confederation of Italy. In Germany, if Schwarzenberg was unsuccessful in gaining the inclusion of the entire Austrian empire within the confederation or the *Zollverein*, he obtained from Prussia a three-year guarantee of the territorial integrity of the Austrian empire (treaty of Dresden, 1851). The following years were to witness a systematic attempt by Austria to gain effective control of the *Bund* by winning the support of a majority of the German states and forcing Prussia to recognize the validity of its decisions. In any case, Prussian ambitions in Germany seemed less dangerous so long as Frederick William lived under his traumatic obsession with the threat of revolution. Even Louis Napoleon, the disquieting ruler of France, seemed firmly aligned in the conservative camp with his restoration of the pope and his coup against the French republic (2 December 1851).

Yet these years following the revolutions constituted no more than the brief Indian summer of Restoration, the twilight of the Holy Alliance, the dying flickerings of the Concert of Europe. The failure of the revolutions marked a transformation of the political climate of Europe, which was soon to be reflected in the relations between the great powers. Among the democrats, the romantic vision of the palingenesis of Europe and humanity to be achieved through the missions of nations was abruptly shaken by France's reversion from republic to empire. A Mazzini, a Kossuth, might remain constant to their ideals, but the evidence of the bourgeoisie's panic reaction to the fear of communism, as well as of the failure of the revolutionary nations to unite in their common task of regeneration, led many democrats to modify their ideas. For a Lamennais, a Montanelli, a Ferrari, revolution had necessarily to be both political and social, and thus transcend national boundaries. As the socialist Proudhon noted: 'If one thing has been shown clearly, it is that Mazzini's policy of unitarianism, Kossuth's nationalism, the teutonic empire of A. Ruge and his friends, failed totally in Italy, Hungary, and Germany' (Saitta, 113, p. 225). Herzen, echoed faintly by Lorenzo Valerio, was convinced by the betrayal of the western bourgeoisie that hope was only to be found among the Slav peoples. The French anarchist, Ernest Coeurderoy even invoked the revolution of the Cossacks. The failure of the revolutions led to doubts about whether the co-existence of nations would prove inevitably peaceful, whether universal tranquillity would emerge spontaneously and induced both republicans and moderates to restrict their ambitions to peace propaganda and congresses in order to achieve the more limited aim of the settlement of disputes between separate, powerful states.

The peace congresses of the 1850s were symptomatic of the changing relationship between the peoples and the states. They constituted both an acknowledgement of the collapse of faith in the solidarity of nations and a recognition that the governments of the states were not necessarily opposed to the aspirations of their peoples. The international confrontation between governments and peoples was beginning to break down. Governments recognized the imprudence of denying the existence of national aspirations. Some leaders of states – Napoleon III, Cavour, Bismarck – were ready to join hands with nationalism, even with national revolutions and become (in Marx's words) their 'legal executors'. In the decades after 1848–9 nationalism ceased to be the monopoly of the revolutionary or liberal opponents of the state authorities and was taken over by governments, which were thus able to appeal for broader popular support. An essential element in this process was the erosion of the former international solidarity of governments, a withdrawal by states from their tacit acceptance of the principles underlying the Concert of Europe.

The moment of change came with the Crimean War of 1854–6, the first armed conflict between the great powers in forty years. It was a war desired by none of the powers, dominated by diplomatic attempts to prevent its outbreak and its continuation, waged with much bloodshed and futility on a battlefield remote from the real interests of any of the participants. Ostensibly the war had broken out because of the rival claims of France and Russia to the protection of Christians in the Ottoman empire and British fears of Russian ambitions over Turkish territory. In practice, the powers slid slowly into war over a period of thirteen months because of their mutual distrust and their inability to draw back for reasons of prestige.

This distrust and abandonment of national self-restraint, which destroyed the powers' earlier willingness to act in concert, were an indirect consequence of the revolutions. The apparent solidity of the Holy Alliance of the three 'northern courts' proved illusory. Unlike Francis Joseph or Frederick William, Nicholas I, the defender of conservatism against 'revolution' in Europe, deliberately snubbed Napoleon III on his assumption of the title of emperor. The Russian tsar erroneously assumed he would be supported by his German fellow sovereigns when he sharply reasserted his claims against France to control Turkey as a buffer state protecting the Black Sea. Prussia, without direct interests at stake, saw neutrality as the most effective way to ensure that its territory did not become a battlefield in a large-scale war. Austria, fearful of French incitement of the revolution in Italy, nevertheless could not tolerate Russian occupation of the Danubian principalities of Moldavia-Wallachia, which threatened its major trade route. The Holy Alliance, reconstructed in defence of the cause of monarchy in Germany, ultimately broke down because of the traditional rivalry of Austria and Russia over the Balkans and the Ottoman empire.

The *agent provocateur* of the Near Eastern crisis was Napoleon III. The ambiguous, conspiratorial, deceitful nephew of the 'great Napoleon' was the emblematic product (and agent) of the new political climate. In his desire to reconcile order, peace and prosperity with the Napoleonic tradition of glory, social conservatism with revolutionary intriguing, the overthrow of the settlement of 1815 by the emergent nationalities with a peaceful congress of the great powers, Napoleon represented a permanent threat to the Concert of Europe. Hostile to Austria as the embodiment of the Vienna treaties, but always concerned to maintain good relations with Britain and so avoid his uncle's major error, Napoleon achieved his object of destroying the Holy Alliance and gaining an agreement with Britain, but at the probably unexpected and at least partly undesired price of a major war.

Britain, determined as ever to prop up the Ottoman empire against Russian expansion, hostile to the repressive methods adopted by Austria and Russia against the revolutions, overcame its traditional distrust of France in an attempt to reassert the Concert of Europe against the hegemony of Russia. As Britain and France blundered into war against Russia, Austria endeavoured repeatedly and ineffectively to mediate in order to avoid committing itself to either side. When Napoleon finally gained an alliance with Francis Joseph at the price of guaranteeing the *status quo* in Italy (December 1854), Austria – which had already occupied the principalities – still avoided a commitment to warfare by initiating further peace proposals. The war dragged to an end after Nicholas' death, despite British reluctance, through Russian exhaustion and French insistence (February 1856). But the Concert of Europe was irrevocably smashed.

The congress held at Paris in 1856, the first congress since that of Verona in 1822, revealed the unwillingness of the powers to collaborate in reconstructing a system for the peaceful settlement of disputes in Europe. Clarendon was unable to gain acceptance for more than a vague statement of the desirability of mediation before any of the powers engaged in war. Russia was forced to accept neutralization of the Black Sea, an imposition of disarmament not inflicted even upon France in 1814–15. Prussia was punished by the Western powers for her policy of neutrality by only being admitted to the congress in its final stages. Austria discovered that it had alienated both France and Russia, could not depend upon Prussia and was reliant upon British support. Napoleon III was unable to redraw the map of Europe in the interests of oppressed nationalities. Britain felt that its costly war had failed to re-establish the Concert of Europe. Sardinia, a secondary power only admitted to the congress as the ally of France and Britain, failed to make any territorial gains.

The years following the congress of Paris were to reveal the drastic consequences of the breakdown of the Concert of Europe. As no great state felt wholly committed to the existing balance of power, the premises upon which the Concert had been based were replaced by new aggressive, bilateral alliances or diplomatic 'understandings' to impose territorial adjustments of existing treaty arrangements. Four wars involving the great powers were to break out in the following fifteen years, resulting in the creation of the new states of Italy and Germany and the downfall of the most restless agent of change, Napoleon III. International conferences were invoked more frequently than before, but either never met (as in 1859 over the Italian war), or failed in their mediation (as in 1864 over the Prussian–Danish dispute, or in 1867 over the French attempt to annex Luxembourg). The territorial changes achieved by war were no longer legitimized by conferences, as had occurred over Greece and Belgium. By 1871 a new, but less stable balance of power had been created in Europe.

In the long term this rapid upheaval in international relations reflected a slow process of change in the distribution of power among the great states: compared to the industrializing countries – Britain, France and now Prussia – the eastern empires of Austria and Russia were undergoing a period of relative decline, which in Austria's case was to prove permanent. But the immediate causes of change were the alliance of governments, especially of Napoleonic France, with the popular forces of nationalism, and the withdrawal from Europe of its former major guarantors, Russia and Britain.

The great powers and Italy

Crimea and the Paris congress were a disappointment to Napoleon: the price of alliance with Britain had been renunciation of his schemes to extend the war from the Black Sea to Italy and the Rhine. The only concrete recognition of the principle of nationalities had been the enforced cession of Bessarabia by Russia in favour of the Danubian principalities and acceptance that the peoples of that region determine their own future by popular vote. Napoleon's ambitions in support of the peoples of Poland, Hungary and Italy had dwindled into acceptance of a denunciation at the Paris congress – by Clarendon, rather than by Napoleon's conservative foreign minister Walewski – of misgovernment in the Papal States and of the undesirability of the foreign armies of occupation there. Italy, where so many members of the Napoleonic family had lived (and were still living), had always constituted the most immediate object of Napoleon's attention, perhaps because of the traditional sympathy towards France of many Italian patriots (in contrast to the unquestioned hostility of Germans towards French ambitions on the Rhine), certainly because of his belief that the overthrow of the 1815 settlement in Italy would lead inevitably to its disintegration without further war elsewhere in Europe.

The congress of Paris had only served to render the Italian question more pressing by the very fact that it had been discussed. Clarendon was aware of Cavour's new-found mood of belligerence and wrote to Palmerston: 'This congress I can see won't separate without leaving behind it the seeds of some mighty pretty quarrels' (Mack Smith, 111, p. 85). In effect, the congress discussion of 8 April had aroused strong pro-Italian sympathy in Britain and France, reinforcing Napoleon's desire to find a solution. As the Prussian ambassador at Paris wrote:

> Before the congress of Paris there were still many possible remedies, which today will no longer be activated nor have any chance of success; for, once it becomes known in Italy that two powers, which have just emerged victoriously from a gigantic struggle and felt themselves so strong as to press their wishes, have declared loudly that Italians have the right to complain, this moral support will prove of incalculable effect, as it will necessarily be linked to the belief that material support will not be lacking at the right time and place. (Di Nolfo, 334, p. 345)

Economic crisis in 1857, with its threat to the stability of the Second Empire, combined paradoxically with Orsini's attempt on Napoleon's life in the cause of Italian liberation (January 1858) to push the emperor into an active alliance with Piedmont aimed at the destruction of Austrian power in Italy (agreement of Plombières, July 1858, and subsequent treaty of 19 January 1859). Sardinia was to receive upper Italy, but cede Savoy and Nice to France; a new kingdom was to be created in central Italy; the Papal States were to lose the Legations, but otherwise remain independent; the Two Sicilies were to remain intact. The radical destruction of the treaty settlements of 1815 implicit in these objectives accounts for Napoleon's concern to provoke Austria into declaring war and so deprive itself of the possibility of invoking the Concert of Europe. The French alliance with Russia (March 1859), hopes of English neutrality, attempts to persuade Prussia to remain neutral, resistance to English proposals of mediation, were all ultimately subordinate steps, dependent upon Franco-Sardinian ability to justify their respect for public law as defined in treaties by provoking Austrian aggression. That Austria now relied on force, rather than on the moral sanction of treaties, had been publicly recognized by the powers by their discussion at Paris of the Austrian army of occupation in Italy. The war of 1859 finally broke out because of Vienna's conviction that Sardinia could only be checked by force and that the war would spread, with Prussian support, to the Rhine.

Once the destruction of international law had commenced with the war, the consequences were difficult to check. Napoleon only managed to keep the war localized by the hastily concluded peace of Villafranca which left Venetia in Austrian hands (July 1859). He had allied himself with nationalism, but was fearful of revolution. It was Cavour's deliberate incitement of revolution in central Italy, supported by British ministers, which forced Napoleon once more to ignore a settlement legitimized by Europe, abandon his plans for an Italian federation and accept Sardinia's annexation of the Duchies, the Legations and Tuscany in exchange for its cession to France of Savoy and Nice (March 1860). By now too deeply involved to turn against Sardinia, always attracted by adventure, Napoleon adopted a policy of benevolent neutrality during Garibaldi's expedition and even during Cavour's invasion of the Papal States, restraining Russia by offering support for a revision of the Black Sea settlement. Rome alone, whose occupation by French troops Napoleon had long regarded as a tragic but insoluble error, was not to be touched, through fear of arousing the hostility of the French clerical party.

The unification of Italy was certainly not the result that Napoleon (or indeed the only other pro-Italian power, Britain) had envisaged when he embarked upon his destruction of the 1815 settlement. His aim, intimated already at the time of the Paris congress and confirmed at the Plombières meeting, had been to create a confederation of Italian states, similar in scope to other, vaguer confederations he envisaged for liberated peoples in his continuous schemes to redraw the map of Europe. The unexpected conclusion of his involvement in Italy was to make him more cautious and conservative in his restless search for prestige in the following years.

The unification of Italy was an unexpected result, because it ran counter to a general belief among statesmen and diplomats that rearrangements of European territories required federative structures: the Swiss confederation had been strengthened by the Concert in 1857, Wallachia and Moldavia had received a federal constitution in 1858, Austria attempted to reinforce the German confederation in the early 1860s. The fundamental explanation of Italian unification is to be found in the clash of moderate and democratic initiatives within Italy, which seized upon the opportunity opened up by France. But the fact that the Italians were able successfully to exploit this opportunity ultimately depended upon the withdrawal of Russia and Britain from active intervention in European disputes.

The transformation of Russian policy after Crimea soon became apparent. With the death of Nicholas I (1855) and the retirement of the old chancellor Nesselrode (1856), Russia abandoned its traditional defence of the solidarity of monarchs and the treaties of 1815 in order to avenge its national honour by a revision of the 1856 settlement of the Black Sea. Resentful of Austria's treachery so soon after Russian aid in suppressing the Hungarian revolution, Alexander II and Gorčakov sought to separate France from Austria and Britain. Russia saw little reason to change the *status quo* in western Europe, where its support of Naples was long-standing, and was committed to conserving Prussia as a protection for its occupation of Poland. But Alexander's obsession with a revision of the 1856 settlement in the Black Sea led him slowly to accept Napoleon III's plans for a revision of the 1815 settlement in western Europe. A meeting between the two sovereigns at Stuttgart in September 1857 paved the way for a secret alliance in March 1859, by which Alexander promised to adopt an attitude of benevolent neutrality during the

Italian war. It was Russia which defeated British efforts at mediation before the war broke out by calling for a conference on Italy (18 March 1859). Although alarmed by the revolutionary expulsion of legitimate rulers from central Italy in 1859, and even more by Garibaldi's attack on the king of the Two Sicilies in 1860, Alexander remained faithful to his alliance with Napoleon, repeatedly tempted by the prospect of winning France away from England and so facilitating a treaty revision in the Near East.

Russia's policy inevitably influenced that of Prussia. Frederick William IV had been prepared to join France and Russia against Austria. Even when he was replaced in 1858, after a mental breakdown, by his brother William, who was initially hostile to Russia and sought a close alliance with Britain, rivalry with Austria kept Prussia neutral. William refused a Franco-Russian guarantee of German federal territory in exchange for Prussian neutrality before the outbreak of the 1859 war; but he also declined to support Austria when Francis Joseph rejected his demand for the supreme command of German federal forces on the Rhine. He only mobilized the Prussian army during the war in an attempt to impose armed mediation because of the pressure of German opinion, outraged by the aggression against 'German' territory in Italy. Cheated of his hopes of military leadership in Germany by the Franco-Austrian agreement at Villafranca, William finally accepted the Russian guarantee of the Rhine frontier in exchange for neutrality over Italy (October 1859). Hostility towards Austria overcame dislike of France and made Prussia more dependent upon Russian policy. St Petersburg exerted pressure on Berlin to recognize Turin's annexation in central Italy in March 1860 and engineered Berlin's rejection of Vienna's proposals to re-form the Holy Alliance, against Sardinia and France, in July 1860. Prussia's hopes of changing the *status quo* in Germany, like Russia's desire to revise the Black Sea settlement, proved essential elements in isolating Austria and allowing Sardinia to wage two wars in Italy.

Britain's withdrawal from Europe was as crucial as that of Russia in facilitating the destruction of the territorial settlement of 1815. The Crimean War had proved a negative experience and left a widespread desire to avoid a similar drift into another war. The ways had passed when Palmerston could voice the aggressive self-confidence of Britain, 'the new Rome', by bullying Greece into compensating a discreditable merchant of British nationality, don Pacifico. The British still believed in their moral obligation to state their opinion to Europe, but were now reluctant to back up their sermons with force. The leading statesmen – Palmerston, Russell, Clarendon, Malmesbury – remained opposed to both Russian and French plans to revise treaty settlements, but failed to appreciate that an intransigent position over the Black Sea would leave them unable to resist Napoleon's manoeuvres in the west. In a period of unusually weak governments, with

divided and disorganized parties, English public opinion – for once concerned about foreign affairs – was able to exert exceptional pressure.
Generic support for liberalism and nationalities had acquired specific tones
among both educated and popular classes in support of a free Italy. For the
educated, Italian culture and the traditional dislike of 'popery' reinforced
both the Gladstonian denunciation of the evils of Neapolitan misgovernment and sympathy for the liberal, free trade reforms of Cavour in Piedmont. For the populace, the sword of honour presented to Garibaldi by the
Newcastle workers in 1854 was the counterpart to the attack in London on
the 'butcher' of Brescia and Hungary, Haynau.

Despite public dislike of Austrian absolutism, British policy at the Paris
congress was to maintain support of Austria as the most effective defence
against Russia; Clarendon indeed persuaded Napoleon to sign a treaty with
Austria and Britain guaranteeing the integrity of the Ottoman empire (15
April 1856). Only over Italy did the British leaders disagree with Austria,
but not to the extent of wishing to upset its territorial settlement. Cavour's
hopes of obtaining compensation for Sardinia in the form of the Italian
duchies – by despatching their rulers to the Danubian principalities – was
vetoed by Clarendon. His ambitions over papal territory had already been
dashed by Napoleon. For Clarendon and Palmerston, the most that could
be done for Italy was to reform or secularize the Papal States by insisting on
a withdrawal of Austrian and French troops and to denounce Neapolitan
repression; in like manner, the most that could be done for Poland was to
appeal to the tsar's humanity. In both cases, as in his public denunciation of
the papacy and Naples on 8 April, Clarendon was far from unaware of the
utility of such a stance in maintaining the support of English public opinion.
As he wrote to Palmerston on 31 March:

> If we can now do anything for Italy and for Greece and for Bomba's victims
> and place an opinion on record about Poland and the expediency of recurring
> to arbitration before the *ultima ratio* of war is resorted to we shall satisfy public
> opinion in England, I hope. (Di Nolfo, 334, p. 504)

But the ineffectiveness of this reluctance to back up protest by force was
rapidly revealed in the pope's refusal to accept reform and the king of
Naples' sharp retort to both Britain and France not to interfere in the
internal affairs of his kingdom (autumn 1856). British leaders remained tied
to their faith in the concession of civil liberties and reforms as the solution
to the Italian problem, and were unwilling to conceive of any war for
independence (and even less for unity). But when the crisis exploded in
1859 their policy of non-intervention tended to isolate Austria yet further:
Britain was prepared to guarantee Piedmont against Austria (but not the
opposite) and warned Prussia and Naples against enlarging the area of
the war. Piedmont could rely on British (and French) determination to

maintain its frontiers even in the event of defeat, because of the importance of the north Italian state to the balance of power.

With the war against Austria, the major British worry remained French
ambitions. But after Austria's ultimatum pro-Italian sympathy grew strong.
Indeed, when returned to power in the general election of May 1859, the
old liberal leaders Palmerston and Russell, supported by Gladstone, were
even prepared to revive the earlier British policy of intervention in order to
support Piedmont and control France. But the years of adventure were now
over and the 'two dreadful old men' (in Victoria's words) were restrained by
the Queen and their cabinet colleagues. As the crisis revived after the war,
Palmerston and Russell moved towards support of Piedmontese annexation
of central Italy, as a strong Sardinia would help to check France. The
cession of Savoy and Nice aroused deep resentment but, if Cavour was now
less trusted, popular and official support for Italy remained strong. Enthusiasm for Garibaldi, as much as uncertainty within the government, lay
behind Britain's benevolent attitude towards the invasion of the Two
Sicilies. But British policy had become hesitant and confused. Only the
threat of revival of the Holy Alliance, with its dangerous implications for
the Near Eastern settlement, led Russell to issue a rhetorical declaration on
27 October 1860 justifying Italian unification in terms of the will of the
people. British refusal to intervene or mediate in these crucial years (in contrast to its attitude in earlier crises) was as much responsible as Russian
neutrality for blocking the normal machinery of international diplomacy,
which facilitated the Italian assault on Austria and the other Italian rulers.

Cavour and Italy

The transformation of the Italian question from a perennially dangerous,
but ultimately secondary, problem of European diplomacy into the dominating issue of international relations in 1859–60 had occurred with great
suddenness. In the years of reaction after 1848–9, Piedmont was regarded
by most European diplomats as a dangerous and revolutionary state, whatever its protestations of moderation and conservatism. The attempts of the
other Italian states to involve Austria in a defensive league derived from
anxiety over Piedmont. Only by deliberate ambiguity was the house of
Savoy able to combine collaboration with democratic forces in Italy with
traditional dynastic ambitions of aggrandizement. Hence it was with some
justification that, until the Crimean war, Piedmont was regarded as conservative and treacherous by democrats in Italy, and as ambitious and revolutionary by diplomats in Europe.

But Savoyard ambitions and the distrust they aroused were only of
relative importance at the European level; the kingdom of Sardinia was,
after all, only a secondary power. As the Crimean crisis developed in 1853–4,

the Piedmontese leaders hoped for a general conflagration, an ideological war of the western powers against Russia and Austria, which would enable a small state like Sardinia to profit from the weakening of the Austrian stranglehold on Italy. Excitement grew, Victor Emanuel was determined on war, the dying Balbo revived his old pipe-dream of an 'orientalizing' of Austria towards the Balkans. The weakness of Piedmont and the inconsistency of these fantasies was revealed by the rapid fluctuations of hopes following each turn of Napoleon's shifting manoeuvres towards Austria. As Margherita Provana di Collegno noted in her diary for 28 February, Napoleon wanted to show Austria that 'he possessed the torch to set light [to Italy] and the hose to extinguish it, as he pleased' (Malvezzi, 305).

France's apparent success in winning an Austrian alliance at the cost of maintaining the *status quo* in Italy (December 1854) meant not only the destruction of Piedmontese – and Cavour's – hopes, but the revival of Piedmont's perennial danger – isolation. Cavour's decision to enter the war, even alongside Austria, pushed through against the hostility of his cabinet (9 January 1855), was taken to escape from this isolation and, even more, to prevent Victor Emanuel sacrificing him in favour of a conservative government of 'diehards'. But the alliance with France and Britain revealed Sardinia's fundamental impotence as a secondary power, unable to lay down terms to the western powers. As Solaro della Margarita, the most intransigent of the diehards, savagely criticized Cavour in parliament:

> Why have France and Britain asked us, so far from the theatre of war, to join the treaty, rather than Denmark which has the keys to the Baltic, rather than putting pressure on Stockholm, where hopes of recovering Finland must certainly be tempting, especially as Sweden can provide an army no less hardy than ours and a sizable fleet? (Valsecchi, 333, p. 470)

The western powers, indeed, were to conclude an alliance with Sweden in November 1855.

The congress of Paris did not increase Sardinia's weight in Europe. Although Sardinia was admitted to the congress and Prussia excluded until late, there were no doubts about the respective importance of the two states. Cavour was expected not to abuse the hospitality extended him by intervening too much in the sessions. He returned empty-handed and was convinced of his failure. If his admittance to the congress signified the acceptance of Sardinia by the great powers as a 'respectable' state, in the months following the congress he threatened, in his desperation, to squander this newly acquired status by revolutionary schemes to spark off a new war. To his surprise, the discussion of the Italian question at Paris had won for Piedmont a prestige in Italy unprecedented since Charles Albert's initial declaration of war on Austria – and uncontaminated by association with revolution. But Austria's unexpectedly conciliatory policy in Lombardy (as in Hungary) threatened to destroy this position. Cavour's public refusal to oppose Austria by revolutionary means (15 January 1857), marked his acceptance of a diplomatic solution to the Italian question. But no longer was Cavour ready passively to await the slow process of diplomacy. The experience he had acquired at the Paris congress was now to be employed to force the hand of European diplomacy. Conspiracy was not excluded, whether with Murattists or democrats, but it was to be carefully controlled and subordinated to what European diplomacy could be forced to accept. At Paris Cavour had wholly misjudged the limits of English support and, ignorant of the Anglo-Austrian treaty, had intrigued with English tory leaders, hoping to provoke a new war against Austria, with English aid. He was now to turn definitively towards France. The total breakdown of the European concert was to offer him his opportunity to exploit the differences among the powers. Even so, it needed the constant threat of the democrats (or what he regarded as a threat) to induce Cavour to accept the possibility of unifying Italy.

The crisis of the political democrats

The democrats had emerged from the revolutions with considerable prestige and much optimism. They had redeemed their loss of the initiative in 1848 by their resistance in 1849, with popular support, in Rome, Venice and Hungary. The moderates had compromised themselves everywhere during the revolutions, and now, after their collapse, had either joined the reaction or been forced into silence or exile. The very harshness of the reaction in all the Italian states except Piedmont (where the situation remained uncertain) encouraged the democrats, because it publicly revealed the illusory bases of giobertism and moderatism, strengthened popular hostility to Austrian domination and dynastic rule, and pointed to revolution as the only effective means of liberation. Even more, the optimism of the Italian democrats was reinforced by their belief, shared by other democratic exiles, that the tide of European revolution had receded only momentarily and would soon, very soon, surge forward with irresistible impulse. The messianic year of revolution was to be 1852, the year in which Louis Napoleon's mandate as president of the French republic expired, when the people would rise of their own accord or defeat an attempted coup by Napoleon. For all the Italian democrats the revival of the revolution thus remained intimately linked to its resurgence in France, although they differed in their assessment of the significance of France's revolutionary mission.

It was, inevitably, Mazzini who took the initiative in organizing for this renewal of revolution. Mazzini's reputation, because of his leadership of the Roman republic, probably stood higher than ever among European as much as among Italian democrats. Although he retained his faith in the mission of peoples who still had to conquer their own nationality, Mazzini also laid his plans in expectancy of an outbreak of revolution in France. But if France was to offer the signal, the success of the revolution would depend on the simultaneous risings of the peoples of central Europe, especially the Slav nationalities of the Austrian empire. Of the four Slav groups identified by Mazzini (Russians, Poles, Bohemian-Moravians, and a heterogeneous group of Serbs, Croats, Slovenes, Montenegrins and Bulgarians), the Poles were destined to act as the guiding nation, while the Bohemians would provoke the collapse of the Austrian empire; even more crucial than the Slavs were the Hungarians, whose rising, timed to coincide with that of the Italians, would destroy Austria. Hence, for his new organization, the European Democratic Committee (1850), Mazzini carefully selected representatives of the different nationalities: Ledru-Rollin (French), Ruge (German), Darasz (Polish), Bratianu (Rumanian). Mazzini's ignorance of central Europe (where he thought the Hungarians were rapidly becoming a Slav nation) led to Kossuth's refusal to join a committee which included a Rumanian, although he was still ready to collaborate with Mazzini in a joint Italian-Hungarian agreement. But more serious was Mazzini's selection of anti-socialist colleagues to represent the French and Germans, which immediately aroused the hostility of the socialist groupings.

The choice, in fact, was prejudicial to Mazzini's hopes of unifying the entire front of democratic forces under his banner. The revolutions had brought to the fore the antithetical positions of socialist and nationalist democrats throughout western and central Europe. Apart from the practical unreality of Mazzini's organization – only in Hungary were there serious possibilities of arousing support among the people – this self-nominated committee merely accentuated the divisions among the *émigrés*, arousing the bitter or contemptuous comments of Blanc, George Sand, Herzen, Marx and Engels. The contemporaneous creation of an Italian National Committee with the Roman triumvirs Saffi, Saliceti and others, provoked the same reaction, despite Mazzini's claims to legitimize the committee with the authority delegated to its leaders by the dying Roman republican assembly. It was Mazzini's exclusive monopoly of the right to create a national party, as much as his programme, that aroused hostility: 'In Italy, since Pius IX's fall, since Charles Albert's fall, and since the word has come forth from Rome, it is necessary to repeat that there is and there can only be one party: the NATIONAL PARTY' wrote Mazzini (257, vol. 39, p. 341). But, as George Sand replied, refuting Mazzini's attacks on socialists: 'You have denounced all doctrines, whatever their kind, with the arrogance of a pope who proclaims: "*Outside of my Church, there is no salvation!*"' (Mazzini, 257, vol. 47, p. 205).

Mazzini's programme had not changed: imbued with the language of religious dedication, he again invoked unity, national insurrection under the guidance of a small group, and a constituent assembly to decide Italy's future once independence had been achieved. No mention was made of the republic, because Mazzini hoped to attract those exiles still undecided in their attitude towards constitutional Piedmont. There is little evidence that Mazzini made much headway among such exiles. Gioberti, in his final book *Of the Moral and Civil Revival of Italy* (1851), also placed his hopes in a democratic revival in France. But, although sceptical, he reluctantly admitted that a constitutional anti-Austrian, anti-clerical, nationally-minded Piedmont might yet save Italy. The Piedmontese monarchy, like Mazzini, continued to attract support. Mazzini's belated assertion of the republic (July 1851) was not merely a response to the criticisms of socialist and federalist democrats, but a recognition of his failure to win over those patriots still inclined towards Piedmont.

But it was Mazzini's criticism of socialism, veiled so long as he hoped to win consensual support, acrimonious after Napoleon's coup of 2 December 1851, which aroused the most violent opposition. Mazzini ascribed the failure of the revolutions as much to the materialistic 'systems' of Fourier, Proudhon, Leroux, and Blanc, as to the treachery of the moderates. Transposing to Europe, as always, his vision of an Italy untroubled by socialism or class conflict, Mazzini cast his renewed anathema against France's revolutionary mission in terms of the perverse effects of its socialists on the true revolutionary fervour of the masses. Inner conviction combined with tactical necessity in his onslaught, because Mazzini – not unjustifiably – feared the efficacy of reactionary and clerical propaganda in identifying him with the social terrors of communism. The new Jesuit journal, *Civiltà Cattolica*, after all, attacked him, as the incarnation of evil, as 'the apotheosis of prostitution and assassination, the abolition of the family, the emancipation of women, the denial of the right of property' (*La Civiltà Cattolica*, vol. 1, 1850). Fearful of losing the support of the middle classes, with their leadership and financial means, for which he now appealed, Mazzini wanted to shelve all discussion of economic and social reform until after the successful revolution:

> There are men who, deceived by the existence of reactionary writers, believe in good faith that we want to march towards our goal by terror, by disorder, to profit from who knows what savage anarchy, which would swallow up all social guarantees. It is to these men that we direct our words. Let them be reassured; we do not hide secret thoughts. (Mazzini, 257, vol. 46, p. 76)

Mazzini's dogmatic dismissal of all opposition as factious, his rigid assertion of a programme unaltered since it first proclamation in 1831, his attack on socialists and federalists, thus immediately destroyed his claims to undisputed leadership of the democratic exiles. Whereas before 1848 his leadership had been challenged because he refused to compromise with moderates or monarchy, and only isolated voices had opposed his dismissal of social issues, now the experiences of the revolutions led many of its former leaders to denounce the political formalism of his programme. For Mazzini the course of the revolutions merely confirmed the righteous certitude of his interpretation of the direction of human progress. For Ferrari and Cattaneo, for Montanelli and Pisacane, for De Boni and Maestri, the failure of the revolutions necessitated self-critical reflection, a deeply personal analysis of past errors in order to achieve future unity. As Montanelli wrote:

> Some would like to adjourn the discussion and declare it untimely and damaging. . . . But why are we divided? Because we agree on neither the end nor the means of the action we wish to undertake together. If we are in good faith, if error divided us, discussion and the search for truth can only remove the misunderstandings and unite us. (Montanelli, 315, pp. 50–1)

Liberty had been sacrificed to independence and unity, the struggle against privilege to the war against the foreigner, wrote Mazzini's critics. In Ferrari's words:

> If one wishes to give the name of foreigner to the enemy, not only the Austrian is a foreigner, but the baron who oppresses the cottager, the prelate who has neither country nor family; the barbarian is not only to be found at Milan and Venice, he rules at Rome, where he represents the supremacy of a cosmopolitan error; not only the Holy See is barbarian, but that part of the population whose privilege of wealth gives it a stake in the dominion of Church and Empire. (Ferrari, 269, p. 1)

The failure to make liberty the motive force of the revolution had led to the containment of the struggle within the restricted boundaries of separated nations. As Cattaneo explained: 'The expansive force of the revolution was thus lessened, in that the idea of universal liberty was not put forward, but only the narrower idea of a solitary independence' (Cattaneo, 265, vol. 1, p. 371).

A national struggle for independence had few chances of success, because of the international character of both papacy and empire. 'This original curse of being born in the land of pope and emperor, of Christ and Caesar', as Ferrari wrote (268, p. 156), made it imperative for Italians, even more than for others, to fight for the only cause shared by all oppressed, irrespective of national differences – liberty. For De Boni as for Maestri, for Montanelli as for Ferrari, reaction inevitably formed a supranational Holy Alliance, in which the cosmopolitanism of the papacy attracted to itself the solidarity of all the privileged classes of Europe.

Mazzini's insistence on unity, as much as on independence, had led to the failure of the revolutions. The federalists, who now made their voice heard, were acutely conscious of the regional and local character which had lain behind the popular movements. For Cattaneo the Lombard rising had demonstrated that the people would fight, but only if they were assured of their own individuality and natural institutions. The revolution had been ruined by the campaign for fusion under a monarchical banner, for which the ground had been unwillingly but unquestionably prepared by Mazzini's invocation of unity.

Mazzinianism was the republican mirror-image of monarchical fusionism, as Ferrari noted acutely, when describing his alternative programme: 'My task was to avoid all polemics with Mazzinianism, but to link it with the Piedmontese system so closely that it could separate itself no more' (Cattaneo, 263, vol. 2, pp. 349–50). Cattaneo had never defined what he understood by federalism, despite Pisacane's appeals to him. But he identified it instinctively with liberty: 'Liberty is republic, and republic is plurality, or federation' (Cattaneo, 263, vol. 2, pp. 122, 157). Unity was artificial, an imposition on the liberty of the individual. Cattaneo did not exclude the gradual unification of Italy, as civil and material progress within a republican federation of communes slowly strengthened the natural bonds between Italians. Ferrari went further: his libertarian cult led him to defend the autonomy of the individual at all costs and to relegate unity to so distant a future as to render it unimaginable. But both Cattaneo and Ferrari elaborated their doctrine of republican federalism in deliberate polemic with Mazzini on the basis of their experiences of the revolutions, as a practical method to reconcile liberty with the struggle for independence.

Against these self-evident truths Mazzini, according to his critics, offered no more than a superficial political cry, a purely formalistic concept of liberty which masked the conservation of inequality. 'Formal liberty . . . protects friend and enemy, good and evil, justice and injustice, truth and error', denounced Ferrari. It explained why Mazzini had abandoned all truly revolutionary principles in 1848, while still expecting the peasants to sacrifice themselves:

> He marches with the *signori*, but wants all the poor to sacrifice themselves for his cause; he fraternises with the executioners of June [1848 at Paris], then claims that the war is a popular one and explosive; he has the ideas of Cavaignac, but expects the miracles of socialism. (Ferrari, 268, pp. 125, 107–8)

The revolution could only succeed if it was a social as well as, even more than, a political revolution. Socialist ideas and experiences, which had begun to circulate on a new scale in Italian democratic circles during the revolutionary years, increased the awareness among Mazzini's critics of the withdrawal of popular support after the initial insurrections. The isolation of the masses, and especially of the peasants, their desire to improve their material condition, the failure to conserve their support by the adoption of a truly revolutionary 'concept', are constantly recurring themes in the flurry of critical, militant publications produced in these years by many minor figures from both north and south, as well as by the former democratic leaders. Some, like Petruccelli della Gattina or La Farina, did not draw radical conclusions from their analysis of the deep class divisions and revolutionary force of the peasantry. Others, particularly Lombards like Maestri or De Cristofaris, turned to Proudhonian ideas of free credit as the solution to the social problem. But for Ferrari, Montanelli and Pisacane (although not for Cattaneo) only socialism could ensure the success of the revolution in Italy.

Giuseppe Ferrari, always eclectic, directly influenced by the experiences of the Revolution in France, as well as by Proudhon, Saintsimonism and Louis Blanc, was acutely conscious of the backwardness of Italian social structures compared with those of France, but deduced from this that only a revolution that was both social and political could succeed in Italy, and then only if it was achieved alongside a socialist, democratic revolution in France. Socialism, for Ferrari, was to be achieved by the triumph of 'irreligion', of reason and science over dogma and religious myth; but equally by an 'agrarian law', justified by man's right to subsistence, 'the right of need', capable of realization by the limitation of private property through the abolition of inheritance. Giuseppe Montanelli, less radical and less conscious of the profound divisions within Italian society than Ferrari, whose atheism he rejected, was equally hostile to Mazzini's political revolution and saw socialism as the only solution for Italy, a Christian socialism of French, particularly Lamennaisian derivation, which attacked the political power of the clergy and was concerned to improve the condition of the peasants and increase the liberty of the individual against the encroachments of the state.

Carlo Pisacane, strongly influenced by his direct contacts with French socialists during his exile in England and possibly also by Ferrari's *Republican Federation* (1851), emerged with the most radically socialist conclusions of all the Italian democrats in his *War Fought in Italy in the Years 1848–9* (1851). More than Ferrari, Pisacane derived his analysis of the failures of 1848–9 and deduced his conclusions of the need for a wholly socialist revolution from his class interpretation of the conditions and aspirations of the Italian bourgeoisie and masses:

> The bourgeoisie in Italy possesses land, capital; it has the monopoly of trade, science, industry and employment; it rules in Italy, as in America, England, France; it only lacks certain franchises which it enjoys in other states; to acquire them it has staged some risings ever since 1815, which have been and always will be in vain. (Pisacane, 324, p. 352)

To succeed, the bourgeoisie needed popular support. But only 'a clear, practical concept, which would promise the people a change in its condition' could retain the enthusiasm of the popular masses after the initial insurrection and create a disciplined, courageous army, an 'armed nation', to defeat the Austrians. Direct democracy, the abolition of private property and (with Proudhonian overtones) the destruction of governmental authority offered the essence of this 'concept', this 'motor' of the revolution. Italy's hopes now lay in the people's consciousness of their oppressed condition:

> The people is aware of its ills, and mutters when it perceives the landowner and capitalist idly enjoying the fruits of the labour of the peasant and worker, who barely earn a living scrap by scrap. The people no longer accepts its state, but suffers it. This first sentiment of disgust with its present condition which is already beginning to emerge among the people, is the seed of the future Italian revolution. (Pisacane, 324, pp. 349–50)

The need for a social revolution, which would win mass support by the promise of material improvement, thus emerged among Italian democrats in the years immediately following 1848–9 as a criticism and alternative to Mazzini's political revolution. It implied, again in contradiction to Mazzini, close links with, if not dependence upon, French revolutionary initiative. For, as Ferrari argued, the French initiative lay in its revolutionary, socialist ideas, not in the geographical area where the first spark of insurrection would catch fire. Only Pisacane, with his strong sense of the need for political independence as a condition of liberty, disagreed with this reliance on the French initiative typical of republican federalists like Ferrari, Montanelli, Cattaneo, or Manin. Indeed, for Pisacane, the weakness of the bourgeoisie and the absence of a strong national army facilitated the revolution in Italy. But for all these opponents of Mazzini, the restriction of the democratic programme to the purely political issue of national independence was outdated and destined to failure because of its inability to arouse popular support.

Mazzini and his democratic opponents

Ferrari took the lead in 1851 in attempting to organize a republican federalist party in opposition to Mazzini among the exiles in France and Piedmont. His *Republican Federation*, published by a Swiss typography at Capolago directed by Cattaneo, was intended as a preliminary manifesto. Federalism, for Ferrari, risked the same accusations of 'formalism' as Mazzini's unity, unless it was integrated with socialism. As he wrote to Cernuschi:

> The federal dialectic (excuse the phrase) is not understood, is not popular; I mean, it is something that can be swept away in false, arid discussions of administrative matters. Socialism linked to this idea throws an instantaneous light upon it, the boldness of telling the truth amidst a bundle of fictions explains everything, even to the slowest. (Della Peruta, 271, p. 440)

Ferrari's hopes rested on Cattaneo, whose prestige alone could challenge that of Mazzini. But Cattaneo, who had only reluctantly taken the lead in the Five Days of Milan, who had then withdrawn in disgust from the republican squabbles at Paris in 1848, was a man of study and not of action. In exile in Switzerland, his entire activity was absorbed in gathering together the materials which would demonstrate the reasons why the Italian revolution had failed. Opinion alone could prepare the future and Cattaneo had thrown himself into a cultural policy directed as much towards the illumination of the middle classes as towards the 'multitudes'. His very faith in the transcendental values of middle-class culture marked his distance from the socialism of Ferrari or Pisacane, as from their belief in popular action:

> Only education, encouraged and promoted in every manner, will be able to produce a remedy to that paralysis of intelligence and will by which our populations have been afflicted, and which leaves the way open for the State to seize possession of the country's forces and become its sole and absolute administrator. . . . When public opinion will be for us, which heaven knows *it is not*, we shall have money, arms, soldiers and everything; undeceive the multitude, and the oppositions fall into nothing. (Cattaneo, 264, vol. 3, p. 132; 263, vol. 2, p. 46)

Despite Cattaneo's reluctance to play an active role, the extent of opposition to Mazzini by mid-1851 seemed likely to bear fruit. Under Lamennais' inspiration a Franco-Spanish-Italian Committee, the Latin Committee, was created in Paris in July as a direct challenge to Mazzini's European Democratic Committee at London. Its social programme, with its defence of property, bore the mark of Lamennais' Christian social humanism. Montanelli's membership of the Committee served to draw together the heterogeneous opposition to Mazzini. His programme for Italy was intransigently republican and confirmed the need to link the Italian to the coming French revolution. Even more, he denied Mazzini's assertion of the need for a single provisional dictatorial power during the period of insurrection, visualizing instead the spontaneous emergence of a plurality of directive centres as each region liberated itself.

The threat to Mazzini was clear, and he tried in vain to reach a compromise. His failure appeared the more marked because of the defection of followers like Sirtori from his own Committee. Manin, Cernuschi and many of the former representatives or ministers of the Roman constituent assembly, including the Bonaparte prince of Canino, rallied to Montanelli. The Sicilian exiles at Paris, previously closely connected to the London committee, began to break away. Ferrari, while contemptuous of its social programme, now planned to take over the Italian section of the Latin committee by placing Cernuschi and Cattaneo as representatives of Lombardy, and Manin as representative of the Veneto. But Cattaneo's renewed refusal, which he justified on this occasion by Ferrari's exaggerated rejection of the ultimate prospect of unity in favour of federalism, left the opposition without a leader. Because of its heterogeneous composition, the anti-Mazzinian agitation rapidly died down, despite Ferrari's efforts to keep it alive. The Napoleonic coup of 2 December and the crisis of French socialism and democracy inevitably reflected negatively on Italians like Ferrari and Montanelli, who had placed their hopes on socialism and France. No democratic alternative, whether federalist or socialist, was to emerge in the following years as a serious challenge to Mazzini's political, unitarian nationalism.

Even before the French coup put paid to their hopes, Ferrari and Montanelli had only succeeded in influencing *émigré* circles, whether in France or in the Sardinian states. By the end of 1851, and especially during 1852, Mazzini had managed to organize a broader network of support in Italy than ever before. Despite the flight or imprisonment of so many leading figures, the revolutions had aroused opposition to the foreigner and the old regimes on so broad a scale within the cities that secret conspiracy revived immediately with the Restoration.

In Rome and throughout the urban centres of the Papal States a highly centralized Mazzinian network was set up in hierarchical manner, consisting of squads and squadrons, centuries and cohorts, town and provincial committees, which recruited wide support among craftsmen and unskilled workers as well as among the middle classes. In Tuscany the Mazzinian leaders of the revolution, such as Cironi and Fenzi, rapidly organized the movement, attempting to establish contact with the moderate constitutionalists who were most hostile to the Restoration. In Lombardy and to a lesser extent in Venetia, the same Mazzinian pattern emerged under local leaders at Milan, Brescia, Pavia, Mantua and Como. In Piedmont, and especially in Liguria, Mazzinianism spread, gaining popular support through the recently formed mutual aid societies. In Sicily, where the experiences of the revolution had taught the democrats to distinguish themselves more clearly from the moderates, the tradition of separatism was abandoned, although the democrats – who now turned to Mazzini – insisted on a high degree of administrative autonomy and decentralization in the unitarian state. Only in the kingdom of Naples was Mazzini unable to organize support, because of the intensity and ferocity of the reaction (since 15 May 1848), which had checked the consolidation of a democratic movement; the repression of the 'Italian unity' sect and (at the end of 1850) of the 'military-carboneria sect' left Mazzini without contact in the Mezzogiorno until after the Milan rising of 1853.

The characteristics of Mazzini's renewed National Association were the wide degree of support it attracted in Italy among the urban populace and its reversion to the extreme form of centralization of the original *Giovine Italia*. Much of its popular support derived from the working-class mutual aid societies which had developed since about 1840, mainly in northern Italy. In Piedmont the moderates' influence was sufficiently strong to restrict the activities of these societies to non-political economic questions, such as insurance against sickness and death. But in Liguria – especially in Genoa – the Mazzinians had consolidated their support through these craftsmens' associations by 1850.

In Milan a secret working-class organization, combining anti-Austrian, patriotic aims with mutual aid purposes, developed independently of Mazzini, under the democratic direction of Carlo De Cristofaris and the hardened conspirator G. B. Carta. Its very name, the Committee of Olona (a department of the Jacobin Cisalpine republic), and its terroristic methods, executing spies, distinguished it from the Mazzinians. And only after Carta's arrest was Mazzini able to make contact and absorb it within his network in 1852. But the overtly class character of this workers' movement, so totally in contrast with Mazzini's anti-socialist, associationist position, was to have negative repercussions on the insurrection because of the fear it inspired in the middle-class Mazzinians. De Cristoforis' friend, Guttièrez, described the worrying effects on the Milanese Mazzinians of the workers' offer to continue their terroristic campaign:

> One suggested bumping off a spy, another proposed a police commissioner, yet another a general, another a banker, another a Jesuit. . . . The leaders energetically rejected these bloody offers. . . . This rejection upset the plans of the infernal archangels, and was the original cause of that sullen hostility to which the genteel members of the association were subjected by the brutal men who had penetrated it; matters reached such a pitch, that the former found themselves caught unawares between two fires, the foreign oppressors and the saviours: and often the latter caused more terror than the former. (Guttièrez, 335, p. 159)

If these social tensions only burst forth at the moment of the insurrection, Mazzini's policy of centralization had aroused resistance already in 1852, as it had done before 1848. Within the National Association, Giuseppe Petroni attempted to transform the Roman Committee into the central organism for the whole peninsula and, with the support of the Tuscan Mazzinians Cironi and Mazzoni, gained the adherence of the Tuscan organization. Petroni's reasons (apart from his authoritarian personality) were to be found in the typical fear of conspirators within an oppressed country that their views over the future problems of government would be ignored by the exiles. He wrote to Mazzini:

> It's sad that you reject all internal work – to the disgust of all the best elements within the country – and that you consider the men of the interior as a passive mass, as cannon fodder. It's regrettable that you continue the system of middle-aged exiles and consider the interior as a land of conquest for the émigrés. (Guglielmetti, 336, pp. 133 ff.)

At Genoa, a 'committee of war' headed by Pisacane and Medici challenged the authority of the London committee; supported by Mazzinians like Mordini and Bertani, they proposed to depose Mazzini and form a broad republican front with federalist and social-minded democratic groups. Other democrats, from Sicily and elsewhere, became more tepid about Mazzini's republican stand. The movement could not be held together for long because of its size and the tensions within it.

By mid-1852 Mazzini began to prepare for an imminent insurrection. His deliberate delay over deciding the localities and tactics of the insurrection had assisted him in overcoming the negative repercussions of the Napoleonic coup in France, in contrast to his federalist rivals. But police arrests in Lombardy, which were to result in the execution of the last martyrs of the Risorgimento at Belfiore, now made action the more urgent. Lombardy-Venetia was to form the strategic centre of the insurrection, as this would paralyse Austria, and could coincide with a revolt in Hungary. A rising in the south was excluded because of the lack of a solid network of support; while the presence of French troops made an initial rising in Rome too dangerous. Support and financial aid was obtained from the Piedmontese parliamentary democrats, Lorenzo Valerio and Agostino Depretis; Lombard and Hungarian exiles in Piedmont, led by Benedetto Cairoli and Stefan Türr, prepared to enter Lombardy. The Milan revolt was to lead to a general rising in Lombardy, cutting off the Austrian supply routes, a mass insurrection in Emilia, Romagna and the Marches to destroy the Austrian lines in Italy, and then an attack upon the kingdom of Naples which was to coincide with a rising in Sicily.

The major difficulty lay in the reluctance of the Lombard middle-class Mazzinians to initiate the revolution, after the arrests which had disorganized their network. But, as Mazzini was forced to admit, their fears ran deeper and were directed towards the danger of the insurrection turning into a social revolt. Mazzini and Saffi, now in Switzerland, tried desperately to reconcile the two social groups, whose reciprocal mistrust negated every principle of patriotic collaboration. In mid-January 1853, Mazzini wrote despairingly to an English friend:

> My followers are admirable people: a middle-class hostile of course to the Austrians, but convinced that a rising would have no chance and consequently preaching against it; and delegates from the popular classes who come to me declaring that they do not want to be led by the gentlemen. (Mazzini, 257, vol. 48, p. 129)

It was fully agreed that the working-class *barabba* of Milan would start the insurrection and the bourgeois 'tail coats' and Genoese 'military' group subsequently join it. The result proved disastrous. Whatever the reasons, only a few hundred of the two to three thousand craftsmen and workers in the Committee of Olona attacked the Austrian garrison at Milan on 6 February 1853 and were soon suppressed.

With the failure of the Milan rising Mazzini's influence in Italy declined definitively. Recriminations and accusations arose louder than ever and the Mazzinian movement fragmented. Cattaneo led the democratic federalists in denouncing the futile shedding of blood and momentarily even spoke of the need to create an autonomous democratic organization. But his profound belief in the need to educate public opinion inhibited the federalists from attempting to force the pace by political action. The Genoese group – Medici, Bertani, Mordini – once more proposed to create a large revolutionary party which would include all the republican groups and could decentralize and democratize activities within the peninsula. The Roman Mazzinian network, which had escaped repression, now split: while Petroni retained the loyalty towards Mazzini of the popular groups, the middle-class conspirators, the 'fusionists', called for the abandonment of all proposals (especially republicanism) which impeded a unified struggle for independence. In Tuscany many Mazzinians moved closer to the moderate constitutionalists, who had already begun to turn towards Piedmont. Throughout northern and central Italy, as well as among the exiles, disillusion with Mazzini led to the demand that the prerequisite of the republic be abandoned in favour of unity with the moderates.

In the following years an increasing number of these democrats were to turn towards Piedmont and join the National Society. Their evolution in this direction was often slow and hesitant; while ready to delay decisions about monarchy or republic, unity or federation, until the war of independence had been won, many remained reluctant to abandon their belief in the right of a national assembly to decide these questions. This was the attitude expressed at Paris in November 1854 by an important group of exiles, including Manin, Sirtori, Maestri, and the Sicilian Amari. Some, like Garibaldi in 1854, broke with Mazzini because of his dogmatic intolerance of all criticism; others, like La Farina or Visconti Venosta, could justify their abandonment of republicanism by pointing to the Master's past oscillations. Mazzini's renewed attempts at insurrection, because of their pitiful failure, accelerated the process. As the Crimean War seemed to open up new prospects for Piedmont, middle-class support for republicanism disintegrated in northern and central Italy.

Mazzini's deliberate subordination of all social issues, his violent hostility towards socialism, his exclusive concern with the purely political issues of independence and unity, benefited the cause of moderate monarchical patriotism as soon as the failure of his insurrectionary tactics could no longer be doubted. 'His faith was dictatorial, Caesarian, Napoleonic', Cattaneo had noted (265, vol. i, p. 250). 'Nowadays we all know that the vote of majorities is decided, in the final analysis, by minorities, and that the principle which makes the revolution is that which establishes itself by force or persuasion in constituent assemblies', Montanelli had warned him at a moment when he seemed ready to abandon the republic (Mazzini, 257, vol. 45, p. 337). By 1855 a tired but perennially combative Mazzini was forced to acknowledge the ease with which his former followers shifted their loyalties to Piedmont. As he wrote in an open letter to Cavour, denouncing the deceits of diplomacy and Piedmont's entry into the Crimean War:

> For thirty-four years *a fatal ambiguity* has contested right, pure sense, logical thought, in the minds of Italians. Despite 1821, despite Milan and Novara, despite the continuous persecutions of men who have striven for the liberty of the country, despite the overwhelming reasons that exclude the monarchy from fraternizing with insurrection, the dream of a liberating Court, of a King captain of insurgent peoples, has appeared again in recent times to many, too many of the men who have consecrated their thoughts to the idea of a Patria. (Mazzini, 257, vol. 55, p. 5)

Mazzini's reaction to the Milan failure had been to reject all criticism and lay the blame entirely on the middle-class republicans who had refused to participate actively: 'After the monarchical doctrinaires of 1848, I found myself faced by the republican doctrinaires' (Mazzini, 257, vol. 51, p. 60). He now placed his hopes on the craftsmen and workers, among whom his influence remained strong. But the Milan insurrection modified his attitude in one crucial respect. He was now convinced that Italy was ready to rise, that the period of 'ideas' was over, that the time had come for 'arms'. His new Party of Action was to consist of a small homogeneous body of convinced unitarian republicans who were to set light to an inflammable Italy. Guerrilla warfare assumed a new importance; the bands were no longer to emerge after the insurrection as a response to an enemy counter-offensive, but were to spark off the insurrection: 'The vast Italian conspiracy has today completed its work and prepared the ground for all eventualities: on this terrain the small conspiracy, the *initiatory* conspiracy assumes an importance that could prove decisive' (Mazzini, 257, vol. 51, p. 103). Hence the four attempts to invade the Lunigiana and the attack on the Valtellina between 1853 and 1856.

Carlo Pisacane

The repeated failure of these episodes accelerated the defections from Mazzini. In 1854 his awareness of the loss of the initiative to the Piedmontese moderates had led him once more to abandon his intransigent republicanism. His new slogan, the 'neutral flag', was an appeal to Manin and his pro-Piedmontese companions not to commit themselves to a monarchy, but to unite in starting an insurrection and forming a provisional government, which would then permit them to negotiate with Piedmont as an equal. But the Mazzinian network began to crumble, as its leaders seceded under the pressure first of the Roman 'fusionists', then of the National Society and the Murattists, in Lombardy, Tuscany, the Papal States, the Mezzogiorno. He failed to win back Garibaldi, the Genoese group of Medici and Bertani, or many others of the 1848–9 leaders – Manin, Sirtori, Tommaseo, Michele Amari.

But he gained Pisacane, convinced, like Mazzini, that Italy was now ready for revolution. Carlo Pisacane believed that the social conditions of the south made it the natural place to start the insurrection. Whereas Fabrizi, still a firm supporter of the southern initiative, based his argument on tactical grounds (the distance from the Austrian army, which would permit the insurrection to consolidate itself before a major battle), Pisacane's conclusions derived from a class analysis, tinged by anarchism. 'I am convinced', he affirmed, 'that in the South of Italy the moral revolution exists; that an energetic drive can push the populations into attempting a decisive movement.' The socialist conclusions of his 'political testament', which he left to the young English journalist Jessie White, an enthusiastic Mazzinian, were to arouse polemical discussions after his death because of some of his more extreme judgements. His faith lay in the revolution 'which, changing the social order, will offer to the advantage of all what is now only to the advantage of some'. His hostility to 'temperate remedies' which, he thought, 'far from furthering the resurgence of Italy, can only delay it', made him reject moderate ideas of economic progress and reforms:

> In my opinion, the domination of the house of Savoy and the domination of the house of Austria are exactly the same thing. I also believe that the constitutional regime of Piedmont is more harmful to Italy than Ferdinand II's tyranny. I believe firmly that if Piedmont had been governed in the same way as were the other Italian states, the revolution of Italy would have been completed by now. (Pisacane, 337, p. 228)

Like Cattaneo, Ferrari, Montanelli and other of the democratic leaders, Pisacane was reacting violently against the disastrous illusions of the moderates during the revolutions. But that Mazzini and Pisacane – with their opposing attitudes towards the class structure of society and national revolutions – should have drawn together again and have planned a major insurrection in the south was a clear indication of the sense of crisis among the republicans.

The conspiratorial network had remained strong in Sicily and had slowly developed in the kingdom of Naples. After Napoleon III's coup, a party supporting the claims of the son of the former French king, Gioacchino Murat, suddenly emerged. It was exiguous in number but well-propagandized by the fears of the Neapolitan court. The presence of this Murattist party in the kingdom of Naples, combined with Anglo-French pressure on Ferdinand after the congress of Paris, created the threat of an alternative moderate solution which would destroy unitarian hopes. Sicily had seemed the most likely region for an insurrection, because of the universal hostility towards the Bourbon government, the survival of the democratic network, and the strong spirit of revolt among the peasants. Indeed, discussions had been held with Garibaldi to lead an expedition there. But the failure of a Sicilian revolt in November 1856 made Pisacane insist on an early insurrection in the southern mainland.

Mazzini gave his full support and planned contemporaneous risings at Leghorn and Genoa. Despite Pisacane's awareness of the weaknesses of the Neapolitan democratic organization, he sailed for Sapri (25 June 1857), increasing the strength of his expedition by freeing the prisoners at Ponza, and relying on a revolt of the whole Cilento region. But a general democratic rising failed to materialize, the peasants who had risen on previous occasions were away harvesting in Apulia, and the rest of the population was terrified by government rumours of the threat of brigands. Pisacane's small following of men was soon dispersed by government militia and the wounded Pisacane killed himself rather than fall prisoner (2 July).

The Sapri expedition marked the end of Mazzinian hopes. As a moderate wrote, 'after the latest movements, which have proved futile . . . one can sing a *requiem aeternam* over Mazzini the *politician*' (Pallavicino, 356, vol. 3, p. 407).

The hegemony of the political liberals

The survival of the Piedmontese Statute after Novara probably owed more to the traditional anti-Austrian policy of this dynastic state than to any other factor. The new king, Victor Emanuel II, the son and husband of Austrian archduchesses, had opposed his father's renewal of the war against Austria, was authoritarian in character, and despised the democratic *canaille*. But Novara left him with a defeated army, a hostile nobility and senate, Genoa in revolt and a strongly patriotic democratic majority in the lower chamber. The revocation of the Statute would have led to civil war, even to a democratic revolution as in Tuscany or Rome. The King's main hopes of regaining prestige and authority for the dynasty lay with D'Azeglio and the moderates, whose anti-Austrian patriotism was by now solidly welded to their belief in constitutionalism. The Statute could be used as a legal and peaceable instrument to curb the democrats, as the king explained to Radetzky at a meeting at Vignale. Radetzky's fear of provoking French intervention by an invasion of Piedmont, his (illusory) hopes of pacifying this most turbulent of all Italian states by drawing the young king within the

Austrian orbit, explain the extremely lenient armistice he granted this twice-defeated enemy.

The protracted negotiations over a peace treaty revealed the contradictory pressures on the king. Schwarzenberg, although determined to rely on force, did not impose impossible conditions through fear of international complications, and could not understand Piedmontese obstinacy, nor indeed French support

> for this government without faith or law, for this frog of the fable, for these men dear to the revolution and abhorred by all the rest of Italy, for this country that corrupts everything it touches and does not know how to make either war or peace. (Moscati, 219, p. 182)

In Piedmont, not only reactionaries like Latour and Solaro della Margarita, but even establishment liberals like Pinelli saw an Austrian alliance and the abolition of the Statute as the only solution. But the moderates rallied alongside D'Azeglio, whom the king had rapidly called to replace the Savoyard general Launay as premier. General Dabormida, who was responsible for the negotiations with Austria, was convinced that the revocation of the Statute would be catastrophic: 'It would be disastrous to return to absolutism, which would bring reaction with it and increase the disaffection of the people for the monarchical regime' (Colombo, 349, p. 91). The dependence upon Austria of the other Italian sovereigns who had abandoned their constitutions offered continuous evidence of the dangers. If Piedmont was to retain its position as the leading state in Italy, it had to resist a humiliating peace and defend the Lombard exiles who had first risen against the Austrians. As Dabormida and Boncompagni wrote at a moment when the negotiations broke down:

> The Piedmontese government must maintain itself within the peninsula as the representative of a sincerely liberal and constitutional policy; show itself ready to oppose with all its forces whomsoever wished to make Italy retreat towards the old absolutism, or rush towards the republic. (Bianchi, 351, vol. 6, p. 310)

The difficulty for D'Azeglio and his colleagues was that the democratic majority in the chamber refused to accept what it regarded as a humiliating peace. D'Azeglio called new elections in July 1849, in which the king appealed to the electorate; but the apathy was such that only 30 000 of the 87 000 electorate voted, returning a democratic majority. The king accepted the peace of Milan (6 August 1849), as lay within his powers according to the Statute, but the democrats delayed its ratification because of the financial indemnity and the question of the Lombard exiles. Constitutional government, as interpreted by D'Azeglio and the king, had become impossible: the hostile majority in the chamber refused to approve the budget for more than a month at a time. Pressure for a coup increased – even Cavour had been tempted before Novara. D'Azeglio was overwhelmingly oppressed by his sense of the strength of the reaction in Europe. As his sister-in-law Costanza wrote: 'Maxime . . . believes . . . that Italy can do nothing by itself; that it is in the middle of Europe as if in a vice, and that Europe, which does not want a perpetual subject of disturbance, will settle matters without us and against us' (D'Azeglio, 341, p. 321). He appealed constantly to the state of emergency, the 'exceptional times', and threatened the opposition with a reactionary government if it did not give support. Finally he dissolved parliament again and stretched the Statute to its limit by issuing in the king's name from Moncalieri a proclamation denouncing the opposition (20 November 1849):

> With the dissolution of the chamber of deputies, the liberties of the country are not in any danger. They are protected by the revered memory of king Charles Albert my father, they are entrusted to the honour of the house of Savoy; they are defended by the religion of my oaths: who would dare to fear for them? . . . But if the country, if the electors deny me their support, the responsibility for the future will no longer fall upon me. (D'Azeglio, 339, vol. 3, pp. 195-6)

Given the example of Neapolitan and Tuscan liberals, who had collaborated in the abolition of their constitutions, the threat was a real one. But, strong in the support of king, army, senate, bureaucracy and nobility, D'Azeglio was merely hammering the last nail in the coffin of the democratic initiative of the revolutionary years. A massive vote returned a solid moderate majority.

The weakness of D'Azeglio's stand against the democrats was that it blurred the distinction between the constitutional moderates and the reactionaries. It also reinforced the autonomy of the king, whose mythical reputation as the 'gentleman King', *il re galantuomo*, who had refused to sign peace at the expense of the constitution, D'Azeglio was carefully creating. Genuine concern for the Statute led D'Azeglio to consolidate his support in the new chamber by eliminating those privileges of the Church that contrasted flagrantly with the constitution's guarantee of civil equality. The Siccardi laws (1850), which abolished the ecclesiastical tribunal and rights of asylum granted in Charles Albert's concordat of 1841, ranged all reactionaries and clericals (even cautious clerical moderates such as Balbo) against the government, thus enabling it to reacquire its distinctive physiognomy as upholder of the Statute.

Cavour, by 1850 the most important liberal deputy not in the government, supported the Siccardi laws precisely because they offered the means of demonstrating to the doubting and the hostile that the Statute was no empty shell, but the basis for reform and progress:

> In many minds, doubt and discouragement arose, because of the belief that our constitutional forms were incapable of producing those effects and reforms

requested by public opinion and which the needs of the times demanded imperiously. . . . On the opposition side, the party which before the Statute was satisfied with the old order of things and which had only accepted the new fundamental pact with resignation, saw that one could live under the constitutional regime without reforming anything, merely conserving the *status quo*. Gradually this party began to think that it was even possible to maintain the Statute, and retreat a little. (Cavour, 286, vol. 2, p. 77)

For D'Azeglio the Statute was adequate protection against both a return to absolutism and a degeneration into republican anarchy. For Cavour it was the starting point for development towards a parliamentary regime, on the English model. But it was the determination of both men which protected the Statute against the attacks of the clericals and reactionaries and the recurrent forays of the king into personal policy-making.

Victor Emanuel II's powers remained strong, and his exercise of them often dubiously constitutional. He collected taxes without parliamentary consent in 1849, imposed his ministers of war on all governments, and dabbled in secret diplomacy with disastrous results. He rid himself of D'Azeglio and tried to rid himself of Cavour by extra-parliamentary intrigues. He forced Cavour into the Crimean War and was on the verge of destroying the Statute in the crisis of 1855 for what D'Azeglio called 'a monkish plot'. Surrounded by army officers, intolerant and contemptuous of the delicate balances of civilian government, 'more like a knight of the Middle Ages who lived by his sword, than a king in present days' as Queen Victoria described him in her private diary (Mack Smith, 346, p. 54), the *re galantuomo* was reluctantly, gradually and partially enmeshed within the workings of a parliamentary system, because of his inability to develop a firm and constant link with the conservative Catholics and his reluctance to lose a popularity largely based on his unjustified political reputation. But the potential threat of his powers and his unpredictability go far towards explaining Cavour's assertions of the primacy of parliament and the somewhat unparliamentary methods by which he ensured it.

Cavour and the reforms in Piedmont

Camillo Benso di Cavour (1810–61), the younger son of the head of police at Turin in the years of the Restoration, had been kept out of power because of the mistrust he aroused. Unfairly described as a *carbonaro* by Charles Albert, Cavour fervently believed in the happy mean, the *juste milieu*. In the long years of absolutism and revolutionary insurrections, this left him in fact little choice but to keep to a private life. His Swiss Protestant relatives – the only unusual element in an otherwise typical Piedmontese noble family – stimulated his faith in rationality, the ethic of work, liberty and conscience. Unlike most of his class, Cavour had occupied his years of isolation with an intensive study of economic and political developments in the western world. He emerged less tied to Italian political-cultural traditions than his contemporaries, and with an unmitigated admiration for the economic and political thought and (what he interpreted as) practices of England and France. Fascinated by the apparent interdependence of economic and civil progress in these countries, he accompanied his studies by wide-ranging – and sometimes imprudent – agricultural, commercial and banking activities; he promoted railways, was one of the founders of the bank of Turin and a leading figure in the Agrarian Association.

Ambitious and extraordinarily self-confident, Cavour had only emerged as a public figure in the years of the moderate influence before the 1848 revolution. But his liberal-conservative credo of the merging of the nobility with the bourgeoisie did not endear him to the Piedmontese aristocracy, nor gain the confidence of middle-class leaders. During the revolution he was kept out of the successive governments by Charles Albert's hostility. His hatred of all revolutionaries had led him to ally with the parochial defenders of 'old Piedmont' against the Casati government and even to approve of the Moncalieri proclamation. His support for the D'Azeglio government was conditioned by his personal ambitions, but also by his conviction of its inadequacy as an instrument to transform Piedmont into the most advanced state in Italy, modelled upon and closely tied to the western powers.

The D'Azeglio government, like its predecessors, was based on no party and held no firm majority in the chamber. Its literary-artistic leader, although far more of a politician than the philosopher-priest Gioberti, had little taste for the humdrum problems of administration, suffered from a wound he had incurred in 1848, and was disinclined to challenge royal authority by extending the legislative influence of parliament. D'Azeglio was, rightly, suspicious of Cavour, and only reluctantly invited him to join the government in a minor post as minister for the navy, agriculture, industry and commerce (November 1850). D'Azeglio was warned by his friend, Diomede Pantaleoni:

> The new minister will be of great help to your ministry. He is active, ambitious, and will introduce into the government's behaviour the energy which perhaps it needs. Note, however, that sooner or later he will want to dominate, to be the first, and perhaps will prove a terrible dissolvent for your ministry. (Faldella, 340, p. 288)

With his enormous energy and activity Cavour immediately became the dominating figure in the government, soon taking over the finance ministry and driving through a series of trade treaties and finance measures, coherently linked to his philosophy of economic development based on free trade. His support came mainly from the constitutional democrats and even from the extreme left, rarely from the conservatives. In contrast to

D'Azeglio, Cavour was prepared to forget what both men regarded as the democrats' responsibility for the renewal of the war in 1849. Independent and ambitious, not too scrupulous about his methods, Cavour used the increased pressure of the conservatives after Napoleon's coup as an excuse to strike a private agreement for support with the leader of the moderate democrats Urbano Rattazzi. The agreement was revealed when Cavour successfully supported Rattazzi's election as president of the chamber, despite Victor Emanuel's belated attempt to intervene (May 1852). When D'Azeglio's proposals to introduce civil marriage into Piedmont were resisted by the king because of religious scruples, Cavour accepted the rejection of the bill by the senate in exchange for his appointment as premier (November 1852). Only the following year did he feel sufficiently strong to bring Rattazzi into the government.

This 'marriage' or *connubio*, as it was called by Pinelli, aroused much resentment at the time and has since frequently been indicted as the first step towards the later parliamentary system of 'transformism'. It was justified by Cavour at first with the example of English leaders who had accepted opposition support to pass necessary measures of reform and, later, because of the need to oppose the rising tide of reaction in Europe. Wellington's decision to accept Catholic emancipation, Grey's support of the reform bill, Peel's split with his party over the repeal of the corn laws were all cited by Cavour; and, although he now criticized the conservatism of Guizot's later years, Cavour retained his admiration for the French politician's parlia mentary methods during the earlier period of the July monarchy. The unusual weakness of clear party lines in England in recent years, and the trend Cavour saw in France to 'transform' parties into centre coalitions against the extremes, thus reinforced his own dislike – shared by most Piedmontese political leaders – of parties, which were regarded as little better than 'factions'. If Balbo in the 1850s finally came to support the free play of opposing parties, it is arguable that this was, at least in part, a reaction against the dissolution of an effective conservative opposition by Cavour's *connubio*. The system, as worked by Cavour, unquestionably strengthened his personal authority by giving him the power to adjust his alliances according to the changing parliamentary situation – even to the extent of sacrificing Rattazzi in 1858 in exchange for support from the sizeable conservative opposition returned in the elections of the previous year. But, as originally conceived and put into practice, the *connubio* was based on a clear programme of internal reforms and commitment to an independent Italy. A witness at the crucial meeting between Cavour and Rattazzi, recalled: 'The programme was quickly arranged: Monarchy, Statute, Independence, civil and political Progress' (Castelli, 343, p. 41).

For Cavour, indeed, the *connubio* – and hence the guarantee of a firm parliamentary majority – was necessary not only to implement his programme, but to weaken the threats from revolutionary democrats, the clerical-conservative amalgam and the Court. Within Piedmont (although not in Italy), the threat from the revolutionaries was mostly imaginary by the time Cavour assumed power. But this remained so, because of Cavour's reforms: 'Reforms, carried out in time, instead of weakening authority, strengthen it; instead of increasing the strength of the revolutionary spirit, reduce it to impotence' (Cavour, 286, vol. 2, p. 84).

The threat from the right was more continuous. The conservatives' strength lay in the enormous influence of the Church (and this very fact was indicative of the backwardness of Piedmont compared to Lombardy, Tuscany or even Naples, where ecclesiastical power had been curbed long before). The struggle to pass legislation restricting the power of the Church had as decisive an effect on the development from limited constitutional government to parliamentary government as the chamber's assumption of full control over public finances. But the fact that such anti-ecclesiastical legislation was put forward, albeit only with partial success, at the very moment when the other Italian states were making concordats with the pope, underlined the determination of the Piedmontese ruling class to achieve a level of secular control befitting a modern, western state. The attack on the Church ranged from measures which asserted the primacy of secular values – abolition of ecclesiastical jurisdictional privileges, civil marriage, state control of education – to more antiquated proposals reminiscent of the later eighteenth century, such as abolition of the monasteries and state stipends for priests. This very confusion reflected the groping development from enlightenment faith in the subordination of Church to State towards the later nineteenth-century belief in the total separation of Church and State.

In the last months of his life Cavour was to enunciate the famous formula of 'a free Church in a free state'. But this was wishful thinking. On the one hand the Piedmontese liberals had failed to pass much of the anti-ecclesiastical legislation of the 1850s. On the other, unification had been achieved at the expense of the pope's temporal power, while Cavour himself had deliberately isolated and persecuted the representatives of the Church in parliament.

This persecution, typical of Cavour's attitude towards those whom he regarded as irreconcilable enemies, was perhaps inevitable, given the venom and danger of the clerical assault on his power. D'Azeglio had fallen over the attempt to introduce civil marriage. In 1855, a fully orchestrated attack directed from Rome against Rattazzi's proposed dissolution of the monasteries seemed on the point of success. The clerical party, led by the Piedmontese bishop and senator Calabiana, wanted the rejection of the bill, offering in compensation a substantial episcopal subsidy, ostensibly in recognition of the burden of the Crimean War. The king was won over to the clericals by his respect for Pius IX's religious authority and his personal dislike of Cavour. He wrote privately to Pius to reassure him of his determination to reject the law on the monasteries:

> Perhaps in a few days this Cavour ministry will fall, I will nominate a right wing one and insist as a condition *sine qua non* that a total adjustment with Rome be reached as soon as possible. Do me the favour of helping me: I for my part have always done what I could. (Pirri, 348, vol. 1, p. 157)

Only the impossibility of forming an alternative government with a majority in the chamber, and pressure from Napoleon III, who feared a clerical-conservative government would turn towards Austria, made the king desist from the temptation of a coup.

The consequences, for the development of liberalism in Piedmont, were of lasting significance: the king was left with a deep resentment of the clericals, because of the embarrassment in which they had placed him; parliamentary government had established itself against the powers of the king. Even though the clericals gained a notable success in the 1857 elections, the gulf which now divided them from the king enabled Cavour to trample rough-shod over them, disqualifying some of their elected deputies. Cavour had asserted the secular power of the State, and was to confirm it with Casati's education law of 1859. But the price he paid was to identify liberalism with anti-clerical feeling, which was to prove a problematic heritage for the newly unified Italy.

If the fight against the Church confirmed the powers of parliament, discussion of Cavour's financial, commercial and administrative proposals trained its deputies as a minute but technically competent ruling class. The submission of the budget to the chamber, begun by Revel in 1848, became the means by which the deputies acquired a detailed knowledge of the mechanism of the state. The extenuating eight-month discussion of the 1851 budget, presented by Cavour, marked the path for the future. Public expenditure for the army, public works and the railways now increased rapidly, as Cavour oscillated between his desire for a balanced budget and his ambitions for a rapid development of the Piedmontese economy. His early *laissez-faire* convictions were modified, following the evolution of post-Ricardian economic thought, from Malthus to Senior and Mill, over the need for and justification of state intervention and public expenditure.

Ideally, according to Cavour, the state should intervene as little as possible, and at all events it should encourage commercial liberty so as to boost exports and hence stimulate productivity. But the state needed to take upon itself the cost of improving roads, waterways and all forms of communication, if private initiative proved reluctant. It had to reform the credit system, developing a central bank as well as encouraging private financial houses and savings banks, in order to finance trading transactions and accelerate monetary circulation. The rise in public expenditure would be covered, Cavour constantly claimed, by increased trade. It was indicative of the growing support for economic liberalism, as much as of Cavour's technical dominance in such discussions, that his fiscal plans – mostly completed by 1853 – were accepted by parliament, despite the alarming rise in the budget deficit and even more alarming growth in the public debt, covered by internal and foreign loans. State income rose from 91 to 164 million lire between 1850 and 1859, and the public debt from 120 millions in 1847 to 725 millions in 1859.

The support came from the small proprietors, the entrepreneurs, the professional classes – the backbone of the constitutional democratic party. The bilateral trade treaties of 1850-1 with England, Austria, France, Belgium, Portugal, Greece, Switzerland, Holland and the *Zollverein*, while not introducing free trade, lowered customs duties. A general tariff reduction in 1851 was followed by the lowering of the duty on the import of grain and, after the riots during the 1853 famine, by its complete abolition. Cavour was consciously opening up Piedmontese markets to western trade: rising international agricultural prices stimulated exports, while the import of raw materials accelerated the mechanization of the woollen and cotton industries; state orders for railways and especially ships stimulated the iron and steel industry. These nuclei of modern mechanized industry developed at the expense of the craftsmen. But Cavour was clear about the need to concentrate on agriculture, for political as well as economic reasons. As he had written in 1845:

> The opening of the richest market in the world [England] to foodstuffs will favour growth of production, the main aim of agricultural industries, which are among our most important industries. . . . As trade becomes an essential element of prosperity for the agricultural classes, they will be driven naturally to join with the supporters of the liberal system. Producers of raw material will then be in the same position *vis-à-vis* privileged manufacturers as are the industrial classes in England at this moment *vis-à-vis* landed proprietors and colonial plantation owners. (Cavour, 283, p. 171)

This courageous innovating economic policy was criticized because of its partial abandonment of free trade. Cavour's banking proposals, in particular, aroused the anger of the leading free trade economist, Francesco Ferrara, and were rejected. The attempt contemporaneously to force the pace of economic development and prepare Piedmont militarily was to leave the future Italy facing financial collapse. But Cavour consolidated his support by his attack on the administrative structure and personnel of the old absolutist state. Control of the budget led to reductions in stipends and the removal of the most overtly hostile aristocratic ambassadors; some steps were taken to ensure the impartiality of the magistracy; even the higher ranks of the army were opened up with La Marmora's reforms, although the tradition of authoritarian discipline remained. The modernization of the foreign office, begun by D'Azeglio, was completed by Cavour (1849–53). The absolutist financial bureaux of the central administration, which had survived parallel to the new ministries, were suppressed (1852). The dominance of the old aristocracy, like that of the Church, was definitively ended.

The effect of these reforms, in a decade of economic uncertainty, undoubtedly made Piedmont economically the most modern state in Italy. Austria, only too conscious of its exclusion from the expanding free trade markets, tried to compete by forming a customs union between Lombardy and the central Italian duchies (1852). It hoped to transform this into a vaster union between the *Zollverein*, the Austrian empire and an Italian customs league excluding Piedmont, which would be consolidated by new railway lines from Lombardy south to the Papal States. But these plans were sabotaged by Prussia and Piedmont, and even Parma – flooded with Lombard products – withdrew from the renewal of the customs agreement in 1857. Verging ever-nearer bankruptcy, Vienna was forced to cut back on its railway plans, which only developed again with private financing in the later 1850s. All the other Italian states, even Naples and the Papal States, were lowering tariffs and seeking foreign capital and entrepreneurs, like Piedmont, in this decade. But the agricultural crisis, precipitated by vine and mulberry tree diseases and worsened by the general recession of 1857, proved disastrous, except where agriculture had been modernized in Piedmont and the Lombard plain. Of all the states perhaps the kingdom of Naples was worst hit, as the country was deprived of its most promising export – crude silk. The weakness of the southern economy, compared with that of the north, became more evident. The economic hegemony of Piedmont, based on its commercial links with foreign countries – not with the other Italian states – was reflected even in the economic discussions in the south, which palely echoed the argument circulating in Piedmont for and against free trade.

Cavour's reforms acquired for Piedmont a renewed reputation among the moderates in the other Italian states. But they suffered both in range and in method of implementation from their author's dominating concern with their political effects. As Cavour became increasingly absorbed by the possibilities of successfully reviving the struggle for independence, his interest in internal renewal declined and his methods became more authoritarian. The reform of legislation and local administration, inevitably lengthy processes, were major victims: his earlier promises of a reform of communal and provincial administration, like that of a new code of civil procedure, went unfulfilled. The democrat Brofferio, admittedly a perpetual critic of Cavour, could rightly complain about the government's failure to update Piedmont's antiquated laws in conformity with the Statute:

You ministers have never wished to harmonise the nation's legal codes with the statute: you have promised much, it is true, but you have done nothing. You nominated commissions, and we have seen traces of them in the budget, but we never saw any results. Until these reforms are completed, our institutions will remain an illusion and nothing else. (Omodeo, 344, vol. 1, p. 218)

Almost inadvertently, Brofferio had pointed to the contradiction inherent in so rapid a process of modernization. The vitality of the Piedmontese legislative assembly was reflected, not least, in the relative freedom of democratic criticisms, at a time when Austria had just abolished its legislative body. But Piedmontese legal codes remained more backward than those of Austrian Italy and were to survive as another legacy to united Italy.

The reforming initiative suffered increasingly from its subordination to political considerations. The drive against the Church had died down because of the king's reservations. Even more inhibiting was Cavour's determination to cultivate French friendship: unfavourable commercial treaties had been accepted, the liberty of the press was cut back, persecution of the Mazzinian democrats stepped up.

Above all, parliament was deprived of the possibility of assuming full political control because of Cavour's fears that it might impede his tortuous manoeuvres and subtle directing of Piedmont's future. The fortification of Casale in 1851 and then of Alessandria in 1857 were decided upon before parliamentary discussions. The decision to enter the Crimean War was taken by Cavour against the cabinet, without reference to parliament. Only one cabinet minister was aware of the French alliance arranged at Plombières. Even the cession of Savoy and Nice in 1860 was agreed to, against the constitution, without parliamentary consent. Control of the chamber by illiberal methods, which recalled those of the July monarchy, was justified by the need for a firm majority: perhaps a third of the deputies were salaried by the state as army officers, magistrates, civil servants; government officers were used to assist official candidates in elections. After the disastrous consequences which resulted from the neglect of the 1857 elections (when the government lost over forty seats), Cavour took over the interior ministry and sent strict electoral instructions to the provincial intendants. Cavour's resignations in 1855 and 1859, and his reappointment in 1860, were made without reference to parliament.

If Cavour trained the two houses in the technical administration of the state, he diseducated them increasingly in political matters. His infinitely superior knowledge and experience gave him a personal mastery over the deputies in the chamber, who changed in large numbers with each legislature. His accumulation of office – foreign minister and minister of the interior, minister responsible for economic and financial matters, even minister of war and navy for some months in 1859 – deprived colleagues of the opportunity of gaining experience. From the Crimean War, and especially from 1856, internal reforms were sacrificed to foreign policy, economic liberalism to political liberalism. National emergency was pleaded increasingly to justify illiberal measures, from the harassment and final suppression of the sole Mazzinian newspaper, *Italia del Popolo*, to the exclusion from Sardinian citizenship of democratic exiles. The overriding national cause became a means by which to absorb within the government ranks all except fringe opposition parties. It was Mazzini who had preached the need to subordinate and delay all non-political problems until after the achievement of independence. It was Cavour, after the Paris congress, who enacted this policy, with deeply negative consequences for united Italy.

The Italian National Society

Cavour's evolution towards an exclusively political vision of the 'Italian problem' was stimulated not only by reaction to the Mazzinian opposition he so loathed, but by the growth of pro-Piedmontese feeling among the moderates both in exile and in the other Italian states. If Mazzini's insurrectionary attempts forced Cavour, at French behest, to adopt more drastic measures against the democrats in Piedmont than he might otherwise have been inclined to use, they also served the purpose of maintaining the image of Piedmontese moderatism as the sole non-revolutionary party which could achieve Italian independence. Austria's reliance on force to repress opposition and revolution facilitated Cavour's task of upholding Piedmont's claim to represent the 'real' Italy. He was able to seize upon the Austrian confiscation of the Lombard exiles' lands, a festering issue since 1849, to unfurl Piedmont's anti-Austrian banner, always the basis of his Italian policy (1856). His earlier fears that Mazzinian insurrection would be the prelude to social revolution would seem to have diminished by the mid-1850s, perhaps because he had begun to recognize the purely political nature of the Mazzinian message, almost certainly because he was so anxious to force the pace after the Paris congress: his government tolerated Mazzini's semi-secret presence at Genoa and was implicated in the attempted attack on the Lunigiana in 1856. By then, it was less the reality of the threat of revolution than its spectre that Cavour was able to use to reinforce his own programme. The Sapri expedition confirmed the impotence of the Party of Action and hastened its disintegration.

While Mazzini served as a bogy, the exiles increased pressure on Cavour to subordinate all to the Italian cause. The attraction of Piedmont had never died, and Gioberti's last book, *Rinnovamento*, had served to consolidate the myth of a national Piedmont (whatever its author's intentions). At Paris Mazzini's authority had been challenged as much by pro-Piedmontese moderates, like Guglielmo Pepe, as by socialists like Ferrari. Piedmontese

hospitality towards the exiles, although discriminating against the democrats almost as much as that of Napoleonic France, attracted many thousands, including the cultural and political leaders of the different Italian
states, from the Sicilian Ferrara to the Neapolitan De Sanctis and the
Tuscan Guerrazzi. Increasingly Turin and Genoa, rather than London or
Paris, became the centres of Italian patriotism. The exiles were ill-tolerated
by the Piedmontese, by liberals as well as by clericals. They were among
the 'Ten plagues of Egypt renewed in Piedmont in the 19th century',
according to a pamphlet published in Turin in 1850. Giorgio Pallavicino,
the 'martyr' of the Spielberg (as he liked to recall), and a whole-hearted
supporter of Piedmont's 'mission', could complain:

> The Piedmontese, all the Piedmontese – from count Solaro della Margarita to
> the lawyer Angelo Brofferio – are tarred with the same brush. In place of an
> Italy with one metropolis, Rome, they prefer an Upper Italy with two capitals:
> *Turin and Milan.* Camillo Cavour is the most Piedmontese of all. (Maineri, 355,
> p. 212)

But as the Crimean War seemed to open up new possibilities, hopes of
Piedmont grew stronger among some of these *italianissimi*. Pallavicino tried
to win over Manin, whose great prestige at Paris would help convince those
exiles who favoured unity but retained their faith in a national assembly,
that the only hope lay in Piedmontese dictatorship:

> To speak now of popular assemblies is not opportune. Having learnt from errors,
> both old and new, I do not want popular assemblies in the first phase of our
> revolution. What use would be these assemblies during the war? They would
> nourish our disagreements at grave cost to the military operations. *During the
> war of independence, I do not want liberty, but dictatorship: the dictatorship of a
> soldier.* In Italy the *nation* does not yet exist, but a *liberal government* exists, which
> represents it. We have no choice between two parties: we must accept this
> government willingly or perforce. (Pallavicino, 356, vol. 3, p. 9)

The resemblance between the Mazzinian and the 'Piedmontese' ideologies
was becoming even closer.

Distrust of Cavour remained, even in a Pallavicino. But the Crimean
battle of the Tchernaia, however small a skirmish, and the Paris congress,
however intangible its results, convinced some exiles that Piedmont had
finally understood its Italian destiny. Other exiles, such as Montanelli and
Sirtori, retained their hopes of France, and encouraged the claims of
Luciano Murat to the Neapolitan throne. The unitarian exiles were outraged. Support for Piedmont grew, but still only a handful were prepared
to organize a party. In 1855 Manin came out firmly for a monarchical-
unitarian solution:

> The republican party, so bitterly slandered, makes a new act of abnegation and
> sacrifice for the national cause. Convinced that before all else it is necessary to

make Italy, that this is the prior and predominant question, it says to the house of Savoy: Make Italy and I am with you. – If not, no. And it says to the constitutionalists [of Piedmont]: Think of making Italy and not of enlarging Piedmont, be Italians and not provincials, and I am with you. – If not, no. (Maineri, 355, p. 323)

By now the pro-Piedmontese exiles were even prepared to replace the revolutionary demand of 'unity' with 'unification', despite its implications of a gradual expansion of Piedmont into an ultimately unified Italy: the traditional dictum that the house of Savoy would eat Italy like the leaves of an artichoke seemed to be coming true.

The creation of a party required three elements: an ideology distinct from that of Mazzini, an organizer, and followers. Manin's public smear against Mazzini, whom he accused of advocating 'the theory of the assassin's dagger' and his abandonment of his earlier insistence on 'all Italy or nothing' achieved the first aim. Giuseppe La Farina's conversion to the new cause gained an able organizer and ensured an effective use of Pallavicino's money. The search for committed followers was to prove more difficult. The survival of the new association was only really guaranteed when Garibaldi, ready to join any patriotic movement and bitterly hostile to Mazzini, offered his support in a typically ingenuous manner. The Italian National Society was born (July 1857). Its small membership did not inhibit it from proclaiming itself the representative of all true patriots. It was in contact with and exerted pressure upon Cavour, once it had been reassured about his coolness towards the Murattian claims over Naples. Its propaganda – for unification and independence – attracted many democrats and some moderates in the other Italian states. As Mazzini's middle-class supporters broke away from him ever-more rapidly after Sapri, and as the Murattian ghost disappeared as mysteriously as it had arisen, Cavour found himself with a new, but somewhat embarrassing support. The leaders of the National Society prised a fairly willing Cavour away from the Piedmontese moderates and democrats, like Rattazzi, whose priority remained the consolidation of reforms within the Sardinian state. Rattazzi's dismissal in 1858 and Cavour's absorption of the moderate right into his government were symptomatic of the new situation. To retain control, Cavour now had to accept a purely political solution to the Italian problem, and to force its pace.

The triumph of political moderatism

Despite his secret contacts with the ex-revolutionary *italianissimi*, and even with some active revolutionaries, Cavour's hopes lay outside Italy, in French military aid against Austria. As the months had dragged on after the Paris congress, his optimism drained away, for tension could not be maintained indefinitely in Italy. In March 1857 his close friend Castelli wrote of

Cavour's belief that 'all plans, all projects are useless, everything depends on an accident, and then we shall see if he [Napoleon] knows how to seize fortune by its hair' (Castelli, 342, vol. 1, p. 158). The 'accident', which occurred soon after, was the attempt on the emperor's life by the dissident Mazzinian Felice Orsini and his dying appeal to Napoleon to achieve Italy's independence (January–February 1858). Displaying that remarkable skill to exploit a new situation which was to characterize his leadership over the next three years, Cavour ably cultivated Napoleon's secret approaches until the meeting at Plombières (July 1858). He then reported with satisfaction to Victor Emanuel about Napoleon's proposed division of Italy into four states: 'As Your Majesty will be sovereign by right of the richest and strongest half of Italy, you will be sovereign in practice of all the peninsula' (364, vol. 1, p. 105).

Cavour's determined reliance on France had finally yielded its results. But the price he paid was the complete subordination of Piedmontese policy to Napoleon. This was immediately visible in the terms of the secret treaty of January 1859, which were distinctly less generous than those of Plombières. It emerged cruelly in the following months, when Anglo-Prussian pressure to mediate forced Cavour to accept Napoleon's decision to abandon the war, only to be saved by Austria's ultimatum (19–23 April). It conditioned Cavour's policy towards the patriots in central Italy. It reached its logical conclusion in the unexpected armistice after the battles of Solferino and San Martino (24 June), decided upon by the French emperor with barely a reference to his fellow sovereign and ally, the king of Sardinia, and none at all to Cavour. Austria's deliberately insulting indirect cession of Lombardy to Sardinia, using Napoleon III as intermediary, symbolized Piedmontese subordination.

But if the limits on Cavour's freedom of action were clearly marked by his dependence on international diplomacy, his alliance with France ensured him unchallenged leadership in Italy. In the Piedmontese parliament his majority, imperilled by the 1857 elections, became overwhelming as opposition was reduced to the representatives of Savoy on the French side of the Alps. Outside parliament, anti-Austrian or anti-absolutist feeling turned towards Piedmont, even if many were still not prepared to offer such unconditional support as La Farina's National Society.

The National Society had extended its organization since its foundation in 1857. Unlike Mazzini's Young Italy a quarter of a century earlier, it relied on local notables, whose social status attracted the support of shopkeepers and officials in the small towns. Its major strength was in the duchies and especially papal Romagna, where its structure – as an organized network of friends – fitted easily into the tradition of clandestine political sects. In Lombardy, where it established important contacts, and in Tuscany, where it created a committee by early 1859, the National Society remained weak compared to local groupings. La Farina's contacts with Cavour became more intense from late 1858, and it was through La Farina that Cavour was assured of Garibaldi's support, a matter of some significance given the general's prestige. Cavour did not confine his contacts to the National Society; indeed, the politicians closest to him, such as Minghetti and Farini, remained suspicious of the association. But he seemed to accept La Farina's assertions that the Society was a highly organized, efficient body, and he willingly acquiesced in its self-appointed mission of organizing the flow of volunteers to Piedmont.

The National Society's ideology, as it evolved from La Farina's flowing pen, fitted in well with Cavour's concern, shared by Napoleon, to insulate the war from revolutionary developments. Unification and national concord were the Society's aims and *raison d'être*; and if unification was in theory to be achieved jointly by Victor Emanuel and the revolution, the latter element was confined to the states outside Sardinian frontiers and increasingly subjected to Piedmontese leadership. The postponement of all other issues until after unification, the inhibition of discussion through fear of dividing opinion, made the Society's leaders intolerant of disagreement, which was regarded at best as heresy, at worst as treachery. The fundamental debate about why Italians should want to be independent, or the purposes to which independence would be put, was reduced to the single practical issue of how to achieve unification. In consequence, the moral fervour, the democratic or social aspirations which had characterized the patriotic movement, were replaced by militaristic faith and social conservatism. The National Society was self-consciously liberal, but in the most limited sense: it looked to the educated middle classes – the industrialists, the traders, the landowners – rejecting both aristocratic claims to social privilege and the threat implicit in an appeal to the masses. It was precisely this conscious restriction of the Society's message to the urban bourgeoisie and country gentry that enabled it to attract so many of the former Mazzinians, tired of their Master's dogmatism and ineffectiveness.

Against this flood of patriotism, the democrats could do little. Cattaneo, disgusted by the dynastic, unitarian war in 1859, but as always unwilling to take a public position, could only warn Bertani, Medici and the dissident Genoese group of democrats against the illiberal character of the war. Yet at the same time – attracted by the prospect of the liberation of Italy – even Cattaneo accepted that they should volunteer. Curiously echoing the reasons put forward by Italian officers half-a-century earlier to justify their service under Napoleon, he advised that: 'Whoever wants to become a soldier, one day or another will also be able to fight for liberty; but meanwhile let him train himself as a soldier' (Cattaneo, 263, vol. 3, p. 107).

Mazzini, disillusioned by the desertion of many of his most faithful followers, disgusted by the readiness to serve Piedmont of the 'notables' of

1848–9 – Manin, Sirtori, Garibaldi and so many others – warned his followers that the war could not but lead to French control of Italy and the defeat of unitarian hopes. After Sapri he had placed increasing stress on the revolutionary drive within the urban proletariat and had developed his theory of association into an ideology of economic co-operation between classes. He now urged the Party of Action to take the initiative and turn the war into a national one, without foreign contamination; if unable to achieve this, its members should keep aloof. But once the war broke out – as he feared it would – he changed his attitude and advised his followers to participate, but to keep themselves separate as a group. This change in Mazzini's position was based on his recognition that the war was, after all, against Austria and his hope that the risings in central Italy and the strength of the volunteers could transform it into an Italian struggle.

Despite the ominous predictions of Cattaneo and Mazzini, enthusiasm for the war reached a level unknown since 1848. Some 20 000 volunteers came to Piedmont. But, as Massari noted with surprise, 'in 1848 there was a mania to command, in 1859 there is a frenzy to obey' (Massari, 366, p. 225). The magnetism of Garibaldi's name lay behind the renewed phenomenon of mass volunteers. But Cavour and the Piedmontese army took care to control it. Garibaldi's Alpine Rifle corps was deliberately limited to 3000 extremely young volunteers or veterans of 1848, whose role was systematically restricted by the regular officers. As Bertani wrote to Cattaneo before the war broke out:

> So far, one can say, Garibaldi has been ridiculed. They are afraid of his name, his influence, of hearing him asked for, chosen, made as a condition by those coming from the other states. . . . La Marmora and the Piedmontese party is inflexible, unapproachable. Garibaldi is heartily disgusted. (Cattaneo, 263, vol. 3, p. 553)

The war, which began towards the end of April 1859, proved a rapid, though massive and bloody affair. The Piedmontese army, which had been reorganized by La Marmora on the French model of an army of 'quality', only numbered 63 000 men, instead of the 100 000 promised in the treaty with France, while the French provided 200 000. Both Napoleon and Victor Emanuel, like their opponent Francis Joseph, personally led their armies, although neither emperor had direct experience of command and the king may have preferred to forget his inglorious part in the defeat of Novara. After the initial Austrian advance beyond the Ticino, which led to the occupation of Biella and Vercelli (early May), there was little action until Garibaldi penetrated into Lombardy and occupied Varese and Como (23 May). Napoleon transported the major part of his army to Novara on the newly constructed railroad in eastern Piedmont (Alessandria-Casale-Vercelli), protected by the Piedmontese troops which occupied Palestro and clashed with the Austrians (30–1 May). The battle of Magenta (4 June) forced the Austrians to withdraw towards the Quadrilateral fortresses, while the allied sovereigns entered Milan and Garibaldi turned north, after occupying Bergamo and Brescia. The Franco-Sardinian forces won the major and most bloody battles of the war at Solferino and San Martino (22 June) and commenced the siege of the Quadrilateral. Unexpectedly, Napoleon proposed an armistic to Francis Joseph and rapidly signed the peace of Villafranca (11 July).

Napoleon's reasons for concluding peace before liberating Venetia and so, according to the terms of the January alliance, gaining Savoy and Nice as compensation, were to be found in developments internationally and in Italy. The growing threat of Prussian armed mediation undoubtedly worried him. But he was certainly as concerned with the repercussions of the war in central Italy, where Cavour's involvement seemed to be provoking revolutionary developments, not only in the duchies and Tuscany, but in papal Romagna. Both Cavour and Napoleon had agreed on the desirability of inciting Kossuth towards a revolution against Austria in Hungary. But insurrection in the Papal States went against the emperor's pledge to Pius IX, contradicted the presence of French troops in Rome, and threatened to arouse dangerous clerical opposition in France.

The annexation of the duchies, and particularly of Parma, were not precluded by the treaty. But Napoleon had always excluded Tuscany and had subsequently withdrawn his initial mention of the Legations at the Plombières meeting. La Farina had followed Cavour's general directives, instructing the National Society committees to prepare to form provisional governments once Piedmontese troops could ensure control, but not to incite popular risings. The Society was excellently equipped to spread propaganda, but was in no way capable – or desirous – of organizing revolution. Indeed, after sending instructions about the organization of the future provisional governments – in which it stressed the importance of maintaining order until the arrival of a Piedmontese authority – the Turin central committee dissolved the National Society on 26 April, convinced that its task was over, now that war had commenced.

But the strength of the National Society depended upon the vicinity of Piedmontese troops and proved inadequate to offer central Italy to Victor Emanuel, as Cavour had seemed to hope. This was shown not only in Tuscany, where the Society was weak, but even in the duchies. At Massa and Carrara, owned by the duke of Modena, the Society had assumed control, with the support of Piedmontese troops, when the duke's representatives withdrew on 27–8 April. At Parma, on the duchess' hasty withdrawal, the Society again created a provisional government, but this was rapidly overthrown by troops who remained loyal to the duchess. Only after Maria Luisa's final decision to withdraw following Magenta (9 June) were new governments formed at Parma and Piacenza by local notables – not by members of the National Society. The offer of the duchy to Victor Emanuel by these provisional governments and the arrival of a Piedmontese commissioner then permitted members of the Society to resurface as prominent members of the administration. Reggio rose against the duke of Modena on 12 June and Modena on the 13, with the evacuation of Austrian troops and the duke's flight. Only after these popular demonstrations did the Society's leader, Luigi Zini, form a provisional government at Modena, offering the city – as Reggio had offered itself – to Victor Emanuel. Cavour's commissioner, Luigi Carlo Farini, arrived soon after. In the duchies the National Society had thus shown itself capable of filling a vacuum and preserving order against possible popular demands for social change, but not of organizing a revolution against the local authorities.

In Tuscany, the first state to revolt against its ruler, the situation was far more complicated and the National Society played little part. Leopold II's decision in 1849 to return only with the support of Austrian troops had undoubtedly alienated the moderate ruling class, the mainstay of the regime. But fearful memories of the democratic republican developments of 1848-9 coloured their attitude. The most active moderates, led by Ricasoli and Ridolfi, had gathered together early in 1858 to publish a series of patriotic pamphlets. Although Ricasoli personally believed in the ultimate unification of Italy, the group were firm supporters of Tuscan autonomy, and, as the leaders of Tuscan society, carried great influence. Like the far weaker Tuscan followers of La Farina, they were fearful of social disorder, but, as patriots, supported sending volunteers to Piedmont.

A far more radical movement began to be organized by a leader of the Florentine populace, Giuseppe Dolfi, and by the Mazzinian Piero Cironi. The moderate nobles, like the members of the National Society, were in contact with Cavour, but were increasingly disillusioned by his indifference towards their opinions. Cavour, under the immense stress of running all the ministries concerned with the war, aware of Napoleon's concern to maintain an independent Tuscany, urged the patriots to detach the grand-duke from his alliance with Austria, ally him to Piedmont, and press for a constitution. As the situation precipitated, the directives changed, confusing the Piedmontese representative in Tuscany, Boncompagni, the moderates and the members of the National Society, who had almost lost direct contact with La Farina. But while Cavour pressed for legal agitation, he excluded a popular rising.

After unsatisfactory contacts with Ricasoli and his followers, Dolfi called for a popular rising on 27 April, still hoping that Ricasoli would take the lead. Ricasoli had hastily left for Turin to seek the aid of Piedmontese troops to control the revolution. The moderates, until the end, hoped to save the Tuscan dynasty by persuading Leopold to join the war against

Austria and appoint a liberal government. They were only defeated by Dolfi's disciplined control of the crowds in Florence which demonstrated throughout the day, demanding the grand-duke's abdication, and Leopold's fear, which led to his sudden decision to leave the country rather than abdicate. The long-standing subordination of the Tuscan democrats to the moderates was once more apparent, as they agreed not to press their claim to membership of the moderate provisional government in the interests of patriotic unity.

The Tuscan request for the dictatorship of Victor Emanuel for the duration of the war was rejected by Cavour, in accordance with French wishes. He agreed only to a protectorate over Tuscany under the Piedmontese diplomatic representative, Boncompagni. Cavour was now primarily concerned to obtain the despatch of a large Tuscan contingent to the front. The Tuscan moderates resisted Boncompagni's attempt to form a non-political administration and forced him to accept a government under Ricasoli, Ridolfi and Salvagnoli (11 May). The moderates, once more in control, were firm in their defence of Tuscan independence, but remained fearful of popular pressure: they requested military aid from the French emperor, who sent a force under his cousin prince Napoleon. Possibly in secret agreement with Cavour, prince Napoleon – always favourable to Piedmont and formerly the major secret contact between Cavour and the emperor – openly declared for Tuscan annexation to Piedmont, while Cavour, changing his plans once more, sent Nigra to agitate for support. The hostile reaction in Tuscany, where only Ricasoli had begun to consider annexation as a step towards the unification of Italy, combined with the disavowal of Cavour's initiative by Napoleon and Victor Emanuel. Napoleon's mistrust of Cavour was reinforced by the open hostility of his foreign minister Walewski. By mid-June even prince Napoleon abandoned Tuscany in disgust at the lack of support, taking with him a Tuscan division, ineffectively reorganized by Cavour's military nominee, general Ulloa.

Ricasoli, a convinced unitarian after Magenta, found his views gaining ground among his reluctant moderate colleagues, as the weakness of the Tuscan state and its vulnerability to a renewal of popular revolution became apparent. The 'iron baron', less inhibited than this colleagues, even sought the democrat Dolfi's assistance to organize petitions from the town councils in support of a strong, united Italy. Fear of 'shopkeepers, piddling doctors, dim lawyers' (Ricasoli, 358, vol. 3, p. 103) drove even the haughty, non-political aristocratic families, such as the Pazzi, Gherardesca and Ginori, to support the new Italian policy. Resentment against the union of civilized Tuscany with the semi-barbarian Piedmont remained strong, but Ricasoli, accepting 'fusion' as a necessary step towards a united Italy, now had a firm control.

The disaffection towards the pope in the Legations and La Farina's assurances about the strength of the National Society there had led Cavour to hope for demonstrations of patriotism without disorder. But there were serious rivalries in the Romagna, where the moderate Marco Minghetti remained distrustful of the National Society and the French emperor's cousin Pepoli could not be ignored. In the event, no spontaneous revolt took place and the local National Society leaders were too worried about maintaining order to incite one. Only after Magenta and the withdrawal of Austrian troops (12 June) was the Society able to form a provisional government in Bologna and to assist the formation of similar governments in the smaller cities of the Romagna. Once more, to avoid an open clash with Napoleon, Victor Emanuel refused the offer of a dictatorship, only agreeing to a protectorate. D'Azeglio, nominated governor by Cavour, arrived on 14 July. The bloodless change of power in the Romagna encouraged the cities of the Papal Marches and Umbria to rise (15-16 June), relying upon support from volunteers organized in Tuscany. But the support failed to materialize, and the pope's Swiss mercenaries reconquered and savaged Perugia (20 June) and the other cities of Umbria and the Marches.

By the time Napoleon signed the peace of Villafranca, revolution had thus followed the withdrawal of Austrian troops in central Italy. But, after the initial insurrection at Florence on 27 April, the old regimes had been replaced by provisional governments composed of moderates and members of the National Society, who had successfully exerted their efforts to repress all signs of disorder or democratic revolution, and claimed to represent the popular desire for rule by Victor Emanuel.

The crisis in central Italy

Napoleon's decision to sign peace signified the crisis of Cavour's policy. Carried away by one of those rare attacks of rage in which he lost all control over himself, Cavour had urged the continuation of the war without France, upbraided the king for his refusal and finally resigned (11 July). As Mazzini had foreseen, Cavour had failed to run in harness the Italian national movement and the diplomatic alliance with Bonapartist France. But the new situation in central Italy jeopardized the agreement of the two emperors, which stipulated the return to their states of the rulers of Modena and Tuscany.

The position of the provisional governments in central Italy remained uncertain after the withdrawal of the Piedmontese commissioners and governors. For it became clear that Austria was in no position to defy the British policy of non-intervention and restore the deposed princes by force. Although Napoleon's attitude remained cold until late 1859, and that of his foreign minister Walewski hostile, it was evident that France would not use force to assist the dukes immediately after a war waged for the independence of Italy. The main threat from France was the possibility that Napoleon press the candidature of his cousin, prince Napoleon, as ruler of an autonomous state of central Italy. Encouraged secretly by Cavour in the few days between his resignation and the formation of a new Sardinian government under La Marmora and Rattazzi, the liberal governments of central Italy took steps to organize themselves against any attempted coups, whether by the former rulers or by democratic forces.

They received little support from Turin, where the new government showed itself above all concerned to obtain French approval. In Tuscany, Ricasoli assumed dictatorial powers and manipulated elections held on a narrowly restricted suffrage (7 August): a massive majority was returned, and only a few democrats, led by Montanelli, were elected. The government even disqualified Guerrazzi's candidature. The new assembly was agreed in its opposition to the old dynasty. But although it voted unanimously in favour of joining a constitutional kingdom under Victor Emanuel, many moderates remained hopeful that the great powers would ensure the state's independence. After this vote, the assembly delegated its powers to the government (20 August). In the duchies and the Legations the same pattern was followed. Farini managed to retain his authority by resigning as Piedmontese governor and assuming dictatorial powers by popular acclamation in Modena (27 July) and then Parma (18 August). Elections were held, on a suffrage of all literate citizens: the new assemblies predictably voted for annexation by Piedmont and confirmed Farini's position as dictator (August–September). In the Legations the most influential notables, Minghetti and Pepoli, obtained the nomination of Leonetto Cipriani as governor general, because of his friendship with Napoleon. As in Tuscany, the suffrage was restricted by the exclusion of all manual labourers. Under Minghetti's leadership the moderate assembly which emerged from the elections justified the end of papal rule and annexation by Piedmont on the grounds of the need for a strong state and civil equality, liberty and national independence (September). A military convention for their joint defence was agreed to by the three governments.

Under pressure from Napoleon, Victor Emanuel reluctantly refused the offers of annexation, until 'Europe' should agree. But the three dictators – Ricasoli, Farini, Cipriani – maintaining strict control within their states, continued to organize public opinion and to claim to speak in the name of the Italians of central Italy. They now got their respective assemblies to vote in favour of the election as regent of the heir to the Sardinian throne, the prince of Carignano (November). Once more Napoleon obliged Victor Emanuel to refuse. In the Romagna the assembly removed the Bonapartist Cipriani and appointed Farini dictator.

Given the diplomatic *impasse*, Farini took matters into his own hands and hastened through a *de facto* unification with Sardinia of Parma, Modena and the Romagna – the 'Royal provinces of Emilia' – by enforcing the adoption of Piedmontese legislation and its administrative system (December 1859 – January 1860). Ricasoli, unitarian but ill-inclined to accept Piedmontese superiority, was far less willing to adopt the rigid centralization of the Sardinian state and would agree to no more than customs unification with Piedmont and the other independent provinces. Farini's action prejudged the diplomatic solution and was to prove of lasting negative influence on the structure of the new state. But Farini could justify his measures by Rattazzi's example in Lombardy. As soon as the annexation of Lombardy had been approved by France and Austria, decree laws had been hastily pushed through in Turin, while parliament was out of session, without consulting Lombard opinion or officials, or even the Lombard members of Rattazzi's own cabinet (October–November). The pattern for the administrative centralization of Italy, which was to arouse such bitter discussion with the annexation of the Mezzogiorno, had already been set by Rattazzi and Farini without public discussion. The price of the exclusive preoccupation with purely political matters was already beginning to be paid.

Despite the severe control exercised by the dictators, the protracted crisis inevitably aroused the criticism of those who saw a need to force the situation. Mazzini came secretly to Florence in August. Convinced that a unique opportunity existed, given the international stalemate, he urged an invasion of the Papal States under Garibaldi, who could then press into the Neapolitan Abruzzo, contemporaneous to a rising in Sicily: 'If matters are allowed to settle, by congresses or in other ways, we shall be at it for another ten years' (Mazzini, 257, vol. 65, p. 60). Garibaldi, who had been called, after the war, to head the forces of the central Italian states, constituted a continuous threat, attracting volunteers and democrats. Indeed, Minghetti had hastened to obtain the nomination of a regular Piedmontese general, Fanti, as Garibaldi's superior.

Mazzini lacked support, Garibaldi lacked direction. But Victor Emanuel's private diplomacy soon aroused new worries among the moderates. The king, as cheerful as a schoolboy on holiday after Cavour's resignation, chafed at the imposition of French control and intrigued with the democrats, even contacting Mazzini. He thought of purchasing Venice from Austria, but also talked of renewing the war against Austria, even without France, in the following spring. In August, he plotted secretly with Garibaldi, who agreed to lead an invasion of the Papal States. By October the invasion seemed probable. It required the combined warnings of Napoleon, Ricasoli, La Farina and Minghetti, and the direct prohibition of Farini and Fanti, reluctantly supported by the king, to dissuade Garibaldi (November). As James Hudson, the British representative at Turin, wrote: 'The King of Sardinia, who has no head for anything but a sword and a horse, looks forward with glee to drawing the one and riding the other, no matter where' (Giarrizzo, 350, vol. 7, p. 302).

The dangers of dissipating the hard-won concord of the early months of 1859 convinced La Farina, incapable of maintaining a passive attitude, to reconstitute the National Society. He had persuaded Garibaldi to act as honorary president, but had been unable to prevent the clash over the invasion of the Papal States. Garibaldi's resignation and subsequent support for Brofferio's democratic rival organization of *Free Assemblies* and its equally short-lived successor, *Armed Nation*, pushed La Farina ever closer to Cavour and accentuated the National Society's dislike of democrats: this time the association included few of the 1848 activists. Once more, the National Society was most effective in those regions where the social prestige of local notables and the traditions of sectarian activities were strongest. As the National Society reconstituted itself (December 1859–January 1860) in the smaller cities of the former duchies and Tuscany, and above all in the Romagna and Marches – where it superimposed itself upon the local anti-papal 'emigration committees' – it consolidated the power of the dictators. By spring 1860 Farini had adapted the Emilian provinces to Piedmontese rule, while Ricasoli's energetic support of a larger Italy had slowly overcome the Tuscan moderates' resentment of annexation by Piedmont.

Diplomacy and the formation of Italy

The solution to the problem of central Italy was decided internationally, but not by the Concert of Europe. It was imposed bilaterally by the Russell-Palmerston whig government and the emperor Napoleon III. British insistence on non-intervention, which had frozen the situation, developed by early January 1860 into strong support for Piedmontese annexation as a counter-weight to French influence. Palmerston even thought of war against Austria to settle the issue, and in any case ensured that Austria would not intervene with force against annexation. Napoleon, slowly obliged to abandon his hopes of an independent Tuscany, unable to convince the pope of the desirability of any change or reform, seized upon the British initiative as a solution to an intolerable situation. Anglo-French friendship reached a new warmth as Napoleon agreed to lower tariffs and signed a trade treaty with Britain (23 January 1860). On 15 January the two governments agreed to exclude outside intervention in the internal affairs of Italy and to allow central Italy to decide its own fate by popular vote. In compensation, Austria was to be left a free hand in Venetia (which, according to Villafranca, included the Quadrilateral fortresses).

In the same days Cavour returned to office. The La Marmora-Rattazzi government had proved ineffective, and Rattazzi had spent increasing energy plotting against Cavour's return. Cavour's position was weak, not only because of the king's antipathy towards him, but because parliament, which – at his suggestion – had handed over full powers to the king at the outbreak of the war, was still suspended. Cavour returned to politics in the autumn and soon became the spokesman for aristocratic and conservative opinion, which was strongly opposed to Rattazzi's policy of centralization, and worried by the king's intrigues with Brofferio and the extreme left and his schemes to make Garibaldi the centre of an anti-Cavourian bloc. D'Azeglio, preoccupied by the royal threat to the constitution, supported Cavour, as did the French and English governments. It was Hudson, indeed, who virtually forced Victor Emanuel to reappoint Cavour (21 January 1860).

Cavour was convinced that Napoleon could be brought to accept the annexation of Tuscany and the Legations, as well as the duchies, in return for Savoy and Nice. Although unhappy about the dangers of holding elections to new assemblies in central Italy by universal suffrage, he – like Ricasoli – accepted this as a necessity to convince foreign opinion:

> As far as we are concerned, universal suffrage will not be without its drawbacks. It will establish a tiresome precedent which could be invoked in a not too distant future either by the ultra-democratic party led by Mazzini, Cattaneo, etc.; or by the clerical party. Despite these objections, if England agrees to universal suffrage and if this were the price for French acceptance of annexation, Sardinia would accept it frankly and without reservations. (364, vol. 3, pp. 46-7)

The National Society threw itself wholeheartedly into organizing the plebiscites, worried about mass abstentions. Its local landowning leaders, traditionally looked up to because of their social position, were ideally placed, as an organized network, to act as a transmission belt for official views. Propaganda and electioneering, bribes and threats, were all employed by the central Italian governments and their supporters. On the appointed holiday, the voters were mobilized in groups by social class – students, craftsmen, landowners, peasants, etc. They were called upon to choose between annexation to a constitutional monarchy under Victor Emanuel and an unspecified 'separate kingdom'. A typical example of the atmosphere of those days is offered by the small city of Sesto Fiorentino, near Florence. Marquess Lorenzo Ginori, chief magistrate of the city and employer of most of its population in his pottery works, explained to his citizen employees, lest they fail to understand, that 'small fish are gobbled up by big fish':

> In 1848, as you all know, we raised our heads, but we didn't all agree; the matter wasn't approached in the right way, there was too much shouting, too little thought; in short, the whole business finished up in the way it did, no one is born a master. But now it's quite a different matter. (Ragionieri, 378, pp. 228-9)

The myth of universal national patriotism was fired in the furnace of the plebiscite: over 80 per cent of the million registered voters turned out, giving over 97 per cent support for annexation (18–22 March).

Napoleon's pound of flesh was agreed to by Cavour and Victor Emanuel in the same month, and announced on 1 April. Few had doubts about the result of a vote in Savoy, increasingly drawn towards neighbouring France and remote from, hostile to, Piedmont's Italian policy. But Nice's population was strongly Italian. The presence of French troops inevitably ensured a favourable vote (15–22 April): the virtual unanimity for annexation by France confirmed the Piedmontese experience about the utility of plebiscites. Nevertheless, the problems created by the cession of these regions, as much as by the annexations in central Italy, revealed the limits of Piedmontese policy and the high price paid for French protection. The revival of the democratic initiative – in a situation which had worsened significantly because of the king's dissatisfaction and the rivalry between the leading moderates – was not only to create the final drive towards unification, but to offer a vigorous confirmation of those deeper needs which had underlain the struggle for independence and which were to make more than diplomatic sense of the creation of the new state.

The final drive of democratic unitarianism

The news of the successful unification of central Italy with Piedmont sparked off insurrection in Sicily. Conspiracy had never ceased in Sicily, where it had been led by the democrats. In the continental kingdom of Naples the democrats, never strong after 1848, had been severely weakened by the failure of the Sapri expedition, while the moderates awaited salvation by a foreign power – Piedmont or Murat. The hopes aroused by the death of Ferdinand II had soon been dashed by his son Francis II (1859–61). In Sicily, despite the viceroy Filangieri's initial attempts to attract support after the 1848–9 revolution, the rumblings of insurrection had never been entirely suppressed by the Bourbons and grew more ominous during 1859. The Sicilian moderates, like their Neapolitan counterparts, awaited a solution from outside the island; even those in favour of autonomy, like the democrats, identified the struggle for Italy with Piedmont. With the war, hopes of an expedition revived, perhaps led by Garibaldi.

Among the Sicilian exiles, Francesco Crispi and Rosolino Pilo, Mazzinian republicans who had refused to participate in the dynastic war of 1859, began to plan an expedition. Crispi, after a secret visit to Sicily in summer 1859, was convinced that conditions were ripe for revolution. But, in his report to Fabrizi, he recognized that unification, not the republic, offered the only hope:

I cannot tell you which flag will be hoisted, if some of our men are there at the decisive moment. You know my principles, and they will not change; but today, as I have told you many times and now repeat, in the present state of affairs the only goal which can and must be reached is that of national unity. (Crispi, 367, pp. 98–9)

Crispi's assessment of conditions in Sicily, like those of all democrats and moderates, referred to the politically conscious elements of the population. In classic Mazzinian style, he conceived of the spirit of revolt among the peasantry in a purely tactical manner, as a means of arousing the passive masses, under the direction of the middle classes, towards the patriotic end of unity. Indeed, little attention was paid to the peasantry, as the revolution was to be an urban affair, with the lawyers, doctors and shopkeepers, the professional democrats, leading the craftsmen. But once insurrection broke out in Palermo (4 April 1860) – where it was rapidly suppressed – it spread into the smaller cities and the countryside on a far wider scale than in 1820 or 1848. Peasant 'squads', led by bandits in attacks on Bourbon police or tax-collectors, were a familiar phenomenon in nineteenth-century Sicily. Class hostility explained much, but not all, of their recurrent revolts. For these 'squads' often consisted of kinship groups and those closely allied to them, waging a private vendetta to avenge a personal injustice. This sometimes obscure intertwining of motives of honour and class had led to a semi-secret pattern of private bands who sought to impose by force their own concepts of law and order. The revolt of peasant 'squads' led automatically to the creation of 'counter-squads' or 'armed companies' of local officials and landowners with their retainers, often playing off one peasant 'squad' against another. This phenomenon was soon to be given the name of the 'mafia'. Hence it was to be expected, unless extraneous elements intervened, that the peasant revolt of Spring 1860 would arouse a counter-movement. The revolt was immediately directed against the government and then turned towards the traditional demands for the division of the communal lands and those illegally usurped by the proprietors. Local government collapsed as the officials fled. The arrival of Pilo and Corrao, a Palermitan popular leader, gave hope to the democrats and even to some of the peasant 'squads' that an expedition was on its way.

The Bourbon government, with 20 000 troops in Palermo, had difficulty in suppressing the revolt because of its very diffusion, and combined measures to calm the urban populations (creating employment through public works, importing flour) with the despatch of repressive mobile columns into the countryside. It appealed for support to the proprietors, who responded – as in the previous revolutions – by the creation of civic guards. By the end of April the revolt was dying out, although the brutality of the Bourbon troops and the continuing activity of some peasant bands disrupted trade in the cities and left the merchants and professional classes hostile.

The expedition to Sicily, planned for so long by the democrats, differed from all previous Mazzinian attempts in that it was not sent to arouse a general insurrection, but to support one: it arrived in time to reinforce a revolt of major proportions, albeit in its dying stages. The number and experience of the troops, the efficiency of the logistics (especially after the initial embarkation of the Mille), which again distinguished this expedition from previous attempts, were rendered possible by the magnetism of Garibaldi's name and the exceptional atmosphere of patriotism generated by the events of the previous twelve months.

The republican reputations of Crispi and Pilo had worked against them in their earlier contacts with the Piedmontese government. Victor Emanuel, once more plotting behind Cavour's back, had also judged the time inopportune and had sent a representative to Sicily at the beginning of 1860 to discourage the moderates from insurrection. Even Garibaldi had displayed little enthusiasm when Rosolino Pilo had appealed to him in March:

> I do not believe the present moment opportune for a revolutionary movement in any part of Italy. Today the fate of the country is in the hands of political meddlers, who want to settle everything by diplomatic negotiations; we must wait until the Italian people recognise the futility of the intrigues of these doctrinaires. That will be the moment to act. (Crispi, 367, pp. 118-19)

But when Bixio and Crispi brought the news of the revolution, Garibaldi threw himself into preparing the expedition, despite Victor Emanuel's refusal to allow him to recruit volunteers from the regular Piedmontese army. The democrats had regained the initiative, but Garibaldi's leadership signified their acceptance of the monarchy as the price of Mazzinian unity: 'In case of action', Garibaldi had written to Pilo already in March, 'remember that the programme is: Italy and Victor Emanuel.'

The legendary Thousand (in reality nearly exactly 1100) represented the democrats in their social composition and geographical origins. About half were middle class, mainly sons of professional men and intellectuals, and half craftsmen and workers; nearly three-quarters came from Lombardy, Venetia and Liguria, with small contingents from Tuscany and Sicily; they included the leading Sicilian democratic exiles – Crispi, the Orlandos – and many who had fought with Garibaldi in the war of the previous year. The *Mille* left Quarto (near Genoa) on two steamships (5 May), stopped for supplies at Talamone, reached Marsala on 11 May and in spectacular manner marched upon and captured Palermo by 30 May. Garibaldi owed his success not only to his remarkable tactical qualities and the courage of his troops, forced to attack by bayonet as their rifles were too old and unreliable for steady gunfire, but to the renewal of the peasant revolt, which effectively masked his movements, reinforced his numbers and demoralized the Bourbon troops.

Crispi and Garibaldi did not undervalue the importance of this peasant support, but – at first – appeared to conceive of it in terms of the 1848 revolution. After nominating himself dictator of the island in the name of Victor Emanuel at Salemi (14 May), Garibaldi had ordered the reconstitution of the local civic councils with the personnel of the 1848–9 revolutions. He had abolished the grist-tax and other taxes imposed since the Bourbon Restoration, as well as the import duty on cereals and vegetables (17 May). The new revolution was clearly meant to be the continuation of the previous one. But the strength of peasant support induced Crispi to move further after the liberation of Palermo: by a decree of 2 June all combatants were to receive a quota of the communal demesnes. The peasant movement assumed vast proportions between June and August, but increasingly revealed its social motivation, remote from Garibaldi's patriotic war, with the demand for the division not only of the communal demesnes but of the usurped lands. The peasant revolt was rapidly developing into a *jacquerie*, directed against the government and the landowners.

Garibaldi and Crispi had absorbed far too much Mazzinian doctrine to tolerate class conflict of this nature. Their decrees reflected their belief in democratic-liberal reforms and class collaboration: free trade, a legal obligation to continue paying interest on all state loans (even those of the deposed government), public works to reduce unemployment, an attempt to fix maximum prices for foodstuffs, even the establishment of nurseries. Property was sacred and order had to be maintained. The early decrees in favour of the peasants were accompanied by others imposing the death penalty for murder, theft or looting. Crispi, authoritarian in character, obsessed by the pursuit of a united Italy, imposed his authority as Garibaldi's representative with a heavy hand. Contemporaries were astonished at the order in Palermo during the days of fighting, especially when compared to the bloodshed of 1848. But outside the capital, particularly in the inland, hilly regions, the peasant rising had swept away the structure of local government and in many places led to savage attacks on the landowners. The old 'armed companies' reappeared to maintain order, the landowners, abandoning both the Bourbons and their hopes of independence, turned to the revolutionary government for support, as the local leaders proved incapable of controlling the mass of the peasants.

Garibaldi's loss of peasant support was accelerated by the attempt to introduce conscription into an island where the Bourbons had acknowledged defeat after the 1820 revolution. By the summer Garibaldi and Crispi had accepted their failure, masking it by decrees allowing exemptions from conscription and then a general prorogation until the harvest was collected. But by this time they had already begun to identify themselves with the traditional local ruling class, the middle-class proprietors and *gabelloti* who had bought up or administered the lands of the bankrupt feudal barons. Crispi had disregarded the decree for the popular election of local councils, in many cases recalling the former Bourbon administrators, as these were the only local notables.

This middle class of *galantuomini*, both in city and countryside, had remained neutral in the early days of Garibaldi's invasion, resenting the Bourbons, but reluctant to identify itself with revolution. It had needed the defeat of the Bourbon army, but even more the threat of the urban masses and peasantry to their property and lives, to transform them into patriots. It was their 'counter-squads', more than Crispi's militia, who were responsible for the restoration of order. Indeed, these landowners remained hostile to the democrat Crispi, challenging such decrees as the reimposition of the land-tax to replace the grist-tax. As a French eye-witness, Marc Monnier, already wrote of Messina in mid-June: 'All roles have been inverted, and the timorous, the alarmists, the good bourgeois, the enemies of revolution, await Garibaldi anxiously, as he alone can save their cash-tills' (Monnier, 368, p. 165). But if the Sicilian merchants and landowners now turned to Garibaldi for economic and social reasons, they were increasingly tempted to shift their allegiance towards Piedmont and annexation, however deep their attachment to Sicilian independence. They were encouraged in this by Cavour's attempt to regain the initiative.

Cavour and Garibaldi

Garibaldi's decision to lead an expedition to Sicily had taken Cavour unawares. His position in Turin was weak, as he had only just agreed to the cession of Savoy and Nice in an unconstitutional manner, without informing parliament. He was worried about the criticism of the representatives of the old Savoyard state, although he remained optimistic that he would hold a majority in parliament through the support of the deputies of the new provinces. Despite Garibaldi's denunciation in the chamber of the cession of his birthplace Nice, Cavour had managed to delay a discussion until after the plebiscites were held in Savoy and Nice: the final vote was only taken on 29 May, when Garibaldi was nearing the conquest of Palermo. Garibaldi's departure had taken place on the day supplementary elections were being held, which were crucial to Cavour. The government was in crisis, as Fanti threatened to resign and bring down the cabinet. Although the king could not but support Cavour over the cessions of Sardinian territory, he was ever-more hostile to his premier. Victor Emanuel was in contact with Garibaldi and had seemed ready to allow him to try his luck, as it might allow the king to assert his authority. While the preparations for the expedition had proceeded, Cavour had done little to help, and indeed had tried to impede them, tacitly accepting the refusal of D'Azeglio, governor of Lombardy, to allow Garibaldi to withdraw the rifles he had collected after Villafranca for a renewal of the war.

But as leader of patriotic Italy, Cavour could not openly oppose an expedition aimed at completing Italian unity and headed by so popular a figure as Garibaldi. He was undoubtedly worried by Garibaldi's republican comrades and feared the bogy of a Mazzinian revival. He had contemplated pre-empting Garibaldi by sending a separate force to Sicily under Ribotti or La Masa, and had then approved La Farina's endeavours to collaborate with the preparation of Garibaldi's expedition, while combating republican infiltrations. But, in the end, Cavour had permitted the preparations at Genoa and Garibaldi's departure, with only an ambiguous message to the Piedmontese admiral Persano to stop Garibaldi if he put in at a Sardinian port. As Hudson wrote to Russell in June:

> At the outset nobody believed in the possibility of Garibaldi's success; and Cavour and *tutti quanti* thought the country well rid of him and of the unquiet spirits who went with him. The argument was, if he fails we are rid of a troublesome fellow, and if he succeeds Italy will derive some profit from his success. (Mack Smith, 346, pp. 181–8)

Cavour's preoccupations were naturally over the international situation. As always, he was most worried about Napoleon, but he did not exclude English hostility, given British resentment over the cession of Savoy and Nice to France. If the two western powers did not prove friendly, there was a serious prospect of Austrian intervention. The danger seemed even greater, as Garibaldi's representative at Genoa, Bertani, threatened to organize an invasion of the Papal States by the volunteers who continued to gather there. Indeed Garibaldi himself, when he had stopped at Talamone to seize the fortress' supplies of arms, had despatched a small force towards the Papal States, which had been easily repelled. As Cavour wrote to Ricasoli on 16 May:

> Garibaldi, detained violently, would become dangerous in the country. Now what will happen? It is impossible to foresee. Will England help him? It is possible. Will France block him? I do not believe it. And we? To support him openly is not possible, but neither is restraint of the individual efforts in his favour. So we have decided not to permit new expeditions from the ports of Genoa and Leghorn, not to impede the dispatch of arms and munitions, as long as it be done somewhat prudently. I am aware of all the inconveniences of this ill-defined line we are following, but I cannot indicate another path which would not present graver dangers. (Cavour, 365, vol. 1, p. 104)

Cavour's worries about the great powers gradually subsided. Palmerston and Russell, voicing British public opinion, supported Garibaldi once they were sure that the expedition would not result in further cessions of territory to France. Napoleon was disinclined to act without British support, which was twice refused him. British assertions of non-intervention effectively checked any threat from Austria. The main danger remained an attack on the Papal States. That this was a reality was clear from Garibaldi's proclamation 'To Italians' at the moment of his departure, in which he stated his intention of achieving the unity of Italy. His instructions to Bertani echoed Mazzini's schemes for provoking insurrection in the Papal States and Naples. Mazzini's arrival at Genoa encouraged Bertani to persist in his plans. Only Garibaldi's constant need for reinforcements (a total of 20 000 volunteers was sent) and La Farina's determined collaboration through the National Society, winning away from Bertani the undecided democrats like Medici and Cosenz, checked the organization of an expedition against the Papal States.

By the beginning of June, Cavour had decided to attempt to regain the initiative by pressing for the immediate annexation of Sicily. Garibaldi and Crispi had refused to proclaim annexation as they regarded Sicily as the necessary strategic base for the invasion of the mainland, and retained the democratic belief in the right of the people to decide their own destiny through an elected assembly. As a Sicilian exile and as leader of the National Society, La Farina was sent to the island by Cavour as his representative (early June). But the choice could not have proved worse. If La Farina reinforced the Sicilian moderates in their new-found enthusiasm for Italy, his tactlessness and open propaganda for immediate annexation revived Crispi's enmity and clashed with Garibaldi's determination to wage a war. One month after his arrival, on 7 July, Garibaldi expelled him as a spy. But La Farina had succeeded in forcing Garibaldi's representatives to decree the compilation of electoral lists, which could serve either for an assembly or a plebiscite, and in gaining a new and more moderate provisional government. The mistrust between Garibaldi and Cavour grew worse. But the Sicilian dictatorship was now ever-more identified with the propertied classes, as Crispi suppressed the peasant insurrections, fearful less they be exploited for a counter-revolution. Bixio's ruthless repression of the Bronte rising (4 August) was to remain notorious. With Garibaldi's victory at Milazzo (20 July) and the Bourbon evacuation of Messina, the probability of an invasion of the mainland became ever-more likely. Peasant agitations increased in an almost messianic expectation of Garibaldi's arrival. Francis II's sudden decision to grant a constitution and open negotiations with Sardinia (25 June) was too late to win support from the Neapolitan liberals, ever-suspicious of Bourbon promises and by now turning towards Savoy as a social guarantee. Indeed, Francis' *volte-face* disoriented the loyal Bourbon administration and army. But it placed Cavour in an embarrassing position. He procrastinated over the negotiations, trying to prevent Garibaldi from

crossing the straits of Messina, and contemporaneously attempted to provoke a pre-emptive moderate revolution in the kingdom of Naples. Victor
Emanuel was induced to write to Garibaldi, to dissuade him from invading
Naples, but managed to leave the general with the impression that he was
not really firmly opposed (22 July). Cavour sent agents to Naples to provoke
an insurrection before Garibaldi's arrival, despite Napoleon III's dis-
approval. But their contacts with the moderates, with the most powerful
Neapolitan minister, Liborio Romano, even with the king's uncle, conte di
Siracusa, failed completely. The moderates were too fearful of Bourbon
repression and the imminent arrival of Garibaldi, while the democratic
Action Committee intensified its preparations to assist Garibaldi. After
insurrections broke out in Calabria and Basilicata, the moderates hastily
joined the democrats in support of Garibaldi's dictatorship. Cavour's only
success was to prevent Bertani from launching the attack on the Papal
States, which he had finally organized in Tuscany, Romagna and Genoa.

Garibaldi's conquest of the kingdom of Naples proved far easier than
that of Sicily. On the mainland, as on the island, popular risings were of
crucial support. After Garibaldi's landing in Calabria on 18 August, the
spontaneous revolt in the peasant villages and towns destroyed the power of
the Bourbon police and administration and led to the defection of many
soldiers in the Neapolitan army. The general's procession through Calabria
and Basilicata proved even more triumphal than that of cardinal Ruffo
sixty years earlier. When the *lazzaroni* of the city of Naples – the *menu
peuple* of porters, petty craftsmen and street traders – rose in revolt, the
Bourbon dynasty lost its traditional support in the capital. On 7 September,
after Francis' withdrawal, Garibaldi entered Naples.

For Cavour the situation had become desperate. If Garibaldi continued
in his successful invasion of southern Italy, he would be in a position to
insist upon a constituent assembly: Mazzini's dreams seemed about to
become reality. If Garibaldi attacked Rome, Napoleon, with his troops
stationed there, could not but intervene. If he proceeded against Venice,
Austria would begin war again. Despite Garibaldi's evident loyalty to
Victor Emanuel, despite the acceptance of the monarchy by Garibaldi's
followers, Cavour was ever-more worried by the threat of Mazzini. As he
wrote to Nigra, before the general crossed the straits of Messina:

> If Garibaldi passes over to the mainland and seizes the kingdom of Naples and
> its capital, as he has done with Sicily and Palermo, he becomes absolute master
> of the situation. King Victor Emanuel loses more or less all his prestige; in the
> eyes of the great majority of Italians he is no more than Garibaldi's friend. . . .
> Garibaldi will not proclaim the republic at Naples; but he will not annex it and
> he will maintain his dictatorship. With the resources of a kingdom of 9,000,000
> inhabitants at his disposal, surrounded as he is by irresistible popular prestige,
> it is impossible for us to struggle against him. (364, vol. 4, p. 122)

Distrustful as ever of the king's intentions, Cavour now had to combat Ricasoli's insistence on the need to take an energetic line, proclaim the king dictator and invade the Papal States. As Cavour complained in a private letter: Ricasoli 'writes and writes again, telegraphs day and night to urge us on with advice, warnings, reprimands, almost I would say with threats' (365, vol. 2, p. 43). Cavour restrained Ricasoli with difficulty and indeed, momentarily, was sufficiently influenced by him to be tempted to challenge Garibaldi's prestige by starting a war against Austria for the liberation of Venice ('the seizure of Verona and Venice would make people forget Palermo and Milazzo', he wrote to Nigra). But he recognized that 'to do something at this hour, Victor Emanuel and Garibaldi must not be made to clash'. As realistic a politician as ever, Cavour was ready to acknowledge that:

> Garibaldi has rendered to Italy the greatest service that a man could render: he has given Italians confidence in themselves. . . . As long as he is faithful to his flag, one has to march along with him. This does not alter the fact that it would be eminently desirable for the revolution of Naples to be accomplished without him. (364, vol. 4, pp. 144–5)

By the end of August Cavour had decided to risk all in order to regain the initiative. With a remarkable *volte-face* he determined to precede Garibaldi in an invasion of the Papal States, occupy the Marches and Umbria and block Garibaldi's advance on Rome. Napoleon was informed and displayed tolerance of this unconventional method of checking a potential revolutionary threat and a real embarrassment to the presence of French troops at Rome. The rupture between Cavour and Garibaldi was complete. Cavour, anticipating the general's reaction, warned the king of the constitutional dangers of dismissing him at Garibaldi's request, so forestalling a letter from Garibaldi (11 September). But, conscious of the king's influence over Garibaldi, Cavour sent Victor Emanuel to head the army of invasion; at the same time, suspicious of the monarch's private diplomacy, he delegated Farini and Fanti, Garibaldi's bitter enemies, to accompany him. By 29 September the Marches and Umbria had been conquered.

With this sudden disregard of diplomatic caution in favour of revolutionary methods, Cavour regained control. Mazzini was the first to recognize this: 'The decision taken by the government, to do what it has stopped us doing, naturally modified the new leadership. So long as they move forward, no-one can oppose them' (257, vol. 70, p. 36). Whether the invasion of the Papal States had been necessary in order to prevent Garibaldi from advancing on Rome was questionable. For Garibaldi was already abandoning the project, despite the arrival at Naples of Mazzini and then (at the general's request) of Cattaneo. Peasant risings in the kingdom of Naples were already assuming a threatening anti-liberal character, as the landowners immediately identified themselves with the dictator and nullified the early measures in favour of the peasants. The Bourbon army of 50 000 remained intact, protecting Francis at Gaeta, and capable of an offensive against Naples. In the battle of the Volturno (1 October) Garibaldi managed to push back, but not to inflict a decisive defeat on the Bourbon army. Victor Emanuel, flushed with pride at his own occupation of all papal territory except Rome and the Lazio, brusquely reasserted his authority, declaring his readiness to use force against Garibaldi if necessary. He ordered the general to await his arrival, then to hand over his power. And Garibaldi obeyed. The meeting between king and general at Teano (25 October 1860) was to offer the scenario for the patriotic legends of national concord. But Farini, in his letter to Cavour describing the scene, hinted at the underlying tensions:

> The king tells me that Garibaldi, with his head still always in the clouds, showed himself ready to obey in everything and all ways: and in fact he immediately went with his men to where the king, on Fanti's advice, had ordered him. . . . Why wish him ill if in the end he gives everything to the king honestly? (Cavour, 365, vol. 3, p. 207)

Cavour had won his battle against Garibaldi. Now confident of his strength, he had summoned parliament to ratify the invasion of the Papal States and the annexation of the new territories. His fear of deliberative assemblies and his haste to complete the unification of Italy made him insist on the Turin parliament's prerogative to accept the newly liberated territories, without conditions, only subject to subsequent favourable plebiscites. It was a legitimation of the new Kingdom of Italy before its formal constitution, but in the shape of further annexations by the kingdom of Sardinia. The annexations of Emilia and Tuscany had only been accepted by the Piedmontese parliament after plebiscites. In his determination to complete the monarchical unification of Italy, Cavour deliberately ignored the strong demand in Sicily for some form of autonomy, despite his earlier readiness to accept that the enlarged kingdom required a less centralized administration than the Piedmontese. The triumph of Cavour's appropriation of Mazzini's programme of unity in the name of the monarchy emerged in the final vote in parliament: 290 in favour against 6 (11 October). As Cattaneo had noted sadly already twelve months earlier: 'The idea of unity is the sole one to have been inculcated and understood. Cavour has driven along the rails laid by Mazzini' (263, vol. 3, p. 209).

After thirty years in the desert, Mazzini finally saw his flock emerge into the promised land. But, unlike Moses, he was to survive and experience disillusionment. His insistence upon unity, to the exclusion of all social issues, had deprived the democrats of any effective alternatives. The transfusion of his faith to the royalist moderates had inhibited even their most able and sensitive leader, Cavour, from serious consideration of the dangers of a unification imposed upon Italy by the minute ruling class of a state whose legislative codes and system of administration were among the most backward of all the pre-unitarian Italian states. As peasant revolt spread and the hostility of the educated classes in southern Italy became ever more evident, Cavour's determination to maintain unity was transformed into a growing rejection of all claims for decentralization. The demand for a 'strong state' of a Ricasoli as of a Crispi, had triumphed over the liberal struggle for an independent Italy.

The plebiscites in the Marches and Umbria, Naples and Sicily were carried out, with the support of the National Society, in the by-now customary manner and obtained the by-now customary results (21 October, 4–5 November). Definitively freed of all threats of a constituent assembly, Cavour had accepted that they be held in favour of 'a single indivisible Italy with Victor Emanuel as constitutional king'. But the Piedmontese hegemony over unified Italy was symbolized by the new Italian parliament's acceptance of the title of its first king: Victor Emanuel II. The ambiguity of the process of unification was confirmed. The cost of independence was to reveal itself immediately.

16

Epilogue

The apparent failures of the unified state of Italy, following upon the struggle for independence, aroused regretful or bitter comment among contemporaries and ever since have formed a recurrent motif among historians. The achievement of national self-determination by Italy, and particularly the romantic figure of Garibaldi, had captured the imagination of liberal and democratic circles in Europe. Because expectations had been raised so high, the military failures and internal difficulties of the young state aroused a corresponding sense of disappointment. Italians, as always too prone to self-criticism, voiced their disillusionment even more than usually sympathetic foreigners. As the decades passed, the weaknesses and problems that emerged were contrasted with an increasingly uncritical and complacent vision of the triumphs that had led to unification: compared to the heroic stature of the men of the Risorgimento, current leaders appeared as the embodiment of mediocrity, while the Italian people seemed to suffer from a congenital incapacity to set their house in order. Inevitably the polemical, often dramatic delivery of such judgements, by exaggerating the contrasts, distorted both past and present. Italy was viewed almost as if it existed in a timeless vacuum, with little regard to the rapid and profound changes in Europe and the world that reflected so directly, and often so harshly, upon the country and its people. But despite the almost exclusively political content of these assessments, they did point to certain weaknesses within the process of unification, to the remoteness of the new state from Italian society.

The creation of Italy had not been a mere accident, the fortunate consequence of international diplomatic support, as the moderates tended to stress. It was as much the result of the patriotic aspirations and drive for independence of (for the most part) educated groups during an age when the belief in self-determination was as yet uncomplicated by questions of ethnic frontiers. Inevitably these groups constituted no more than a minority within the nation. Only some tens of thousands had participated as volunteers in the risings, movements and wars of the Risorgimento, and merely a few thousand had been involved actively in these movements as a 'political class'. But even though the patriots never represented more than a minute proportion of the population, their numbers had increased significantly over the period and their influence within the cities had trickled down socially, as much through the experiences of the insurrections as through propaganda or education. Without this diffusion of a patriotic drive, it would be difficult to explain how the country was ever unified and impossible to account for the romantic episode of Garibaldi's 'Thousand'.

If a basic consensus about the desirability of independence held the patriots together, the political divisions over the form the new state should take – monarchy or republic, unity or federation – remained deep, not least because of the manner in which unification had finally been achieved. Although the democratic forces – divided between Mazzinians and Garibaldians – were never able to organize a viable republican alternative, republicanism remained an undercurrent within the body politic, surfacing at moments of crisis, particularly when military defeat (as at Custoza and Lissa in 1866 or Adua in 1896) appeared to destroy the prestige of the monarchy. In similar manner, although the administratively centralized form of unity proved irrevocable, decentralization and regionalism, which derived directly from federalism, remained constants of democratic opposition within the state.

In the first decade of unity, these divisions were compounded by opposing visions of how to gain Venetia and Rome and so complete the territorial integrity of the nation-state. The moderates had been won over to Mazzini's myth of Rome as the necessary capital of Italy. But the diplomatic caution of Cavour's successors, conscious of their dependence on the great powers and especially France, clashed with the impatience of the democratic patriots, ever ready under the leadership of the national hero Garibaldi to force the pace by revolutionary initiatives. The débacles at Mentana (1862) and Aspromonte (1867) that frustrated Garibaldi's attempts to repeat his Sicilian exploit and liberate Venetia and Rome by military force increased the resentment of the democrats; the humiliating manner in which Italy acquired these territories (despite military and naval defeat at Austrian hands) through Prussian victory over Austria (1866) and then France (1870) did little to re-establish the prestige of the moderate governments. Irredentism, the patriotic desire to free the 'unredeemed' lands of the Trentino and Trieste, remained (like republicanism) an undercurrent, incapable of achieving its aims of its own, but a source of division and potentially dangerous at moments of crisis.

Purely political solutions can only hope to be successful in highly exceptional circumstances, such as prevailed in 1859–61. Hence the ideology imposed by the National Society and accepted by the Garibaldian Party of Action – political unity under Victor Emanuel, to the exclusion of all other factors – soon proved inadequate. The demands of economic, social and cultural elements over the purely political were soon asserted, as a more normal pattern of political life was re-established. It was hardly surprising, given its minute numbers and the manner in which it had imposed unity upon the country, that the moderate ruling class should have had an elitist attitude towards the problems of government and participation. Only too conscious of the enormity of the tasks that lay ahead, but truly Victorian in their confidence in their own capacities and in the sober austerity of their standards of public morality, these followers of Cavour (after the statesman's unexpected death on 6 June 1861) saw their duties in enlightened liberal manner as guiding an immature nation towards an ultimately tranquil, but ever-distant, future. Their cultural formation and the predominance of leaders from the north and centre explained their remoteness from the particular problems of the south, if not from those of the peasantry in general.

This remoteness was accentuated by the moderates' isolation even as a political class. The hostility of the Church, inevitable given the creation of the Italian state at the expense of the pope's temporal possessions, but rendered the more obdurate by the analogous (and sometimes petty) anti-clericalism of the secular authorities, deprived the moderates of the support of both priests and Catholic laity. Indeed, papal intransigence obliged the secular rulers to proclaim the authority of the state in assertive fashion through persistent fear of the deep and potentially subversive influence of the Church among the Italian people. The consequent brusqueness with which the 'legal' Italy imposed its power further isolated the moderates from the 'real', especially the rural, Italy. The high property requirement for voting rights reduced the social base of the moderates as it excluded many middling groups with appropriate educational qualifications. Ostracism of extreme democrats, especially republicans, cut off the ruling class of the Destra from precisely those patriots with the strongest links among the urban lower-middle classes and artisans. The Italian moderates, similar in so many respects to their peers in imperial France (except over their anti-clericalism), accentuated their separateness and remoteness from the great mass of the population both by choice and by policies.

Unification, however, had by no means given the Italian ruling class full autonomy in its actions. The newly independent state remained deeply conditioned by the international situation, not merely in the early years, but over the longer term. Italy had established its status as a great power, in terms of its population and geographical location in the Mediterranean, but it remained far weaker than the other great powers, England, France, Russia, Germany and Austria. Even after Italy asserted its independence of

France by its seizure of Rome at the moment of France's defeat (1870), the country could not run the risk of war against any of the major powers. The completion of the Suez canal (1869) raised expectations far higher than subsequent reality justified, and had the dubious consequence of forcing Italy – because of its status and central involvement in the Mediterranean – to participate more actively than it might otherwise have wished in an international scene soon characterized by growing tension. The policy of independence without isolation laid down by the Destra's leading foreign minister, Emilio Visconti Venosta, became ever-less possible as the breakdown of the Concert of Europe became more apparent. Between Crimea and the final unification of Germany, the great powers which had upheld the Concert of Europe for nearly forty years were all involved in wars on the continent, which left a legacy of diffidence and rivalry. The new balance of power, soon marked by imperialism and a system of opposing alliances, left little autonomy for an independent Italy which wished to play its role as a great power.

The policy of more direct involvement in international affairs, which resulted from Italy's emergence from the congress of Berlin with 'clean but empty hands' (1878) and France's occupation of Tunisia (1881), revealed Italy's dependence on the relations between the other great powers. Both entry into the Triple Alliance (1882) and the Italian quest for territory in Africa required the benevolence of these powers. The acquisition of the Red Sea port of Massawa (1885), Crispi's grandiose schemes for an east African empire in the 1890s, like Giolitti's conquest of Libya (1912), were only possible through the support or tacit acceptance of England, Germany and (later) France. The imperialism of an ex-democrat like Francesco Crispi was not so dissimilar, in ideological terms, from that of former radicals like Jules Ferry or Joseph Chamberlain. But it was far more dangerous, because Italy's weakness constrained its liberty of action. Imperialism, like the bouts of direct monarchical intervention in foreign affairs and the sporadic popular waves of irredentism, imperilled Italy's careful balancing between potentially hostile powers, threatening to engulf the country in conflicts it was unable to sustain. The crisis of intervention following the outbreak of the First World War offered the final proof of the contradiction between Italy's status as a great power and its incapacity to uphold this status.

Economic weakness is the basic reason for Italy's relative failure in international diplomacy and offers a further example of how the country's internal development was conditioned by factors outside its control. The unification of Italy occurred at a time when technological innovation significantly raised the level and cost of industrialization. Coal and iron, the primary raw materials of this new phase of industrial development, were virtually lacking in Italy, while capital was scarce; the sharp drop in transport costs, already induced by the rapid spread of railways, soon precipitated a crisis in European agriculture, unable to sustain American competition. Cavour's belief in an international division of production, in which Italy would rely primarily for its exports on a modernized farming sector, had already by the late 1870s become untenable as agricultural prices collapsed.

Free trade, pursued dogmatically in the years after unification, left Italy highly vulnerable to cyclical movements in the international economy. If external demand in the first decade encouraged capital investment and specialization in scattered areas of the countryside in a few, selected products (wine, olive oil, citrus fruit, rice), the commercial treaties of these years worked against manufacturing industries. The moderate politicians clung tenaciously to their faith in progress as the direct product of liberalism and free trade, and remained suspicious of the self-interested protests of the manufacturing-trading groups, as well as fearful of the negative social consequences of rapid industrialization. It would be mistaken to underestimate the unusual intensity of ideological commitment, based on the assumption that the creation of a national market of some twenty-five millions would automatically offset the initial disadvantages of foreign competition by selective encouragement of 'healthy' manufacturing firms. But the high borrowing requirements of the state, to service the perilously large national debt and heavy military establishment and to guarantee the extension of the railway network, also deflected the scarce flow of capital away from industry. The effects of this policy were to destroy the highly protected industries in the south, while weakening even the more modern textile and metal-working factories and workshops of Lombardy and Piedmont. Silk, the major Italian export, was of benefit primarily to the north; the south, whose artisan industries were unable to withstand foreign manufactured imports, found its agricultural exports threatened by northern competition. The economic gap between north and south, already existent at the time of unification because of the north's structural advantages, increased in these early years, and was to assume disastrous dimensions with the agricultural crisis from the late 1870s. Italy's economic development, like its great power status, remained closely dependent upon international conditions.

Growing awareness of Italy's vulnerability in a world economy characterized increasingly by the dominance of industrialized states and the adoption of protectionist policies explains the abandonment of free trade by the Sinistra as well as by sectors of the moderate Destra, with the adoption of the mild tariff of 1878 and especially the extremely high, selective tariff of 1887. Foreign capital, on which Italy for long depended, had been invested in banking, railway construction, mines and urban services, at the expense of local manufacturing industries. The short-lived boom of the 1880s, based primarily on speculative urban building, already revealed two aspects of the future path of Italian industrial development: the close links between private industrialists and the public administration, regarded almost as a necessary condition for entrepreneurial success; and the deep involvement of the banks in speculative activities, which was to lead to those spectacular bank crashes which recurrently mark the history of the Italian economy. The 1887 tariff, justified in terms of the need to equip a 'strong' Italy with its own steel and shipbuilding industries as well as to save agriculture, extended protection from the cotton to the metal-working industries and in the agricultural sector to wheat and sugar. Although it prepared the base for Italy's subsequent industrialization, it is arguable that it failed in its ostensible overall purpose, namely to lessen the Italian economy's dependence on international cyclical movements: the deep recession from the later 1880s, the recovery from 1896, the rapid growth of the Giolittian years and the crisis of 1907, all coincided with and were directly linked to analogous movements in the world economy.

The long-term structural consequences of the 1887 tariff are difficult to underestimate. Protection for wheat discouraged the development of a capitalist, intensive agriculture, which still only covered a mere fifth of the cultivated area in the mid-1880s. The backwardness of the south, not just relative to the north and centre but in absolute terms, became a permanent feature of the Italian scene. The dualism of the Italian economy, marking off the south from the rest of the country, most of the countryside from the cities, deepened within the manufacturing sector through the development of a modern, mechanized, mostly capital-intensive industrial sector. This structural imbalance had a depressive effect on the growth of internal demand and above all on employment. As population grew, emigration, initially mostly from the rural areas of northern Italy, shifted increasingly and decisively to the south. From about 100 000 a year in the early 1870s, overall emigration rose to 300 000 annually by the 1890s and over 500 000 annually in the years of rapid industrial growth after 1900. Within the manufacturing sector, the links between the state and protected heavy industry (steel, shipbuilding, armaments) grew ever closer, encouraging oligopolistic tendencies within these industries. The protected mechanized cotton industry expanded at the expense of artisan production, but in general small workshops and minute family firms remained the dominant characteristic of Italian manufacturing. By 1914 the structure of the Italian economy – accentuated dualism and dependence on the state – had crystallized, but the possibilities of growth remained primarily dependent upon the international economy.

The political act of unification brought no sudden change in social relations in Italy. The pace of social change is inherently slower than that of political decisions, unless such decisions are deliberately directed towards encouraging a social revolution. In Italy political unity had been achieved by the conscious exclusion of social upheaval. Hence it is not surprising that social change, in both countryside and city, only became apparent some decades later, as industrialization and the agricultural crisis finally broke the fragile equilibrium of family structures. Until the 1880s fertility rates declined only marginally, remaining higher in the south than in the north and in the countryside than in the cities, everywhere exerting growing pressure on resources, only marginally relieved by emigration or the terrible cholera epidemic of 1865–7.

The absolute primacy of politics in the final drive for unification, by its deliberate exclusion of social issues, had led in practice to an acceptance of existing social relations. Until Garibaldi's expedition to the south, the Catholic humanitarianism of the landowners in the north and centre offered a significant safeguard against social disruption in the countryside, as the effective organization of the plebiscites showed. The inclusion of Sicily and Naples within the new kingdom of Italy created far graver threats of disorder, as Cavour recognized. His belief that severe but free and honest government would be sufficient to restore a naturally fertile south to its former prosperity was based upon the false assumption that its unhappy condition derived purely from the inefficient and corrupt rule of the Bourbons. But the class hatreds between the poor and the *signori*, the desperate land famine of the peasantry, the absence of a capitalist-oriented urban middle class such as existed in the north, would have undermined Cavour's proposed method of government, even if his successors had not reduced it to a mockery by the abuse of liberty in favour of privilege. The civil war that raged through the south between 1861 and 1865 – described as brigandage by the authorities – was a mass social protest against the new state more than a demonstration of loyalty for the deposed Bourbon ruler. Despite the 100 000 soldiers employed to repress these brigands, the moderate leaders were forced to turn to the network of intermediaries, the *gabelloti*, mafia and camorra leaders, the landowners with their private retinues, who alone were able to buy off the bandit leaders, terrorize and patronize the peasant poor, recruiting them to their own bands. The price paid by the state for this co-operation was acceptance of the authority and privileges of these local landowning notables. The sale of ecclesiastical property in 1866–7 to these same groups, rather than to the land-hungry peasantry, consolidated the loyalty of the southern *galantuomini* to the new state, but also guaranteed the survival of the system of clientelism.

Although social upheaval had been avoided or repressed, the administrative presence of the new state inevitably affected the life of the population, whether rural or urban. The extension to all Italy in uniform manner of the Piedmontese pattern of government meant the imposition of new laws and administrative practices, replacing those of the pre-unitarian states. The initial fears of counter-revolution, the bitter struggle against a hostile

Church, the desperate financial needs (particularly following the near-bankruptcy of 1866), the weight of the military establishment, the administrative centralization, all contributed to broadening the scale and deepening the intensity of the activities of the new state, compared to those of the previous governments. Overt manifestations of these activities were the vast powers of the prefects at the provincial level; the heavy land and consumption taxes, which underlay the civil war in the south and sparked off the riots of the Emilian peasantry against the grist-tax in 1869–70; conscription, which caused an insurrection at Palermo in 1866; and the state's aggressive support for private property, which encouraged the legal and illegal appropriation of commonlands. But in an infinite number of ways, through its regulation of local government, its appointment of mayors and communal secretaries, doctors and primary school teachers, its choice of location for railway lines and administrative offices, its despatch of *carabinieri* as representatives of the law to remote towns and villages, the state made its presence felt at the level of the community, the family and the individual.

It was a hostile presence, particularly for the peasantry, not merely in terms of the identification of the state with the landowner, the tax-collector and the *carabiniere*, but because of the paucity of intermediary strata attached to the values of the state and in continuous contact with the people. Of a population of twenty-three million in 1861, seventeen million were illiterate; and in a country where dialect accurately reflected deep-rooted regionalism and particularism, only 2.5 per cent of the population could confidently speak the national language – Italian. Although the state placed strong emphasis on education as an essential means of unifying the nation (like the railways were to unify the country), the appointment of primary school teachers depended upon the availability of communal funds, always insufficient and inevitably even less adequate in the south where the need was greatest; the teachers themselves, for the most part without proper qualifications, were badly paid and easily subject to dismissal. Even in the Giolittian years, the Italian village *maestri* never effectively performed the function of the French *instituteurs* in transmitting the values of the state to the mass of the rural population. This, as much as the continuing active presence of the Church and the absence of a substantial stratum of independent peasant landowners, explains the lack of political involvement among the Italian rural population. Emigration rapidly became the response to state pressure and agricultural crisis. It is significant that political involvement – leading to the creation of an agricultural workers' trade union – was to emerge after 1900 only in the area of the lower Po valley, where capitalist agriculture had led to a class-conscious workforce of *braccianti*.

Alongside, and often in the place of the village *maestri*, the parish priests retained their traditional influence. The refusal to recognize the new state led to a greater effort on the part of the Church to identify itself with the Italian people. Through their pastoral, educational and welfare activities, the parish priests – the majority of the 130 000 clergy in the 1860s – acted as intermediaries between the state and the peasants, upholding the values of the family and religion against the encroaching threat of a secular society and urban industrialization.

The landowners and their representatives formed the other main category of intermediaries between the state and the rural population. In the regions of *mezzadria* in northern and central Italy unification brought little change in the structure of authority. The new administrative posts – mayor and communal council – were filled by the same landowners as before; the few state-appointed employees – such as communal secretary and doctor – were soon absorbed within the network of local notables. The family and household remained the fundamental unit of rural life. The community continued to be structured around an informal hierarchy, based upon 'respect' for those wealthier families, of long-standing residence, willing to assume public responsibilities.

In the south, the sharp division between the peasants and the *galantuomini* increased after unification. The propertied classes controlled local government, charities and justice, and manipulated taxation and electoral lists in their own interests. A deep chasm separated the *signori* from the manual labourers. Kinship, friendship and a corporate sense of community counted for little in the peasant villages and small towns of the south, where families, dependent upon short-term leases, were forced to engage in a variety of economic activities, and constantly changed properties and occupations. As foreign and then north Italian cotton manufactures entered the south, rural domestic textile industry collapsed; the fall in wine prices broke the independence of many subsistence smallholders; the system of extensive wheat cultivation, consolidated by tariff protection, only encouraged population growth, since human labour substituted, with antiquated tools, for the lack of animals. But the continuous alien presence of the state obliged the peasants to seek some form of mediation. The notables and intermediaries, landowners, *gabelloti* and *galantuomini*, possessed the personal contacts and legal skills to obtain 'favours' from the state authorities for the peasants they protected. It was not accidental that the heaviest concentration of lawyers was to be found in the south. For a legal qualification gave the necessary status and knowledge to operate the system of clientelism and patronage, which acted as the main channel of communication between a distant, hostile state and the abject peasant citizens of the south.

The presence of the new state had a different and more immediate impact on Italian cities and the composition of their populations. The requirements of government rapidly transformed the appearance of the cities, with the construction of new prefectures and post offices and the conversion of ecclesiastical buildings into administrative offices. Following the pattern of other European countries, Italy remodelled its major cities by bureaucratic decree and private speculation. Florence, during its brief years as capital of Italy (1864–70) was deemed worthy – like Haussmann's Paris – of a more dignified appearance, to be achieved by the demolition of the medieval dwellings of the city centre and their replacement with the heavy, austere apartment houses of later nineteenth-century taste, plastered, in imitation of Savoyard Turin, in sombre ochre colour. Rome was subjected to massive, uncontrolled speculative building, financed by Piedmontese, Florentine and international capital, which led to the destruction of large areas of the ancient city. But all the major and many of the minor cities acquired a new physiognomy, as their outer walls were knocked down and much of the historic inner quarters of cramped artisan dwellings and tortuous narrow streets were destroyed to make way for broad avenues and large middle-class apartment houses. The railway stations often formed the starting point for this development of a new urban topography, especially in central and southern Italy, where the location of the lines frequently ignored traditional routes, isolating some historic centres, cutting off others from their natural outlets.

Within the cities, unification rapidly confirmed the leading role of the bourgeoisie, whether of industry, commerce or the professions, over that of the old aristocracy. Even before the urbanizing effects of economic change in the north (from the 1880s), the machinery of government led to the emergence of a petty bourgeoisie of white-collar workers, clerks and minor employees, separated from the propertied middle classes by their lack of resources and total dependence on salaries, but whose life-style asserted their distance from the manual workers.

In northern Italy, in Lombardy, Piedmont and Liguria, the composition of the urban labouring poor changed, particularly from the 1880s, as mechanization in the textile industries degraded skills and for many years increased domestic outwork. The textile and building industries, railway construction and public works offered employment to at least some of the rural population expelled by the agricultural crisis. The distinction, always present, between the urban working class and the immigrants became more marked, with the growth in the numbers of migrants, most of whom for long maintained strong links with the countryside. Seasonal employment, daily or weekly commuting from the countryside, temporary residence within the cities, all pointed to the fundamental division between regular employment and casual or intermittent labour, typical of these newly industrializing cities of northern Italy, as of London or Paris. Mutual aid societies, sometimes perhaps connected with earlier traditions of confraternities and guilds, had developed in Piedmont and Liguria already in the 1850s and spread, especially to Lombardy, after unification. But their Mazzinian tone, with its stress on class association, as well as the high cost of membership and their exclusive craft orientation, limited their influence among the labouring poor for some decades after unity. The formation of a class-conscious urban proletariat was to prove slow and difficult precisely because of the pressure on employment of these unskilled poor, often without fixed abode.

Within these industrializing cities of north Italy, a process of segregation resulted, as high rents and the middle-class apartment houses forced the urban working class out of the centre of the city, into new zones near the factories, and the casual and migrant workers into unsanitary rooms on the expanding periphery. In the southern cities, where no proletariat was to develop except in isolated pockets near Naples, the same phenomenon of building speculation worsened the already appalling living conditions of the poor. But in almost all the Italian cities of any size, over the decades the creation of the new state deepened the social divisions between the propertied classes and the propertyless.

The remoteness of the state from civil society remained the most significant characteristic of united Italy and conditioned the forms of its economic and social development. Although it would be a distortion to ascribe all the subsequent problems of the country solely to the hasty and exclusively political manner in which Italy was unified, the incapacity of the extremely small ruling class to attract to its own values broad sectors of the population reflected the constraints on purely political action imposed by lethargic social change. The extremely restricted suffrage, which gave the vote to a mere 2 per cent of the population, the excessive centralization, and the heavy controls imposed to repress manifestations of hostility, worked against the rapid emergence of intermediary groups capable of bridging the gulf and encouraging the identification of nation and state. Unlike Prussia, neither army nor nobility were able to substitute for the weakness of the political class, as the former was too dominantly Piedmontese and the latter, merging increasingly into bourgeois financial circles, remained fragmented through regional loyalties. The monarchy, although able to exert considerable political influence because of the isolation of the political system, remained too remote to act as a unifying catalyst at the level of the population.

In these conditions, the political practice of 'transformism' did not simply derive from a decline in the standards of public morality, following the assumption of power by the Left in 1876. 'Transformism', the replacement of distinctive parties and programmes by fluid personalistic parliamentary groupings negotiating their support for a government in terms of purely local and sectional interests, became a system peculiar to Italy because of its persistent survival. But it should be regarded as a direct consequence of the social constraints on political change. The exclusion of the vast majority of the population, progressively greater moving from the north to the south of the country, and the deep division between the propertied classes and the peasantry and urban poor, created the essential basis for 'transformism': an archaic social structure, carefully conserved in the south, provided the necessary framework for the continuing practice of clientelism.

The economic and accompanying social changes between the 1880s and the First World War led to developments, of which the most significant were the emergence of socialist and Catholic political and union organizations representing the excluded masses. But the permanence of the dualism between north and south, the dependence of a large portion of industry on state support, the rising flood of emigration, and the strengthening of southern clientelism, were all indicative of structural weaknesses related to the process of creation of the unified Italian state. The strength of Italy was to be found in the resilience of its people, ready to search for employment throughout the world and to work hard to create for themselves and their children those opportunities denied them by their rulers.

Glossary

Abate, cleric, abbé
Annona, victualling board (usually municipal) to ensure adequate food supplies for a large city
Anti-curialist, opponent of Papal claims
Arrendamenti, taxes of the kingdom of Naples alienated to private individuals or institutions as guarantees of loans to the State.
Arrendatari, owners of *arrendamenti*

Babouvist (babouvism), follower of the radical ideas of the French revolutionary Gracchus Babeuf (1760–97)
Barnabotti, poor Venetian nobles
Biens nationaux, national properties, confiscated mainly from the Church, by the revolutionary and Napoleonic administrations
Bifolco, Venetian peasant
Bracciante, landless day-labourer

Cadastral register, land register
Capitazione, capitation tax
Cascina, farm-house (and, by extension, farm), run by peasant, term usually employed in Piedmont
Catasto, land register, usually including measurement, taxable value and changes in ownership of properties
Catasto 'onciario', kingdom of Naples *catasto*, of 1741–54
Censimento, census, often used to describe the compilation of a land register
Charte octroyée, constitutional charter granted by Louis XVIII in 1814
Colonia parziaria, agricultural lease on a profit-sharing basis, similar to share-cropping
Colono, share-cropper, peasant tenant
Common lands, rights of pasturage on lands owned by village community
Comunanze, common lands of village community
Congregazione, main consultative organ of duchy of Milan, with membership principally restricted by birth
Contratti alla voce, loan to peasant (usually of wheat), made when price was high

through seasonal scarcity, and repaid at harvest-time; typical of southern Italy

Country merchants, lease-holders of large and extensively cultivated Roman estates, whose prime interest was in the marketing of wheat and sheep

Curia, papal administration and court

Donativo, direct tax, originally granted to rulers by their estates, but regularly exacted by the seventeenth century

Emphyteusis, perpetual lease of property

Entail, legal settlement of property, preventing successors from freely disposing of it

Exequatur, approval by state authorities for the publication of Papal decrees within its boundaries

Fattoria, usually Tuscan estate, consisting of different farms (*poderi*), but managed as a single unit

Fedecommesso, legal settlement of property, preventing successors from freely disposing of it

Fermiere, fermier, tax-farmer, with right to collect State revenues in return for payment of a fixed sum

Feudal property, land or seigneurial rights held by feudal title and usually exempt from land-taxes

Fief, property (land usually with noble title), held by feudal investiture of sovereign

Fittabile, fittavolo, tenant farmer, usually peasant

Fittanziere, intermediary between landowner and peasant cultivator, paying fixed rental to former and exacting rental and dues from latter

Gabella, tax, usually a toll, exacted by either public authorities or feudatories.

Gabelloto, cf. *fittanziere*

Gallican (gallicanism), right of French church (and by extension other national churches) to be free in certain respects of Papal control

Ghibelline (ghibellinism), of lay tendencies, usually anti-clerical

Guelph, theocratic tendency in politics, supporter of Papacy; in nineteenth century, usually called neo-guelph and an advocate of Gioberti's ideas

Illuminato, member of radical secret sect of later eighteenth century

Jansenist (Jansenism), follower of bishop Jansen (d. 1638), whose doctrine limited free will by asserting that grace was assigned at birth only to some human beings

Josephism, autocratic imposition of Enlightened despotic reforms, named after Joseph II (1741–90)

Jurisdictionalist (jurisdictionalism), promoter of authority of State in disputes over legal boundaries between Church and State

Latifondo, latifundium, vast, privately-owned estate in southern Italy, cultivated by extensive methods

Livello, land held as emphyteusis (on perpetual lease, with nominal rent)

Masseria, farm-house (and, by extension, farm) of peasant cultivator, term usually employed in northern Italy

Menu peuple, small urban artisans; also used more extensively for pre-industrial urban working classes

Mercantilist, advocate of economic doctrine that money alone is wealth and that a fixed stock of bullion exists; opposed to free trade

Mezzadria, share-cropping lease (French: *métayage*)

Mezzadro, share-cropper

Mortmain, literally 'dead hand', property owned inalienably by (usually) religious institutions, with privileges such as tax exemptions

Pedaggio, toll

Pensionatico, grazing rights of village community

Perequazione, compilation of a land register as the basis for a land-tax in Piedmont, by Victor Amadeus II (1684–1732)

Physiocrat (physiocracy), eighteenth-century follower of Quesnay, believing that land is the sole source of wealth, and in freedom of property, industry and trade

Placet, assent by State authorities to a Papal appointment or ruling

Podere, share-cropping farm, usually in Tuscany

Polenta, maize-flour, cooked with water like porridge

Poll tax, tax on every head of population

Popolo grasso, originally merchants, bankers and some skilled artisans; more generally wealthier citizens, in contrast to the *populo minuto*

Populo minuto, small urban artisans, also used more extensively for pre-industrial urban working classes

Promiscuous rights, grazing rights of village community on stubble

Provisioning system, administrative structure to ensure adequate food supplies for a large city

Quit-rent, nominal rent paid for an emphyteusis

Regalie, certain payments to a sovereign regarded as his prerogatives; payments in kind (of chickens, eggs, etc.) by a peasant farmer to his landlord

Regalist (regalism), advocate of the supremacy of the sovereign in ecclesiastical matters

Reggitore, administrator of estate, usually in Venetia

Sedili, consultative organ of city of Naples, with representatives appointed by district

Serenissima, Venetian Republic

Signoria, domination of a lord of a city-republic in the later medieval period in north-central Italy

Terziario, peasant cultivator, paying one-third of his produce to landowner

Tithe, due paid to ecclesiastical or lay lord of portion of annual produce of agriculture, initially calculated as one-tenth

Testatico, poll tax

Ultramontanist (ultramontanism), supporter of the absolute supremacy of the Pope

Usi civici, customary communal rights, usually of grazing

Bibliography

The following bibliography is highly selective. It lists books and articles which were either of direct use to me, or which I believe may be of value to readers if they wish to pursue certain themes. In addition, the full references to the notes have been included; the numbers following the names of authors in the notes refer to this bibliography. I have divided the bibliography into sections, according to broad themes or periods; works relating to more than one chronological section have usually been included in the first section.

General histories, with bibliographies

1. G. Candeloro, *Storia dell'Italia moderna*, 6 vols, Milan, 1956–70.
2. *Storia d'Italia Einaudi*, 6 vols, Turin, 1972–6.
3. C. Spellanzon and E. Di Nolfo, *Storia del Risorgimento e dell'Unità d'Italia*, 8 vols, Milan, 1936–65.
4. N. Valeri (ed.), *Storia d'Italia*, 5 vols, Turin, 1959–60.

Pre-eighteenth century and longer-term trends

5. P. J. Jones, 'Per la storia agraria italiana nel medio evo: lineamenti e problemi', *Rivista Storica Italiana*, LXXVI, 1964.
6. R. Romano, *Tra due crisi: l'Italia del Rinascimento*, Turin, 1971.
7. G. Quazza, *La decadenza italiana nella storia europea*, Turin, 1971.
8. G. Giorgetti, *Contadini e proprietari nell'Italia moderna*, Turin, 1974.
9. R. Zangheri, *Agricoltura e contadini nella storia d'Italia*, Turin, 1977.
10. E. Sereni, *Storia del paesaggio agrario italiano*, Bari, 1962.
11. G. Chittolini, 'Un problema aperto. La crisi della proprietà ecclesiastica fra Quattrocento e Cinquecento', *Rivista Storica Italiana*, LXXXV, 1973.
12. P. J. Jones, 'Communes and despots: the city-state in late medieval Italy', *Transactions of the Royal Historical Society*, 5th ser., XV, 1965.
13. A. De Maddalena, 'Il mondo rurale italiano nel Cinque e nel Seicento. (Rassegna di studi recenti)', *Rivista Storica Italiana*, LXXVI, 1964.

14. F. McArdle, *Altopascio. A study in Tuscan rural society, 1587–1784*, Cambridge, 1978.
15. G. Delille, *Croissance d'une société rurale. Montesarchio et la Vallée Caudine au XVIIe et XVIIIe siècles*, Naples, 1973.
16. L. Del Panta and M. Livi-Bacci, 'Chronologie, intensité et diffusion des crises de mortalité en Italie: 1600–1850', *Population*, XXXII, 1977.

Italy in the eighteenth century: general

17. G. Quazza, *Il problema italiano e l'equilibrio europeo 1720–1738*, Turin, 1965.
18. A. Battistella, 'La guerra di successione polacca in Italia desunta da lettere private del tempo', *Atti del R. Istituto Veneto di Scienze Lettere ed Arti*, LXXIV, 1914–15.
19. F. Valsecchi, *L'Italia nel Settecento dal 1714 al 1788*, Milan, 1959.
20. C. Tivaroni, *L'Italia prima della rivoluzione*, Turin, 1888.
21. F. Borlandi, 'Italia e Mediterraneo nel secolo XVIII', *Annali della Facoltà di Scienze Politiche dell'Università di Pavia*, 1932.
22. A. Annoni, *L'Europa nel pensiero italiano del Settecento*, Milan, 1959.
23. L. Dal Pane, *Il tramonto delle corporazioni in Italia (secoli XVIII e XIX)*, Milan, 1940.
24. L. Dal Pane, *Storia del lavoro in Italia (dal sec. XVIII al 1815)*, Milan, 1944.
25. P. Villani, 'Il capitalismo agrario in Italia (secoli XVII–XIX)', in P. Villani, *Feudalità, riforme, capitalismo agrario*, Bari, 1968.
26. L. A. Muratori, *Annali d'Italia dal principio dell'era volgare sino all'anno 1749*, 12 tomes, Milan, 1744–9.
27. F. Venturi (ed.), *Illuministi italiani*, t.3: *Riformatori lombardi piemontesi e toscani*, Milan-Naples, 1958.
28. F. Venturi (ed.), *Illuministi italiani*, t.5: *Riformatori napoletani*, Milan-Naples, 1962.
29. G. Giarrizzo, G. F. Torcellan and F. Venturi (eds), *Illuministi italiani*, t.7: *Riformatori delle antiche repubbliche, dei ducati, dello stato pontificio e delle isole*, Milan-Naples, 1965.
30. F. Venturi, *Settecento riformatore. I. Da Muratori a Beccaria*, Turin, 1969.
31. F. Venturi, *Settecento riformatore. II. La chiesa e la repubblica dentro i loro limiti*, Turin, 1976.
32. F. Venturi, *Italy and the Enlightenment*, London, 1972.
33. F. Venturi, *Utopia and reform in the Enlightenment*, Cambridge, 1971.
34. F. Venturi, 'La circolazione delle idee', *Rassegna Storica del Risorgimento*, XLI, 1954.
35. F. Venturi, 'Illuminismo italiano e illuminismo europeo', in M. Fubini (ed.), *La cultura illuministica in Italia*, Turin, 1957.
36. E. Garin, *Storia della filosofia italiana*, 3 vols, Turin, 1966.
37. C. Morandi, 'Il problema delle riforme nei risultati della recente storiografia', in C. Morandi, *Problemi storici italiani ed europei del XVIII e XIX secolo*, Milan, 1937.
38. E. Codignola, *Illuministi, giansenisti e giacobini nell'Italia del Settecento*, Florence, 1947.

39. E. Passerin d'Entrèves, 'La politica dei giansenisti in Italia nell'ultimo Settecento', *Quaderni di Cultura e Storia Sociale*, I–III, 1952–4.

The Italian states in the eighteenth century

Piedmont and kingdom of Sardinia

40. G. Quazza, *Le riforme in Piemonte nella prima metà del Settecento*, Modena, 1957.
41. S. Pugliese, *Due secoli di vita agricola, produzione e valore dei terreni, contratti agrari, salari e prezzi nel Vercellese nei secoli XVIII e XIX*, Turin, 1908.
42. G. Prato, *La vita economica in Piemonte a metà del secolo XVIII*, Turin, 1908.
43. G. Prato, 'L'evoluzione agricola nel secolo XVIII e le cause economiche dei moti del 1792–98 in Piemonte', *Memorie della R. Accademia delle Scienze di Torino*, LX, 1910.
44. F. Venturi, *Dalmazzo Francesco Vasco (1732–1794)*, Paris, 1940.
45. G. Levi, 'La seta e l'economia piemontese del Settecento. A proposito di un saggio inedito di Dalmazzo Francesco Vasco', *Rivista Storica Italiana*, LXXIX, 1967.
46. L. Bulferetti (ed.), *Il riformismo settecentesco in Sardegna*, Cagliari, 1966.

Genoa and Corsica

47. G. Doria, *Uomini e terre di un borgo collinare dal XVI al XVIII secolo*, Milan, 1968.
48. G. Levi, 'Famiglie contadine nella Liguria del Settecento', *Miscellanea Storica Ligure*, V, 1974.
49. P. Nurra (ed.), 'Girolamo Serra: Memorie per la storia di Genova, dagli ultimi anni del secolo XVIII alla fine dell'anno 1814', *Atti della Società Ligure di Storia Patria*, LVIII, 1930.
50. W. Maturi, 'La Corsica nel carteggio del Tanucci, del Galiani e del Caracciolo (1763–4 e 1768–9)', *Archivio Storico di Corsica*, III, 1927.

Lombardy

51. S. Pugliese, 'Condizioni economiche e finanziarie della Lombardia nella prima metà del secolo XVIII', *Miscellanea di Storia Italiana*, XXI, 1924.
52. M. Romani, *L'agricoltura in Lombardia dal periodo delle riforme al 1859*, Milan, 1957.
53. B. Caizzi, *Il Comasco sotto il dominio austriaco fino alla redazione del catasto teresiano*, Como, 1955.
54. B. Caizzi, *Industria, commercio e banca in Lombardia nel XVIII secolo*, Milan, 1968.
55. M. Romani, 'Gian Luca Pallavicini e le riforme economiche nello stato di Milano', *Annali dell'Università Cattolica del Sacro Cuore*, 1957–9.
56. J. M. Roberts, 'Lombardy', in A. Goodwin (ed.), *The European nobility in the eighteenth century*, London, 1953.

488 BIBLIOGRAPHY

57. N. Valeri, *Pietro Verri*, Milan, 1937.
58. S. Romagnoli (ed.), *Il Caffè ossia brevie vari discorsi distribuiti in fogli periodici*, Milan, 1960.
59. F. Valsecchi, *L'Assolutismo illuminato in Austria e Lombardia*, vol. 2, part 1, *La Lombardia. La politica interna*, Bologna, 1934.
60. F. Venturi, 'La corrispondenza letteraria di Auguste de Keralio e Paolo Frisi', in H. Friedrich and F. Schalk (eds), *Europäische Aufklärung. Festschrift für Herbert Dickmann*, Munich, 1966.
61. B. Peroni, 'La politica scolastica dei principi riformatori in Italia', *Nuova Rivista Storica*, XII, 1928.
62. C. Vivanti, *Le Campagne mantovane nell'età delle riforme*, Milan, 1959.

Venice

63. M. Berengo, *La Società veneta alla fine del Settecento*, Florence, 1956.

Tuscany

64. A. Anzilotti, *Movimenti e contrasti per l'unità italiana*, Milan, 1964.
65. N. Carranza, 'L'università di Pisa e la formazione culturale del ceto dirigente toscano del Settecento', *Bollettino Storico Pisano*, XXIII–XXV, 1964–6.
66. L. Dal Pane, *La Questione del commercio dei grani nel Settecento in Italia*, vol. 1, *Parte generale. Toscana*, Milan, 1932.
67. M. Mirri, 'Considerazioni su "moderni" e "illuministi" ', *Critica Storica*, II, 1963.
68. M. Mirri, 'Ancora qualche idea su "moderni" e "illuministi" ', *Critica Storica*, VII, 1968.
69. M. Mirri, 'Per una ricerca sui rapporti tra "economisti" e riformatori toscani. L'abate Niccoli a Parigi', *Annali dell'Istituto Giangiacomo Feltrinelli*, II, 1959.
70. M. Mirri, *La lotta politica in Toscana intorno alle 'riforme annonarie'* (*1764–1775*), Pisa, 1972.
71. M. Mirri, 'Proprietari e contadini toscani nelle riforme leopoldine', *Movimento Operaio*, VII, 1955.
72. F. Diaz, *Francesco Maria Gianni. Dalla burocrazia alla politica sotto Pietro Leopoldo di Toscana*, Milan-Naples, 1966.
73. F. Diaz, 'La "philosophie" ed il riformismo leopoldino', *Rassegna Storica Toscana*, XI, 1965.
74. M. Rosa, 'Intervento' to Diaz, 73, *Rassegna Storica Toscana*, XI, 1965.
75. M. Rosa, 'Giurisdizionalismo e riforma religiosa nella politica ecclesiastica leopoldina', *Rassegna Storica Toscana*, XI, 1965.
76. E. Codignola, *Il giansenismo toscano nel carteggio di Fabio de' Vecchi*, 2 vols, Florence, 1944.
77. E. Passerin d'Entrèves, 'L'istituzione dei patrimoni ecclesiastici e il dissidio tra il vescovo Scipione de' Ricci e i funzionari leopoldini (1785–1789)', *Rassegna Storica Toscana*, I, 1955.
78. E. Cochrane, *Florence in the forgotten centuries (1527–1800)*, Chicago, 1973.

Modena and Parma

79. L. Ricci, *Riforma degl'istituti pii della città di Modena*, Modena, 1787.
80. C. Poni, 'Aspetti e problemi dell'agricoltura modenese dall'età delle riforme alla fine della Restaurazione', in *Aspetti e problemi del Risorgimento a Modena*, Modena, 1963.
81. P. L. Spaggiari, *Economia e finanza negli stati parmensi*, Milan-Varese, 1961.

Papal States

82. L. Dal Pane, *Lo Stato pontificio e il movimento riformatore del Settecento*, Milan, 1959.
83. A. Caracciolo, *Ricerche sul mercante italiano del Settecento*, I, *Fortunato Cervelli*, Milan, 1962.
84. A. Caracciolo, *Ricerche sul mercante italiano del Settecento*, II, *Francesco Trionfi*, Milan, 1962.
85. A. Caracciolo, *Domenico Passionei tra Roma e la repubblica delle lettere*, Rome, 1968.
86. F. Venturi, 'The Enlightenment in the Papal States', in F. Venturi, *Italy and the Enlightenment*, London, 1972.
87. C. Capra, *Giovanni Ristori da illuminista a funzionario 1775–1830*, Florence, 1968.

Naples and Sicily

88. P. Colletta, *Storia del reame di Napoli*, 3 vols, Naples, 1951–7.
89. L. Marini, 'Il Mezzogiorno d'Italia di fronte a Vienna e a Roma (1707–1734)', *Annali dell'Istituto Storico Italiano per l'Età Moderna e Contemporanea*, V, 1953.
90. R. Ajello, *Il problema della riforma giudiziaria e legislativa nel regno di Napoli durante la prima metà del secolo XVIII*, 2 vols, Naples, 1961–5.
91. C. Grimaldi, *Memorie di un anticurialista del Settecento*, Florence, 1964.
92. G. Ricuperati, *L'esperienza civile e religiosa di Pietro Giannone*, Milan-Naples, 1970.
93. P. Villani, *Mezzogiorno tra riforme e rivoluzione*, Bari, 1962.
94. P. Villani, 'La feudalità dalle riforme all'eversione', *Clio*, 1965.
95. P. Villani, 'Il dibattito sulla feudalità nel regno di Napoli dal Genovesi al Canova', in *Studi e Ricerche sul Settecento*, Naples, 1968.
96. R. Villari, 'Rapporti economico-sociali nelle campagne meridionali', *Quaderni di Cultura e di Storia Sociale*, II, 1953.
97. R. Villari, *Mezzogiorno e contadini nell'età moderna*, Bari, 1961.
98. P. Chorley, *Oil, silk and enlightenment*, Naples, 1965.
99. L. De Rosa, *Studi sugli arrendamenti del regno di Napoli*, Naples, 1958.
100. R. Romano, *Le commerce du royaume de Naples avec la France et les pays de l'Adriatique au XVIIIe siècle*, Paris, 1951.
101. F. Venturi, 'Alle origini dell'illuminismo napoletano. Dal carteggio di Bartolomeo Intieri', *Rivista Storica Italiana*, LXXI, 1959.

102. F. Venturi, '1764: Napoli nell'anno della fame', *Rivista Storica Italiana*, LXXXV, 1973.
103. F. Venturi, 'The Enlightenment in southern Italy', in F. Venturi, *Italy and the Enlightenment*, London, 1972.
104. B. Croce, 'Sentenze e giudizi di Bernardo Tanucci', in B. Croce, *Uomini e cose della vecchia Italia*, 2nd series, Bari, 1927.
105. E. Pontieri, *Il riformismo borbonico nella Sicilia del Sette e dell'Ottocento*, Rome, 1945.
106. E. Pontieri, *Il tramonto del baronaggio siciliano*, Florence, 1943.
107. V. Titone, *Economia e politica nella Sicilia del Sette e Ottocento*, Palermo, 1947.
108. B. Croce, 'Il marchese Caracciolo', in B. Croce, *Uomini e cose della vecchia Italia*, 2nd series, Bari, 1927.
109. L. Genuardi, *Terre comuni ed usi civici in Sicilia*, Palermo, 1911.

The Risorgimento: general

110. D. Mack Smith, *The making of Italy, 1796–1870*, London, 1968.
110a. D. Mack Smith, *Il Risorgimento italiano*, Bari, 1968.
111. D. Mack Smith, 'An outline of Risorgimento history, 1840–1870', in D. Mack Smith, *Victor Emanuel, Cavour and the Risorgimento*, Oxford, 1971.
112. A. Gramsci, *Sul Risorgimento*, Rome, 1967, partly transl. in A. Gramsci, *Selections from the prison notebooks*, London, 1971.
113. A. Saitta, *Aspetti e momenti della civiltà europea*, Naples, 1971.
114. C. Morandi, *I partiti politici nella storia d'Italia*, Florence, 1945.
115. C. Morandi, 'Aspetti del Risorgimento come problema politico europeo', in C. Morandi, *Problemi storici italiani ed europei del XVIII e XIX secolo*, Milan, 1937.
116. G. Salvemini, *Scritti sul Risorgimento*, Milan, 1961.
117. A. Omodeo, *Figure e passioni del Risorgimento italiano*, Palermo, 1932.
118. A. Omodeo, *Difesa del Risorgimento*, Turin, 1951.
119. G. Quazza, *La lotta sociale nel Risorgimento*, Turin, 1951.
120. N. Rosselli, *Saggi sul Risorgimento*, Turin, 1946.
121. F. Catalano, R. Moscati and F. Valsecchi, *L'Italia nel Risorgimento dal 1789 al 1870*, Milan, 1964.
122. P. Pieri, *Storia militare del Risorgimento*, Turin, 1962.
123. P. Gobetti, *Risorgimento senza eroi*, Turin, 1926.

The revolutionary years

124. B. Peroni, 'Gli italiani alla vigilia della dominazione francese 1793–1796', *Nuova Rivista Storica*, XXXV, 1951.
125. B. Peroni, *Fonti per la storia d'Italia dal 1789 al 1815 nell'Archivio Nazionale di Parigi*, Rome, 1936.
126. D. Cantimori (ed.), *Giacobini italiani*, vol. 1, Bari, 1956.
127. D. Cantimori and R. De Felice (eds), *Giacobini italiani*, vol. 2, Bari, 1964.
128. A. Saitta (ed.), *Alle origini del Risorgimento: i testi di un 'celebre' concorso (1796)*, 3 vols, Rome, 1964.

129. M. Gioia, *Apologia al quadro politico di Milano*, Milan, 1798.
130. D. Cantimori, *Utopisti e riformatori italiani*, Florence, 1943.
131. A. Saitta, *Filippo Buonarroti*, 2 vols, Rome, 1950.
132. A. Saitta, 'La questione del "giacobinismo" italiano', *Critica Storica*, IV, 1965.
133. A. Galante Garrone, *Buonarroti e Babeuf*, Turin, 1948.
134. G. Romano-Catania, *Filippo Buonarroti*, Palermo, 1902.
135. C. Francovich, *Albori socialisti nel Risorgimento. Contributo allo studio delle società segrete (1776–1835)*, Florence, 1962.
136. J. Godechot, 'Le babouvisme et l'unité italienne, 1796–1799', *Revue des Etudes Italiennes*, 1938.
137. J. Godechot, 'Les jacobins italiens et Robespierre', *Annales Historiques de la Révolution Française*, XXX, 1958.
138. J. Godechot, *Les commissaires aux armées sous le Directoire*, 2 vols, Paris, 1937–41.
139. J. Godechot, *La grande nation. L'expansion révolutionnaire de la France dans le monde. 1789–1799*, 2 vols, Paris, 1956.
140. J. Godechot, 'I francesi e l'unità italiana sotto il Direttorio', *Rivista Storica Italiana*, LXIX, 1952.
141. C. Zaghi, *La rivoluzione francese e l'Italia*, Naples, 1966.
142. C. Zaghi, *Bonaparte e il Direttorio dopo Campoformio. Il problema italiano nella diplomazia europea, 1797–1798*, Naples, 1956.
143. C. Ghisalberti, *Le costituzioni giacobine del triennio 1797–99*, Milan, 1959.
144. G. Vaccarino, *I patrioti 'anarchistes' e l'idea dell'unità italiana (1796–1799)*, Turin, 1955.
145. C. Montalcini and A. Alberti (eds), *Assemblee della Repubblica Cisalpina*, 11 vols, Bologna, 1917–48.
146. U. Marcelli, *La vendita dei beni nazionali nella Repubblica Cisalpina*, Bologna, 1967.
147. U. Marcelli, *La crisi economica e sociale di Bologna nel 1796*, Bologna, 1953.
148. B. Peroni, 'La passione dell'independenza nella Lombardia occupata dai francesi 1796–1797', *Nuova Rivista Storica*, XV, 1931.
149. B. Peroni, 'La Società Popolare di Milano (1796–99)', *Rivista Storica Italiana*, LXVI, 1954.
150. 'Politica estera del governo provvisorio di Lombardia (1796–1797)', *Annuario del R. Liceo-Ginnasio 'Ugo Foscolo' di Pavia*, 1931–4.
151. S. Romagnoli, 'Melchiorre Cesarotti', in S. Romagnoli (ed.), *Ottocento tra letteratura e storia*, Padua, 1961.
152. R. Soriga, *L'idea nazionale italiana dal secolo XVIII all'unificazione*, Modena, 1941.
153. A. Frugoni, *Breve storia della repubblica bresciana (1797)*, Brescia, 1947.
154. V. E. Giuntella (ed.), *Assemblee della Repubblica Romana (1798–99)*, Bologna, 1954.
155. V. E. Giuntella, 'La giacobina repubblica romana (1798–1799). Aspetti e momenti', *Archivio della Società Romana di Storia Patria*, LXXIII, 1950.
156. R. De Felice, *La vendita dei beni nazionali nella Repubblica Romana del 1798–99*, Rome, 1960.

157. V. Cuoco, *Saggio storico sulla rivoluzione napoletana del 1799*, Milan, 1800.
158. B. Croce, *La rivoluzione napoletana del 1799*, Bari, 1948.
159. G. Cingari, *Giacobini e sanfedisti in Calabria nel 1799*, Messina-Florence, 1957.
160. G. Turi, *'Viva Maria'. La reazione alle riforme leopoldine (1790–1799)*, Florence, 1969.
161. B. Peroni, ' "Le cri de l'Italie" 1799', *Quaderni della Rivista Storica Italiana*, 1953.

Napoleonic Italy

162. C. Zaghi, *Napoleone e l'Italia*, Naples, 1966.
163. W. Maturi, *Interpretazioni del Risorgimento*, Turin, 1962.
164. G. Bourgin and J. Godechot, *L'Italie et Napoléon (1796–1814)*, Paris, 1936.
165. F. Melzi d'Eril, *I carteggi di Francesco Melzi, duca di Lodi*, 8 vols, Milan, 1958–65.
166. A. Pingaud, *La domination française dans l'Italie du Nord (1796–1805). Bonaparte président de la République Italienne*, 2 vols, Paris, 1914.
167. A. Pingaud, *Les hommes d'état de la République Italienne 1802–1805*, Paris, 1914.
168. M. Roberti, *Milano capitale napoleonica. La formazione di uno stato moderno 1796–1814*, 3 vols, Milan, 1946–7.
169. R. Zangheri, *La proprietà terriera e le origini del Risorgimento nel Bolognese*, I, *1789–1804*, Bologna, 1961.
170. M. Romani, 'L'economia milanese nell'età napoleonica', in *Storia di Milano*, Vol. XIII, *L'età napoleonica (1796–1814)*, Milan, 1959.
171. R. Monteleone, *L'economia agraria del Trentino nel periodo italico (1810–1813)*, Modena, 1964.
172. E. Sestan (ed.), *Opere di Giandomenico Romagnosi Carlo Cattaneo Giuseppe Ferrari*, Milan-Naples, 1957.
173. E. Federigo, 'Lettere', in *Nozze Folco-Clementi*, Vicenza, 1884.
174. R. Davico, 'Démographie et économie. Ville et campagne en Piémont à l'époque française', *Annales de Démographie Historique*, IV, 1968.
175. J. Borel, *Gênes sous Napoléon*, Paris, 1929.
176. B. Farolfi, *Strumenti e pratiche agrarie in Toscana dall'età napoleonica all'unità*, Milan, 1969.
177. G. Catoni, *Archivi del Governo francese nel dipartimento dell'Ombrone*, Rome, 1971.
178. S. J. Woolf, 'The treatment of the poor in Napoleonic Tuscany 1808–1814', *Annuario dell'Istituto Storico Italiano per l'Età Moderna e Contemporanea*, XXIII-XXIV, 1971–2.
179. G. Orlandi, *Le campagne modenesi fra rivoluzione e restaurazione (1790–1815)*, Modena, 1967.
180. R. Paci, *L'ascesa della borghesia nella Legazione di Urbino dalle riforme alla restaurazione*, Milan, 1966.

181. J. Rambaud, *Naples sous Joseph Bonaparte 1806–1808*, Paris, 1911.
182. V. Ricchioni, *La statistica del Reame di Napoli nel 1811. Relazioni sulla Puglia*, Trani, 1942.
183. P. Villani, *La vendita dei beni dello stato nel Regno di Napoli (1806–1815)*, Milan, 1963.
184. U. Caldora, *Calabria napoleonica (1806–1815)*, Naples, 1960.
185. A. Valente, *Gioacchino Murat e l'Italia meridionale*, Turin, 1965.
186. R. J. Rath, *The fall of the Napoleonic Kingdom of Italy, 1814*, New York, 1941.
187. L. Mercuri and C. Tuzzi, *Canti politici italiani 1793–1945*, 2 vols, Rome, 1962.

Restoration Italy

188. E. Hobsbawm, *The age of revolution 1789–1848*, London, 1964.
189. C. K. Webster, *The Congress of Vienna 1814–1815*, London 1919.
190. A. Reinermann, 'Metternich, Italy and the Congress of Verona, 1821–1822', *Historical Journal*, XIV, 1971.
191. F. H. Hinsley, *Power and the pursuit of peace*, Cambridge, 1963.
192. C. A. Macartney, *The Habsburg Empire 1790–1918*, London, 1969.
193. A. Omodeo, *Studi sull'età della Restaurazione*, Turin, 1970.
194. R. J. Rath, 'The Carbonary: their origins, initiation rites and aims', *American Historical Review*, LXIX, 1964.
195. J. M. Roberts, *The mythology of the secret societies*, London, 1972.
196. R. Soriga, *Le società segrete, l'emigrazione politica e i primi moti per l'indipendenza italiana*, Modena, 1942.
197. G. Spini, *Mito e realtà della Spagna nelle rivoluzioni italiane del 1820–21*, Rome, 1950.
198. A. Galante Garrone, 'L'emigrazione politica italiana del Risorgimento', *Rassegna Storica del Risorgimento*, XLI, 1954.
199. R. Romeo, *Dal Piemonte sabaudo all'Italia liberale*, Turin, 1963.
200. A. Aquarone, 'La politica legislativa della restaurazione nel regno di Sardegna', *Bollettino Storico-Bibliografico Subalpino*, LVII, 1959.
201. S. Santarosa, *La Rivoluzione piemontese del 1821*, Turin, 1920.
202. C. Torta, *La Rivoluzione piemontese nel 1821*, Rome-Milan, 1908.
203. T. Rossi and C. Demagistris (eds), *La Rivoluzione piemontese dell'anno 1821*, 2 vols, Turin, 1927.
204. F. Lemmi, *Carlo Felice (1755–1931)*, Turin, 1931.
205. E. Passerin d'Entrèves, *La giovinezza di Cesare Balbo*, Florence, 1940.
206. A. Omodeo, *La leggenda di Carlo Alberto nella recente storiografia*, Turin, 1940.
207. N. Rodolico, *Carlo Alberto negli anni di regno, 1831–43*, Florence, 1943.
208. N. Rodolico, *Carlo Alberto negli anni 1843–49*, Florence, 1943.
209. R. J. Rath, *The provisional Austrian regime in Lombardy-Venetia, 1814–15*, Austin, 1969.
210. A. Sandonà, *Il Regno Lombardo-Veneto. La costituzione e l'amministrazione (1814–59)*, Milan, 1912.

211. V. Branca (ed.), *Il Conciliatore*, 3 vols, Florence, 1948–54.
212. M. Gioia, *Del merito e delle ricompense*, 2 vols, Lugano, 1830.
213. R. Ciampini, *Gian Pietro Vieusseux. I suoi viaggi, i suoi giornali*, Turin, 1953.
214. R. Ciampini, *Due campagnoli dell'800: Lambruschini e Ridolfi*, Florence, 1946.
215. E. Morelli, *La politica estera di Tommaso Bernetti segretario di stato di Gregorio XVI*, Rome, 1953.
216. D. Demarco, *Il tramonto dello stato pontificio. Il papato di Gregorio XVI*, Turin, 1949.
217. A. Solmi, *Ciro Menotti e l'idea unitaria nell'insurrezione del 1831*, Modena, 1931.
218. *L'Apporto delle Marche al Risorgimento nazionale. Att idel congresso di storia, 29–30 settembre-2 ottobre 1960*, Ancona, 1961.
219. R. Moscati, *Il Mezzogiorno d'Italia nel Risorgimento*, Messine-Florence, 1953.
220. A. Lepre, *Storia del Mezzogiorno nel Risorgimento*, Rome, 1969.
221. R. Romeo, *Mezzogiorno e Sicilia nel Risorgimento*, Naples, 1963.
222. A. Lepre, *La rivoluzione napoletana del 1820–21*, Rome, 1967.
223. G. Cingari, *Mezzogiorno e Risorgimento. La Restaurazione a Napoli dal 1821 al 1830*, Bari, 1970.
224. A. Lepre, *Contadini, borghesi ed operai nel tramonto del feudalesimo napoletano*, Milan, 1963.
225. R. Romeo, *Il Risorgimento in Sicilia*, Bari, 1950.
226. S. F. Romano, *Momenti del Risorgimento in Sicilia*, Messine-Florence, 1952.

Economy and society in Restoration Italy

227. D. Bertolotti, *Descrizione di Torino*, Turin, 1840.
228. G. Stefani and G. Mondo, *Torino e i suoi dintorni*, Turin, 1852.
229. M. Cevasco, *Statistique de la ville de Gênes*, 2 vols, Genoa, 1838–40.
230. A. Fossati, *Pagine di storia economica sabauda (1815–1860)*, Turin, 1940.
231. G. Quazza, *L'industria laniera e cotoniera in Piemonte dal 1831 al 1861*, Turin, 1961.
232. *Otto giorni a Milano, ossia guida pel forestiere*, Milan, 1838.
233. A. Cossa, *Della condizione di Milano dall'anno 1796 al 1840*, Milan, 1840.
234. *Atti della sesta riunione degli scienziati italiani convocati in Milano nel settembre 1844*, Milan, 1844.
235. *Topografia storica di Milano*, 3 vols, Milan, 1846.
236. A. Gaspari, *Statistica della regia città di Milano*, Milan, 1854.
237. C. Cattaneo, *Notizie naturali e civili su la Lombardia*, Milan, 1844.
238. S. Jacini, *La proprietà fondiaria e le popolazioni agricole in Lombardia*, Milan, 1854.
239. G. De Finetti, *Milano. Costruzione di una città*, Milan, 1969.
240. K. R. Greenfield, *Economics and liberalism in the Risorgimento*, Baltimore, 1934.
241. L. Cafagna, 'La "rivoluzione agraria" in Lombardia', *Annali dell'Istituto Giangiacomo Feltrinelli*, II, 1959.

242. F. Della Peruta, 'Le campagne lombarde nel Risorgimento', in F. Della Peruta, *Democrazia e socialismo nel Risorgimento*, Rome, 1965.
243. F. Della Peruta, 'Per la storia della società lombarda nell'età del Risorgimento', *Studi Storici*, XVI, 1975.
244. K. R. Greenfield, 'Commerce and new enterprise at Venice, 1830–48', *Journal of Modern History*, XI, 1939.
245. M. Berengo, *L'agricoltura veneta dalla caduta della Repubblica all'Unità*, Milan, 1963.
246. A. Zuccagni Orlandini, *Atlante geografico fisico e storico del Granducato di Toscana*, Florence, 1832.
247. L. Bortolotti, *Livorno dal 1748 al 1958*, Florence, 1970.
248. L. Dal Pane, *Industria e commercio nel Granducato di Toscana nell'età del Risorgimento*, Bologna, 1971.
249. C. Pazzagli, *L'agricoltura toscana nella prima metà dell'800*, Florence, 1973.
250. G. Biagioli, 'Vicende dell'agricoltura nel Granducato di Toscana nel secolo XIX: le fattorie di Bettino Ricasoli', in *Agricoltura e sviluppo del capitalismo*, Rome, 1970.
251. M. Mirri, 'Mercato regionale e internazionale e mercato nazionale capitalistico come condizione dell'evoluzione interna della mezzadria in Toscana', in *Agricoltura e sviluppo del capitalismo*, Rome, 1970.
252. L. Dal Pane, *Economia e società a Bologna nell'età del Risorgimento*, Bologna, 1969.
253. S. De Renzi, *Sullo stato della medicina nell'Italia meridionale, e sui mezzi per migliorarlo*, Naples, 1842.
254. S. De Renzi, *Topografia e statistica medica della città di Napoli*, Naples, 1845.
255. S. De Renzi, *Intorno al colera di Napoli dell'anno 1854*, Naples, 1854.
256. C. Petraccone, *Napoli dal '500 all'800*, Naples, 1974.

Mazzini and the democrats

257. G. Mazzini, *Scritti editi ed inediti*, 98 vols, Imola, 1906–40.
258. F. Della Peruta (ed.), *Giuseppe Mazzini e i democratici*, Milan-Naples, 1969.
259. F. Della Peruta, *Democrazia e socialismo nel Risorgimento*, Rome, 1965.
260. F. Della Peruta, *Mazzini e i rivoluzionari italiani. Il Partito d'Azione, 1830–1845*, Milan, 1974.
261. G. Berti, *I democratici e l'iniziativa meridionale nel Risorgimento*, Milan, 1962.

Cattaneo

262. C. Cattaneo, *Opere scelte*, 4 vols, Turin, 1972.
263. C. Cattaneo, *Epistolario*, 4 vols, Florence, 1949–56.
264. C. Cattaneo, *Scritti politici*, 4 vols, Florence, 1964–5.
265. C. Cattaneo, *Scritti politici ed epistolario*, Florence, 1892.
266. N. Bobbio, *Una filosofia militante. Studi su Carlo Cattaneo*, Turin, 1971.
267. R. G. Murray, 'Carlo Cattaneo and his interpretation of the Milanese insurrection of 1848', unpublished Ph.D. thesis, Cambridge, 1963.

268. G. Ferrari, *La Federazione repubblicana*, London (but Lugano), 1851.
269. G. Ferrari, *L'Italia dopo il colpo di stato del 2 dicembre 1851*, Capolago, 1852.
270. S. Rota Ghibaudi, *Giuseppe Ferrari. L'evoluzione del suo pensiero (1838–1860)*, Florence, 1969.
271. F. Della Peruta, *I democratici e la rivoluzione italiana*, Milan, 1958.

The moderates

272. C. Balbo, *Delle speranze d'Italia*, Capolago, 1844.
273. C. Balbo, *Pensieri sulla storia d'Italia*, Florence, 1858.
274. G. Prato, *Giacomo Giovanetti ed il protezionismo agrario nel Piemonte di Carlo Alberto*, Turin, 1919.
275. C. I. Petitti di Roreto, *Opere scelte*, 2 vols, Turin, 1969.
276. C. Correnti, *L'Austria e la Lombardia*, Italia [sic], 1847.
277. F. Ferrara, *Opere complete*, 8 vols, Rome, 1970.
278. R. Ciasca, *Le origini del programma per l'opinione nazionale italiana del 1847–48*, Milan-Rome-Naples, 1916.
279. F. Sirugo, 'Intorno alla relazione tra cultura economica e pensiero civile del Risorgimento. L'opera di preparazione nel Settecento', *Annali dell'Istituto Giangiacomo Feltrinelli*, II, 1959.
280. G. Mori, 'Osservazioni sul libero-scambismo dei moderati nel Risorgimento', *Problemi dell'Unità d'Italia. Atti del II convegno Gramsci*, Rome, 1962.

Cavour

281. C. Cavour, *Epistolario*, vol. 1, *1815–1840*, Bologna, 1962.
282. D. Berti (ed.), *Diario inedito con note autobiografiche del Conte di Cavour*, Rome-Voghera, 1888.
283. C. Cavour, *Scritti di economia 1835–1850*, Milan, 1962.
284. C. Cavour, *Lettere edite ed inedite*, 6 vols, Turin, 1883–7.
285. C. Cavour, *Nouvelles lettres inédites*, Rome-Turin-Naples, 1889.
286. C. Cavour, *Discorsi parlamentari*, 11 vols, Florence, 1863–72.
287. C. Cavour, *Scritti politici*, Rome, 1930.
288. R. Romeo, *Cavour e il suo tempo*, 2 vols, Laterza, 1969–77.
289. F. Ruffini, *La giovinezza di Cavour*, 2 vols, Turin, 1937.
290. F. Sirugo, 'L'Europa delle riforme. Cavour e lo sviluppo economico del suo tempo (1830–1850)', in Cavour, 283.
291. G. Prato, *Fatti e dottrine economiche alla vigilia del 1848. L'Associazione Agraria Subalpina e Camillo Cavour*, Turin, 1921.

Gioberti

292. V. Gioberti, *Del primato morale e civile degli italiani*, 2 vols, Brussels, 1843.
293. V. Gioberti, *Epistolario*, 8 vols, 1927–36.
294. V. Gioberti, *Prolegomeni del primato civile e morale degli italiani*, 2 vols, Turin, 1926.
295. V. Gioberti, *Del rinnovamento civile d'Italia*, 2 vols, Paris-Turin, 1851.

296. A. Omodeo, *Vincenzo Gioberti e la sua evoluzione politica*, Turin, 1941.
297. A. Anzilotti, *Gioberti*, Florence, 1922.

The revolutions of 1848–9

298. *Correspondence respecting the affairs of Italy 1846–47, presented to both Houses of Parliament*, London, 1849.
299. A. J. P. Taylor, *The Italian problem in European diplomacy, 1847–1849*, Manchester, 1934.
300. R. Moscati, *La diplomazia e il problema italiano nel 1848*, Florence, 1947.
301. D. Cantimori, 'Italy in 1848', in F. Fejtö (ed.), *The opening of an era: 1848*, London, 1948.
302. A. Codignola, *Dagli albori della libertà al proclama di Moncalieri. Lettere del conte Ilarione Petitti di Roreto a Michele Erede dal marzo 1846 all'aprile 1850*, Turin, 1931.
303. M. D'Azeglio, *I miei ricordi*, Turin, 1971.
304. C. Pischedda, C. Baudi di Vesme and G. Quazza (eds), *La diplomazia del Regno di Sardegna durante la prima guerra d'independenza*, 3 vols, Turin, 1949–52.
305. A. Malvezzi (ed.), *Diario politico di Margherita Provana di Collegno*, Milan, 1926.
306. E. Grendi, 'Genova nel Quarantotto. Saggio di storia sociale', *Nuova Rivista Storica*, XLVIII, 1964.
307. *Archivio Triennale delle cose d'Italia*, 3 vols, Capolago-Chieri, 1850–5.
308. V. Ferrari (ed.), *Carteggio Casati-Castagnetto: 19 marzo-14 ottobre 1848*, Milan, 1909.
309. M. Cessi Drudi, R. Cessi, and G. Gambarin (eds), *La Repubblica di Venezia nel 1848–49. Documenti diplomatici*, 4 vols, Padua, 1949–54.
310. G. Renier, *La cronaca di Mestre degli anni 1848–49*, Treviso, 1896.
311. P. Ginsborg, *Daniel Manin and the Venetian revolution of 1848–49*, Cambridge, 1979.
312. P. Ginsborg, 'Peasants and revolutionaries in Venice and the Veneto, 1848', *Historical Journal*, XVII, 1974.
313. A. Bernadello, 'La paura del comunismo e dei tumulti popolari a Venezia e nelle provincie venete nel 1848–49', *Nuova Rivista Storica*, LIV, 1970.
314. G. Capponi, *Scritti editi ed inediti*, 2 vols, Florence, 1877.
315. G. Montanelli, *Introduzione ad alcuni appunti storici sulla rivoluzione d'Italia*, Turin, 1945.
316. G. Montanelli, *Nel processo politico contro il ministero democratico toscano. Schiarimenti*, Florence, 1852.
317. G. Montanelli, *Memorie sull'Italia e specialmente sulla Toscana dal 1814 al 1850*, 2 vols, Turin, 1853.
318. F. D. Guerrazzi, *Apologia della vita politica, scritta da lui medesimo*, Florence, 1852.
319. G. Andriani, 'Socialismo e comunismo in Toscana tra il 1846 e il 1849', *Nuova Rivista Storica*, V, 1921.
320. C. Ronchi, *I democratici fiorentini nella rivoluzione del '48-'49*, Florence, 1963.

321. N. Badaloni, 'Premesse del '48 livornese', in *Problemi dell'Unità d'Italia. Atti del II convegno Gramsci*, Rome, 1962.
322. L. C. Farini, *Lo Stato Romano dall'anno 1815 al 1850*, 4 vols, Florence, 1853.
323. L. C. Farini, *Epistolario*, 4 vols, Bologna, 1911–35.
324. C. Pisacane, *Guerra combattuta in Italia negli anni 1848–49*, Genoa, 1851.
325. M. Minghetti, *I miei ricordi*, 3 vols, Turin, 1888–90.
326. D. Demarco, *Pio IX e la rivoluzione romana del 1848*, Modena, 1947.
327. D. Demarco, *Una rivoluzione sociale. La repubblica romana del 1849*, Naples, 1948.
328. *Il 1848 nell'Italia meridionale*, Naples, 1950.
329. Camera dei Deputati (ed.), *Le Assemblee del Risorgimento. Sicilia*, 4 vols, Rome, 1911.
330. A. Aquarone, M. D'Addio and G. Negri (eds), *Le costituzioni italiane*, Milan, 1958.
331. D. Bertoni Jovine (ed.), *I periodici popolari del Risorgimento*, 2 vols, Milan, 1959.

1849–61

332. A. J. P. Taylor, *The struggle for the mastery in Europe 1848–1918*, Oxford, 1954.
333. F. Valsecchi, *Il Risorgimento e l'Europa. L'alleanza di Crimea*, Florence, 1968.
334. E. Di Nolfo, *Europa e Italia nel 1855–56*, Rome, 1967.
335. G. Guttièrez, *Il capitano Decristoforis*, Milan, 1860.
336. S. Guglielmetti, 'Giuseppe Mazzini e i suoi seguaci di Roma dal luglio 1849 alla fine del 1853', *Rassegna Storica del Risorgimento*, XVI, 1929.
337. C. Pisacane, *La Rivoluzione*, Turin, 1970.
338. G. Manacorda, 'Sulle origini del movimento operaio in Italia', *Società*, III, 1947.
339. M. D'Azeglio, *Scritti e discorsi politici*, 3 vols, Florence, 1933–7.
340. G. Faldella (ed.), *M. D'Azeglio e D. Pantaleoni. Carteggio inedito*, Turin, 1888.
341. C. D'Azeglio, *Souvenirs historiques*, Turin, 1884.
342. M. Castelli, *Carteggio politico*, 2 vols, Rome-Turin-Naples, 1890–1.
343. M. Castelli, *Il conte di Cavour*, Turin, 1886.
344. A. Omodeo, *L'opera politica del conte di Cavour. Parte I (1848–1857)*, 2 vols, Florence, 1941.
345. R. E. Cameron, 'French finance and Italian unity. The Cavourian decade', *American Historical Review*, LXII, 1956–7.
346. D. Mack Smith, *Victor Emanuel, Cavour and the Risorgimento*, London, 1971.
347. D. Mack Smith, *Vittorio Emanuele II*, Bari, 1972.
348. P. Pirri (ed.), *Pio IX e Vittorio Emanuele II dal loro carteggio privato*, 3 vols, Rome, 1944–51.
349. A. Colombo, *Gli albori del regno di Vittorio Emanuele II*, Rome, 1937.

350. G. Giarrizzo (ed.), *Le relazioni diplomatiche fra la Gran Bretagna e il Regno di Sardegna. 1848–1860*, III ser., vol. 7, Rome, 1962.

351. N. Bianchi, *Storia documentata della diplomazia europea in Italia dall'anno 1814 all'anno 1861*, 8 vols, Turin, 1865–72.

352. F. Bartoccini, *Il Murattismo*, Milan, 1959.

353. P. L. Spaggiari, *Il Ducato di Parma e l'Europa 1854–59*, Parma, 1957.

354. R. Grew, *A sterner plan for Italian unity. The Italian National Society in the Risorgimento*, Princeton, 1963.

355. B. E. Maineri (ed.), *D. Manin e G. Pallavicino. Epistolario politico, 1855–1857*, Milan, 1878.

356. G. G. Pallavicino Trivulzio, *Memorie*, 3 vols, Turin, 1882–95.

357. R. Grew, 'La Società Nazionale in Toscana', *Rassegna Storica Toscana*, II, 1956.

358. B. Ricasoli, *Lettere e documenti*, 11 vols, Florence, 1887–96.

359. W. K. Hancock, *Ricasoli and the Risorgimento in Italy*, London, 1926.

360. R. Ciampini, *Il '59 in Toscana*, Florence, 1958.

361. R. Ciampini, *I toscani del '59*, Rome, 1959.

362. D. Mack Smith, *Cavour and Garibaldi 1860: A study in political conflict*, Cambridge, 1954.

363. D. E. D. Beales, *England and Italy 1859–60*, London, 1961.

364. *Il Carteggio Cavour-Nigra dal 1858 al 1861*, 4 vols, Bologna, 1926–9.

365. C. Cavour, *La liberazione del Mezzogiorno e la formazione del Regno d'Italia, Carteggi*, 5 vols, Bologna, 1949–54.

366. G. Massari, *Diario dalle cento voci, 1858–1860*, Bologna, 1959.

367. F. Crispi, *I Mille*, Milan, 1927.

368. M. Monnier, *Garibaldi. Histoire de la conquête des deux Siciles*, Paris, 1861.

369. D. Mack Smith, *Garibaldi*, London, 1957.

370. R. Villari, *Problemi dell'economia napoletana alla vigilia dell'unificazione*, Naples, 1959.

371. T. Pedio, 'La borghesia lucana nei moti insurrezionali del 1860', *Archivio Storico per le Province Napoletane*, XL, 1960.

372. D. Demarco, 'L'economia degli Stati italiani prima dell'unità', *Rassegna Storica del Risorgimento*, XLIV, 1957.

Epilogue

373. D. Mack Smith, *Italy. A modern history*, Ann Arbor, 1959.

374. C. Seton Watson, *Italy from liberalism to fascism*, London, 1967.

375. R. Grew, 'How success spoiled the Risorgimento', *Journal of Modern History*, XXXIV, 1962.

376. N. Blakiston, *The Roman question. Extracts from the despatches of Odo Russell from Rome 1858–1870*, London, 1962.

377. F. Chabod, *Storia della politica estera italiana*, I, *Le premesse*, Bari, 1951.

378. E. Ragionieri, *Un comune socialista. Sesto Fiorentino*, Rome, 1953.

379. A. Caracciolo, *Stato e società civile. Problemi dell'unificazione italiana*, Turin, 1960.

380. C. Pavone, *Amministrazione centrale e amministrazione periferica da Rattazzi a Ricasoli (1859–1866)*, Milan, 1964.

381. A. Porro, *Il prefetto e l'amministrazione periferica in Italia. Dall'intendente subalpino al prefetto italiano (1842–1871)*, Milan, 1972.

382. E. Ragionieri, *Politica e amministrazione nella storia dell'Italia unita*, Bari, 1967.

383. *Problemi dell'Unità d'Italia. Atti del II Convegno Gramsci*, Rome, 1962.

384. G. Are, *Il problema dello sviluppo industriale nell'età della Destra*, Pisa, 1965.

385. L. Cafagna, 'Industrialismo e politica economica dopo l'unità d'Italia', *Annali dell'Istituto Giangiacomo Feltrinelli*, V, 1962.

386. L. Cafagna, 'The industrial revolution in Italy, 1830–1914', in C. Cipolla (ed.), *The Fontana Economic History of Europe*, IV, 1971.

387. A. Caracciolo (ed.), *La formazione dell'Italia industriale*, Bari, 1971.

388. A. Caracciolo, *Roma capitale. Dal Risorgimento alla crisi dello stato liberale*, Rome, 1956.

389. J. W. Cole and E. R. Wolf, *The hidden frontier. Ecology and ethnicity in an Alpine valley*, New York-London, 1974.

390. J. Davies, *Land and family in Pisticci*, London, 1973.

391. S. Silverman, *Three bells of civilization. The life of an Italian hill town*, New York, 1975.

392. G. Delille, *Agricoltura e demografia nel regno di Napoli nei secoli XVIII e XIX*, Naples, 1977.

393. J. C. Schneider, 'Patrons and clients in the Italian political system', unpublished Ph.D. thesis, Michigan, 1965.

Index

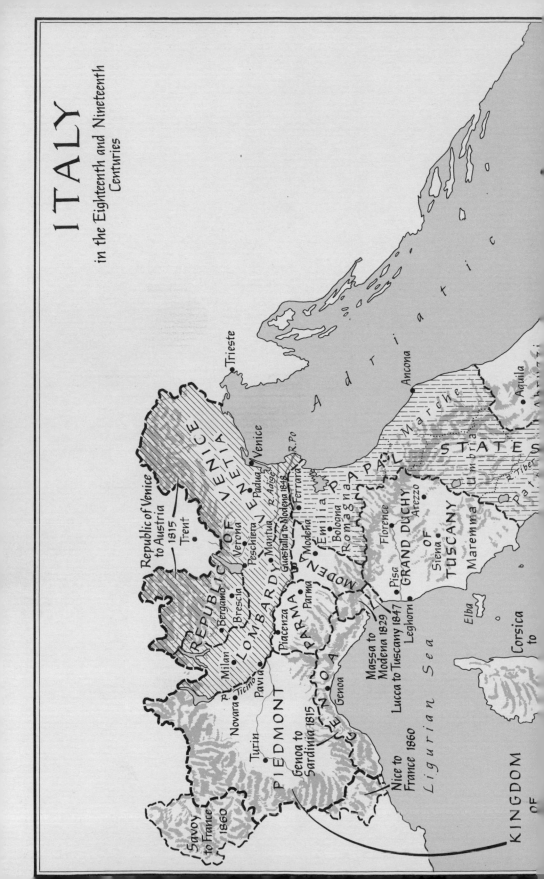

ITALY

in the Eighteenth and Nineteenth
Centuries

Trieste

A d r i a t i c

Ancona

Republic of Venice
to Austria
1815

Trent

REPUBLIC OF VENICE

VENETIA

Venice

Padua

R. Adige

Verona

Ferrara

Peschiera

Mantua to Modena 1848

R. Po

Bergamo

Brescia

PAPAL
STATES

Marche

Milan

LOMBARDY

Guastalla to Modena

Modena

Bologna

Emilia

Romagna

Umbria

R. Tiber

P.

Ticino

Pavia

Piacenza

Parma

MODENA

Florence

Arezzo

Pat

Novara

PARMA

Parma

GRAND DUCHY

Siena

GENOA

Pisa

OF

Turin

PIEDMONT

Massa to
Modena 1829

Leghorn

TUSCANY

Maremma

Savoy
to France
1860

Genoa to
Sardinia 1815

Genoa

Lucca to Tuscany 1847

Elba

Corsica
to

Nice to
France 1860

L i g u r i a n   S e a

KINGDOM

OF